SO-CIG-644

Magazine Markets
for
Children's Writers
2008

Writer's Institute Publications

Acknowledgments

The editors of this directory appreciate the generous contributions of our instructors and students and the cooperation of the magazine editors who made clear their policies and practices.

MARNI McNIFF, Editor

SUSAN TIERNEY, Articles Editor

BARBARA COLE, Assistant Editor

SHERRI KEEFE, Assistant Editor

BECKY FORSTROM, Assistant Editor

Contributing Writers: SUSAN ANDERSON, EILEEN BYRNE, JENNIFER PONTE CANNING, BARBARA COLE, CAROLINE LaFLEUR, NOREEN GUMAN, SUSAN TARRANT, KATHY VARDA

Cover Design: JOANNA HORVATH
Cover illustrations supplied by Getty Images

International Standard Book Number 978-1-889715-37-7

1-800-443-6078. www.writersbookstore.com
email: services@writersbookstore.com
Printed in Canada.

Contents

Submissions Guide   5

This section offers tips and step-by-step instructions for researching the market; writing query letters; preparing manuscript packages and bibliographies; initiating follow-up; and understanding copyrights, permissions, and other common publishing terms.

Gateway to the Markets   31

Contents (cont.)

 # Step-by-Step through the Submissions Process

The Perfect Pitch

You've just come up with a brilliant idea for a magazine article while taking your dog for a walk. Do you a) pitch it to the next person who passes you on the street; b) write a letter to *Highlights* as soon as you get home; or c) research the topic—and possible markets—over the next few weeks?

Ideas are all around us. As writers, it's hard to contain our excitement when new ideas take hold. We tend to share them with everyone, which can sometimes be beneficial, providing valuable feedback and constructive criticism. But there's more to making a sale than just the germ of an idea. Usually, the success of any new idea requires some degree of nurturing, starting with a great sales pitch. Creating the perfect pitch requires time, research—and a plan. (In other words, the answer is 'c'!)

In the world of magazine writing, the plan focuses on creating a perfect match between your idea and a target publication. You'll want to offer that publication's editor an irresistible match of quality, topic, and reader interest. Your goal is to identify the subjects those readers enjoy and then create material that engages them. Such information gathering will help support and complete your idea, so don't make your pitch until it is ready. Following are some tips to launch your research.

What Captivates Young Readers?

You'll increase your publication odds if you know what topics interest children. Consider how a child views the world. What kinds of things are they interested in? What is their typical day like? Researching current publications also goes a long way toward understanding your target audience.

Researching potential subjects can begin by surveying the categories of magazines in *Magazine Markets for Children's Writers*. Start with the Category Index on pages 347–372, an excellent guide to finding magazines that publish the types of articles or stories you write on the subjects that interest you.

You'll find general interest publications, like *Highlights for Children* or *Spider*, and also special interest periodicals on topics such as health, sports, science, fiction, college, religion, history,

and so on. Continue your research online or at libraries. Do Internet searches, and check the library or bookstores. What magazines are out there, for what ages, and what subjects do they cover? Along with magazines targeted specifically to children, be sure to check parenting, educational, and regional magazines.

You'll find that each magazine covers numerous subjects from month to month or year to year, even special interest publications that cover a niche more deeply than widely. Read several issues of each magazine to research which subjects a potential target magazine has covered recently and how it has approached particular subjects in the past. Begin to make a list of the magazines that cover subjects of interest to you. Use the Magazine Match List on page 7.

Roll Call: Who Are Your Readers?

Researching readers is intricately tied to subjects, but a magazine's target age and how the publication speaks to that age—voice and purpose—are important factors in the market research you perform. Select subjects and slants based on age-appropriateness. If you'd like to take on the subject of animals' sleep habits, for example, you'd write an article or story for early readers with less specific information than you would for a middle-grader, and with a different tone.

Once again, go to the Internet and other media, as well as to schools and children's activities, to get a feel for the interests and developmental levels of the readership that is drawing you. For example, go to www.google.com and select the directory. Click Kids and Teens. Look at the websites under preschool, school time, teen life, and other categories. The arts section has many interesting sites that can give you additional insights into every age group.

Look Deeper: Magazine Specifications

Create a magazine market file that seems to be a match with your interests. Use index cards, a notebook, or your computer to develop a file for each magazine for your initial list of publications. Request sample issues for the magazines and read them. Listings in *Magazine Markets for Children's Writers* will tell you if writers' guidelines, an editorial calendar, or a theme list are available, as well as the cost of a sample copy and the size of the envelope to send with your request. (See page 59 for a sample listing.)

You may find the magazines you're targeting at your local library or newsstand, which will save you time and postage. Or, go to their websites—Web addresses are included in the listings.

Review each of the magazines in more detail for subjects related, or comparable, to yours. You should also check the Reader's Guide to Periodical Literature in your library to see if a target magazine has printed a piece similar to yours within the past two years. You may want to find another magazine or, depending on the publication, develop a new slant if you find that your topic is already well covered.

Study the Magazine and Its Guidelines

Sample issues. Use the Magazine Description Form (see example on page 8) to continue your detailed analysis of the publications, especially those you're beginning to hone in on as good matches. Record what you learn about each magazine. Evaluate how you could shape or present your manuscript to improve your chances of getting it published. If a particular idea or target magazine doesn't work out now, it may in the future—or it may lead to other ideas, angles, or possible markets. Review your market files periodically to generate ideas.

Writers' Guidelines. If the listing notes that a magazine offers writers' guidelines, you should send a letter requesting them with an SASE (see sample on page 9). Many magazines also list their writers' guidelines on their websites. This is specified in the listing. Read writers' guidelines, editorial calendars, and theme lists carefully. They may give you specific topics to write about, but even if you're creating your own, take the guidelines seriously. They are key to the needs of publications and often new writers give them too little weight.

Some guidelines are more detailed and helpful than others, but virtually all will tell you something about the readership, philosophy, and voice, as well as word length requirements, submissions format, and payment. More than that, some guidelines can give writers specific insights into the immediate needs of a magazine. For example, *The Magazine of Science Fiction and Fantasy* guidelines say, "We prefer character-driven stories; we receive a lot of fantasy fiction, but never enough science fiction or humor," while *Junior Baseball* guidelines are directive in another way: "A well-detailed story, full of supporting facts, figures, and anecdotes, makes for a better feature."

Magazine Match List: Subjects

Idea Topic: _____

	Magazine	Audience Age	Similar/Related Subject	Slant	Date Published
1.	_____				
2.	_____				

The guidelines will also indicate the rights a publication purchases, payment policies, and many more specifics—factors you'll consider as you get closer to submission. Many experienced writers do not sell all rights, unless the fee is high enough to be worth it; reselling articles or stories for reprint rights can be an additional source of income. (See the discussion of rights on page 24.)

Read with a Writer's Eye

Your review of sample magazines and guidelines should include:

• **Editorial objective.** Turn to the issue masthead, where the names of the editors are listed. Sometimes the magazine's editorial objective is also stated here. Does your story or article fit its purpose?

• **Audience.** What is the age range of the readers and the characters or children portrayed? For fiction, is your main character at the upper end of that range? Kids want to read about characters their own age or older.

• **Table of contents.** Study the table of contents. Usually, the stories and articles with bylines were written by freelancers like you. Compare the author names there with the editors and staff listed in the masthead to make sure that the publication is not primarily staff-written.

• **Article and story types.** Examine the types of articles and stories in the issue. Does one theme tie the articles and stories together? For example, does every article in a science magazine focus on plants, or do the articles cover a broader range of subjects? If the magazine issues a theme list, review it to see the range of topics. Think about the presentation as well: Is the magazine highly visual or does it rely primarily on text? Will photographs or illustrations be a consideration for you? Are there sidebars, and are you willing to provide those?

• **Style.** How is the writing impacted by the age of the audience? Read each story and

---

Magazine Description Form

Name of Magazine: *Plays*　　　　　　　**Editor:** Elizabeth Preston
Address: P.O. Box 600160, Newton, MA 02460

Freelance Percentage: 100%　　　　**Percentage of Authors Who Are New to the Magazine:** 50%

Description
What subjects does this magazine cover? *Plays* features easy-to-perform, one-act plays for students in elementary school through high school.

Readership
Who are the magazine's typical readers? Teachers, librarians, drama coaches, and home schoolers use this magazine for performance purposes and as part of the curriculum.

Articles and Stories
What particular slants or distinctive characteristics do its articles or stories emphasize? The editor is looking for "wholesome and entertaining" dramatic material.

Potential Market
Is this magazine a potential market? Yes. I have a simple, one-act play for high school students.

Ideas for Articles or Stories
What article, story, or department idea could be submitted? A drama about a chilling fortune-telling episode that leads a group of teens to understand the meaning of self-fulfilling prophecy.

article to get an idea of the style and tone the magazine prefers. Are there numerous three-syllable words, or mostly simple words? Are most sentences simple or complex, or a mixture of both? Is the tone upbeat and casual, or informative and educational? Do the writers speak directly to readers in a conversational way, or is the voice appropriately authoritative?

• **Editor's comments.** Note in the writers' guidelines particularly what *feel* for the magazine the editors provide. *Ladybug*'s guidelines include this important request: "(We) look for beauty of language and a sense of joy or wonder." *Magazine Markets for Children's Writers* includes a section called Editor's Comments in each listing. Study this section carefully as well. The editors give you tips on what they most want to see, or don't need.

Refine Your Magazine List

After you analyze your selected magazines, rank them by how well they match your idea, article or story's subject, style, and target age. Then return to the listings to examine other factors, such as the magazine's freelance potential, its receptivity to new or unpublished writers, rights purchased, and payment.

These facts reveal significant details about the magazine that you can use to your advantage as a freelance writer. For example, many published writers prefer magazines that:

- Publish a high percentage of authors who are new to the magazine;
- Respond in one month as opposed to three;
- Pay on acceptance rather than on publication.

If you're not yet published, however, writing for a nonpaying market may be worth the effort to earn the clips to build published credits. Once you've acquired credentials in these markets, you can list these published pieces in your queries to paying markets.

Ever written for a school or church newsletter, or a volunteer organization? If you don't have published 'clips,' writing samples such as these can also serve to showcase your writing skills and style.

Sample Guidelines Request

> Name
> Address
> City, State ZIP
>
> Date
>
> Dear (Name of Current Editor):
>
> I would like to request a copy of your writers' guidelines and editorial calendar. I have provided a self-addressed, stamped envelope for your convenience.
>
> Sincerely,
>
> Your name

Submitting Your Work to an Editor

Your market study will prepare you to draft a query or cover letter that convinces the right editor of why your idea is suitable for the magazine and why you are the person to write it. When do you send a query, and when should you send a cover letter and manuscript? Should a query be accompanied by an outline or synopsis or other materials? Is a query ever appropriate for fiction?

In your research, you should already have begun to see the variety of submission possibilities. Let's sort them out.

Know What Editors Want

Some editors want the query alone; it's efficient and provides them with enough information to make a decision about the article's appeal to their readers. Others want queries accompanied by a synopsis, outline, or other information for an article. Yet other editors prefer to have a complete article or story to get a full sense of the work you do and whether the subject is a match for them. Expect that the editor who accepts a complete, unsolicited manuscript may require even more revisions or rewrites than if you had queried first.

In reality, queries for magazine fiction are rare, although they've become somewhat more common for book-length fiction. Magazine stories are short enough without being too much for an editor to review.

If the editor asks for a:	*Send:*
Query (nonfiction)	• One-page letter indicating article topic, slant, target readership, word count • Bibliography of research sources • One-page résumé (if requested) • SASE
Query (fiction)	• One-page letter containing a brief synopsis of the plot, indicating target readership and word count • SASE
Complete manuscript (nonfiction)	• Brief cover letter • Manuscript • Bibliography of research sources • List of people interviewed • SASE
Complete manuscript (fiction)	• Brief cover letter • Manuscript • SASE

Keys to Writing a Query Letter

Imagine you're at a writing conference and you step onto an elevator with the editor of a major children's magazine. The editor smiles and asks if you're a writer, and you find yourself in the perfect position to make a pitch for your latest article. The problem: You've only got fifteen seconds, about the time it takes for the elevator to go up one floor.

Just as an "elevator speech" is a key concept in the marketing world, a query letter is the writer's equivalent. Editors look at hundreds of submissions, and a query is your chance to get his or her attention and make a positive impression. In the space of a page, a query tells the editor why your article will benefit that particular magazine and why you are the best person to write it. A good query is not about you; instead, it should focus on the needs of the magazine and how your article addresses those needs.

You may have already written an article and want to sell it to a magazine that only reviews query letters. Or, you may be writing a query in advance of writing an article. Either way, there are several advantages to using a query letter:

- Editors generally respond faster to queries than manuscripts.

- Your chances for a sale increase because, at this early stage, the editor is still able to help mold your manuscript to fit the magazine.

- You save research and writing time by knowing exactly what the editor wants.

Do Your Homework

Before you write your query letter, know the magazine inside and out. Review several sample issues and the guidelines, then tailor your idea to work specifically for that publication. Know the word limit the magazine prefers and whether or not it requires a bibliography of sources. Most editors like articles with quotes from experts in the field you're writing about. Be prepared to tell the editor who you'll interview for the piece. For example, if you want to write an article about robots, you might plan to interview robot designers and include their names in your query letter. Or, if the magazine uses primarily articles from a kid's point of view, track down members of a science club or other youth organization who have experience making robots of their own. It may also help to name an expert who can vet the final manuscript and vouch for its accuracy. Lastly, know whether you can obtain photos—this can often swing a sale.

What Makes a Good Query Letter

A good query letter is short and to the point. If you can't get your idea across in one page or less, your article may not be as tightly focused as it should be.

Below are the basic steps in writing a query (see the examples on pages 13–16):

- Direct your query to a specific editor.

- Begin with a lead paragraph that grabs the editor's interest and conveys your slant. Attention-grabbing techniques like statistics or an unusual "twist" on a topic make an editor want to keep reading.

- Include a brief description of your article that conveys your central idea. This should be very narrow in focus.

- Show how your idea meets the editorial goals of the targeted magazine.

- Indicate approximate word length.

- Provide specific details as to what will be in the article—anecdotes, case histories, statistics, etc.

- Cite sources, research resources, and planned interviews.

- Indicate number and type of photographs or illustrations available. If you can't provide any, don't mention them at all.

- List your publishing credits briefly and, if enclosed, refer to your resume, clips, or writing samples. If you are unpublished, don't draw attention to it. Instead, emphasize relevant or unique experience you may have in regard to the subject.

- Close by asking if the magazine is interested; mention whether your query represents a simultaneous submission.

- Include other information if requested, such as an outline or bibliography.

A Good First Impression

Your query is the first impression the editor will have of you and your work, so take a few extra minutes to make sure it's ready to send.

- Use good quality bond paper.

- The font should be close to Times Roman 12 point.

- Use a letter-quality printout, with crisp, dark type.

- Leave 1 to 1¼-inch margins on all four sides. Single spacing is preferred.

- A query is meant to showcase your writing skills, so proofread for grammar, spelling, typos, etc.

- Make sure your contact information is included in the query in case the editor wants to contact you, along with a self-addressed, stamped envelope or postcard for the editor's reply.

Submitting kid-friendly photos with your manuscript can increase the likelihood of a sale. If you don't have a knack for photography, look for images from trade associations, PR departments, or government organizations—whatever is appropriate for your article.

Email or Snail Mail?

If your target magazine accepts both hard copy and email queries, which should you choose? Email does not always mean faster response times, but it does cut down on the time and cost involved in preparing and mailing a traditional submission package.

It also presents new challenges. Email has changed the style of queries somewhat because it is less formal than print. While this is a welcome change in most cases, be watchful that the tone of your email remains professional at all times. Also, avoid using cutesy email addresses and a too-familiar tone, which turns off editors.

If you do submit via email, check each publisher's guidelines to determine their preferences for the following:

- **File attachments.** Most publishers prefer that submissions be included in the main body of the email, not as an attachment. Once an editor gets to know you, attachments may then be preferable.

- **Electronic format.** Rich text format (RTF), Microsoft Word, and HTML are most commonly used for sending documents electronically; postscript and PDF files are also sometimes accepted.

- **Contact information.** Don't forget to include your contact information in the body of your email, as well as the full title of your work.

- **Subject line.** Unless a publisher has specific directions for the subject line, make yours as informative as possible, i.e., "Submission—How to Write Children's Books."

Query Letter—Checklist

Your query letter will make the difference between a sale and a rejection in today's magazine market. The following checklist and sample query letter offer tips on how to avoid simple mistakes that can cost you a sale.

• Verify that you are writing to the current editor and correct address; double-check the spelling of the name and address.

• Phrase the letter as if the article is in the planning stage. Editors prefer pieces written specifically for their publication, not generic articles.

• Give enough examples of what you will cover to allow the editor to get a feel for the article. Include any unique material, interviews, or primary sources that you will use.

• Note any background or experience you have that gives you credibility in writing this piece for this particular audience. **Include publishing credits if available.** No need to tell the editor if you are unpublished; let your work speak for you. If you have been published, briefly give the editor your publishing history.

• Keep the closing brief and professional; remember to include an SASE.

Address
Phone Number
Email
Date

Jennifer Reed, Editor
Wee Ones E-Magazine
1321 Ridge Road
Baltimore, MD 21228

Dear Ms. Reed:

Imagine in the darkness you see a small white bird with bright yellow eyes. You stare in amazement. Have you ever seen snowy owl chicks? Do you know how they change and grow? Do you know what their favorite food is?

I have written a 436-word article about snowy owl chicks for children six to ten years old. I have read many issues of your magazine and feel that "Babes in the Snow" would make a nice addition. Children love animals and babies, and they will enjoy reading about snowy owl chicks. Children are especially interested in these amazing birds because of the Harry Potter books and movies, which feature a snowy owl named Hedwig. My research on this topic includes an interview with Elaine Gruin, the Education Coordinator at ZOOAMERICA North American Wildlife Park in Hershey, Pennsylvania.

Also included are interesting facts about Harry Potter's snowy owl, a list of material for further reading, a word list, and a word search puzzle. A photo of a male snowy owl is attached for review and possible inclusion. A bibliography is available upon request.

I have had material published in *Kids Holiday Crafts Magazine*, and I am a member of the Society of Children's Book Writers and Illustrators.

This article is available upon request.

Thank you for your consideration.

Sincerely,

Suzanne Miles

Sample Query & Article Outline

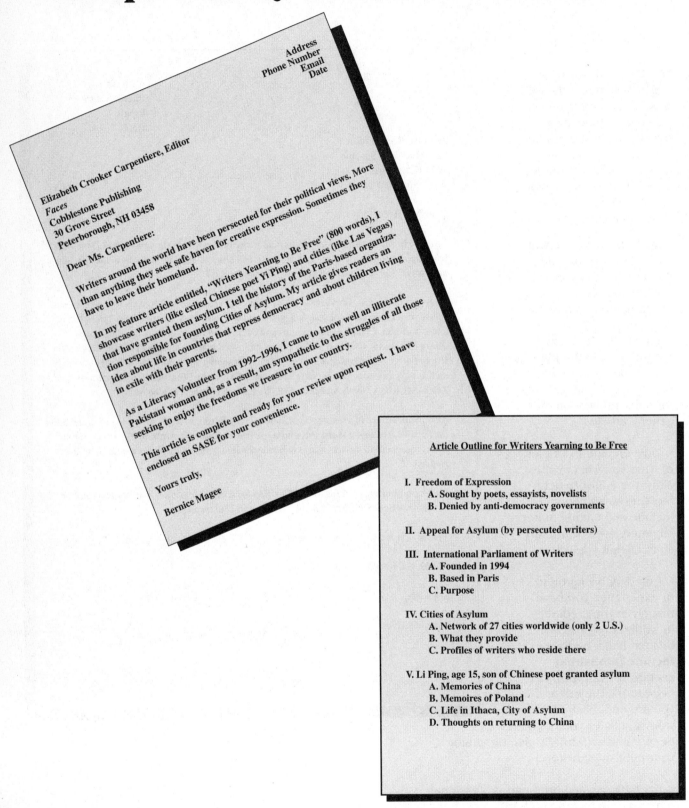

Address
Phone Number
Email
Date

Elizabeth Crooker Carpentiere, Editor
Faces
Cobblestone Publishing
30 Grove Street
Peterborough, NH 03458

Dear Ms. Carpentiere:

Writers around the world have been persecuted for their political views. More than anything they seek safe haven for creative expression. Sometimes they have to leave their homeland.

In my feature article entitled, "Writers Yearning to Be Free" (800 words), I showcase writers (like exiled Chinese poet Yi Ping) and cities (like Las Vegas) that have granted them asylum. I tell the history of the Paris-based organization responsible for founding Cities of Asylum. My article gives readers an idea about life in countries that repress democracy and about children living in exile with their parents.

As a Literacy Volunteer from 1992–1996, I came to know well an illiterate Pakistani woman and, as a result, am sympathetic to the struggles of all those seeking to enjoy the freedoms we treasure in our country.

This article is complete and ready for your review upon request. I have enclosed an SASE for your convenience.

Yours truly,

Bernice Magee

Article Outline for Writers Yearning to Be Free

I. Freedom of Expression
   A. Sought by poets, essayists, novelists
   B. Denied by anti-democracy governments

II. Appeal for Asylum (by persecuted writers)

III. International Parliament of Writers
   A. Founded in 1994
   B. Based in Paris
   C. Purpose

IV. Cities of Asylum
   A. Network of 27 cities worldwide (only 2 U.S.)
   B. What they provide
   C. Profiles of writers who reside there

V. Li Ping, age 15, son of Chinese poet granted asylum
   A. Memories of China
   B. Memoires of Poland
   C. Life in Ithaca, City of Asylum
   D. Thoughts on returning to China

Sample Query Letters

Ms. Marileta Robinson
Highlights for Children
803 Church Street
Honesdale, PA 18431

Address
Phone Number
Email
Date

Dear Ms. Robinson:

Pat Acton's artwork is displayed in fifteen different Ripley's Believe It or Not museums all around the world. What makes his models so unusual is that they are constructed from matchsticks—the same wooden matchsticks that readers may have used to light a campfire.

Pat has had a longtime interest in woodworking beginning with the fully enclosed treehouse he built as a child, complete with glass windows and a wood stove for heating. My article, "Stick by Stick," will include information about Pat's handiwork as a child and how he got started with matchstick models. It will also highlight projects that I believe would be of special interest to children. They include built-to-scale models of the U.S. Capitol and the *Challenger* space shuttle. I think children will be fascinated with details such as the fact that the 12-foot-long U.S. Capitol model took 478,000 matchsticks, ten gallons of carpenter's glue, and over 2,000 hours to construct.

Could I send you the completed article for your consideration? My writing experience includes 14 biographies for children and young adults. My article, "Fit to Be President," was published in the January 2003 issue of *Highlights for Children*.

Thank you for your time and I look forward to hearing from you.

Sincerely,

Barbara Kramer

Address
Phone Number
Email
Date

Nancy Cavanaugh, Editor
Fandangle Magazine
14 Schult Street
Keene, NH 03431

Dear Ms. Cavanaugh:

Molly Moose is hungry for the scrumptious berries that grow in the meadow. But when she arrives in the meadow, she discovers that all the delicious berries are gone. Travel through the forest with Molly Moose as her wildlife friends try to help her figure out the mystery of the missing berries. Help Molly Moose discover that the missing berries were right "under her nose" all along!

I noticed on your editorial calendar that you have a need for stories about berries in your July issue. I believe "Molly Moose and the Missing Berries" would make a fun story for this theme.

Would you be interested in reviewing this 700-word story? I look forward to your response. I have enclosed a writing sample and an SASE for your convenience.

Sincerely,

Shelly Nicholson

Sample Query Letters

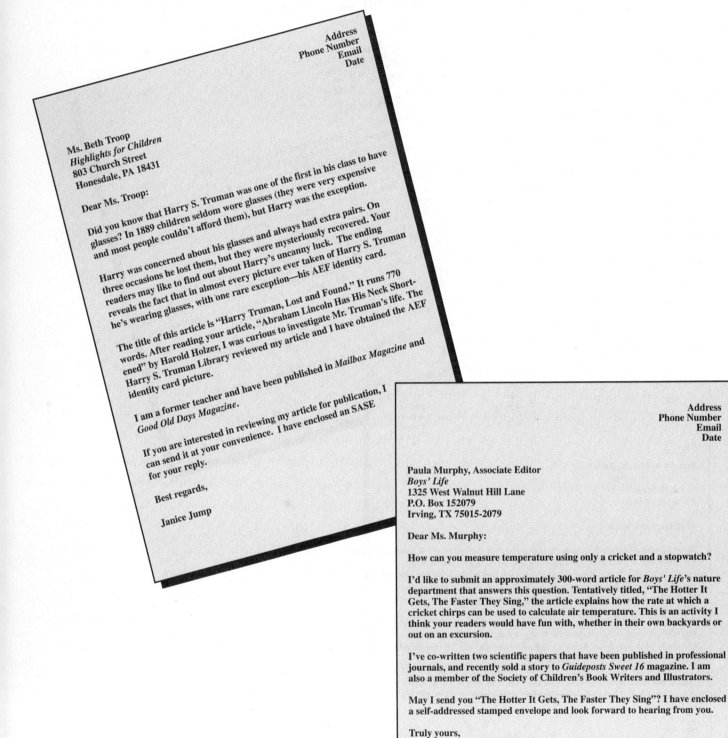

Address
Phone Number
Email
Date

Ms. Beth Troop
Highlights for Children
803 Church Street
Honesdale, PA 18431

Dear Ms. Troop:

Did you know that Harry S. Truman was one of the first in his class to have glasses? In 1889 children seldom wore glasses (they were very expensive and most people couldn't afford them), but Harry was the exception.

Harry was concerned about his glasses and always had extra pairs. On three occasions he lost them, but they were mysteriously recovered. Your readers may like to find out about Harry's uncanny luck. The ending reveals the fact that in almost every picture ever taken of Harry S. Truman he's wearing glasses, with one rare exception—his AEF identity card.

The title of this article is "Harry Truman, Lost and Found." It runs 770 words. After reading your article, "Abraham Lincoln Has His Neck Shortened" by Harold Holzer, I was curious to investigate Mr. Truman's life. The Harry S. Truman Library reviewed my article and I have obtained the AEF identity card picture.

I am a former teacher and have been published in *Mailbox Magazine* and *Good Old Days Magazine*.

If you are interested in reviewing my article for publication, I can send it at your convenience. I have enclosed an SASE for your reply.

Best regards,

Janice Jump

Address
Phone Number
Email
Date

Paula Murphy, Associate Editor
Boys' Life
1325 West Walnut Hill Lane
P.O. Box 152079
Irving, TX 75015-2079

Dear Ms. Murphy:

How can you measure temperature using only a cricket and a stopwatch?

I'd like to submit an approximately 300-word article for *Boys' Life*'s nature department that answers this question. Tentatively titled, "The Hotter It Gets, The Faster They Sing," the article explains how the rate at which a cricket chirps can be used to calculate air temperature. This is an activity I think your readers would have fun with, whether in their own backyards or out on an excursion.

I've co-written two scientific papers that have been published in professional journals, and recently sold a story to *Guideposts Sweet 16* magazine. I am also a member of the Society of Children's Book Writers and Illustrators.

May I send you "The Hotter It Gets, The Faster They Sing"? I have enclosed a self-addressed stamped envelope and look forward to hearing from you.

Truly yours,

Jodie Mangor

Preparing a Manuscript Package

The following guide shows how to prepare and mail a professional-looking manuscript package. However, you should always adhere to an individual magazine's submission requirements as detailed in its writers' guidelines and its listing in this directory.

Cover Letter Tips

Always keep your cover letter concise and to the point. Provide essential information only.

If the letter accompanies an unsolicited manuscript submission (see below), indicate that your manuscript is enclosed and mention its title and word length. If you're sending the manu-script after the editor responded favorably to your query letter, indicate that the editor requested to see the enclosed manuscript.

Provide a brief description of the piece and a short explanation of how it fits the editor's needs. List any publishing credits or other pertinent qualifications. If requested in the guidelines or listing, note any material or sources you can provide. Indicate if the manuscript is being sent to other magazines as well (a simultaneous submission). Mention that you have enclosed a self-addressed, stamped envelope for return of the manuscript.

Address
Phone Number
Email
Date

Lacey Louwagie, Senior Editor
New Moon Magazine
2 W. First St. #101
Duluth, MN 55802

Dear Ms. Louwagie,

Did you know that the first known martyr for women's rights was an Iranian woman? Step back in time to the mid-1800s and discover the fearless efforts of a great heroine who paid the ultimate price to make life better for women everywhere.

My profile/biography titled, "She Died for Women's Rights," is 1,030 words. It reveals the life of Tahirih and how she traveled throughout the Middle East to empower women to reject their oppressed status during a time when they were considered lower than dirt.

Young women will learn some Middle Eastern history and gain inspiration to advance even further. This article is a great fit for *New Moon*'s Herstory section and your upcoming theme focusing on pride and prejudice.

As an Iranian woman, I grew up reading and hearing about Tahirih and now I wish to share her story with other young women. I have been published in *Skipping Stones* magazine and in several local publications here in San Diego.

I have enclosed the manuscript along with a bibliography. I look forward to hearing from you.

Sincerely,

Celia Taghdiri

*Subject/
Specifications:*
A brief description of the topic and its potential interest to the magazine's readers. Word length, age range, availability of photos, and other submission details.

*Publishing
Credits or
Relevant
Experience*

Closing:
Be formal and direct.

Standard Manuscript Format

The format for preparing manuscripts is fairly standard—an example is shown below. Double-space manuscript text, leaving 1- to 1½-inch margins on the top, bottom, and sides. Indent 5 spaces for paragraphs.

In the upper left corner of the first page (also known as the title page), single space your name, address, phone number, and email address. In the upper right corner of that page, place your word count.

Center the title with your byline below it halfway down the page, approximately 5 inches. Then begin the manuscript text 4 lines below your byline.

In the upper left corner of the following pages, type your last name, the page number, and a word or two of your title. Then, space down 4 lines and continue the text of the manuscript.

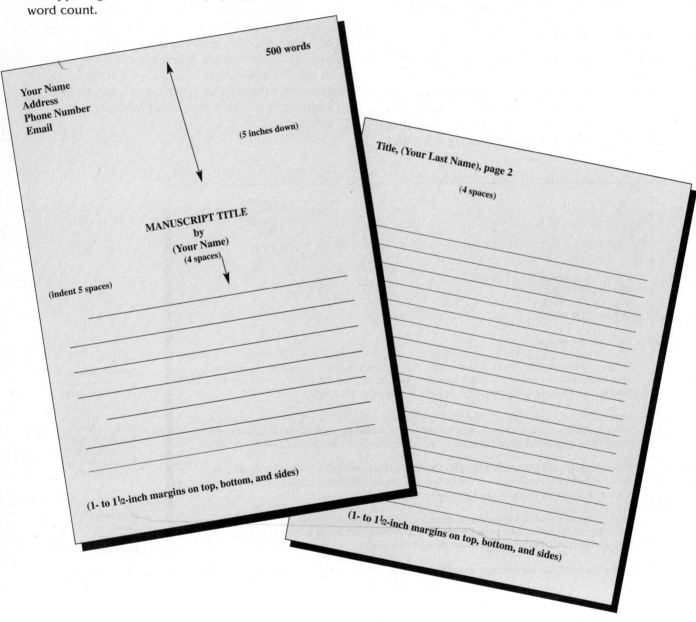

500 words

Your Name
Address
Phone Number
Email

(5 inches down)

MANUSCRIPT TITLE
by
(Your Name)
(4 spaces)

(indent 5 spaces)

(1- to 1½-inch margins on top, bottom, and sides)

Title, (Your Last Name), page 2

(4 spaces)

(1- to 1½-inch margins on top, bottom, and sides)

Sample Cover Letters

Mr. Marvin Wengerd, Editor
Nature Friend
2673 Township Road 421
Sugarcreek, OH 44681

Address
Phone Number
Email
Date

Dear Mr. Wengerd:

What can fly but would rather run, lives in the wild in almost every area of the United States, was once thought to be noble enough to be our national bird, and is the staple of Thanksgiving dinners throughout the nation?

You have most likely guessed the turkey and you are correct. Enclosed is an article of about 800 words tentatively titled "My Neighbors Are a Bunch of Turkeys," as well as a sidebar titled "Ten Strange Turkey Facts" of about 370 words.

Wild turkeys are the only domesticated animal native to North America and thus quite an important part of our history and environment. Living on a farm, I have seen all sorts of wildlife roaming the meadows, fields, and woods. This is the first time I was able to observe a species so close and so often as to be able to research my field notes. I think your young readers will be as intrigued as I have been about this bird that can be found in their backyards.

Thank you for your time and I look forward to hearing from you.

Sincerely,

Jan E. Fetherolf-Shick

Enc.: Manuscript, SASE

Marileta Robinson, Senior Editor
Highlights for Children
803 Church Street
Honesdale, PA 18431

Dear Ms. Robinson:

I was first introduced to the Russian folktale, "The Giant Turnip," when I was in my junior-high Russian language class. Our teacher showed a film and I can still remember the playful repetition of the words in the story: *"Tan-yet, potan-yet, vee-tan-yet nee mogoot"* (which roughly translates to "They pulled and they pulled, but weren't able to pull the turnip out"). Since then, I have come across this story in many places. I have retold this traditional tale in rebus format and hope that you might consider it for use in *Highlights for Children*.

The main theme of "The Giant Turnip" is a reminder that even the smallest of all can make a difference. The story also shows how a great goal can be accomplished by working together. But what beginning readers might find most appealing is the playful repetition that is as much a part of the story as the plot.

My great-grandmother and great-grandfather were from an area near St. Petersburg, Russia, and I grew up influenced by the language and traditions that they brought with them to America.

I hope you will like the story of "The Giant Turnip." I have enclosed a bibliography and an SASE for your convenience.

Best regards,

Diana Calio

Sample Cover Letters

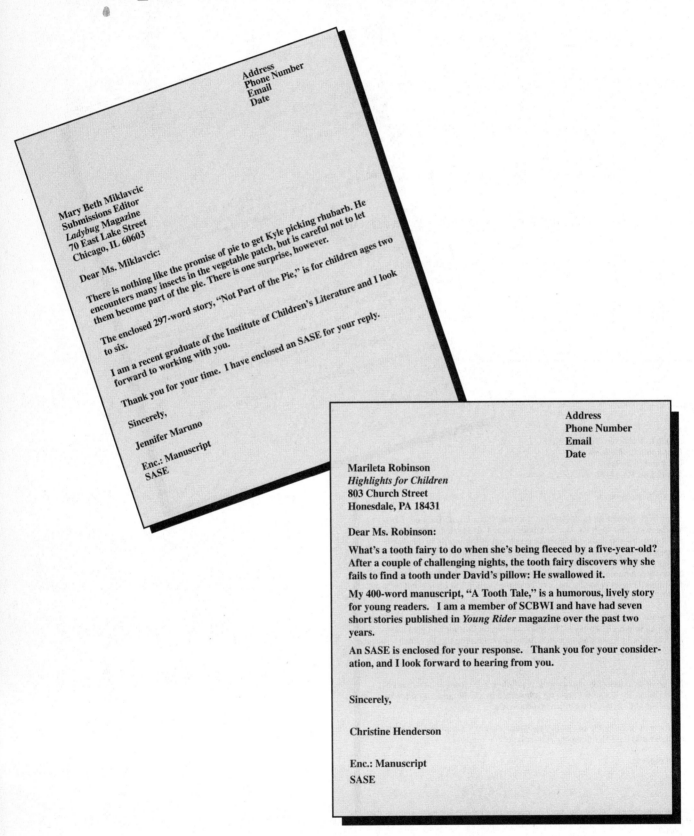

Address
Phone Number
Email
Date

Mary Beth Miklavcic
Submissions Editor
Ladybug Magazine
70 East Lake Street
Chicago, IL 60603

Dear Ms. Miklavcic:

There is nothing like the promise of pie to get Kyle picking rhubarb. He encounters many insects in the vegetable patch, but is careful not to let them become part of the pie. There is one surprise, however.

The enclosed 297-word story, "Not Part of the Pie," is for children ages two to six.

I am a recent graduate of the Institute of Children's Literature and I look forward to working with you.

Thank you for your time. I have enclosed an SASE for your reply.

Sincerely,

Jennifer Maruno

Enc.: Manuscript
SASE

Address
Phone Number
Email
Date

Marileta Robinson
Highlights for Children
803 Church Street
Honesdale, PA 18431

Dear Ms. Robinson:

What's a tooth fairy to do when she's being fleeced by a five-year-old? After a couple of challenging nights, the tooth fairy discovers why she fails to find a tooth under David's pillow: He swallowed it.

My 400-word manuscript, "A Tooth Tale," is a humorous, lively story for young readers.   I am a member of SCBWI and have had seven short stories published in *Young Rider* magazine over the past two years.

An SASE is enclosed for your response.   Thank you for your consideration, and I look forward to hearing from you.

Sincerely,

Christine Henderson

Enc.: Manuscript
SASE

Sample Cover Letter & Bibliography

Address
Phone Number
Email
Date

Ms. Julia M. Messina
Cricket Magazine
P.O. Box 300
Peru, IL 61354

Re: Manuscript "Born to Draw: James McNeill Whistler"

Dear Ms. Messina,

It has been 100 years since American painter James Abbott McNeill Whistler died. Most Americans know little more about him than that he painted a portrait of his mother. Yet Whistler was a fascinating character and one of the most original painters of his time.

Enclosed is my manuscript intended for eight- to twelve-year-olds that I think *Cricket* readers will enjoy. I am always willing to discuss changes that would make the manuscript stronger or a better fit for your magazine. Copies of my sources are available upon request.

My nonfiction work has been published in newspapers, anthologies, and magazines, including *Cricket*. I am writing a young adult biography of Whistler and received a Letter of Merit for it from SCBWI, of which I am a member. Note: This article is not taken from the book.

Thank you for your time and consideration. I look forward to hearing from you.

Sincerely,

Kristina Cliff-Evans

Enc: bibliography/ms/SAE/IRC

Bibliography for "Born to Draw"

Books

Anderson, Ronald and Anne Koval. *James McNeill Whistler: Beyond the Myth.* New York: Carroll & Graf Publishers, Inc., 1994.

Curry, David Park. *James McNeill Whistler: Uneasy Pieces.* Richmond, VA: Virginia Museum of Fine Arts with the Quantuck Lane Press, New York, 2004.

Dorment, Richard and Margaret F. MacDonald. *James McNeill Whistler.* London: Tate Gallery Publications, 1994.

Fleming, Gordon. *James Abbott McNeill Whistler, A Life.* New York: St. Martin's Press, 1991.

Peters, Lisa N. *James NcNeill Whistler.* New York: Todtri Book Publishers, 1996.

Web Sites

Economic History Services, EH.Net, 2002. http://www.eh.net/hmit/exchanger-ates/. Lawrence H. Officer, "Exchange rate between the United States dollar and forty other countries, 1913-1999." Accessed 5/08/2005.

Traditional Fine Arts Organization, Inc. http://www.tfaoi.com/aa/4aa/4aa170.htm. Mr. Whistler's Galleries: Avant-Garde in Victorian London." Accessed 6/3/2005.

Bibliography

Nothing inspires more confidence in you as a writer than a thorough bibliography. More than just a list of materials you plan on using (or have already used) to prepare your article, a well-rounded, diverse bibliography can be an important tool to help sell your writing. Not only does it show that you've properly acknowledged and credited your sources of information, but also that the finished piece is likely to be supported by strong evidence found in a variety of credible sources. For many editors, extensive research often indicates originality in a manuscript.

Some magazines require a bibliography as part of a submission package for nonfiction articles. (Bibliographies are rarely required for fiction, with the possible exception of historical fiction.) Unique research methods are required for every project but, in general, the bibliography should be made up of resources that are both historical and current, target adults and children, and cover primary and secondary sources. It should also show that you plan on culling information from other sources, such as interviews with experts or other relevant individuals (a profile subject and those who know him or her, for example), websites, and museums. And don't hesitate to think outside the box when it comes to information gathering: maps, court documents, diaries, old photographs, song lyrics, census data, and other sources offer a wealth of information that can make your work shine.

Citation styles vary greatly, but several references are available and generally accepted for bibliographic format. Among these are: *The Chicago Manual of Style; Modern Language Association (MLA) Handbook*; or handbooks by news organizations such as the *New York Times*.

Need an expert interview to enhance your bibliography? Professional member associations, consumer advocacy organizations, and large corporations offer a host of potential interview subjects.

Sample Bibliography

Bibliography for "The Doctor is In: Cleaner Fish on the Coral Reef"

Copley, Jon. "Coral Reefs Operate Free Market Economy." *New Scientist*, April 2002.

Dr. James D. Franklin, Scientist, National Coral Reef Institute, interview.

Murphy, Richard C. *Coral Reefs: Cities Under the Sea.* Princeton, NJ: Darwin Press, 2002.

Natural History Museum, "Life on the Reef." http://www.nhm.ac.uk/nature-online/life.html

Sale, Peter F. *Coral Reef Fishes: Dynamics and Diversity in a Complex Ecosystem.* Burlington, MA: Academic Press, 2002.

Preparing a Résumé

S everal publications in this directory request that prospective writers send a list of publishing credits or enclose a résumé with their submission. As you read through the listings, you will notice that some editors want to see a résumé only, while others may request a résumé with a query letter, writing samples, or a complete manuscript.

By reviewing a résumé, an editor can determine if a prospective writer has the necessary experience to research and write material for that publication.

A résumé that you submit to a magazine is different from one you would submit when applying for a job, because it emphasizes writing experience, memberships in writing associations, and education. This type of résumé does not list all of your work experience or every association to which you belong, but should include only those credentials that demonstrate experience related to the magazine's editorial requirements. In the case of educational or special interest publications, be sure to include pertinent work experience.

No one style is preferred, but make sure your name and email address (if you have one) appear at the top of the page. Keep your résumé short and concise—it should not be more than one page long.

Sample Résumés

Joanna Coates
Address
Phone
Email

EDUCATION:

University of Missouri, Columbia, MO
1980   M.Ed. Reading
1975   B.A. English Education

Missouri Certified Teacher of English and Reading Specialist

TEACHING EXPERIENCE:
1997–present   Instructor
                Adult Continuing Education ESL Classes
                Springfield College, Springfield, MO

1981-1995   Classroom Teacher
             Middle School English and Reading
             John Jay Middle School, Thornfield, MO

EDUCATIONAL MATERIAL PUBLISHED:
             Educational Insights
1995   FUN WITH READING II
             Story/activity kit
1993   FUN WITH READING I
             Story/activity kit

MEMBERSHIP:
Society of Children's Book Writers and Illustrators

Maria Lital
Address
Phone
Email

EDUCATION:
1989   Bachelor of Arts
            History/Journalism
            University of North Carolina,
            Chapel Hill, North Carolina

WORK EXPERIENCE:
1998–present   Media Sales Representative,
                Clarkson Ledger; Ripley, Tennessee

1996-1998   Researcher/Librarian, Station WBXI;
                Danville, Kentucky

1993–1996   Researcher, *Family News*; Raleigh, North
                Carolina

1990–1993   Assistant Librarian, Public Library; Edenton,
                North Carolina

RELATED ACTIVITIES:
1998–present   Newsletter Editor; St. James Church, Ripley,
                Tennessee

1998–present   Historical Tour Guide; Ripley,
                Tennessee, Historical Association

1996–present   Active in Civil War Reenactments

MEMBERSHIP:
1996–present   American Library Association

Copyright and Permissions

Just like the movie you watched last night and the CD you listened to on the way to work this morning, your magazine article is one of many creative works that is afforded the protection of copyright. As one of the nation's "copyright-based industries," publishing relies heavily on the concept of obtaining legal ownership of written works. When you write an article, you own the legal rights to the manuscript, as well as the right to decide how it is reproduced and, for certain works, how it is performed or displayed.

As of 1998, your heirs can also enjoy the fruits of your labor: That's when Congress passed the Copyright Term Extension Act, which offers you copyright protection for your work created during or after 1978 for your lifetime plus 70 years, until you choose to sell all or part of the copyright for this work.

Do You Need to Register Your Work?

Thanks to copyright law, your work is protected from the moment it is recorded in a tangible medium, such as a computer file or on paper, without any need for legal action or counsel. You don't even need to register your work with the United States Copyright Office; in fact, most editors view an author's copyright notice on manuscripts as the sign of an amateur, or a signal that the author doesn't trust the publication. A copy of the manuscript and a dated record of your submission will provide proof of creation, should the need arise.

If you do decide to register your work, obtain an application form and directions on the correct way to file your copyright application. Write to the Library of Congress, Copyright Office, 101 Independence Ave. S. E., Washington, DC 20559-6000. These forms and directions are also available online in Adobe Acrobat format at: www.copyright.gov/forms. Copyright registration fees are currently $30.

If you have registered your unpublished manuscript with the Library of Congress, notify your editor of that fact once it is accepted for publication.

Rights Purchased by Magazines

As a writer and copyright holder, you have the right to decide how your work should be shared with the world. By agreeing to publication in a magazine, you also agree to transfer some of your rights over to the magazine so that your article can be printed and distributed as part of that publication. A publisher is restricted, however, on when, how, and where he or she may publish your manuscript—terms that are set down in a publishing contract. Below is a list of common rights that are purchased by magazines:

All World Rights: The publisher purchases all rights to publish your work anywhere in the world any number of times. This includes all forms of media (both current and those which may be developed later). The publisher also has the right to all future use of the work, including reprints, syndication, creation of derivative works, and use in databases. You no longer have the right to sell or reproduce the work, unless you can negotiate for the return of certain rights (for example, book rights).

All World Serial Rights: The publisher purchases all rights to publish your work in newspapers, magazines, and other serial publications throughout the world any number of times. You retain all other rights, such as the right to use it as a chapter in a book.

First Rights: A publisher acquires the right to publish your work for the first time in any specified media. Electronic and nontraditional markets often seek these rights. All other rights, including reprint rights, belong to you.

Electronic Rights: Publishers use this as a catch-all for inclusion in any type of electronic publication, such as CD-ROM, websites, ezines, or in an electronic database.

First North American Serial Rights: The publisher can publish your work for the first time in a U.S. or Canadian periodical. You retain the book and North American reprint rights, as well as first rights to a foreign market.

Second or Reprint Rights: This allows a publication non-exclusive rights to print the material for the second time. You may not authorize second publication to occur until after the work has appeared in print by the publisher who bought first rights.

One-time Rights: Often bought by regional publications, this means the publication has bought the right to use the material once. You may continue to sell the material elsewhere; however, you should inform the publisher if this work is being simultaneously considered for publication in a competing magazine.

You should be aware that an agreement may limit a publisher to the right to publish your work in certain media (e.g., magazines and other periodicals only) or the agreement may include wider-ranging rights (e.g., the right to publish the manuscript in a book or an audiocassette). The right may be limited to publishing within a specific geographic region or in a specific language. Any rights you retain allow you to resell the manuscript within the parameters of your agreement.

It is becoming increasingly common for magazines to purchase all rights, especially those that host Internet sites and make archives of previously published articles available to readers. Unless you have extensive publishing credentials, you may not want to jeopardize the opportunity to be published by insisting on selling limited rights.

E-zines typically purchase both exclusive and non-exclusive electronic rights. They may want to publish your article exclusively for a particular period of time (usually one year). After that you may be free to sell it elsewhere or place it on your own website, while the original e-zine continues to display or archive the article.

Contracts and Agreements

Typically, when a publisher indicates an interest in your manuscript, he or she specifies what rights the publication will acquire. Then usually, but not always, a publisher will send you a letter of agreement or a standard written contract spelling out the terms of the agreement.

If a publisher does not send you a written contract or agreement and appears to be relying on oral consent, you need to consider your options. While an oral agreement may be legally binding, it is not as easy to enforce as a written one. To pro-tect your interests, draft a letter outlining the terms as you understand them (e.g., a 500-word article without photos, first North American serial rights, paying on acceptance at $.05 a word). Send two copies of the letter to the editor (with a self-addressed, stamped envelope), asking him or her to sign one and return it to you if the terms are correct.

Work Made for Hire

Another term that is appearing more frequently in contracts is work made for hire. As a freelance writer, most editors treat you as an independent contractor (not an employee) who writes articles for their publication. Magazine editors can assign or commission articles to freelancers as works made for hire, making the finished article property of the publisher.

Under current copyright laws, only certain types of commissioned works are considered works made for hire, and only when both the publisher and the commissioned writer agree in writing. These works typically include items such as contributions to "collective works" such as magazines. A contract or agreement clearly stating that the material is a work made for hire must be signed by both parties and be in place before the material is written. Once a writer agrees to these terms, he or she no longer has any rights to the work.

Note that a pre-existing piece, such as an unsolicited manuscript that is accepted for publication, is not considered a commissioned work.

Guidelines for Permission to Quote

When you want to quote another writer's words in a manuscript you're preparing, you must get that writer's permission. If you don't, you could be sued for copyright infringement. Here are some guidelines:

- Any writing published in the U.S. prior to 1923 is in the public domain, as are works created by the U.S. government. Such material may be quoted without permission, but the source should be cited.

- No specific limits are set as to the length of permitted quotations in your articles: different publishers have various requirements. Generally, if you quote more than a handful of words, you should seek permission. Always remember to credit your sources.

- The doctrine of "fair use" allows quoting portions of a copyrighted work for certain purposes, as in a review, news reporting, nonprofit educational uses, or research. Contrary to popular belief, there is no absolute word limit on fair use. But as a general rule, never quote more than a few successive paragraphs from a book or article and credit the source.

- If you're submitting a manuscript that contains quoted material, you'll need to obtain permission from the source to quote the material before it is published. If you're uncertain about what to do, your editor should be able to advise you.

It's important for freelance writers to be as knowledgeable about selling their work as they are about creating it. For real-world advice, check out writers' groups (such as the Authors Guild), which sometimes offer contract advice, sample contracts, and tips on contract negotiation.

Resources

Interested in finding out more about writers and their rights under the law? Check these sources for further information:

The Publishing Law Center
www.publaw.com/legal.html

The Copyright Handbook: What Every Writer Needs to Know, 9th Edition by Attorney Stephen Fishman. Nolo, 2006.

The Writer's Legal Guide, 3rd Edition by Tad Crawford. Allworth Press, 2002.

Last Steps and Follow Up

Before mailing your manuscript, check the pages for neatness, readability, and proper page order. Proofread for typographical errors. Redo pages if necessary. Keep a copy of the manuscript for your records.

Mailing Requirements

Assemble the pages (unstapled) and place your cover letter on top of the first page.

Send manuscripts over 5 pages in length in a 9x12 or 10x13 manila envelope. Include a same-size SASE marked "First Class." If submitting to a foreign magazine, enclose the proper amount of International Reply Coupons (IRC) for return postage. Mail manuscripts under 5 pages in a large business-size envelope with a same-size SASE folded inside.

Package your material carefully and address the outer envelope to the magazine editor. Send your submission via first-class or priority mail. Don't use certified or registered mail. (See Postage Information, page 30.)

Follow Up with the Editor

Some writers contend that waiting for an editor to respond is the hardest part of writing. But wait you must. Editors usually respond within the time period specified in the listings.

If you don't receive a response by the stated response time, allow at least three weeks to pass before you contact the editor. At that time, send a letter with a self-addressed, stamped envelope requesting to know the status of your submission.

The exception to this general rule is when you send a return postcard with a manuscript. In that case, look for your postcard about three weeks after mailing the manuscript. If you don't receive it by then, write to the editor requesting confirmation that it was received.

If more than two months pass after the stated response time and you don't receive any response, send a letter withdrawing your work from consideration. At that point, you can send your query or manuscript to the next publication on your list.

What You Can Expect

The most common responses to a submission are an impersonal rejection letter, a personalized rejection letter, an offer to look at your material "on speculation," or an assignment.

If you receive an impersonal rejection note, revise your manuscript if necessary, and send your work to the next editor on your list. If you receive a personal note, send a thank-you note. If you receive either of the last two responses, you know what to do!

Set Up a Tracking System

To help you keep track of the status of your submissions, you may want to establish a system in a notebook, in a computer file, or on file cards (see below).

This will keep you organized and up-to-date on the status of your queries and manuscripts and on the need to follow up with certain editors.

SENT QUERIES TO THE FOLLOWING PUBLICATIONS						
Editor	Publication	Topic	Date Sent	Postage	Accepted/ Rejected	Rights Offered

SENT MANUSCRIPTS TO THE FOLLOWING PUBLICATIONS						
Editor	Publication	Title	Date Sent	Postage	Accepted/ Rejected	Rights Offered

Frequently Asked Questions

How do I request a sample copy and writers' guidelines?

Write a brief note to the magazine: "Please send me a recent sample copy and writers' guidelines. If there is any charge, please enclose an invoice and I will pay upon receipt." The magazine's website, if it has one, offers a faster and less expensive alternative. Many companies put a part of the magazine, writers' guidelines, and sometimes a theme list or editorial calendar on the Internet.

How do I calculate the amount of postage for a sample copy?

Check the listing in this directory. In some cases the amount of postage will be listed. If the number of pages is given, use that to estimate the amount of postage by using the postage chart at the end of this section. For more information on postage and how to obtain stamps, see page 30.

Should my email submission 'package' be different than a submission via snail mail?

In general, an email submission should contain the same elements as a mailed one—i.e. a solid article description, sources, etc. In all cases, writers' guidelines should be followed to the letter when it comes to sending writing samples, bibliographies, and other requirements, either as separate file attachments or embedded in the email text.

What do I put in a cover letter if I have no publishing credits or relevant personal experience?

In this case, you may want to forego a formal cover letter and send your manuscript with a brief letter stating: "Enclosed is my manuscript, (Insert Title), for your review." For more information on cover letters, see pages 17–20.

How long should I wait before contacting an editor after I have submitted my manuscript?

The response time given in the listings can vary, and it's a good idea to wait three to four weeks after the stated response time before sending a brief note to the editor asking about the status of your manuscript. You might use this opportunity to add a new sales pitch or include additional material to show that the topic is continuing to generate interest. If you do not get a satisfactory response or you want to send your manuscript elsewhere, send a certified letter to the editor withdrawing the work from consideration and requesting its return. You are then free to submit the work to another magazine.

I don't need my manuscript returned. How do I indicate that to an editor?

With the capability to store manuscripts electronically and print out additional copies easily, some writers keep postage costs down by enclosing a self-addressed, stamped postcard (SASP) saying, "No need to return my manuscript. Please use this postcard to advise me of the status of my manuscript. Thank you."

Common Publishing Terms

All rights: Contractual agreement by which a publisher acquires the copyright and all use of author's material (see page 24).

Anthology: A collection of selected literary pieces.

Anthropomorphization: Attributing human form or personality to things not human (i.e., animals).

Assignment: Manuscript commissioned by an editor for a stated fee.

Bimonthly: A publication that appears every two months.

Biweekly: A publication issued every two weeks.

Byline: Author's name credited at the heading of an article.

Caption: Description or text accompanying an illustration or photograph.

CD-ROM (compact disc read-only-memory)**:** Non-erasable compact disc containing data that can be read by a computer.

Clip: Sample of a published work.

Contributor's copies: Copies of the publication issue in which the writer's work appears.

Copyedit: To edit with close attention to style and mechanics.

Copyright: Legal rights that protect an author's work (see page 24).

Cover letter: Brief letter sent with a manuscript introducing the writer and presenting the materials enclosed (see page 17).

Disk submission: Manuscript that is submitted on a computer disk.

Early readers: Children 4 to 7 years.

Editorial calendar: List of topics, themes, or special sections that are planned for upcoming issues for a specific time period.

Electronic submission: Manuscript transmitted to an editor from one computer to another through a modem.

Email (electronic mail)**:** Messages sent from one computer to another via computer network or modem.

English-language rights: The right to publish a manuscript in any English-speaking country.

Filler: Short item that fills out a page (e.g., joke, light verse, or fun fact).

First serial rights: The right to publish a work for the first time in a periodical; often limited to a specific geographical region (e.g., North America or Canada) (see page 24).

Genre: Category of fiction characterized by a particular style, form, or content, such as mystery or fantasy.

Glossy: Photo printed on shiny rather than matte-finish paper.

Guidelines: See **Writers' guidelines.**

In-house: See **Staff written.**

International Reply Coupon (IRC): Coupon exchangeable in any foreign country for postage on a single-rate, surface-mailed letter.

Kill fee: Percentage of the agreed-upon fee paid to a writer if an editor decides not to use a purchased manuscript.

Layout: Plan for the arrangement of text and artwork on a printed page.

Lead: Beginning of an article.

Lead time: Length of time between assembling and printing an issue.

Libel: Any false published statement intended to expose another to public ridicule or personal loss.

Manuscript: A typewritten or computer-printed version of a document (as opposed to a published version).

Masthead: The printed matter in a newspaper or periodical that gives the title and pertinent details of ownership, advertising rates, and subscription rates.

Middle-grade readers: Children 8 to 12 years.

Modem: An internal device or a small electrical box that plugs into a computer; used to transmit data between computers, often via telephone lines.

Ms/mss: Manuscript/manuscripts.

One-time rights: The right to publish a piece once, often not the first time (see page 25).

On spec: Refers to writing "on speculation," without an editor's commitment to purchase the manuscript.

Outline: Summary of a manuscript's contents, usually nonfiction, organized under subheadings with descriptive sentences under each.

Payment on acceptance: Author is paid following an editor's decision to accept a manuscript.

Payment on publication: Author is paid following the publication of the manuscript.

Pen name/pseudonym: Fictitious name used by an author.

Pre-K: Children under 5 years of age; also known as *preschool.*

Proofread: To read and mark errors, usually in printed text.

Query: Letter to an editor to promote interest in a manuscript or an idea.

Rebus story: A "see and say" story form, using pictures followed by the written words; often written for pre-readers.

Refereed journal: Publication that requires all manuscripts be reviewed by an editorial or advisory board.

Reprint: Another printing of an article or story; can be in a different magazine format, such as an anthology.

Reprint rights: See **Second serial rights.**

Response time: Average length of time for an editor to accept or reject a submission and contact the writer with his or her decision.

Résumé: Account of one's qualifications, including educational and professional background, as well as publishing credits.

SAE: Self-addressed envelope (no postage).

SASE: Self-addressed, stamped envelope.

SASP: Self-addressed stamped postcard.

Second serial rights: The right to publish a manuscript that has appeared in another publication; also known as *Reprint rights* (see page 24).

Semiannual: Occurring every six months or twice a year.

Semimonthly: Occurring twice a month.

Semiweekly: Occurring twice a week.

Serial: A publication issued as one of a consecutively numbered and indefinitely continued series.

Serial rights: See **First serial rights.**

Sidebar: A short article that accompanies a feature article and highlights one aspect of the feature's subject.

Simultaneous submission: Manuscript submitted to more than one publisher at the same time; also known as multiple submission.

Slant: Specific approach to a subject to appeal to a certain readership.

Slush pile: Term used within the publishing industry to describe unsolicited manuscripts.

Solicited manuscript: Manuscript that an editor has requested or agreed to consider.

Staff written: Prepared by members of the magazine's staff; also known as *in-house.*

Syndication rights: The right to distribute serial rights to a given work through a syndicate of periodicals.

Synopsis: Condensed description or summary of a manuscript.

Tabloid: Publication printed on an ordinary newspaper page, turned sideways and folded in half.

Tearsheet: A page from a newspaper or magazine (periodical) containing a printed story or article.

Theme list: See **Editorial calendar.**

Transparencies: Color slides, not color prints.

Unsolicited manuscript: Any manuscript not specifically requested by an editor.

Work-made-for-hire: Work specifically ordered, commissioned, and owned by a publisher for its exclusive use (see page 25).

World rights: Contractual agreement whereby the publisher acquires the right to reproduce the work throughout the world (see page 24); also known as *all rights.*

Writers' guidelines: Publisher's editorial objectives or specifications, which usually include word lengths, readership level, and subject matter.

Writing sample: Example of your writing style, tone, and skills; may be a published or unpublished piece.

Young adult: Readers 12 to 18 years.

Postage Information

How Much Postage?

When you're sending a manuscript to a magazine, enclose a self-addressed, stamped envelope with sufficient postage; this way, if the editor does not want to use your manuscript, it can be returned to you. To help you calculate the proper amount of postage for your SASE, here are the U.S. postal rates for first-class mailings in the U.S. and from the U.S. to Canada based on the latest increase (2007). Rates are expected to increase again, so please check with your local Post Office, or check the U.S. Postal Service website at usps.com.

Ounces	9x12 Envelope (Approx. no. of pages)	U.S. First-Class Postage Rate	Rate from U.S. to Canada
1	1–5	$ 0.41	$ .69
2	6–10	0.58	1.00
3	11–15	0.75	1.31
4	16–20	1.31	1.62
5	21–25	1.48	1.93
6	26–30	1.65	2.24
7	31–35	1.82	2.86
8	36–40	1.99	2.86

The amount of postage and size of envelope necessary to receive a sample copy and writers' guidelines are usually stated in the magazine listing. If this information is not provided, use the chart above to help gauge the proper amount of postage.

How to Obtain Stamps

People living in the U.S., Canada, or overseas can acquire U.S. stamps through the mail from the Philately Fulfillment Service Center. Call 800-STAMP-24 (800-782-6724) to request a catalogue or place an order. For overseas, the telephone number is 816-545-1100. You pay the cost of the stamps plus a postage and handling fee based on the value of the stamps ordered, and the stamps are shipped to you. Credit card information (MasterCard, Visa, and Discover cards only) is required for fax orders. The fax number is 816-545-1212. If you order through the catalogue, you can pay with a U.S. check or an American Money Order. Allow 3–4 weeks for delivery.

Articles

Thriving in Many Environments: Animal & Nature Writing

The animal kingdom spreads nearly as widely across magazines as it does across the globe. Stories about pets are a staple at general interest publications and specialized magazines. Wild kingdoms reign in magazines as varied as *National Geographic Kids* and *Cousteau Kids*, both affiliated with major conservation organizations; *Nature Friend,* a Christian publication; science magazines such as *KNOW*; and general interest magazines like *Boys' Quest.*

The great popularity of animals and nature also means that many topics in the category have already been well-covered, yet editors always want something fresh. The formula for success in this market is to find an appealing focus, base it on solid science (especially new science or discoveries, when possible), and meet each magazine in its own environment.

Across the Field

"In *National Geographic Kids* feature stories," says Catherine Hughes, Senior Editor, Science, "we cover animals and nature in a non-encyclopedic way. Instead of 'a day in the life of animal X,' we now tend to cover wildlife stories in one of three main ways: (1) choose a main behavior or feature of an animal (such as the stripes of a tiger, or the body build of a cheetah), and focus the story on that, weaving in other facts about their natural history as a secondary part of the story; or, (2) pick a type of behavior and then tell a collection of anecdotes about specific animals exhibiting that

behavior; or, (3) use a top ten list approach, such as 'Ten Cool Things about Great White Sharks.'"

Similarly interested in wildlife, but from a Christian perspective, *"Nature Friend* is almost entirely about wild nature as opposed to domestic animals, plants, and birds," says Editor and Publisher Kevin Shank. "We are also about wild settings, as opposed to zoos. This does not mean children are not very much  interested in pets and farm animals; we just do not attempt to cover all aspects as thoroughly as we do the wild side. We are worldwide in region, so content can be about any wild bird, animal, or plant, not only those in North America."

KNOW is a Canadian science magazine, and looks particularly for pieces on developments in the field. Editor Adrienne Mason says, "We might try to come at the story using new research about an animal. You still would need the basics about that animal, but the breaking science news tack would give the information an up-to-date feel. Is someone doing some fascinating research? Is that animal endangered?"

Editor Marilyn Edwards describes the general interest publication *Boys' Quest,* as well as its companion publications *Hopscotch* and *Fun For Kidz,* as "old-fashioned. We like to publish things that are long-lasting." But within that context, fresh approaches to designated themes are desirable. *"Boys' Quest* will do an entire issue on a theme such as war time heroes, and cover animals like dogs and pigeons that helped during the war. Other themes are animals from down under, or owners and dogs that helped someone."

Even as the editor of a theme magazine, Edwards says she doesn't have set preferences and is very open. In fact, she says, even if a good idea doesn't fit a theme yet, send it along and she might create a theme issue around it.

Nature Friend also follows themes, but Shank acknowledges that ideas from freelance writers have an important influence on what those themes may be. "We recognize that if we relied on our own ideas for a theme list, the quality of the magazine would suffer. The first place to start is to know our magazine. Second, use your knowledge to bring us fresh material; don't rely on us to dictate what we want. For example, we ran an article on Arctic beetles. I did not know they existed and could not have asked for an article on that topic, but when factual material was submitted, the topic caught our interest," Shanks says.

In Harmony

Factual articles come with different slants, however.

At *KNOW,* says Mason, "We publish short news stories. If our theme is animals or nature, we could approach it in many ways.

For instance, in our issue on dogs, we had spreads on dog evolution, wild dogs, dogs with jobs, and dog superlatives (largest litter, smallest, etc.). We try to come at a topic from a variety of angles. I'm most interested in new research and discoveries for our *KNOW* News column."

Shank stresses, "Accuracy of content is very important to us, so writers knowledgeable on the subjects they are writing about are certainly important, but accurate facts alone do not make for interesting reading. If it did, we would be content to read field guides." Underpinning all content in this Christian publication is the faith foundation. "We believe in Divine Creation as God has

---

A breaking science news tack gives information an up-to-date feel.

---

revealed to us in Genesis. Our articles and content will always be in harmony with this truth. In all cases, we remember that God created man above the animal kingdom. We are to be wise stewards of it, but not put animals on the same level of importance as man." *Nature Friend,* he says, does "not use talking animal stories; however, we may consider stories written from an animal's perspective."

National Geographic Kids readers want accurate details presented in a narrative style, says Hughes. "Telling a story through the use of anecdotes—specific stories about specific observations about a specific animal—is very popular with our readers. We might pose the question of whether animals have a sense of humor and then present five to ten anecdotes about different species suggesting that they may. In these stories, our writer finds people to interview who have observed the behavior, and then writes up the anecdotes using quotes from the observers, making them very immediate and specific. This pulls the reader in. It makes them care about a particular animal, and that care then extends to the species. It also makes the reader think about animal behavior."

In what seems an interesting shift from recent years for *National Geographic Kids* and other magazines, Hughes does not entirely frown on a certain degree of anthropomorphizing. "We used to stay away from anthropomorphizing altogether, but now we use it in a balanced way as a valid and intriguing technique to invite kids to get involved with a story," she says. "We've had the support of a number of wildlife biologists and animal behaviorists who participate with us on the telling of these stories."

Close-up

To make a connection to a particular creature and species, close-up looks at one aspect of an animal or nature subject are often a strong option.

"For my needs, the approach should be very focused," says Mason. "A writer isn't going to be able to tell everything they know about cheetahs, for instance, in a 250-word article. A writer needs to narrow and tighten their scope. Try to focus in on questions young children might ask."

Boys' Quest wants nonfiction and good supporting photography. Edwards likes to see each piece include an activity, which "needs to be educational but disguised well so the readers don't realize it's educational!" In particular she would like more "illustrated crafts, clever cooking, and rhyming stories." Query or send complete manuscripts by mail to Associate Editor Bethany Sneed. Do not email. The importance of good photos cannot be overstated.

In addition to articles, *Nature Friend* uses "activities, puzzles, and projects. Our guide-lines go into more detail, but in brief, we do not use projects that teach the making of ornaments and jewelry," says Shanks. He prefers manuscripts over queries. "Unfortunately, we do not have the space to use every good manuscript we receive. So, just because a good manuscript is presented in an attractive way does not guarantee we will be able to use it. The more familiar a writer is with us, the greater their chances of being able to submit material in harmony with the type we select and use." Articles should be no longer than 750 words.

At *KNOW*, Mason wants mail or email with clips (small attachments are accepted) from nonfiction writers. "I assign almost everything, so if I like what I see and have space, I'll assign a story. However, if a writer has an

Markets

- *Fun For Kidz, Boys' Quest, Hopscotch*: P.O. Box 227, Bluffton, OH 48517-0227. www.funforkidz.com

- *KNOW*: 501-3960 Quadra St., Victoria, British Columbia V8X 4A3 Canada. www.knowmag.ca

- *National Geographic Kids*: 1145 17th St. NW, Washington, D.C. 20036-4688. http://kids.nationalgeographic.com

- *Nature Friend*: 4253 Woodcock Lane, Dayton, VA 22821. www.naturefriendmagazine.com

Other Markets

- *Click*: 70 E. Lake St., Suite 300, Chicago, IL 60601. www.cricketmag.com

- *Crinkles*: 3401 Stockwell St., Lincoln, NE 68506. www.crinkles.com

- *Fandangle*: 14 Schult St., Keene, NH 03431. www.fandanglemagazine.com

- *JAKES Magazine*: P.O. Box 530, Edgefield, SC 29824. www.nwtf.org/jakes

idea, it's okay to send me a short email. I have bought some stories this way. Occasionally, we have bought poetry and will consider short fiction (to 500 words), if it relates to our theme."

Most ideas for stories at *National Geographic Kids* originate in-house, Hughes says, as do the activities and puzzles in the back of the magazine. Writers may mail a résumé and clips of articles they have had published for children.

"What doesn't come our way often enough is a story proposal that indicates the sender has really familiarized themselves with our magazine," says Hughes. "Our natural history and wildlife stories are tightly focused, and any query should reflect that as well. Proposing 'a story about lions' isn't going to fly. Nor is a catalogue story such as 'how animals catch their prey.'"

Hughes says to address materials to Executive Editor Julie Agnone, who then routes materials to appropriate editors. "A distinctive style, a sense of humor, a number of clips from other children's magazines, these are all things that will get your résumé and clips routing among the editors. We do not encourage unsolicited manuscripts," says Hughes, "but we welcome strong ideas for a story topic."

Connect with People in Profiles

Connection is the mark of a good profile. Whether the reader feels that the subject is much like him or herself, or is a personal hero, or even if the subject's life offers cautionary lessons that hit home, the direct human link with the audience is key in the selection of a profile subject. Writing style should bolster that connection.

A Heart Tug

"The best profiles tell a story. They have a hook and a narrative flow that keeps the reader engaged and interested," says longtime editor Betsy Kohn, who was Managing Editor of *Guideposts Sweet 16* before it closed late last year. "They show the person to the reader (often through anecdotes), rather than simply telling the reader about him or her. You come away from the piece feeling like you care about this person. You are inspired or feel a heart tug. The best profiles also have a wow factor—'Wow—I read about this girl in a magazine!'"

That sense of the real, of caring, and of the extraordinary found in the ordinary reflects the authenticity essential to profiles today. Jill Ewert, Editor of *Sharing the Victory,* a magazine for teens published by the Fellowship of Christian Athletes (FCA), says, "Profiles are becoming more authentic— especially in the Christian publishing world. People have stopped pretending that Christians are perfect, and are taking off their masks and getting real. That's refreshing.

Everyone has struggles and challenges. Profiles can't pretend that everything is fine in a person's life. The more real, the better."

Deborah Vetter, Senior Contributing Editor of *Cricket,* offers an illustration from the February 2006 issue. "Getting There Is Half the Fun: An Interview with Pilot Kathy McCullough," conducted by Heather A. Delabre and Julia Messina, reveals that McCullough's "mother wasn't too keen on her pilot career," says Vetter, "so she had to overcome her reservations and get a four-year

Profiles are becoming more authentic. The more real, the better.

college education, which the airlines require. She tells humorous anecdotes of her time in the sky. Imagine carrying giraffes, Brahma bulls, an escape artist zebra—and a load of pigs! These anecdotes humanize Kathy and make her seem like a real person."

The Early Years

For their young audiences, children's magazine editors generally want a profile subject's early years to come into play.

"It's always good to know something about a subject's childhood, especially if it shows what led him or her to enter a certain profession or make a certain discovery," says Vetter. An August 2007 profile of Wendy Welsh was a good example. "She's an underwater archaeologist working on what is believed to be *Queen Anne's Revenge,* Blackbeard's pirate ship, which sank off the North Carolina coast in 1718. The article's author, Shannon Hitchcock, asked Wendy about her childhood and school. Wendy loved math and physical education and her least favorite subject was writing. Guess what? She uses what she learned in all three subjects in her work: As a diver, physical fitness is essential. She needs math to mix up solutions, measure artifacts, and budget for supplies. She uses writing to document artifacts. Even though paperwork is her least favorite part of the job, she knows she must do a good job. In other words, kids learn that every job has both its upside and downside. They also learn that it takes hard work and a willingness to overcome obstacles to achieve your goals."

Role models seem to be in high favor among readers and editors. At *Cobblestone,* a U.S. history magazine, Editor Meg Chorlian has "noticed an increased interest in profiles

about heroes or historical figures that command respect and admiration for the things they accomplished or what they represented or stood up for—basically, good role models to offer readers."

Still, however large the subject's place on the stage of history, struggles help make profiles interesting. Chorlian explains, "When *Cobblestone* creates a biographical issue, we focus on someone who achieved a certain level of fame—the first woman doctor, a Civil War general, famous inventors, presidents, etc. The best profiles make sure our readers understand that these famous people also were human and were not perfect. They did amazing things, yes, but they also were children once, or they experi-

enced difficulties in life. I'm not suggesting that these things should be dominant, but the mention of them makes the person being highlighted more real and more likely someone to whom a 10-year-old can relate. An anecdotal story about a young Thomas Edison burning down his father's barn, or George Washington's attempts to master good spelling habits, doesn't make them less heroic, but it does make them more human."

Free-Flying Inspiration

Cricket, says Vetter, is always interested in profiles on scientists, classical and jazz musicians, or "anyone who has participated in a discovery or met an important challenge or done something interesting." A January 2007 article by Naomi Wallace profiled Matthew Stinemetze, a spacecraft engineer in a private manned space program. "He flew on the mother ship *White Knight* and pulled the lever that released *SpaceShipOne,* the privately funded spacecraft that broke the barriers of space and won the Ansari X Prize."

Sometimes inspiration flies a little closer to home. At *Next Step,* a college and career planning magazine, Vice President and Editor in Chief Laura Jeanne Hammond says, "The best career profiles show how the subjects got to their present careers, and are inspirational in tone. Profiles should be conversational for our readers, who are primarily high school juniors and seniors." The magazine also "looks for career profiles that feature several people and careers in one article. For example, a pitch for an article about culinary careers might include a chef, a restaurant buyer, a business owner, etc." *Next Step* runs about 10 career profiles of 850 to 1,000 words each year.

American history profiles for *Cobblestone* should follow the designated monthly themes. Chorlian cites the November 2007 issue on George Washington. "It includes articles on his childhood, his interest in farming, his presidency, and his French and Indian War experience, to name just a few—a series of mini-profiles that cover as much of his life as possible." The magazine may have a different make-up at other times, however. "An issue on citizenship might cover a broad view of how we define citizenship as a nation, from our Founding Fathers to a remarkable public servant of the twenty-first century," she says. "In this case, I would probably ask someone to do an interview of a contemporary person."

The link between history and contemporary times can offer another opportunity for a profile in *Cobblestone*. "We have a department called The Past Is Present, in which we

When the profile subject is deceased, go diving for primary source documents.

try to make a connection between the historical topic of the issue and today," says Chorlian. "This department often works well as an interview with a person (an archaeologist, for example) who has done work that connects to our theme for an issue."

Dive In

Profiles can take a narrative or question-and-answer form, but in either case, interviews are essential for research on a living subject.

"We use both straight narrative profiles (with quotes from the subject) or interview style with question and answer," says Vetter at *Cricket*.

When the profile subject is deceased, says Vetter, "as was the case with Stephen Whitt's 'To Catch a Light Beam: The Story of James Clerk Maxwell' (September 2006), then go diving for primary documents, as well as reading what other authors have written about the subject. Sometimes an author can interview people who knew a subject if the subject is no longer living." Vetter praises Whitt, a science writer who likes to profile scientists and their ground-breaking discoveries, because "he understands his subject and is able to explain difficult concepts so they are accessible for young people. He also consults with experts in the field."

Do not rely solely on information gathered from group interviews, speeches, or panel discussions, or on information already in print or on the Internet, Chorlian stresses. "Since *Cobblestone* is mostly used in schools and libraries, we have a responsibility to make sure the material that appears in the magazine is as accurate as possible and uses the most current information, books, and other resources. We encourage the use of primary sources whenever available."

Kohn says that when profiling a young person, often "not much research is required beyond an interview of the teen, though if there is an unusual aspect to the story, you need to prepare well for the interview. For example, a writer who profiled a teen racing the Iditarod had to research the race and know the basics of dog sled racing in order to conduct the interview and write the piece."

Editor-Specific

Research sources should be included with submissions, along with other components listed in the writers' guidelines. Follow editors' specific preferences closely.

Cricket's Vetter prefers "complete manuscripts, as they allow us to best judge the quality of the overall interview. If we feel the author needs to go back and ask more questions or do more research, we can indicate exactly where that should be. Include something about the subject's childhood; let the subject's personality, quirks, and sense of humor come through; include anecdotes that humanize the subject and inspire young readers to learn more about a field or a subject. We received a letter from a woman who was inspired to enter the field of animal behavior from a profile that appeared in *Cricket* when she was a child. The scientist we profiled became her mentor."

Photographs are always a plus for *Cricket* submissions. If possible, send copies of the photos with the profile or provide online sources. Indicate if you can provide publication-quality photographs, or a contact for obtaining them.

Queries are preferred at *Next Step* and

Markets

- *Cobblestone*: 30 Grove St., Suite C, Peterborough, NH 03458. www.cobblestonepub.com

- *Cricket*: 70 East Lake St., Suite 300, Chicago, IL 60601. www.cricketmag.com

- *Next Step*: 86 West Main St., Victor, NY 14564. www.nextSTEPmag.com

- *Sharing the Victory*: 8701 Leeds Rd., Kansas City, MO 64129. www.sharingthevictory.com

Other Markets

- *Insight*: 55 West Oak Ridge Dr., Hagerstown, MD 21740-7390. www.insightmagazine.org

- *Jack And Jill*: 1100 Waterway Blvd., P.O. Box 567, Indianapolis, IN 46206. www.jackandjillmag.org

- *Kaleidoscope*: 701 South Main St., Akron, OH 44311-1019. www.udsakron.org

Sharing the Victory. "I love a good query letter. A letter that is well thought out and includes the names of potential sources and their careers shows me the author will present what I need," says Hammond.

A link between history and contemporary times can offer an opportunity for a profile.

Kohn suggests that snapshots of the subject often help profile submissions to sell. She also advises writers to study a magazine to know the types of teens and other people it profiles, but remember, she says, "Something out of the ordinary always catches an editor's eye! I saw too many manuscripts about girls and boys overcoming illnesses and injuries, so if someone submitted one of those it had to be really, really unusual and inspirational."

Ewert wants email queries for *Sharing the Victory,* about "profile articles on professional athletes and coaches who have a tie to the FCA ministry. We have a variety of lengths, anywhere from 1,100 to 2,000 words. We typically purchase about 15 profiles every year."

The best submission for *Cobblestone,* says Chorlian, "consists of a cover letter that tells me the idea for an article (and might even include a creative title), accompanied by a brief outline, a bibliography, and an SASE. But the cover letter is what I read first, and any effort to give me a taste of a good writing style, as well as evidence that the writer knows what kids like and can compose an engaging article aimed at their reading level, helps a lot. Think about a way to let me know that you have a good writing style. Ask a question. Start your cover letter with a good hook, a great quote. Relate it to the article you'd like to write for *Cobblestone,* not to your love of the topic. I assume you are interested in the topic since you are sending in a query for it."

Cobblestone articles range in length from 400 to 900 words. The number of profiles purchased annually varies. Chorlian explains, "We did an issue on women in World War I (March 2006), and we filled it with profiles of varying lengths. There were longer general articles on groups of women, such as women in the Navy, nurses, and suffragists, but there were quite a few shorter articles (about 400 words) on female performers Elsie Janis and Mary Pickford, peace activist Jeannette Rankin, writer Edith Wharton, sculptor Anna Coleman Ladd, and First Lady Edith Wilson.

Every issue benefits from some biographical sketches and articles, some just require less. An issue on Yorktown (October 2006), the siege that effectively ended the Revolutionary War, had fewer profiles of specific people and more articles devoted to the events that came before and after the siege."

The spectrum of people who can be profiled—whether in a particular time period, like World War I women, or contemporary subjects such as cute teen boys—is wide. Who interests you? Who will appeal to your young audience? What makes the subject worthy of a story, exceptional or unique as a person? Connect the dots for a profile filled with authenticity and color.

Holidays Out of the Ordinary

Happy holidays, whichever they may be. While fiction and nonfiction about big yearly celebrations like Christmas and Passover may be joyously anticipated—and always have a place in magazines—editors seem to prefer seeing submissions about smaller or different festivities.

"*Fun For Kidz* looks for unfamiliar holidays," says Editor Marilyn Edwards. "Children hear the same thing all the time about regular holidays." These other celebrations may not be truly unfamiliar, simply less often covered in articles and stories. For example, Edwards cites a *Fun For Kidz* issue on mothers and daughters and how Mother's Day came about.

Different traditions can also expose children to holidays new to them. "In an increasingly globalized world, it is more important than ever for young readers to understand and have an appreciation for other cultures," says Elizabeth Crooker Carpentiere, *Faces* Editor. "Because we focus on a different world culture each month, we have an opportunity to explore different holidays and festivals in each issue."

Religious holidays offer options beyond the obvious. "I'd like to see submissions on holidays other than Christmas/Hanukkah and Easter/Passover," says Mary Helene Rosenbaum, Director and Editor of *Dovetail: A Journal by and for Jewish/Christian Families*, a publication for interfaith couples and families. "A comparison of Halloween and Purim, which have costumes and sweets and door-to-door visits in common but which have very different tones and religious significance, would be fun. Or perhaps a writer could explore a religious holiday and its possible relationship to a secular observance that occurs around the same time—I'm thinking of Martin Luther King Jr. Day and Tu B'Shevat, or Thanksgiving and Sukkot."

"Of most interest to us," says *BabagaNewz* Managing Editor Aviva Werner, "are articles that help our readers find new messages in a holiday observance." This newsmagazine for Jewish preteens wants articles with "new angles. We don't provide basic information on observance or history. In addition, our articles encourage family involvement and discussion."

Impact

Holiday writing can be done on many levels. It can be simple fun, straightforward and joyful. But it can also convey ideals and cultural truths to children.

Editor of the small Canadian literary newsletter *Mr. Marquis' Museletter*, Kalen Marquis says, "The best writing in this category fits the season or holiday and yet is consistent with our overall mission as a publisher to promote wisdom, wonder, and wellness, often through humor and heartstrings." The *Museletter* publishes fiction and nonfiction, and in both, he says, "There tends to be a dreamy or nostalgic voice present in our pieces. This is especially so with holiday and seasonal works that tend to have great emotional or affective impact on both writer and reader."

In *Fun For Kidz* and its companion publications *Hopscotch* and *Boys' Quest,* Edwards promotes the idea of kids being kids and the importance of wholesome activities. She "would like good values to stay the same. If there are any good values in holidays, I want to preserve them."

Carpentiere prefers "articles that tell the story of a holiday or festival through the eyes of a child, especially if children play a special role in the festivities. *Faces* authors should be non-judgmental and not make a holiday seem exotic or strange."

At *Highlights for Children,* says Managing Editor Judy Burke, "We have always represented a wide variety of holidays, traditions, and festivals in the pages of our magazine. We feel that it's important to encourage an appreciation for the world's different cultures and religions, so we'll continue to do that."

Religious publications are a natural niche for exploring celebrations or commemorations. "Holiday fiction is often a metaphor for, or illustration of, the meaning and values of the holiday," says Werner. For example, last year before Rosh Hashanah, *BabagaNewz* published a story centered on the theme of character improvement. It took the form of a spy story. "A special agent is on a mission to discover and eradicate evil (ultimately, inside himself) using high-tech surveillance technology and terminology. This year, we did an article around the same theme of improving

---

Tell the story of a holiday through the eyes of a child, especially if children have a special role in the festivities.

---

one's character traits before Rosh Hashanah, but this time the hook was juggling. We presented 10 steps to learning to juggle that paralleled 10 steps to character improvement."

BabagaNewz publishes some fiction, but tends toward more nonfiction. "As a Jewish children's magazine, we have always given holidays a prominent place. Each issue has a holiday feature plus other departments devoted to the upcoming holidays," says Werner. *BabagaNewz* publishes 500- to 1,000-word pieces on Rosh Hashanah, Yom Kippur, Sukkot, Hanukkah, Tu B'Shevat, Purim,

Markets

- *BabagaNewz*: 90 Oak St., Newton, MA 02464. www.babaganewz.com

- *Dovetail*: 775 Simon Greenwell Lane, Boston, KY 40107. www.dovetailinstitute.org

- *Faces*: 30 Grove St., Suite C, Peterborough, NH 03458. www.cobblestonepub.com

- *Fun For Kidz*: P.O. Box 227, Bluffton, OH 48517-0227. www.funforkidz.com

- *Highlights for Children*: 803 Church St., Honesdale, PA 18431. www.highlights.com

- *Mr. Marquis' Museletter*: Box 29556, Maple Ridge, British Columbia V2X 2V0 Canada.

- *Pack-o-Fun*: 2400 Devon, Suite 292, Des Plaines, IL 60018-4618. www.pack-o-fun.com

Pesach, Yom Ha'atzmaut, and Yom Yerushalayim.

BabagaNewz works at least three months in advance, and needs holiday-related features, crafts, recipes, puzzles, and other submissions very early. Werner prefers manuscripts. "However, because our needs are specific, we often assign our holiday content to freelancers."

Dovetail's Rosenbaum is "interested in seeing material exploring the specifically religious, as opposed to the social or cultural, questions that children of interfaith parents have. This area has to be approached with great sensitivity and deep knowledge to avoid oversimplification on the one hand, or proselytization on the other. Examples would be how a child with one Christian and one Jewish parent thinks about Jesus, or how a child with a monotheist parent and a parent from an Asian faith tradition deals with the crosscurrents of tolerance and exclusivism."

Writers should submit material to *Dovetail* that "deals in a positive way with the challenges faced by children in interfaith families while emphasizing the benefits (having two sets of holidays, for instance). Still, writers should avoid glossing over religious differences: Don't pretend that hanging Stars of David on your Christmas tree solves everything."

The Dovetail Institute publishes for both adults and children. "Our publications for children contain primarily fictional narratives or treatments of nonfiction themes (Winston the Bear explores different religions by visiting their places of worship, for instance) but we're open to non-narrative nonfiction for children, especially older children," says Rosenbaum. "Again—I can't emphasize this enough—it must be from the perspective of someone who knows about and values more than one faith tradition. While a broad range of ideas are possible, whatever topic is being treated in the piece must be clearly discussed in a knowledgeable but non-judgmental way."

Keep Listening

Werner describes the best writing on holidays as "fun, interesting, and engaging—not preachy or too old-fashioned. We want to encourage young people to see the holidays from perspectives that are novel, thought-provoking, and exciting, and that will encourage them to continue these explorations with the full power of their imaginations and reflections. Kids stop listening, though, if they feel they sense sermonizing."

Burke looks for strong writing and an "insider's feel" about the cultures represented in holiday stories. "Articles and stories that have an us/them feel don't usually work for *Highlights*. This is not to say that the author must celebrate the holiday or be of

> Encourage young people to see the holidays from perspectives that are novel, thought-provoking, and exciting.

the culture or religion being represented in a story or article, but it must ring true for readers of that culture or faith. For this reason, whatever their cultural or religious background, we ask authors to have an expert review holiday and cultural pieces for accuracy and sensitivity."

Whether the writing is fiction or nonfiction, Burke says, "The tone of these pieces is the most important factor. The tone should be respectful. It sometimes helps when authors focus on what people of a certain culture or religion have in common with people not of that group, as opposed to noting how they're different. Preachiness and patronizing or condescending language are common problems that we see."

In addition to pieces based on different world traditions told in the first person, *Highlights* would like U.S. history nonfiction articles that focus on holidays, particularly Christmas and Thanksgiving; anecdotal nonfiction articles about George Washington and Abraham Lincoln; nonfiction articles with patriotic themes; and fictional Kwanzaa, Ramadan, Hanukkah, Passover, and Easter stories (no Easter bunnies); and seasonal crafts and activities.

Burke says that the most successful seasonal and holiday fiction conveys the true spirit of a holiday, with "engaging characters, compelling conflict, and all the other traits of good fiction in general." She sees "some authors trying to disguise nonfiction as fiction—having a fictional character experience a particular holiday, but with no plot, for

example—but those manuscripts are often best rewritten as straight nonfiction."

The qualities Marquis wants to see most arise from voice. "While artistry and craftsmanship can be enchanting, the honesty and integrity of the writer's voice and meaning are paramount." The newsletter is "receptive to more mainstream traditional North American celebrations but is just as likely to publish multicultural or multi-faith works as well. It is a joy to be inclusive and representative."

Whether poetry or prose, material should

be fresh. "Shorter poetic works are easy to place in our newsletter as space is so limited. Creative or literary nonfiction, as well as traditional nonfiction articles suitable for our audience, are of particular interest," Marquis says.

Focus on what people of a certain culture or religion have in common with others, as opposed to noting how they're different.

The *Museletter* also uses inspirational nonfiction and biography. Send complete manuscripts (300 to 500 words or up to five poems of 4 to 16 lines).

Artful Activities

Fiction, nonfiction, and activities for unfamiliar holidays for *Fun For Kidz* should be unique, wholesome, "and speak to setting a good example, being very careful not to alienate anyone," says Edwards. Good accompanying photos are always a big plus. Articles should be around 500 words. Edwards says she doesn't receive very many seasonal articles, but even these must be tied to designated themes, available on the website.

All submissions must relate to the theme at *Faces*, too. "We use mainly nonfiction. However, that does not mean I would automatically reject a fiction piece," Carpentiere says. "Because *Faces* is used in a classroom setting, any projects or cooking activities must use materials that would be readily accessible to a teacher." A query to *Faces* must include a brief cover letter stating the subject and word length of the proposed article, which should be 600 to 800 words; a detailed one-page outline explaining the information to be presented; an extensive bibliography of materials the author intends to use in preparing the article (if appropriate); a writing sample; and a self-addressed stamped envelope.

Pack-o-Fun looks for holiday crafts and

activities year-round. Editor Annie Niemiec says, "*Pack-o-Fun* is based predominantly on the seasons and therefore we feature seasonal crafting. We find that our readers (whether moms, teachers, or group leaders) have little time to craft on a regular basis. The majority do make time around the holidays to craft gifts, favors, or decorations with kids. We focus on providing projects based around Valentine's Day, Easter, Halloween, Christmas/Hanukkah, and also on more broad seasonal times like back-to-school, summer, winter, and spring."

Other needs include Halloween costumes; homemade gift ideas for parents, siblings, teachers, and grandparents; Bible crafts; Scout crafts; and activities that teach a science, math, reading, or art concept. Arts and crafts projects should use low-cost materials, minimal supplies, and recycled items. *Pack-o-Fun* purchases roughly 200+ seasonal arts and crafts projects each year.

Mail editors those holiday greetings—in the form of winning fiction, nonfiction, or activities—and give them reason to celebrate.

The Wide Multicultural World

Far from being the narrow niche it was once considered, multicultural writing today consists of a "broad variety of pieces, ranging from those that simply use multicultural names for characters to pieces that go deep into cultural exploration," *Skipping Stones* Editors Arun Toké, Nicole Esposti, and Nina Forsberg explain. "Publications have gone beyond the simple travel story in which the writer is a tourist observing a different culture without making points of cultural contact. There are also more writings from people of color about their own cultural experiences, which doesn't promote stereotypes as easily."

Skipping Stones identifies itself as a resource in multicultural education "that encourages cooperation, creativity, and celebration of cultural and environmental richness." Among its current interests today are "explorations of multiple heritage backgrounds."

A range of other publications have cultural missions of their own, making multicultural writing one of the most open-armed of children's markets.

On a Mission

"Since its inception, *New Moon* has striven to be a magazine that represents and appeals to *all* girls, so we've always been aware of the need for multicultural stories," says Senior Editor Lacey Louwagie. "I see other publishers becoming more aware of the need to reflect that we live in a multicultural world. Several specific niche publications have cropped up to cater to kids of specific ethnic backgrounds, such as the wonderful *Kahani* for South Asian kids. More multiculturalism in mainstream publications and specific multicultural niche markets are positive changes; we all live in this world and all need to see ourselves reflected in the media."

Louwagie continues, "*New Moon* is always very interested in anything written by a girl (ages 8 to 14) from a multicultural standpoint. From adults, we're interested in fiction from a multicultural perspective. This can include stories about girls living outside North America, stories about girls in immigrant families, or stories about girls who belong to any type of subculture. We're also interested in stories about career women from different cultures and working with different cultures, and biographies of historical women from diverse cultural backgrounds. We actively solicit multicultural work and would love to see more of it come through in our submissions process."

Faces, from Cobblestone Publishing, entertains and educates readers 9 to 14 about countries and cultures around the globe. Recent themes have been China, India, Portugal, Islam in Africa, and Ireland. "Our magazine has always had multicultural themes. Each month we focus on a different world culture or topic," says Editor Elizabeth Crooker Carpentiere. "The best multicultural writing presents cultures in a way that is neither condescending nor judgmental. With 48 pages a month dedicated to a specific culture, it is our goal to create a full picture of life within a culture. Kids want to know how other kids live—what do they do for fun, what is school like for them, what kind of music do they listen to, etc. If you can relate the subject matter to the readers, you are more likely to keep their interest."

The mission of *MultiCultural Review* is to help educators expose young readers to places and people of many traditions. "We publish articles geared to librarians and teachers who are selecting multicultural books. We always look for reviewers who are specialists in the culture or region of the books that publishers send us for review," says Lyn Miller-Lachmann, Editor in Chief. "We also publish feature articles that evaluate the literature of a given cultural group or part of the world. For instance, several years ago, we published an article that evaluated young adult fiction that focused on the body image and beauty aesthetics of African-American teenage girls."

The quarterly is continuing to look "for bibliographic articles focusing on children's and young adult books, fiction and nonfiction, about the Middle East and about places where Islam is a major religion. There are many titles being published now, but our readers would like to know which ones present a compelling and nuanced portrait and which ones merely reinforce prejudices and stereotypes," says Miller-Lachmann.

Making Contact

Multicultural writing tries to make the foreign familiar—to make the unknown universal in some way—while at the same time acknowledging what remains distinct and unique culturally and personally. Louwagie puts it this way: "The best multicultural writing and

publishing acknowledges the diversity within any cultural subset. It realizes that a story about an Indian girl does not represent the experience of all Indian girls. It goes beyond tokenism and embraces diversity within diversity."

The best multicultural writing recognizes that a story about an Indian girl does not represent all Indian girls. It embraces diversity within diversity.

Who should author multicultural fiction is the subject of ongoing discussion. Miller-Lachmann says, "There's a long debate over whether a cultural outsider can write authentically about a given culture. Certainly, insiders have an advantage, and there's a social justice issue at play here for groups both in the United States and throughout the world who have traditionally been denied a voice in the mainstream publishing industry. However, a writer with extensive knowledge of another culture and the skill of inhabiting the life of another (which someone who doesn't simply write memoirs or thinly veiled autobiographies should be able to do) should not be automatically disqualified from creating a cross-cultural or multicultural story."

Carpentiere welcomes submissions for *Faces* from writers who come from the culture being covered, but shared heritage is not a requirement.

At *Skipping Stones*, "The writer may be outside the culture being observed but make points of genuine cultural contact, consistent with the objective or goal of the piece and the target audience age group," say the editors. For them, good "multicultural writing finds a balance between the subject and style of writing; shows sensitivity to the language of the culture of focus, as well as a feel for authentic, well-written dialogue; and exemplifies different ways that people can tell a story (such as circular or linear storytelling), in a way that makes sense to the average reader."

Authors may lean too easily toward food and holidays for multicultural subjects. Writers should "go deeper than food or holidays, and explore the unifying aspects of the culture in which the story takes place," say Toké, Esposti, and Forsberg. "Personal, authentic experiences are more valuable than general-izations and assumptions about a culture that may rely on, and perpet-uate, stereotypes. At *Skipping Stones*, we like authors to disclose in their cover letters where information was obtained. In each issue, we strive for different points of view on the same or closely related topics."

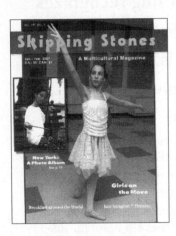

Louwagie "definitely prefers for multicul-tural pieces to come from an author within that cul-ture. If not, the author should have strong connec-tions to the culture she's writing about, whether she works with girls from that culture, has lived within that culture, or has had extensive interviews or con-versations with people in the culture. We'd also prefer for an author writing about a culture that isn't her own to check the piece with someone who is—for accuracy and respect—before submitting to us."

New Moon, says Louwagie, "rarely pub-lishes seasonal work (i.e.: stories about holi-days, etc.), but we are interested in publishing stories in which girls talk about certain aspects of their lives and why these aspects are important, and this can include holidays or religious or spiritual practices."

Personalized

"While we do like when *Skipping Stones* authors write about their own cultures," say the editors, "we also appreciate submissions that have a personal aspect to the story, or that encourage cross-cultural communication. When an author writes from his or her authen-tic cultural immersion experience, it shows up strongly in the writing and makes the piece genuinely educational. Our March/April 2007 issue featured an unusual love story by a Tibetan youth in People's Republic of China, which brings in beautifully and effortlessly the traditional Tibetan culture as the story is told."

Carpentiere looks for articles for *Faces* "that personalize a topic. For example, rather than telling me about different art styles in Portugal, interview an artist. Instead of telling readers about a typical school day in Portugal, have an actual student tell you about their day. Go beyond what kids are going to read about in their textbooks or in an encyclope-dia. In our issue on the U.S. West Coast, a log-ical topic was Hollywood and I did receive

---

For multicultural subjects, authors should go deeper than food or holidays, and instead explore personal, authentic experiences that encourage cross-cultural communication.

---

numerous queries relating to Hollywood. However, the query that I chose describes dream jobs of the West Coast—profiles of sev-eral different people, including three who work in the entertainment field." *Faces* pub-lishes nonfiction, and fiction in the form of retold folktales or legends.

Miller-Lachmann helps clarify what makes writing about different cultures full of vitality. "Good multicultural writing is fresh and hon-est. It captures the experience of living within a given culture without preaching, overtly teaching, or overwhelming the reader with detail. Authors of multicultural books should have intimate knowledge of the culture. The writing should be vivid and, like each scene in the story, the writing should evoke the sense of a culture—of a language (the rhythm, slang, sense of humor, etc.)—even if it's a different language and the book is in English."

Speaking the Language

Making language, style, and story structure reflect the subject can be especially exciting for writers in this genre.

Skipping Stones editors like to see "a multicultural theme woven into a story in an unexpected or complex way, with some ambiguity in the resolution. A story appeals more when it is not linear or how it concludes is not that obvious."

The magazine likes to mix its multicultural content: "We enjoy reading diverse submissions. In each issue we have one article with information for parents and teachers and one on health. Articles about nature conservation, ecological approaches to day-to-day living, and healthy practices in different cultures are very much encouraged." *Skipping Stones* authors must remember that "a multicultural story goes beyond just using a different setting or character name. The reader must feel like she or he is genuinely exploring some aspect of a culture. Sometimes, multicultural fiction uses words or phrases from the language of the culture where the story takes place. We like a personal, accessible style or touch rather than a distanced, authoritative voice. The reader should not feel talked down to."

New Moon publishes fiction and nonfiction, but limits the types of nonfiction it accepts from adults. "We prefer writing in our magazine to have a down-to-earth, conversational tone," says Louwagie. "For multicultural fiction, as with all fiction, we prefer a show, don't tell approach. Rather than coming out and explaining anything that may not be familiar to girls outside the culture being written about, the writer should paint a vivid enough picture of the protagonist's life that we feel a part of it and don't need explanations inserted into the text. We definitely prefer multicultural work coming from a girl or woman within the culture she writes about, or at least a girl or woman who understands deeply the nuances of the particular culture."

Although *MultiCultural Review* reviews but doesn't publish fiction, Miller-Lachmann thinks, "The challenge for someone who wants to write a multicultural story that will be read by a broad audience, or a story about a completely unfamiliar culture, is to fill in the knowledge gaps while creating an engaging plot with characters who have universal

Markets

- *Faces*: 30 Grove St., Suite C, Peterborough, NH 03458. www.cobblestonepub.com

- *MultiCultural Review*: 194 Lenox Avenue, Albany, NY 12208. www.mcreview.com

- *New Moon*: 2 West First St., Suite 101, Duluth, MN 55802. www.newmoon.org

- *Skipping Stones*: P.O. Box 3939, Eugene, OR 97403. www.skippingstones.org

Other Markets

- *AIM Magazine*: P.O. Box 856, Forest Grove, OR 97116. www.aimmagazine.org

- *Breakaway*: 8605 Explorer Dr., Colorado Springs, CO 80920. www.breakawaymag.com

- *Children's Playmate*: 1100 Waterway Boulevard, P.O. Box 567, Indianapolis, IN 46206. www.childrensplaymatemag.org

- *InTeen*: P.O. Box 436987, Chicago, IL 60643. www.urbanministries.com

appeal." She explains further: "When a story comes from a majority culture, one reflected in the media and in the experience of the majority of readers, a lot of background is assumed and therefore doesn't appear in the story. Readers can read between the lines. This is also true for some multicultural fiction that is directed specifically to readers within that culture. I'm thinking here of several new

The writing should evoke a sense of the culture and language—the rhythm, slang, sense of humor.

series of urban fiction with African-American characters and a predominantly African-American audience, such as Drama High (Dafina Books) and the Bluford series (Townsend Press, now published by Scholastic)."

Clear Connections

Whether writing articles for educators or for preteen girls or for a range of young readers, authors have many format choices in the multicultural market.

Skipping Stones is looking for more submissions with interviews, which must be age-appropriate. It also wants tested crafts and recipes, puzzles, crosswords, or board games that "encourage readers to explore cultural geography or ecological awareness of a region of the country or world." Send complete manuscripts with an SASE. Even if submitting by regular mail, please include your email address. Cover letters should explain context and the author's background. Artwork and photographs are a plus. Articles and stories are 750 to 1,000 words. The magazine uses 50 to 100 multicultural pieces a year.

New Moon gives preference to multicultural pieces, "especially if they are clearly coming from a deep understanding of the culture being explored and especially if they come from a writer within the culture," says

Louwagie. It accepts queries, manuscripts, and outlines for nonfiction, and complete manuscripts only for fiction. "The pieces that stand out are the ones that have a clear connection with girls' real lives and voices. Anything submitted to *New Moon* should not stereotype, simplify, or preach to girls." Nonfiction is 600 words, and fiction is 1,200 words. Louwagie says the magazine publishes six fictional stories, six historical biographies, and six profiles of women in their chosen careers each year. "We will gladly consider multicultural pieces for any of these departments."

She does not purchase activities, puzzles, how-to's, or projects by adults, but does accept historical profiles from adult writers. "A historical profile in *New Moon* should show a well-rounded woman. Many writers have a tendency to put the woman they're profiling on a pedestal. This is understandable and it's appropriate to be in awe of great historical women. But it's also especially fitting with *New Moon*'s mission for us to see that great women are still real women. It's okay to disclose faults, controversy, or hardship associated with the woman profiled, as well as her talents and accomplishments. This is true of women profiled from any culture," says Louwagie.

Theme is important at *Faces*, so check the theme list available on its website. In addition to articles, Carpentiere is "most interested in logic problems. Recipes are a great way to introduce readers to the food of a country, just keep in mind that most of our activities are done in a classroom setting so the ingredients and materials should be easy to obtain (and relatively inexpensive). The directions should be clear and easy to follow. Define any cooking terms." Queries should include a brief cover letter stating the subject and word length of the proposed article; a detailed one-page outline explaining the information to be presented in the article; an extensive bibliography of materials the author intends to use; a writing sample; and a self-addressed stamped envelope. "Topics should be well researched.

If the bibliography has only two or three sources, I'm apt to disregard it," Carpentiere says.

MultiCultural Review is a professional journal that only publishes nonfiction. "We appeal to people who are college graduates but not necessarily scholars," says Miller-Lachmann. She likes articles "that use case studies so that readers get a sense of the classroom where the highlighted program is taking place. Two models for this kind of article are Daniel A. Kelin's 'Integrating Drama into the ESL Classroom' (Fall 2006), and Martha Casas's 'Mother Goose Teaches on the Wild Side' (Winter 2006)."

Miller-Lachmann prefers to see the full manuscript. "I don't get enough articles that are written in an interesting way—that capture the reader's attention rather than simply convey information. Most of our readers are practitioners rather than scholars, but too many of the articles we receive suffer from dry, pedestrian writing and are too scholarly or theoretical. Our contributors are, for the most part, experts in their given area. Most of them are from the culture about which they write (or review), though relevant coursework and professional experience are also important."

Feature articles at *MultiCultural Review* run from 2,000 to 6,000 words. Miller-Lachmann recommends the 1,000- to 1,500-word opinion column, Parting Words, as a good place for a writer to break in. Book reviews are about 200 words; all books are assigned to reviewers. "If you would like to review, please contact me with a list of your areas of interest, a vitae, and writing samples," she says. "We are open to beginning writers as reviewers, as long as you have familiarity with the culture and genre in which you would like to review, and we've worked with beginning reviewers to polish their work."

Walk Through the Door with Early Readers

That threshold children cross from pre-reading to reading is receiving a fresh coat of paint. Editors are brushing up this important developmental stage by publishing bright new fiction and nonfiction that opens the door wide to early readers.

"Publishing for emergent and early readers today is vibrant," says Alice Letvin, Editorial Director of Cricket Magazine Group. "Our particular focus is on literature that cultivates children's imaginations, rather than on basic literacy. It seems to me that there's a lot of fresh, poetic work being done now. I'm also seeing greater openness to international illustrators and writers, who are bringing new ideas, styles, and attitudes toward childhood—free-spirited and less protectionist—to publishing in the U.S."

At the Christian magazine *Clubhouse, Jr.*, Associate Editor Suzanne Hadley acknowledges the educational dimension of publishing for early readers, but also notes a change in religious publishing for this audience. "Fiction for this age group must delight and educate. Stories used to be more preachy. Now, we prefer that lessons emerge naturally from a well-told story. Our magazines are competing with educational video games, so stories must not only entertain but also teach," she says.

Writing for early readers has distinct characteristics, but also shares much in common with other kinds of children's writing—above all, the need for high quality and a joyful understanding of the children and what interests them. New readers always learn more from inviting, genuine writing than from the pedantic or commonplace.

Hold the Sugar

"The best writing for young children is distinguished by a sense of authenticity. It reflects the truth of childhood experience, and is not sugarcoated, well-meaning, or didactic," says Letvin. "Another way of putting this is that the best children's literature is written from the *inner child* rather than from an adult perspective. Quality literature also initiates children into the pleas-

ures of language, shows them they're not alone in their thoughts and feelings, tickles their funny bones, and encourages them to see that there's no limit to what imagination can accomplish."

Marileta Robinson, Senior Editor of *Highlights for Children,* says, "When I see that a writer has thought of a fresh, new idea, I get excited. A strong beginning is important, with energy, humor, an engaging voice, an element of suspense. I look for a sense that the writer knows what children of this age like, and also knows what's appropriate for us (no potty humor, for example). Stories that incorporate some repetition or a repetitive pattern work well, if they are not too babyish."

Repetition is clearly one of the elements that is important to reading skill development in early readers. Rather than seeing repetition as a boring essential, writers should use the device for its strengths. "A whimsical and lyrical storytelling style marks the best writing for early readers. Repetition of ideas is also important," says Hadley. "For example, in a story called 'Amazing Maizy' (January 2007), by Kathryn Umbarger, Caitlin is jealous of her best friend's new neighbor. Throughout the story, Caitlin's friend Paige tells Caitlin about what Maizy can do and gushes, 'Isn't that amazing?' Caitlin begins to feel like she is not as special as Maizy, but in the end we learn that Maizy is seeing-impaired. When Caitlin meets Maizy for the first time, we are delighted to hear her say, 'That's amazing.' Children will pick up on repetitive language."

At the same time, the language should have fluency and, whether fiction or nonfiction, the content should have substance. While simple can be good, the writing should never be simplistic.

"At *Highlights* we seek stories that are appropriate for beginning readers, and that younger children (and older children) will enjoy listening to. The writing should flow well, and not be choppy. We don't use word lists. We expect the sentences and vocabulary to be reasonably simple," says Robinson. "Writing for this age should be fun and lively, but the writer needs to be aware of the level of sophistication of the audience. This means appropriate sentence structure and vocabulary and also appropriate humor and story messages. What is funny to a nine-year-old might not be funny to a five-year-old. Children are also dealing with different social and developmental issues at different ages."

Imagination and Shape

Despite common needs for beginning readers, the doors that open over that early reader threshold come in many shapes and colors.

Highlights is "open to talking animal stories if they are done with humor, imagination, and

a fresh approach. We like to see stories about real children in which the main character solves the problem. The main characters should be in the upper end of the age range— six or seven. We need humorous stories and stories that appeal to boys," says Robinson.

A whimsical and lyrical storytelling style marks the best writing for early readers.

Letvin, at *Ladybug*, "would like to see more stories written from a genuine, child's point of view; more fully shaped stories with a beginning, middle, and end (rather than slice-of-life vignettes), which is a challenge given our word limit (no more than 700 words); and more folktales and fantasy. We're also eager to see brief, humorous stories for the younger set that lend themselves to panel or spot illustrations, such as 'That's Strange,' by Suzanne Hardin (November 2006)."

She continues, "Similarly, we're interested in poems that capture a child's perceptions. See, for instance, 'I Found a Stick,' by Jane Dauster (April 2007) and 'Mercy,' by Claire Boiko (April 2007). We'd love also to see more nonsense verse in the tradition of Edward Lear or Dr. Seuss."

Settings can give a story a fresh, inviting approach. "Oddly enough, we receive many more submissions about farm life than city life. We could really use more of the excitement of the city in *Ladybug*. Autumn and winter features are also few and far between," says Letvin. *Ladybug* is also "currently short on our World Around You or nonfiction features, which focus on either natural or cultural phenomena—anything a child might wonder about. In nature pieces, we favor a literary approach (empathic, poetic, or humorous) combined with depth and accuracy of research and observation. 'Baby Blue,' by Eileen Spinelli (August 2007) is an example of how a very pared-down presentation can reflect solid research and attention to the clar-

ifying detail: 'Can you imagine five bathtubs in a row? That's how big a bay blue whale is at birth.' Finally, activity ideas and action rhymes are always welcome, particularly those with an imaginative or storytelling component."

Clubhouse, Jr. has some similar nonfiction needs. "We are always looking for nature factoids about unusual animals or natural wonders," says Hadley. "Recently, we published features on ostriches, hedgehogs, and okapis. We've also published stories about Titan, why leaves change color, animal eyes, and lightning. We look for stories that give children a better understanding of their world.

"In the way of fiction, we love stories that introduce children to people different from themselves" as in "Amazing Maizy," continues Hadley. "We are also interested in historical biographies of great people, particularly those of the Christian faith, told with fictional technique." Finally, *Clubhouse, Jr.* needs rebus stories of 200 words, with 10 to 12 repeated pictures. These may be fiction, or nonfiction about nature. "Pre-readers love to help Mom or Dad *read* as they enjoy these stories together," she says.

Send It On

Clubhouse, Jr. is composed almost entirely of freelance stories. It purchases up to 20 pieces of fiction and 10 nature features

annually, in addition to rebuses. "Amazing Maizy" works, Hadley says, "because the vocabulary is just right for the audience and the dialogue is enchanting. Children will identify with Caitlin's struggle of feeling replaced by Maizy. The resolution of the story is especially sweet."

Hadley cites some other past favorites: "Left-Handed Louie," by Ed Butts (June 2006) "uses clever wording to delight readers. When Louie, a southpaw, plays in the big baseball game his coach encourages him to do things *right*. But every time Louie tries to do things right, he meets with disaster. Finally, the coach tells Louie to give it everything he has *left*. Louie leads his team to victory." Kristi Butler's "Gracie's Groundhog Day Surprise" (February 2007) "teaches children about Groundhog Day and resolving sibling rivalry. When Gracie is selected to be the special groundhog to look for her shadow, her jealous brother Grover digs a fake burrow so Gracie will miss the event. With sound effects, vivid description, and cute dialogue, this story helps children

Markets

- *Clubhouse, Jr.*: 8605 Explorer Dr., Colorado Springs, CO 80920. www.clubhousemagazine.org

- *Highlights for Children*: 803 Church St., Honesdale, PA 18431. www.highlights.com

- *Ladybug*: 70 East Lake St., Suite 300, Chicago, IL 60601. www.cricketmag.com

Other Markets

- *Current Health 1*: Weekly Reader Publishing, 1 Reader's Digest Rd., Pleasantville, NY 10570. www.weeklyreader.com/ch1

- *Kids Hall of Fame News*: 3 Ibsen Court, Dix Hills, NY 11746. www.thekidshalloffame.com

- *Pockets*: 1908 Grand Ave., P.O. Box 340004, Nashville, TN 37203. www.pockets.org

identify with Gracie and Grover as they solve their differences and forgive."

Highlights purchases about 50 early reader pieces each year. They should be no longer than 500 words; rebus stories are no longer than 120 words. Stories that have worked for the magazine include "Goose Says Good-Bye," by Debra Friedland Katz (March 2007). Robinson says, "The story takes the familiar idea of birds migrating and makes it moving and memorable." In Janice Tingum's "Grandma's Purse" (December 2006), "the silly exaggeration is fun to read, but the story also has a clever twist," and "Stinky Treasure," by Jacqueline Adams (April 2006) "has a wonderful, original voice."

All the Cricket "bug" magazines accept unsolicited manuscripts. *Ladybug* would "happily accept 20 or more full-length read-aloud stories this year, 10 or more picture stories, 20 or more nonfiction articles, and 30 poems, action rhymes, and activities—well beyond our present acceptance rate," says Letvin. One that was happily published was Jody Kapp's "Two Places to Call Home," a story about a little boy's trip to see his relatives in Ghana, with a related activity, "Kente Cloth Frame" (March 2007).

"It's helpful to include a brief cover letter indicating your credentials, any relevant expertise or background on the story, and sources as appropriate, particularly for folktales and nonfiction," says Letvin. "We're much more likely to accept a piece that needs significant revision if we see that the author has put serious effort into research. We're apt to dismiss an article, even on a very appealing topic, if the author cites only Web sources and encyclopedias. A crisp presentation without typos will always have an edge."

Listings

How to Use the Listings

The pages that follow feature profiles of 636 magazines that publish articles and stories for, about, or of interest to children and young adults. Throughout the year, we stay on top of the latest happenings in children's magazines to bring you new and different publishing outlets. This year, our research yielded over 60 additional markets for your writing. They are easy to find; look for the listings with a star in the upper right corner.

A Variety of Freelance Opportunities

This year's new listings reflect the interests of today's magazine audience. You'll find magazines targeted to readers interested in nature, the environment, computers, mysteries, child care, careers, different cultures, family activities, and many other topics.

Along with many entertaining and educational magazines aimed at young readers, we list related publications such as national and regional magazines for parents and teachers. Hobby and special interest magazines generally thought of as adult fare but read by many teenagers are listed too.

In the market listings, the Freelance Potential section helps you judge each magazine's receptivity to freelance writers. This section offers information about the number of freelance submissions published each year.

Further opportunities for selling your writing appear in the Additional Listings section on page 283. This section profiles a range of magazines that publish a limited amount of material targeted to children, young adults, parents, or teachers. Other outlets for your writing can be found in the Selected Contests and Awards section, beginning on page 331.

Using Other Sections of the Directory

If you are planning to write for a specific publication, turn to the Magazine and Contest Index beginning on page 372 to locate the listing page. The Category Index, beginning on page 347, will guide you to magazines that publish in your areas of interest. This year, the Category Index also gives the age range of each publication's readership. To find the magazines most open to freelance submissions, turn to the Fifty+ Freelance index on page 346, which lists magazines that rely on freelance writers for over 50% of the material they publish.

Check the Market News, beginning on page 344, to find out what's newly listed, what's not listed and why, and to identify changes in the market that have occurred during the past year.

About the Listings

We revisited last year's listings and, through a series of mailed surveys and phone interviews, verified editors' names, mailing addresses, submissions and payment policies, and current editorial needs. All entries are accurate and up-to-date when we send this market directory to press. Magazine publishing is a fast-moving industry, though, and it is not unusual for facts to change before or shortly after this guide reaches your hands. Magazines close, are sold to new owners, or move; they hire new editors or change their editorial focus. Keep up to date by requesting sample copies and writers' guidelines.

Note that we do *not* list:

- Magazines that did not respond to our questionnaires or phone queries. Know that we make every effort to contact each editor before press date.

- Magazines that *never* accept freelance submissions or work with freelance writers.

To get a real sense of a magazine and its editorial slant, we recommend that you read several recent sample issues cover to cover. This is the best way to be certain a magazine is right for you.

Kid Zone

 — New listing

801 W. Norton Avenue, Suite 200
Muskegon, MI 49441

Editor: Anne Huizenga

— Who to contact

Description and Interests
This magazine offers a great way for kids to have fun reading, creating, learning, and exploring. Each issue is chock full of informational articles on topics such as animals, science, and history, as well as games, recipes, trivia, puzzles, and crafts.
- **Audience:** 4–12 years
- **Frequency:** 6 times each year
- **Circulation:** 65,000
- **Website: www.scottpublications.com**

— Profiles the publication, its interests, and readers

Freelance Potential
90% written by nonstaff writers. Publishes 20–30 freelance submissions yearly; 25% by authors who are new to the magazine. Receives 60–100 queries and unsolicited mss yearly.

— Designates the amount and type of freelance submissions published each year; highlights the publication's receptivity to unpublished writers

Submissions
Query or send complete ms. Accepts hard copy and email to ahuizenga@scottpublications.com. Availability of artwork improves chance of acceptance. SASE. Responds to queries in 1 month, to mss in 1 year.
Articles: 500 words. Factual and informational articles. Topics include animals, food, culture, holiday and seasonal topics, science, and safety.
Artwork: Color prints or transparencies.
Other: Submit seasonal material 4–6 months in advance. See guidelines for specifics.

— Provides guidelines for submitting material; lists word lengths and types of material accepted from freelance writers

Sample Issue
50 pages (no advertising): 7 articles; 3 depts/columns; 10 puzzles and activities. Sample copy, $4.99 with 9x12 SASE. Guidelines and theme list available.
- "Grits." Article explores the history of grits and offers several recipes for making grits dishes.
- "Purple Gallinule." Article describes the characteristics of this dark green and purple bird.
- "The Diary." Story tells how animals learn about privacy when they read a friend's diary.

— Analyzes a recent sample copy of the publication; briefly describes selected articles, stories, departments, etc.

Rights and Payment
World rights. All material, payment rates vary. Pays on publication. Provides 2 author's copies.

— Lists types of rights acquired, payment rate, and number of copies provided to freelance writers

Editor's Comments
We look for writing using "kid slang." We are interested in articles for our "Zones," including "Culture Zone," "Chop Zone," "Fun Zone," and "Critter Zone." You don't need to provide everything for the feature, you may provide just the information, but extras (games, projects, etc.) will increase your chances of acceptance.

— Offers advice from the editor about the publication's writing style, freelance needs, audience, etc.

Icon Key

 New Listing 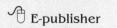 E-publisher 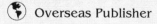 Overseas Publisher

Accepts agented submissions only   ✗ Not currently accepting submissions

Abilities

340 College Street, Suite 401
Toronto, Ontario M5T 3A9
Canada

Managing Editor: Jaclyn Law

Description and Interests
This Canadian lifestyle magazine for people with disabilities seeks to inform, empower, and inspire its readers with conversational articles about all aspects of life, from housing to careers to sports. It also offers advice on parenting a disabled child.
• **Audience:** Families with disabled members
• **Frequency:** Quarterly
• **Circulation:** 20,000
• **Website: www.abilities.ca**

Freelance Potential
80% written by nonstaff writers. Publishes 30–40 freelance submissions yearly; 5–10% by unpublished writers, 50% by authors who are new to the magazine. Receives 120 queries, 504 unsolicited mss yearly.

Submissions
Prefers query with writing samples; will accept complete ms. Accepts email to ray@abilities.ca. No simultaneous submissions. Responds in 2–3 months.
Articles: 1,500–2,000 words. Informational, self-help, and how-to articles; profiles; and interviews. Topics include health, technology, careers, and social issues.
Depts/columns: 500–1,200 words. News, media and product reviews, profiles, family life, parenting, education, sports, travel, health, relationships, employment, housing, sexuality, and humor.

Sample Issue
54 pages (50% advertising): 5 articles; 8 depts/columns. Guidelines available.
• "Intelligent Tools." Article reports on assistive technology—products and equipment that help people with disabilities work, play, and communicate more effectively.
• Sample dept/column: "Relationships" discusses love connections between people with disabilities.

Rights and Payment
First-time serial and non-exclusive electronic rights. Written material, $25–$350. Kill fee, 50%. Pays 2 months after publication. Provides 2 contributor's copies.

Editor's Comments
Our readers know what it is like to acquire and live with a disability. We encourage writers to draw on their experiences to illustrate a broader topic and provide practical information that can be applied to daily life.

Ad Astra

1620 I Street NW, Suite 615
Washington, DC 20006

Editor: Anthony Duignan-Cabrera

Description and Interests
Published by the National Space Society, *Ad Astra* covers a broad realm of space exploration and aerospace science topics. Its readers are avid space enthusiasts, scientists, and technologists who are interested in every aspect of this industry.
• **Audience:** Adults and college students
• **Frequency:** Quarterly
• **Website: www.imaginova.com**

Freelance Potential
95% written by nonstaff writers. Publishes 50 freelance submissions yearly. Receives 65 queries and unsolicited mss yearly.

Submissions
Query or send complete ms with résumé. Accepts disk submissions and email submissions to aduignan@hq.space.com. SASE. Response time varies.
Articles: Word lengths vary. Informational and factual articles; profiles; and interviews. Topics include science and technology related to space exploration and issues related to the aerospace industry.
Depts/columns: Word lengths vary. Reviews and opinion pieces.

Sample Issue
48 pages (14% advertising): 7 articles; 5 depts/columns. Sample copy, $11.25 ($4 postage). Guidelines and editorial calendar available.
• "Moon Base: The Next Step in the Exploration of the Solar System." Article details how NASA plans to return to the moon.
• "Parom: Russia's Response to a Retiring Shuttle Fleet." Article examines Russia's efforts to create a new workhorse for low Earth orbit.
• Sample dept/column: "Opinion" tells how tax incentives can be used to enable private space enterprise.

Rights and Payment
First North American serial rights. No payment.

Editor's Comments
All sections of our magazine are open to new writers with the exception of our "Spotlight" and "Community" departments. Our mission is to educate the public about space exploration and science. We will consider well-written articles that appeal to people who are passionate about our subject.

ADDitude

39 West 37th Street, 15th Floor
New York, NY 10018

Submissions Editor

Description and Interests
This magazine for parents of children with Attention-Deficit Disorder (as well as adults with ADD) publishes useful articles on managing its symptoms and helping kids to live fulfilling lives.
• **Audience:** Parents
• **Frequency:** 6 times each year
• **Circulation:** 40,000
• **Website:** www.additudemag.com

Freelance Potential
80% written by nonstaff writers. Publishes 15–20 freelance submissions yearly; 30% by unpublished writers, 30% by authors who are new to the magazine. Receives 96 queries yearly.

Submissions
Query. Accepts email queries to submissions@additudemag.com. Response time varies.
Articles: To 2,000 words. Informational articles and personal experience pieces. Topics include ADD and ADHD, education, medication, recreation, organization, parenting, and child development.
Depts/columns: Word lengths vary. Profiles of students, teachers, and schools; first-person essays; healthy living; organization; product reviews; and ADD/ADHD news and notes.

Sample Issue
62 pages (33% advertising): 3 articles; 21 depts/columns. Sample copy, $6.95. Guidelines available.
• "How to Raise a Superstar." Article profiles the mothers of TV host Ty Pennington, Olympic swimmer Michael Phelps, and mountain-climber Danielle Fisher—all of whom were diagnosed with ADHD.
• "Helping the Teacher Help Your Child." Article gives tips for effectively working with a school to arrange for special services.
• Sample dept/column: "The Effective Parent" provides eight rules to help children stay motivated.

Rights and Payment
First rights. Written material, payment rates vary. Kill fee, $75. Pays on publication.

Editor's Comments
Writers of the personal essays we publish generally receive a one-year subscription to the magazine. Payment for reported articles varies. We're a small magazine; our pay rates are scaled accordingly. We consider all submissions on a speculative basis.

Adoptalk

North American Council on Adoptable Children
970 Raymond Street, Suite 106
St. Paul, MN 55114-1149

Editor: Diane Riggs

Description and Interests
Factual, substantive articles about adoption and foster care—particularly those related to special needs children—appear in this newsletter, which also features news and updates from NACAC.
• **Audience:** Adults
• **Frequency:** Quarterly
• **Circulation:** 3,700
• **Website:** www.nacac.org

Freelance Potential
30% written by nonstaff writers. Publishes 6–8 freelance submissions yearly; 5% by unpublished writers, 40% by authors who are new to the magazine. Receives 10 queries and unsolicited mss yearly.

Submissions
Query or send complete ms with bibliography. Accepts hard copy and email to dianeriggs@nacac.org. Responds in 2–3 weeks.
Articles: To 2,000 words. Informational articles; personal experience pieces; profiles; and interviews. Topics include adoptive and foster care, parenting, recruitment, adoption news, conference updates, and NACAC membership news updates.
Depts/columns: Word lengths vary. Book reviews and first-person essays.

Sample Issue
20 pages (no advertising): 8 articles; 6 depts/columns. Sample copy, free with 9x12 SASE ($.87 postage). Guidelines available.
• "Now Is the Time for Foster Care Reform." Article stresses reform for the safety, permanency, and well-being of children.
• "Taunting Nightmare." Personal experience piece recounts an adopted child's experiences of abuse and her subsequent rescue.
• "Parenting Children from Substance Abusing Families." Article lists different personality styles children use to relate to authority figures.

Rights and Payment
Rights vary. No payment. Provides 5 author's copies.

Editor's Comments
We promote the welfare of adopted and foster children. Currently, we are particularly seeking articles on parenting children who have special needs due to past trauma or loss. Another issue of interest to our readers is diversity in race, background, and lifestyle.

Adoptive Families

39 West 37th Street, 15th Floor
New York, NY 10018

Editorial Assistant: Joanna Yeung

Description and Interests
This magazine covers the unique issues faced by families before, during, and after adoption, while also tackling routine parenting topics from an adoptive angle.
- **Audience:** Adoptive parents
- **Frequency:** 6 times each year
- **Circulation:** 40,000
- **Website:** www.adoptivefamilies.com

Freelance Potential
75% written by nonstaff writers. Publishes 100 freelance submissions yearly; 20% by unpublished writers, 50% by authors who are new to the magazine. Receives 500–600 queries and unsolicited mss yearly.

Submissions
Query with clips for articles; send complete ms for personal essays. Prefers email to submissions@ adoptivefamilies.com (Microsoft Word attachments). Will accept hard copy. SASE. Responds in 6–8 weeks.
Articles: 500–1,800 words. Informational, self-help, and how-to articles; and personal experience pieces. Topics include preparing for adoption; health; school and education; family, friends, and community; birth families; talking about adoption; and parenting tips.
Depts/columns: To 1,200 words. "The Waiting Game," "Parenting the Child Who Waited," "About Birthparents," "Been There," "Adoption and School," "In My Opinion," "At Home," "Single Parent," "Living with Diversity," and "Parent Exchange."

Sample Issue
74 pages (40% advertising): 3 articles; 11 depts/ columns. Sample copy, $6.95. Guidelines available at website.
- "The Facts of Life." Article provides expert advice on answering kids' questions about sex and adoption.
- "Perception & Reality." Article debunks the myths surrounding modern domestic adoption.
- Sample dept/column: "About Birthparents" is a woman's account of how her child's birth mother put her at ease.

Rights and Payment
All rights. Written material, payment rates vary. Payment policy varies. Provides 2 contributor's copies.

Editor's Comments
We are currently looking for articles that cover the middle-school and teen years; adoptive parents of color; and foster, transracial, and domestic adoption.

Advocate

1881 Little Westkill Road
Prattsville, NY 12468

Publisher: Patricia Keller

Description and Interests
Since 1987, *Advocate* has offered aspiring writers of original, previously unpublished short stories, essays, poetry, and profiles an opportunity to begin, or promote, their careers.
- **Audience:** YA–Adult
- **Frequency:** 6 times each year
- **Circulation:** 10,000

Freelance Potential
90% written by nonstaff writers. Publishes 150 freelance submissions yearly; 65% by unpublished writers, 35% by authors who are new to the magazine. Receives 1,500 unsolicited mss each year.

Submissions
Send complete ms. Accepts hard copy. No simultaneous submissions. SASE. Responds in 6–10 weeks.
Articles: To 1,500 words. Topics include horses, animals, arts, humor, nature, and recreation.
Fiction: To 1,500 words. Genres include adventure; fantasy; folktales; folklore; romance; historical, contemporary, realistic, and science fiction; humor; mystery; suspense; and stories about animals, nature, and the environment.
Artwork: All forms of prints and illustrations.
Other: To 1,500 words. Submit items for the included "Gaited Horse Association Newsletter." Poetry, lengths vary.

Sample Issue
20 pages (50% advertising): 3 articles; 2 stories; 30 poems. Sample copy, $4. Guidelines available.
- "O'Brannigan's Horse." Story tells of the relationship between the author and a larger-than-life horseman named O'Brannigan.
- "The Continuing Saga of Fettuccine and Alfredo." Story relates the perilous adventures of a herd of wild horses told from the perspective of the animals themselves.

Rights and Payment
First rights. No payment. Provides 2 copies.

Editor's Comments
We are interested in high-quality writing on a variety of topics, but particularly on horses, nature, and the environment. We are absolutely not interested in any unwholesome material. Keep in mind that we currently have a backlog of short stories. Poetry and cartoons are always sought, and may be sent individually or in batches.

African American Family

22041 Woodward Avenue
Ferndale, MI 48220

Editor: Denise Crittendon

Description and Interests
This magazine was created specifically for African American families living in Detroit and its surrounding communities. It addresses parenting and child development issues, while also publishing features on entertainment, travel, and education. Regional community projects and current events are also covered, and profiles of local leaders appear regularly.
- **Audience:** Parents
- **Frequency:** Monthly
- **Circulation:** Unavailable
- **Website:** www.metroparent.com

Freelance Potential
20% written by nonstaff writers. Publishes 20 freelance submissions yearly.

Submissions
Query through website only. Accepts simultaneous submissions if identified. Response time varies.
Articles: Word lengths vary. Informational and self-help articles; profiles; interviews; personal experience pieces; and reviews. Topics include current events, education, history, nature, the environment, recreation, social issues, sports, and travel.
Depts/columns: Word lengths vary. Discussions of community issues; regional resources and events; and health and fitness.

Sample Issue
46 pages: 2 articles; 7 depts/columns. Guidelines available at website.
- "Traveling Up North on Less." Article offers descriptions of resorts and campsites that let you vacation in northern Michigan for less than $100 per night.
- "From Wrecked to Rockin'." Article features ideas for doing a total makeover on a child's bedroom.
- "The Birds and the Bees . . . and a Thing Called Love." Article offers advice for talking to your kids about sex.

Rights and Payment
Rights vary. Written material, payment rates vary. Pays on publication.

Editor's Comments
All submissions must come through our website. Work must be professional, reflecting solid reporting and writing skills. We very much prefer writers who use sources and ideas from the greater Detroit metropolitan area.

AIM Magazine

P.O. Box 856
Forest Grove, OR 97116

Editor: Kathleen Letham

Description and Interests
The mission of this publisher is "to purge racism from the human bloodstream." Its articles, stories, and poems are intended to bridge the gap between races, cultures, and religions.
- **Audience:** Educators
- **Frequency:** Quarterly
- **Circulation:** 2,000
- **Website:** www.aimmagazine.org

Freelance Potential
95% written by nonstaff writers. Publishes 50 freelance submissions yearly; 50% by unpublished writers, 80% by authors who are new to the magazine. Receives 98 unsolicited mss yearly.

Submissions
Send complete ms. Accepts email submissions only to submissions@aimmagazine.org (attach document). No simultaneous submissions. SASE. Responds in 3–4 months.
Articles: To 4,000 words. Informational articles; personal experience and opinion pieces; essays; profiles; and interviews. Topics include race, social issues, bigotry, culture, ethnic holidays, politics, and humor.
Fiction: To 4,000 words. Genres include inspirational, historical, contemporary, ethnic, multicultural, humorous, and literary fiction.
Poetry: To 100 lines; limit 5 poems per submission.
Artwork: B/W or color prints. Line art. JPG, TIF, or BMP images at 300 dpi.

Sample Issue
50 pages: 1 article; 9 stories; 2 essays; 4 poems. Sample copy, $5 with 9x12 SASE (5 first-class stamps). Guidelines, editorial calendar, and theme list available.
- "Mordecai's Grave." Story depicts the friendship between an old black woman and a white girl.
- "Eradicating Racism—One Person at a Time." Essay talks about individual responsibility.

Rights and Payment
First rights. Articles, $15–$25. Short stories, $100. Pays on publication. Provides 1 contributor's copy.

Editor's Comments
Please provide an introduction to yourself and your work in a concise statement that includes your contact information. All editorial decisions are based on the content and quality of the work submitted.

Alateen Talk

Al-Anon Family Group
1600 Corporate Landing Parkway
Virginia Beach, VA 23454-5617

Associate Director: Mary Lou Mahlman

Description and Interests
Published by Al-Anon Family Group, this newsletter acts as a forum for young people who have had their lives affected by someone else's drinking. It shares members' experiences, hopes, and strengths through its articles and letters.
• **Audience:** 6–18 years
• **Frequency:** Quarterly
• **Circulation:** 4,000
• **Website:** www.al-anon.alateen.org

Freelance Potential
90% written by nonstaff writers. Publishes 85–120 freelance submissions yearly; 80% by unpublished writers, 75% by authors who are new to the magazine. Receives 100–150 unsolicited mss yearly.

Submissions
Accepts complete ms from Alateen members only. Accepts hard copy. SASE. Responds in 2 weeks.
Articles: Word lengths vary. Self-help and personal experience pieces. Topics include alcoholism and its effects on relationships, social issues, and family life.
Depts/columns: Staff written.
Artwork: B/W line art.
Other: Poetry.

Sample Issue
8 pages (no advertising): 2 articles; 15 letters; 2 activities. Sample copy, free with 9x12 SASE ($.87 postage). Guidelines available to Alateen members.
• "From a Workshop at Komaic 2006." Article compares how Alateen groups from the past and present perform outreach.
• "Sharing from Alateen Meetings." Article describes what the Alateen program is and how teens can reach out to others in need.
• "Serenity Island." Activity offers a game to be used at meetings that centers on the Twelve Steps and Twelve Traditions for Alateen.

Rights and Payment
All rights. No payment.

Editor's Comments
All of our material is written by young Al-Anon members, who are usually teens. We look for personal sharings that act as recovery tools that can help young people deal with their problems and live better lives.

Alfred Hitchcock Mystery Magazine

475 Park Avenue South
New York, NY 10016

Editor: Linda Landrigan

Description and Interests
This mystery magazine named for the acclaimed movie director features every type of crime story, from police procedurals, to private eyes, suspense, courtroom dramas, and espionage.
• **Audience:** YA–Adult
• **Frequency:** 10 times each year
• **Circulation:** 150,000
• **Website:** www.themysteryplace.com

Freelance Potential
97% written by nonstaff writers. Publishes 90–100 freelance submissions yearly; 5% by unpublished writers, 10% by authors who are new to the magazine. Receives 1,000–1,500 unsolicited mss yearly.

Submissions
Send complete ms. Accepts hard copy. No simultaneous submissions. SASE. Responds in 3–5 months.
Fiction: 12,000 words. Classic crime mysteries, detective stories, suspense, private-eye tales, courtroom drama, and espionage.
Depts/columns: Word lengths vary. Reviews, puzzles, and bookstore profiles.

Sample Issue
146 pages (2% advertising): 10 stories; 7 depts/columns. Sample copy, $5. Guidelines available.
• "Ten Little Gangsters." Depression-era crime story features Al Capone and his henchmen.
• "The Limner's Masterpiece." Story revolves around an artist who is called to a family's home to record a tragic death.
• Sample dept/column: "Booked & Printed" features reviews of new mystery books.

Rights and Payment
First serial, anthology, and foreign rights. Written material, payment rates vary. Pays on acceptance. Provides 3 contributor's copies.

Editor's Comments
Finding new authors is a great pleasure for us, and we look forward to reading the fiction you send. Since we do read all submissions, there is no need to query first; please send the entire story. Our one requirement is that the story must be about a crime, the threat of a crime, or the fear of a crime. We are a mystery magazine and your work must fit into that genre. We occasionally accept ghost stories or supernatural tales, as long as they involve a crime.

American Baby

375 Lexington Avenue, 9th Floor
New York, NY 10017

Editorial Assistant: Katie Rockman

Description and Interests
This is a magazine for first-time parents who are looking for guidance from pregnancy through toddlerhood. Its motto is "Mom to Mom—Woman to Woman," yet it covers fatherhood as well.
- **Audience:** Parents
- **Frequency:** Monthly
- **Circulation:** 2.1 million
- **Website:** www.americanbaby.com

Freelance Potential
55% written by nonstaff writers. Publishes 24 freelance submissions yearly; 20% by unpublished writers. Receives 996 unsolicited mss each year.

Submissions
Query with clips or writing samples; or send complete ms. Accepts hard copy and simultaneous submissions if identified. SASE. Responds in 2 months.
Articles: 1,000–2,000 words. Informational and how-to articles; profiles; interviews; humor; and personal experience pieces. Topics include health, fitness, nutrition, child care, child development, religion, and travel.
Depts/columns: 1,000 words. Health briefs, fitness, new products, and fashion.
Other: Submit seasonal material 3 months in advance.

Sample Issue
72 pages (50% advertising): 3 articles; 9 depts/columns. Guidelines available.
- "How Much Should Babies Eat?" Article gives stage-by-stage advice on introducing solids.
- "Bedtime Story." Feature details pleasant ways to put a child to sleep.
- Sample dept/column: "In Your Words: Girl of My Dreams" is a mother's reflection on the daughter she never had.

Rights and Payment
First serial rights. Articles, to $2,000. Depts/columns, to $1,000. Pays on acceptance. Provides 5 contributor's copies.

Editor's Comments
We cover health, medical, and child-care concerns for expectant and new parents, particularly those having their first child or those whose child is between the ages of birth and two years. Mothers are the primary readers, but fathers' issues are equally important.

American Careers

6701 West 64th Street
Overland Park, KS 66202

Editor: Mary Pitchford

Description and Interests
This magazine offers the latest career information, how-to articles, self-assessments, and other articles that help middle school and high school students choose and develop future careers. Two age-appropriate editions are published.
- **Audience:** 12–18 years
- **Frequency:** Annually
- **Circulation:** 400,000
- **Website:** www.carcom.com

Freelance Potential
20% written by nonstaff writers. Publishes 10 freelance submissions yearly; 20% by authors who are new to the magazine. Receives 240+ queries yearly.

Submissions
Query with résumé and clips. Accepts hard copy. SASE. Responds in 2 months.
Articles: 300–750 words. Informational and how-to articles; personal experience pieces; and profiles. Topics include specific careers, career clusters, self-evaluation, and entrepreneurs.
Depts/columns: 300–750 words. Educational opportunities, employability and life skills, careers.
Artwork: Color prints or digital images.
Other: Quizzes and self-assessments.

Sample Issue
64 pages (no advertising): 17 articles; 8 depts/columns. Sample copy, $4 with 9x12 SASE (5 first-class stamps). Guidelines available.
- "Interesting Careers in Economics." Article presents an overview of finance-related careers.
- "Substance Abuse Counselors Help Addicts Find Their Way Back." Article profiles three substance abuse counselors, who talk about their jobs.
- Sample dept/column: "4 Tips for Planning a Life" gives advice on turning fear of the unknown into a plan for success.

Rights and Payment
All rights. All material, payment rates vary. Pays on publication. Provides 2 contributor's copies.

Editor's Comments
Articles should be written at a seventh-grade reading level. Most of the assignments that we make are for short career profiles. Some topics may require additional space for impact and clarity; these topics are discussed on an individual basis.

American Cheerleader

110 William Street, 23rd Floor
New York, NY 10038

Editor-in-Chief: Marisa Walker

Description and Interests
Teens who are passionate about cheerleading read this magazine for training ideas, profiles of cheerleaders and squads, competition reports, and updates on style and beauty.
- **Audience:** 13–18 years
- **Frequency:** 6 times each year
- **Circulation:** 150,000
- **Website:** www.americancheerleader.com

Freelance Potential
40% written by nonstaff writers. Publishes 15 freelance submissions yearly; 20% by unpublished writers, 10% by authors who are new to the magazine. Receives 12–24 queries and unsolicited mss yearly.

Submissions
Query with clips; or send complete ms. Prefers email submissions to mwalker@americancheerleader.com. Will accept hard copy. SASE. Responds in 3 months.
Articles: To 1,000 words. Informational and how-to articles; profiles; personal experience pieces; and photo-essays. Topics include cheerleading, workouts, competitions, scholarships, fitness, college, careers, and popular culture.
Depts/columns: Word lengths vary. Safety issues, health, nutrition, beauty, fashion, fundraising, and new product information.
Artwork: High resolution digital images; 35mm color slides.

Sample Issue
112 pages (40% advertising): 19 articles; 6 depts/columns; 1 quiz. Sample copy, $3.99 with 9x12 SASE ($1.70 postage). Editorial calendar available.
- "Moving Forward." Article describes how a cheerleading squad dealt with a tragedy after a devastating tornado.
- "Long Lean Legs." Article offers tips to tone down muscular legs.
- Sample dept/column: "What's Going On" features short news items from the world of cheerleading.

Rights and Payment
All rights. All material, payment rates vary. Pays 2 months after acceptance. Provides 1 author's copy.

Editor's Comments
We're always looking for more fun articles on topics related to cheerleading. Write in a style that will engage our teenage audience.

American Girl

American Girl Publishing
8400 Fairway Place
Middleton, WI 53562

Editorial Assistant

Description and Interests
With the mission of celebrating girls of yesterday and today, *American Girl* publishes historical and contemporary fiction and nonfiction, as well as short profiles, activities, crafts, and games. Its target audience is girls in the "tween" years.
- **Audience:** 8–12 years
- **Frequency:** 6 times each year
- **Circulation:** 700,000
- **Website:** www.americangirl.com

Freelance Potential
10% written by nonstaff writers. Publishes 5 freelance submissions yearly; 5% by unpublished writers, 5% by authors who are new to the magazine. Receives 648 queries and unsolicited mss yearly.

Submissions
Query for nonfiction. Send complete ms for fiction. Accepts hard copy and simultaneous submissions if identified. SASE. Responds in 4 months.
Articles: 500–1,000 words. Informational articles; profiles; and interviews. Topics include history, nature, food, hobbies, crafts, sports, and culture.
Fiction: To 2,300 words. Contemporary, historical, and multicultural fiction and mystery.
Depts/columns: 175 words. Profiles, how-to pieces, and craft ideas.
Other: Word games and puzzles.

Sample Issue
48 pages (no advertising): 4 articles; 1 story; 6 depts/columns; 1 poster; 1 quiz. Sample copy, $4.50 at newsstands. Guidelines available.
- "Talk to Your Parents About Anything." Article suggests the best ways to approach parents about important issues.
- "The Misadventures of Average Girl." Story features a girl who overcomes disappointment.
- Sample dept/column: "Girls Express" offers short profiles, fun ideas, and easy crafts.

Rights and Payment
First North American serial rights. Written material, payment rates vary. Pays on acceptance. Provides 1 contributor's copy.

Editor's Comments
The "Girls' Express" section is most open to new writers. Send short profiles of girls who are into sports, the arts, interesting hobbies, and cultural activities.

American Libraries

American Library Association
50 East Huron Street
Chicago, IL 60611

Acquisitions Editor: Pamela Goodes

Description and Interests
Professional librarians and media specialists read this 100-year-old publication of the American Library Association (ALA) for news and information about library programming and management.
- **Audience:** Librarians and library media specialists
- **Frequency:** 11 times each year
- **Circulation:** 56,000
- **Website:** www.ala.org/alonline

Freelance Potential
60% written by nonstaff writers. Publishes 50 freelance submissions yearly; 50% by authors who are new to the magazine. Receives 492 mss yearly.

Submissions
Send complete ms. Accepts hard copy, IBM disk submissions (Microsoft Word), and email submissions to americanlibraries@ala.org. No simultaneous submissions. SASE. Responds in 8–10 weeks.
Articles: 600–2,000 words. Informational articles; profiles; interviews; and personal experience pieces. Topics include modern libraries, library and ALA history, technology, leadership, advocacy, funding, and privacy.
Depts/columns: Word lengths vary. News, opinion, profiles, book and media reviews, information technology, ALA events, career leads, professional development, and Internet updates.

Sample Issue
152 pages (27% advertising): 11 articles; 23 depts/columns. Sample copy, $6. Guidelines available.
- "Archiving America." Personal essay by documentary filmmaker Ken Burns discusses his lifelong love of learning and libraries.
- "Capital Improvements." Article describes a comprehensive plan to revamp the District of Columbia Public Library System and its facilities.
- Sample dept/column: "Youth Matters" recalls the joy of discovery through encyclopedias.

Rights and Payment
First North American serial rights. Written material, $50–$400. Pays on acceptance. Provides 1+ contributor's copies.

Editor's Comments
Articles should be factually based and written in a conversational style. We do not publish scholarly articles with excessive footnotes.

American School & University

9800 Metcalf Avenue
Overland Park, KS 66212

Executive Editor: Susan Lustig

Description and Interests
The focus of this magazine is on educational facilities, including building design, construction, and maintenance. Read by school administrators and architects, it features how-to articles, industry reports, case histories, and new product information.
- **Audience:** School administrators and architects
- **Frequency:** Monthly
- **Circulation:** 65,000
- **Website:** www.asumag.com

Freelance Potential
35% written by nonstaff writers. Publishes 40 freelance submissions yearly; 30% by authors who are new to the magazine. Receives 180 queries yearly.

Submissions
Query with outline. Prefers email queries to slustig@asumag.com. Will accept hard copy. SASE. Responds in 2 weeks.
Articles: 1,200 words. Informational and how-to articles. Topics include facilities management, maintenance, technology, energy, furnishings, and security.
Depts/columns: 250–350 words. New technologies, new product information, and construction and planning issues.

Sample Issue
58 pages (55% advertising): 5 articles; 7 depts/columns. Sample copy, $10. Guidelines and editorial calendar available.
- "Water Ways." Article reports on the new technologies that will maximize water efficiency and improve student hygiene in new school buildings.
- "Adjusting to Technology." Article explains why classroom furniture selection should depend on the kind of technology students will be using.
- Sample dept/column: "Know-How" examines different types of door/entry systems.

Rights and Payment
All rights. Written material, payment rates and payment policy vary. Provides 2 contributor's copies.

Editor's Comments
Most of the articles that we accept for publication correspond to our editorial calendar. We look for articles that give readers new insight into the market, provide tips and pointers, and help them through the design or renovation process. Remember that we don't target teachers or students.

American Secondary Education

Ashland University, Schar College of Education
401 College Avenue
Ashland, OR 44805

Editor: Dr. James A. Rycik

Description and Interests
Educational practitioners and researchers contribute to this scholarly journal, which focuses on current theories and practice related to secondary education. It covers topics of relevance to both teachers and school administrators.
- **Audience:** Secondary school educators and researchers
- **Frequency:** 3 times each year
- **Circulation:** 450
- **Website: www3.ashland.edu/ase.html**

Freelance Potential
95% written by nonstaff writers. Publishes 20 freelance submissions yearly; 10% by unpublished writers, 80% by authors who are new to the magazine. Receives 40–50 unsolicited mss yearly.

Submissions
Send 3 copies of complete ms with 100-word abstract. No simultaneous submissions. SASE. Response time varies.
Articles: 10–30 double-spaced manuscript pages. Informational articles. Topics include secondary and middle school education research and practice.
Depts/columns: Book reviews, word lengths vary. "In the Schools" provides a look at innovative programs that are unique to a particular school district.

Sample Issue
118 pages (no advertising): 8 articles. Sample copy, free. Guidelines available.
- "Classroom Management in Secondary Schools: A Study of Student Teachers' Successful Strategies." Article looks at different ways student teachers managed discipline problems and chronically disruptive children.
- "Moral Aspects of Grading: A Study of High School English Teachers' Perceptions." Article explores a framework that considers the grading process in terms of truth, worthiness, and trust.

Rights and Payment
All rights. No payment. Provides 1 contributor's copy.

Editor's Comments
We are now willing to consider articles that address middle school issues, as well as current theory, research, and practice in secondary schools. We usually offer a mix of research reports and informed commentary from educational professionals.

American String Teacher

4153 Chain Bridge Road
Fairfax, VA 22030

Editor: Mary Jane Dye

Description and Interests
This magazine presents articles and news to assist string teachers in private studios and schools in their professional development. Published by the American String Association, it covers topics such as teaching, methodology, techniques, and performing.
- **Audience:** String teachers and performers
- **Frequency:** Quarterly
- **Circulation:** 11,500
- **Website: www.astaweb.com**

Freelance Potential
75% written by nonstaff writers. Publishes 30 freelance submissions yearly; 5% by unpublished writers, 50% by authors who are new to the magazine. Receives 24–36 queries yearly.

Submissions
Prefers query. Will accept 5 copies of complete ms. Prefers email submissions to komortension@cox.net. Will accept hard copy. No simultaneous submissions. SASE. Responds in 3 months.
Articles: 1,000–3,000 words. Informational and factual articles; profiles; and association news. Topics include teaching, methodology, techniques, competitions, and auditions.
Depts/columns: Word lengths vary. Teaching tips, opinion pieces, and industry news.

Sample Issue
108 pages (45% advertising): 5 articles; 12 depts/columns. Sample copy, free with 9x12 SASE ($3.25 postage). Guidelines available.
- "Getting the Most from Your Competition Experience." Article offers advice on performing in competitions and auditions.
- "411 for College String Teachers." Article offers information on how to use electronic databases for research.
- Sample dept/column: "Teaching Tips" looks at the Practice Factory analogy as a tool for students.

Rights and Payment
All rights. No payment. Provides 5 author's copies.

Editor's Comments
We prefer to publish articles that are based on research rather than the presentation of the results of the research, and that present a national perspective rather than that of one area of the country. We accept articles from members only.

Analog Science Fiction and Fact

Dell Magazine Fiction Group
475 Park Avenue South
New York, NY 10016

Editor: Stanley Schmidt

Description and Interests
This journal publishes a broad range of science fiction stories as well as factual articles about real-life scientific breakthroughs.
- **Audience:** YA–Adult
- **Frequency:** 10 times each year
- **Circulation:** 40,000
- **Website:** www.analogsf.com

Freelance Potential
100% written by nonstaff writers. Publishes 80–90 freelance submissions yearly; 10% by unpublished writers, 10% by authors who are new to the magazine. Receives 6,000 unsolicited mss yearly.

Submissions
Query for serials. Send complete ms for shorter works. Accepts hard copy. SASE. Responds in 6 weeks.
Articles: To 6,000 words. Informational articles. Topics include science and technology.
Fiction: Serials, 40,000–80,000 words. Novellas and novelettes, 10,000–20,000 words. Short stories, 2,000–7,000 words. Physical, sociological, psychological, and technological science fiction.
Depts/columns: Staff written.

Sample Issue
144 pages (7% advertising): 1 article; 1 serial; 1 novella; 1 novelette; 2 short stories; 6 depts/columns. Guidelines available.
- "Toward a Not-Just-Diamond Age." Article describes the disadvantages of carbon and the promise of other nanotechnological materials.
- "Cool Neighbor." Novelette chronicles the legacy of a space-station physicist who is killed by a supernova.
- "Trucks." Short story details a mother's realization that her young son is not like everyone else.

Rights and Payment
First North American serial and non-exclusive rights. Serials, $.04 per word; other written material, $.05–$.08 per word. Pays on acceptance. Provides 2 contributor's copies.

Editor's Comments
An author's name, reputation, or publishing history has *absolutely no effect* on our decision about whether to buy a story. We consider material solely on the basis of merit. We are eager to find and develop new, capable writers.

Aquila

P.O. Box 2518
Eastbourne, East Sussex BN21 2BB
United Kingdom

Editor: Jackie Berry

Description and Interests
Created for British children with lively minds, *Aquila* fills its pages with word and math games, puzzles, art and activity ideas, and articles about science and the world around us. It is written to appeal to readers in the middle grades.
- **Audience:** 8–13 years
- **Frequency:** Monthly
- **Circulation:** 7,500
- **Website:** www.aquila.co.uk

Freelance Potential
30% written by nonstaff writers. Publishes 24 freelance submissions yearly; 1% by unpublished writers, 1% by authors who are new to the magazine. Receives 492 queries yearly.

Submissions
Query with résumé. Accepts hard copy and email to info@aquila.co.uk (Microsoft Word attachments). SAE/IRC. Responds in 2–4 months.
Articles: 750–800 words. Informational and how-to articles; profiles; and interviews. Topics include pets, animals, the arts, crafts, hobbies, math, history, nature, the environment, science, and technology.
Fiction: To 1,000 words. Genres include historical and contemporary fiction, science fiction, folklore, folktales, mystery, and adventure.
Artwork: Color prints and transparencies. JPEG digital images.
Other: Arts and crafts activities. Submit seasonal material 3 months in advance.

Sample Issue
20 pages (no advertising): 5 articles; 1 story; 7 activities; 1 joke page. Sample copy, £5 with 9x12 SAE/IRC; also available at website. Writers' guidelines available.
- "Fish for All." Article investigates the problem of dwindling fish stocks and what we can do about it.
- "Edward Elgar." Article examines the life of one of England's greatest composers.

Rights and Payment
First rights. Articles and fiction, £60–£80. Artwork, payment rates vary. Pays on publication. Provides up to 6 contributor's copies.

Editor's Comments
We have a good pool of freelancers now, but if you send us something original we will consider it.

Art Education

Virginia Commonwealth University
Department of Art Education
P.O. Box 843084
Richmond, VA 23284

Editor: Dr. Pam Taylor

Description and Interests
This journal of the National Art Education Association keeps art teachers at all grade levels apprised of developments in their field while also providing them with instructional resources and curricula.
- **Audience:** Art educators
- **Frequency:** 6 times each year
- **Circulation:** 20,000
- **Website:** www.naea-reston.org/publications.html

Freelance Potential
100% written by nonstaff writers. Publishes 36 freelance submissions yearly; 25% by unpublished writers, 5% by authors who are new to the magazine. Receives 120 unsolicited mss yearly.

Submissions
Send 3 copies of complete ms. Accepts hard copy, disk submissions, and simultaneous submissions if identified. SASE. Responds in 8–10 weeks.
Articles: To 3,000 words. Informational articles; personal experience pieces; interviews; and profiles. Topics include the visual arts, curriculum planning, art history, and art criticism.
Depts/columns: To 2,750 words. "Instructional Resources" features lesson plan ideas.
Artwork: 8x10 or 5x7 B/W prints or slides. Digital images.

Sample Issue
52 pages (3% advertising): 2 articles; 5 depts/columns. Sample copy, $1.25 with 9x12 SASE ($.87 postage). Guidelines available.
- "Principles of Possibility." Article discusses establishing a quality art and culture curriculum.
- "Contemporary Approaches to Critical Thinking and the World Wide Web." Article summarizes research into using the Internet to teach critical thinking.
- Sample dept/column: "Instructional Resources" includes a curriculum for grades 9 to 12 built around artists' books.

Rights and Payment
All rights. No payment. Provides 2 author's copies.

Editor's Comments
Anyone with access to museum objects and artworks and curriculum-writing expertise is welcome to submit a manuscript to our "Instructional Resources" department. In the past, such manuscripts have come from individuals or teams of teachers and museum educators.

Arts & Activities

12345 World Trade Drive
San Diego, CA 92128

Editor-in-Chief: Maryellen Bridge

Description and Interests
Art educators at all grade levels rely on the advice and fresh ideas presented in this magazine. It features descriptions of successful teaching programs from professionals working in kindergarten through high school classrooms.
- **Audience:** Art educators, grades K–12
- **Frequency:** 10 times each year
- **Circulation:** 20,000
- **Website:** www.artsandactivities.com

Freelance Potential
90% written by nonstaff writers. Publishes 60–90 freelance submissions yearly; 30% by unpublished writers, 30% by authors who are new to the magazine. Receives 144+ unsolicited mss yearly.

Submissions
Send complete ms. Accepts disk submissions with hard copy. No simultaneous submissions. SASE. Responds in 4–8 months.
Articles: Word lengths vary. Informational, how-to, and practical application articles; and personal experience pieces. Topics include art education, program development, collage, printmaking, art appreciation, and composition.
Depts/columns: Word lengths vary. New product information, short news items, and book reviews.
Artwork: Color photos; digital images, minimum 2550 x 3400 pixel resolution.
Other: Lesson plans for classroom projects.

Sample Issue
54 pages (29% advertising): 10 articles; 6 depts/columns. Sample copy, $3 with 9x12 SASE ($2 postage). Guidelines and theme list available.
- "Pastel Picasso." Article describes a unit that teaches students about the Cubist movement and helps them celebrate old masters in a new way.
- Sample dept/column: "Forum" recounts one art teacher's experiences in Russia.

Rights and Payment
First North American serial rights. All material, payment rates vary. Pays on publication. Provides 2 contributor's copies.

Editor's Comments
Please note that our magazine is for art teachers; we do not publish craft projects written for kids. Your article should be presented in a conversational style.

Asimov's Science Fiction

Dell Magazine Group
475 Park Avenue South, 11th Floor
New York, NY 10016

Editor: Sheila Williams

Description and Interests
This award-winning journal publishes character-driven science fiction and fantasy stories that examine or illuminate some aspect of human existence.
- **Audience:** YA–Adult
- **Frequency:** 10 times each year
- **Circulation:** 60,000
- **Website:** www.asimovs.com

Freelance Potential
97% written by nonstaff writers. Publishes 85 freelance submissions yearly; 10% by unpublished writers, 30% by authors who are new to the magazine. Receives 8,400 unsolicited mss yearly.

Submissions
Send complete ms. Accepts hard copy. No simultaneous submissions. SASE. Responds in 6–8 weeks.
Fiction: To 20,000 words. Genres include science fiction and "borderline" fantasy.
Depts/columns: Word lengths vary. Book and website reviews.
Other: Poetry, to 40 lines.

Sample Issue
144 pages (10% advertising): 2 novelettes; 6 stories; 6 depts/columns. Sample copy, $5 with 9x12 SASE ($.77 postage). Guidelines available.
- "Nano Comes to Clifford Falls." Story describes how machines that can instantly create anything transform life in a small town.
- "The Djinn's Wife." Novelette set in near-future India tells of a woman who falls in love with a supernatural being.
- Sample dept/column: "Thought Experiments" provides an insider's view of the Science Fiction Museum and Hall of Fame.

Rights and Payment
First worldwide English-language serial rights. Fiction, $.06–$.08 per word. Poetry, $1 per line. Depts/columns, payment rates vary. Pays on acceptance. Provides 2 contributor's copies.

Editor's Comments
Serious, thoughtful, yet accessible stories constitute the majority of our purchases, but there's always room for the humorous as well. Unfortunately, due to time limitations, we are unable to provide specific criticism of each story that is submitted to us for review.

ASK

Carus Publishing
70 East Lake Street, Suite 300
Chicago, IL 60601

Submissions Editor: Romana Profopin

Description and Interests
This magazine is designed for curious kids who want to know more about their world. Through engaging articles, vivid photography and illustrations, activities, and cartoons, children get a better understanding of living creatures and the environment.
- **Audience:** 7–10 years
- **Frequency:** 9 times each year
- **Circulation:** 42,000
- **Website:** www.cricketmag.com

Freelance Potential
80% written by nonstaff writers. Of the freelance submissions published yearly, 2% are by unpublished writers and 10% are by new authors.

Submissions
All material is commissioned from experienced authors. Send résumé and clips.
Articles: To 1,500 words. Informational articles; interviews; and photo-essays. Topics include animals, science, the environment, nature, computers, technology, history, math, and the arts.
Depts/columns: Word lengths vary. News items and contests.

Sample Issue
34 pages (no advertising): 5 articles; 7 depts/columns. Sample copy available at website.
- "Ocean Pathfinders." Article describes how sailors and scientists studied the tides and currents of the Atlantic Ocean.
- "The Long Swim." Article follows a pregnant humpback whale as she stores up food for her long journey to warmer waters where she will give birth to her calf.
- Sample dept/column: "Scoops" provides the latest news on animals and the environment.

Rights and Payment
Rights vary. Written material, payment rates vary. Payment policy varies.

Editor's Comments
All articles are assigned to experienced writers who understand our young audience and are able to convey complex ideas and theories in language that challenges and engages young readers. We are interested in seeing more pieces on engineering, technology, physics, and chemistry. We would like fewer submissions about animals and the animal world.

Atlanta Baby

2346 Perimeter Park Drive, Suite 101
Atlanta, GA 30341

Editor: Liz White

Description and Interests
This "guide for new and expectant parents" in Atlanta covers all the bases from pregnancy through age two, including local childbirth classes, pediatricians, support groups, and other family resources.
• **Audience:** Parents
• **Frequency:** Quarterly
• **Circulation:** 25,000
• **Website: www.atlantaparent.com**

Freelance Potential
25% written by nonstaff writers. Publishes 50 freelance submissions yearly; 5% by unpublished writers, 30% by authors who are new to the magazine. Receives 2,400 unsolicited mss yearly.

Submissions
Send complete ms. Prefers email submissions to lwhite@atlantaparent.com. Will accept hard copy. SASE. Responds in 2 months.
Articles: 600–1,200 words. Informational and how-to articles; and humor. Topics include pregnancy, childbirth, child development, early education, health, fitness, and parenting.
Depts/columns: Word lengths vary. Short essays and resources guides.
Other: Submit seasonal material 6 months in advance.

Sample Issue
34 pages (50% advertising): 7 articles; 3 depts/columns. Sample copy, $2 with 9x12 SASE. Guidelines available.
• "Your Toughest Baby Products Questions Answered." Article provides expert advice on using everything from breast pumps to car seats.
• "All About the First Trimester." Article gives an overview of the physiological changes that occur during the first three months of pregnancy.
• Sample dept/column: "Baby Bits" includes reviews of maternity and baby products.

Rights and Payment
One-time rights. Written material, $35–$50. Pays on publication. Provides 1 tearsheet.

Editor's Comments
When writing about a problem, give parents the symptoms or signs of the problem and then the solution. We encourage you to include the addresses and phone numbers for national or Atlanta-based resources.

Atlanta Parent

2346 Perimeter Park Drive, Suite 101
Atlanta, GA 30341

Publisher: Liz White

Description and Interests
This sister publication of *Atlanta Baby* offers service-oriented articles about raising children from birth through age 18.
• **Audience:** Parents
• **Frequency:** Monthly
• **Circulation:** 120,000
• **Website: www.atlantaparent.com**

Freelance Potential
40% written by nonstaff writers.

Submissions
Send complete ms. Accepts hard copy, disk submissions, and email submissions to lwhite@ atlantaparent.com. SASE. Response time varies.
Articles: 800–1,200 words. Informational and how-to articles; and humor. Topics include education, child care, child development, health, and parenting issues.
Depts/columns: Word lengths vary. "News You Can Use," "Community Corner," "Ask a Teacher," "Hip Mom," "Family Fun Guide," and "Humor in the House."
Other: Submit secular holiday material 6 months in advance.

Sample Issue
98 pages (55% advertising): 7 articles; 6 depts/columns. Sample copy, $3 with 9x12 SASE. Guidelines available.
• "A Giving Spirit." Article provides ideas for raising compassionate kids.
• "Holiday 'Ex' Etiquette." Article tells how fractured families can find peaceful solutions for holiday gatherings.
• "Skiing Down Easy Street." Article gives tips for hitting the slopes with the entire family.
• Sample dept/column: "Hip Mom" provides fashion and beauty advice for busy mothers.

Rights and Payment
One-time print and Internet rights. Written material, $35–$50. Pays on publication. Provides 1 tearsheet.

Editor's Comments
All of our articles are very down-to-earth—we do not publish philosophical or theoretical articles. Most are third person; we rarely publish first-person pieces, with the exception of humor pieces. We do not publish short stories or poetry. If we like your article but have no immediate plans to use it, our normal procedure is to keep your article on file for possible future publication.

Atlanta Sporting Family

240 Prospect Place
Alpharetta, GA 30005

Editor: Jennifer Morrell

Description and Interests
Families interested in leading active, healthy lifestyles turn to this publication for ideas on getting involved in local sports and recreational activities. Directed toward families in the Atlanta region, it also covers local events and resources.
- **Audience:** Parents
- **Frequency:** 8 times each year
- **Circulation:** 10,000
- **Website:** www.sportingfamily.com

Freelance Potential
30% written by nonstaff writers. Publishes 10 freelance submissions yearly; 10% by authors who are new to the magazine. Receives 600 queries, 120 unsolicited mss yearly.

Submissions
Query or send complete ms. Accepts email submissions to jennifermorrell@sportingfamily.com (Microsoft Word attachments for mss; no attachments for queries). Responds in 1 month.
Articles: Word lengths vary. Informational and how-to articles; profiles; and personal experience pieces. Topics include health, fitness, recreation, social issues, and sports.
Depts/columns: Word lengths vary. News, short profiles, health and wellness, and recreation ideas.

Sample Issue
48 pages: 4 articles; 6 depts/columns. Writers' guidelines available.
- "Getting Into the Swing of Golf." Article describes the growing popularity of this sport, and tells how more kids and moms are getting involved.
- "Prep Baseball Arrives." Article reports that the season for high school baseball has been extended, and that it has become a force in prep athletics.
- Sample dept/column: "Health & Wellness" offers tips for fueling up with the right foods to produce energy and speed recovery after long workouts.

Rights and Payment
First and electronic rights. Written material, payment rates vary. Pays on publication.

Editor's Comments
We're always looking for up-to-date information on Atlanta-area sports, recreation, and local events of interest to active families. Articles on healthy living are also considered.

Autism Asperger's Digest

P.O. Box 337
Little Falls, NY 13365

Managing Editor: Veronica Zysk

Description and Interests
This magazine addresses a wide range of issues related to autism spectrum disorders, including recent research, useable strategies, and practical solutions. Readers include parents, education professionals, and service providers.
- **Audience:** Parents and professionals
- **Frequency:** 6 times each year
- **Circulation:** 12,000
- **Website:** www.autismdigest.com

Freelance Potential
90% written by nonstaff writers. Publishes 30 freelance submissions yearly; 60% by unpublished writers. Receives 50–75 queries yearly.

Submissions
Query. Accepts hard copy and email queries to editor@ autismdigest.com. SASE. Responds in 2–4 weeks.
Articles: To 2,000 words. Informational and how-to articles; personal experience pieces; profiles; and interviews. Topics include life with autism, strategies for professionals, current research, and practical solutions.
Depts/columns: News items, 50–300 words. "Autism Around the World," 600–1,500 words.

Sample Issue
50 pages: 6 articles; 5 depts/columns. Writers' guidelines available.
- "New Addition to the Family." Article discusses hiring in-home support for individuals on the autism spectrum.
- "Drafted without Warning." Article reveals the challenges faced by military families who have children with autism.
- Sample dept/column: "Simply Good Ideas" weighs the pros and cons of inclusive educational programs.

Rights and Payment
First rights. No payment. Provides a 1-year subscription.

Editor's Comments
We are primarily looking for articles on behavior strategies, sensory issues, bullying strategies, and transition to middle school. We're seeing too much on social skills and the vaccine controversy. First-person pieces by parents or individuals with autism are also welcome, but they must be written in a way that is appealing and unique among the hundreds of other stories that can be found in newsletters or on the Internet.

BabagaNewz

90 Oak Street
Newton, MA 02464

Editor: Mark Levine

Description and Interests
Used primarily in the classroom (each issue includes a teacher's guide), this magazine features articles on current events, popular culture, religious holidays, and cultural events that impact Jewish teenagers.
- **Audience:** 9–13 years
- **Frequency:** 8 times each year
- **Circulation:** 41,029
- **Website: www.babaganewz.com**

Freelance Potential
30% written by nonstaff writers. Publishes 20 freelance submissions yearly; 10% by authors who are new to the magazine.

Submissions
Query. All material is written on assignment. Accepts hard copy. SASE. Response time varies.
Articles: Word lengths vary. Informational and how-to articles; profiles; and interviews. Topics include friendship, renewal, personal satisfaction, peace, caring for the environment, truth, responsibility, heroism, health, the Torah, Jewish holidays, history, political science, social studies, geography, and sports.
Depts/columns: Word lengths vary. World news, short profiles, and science news.

Sample Issue
22 pages (no advertising): 6 articles; 2 depts/ columns; 3 activities. Sample copy and guidelines available by email request to aviva@babaganewz.com.
- "Elie Schram Adopts a New Attitude." Article describes how an adolescent boy came to terms with his family's adoption of a Chinese baby girl.
- "All in the Family." Article tells of three families and how they overcame obstacles together.
- Sample dept/column: "W.O.W. (World of Wonders)" examines the wonders of nature.

Rights and Payment
All rights. Written material, payment rates vary. Pays on acceptance. Provides contributor's copies upon request.

Editor's Comments
Schools and teachers use our magazine because each issue focuses on a central theme that is relevant to young people today. We prefer assigning pieces to writers we are familiar with, but if you have an interesting idea that speaks to our Jewish readers, send us your query.

Babybug

70 East Lake Street, Suite 300
Chicago, IL 60601

Submissions Editor: Jenny Gillespie

Description and Interests
This magazine is for babies who love to be read to and for the adults who love to read to them. It features colorfully illustrated short stories, poems, and simple concept pieces that help the youngest listeners learn about the world around them.
- **Audience:** 6 months–2 years
- **Frequency:** 10 times each year
- **Circulation:** 50,000
- **Website: www.cricketmag.com**

Freelance Potential
100% written by nonstaff writers. Publishes 30–40 freelance submissions yearly; 50% by authors who are new to the magazine. Receives 2,400 unsolicited mss yearly.

Submissions
Send complete ms. Accepts hard copy and simultaneous submissions if identified. SASE. Responds in 6 months.
Articles: 10 words. Features material that conveys simple concepts and ideas.
Fiction: 3–6 short sentences. Age-appropriate humor and short stories.
Other: Rhyming and rhythmic poetry, to 8 lines. Parent/child activities, to 8 lines.

Sample Issue
24 pages (no advertising): 1 story; 6 poems. Sample copy, $5. Guidelines available.
- "Good Night and Good Morning." Poem and illustrations describe the daily rhythms of farm life.
- "Wagon Ride." Poem takes the listener on a fun ride full of sound and movement.
- "Two Poodles." Poem compares a little poodle to a big poodle as they splash through puddles.

Rights and Payment
Rights vary. Written material, $25 minimum. Pays on publication. Provides 6 author's copies.

Editor's Comments
We consider *Babybug* to be a listening *and* looking magazine, so all submitted material should lend itself to illustration as well as to sounds and voices. Because babies and toddlers love to laugh, humor is always welcome; and your work should be fun for the adult reader as well. We are always looking for a fresh approach to the everyday things that populate their world; however, we currently have enough bath and bedtime stories.

Baby Dallas

Lauren Publications
4275 Kellway Circle, Suite 146
Addison, TX 75001

Editorial Director: Shelley Hawes Pate

Description and Interests
The latest information about pregnancy, childbirth, and parenting through the first year can be found in *Baby Dallas*. It is distributed free to expectant and new parents living in the Dallas, Texas, region.
- **Audience:** Parents
- **Frequency:** Twice each year
- **Circulation:** 120,000
- **Website:** www.babydallas.com

Freelance Potential
25% written by nonstaff writers. Publishes 12–15 freelance submissions yearly; 20% by authors who are new to the magazine. Receives 240 queries yearly.

Submissions
Query with résumé. Accepts hard copy, simultaneous submissions if identified, and email queries to editorial@dallaschild.com. SASE. Responds in 2–3 months.
Articles: 1,000–2,500 words. Informational, self-help, and how-to articles; profiles; interviews; humor; and personal experience pieces. Topics include pregnancy, parenting, education, current events, social issues, multicultural and ethnic issues, health, fitness, crafts, and computers.
Depts/columns: 800 words. Parenting resources, health information, and health updates.

Sample Issue
38 pages (14% advertising): 2 articles; 6 depts/columns. Sample copy, free with 9x12 SASE. Writers' guidelines available.
- "Chilled Out Childbirth." Article discusses the new role that hypnosis is playing in labor and delivery, and its pleasant side effects.
- "Your 9 Toughest Baby Product Questions Answered!" Article features advice on purchasing cribs, strollers, car seats, and other baby products.
- Sample dept/column: "The First Year" offers insights into baby sign language.

Rights and Payment
First serial rights. Written material, payment rates vary. Pays on publication. Provides contributor's copies upon request.

Editor's Comments
In addition to up-to-date information on health and safety, we want articles that offer guidelines, advice, comfort, and a sense of humor.

Baby Talk

The Parenting Group
135 West 50th Street, 3rd Floor
New York, NY 10020

Senior Editor: Patty Onderko

Description and Interests
Offering "straight talk for new moms," *Baby Talk* advises its readers on all aspects of pregnancy, baby care, and infant health, growth, and development. It is written primarily for women who are expecting a child or have a child under the age of 18 months.
- **Audience:** Parents
- **Frequency:** 10 times each year
- **Circulation:** 2 million
- **Website:** www.babytalk.com

Freelance Potential
50% written by nonstaff writers. Publishes 40 freelance submissions yearly; 20% by authors who are new to the magazine. Receives 504 queries yearly.

Submissions
Query with clips or writing samples. No simultaneous submissions. SASE. Responds in 2 months.
Articles: 1,500–2,000 words. Informational and how-to articles; and personal experience pieces. Topics include pregnancy, baby care, infant health and development, juvenile equipment and toys, day care, marriage, and relationships.
Depts/columns: 500–1,200 words. Humor, finances, women's and infant health, advice, and personal experiences from new parents.

Sample Issue
100 pages (50% advertising): 7 articles; 14 depts/columns. Sample copy, free with 9x12 SASE ($1.60 postage). Guidelines and theme list available.
- "Owning Your C-Section." Article asks readers if they are emotionally and physically ready to have a c-section if necessary.
- "Mealtime Mayhem." Article lists three strategies for making dinner less hectic and more fun.
- Sample dept/column: "Baby Check-Up" offers a collection of short articles on everything from infant weight gain to "outie" belly buttons.

Rights and Payment
First rights. Articles, $1,000–$2,000. Depts/columns, $300–$1,200. Pays on acceptance. Provides 2–4 contributor's copies.

Editor's Comments
Lately we've been receiving a lot of submissions on topics we've already covered. Read back issues, then send us something fresh and different, written in a smart, crisp style.

Baltimore's Child

11 Dutton Court
Baltimore, MD 21228

Editor: Dianne R. McCann

Description and Interests
This free parenting tabloid mixes general features on family issues and child raising with departments on more specific topics, such as food, fatherhood, parenting teens, and family health and fitness. It is distributed throughout Baltimore, Carroll, Harford, and Howard counties, as well as in Baltimore City.
- **Audience:** Parents
- **Frequency:** Monthly
- **Circulation:** 50,000
- **Website: www.baltimoreschild.com**

Freelance Potential
95% written by nonstaff writers. Publishes 250 freelance submissions yearly; 5% by unpublished writers, 10% by authors who are new to the magazine.

Submissions
Prefers query; will accept complete ms. Accepts hard copy and email submissions to dianne@baltimoreschild.com. SASE. Response time varies.
Articles: 1,000–1,500 words. Informational articles. Topics include parenting issues, education, health, fitness, child care, social issues, and regional news.
Depts/columns: Word lengths vary. Music, family cooking, pet care, baby and toddler issues, parenting children with special needs, parenting teens, and family finances.

Sample Issue
96 pages: 4 articles; 17 depts/columns; 4 calendars; 1 annual party directory. Sample copy, $4 with 9x12 SASE ($.77 postage). Guidelines and sample copy available at website.
- "Their Home Isn't Their Castle, It's Their Office." Article profiles women who are successfully working out of their homes.
- "From Barbie to Bratz: Are Fashion Dolls Getting Too Grown-Up for Little Girls?" Article analyzes the effect fashion dolls can have on young children.
- Sample dept/column: "Your Special Child" examines issues of aggression in children with disabilities.

Rights and Payment
One-time rights. Written material, payment rates vary. Payment policy varies.

Editor's Comments
Our goal is to help Baltimore-area families find activities, services, and resources. Send positive, practical material that will help us meet that goal.

Baseball Youth

P.O. Box 983
Morehead, KY 40351

President: Scott Hacker

Description and Interests
Young baseball enthusiasts find profiles of their favorite Major and Minor League players and rising superstars in this magazine. It also provides training tips, information on baseball-related video games, and news for card collectors.
- **Audience:** Youth baseball enthusiasts
- **Frequency:** 6 times each year
- **Circulation:** 100,000
- **Website: www.baseballyouth.com**

Freelance Potential
50% written by nonstaff writers. Publishes 10–20 freelance submissions yearly.

Submissions
Query or send ms. Accepts email submissions to mailbox@baseballyouth.com. Response time varies.
Articles: Word lengths vary. Informational and how-to articles; profiles; interviews; photo-essays; and personal experience pieces. Topics include youth baseball, Major League and Minor League Baseball, video games, baseball equipment and gear, ballparks, and baseball players and personalities.
Depts/columns: Word lengths vary. Baseball cards, drills, new product information, and player and stadium profiles.
Other: Puzzles and games.

Sample Issue
46 pages: 3 articles; 8 depts/columns; 1 poster. Sample copy, $3.95 at newsstands. Guidelines available.
- "Green Light, Red Light." Article offers tips on the art of base stealing, with special instructions for stealing from right-handed and left-handed pitchers.
- "A Fan, a Journalist, and a Batboy." Article describes the experiences of a young fan who attended spring training for the Mets.
- Sample dept/column: "College Profile" features facts about the Clemson Tigers.

Rights and Payment
All rights. Written material, payment rates vary.

Editor's Comments
We're trying to bring excitement back to youth baseball. After reading our magazine, our readers should be inspired and motivated to play ball. One of our biggest needs is for articles about teaching the game of baseball. We can always use well-written pieces on baseball teams and clubs, as well.

Bay State Parent

124 Fay Road
Framingham, MA 01702

Editor: Susan S. Petroni

Description and Interests
This award-winning parenting magazine targets teachers, childcare providers, child advocates, and parents. Reaching more than 100 towns in eastern and central Massachusetts, it just celebrated its tenth year in publication.
- **Audience:** Parents
- **Frequency:** Monthly
- **Circulation:** 42,000
- **Website:** www.baystateparent.com

Freelance Potential
100% written by nonstaff writers. Publishes 84–120 freelance submissions yearly; 5% by unpublished writers, 30% by authors who are new to the magazine. Receives 120 queries yearly.

Submissions
Query. Accepts email queries to editor@baystateparent.com (Microsoft Word attachments). Availability of artwork improves chance of acceptance. Responds in 1 month.
Articles: To 2,000 words. Informational and how-to articles; and humor. Topics include regional and local events, travel, books, arts and crafts, family finance, and computers.
Depts/columns: To 1,500 words. Accepts seasonal material 4 months in advance.
Artwork: B/W and color prints. JPEG images at 200 dpi.

Sample Issue
88 pages (15% advertising): 14 articles; 12 depts/columns. Sample copy, free. Guidelines available.
- "Battle Against the Battery." Article takes a look at infant toys and play.
- "Consuming Kids." Article discusses how to limit marketing influences on children.
- Sample dept/column: "Mom's Playdate" reports on moms who are heading back to college.

Rights and Payment
Massachusetts exclusive rights. Articles, $50–$100. Kill fee varies. Pays on publication.

Editor's Comments
We prefer to work with locally-based writers from New England or those who have a good familiarity with this area. We have no staff writers; all of our material is written by freelancers, so if you know our area and our publication, please send a query.

BC Parent News Magazine

Sasamat RPO 72086
Vancouver, British Columbia V6R 4P2
Canada

Editor: Elizabeth Shaffer

Description and Interests
The editors of *BC Parent News Magazine* strive to offer reliable, leading-edge information about a broad spectrum of parenting topics for people living in British Columbia. Popular topics are pregnancy, baby care, parenting teens, women's health, finances, and family travel and activities.
- **Audience:** Parents
- **Frequency:** 9 times each year
- **Circulation:** 45,000
- **Website:** www.bcparent.ca

Freelance Potential
80% written by nonstaff writers. Publishes 25 freelance submissions yearly; 10–30% by authors who are new to the magazine.

Submissions
Send complete ms. Accepts email submissions to bcparent@show.ca (RTF file attachments) and IBM disk submissions. SAE/IRC. No simultaneous submissions. Responds in 2 months.
Articles: 500–1,000 words. Informational articles. Topics include health care, education, pregnancy and childbirth, adoption, computers, sports, money matters, the arts, community events, teen issues, baby and child care, and family issues.
Depts/columns: Word lengths vary. Parent health, family news, and media reviews.

Sample Issue
30 pages: 4 articles; 3 depts/columns; 1 camp guide; 1 activity guide. Writers' guidelines and editorial calendar available.
- "The Parents at the Park." Article offers a humorous look at how having children can dramatically change your social life.
- "Healthy Choices, Healthy Children." Article discusses how parents' nutrition and behavior choices affect their children's health.
- Sample dept/column: "Parent News" stresses the importance of properly installing car seats.

Rights and Payment
First rights. Articles, $85; reprints, $50. Depts/columns, payment rates vary. Pays on acceptance.

Editor's Comments
If you can supply us with well-written, up-to-date information of interest to parents in British Columbia, we encourage you to contact us.

Better Homes and Gardens

1716 Locust Street
Des Moines, IA 50309-3023

Department Editor

Description and Interests
Known for its beautiful, full-color spreads of home decorating and gardening features, this magazine also has departments devoted to a variety of family-related matters such as parenting, health, nutrition, travel, recreation, and education.
- **Audience:** Adults
- **Frequency:** Monthly
- **Circulation:** 7.6 million
- **Website:** www.bhg.com

Freelance Potential
10% written by nonstaff writers. Publishes 25–30 freelance submissions yearly; 25% by authors who are new to the magazine. Receives 240 queries yearly.

Submissions
Query with résumé and clips or writing samples. No unsolicited mss. Accepts hard copy. SASE. Responds in 1 month.
Articles: Word lengths vary. Informational and how-to articles; personal experience pieces; and profiles. Topics include food and nutrition, home design, gardening, outdoor living, travel, the environment, health and fitness, holidays, education, parenting, and child development.

Sample Issue
308 pages (48% advertising): 48 articles. Sample copy, $3.49 at newsstands. Guidelines available.
- "Garden Sentiments." Article shows how a wife and mother turned her garden into a collection of living memories for her family.
- "Cruising Along." Article explains how bicycling can help make families healthier and bring them closer together.
- "A Job Well Done." Article proves how working hard teaches kids important life lessons and enhances their self-esteem.

Rights and Payment
All rights. Written material, payment rates vary. Pays on acceptance. Provides 1 contributor's copy.

Editor's Comments
The best opportunities for writers new to our magazine are with items submitted on parenting, education, health, and travel. Review an issue and look at our "Family Fun," "Family Matters," and "Family Health" sections to see the types of articles we have published. We do not accept works of fiction or poetry.

Beyond Centauri

P.O. Box 782
Cedar Rapids, IA 52406

Managing Editor: Tyree Campbell

Description and Interests
Beyond Centauri publishes science fiction, fiction and "ewww–gross" stories and poems by young adults and adults, as well as a few short articles.
- **Audience:** 9–18+ years
- **Frequency:** Quarterly
- **Circulation:** 100
- **Website:** www.samsdotpublishing.com

Freelance Potential
100% written by nonstaff writers. Publishes 50–60 freelance submissions yearly; 20% by unpublished writers, 50% by authors who are new to the magazine. Receives 500 unsolicited mss yearly.

Submissions
Query or send complete ms. Accepts hard copy and email submissions to beyondcentauri@samsdotpublishing.com (RTF attachments). SASE. Responds to queries in 2 weeks, to mss in 2–3 months.
Articles: To 500 words. Informational articles; opinion pieces; and book and movie reviews. Topics include space exploration, science, and technology.
Fiction: To 2,500 words. Science fiction; fantasy; and stories about adventure and exploration.
Other: Poetry, to 50 lines. Science fiction, fantasy, and insect themes.

Sample Issue
36 pages (no advertising): 8 stories; 25 poems. Sample copy, $6 with 9x12 SASE. Writers' guidelines available.
- "My Pretty Painted Pony." Story describes how a little girl's fondness for a carousel horse takes her away from her troubles.
- "Dodo Dobbins' Gift." Story depicts the humorous adventures of a boy born with the ability to grant wishes.

Rights and Payment
First North American serial rights. Articles, $3. Fiction, $5. Poetry, $2. B/W illustrations, $5. Pays on publication. Provides 1 contributor's copy.

Editor's Comments
It is our intent to nurture imagination and creativity in the next generation. We want stories and poems that depict adventure, problem-solving, courage, curiosity, compassion—all the qualities that make us human, that make us explorers.

Big Apple Parent

350 Fifth Avenue, Suite 2420
New York, NY 10118

Editor: Helen Freedman

Description and Interests
This New York City-based tabloid provides current news and information on parenting, children's health, education, sports, and other issues of interest to families living in and around Manhattan.
• **Audience:** Parents
• **Frequency:** Monthly
• **Circulation:** 70,000
• **Website: www.nymetroparents.com**

Freelance Potential
25% written by nonstaff writers. Publishes 5 freelance submissions yearly; 20% by unpublished writers, 10% by authors who are new to the magazine. Receives 300 queries and unsolicited mss yearly.

Submissions
Query or send complete ms. Accepts hard copy and email submissions to hfreedman@davlermedia.com. Responds in 1 month.
Articles: 800–1,000 words. Informational and how-to articles; profiles; interviews; and personal experience pieces. Topics include family issues, health, nutrition, fitness, crafts, current events, gifted and special education, nature, sports, and regional news.
Depts/columns: 750 words. News and reviews.
Other: Submit seasonal material 4 months in advance.

Sample Issue
64 pages: 9 articles; 4 directories; 1 calendar; 10 depts/columns. Sample copy, free with 10x13 SASE. Guidelines available at website.
• "What Your Kids Aren't Telling You." Article provides parents with tools for decoding what their struggling students really mean when they complain about school.
• "More Vegetables, Please!" Article explains how a grade school is teaching children to enjoy eating healthful food.
• Sample dept/column: "In the Arts" offers information on new programming and entertainment designed for children and families.

Rights and Payment
First serial rights. No payment. Provides 2 copies.

Editor's Comments
We would like to see more submissions that provide information on local activities, people, places, and events that impact New York families. We see too many humor and travel pieces.

Birmingham Christian Family

P.O. Box 383203
Birmingham, AL 35238

Editor: Dee Branch Park

Description and Interests
Each complimentary issue of *Birmingham Christian Family* includes departments on family books, healthy living, music, and mission work. It addresses parenting issues from a Christian perspective and features the work of individuals and organizations seeking to improve the lives of Birmingham families.
• **Audience:** Families
• **Frequency:** Monthly
• **Circulation:** 35,000

Freelance Potential
30% written by nonstaff writers. Publishes 100 freelance submissions yearly; 5% by unpublished writers, 2–3% by authors who are new to the magazine. Receives 240 queries yearly.

Submissions
Query with artwork if applicable. Accepts email queries to editor@birminghamchristian.com. Availability of artwork improves chance of acceptance. Responds in 1 month.
Articles: To 500 words. Informational, self-help, and how-to articles; profiles; and personal experience pieces. Topics include family life, parenting, religion, animals, pets, the arts, crafts, hobbies, current events, fitness, music, recreation, religion, travel, and sports.
Fiction: To 500 words. Inspirational and humorous fiction.
Depts/columns: To 500 words. Book, movie, and restaurant reviews; family finances; health issues.
Artwork: B/W or color prints.

Sample Issue
30 pages (25% advertising): 2 articles; 21 depts/columns; 1 calendar. Sample copy, free with 9x12 SASE ($3 postage). Editorial calendar available.
• "Joey Jones." Article profiles the head coach of the Birmingham Southern Panthers.
• Sample dept/column: "Money Matters" reports on upcoming conferences for adults who want to give back to the community.

Rights and Payment
Rights vary. No payment.

Editor's Comments
Ours is a local publication designed to promote positive living by sharing with readers the latest news on entertainment, healthy living, and parenting. Most material has a strong local focus.

The Black Collegian

140 Carondelet Street
New Orleans, LA 70130

Chief Executive Officer: Preston J. Edwards, Sr.

Description and Interests

African American college students read this publication for its timely and inspiring articles on careers and self-development. It also offers profiles of successful African Americans from all walks of life.
- **Audience:** African Americans, 18–30 years
- **Frequency:** Twice each year
- **Circulation:** 121,000
- **Website:** www.blackcollegian.com

Freelance Potential

95% written by nonstaff writers. Publishes 20 freelance submissions yearly; 33% by authors who are new to the magazine. Receives 24 queries yearly.

Submissions

Query. Prefers email queries to pres@imdiversity.com. Accepts hard copy. SASE. Responds in 3 months.
Articles: 1,500–2,000 words. Informational, self-help, and how-to articles; profiles; and personal experience pieces. Topics include careers, personal development, job hunting, colleges, financial aid, history, technology, and multicultural and ethnic issues.
Depts/columns: Word lengths vary. Health issues and African American book and art reviews.
Artwork: 5x7 and 11x14 B/W and color transparencies. B/W and color line art.

Sample Issue

88 pages: 18 articles; 1 dept/column. Writers' guidelines available.
- "Will Smith: In Pursuit of Excellence." Article profiles the actor whose sharp wit, talent, and determination have propelled him to success.
- "Ten Keys to Unlocking and Evaluating a Job Offer." Article describes the steps necessary to identifying and choosing the right job.
- "The On-Campus Interview." Article explains how a successful on-campus interview can lead to an invitation to an on-site interview.

Rights and Payment

One-time rights. Written material, payment rates vary. Pays after publication. Provides 1 contributor's copy.

Editor's Comments

Articles should be well-researched and full of practical advice on career-related topics such as writing résumés, job-hunting, and successful job interview tactics, as well as timely information about emerging career opportunities.

Blaze Magazine

P.O. Box 2660
Niagara Falls, NY 14302

Editor: Brenda McCarthy

Description and Interests

Now in its fourth year, *Blaze Magazine* is designed specifically for kids who love horses. It provides interactive content, such as games and crafts, as well as articles offering fascinating facts on all aspects of caring for and riding horses.
- **Audience:** 8–14 years
- **Frequency:** 4,000
- **Circulation:** Unavailable
- **Website:** www.blazekids.com

Freelance Potential

50% written by nonstaff writers. Publishes 25–30 freelance submissions yearly.

Submissions

Query. Accepts email queries to brenda@blazekids.com. Availability of artwork improves chance of acceptance. Response time varies.
Articles: 200–500 words. Informational and how-to articles; and profiles. Topics include horseback riding, training, and breeds.
Fiction: Word lengths vary. Stories about horses.
Depts/columns: Word lengths vary. Short news items, arts and crafts.
Artwork: B/W and color prints and transparencies.
Other: Puzzles and games.

Sample Issue

42 pages (15% advertising): 3 articles; 1 story; 7 depts/columns; 1 comic. Sample copy, $3.75.
- "Opera Horses: Stars on Stage." Article talks about the horses at New York City's Claremont Riding Academy that perform at the opera when needed.
- "Dancing With Horses: Boo Boo Stewart." Article profiles a 13-year-old world champion in martial arts who has a herd of horses.
- Sample dept/column: "Friend or Foe" features facts about barn spiders.

Rights and Payment

Rights vary. Written material, $.25 per word. Artwork, payment rates vary. Payment policy varies.

Editor's Comments

Our needs include profiles of people involved in the world of horses, as well as descriptions of programs involving horses. Don't send breed profiles—we only use one in each issue and we have too many. Remember that kids want creativity and challenges—and they want to have fun.

bNetS@vvy

Tools for Adults to Help Kids Connect Safely

1201 16th Street NW, Suite 216
Washington, DC 20036

Editor: Caitlin G. Johnson

Description and Interests
A joint effort between the National Education
Association and Sprint, this new publication provides
parents, guardians, and teachers with the tools they
need to help kids between the ages of 9 and 14 stay
safe online. Primarily an online publication, it looks for
positive, solutions-based approaches that bring youth
and adults together.
• **Audience:** Parents, guardians, and teachers
• **Frequency:** 6 times each year
• **Hits per month:** Unavailable
• **Website:** www.neahealthinfo.org/net–savvy/
  nsindex.html

Freelance Potential
85–90% written by nonstaff writers. Publishes 25 freelance submissions yearly.

Submissions
Query. Accepts email queries to internetsafety@
nea.org; include clips or links. Responds in 2 weeks.
Articles: 600–950 words. Informational and how-to
articles; and reviews. Topics include the Internet and
Internet safety, and social networking sites.
Depts/columns: 600–950 words. Expert advice and
ideas from parents and teens.

Sample Issue
Sample copy available at website. Writers' guidelines
available.
• "Let's Talk About Social Networking." Article offers
  expert observations on keeping kids safe at social
  networking sites and keeping the lines of real-world
  communication open.
• Sample dept/column: "Parents' Corner" explains how
  one parent used the Internet to get the word out
  about burglaries in her neighborhood.

Rights and Payment
All rights. Written material, payment rates vary.
Payment policy varies.

Editor's Comments
Our publication seeks to go beyond personal stories
to equip young people, their parents and teachers,
and other adults to understand and work together to
positively ensure the safe use of technologies. Send
us informative, compelling queries for stories that link
to action ideas, tips, and solutions. We are not interested in sensationalized or salacious coverage.

Book Links

American Library Association
50 East Huron Street
Chicago, IL 60611

Editor: Laura Tillotson

Description and Interests
Book Links explores ways to connect children with
literature. It publishes bibliographies, essays that link
books on a similar theme, and retrospective reviews
for an audience that includes teachers, librarians,
media specialists, and parents.
• **Audience:** Adults
• **Frequency:** 6 times each year
• **Circulation:** 20,577
• **Website:** www.ala.org/booklinks

Freelance Potential
90% written by nonstaff writers. Publishes 60 freelance
submissions yearly; 20% by unpublished writers, 30%
by authors who are new to the magazine. Receives 96
queries yearly.

Submissions
Query. No unsolicited mss. Accepts hard copy. SASE.
Response time varies.
Articles: Word lengths vary. Informational articles;
profiles; interviews; and personal experience pieces.
Topics include children's books, current and historical
events, nature, the environment, and ethnic and multicultural subjects.
Depts/columns: Classroom ideas for curriculum
enrichment; 800–1,200 words. Book lists for specific
countries, locales, or themes; 250–300 words.
Interviews with authors and illustrators; word lengths
vary.

Sample Issue
64 pages (28% advertising): 11 articles; 5 depts/
columns. Sample copy, $6. Writers' guidelines and
theme list available.
• "A Trip Around the Solar System." Article features
  reviews of astronomy books for children in the lower
  grades.
• "From Seed to Harvest." Article offers an overview of
  titles related to growing food.
• Sample dept/column: "Points of View" tells how one
  author gets ideas for her stories.

Rights and Payment
All rights. Articles, $100. Pays on publication. Provides
2 contributor's copies.

Editor's Comments
Most of our articles consist of one or two brief, upbeat
paragraphs that introduce a topic and set the tone, followed by a list of 20 to 30 titles that advance the subject.

Bop

330 North Brand
Glendale, CA 91203

Editor-in-Chief: Leesa Coble

Description and Interests

This magazine is a must for teens and tweens who love to devour details about their favorite young stars. The collage-like layout is packed with photos and punctuated by short articles and quizzes that make readers feel up close and personal with teenage celebrities.
- **Audience:** 10–16 years
- **Frequency:** Monthly
- **Circulation:** 200,000+
- **Website:** www.bopmag.com

Freelance Potential

1% written by nonstaff writers. Receives 20 queries each year.

Submissions

Query with résumé and clips for celebrity-related pieces only. Prefers email submissions to leesa@laufermedia.com. Will accept hard copy. SASE. Responds in 2 months.
Articles: To 700 words. Celebrity interviews and profiles; and behind-the-scenes reports on the entertainment industry.
Depts/columns: Staff written.

Sample Issue

84 pages (15% advertising): 17 articles; 13 depts/columns, 8 quizzes, 15 posters. Sample copy, $3.99 at newsstands.
- "A Letter to Myself." Interview with actress Miley Cyrus reveals what she wrote in a time capsule.
- "Where Is Zac?!" Article talks about what actor Zac Efron has been up to recently.
- "How My Dream Came True!" Article interviews actress Vanessa Hudgens about her big break.
- "The Party's Just Begun." Article describes the favorite pastimes of the multimedia group, the Cheetah Girls.

Rights and Payment

All rights. Written material, payment rates vary. Pays on publication. Provides 2 contributor's copies.

Editor's Comments

We no longer accept freelance submissions for text. We do accept freelance submissions of Hollywood event coverage and interview transcripts with relevant celebrities: the young television, film, and music personalities who are adored by our readers. Our goal is to pack each issue of our magazine with the best celebrity news, features, quizzes, contests, and games.

The Boston Parents' Paper

670 Centre Street
Jamaica Plain, MA 02130

Editor: Alison O'Leary Murray

Description and Interests

The Boston Parents' Paper claims to be Massachusetts' number-one parenting magazine. It covers the basics of child rearing while also offering discussions of contemporary challenges faced by families. Information on local resources is also a large part of its editorial content.
- **Audience:** Parents
- **Frequency:** Monthly
- **Circulation:** 70,000
- **Website:** www.bostonparentspaper.com

Freelance Potential

50% written by nonstaff writers. Publishes 36 freelance submissions yearly; 10% by unpublished writers, 50% by authors who are new to the magazine. Receives 36 queries yearly.

Submissions

Query with clips or writing samples. Accepts hard copy. Availability of artwork improves chance of acceptance. SASE. Response time varies.
Articles: Word lengths vary. Informational articles; profiles; and interviews. Topics include child development, education, parenting, family issues, and health.
Depts/columns: To 1,800 words. Short news items, parenting tips, and profiles.
Artwork: B/W prints. Line art.
Other: Submit seasonal material 6 months in advance.

Sample Issue

66 pages (45% advertising): 3 articles; 7 depts/columns; 1 calendar. Writers' guidelines and theme list available.
- "The Truth About Birthday Parties." Article offers advice about what works and what doesn't.
- "See Us As a Family." Article examines the difficulties and rewards of gay parenting.
- Sample dept/column: "Education" explores possibilities for summer learning experiences.

Rights and Payment

First North American serial and electronic rights. All material, payment rates vary. Pays within 30 days of publication. Provides 5 contributor's copies.

Editor's Comments

We look for writing that offers fresh insights on the everyday joys and challenges of raising children, as well as analysis of more complex parenting issues.

Boys' Life

Boy Scouts of America
1325 West Walnut Hill Lane
P.O. Box 152079
Irving, TX 75015-2079

Senior Writer: Aaron Derr

Description and Interests
Published by the Boy Scouts since 1911, *Boys' Life* covers a broad array of topics of interest to boys, including outdoor activities, science topics, and history. Fiction featuring boys is also published regularly.
• **Audience:** 6–18 years
• **Frequency:** Monthly
• **Circulation:** 1.3 million
• **Website: www.boyslife.org**

Freelance Potential
80% written by nonstaff writers. Publishes 50 freelance submissions yearly; 1% by unpublished writers, 2% by new authors. Receives 96+ queries yearly.

Submissions
Query for articles and depts/columns. Query or send complete ms for fiction. Accepts hard copy. SASE. Responds to queries in 4–6 weeks, to mss in 6–8 weeks.
Articles: 500–1,500 words. Informational and how-to articles; profiles; and humor. Topics include sports, science, American history, geography, animals, nature, and the environment.
Fiction: 1,000–1,5000 words. Genres include science fiction, humor, mystery, and adventure.
Depts/columns: 300–750 words. Advice, humor, collecting, computers, and pets.
Other: Puzzles and cartoons.

Sample Issue
62 pages (18% advertising): 5 articles; 1 story; 5 depts/columns; 9 comics. Sample copy, $3.60 with 9x12 SASE. Guidelines available.
• "Northern Exposure." Article recounts the adventures of a Las Vegas Scout Troop that explored the Alaskan wilderness.
• "A River Runs Through It." Article profiles the people who keep America's waterways clean.
• Sample dept/column: "Heads Up" features the latest news of interest to boys.

Rights and Payment
First rights. Articles, $400–$1,500. Fiction, $750+. Depts/columns, $150–$400. Pays on acceptance. Provides 2 contributor's copies.

Editor's Comments
The current list of the Boy Scouts of America's more than 100 merit badge pamphlets offer an idea of the wide range of subjects we cover. Fiction and departments offer the best opportunities for new writers.

Boys' Quest

P.O. Box 227
Bluffton, OH 45817-0227

Editor: Marilyn Edwards

Description and Interests
The publishers of *Boys' Quest* strive to foster literacy and instill traditional family values in boys through exciting articles and hands-on projects.
• **Audience:** 5–14 years
• **Frequency:** 6 times each year
• **Circulation:** 12,000
• **Website: www.boysquest.com**

Freelance Potential
90% written by nonstaff writers. Publishes 100–150 freelance submissions yearly; 60% by unpublished writers, 40% by authors who are new to the magazine. Receives 2,000–3,000 queries and mss yearly.

Submissions
Prefers complete ms. Will accept queries. Accepts hard copy and simultaneous submissions if identified. SASE. Responds to queries in 1–2 weeks, to mss in 2–3 months.
Articles: 500 words. Informational and how-to articles; profiles; personal experience pieces; and humor. Topics include pets, nature, hobbies, science, sports, careers, family, and cars.
Fiction: 500 words. Genres include adventure, mystery, and multicultural fiction.
Depts/columns: 300–500 words. Science projects and experiments.
Artwork: Prefers B/W prints; will accept color prints.
Other: Puzzles, activities, and riddles. Poetry.

Sample Issue
48 pages (no advertising): 11 articles; 9 depts/columns; 6 puzzles; 3 poems; and 2 comics. Sample copy, $6 with 9x12 SASE. Writers' guidelines and theme list available.
• "The Gentle Giant of Galapagos." Article introduces readers to these amazing tortoises, particularly one who is the last of his subspecies.
• Sample dept/column: "Science" includes an experiment to explain what is meant by hot- and cold-blooded animals.

Rights and Payment
First and second rights. Articles and fiction, $.05 per word. Depts/columns, $35. Poems and activities, $10+. Artwork, $5–$10. Pays on publication. Provides 1 copy.

Editor's Comments
We have enough fiction. We are more interested in high-quality nonfiction with supportive artwork.

Bread for God's Children

P.O. Box 1017
Arcadia, FL 34265-1017

Editorial Secretary: Donna Wade

Description and Interests
This magazine publishes fictional stories and articles aimed at helping parents teach biblical principles to their children.
- **Audience:** Families
- **Frequency:** 6–8 times each year
- **Circulation:** 10,000
- **Website:** www.breadministries.org

Freelance Potential
10% written by nonstaff writers. Publishes 15–20 freelance submissions yearly; 70% by unpublished writers, 80% by authors who are new to the magazine. Receives 1,200 unsolicited mss each year.

Submissions
Send complete ms. Accepts hard copy and simultaneous submissions. SASE. Responds in 2–3 months.
Articles: To 800 words. Informational, self-help, and personal experience pieces. Topics include religion and spirituality.
Fiction: Stories for younger children, to 800 words. Stories for middle-grade and young adult readers, to 1,800 words. Tales that demonstrate Christian values.
Depts/columns: To 800 words. Bible study, ministry highlights, family activities, living memorials, and book recommendations.
Other: Filler and crafts.

Sample Issue
28 pages (no advertising): 4 stories; 5 depts/columns. Guidelines available.
- "Christmas Is for Giving." Story aimed at teens depicts a boy who discovers the joy of giving.
- "Janelle's Different Christmas." A little girl and her parents host a disadvantaged family for the holiday in this story aimed at young children.
- Sample dept/column: "Keep a Family History" encourages parents to assemble a scrapbook of annual holiday newsletters and photos.

Rights and Payment
First rights. Fiction, $40–$50. Articles, $25. Filler, $10. Pays on publication. Provides 3 copies.

Editor's Comments
Stories must be written from a child's viewpoint, with the story itself getting the message across—no preaching, moralizing, or tag endings. The plot and characters need to be realistic. We would like to see more stories of healing.

Breakaway

Life. God. Truth. For Guys.

Focus on the Family
8605 Explorer Drive
Colorado Springs, CO 80920

Editor: Mike Ross

Description and Interests
This magazine from Focus on the Family targets teenage boys with fast-paced articles on religion, sports, and other topics of interest to this age group. Its articles and stories present good role models, promote self-esteem, and make the Bible relevant to contemporary society.
- **Audience:** 12–18 years
- **Frequency:** Monthly
- **Circulation:** 95,000
- **Website:** www.breakawaymag.com

Freelance Potential
20% written by nonstaff writers. Publishes 5 freelance submissions yearly; 1% by unpublished writers, 1% by authors who are new to the magazine. Receives 600 unsolicited mss yearly.

Submissions
Send complete ms. Accepts hard copy and email submissions through website. SASE. Responds in 8–10 weeks.
Articles: 600–1,200 words. How-to and self-help articles; personal experience pieces; profiles; interviews; and humor. Topics include religion, sports, and multicultural issues.
Fiction: 1,500–2,200 words. Contemporary, religious, and inspirational fiction; suspense; adventure; humor; and sports fiction.
Depts/columns: Word lengths vary. Scripture readings, Bible facts, and advice.
Other: Filler. Submit seasonal material about religious holidays 6–8 months in advance.

Sample Issue
32 pages (9% advertising): 5 articles; 5 depts/columns. Sample copy, $2 with 9x12 SASE (2 first-class stamps). Guidelines available.
- "Time to Dig Deeper." Article tells how boys can defend and explain their faith to others.
- Sample dept/column: "Gameface" reviews an amusement park management game.

Rights and Payment
First or one-time rights. Written material, $.15 per word. Pays on acceptance. Provides 5 author's copies.

Editor's Comments
We rarely publish unsolicited material. If you do feel you have something valuable for us, please go to our website and follow the submissions guidelines.

Brilliant Star

1233 Central Street
Evanston, IL 60201

Associate Editor: Susan Engle

Description and Interests
Brilliant Star invites children of all faiths to explore the teachings of the Bahá'í Faith. It presents middle-grade readers with this faith's history and principles through stories, articles, activities, games, music, and art.
• **Audience:** 8–12 years
• **Frequency:** 6 times each year
• **Circulation:** 7,000
• **Website:** www.brilliantstarmagazine.org

Freelance Potential
35% written by nonstaff writers. Publishes 5 freelance submissions yearly; 5% by unpublished writers, 80% by new authors. Receives 100 unsolicited mss yearly.

Submissions
Query with clips for nonfiction. Send complete ms for fiction. Accepts hard copy, email queries to brilliant@usbnc.org, and simultaneous submissions. SASE. Responds in 6–8 months.
Articles: To 700 words. Informational and how-to articles; personal experience pieces; profiles; and biographies. Topics include the Bahá'í Faith, historical Bahá'í figures, religion, history, ethnic and social issues, travel, music, and nature.
Fiction: To 700 words. Early reader fiction. Genres include ethnic, multicultural, historical, contemporary, and problem-solving fiction.
Depts/columns: To 600 words. Profiles of kids, religion, and ethics.
Other: Puzzles, activities, games, and recipes.

Sample Issue
30 pages: 6 articles; 1 story; 2 depts/columns; 12 activities; 1 comic; 2 contests; 1 song; 1 calendar. Sample copy, $3 with 9x12 SASE (5 first-class stamps). Guidelines, theme list, and editorial calendar available.
• "Riley's Rainforest." Article tells why gratitude is good for you.
• "The Birthday List." Story shows how prayer helped a family through a difficult situation.

Rights and Payment
All or one-time rights. No payment. Provides 2 copies.

Editor's Comments
Submissions must demonstrate a working knowledge of the Bahá'í Faith and its basic principles, such as the oneness of humanity, equality of men and women, the oneness of God and religion, and the oneness of science and religion.

Brio

Focus on the Family
8605 Explorer Drive
Colorado Springs, CO 80920

Associate Editor: Martha Krienke

Description and Interests
Brio is filled with articles and stories that challenge and inspire Christian teen girls to live faith-filled lives. It also features items on fashion and lifestyle with a focus on a healthy self-concept.
• **Audience:** 12–15 years
• **Frequency:** Monthly
• **Circulation:** 150,000
• **Website:** www.briomag.com

Freelance Potential
65% written by nonstaff writers. Publishes 75 freelance submissions yearly; 1% by unpublished writers, 5% by authors who are new to the magazine. Receives 300 queries, 300 unsolicited mss yearly.

Submissions
Query or send complete ms. Accepts hard copy. SASE. Responds in 4–6 weeks.
Articles: To 2,000 words. Informational and how-to articles; profiles; interviews; and personal experience pieces. Topics include Christian living, peer relationships, family life, and contemporary issues.
Fiction: To 2,000 words. Genres include contemporary fiction, romance, and humor with Christian themes.
Depts/columns: Staff written.
Other: Cartoons, anecdotes, and quizzes.

Sample Issue
38 pages (6% advertising): 9 articles; 1 story; 9 depts/columns. Sample copy, $2 with 9x12 SASE (2 first-class stamps). Guidelines available.
• "God Knows Best." Article explains that submitting to God's will reaps great rewards.
• "The Great Alexander." Article profiles the Seattle Seahawks' running back who uses his gifts for the good of others.
• "Parties, Principles, and Paul." Story tells how a girl learns to appreciate her disabled brother.

Rights and Payment
First rights. Written material, $.08–$.15 per word. Pays on acceptance. Provides 3 contributor's copies.

Editor's Comments
We are always looking for spiritually enriching material that will appeal to teenage girls, including profiles of positive Christian role models, both well known and everyday, who share their faith with others. Keep the tone teen-friendly, not preachy.

Brio & Beyond

Focus on the Family
8605 Explorer Drive
Colorado Springs, CO 80920

Associate Editor: Martha Krienke

Description and Interests
This sister publication of *Brio* magazine is for older teen girls. Its articles also focus on Christian values as they pertain to the issues important to its readers.
- **Audience:** 16–19 years
- **Frequency:** Monthly
- **Circulation:** 50,000
- **Website: www.briomag.com**

Freelance Potential
65% written by nonstaff writers. Publishes 75 freelance submissions yearly; 70% by unpublished writers, 50% by authors who are new to the magazine. Receives 800 queries yearly.

Submissions
Send complete ms. Accepts hard copy, disk submissions, and email submissions to marthakrienke@fotf.org. Availability of artwork improves chance of acceptance. SASE. Responds in 1 month.
Articles: Word lengths vary. Informational and how-to articles; profiles; interviews; reviews; personal experience pieces; and humor. Topics include religion, multicultural and social issues, college, careers, crafts, hobbies, health, fitness, music, popular culture, sports, and travel.
Fiction: Word lengths vary.
Depts/columns: Staff written.
Artwork: Color prints or transparencies. Line art.
Other: Submit seasonal material 6 months in advance.

Sample Issue
34 pages (no advertising): 7 articles; 12 depts/columns. Sample copy, free. Guidelines available.
- "Inside the Male Mind." Article reveals what respect looks like to a guy, and how important it is for girls to treat guys with respect.
- "As Fast As She Can!" Article profiles successful drag car racer Mallori McCullar.

Rights and Payment
First or second rights. All material, payment rates vary. Pays on acceptance. Provides 2 contributor's copies.

Editor's Comments
We are looking for material of interest to older teen girls presented in a way that supports them in their Christian faith. Review one of our recent issues to become familiar with the subjects we cover, and how we cover them.

Brooklyn Parent

350 Fifth Avenue, Suite 2420
New York, NY 10118

Editor: Judy Antell

Description and Interests
This magazine provides parents living in Brooklyn with the latest regional news about parenting, child rearing, health, and education. It also provides news on family entertainment, a calendar of events, and a camp guide.
- **Audience:** Parents
- **Frequency:** Monthly
- **Circulation:** 50,000
- **Website: www.nymetroparents.com**

Freelance Potential
25% written by nonstaff writers. Publishes 5 freelance submissions yearly; 20% by unpublished writers, 10% by authors who are new to the magazine. Receives 300 queries and unsolicited mss yearly.

Submissions
Query or send complete ms. Accepts hard copy and email submissions to hellonwheels@parentsknow.com or judy@parentsknow.com. SASE. Responds in 1 week.
Articles: 800–1,000 words. Informational articles; profiles; interviews; and personal experience pieces. Topics include family issues, health, nutrition, fitness, crafts, current events, gifted and special education, humor, nature, and regional news.
Depts/columns: 750 words. News and reviews.
Other: Submit seasonal material 4 months in advance.

Sample Issue
48 pages: 8 articles; 6 depts/columns. Sample copy, free with 10x13 SASE. Guidelines available at website.
- "A Near-Disaster Sets Mom on a Mission." Article describes how the near-drowning of her daughter encouraged a mom to start a group to train parents in life-saving techniques.
- "A Spoon Full of Sugar." Article provides helpful hints for getting children to take their medicine.
- Sample dept/column: "Family Health" discusses what to expect during baby's first year.

Rights and Payment
First New York area rights. No payment.

Editor's Comments
If you live in Brooklyn or know the area and have an idea for an article that emphasizes the local character and the families that live here, please submit your piece for our review.

ByLine

P.O. Box 111
Albion, NY 14411–0111

Editor: Robbi Hess

Description and Interests
ByLine, calling itself "the best little writers' magazine in America," publishes articles on the craft and business of writing, as well as short fiction and poetry.
- **Audience:** Writers
- **Frequency:** 11 times each year
- **Circulation:** 3,500
- **Website:** www.bylinemag.com

Freelance Potential
80% written by nonstaff writers. Publishes 198 freelance submissions yearly. Receives 3,600 queries and unsolicited mss yearly.

Submissions
Query or send complete ms. Accepts hard copy and email queries to robbi@bylinemag.com. Do not email mss. SASE. Responds in 1–2 months.
Articles: 1,500–1,800 words. Informational and how-to articles; personal experience pieces; and interviews with editors. Topics include writing and marketing fiction, nonfiction, poetry, and humor; finding an agent; research; grammar; and writers' conferences.
Fiction: 2,000–4,000 words. Genres include mainstream and literary fiction.
Depts/columns: "End Piece," 700 words. "First Sale," 250–300 words. "Only When I Laugh," 50–400 words. "Great American Bookstores," 500–600 words.
Other: Poetry about the creative experience.

Sample Issue
34 pages (8% advertising): 3 articles; 1 story; 10 depts/columns; 5 poems. Sample copy, $5 with 9x12 SASE. Guidelines available.
- "Self-Promotion from a Shy Writer." Article provides tips for overcoming doubt and apprehension about being in the spotlight.
- "The Library." Story depicts a delivery boy's visits to a mysterious mansion.
- Sample dept/column: "End Piece" is about a woman's foray into a writing career, despite a lack of training.

Rights and Payment
First North American rights. Articles, $75. Depts/columns, $15–$40. Poetry, $10. Pays on acceptance. Provides contributor's copies.

Editor's Comments
Our message to writers is a simple one: Believe in yourself and keep trying.

BYU Magazine

218 UPB
Provo, UT 84602

Editor: Jeff McClellan

Description and Interests
All members of the Brigham Young University community—including students, alumni, and staff—read this magazine for a picture of current campus life and thought-provoking, inspirational articles about contemporary life and faith.
- **Audience:** YA–Adult
- **Frequency:** Quarterly
- **Circulation:** 200,000
- **Website:** www.magazine.byu.edu

Freelance Potential
45% written by nonstaff writers. Publishes 10 freelance submissions yearly; 5% by authors who are new to the magazine. Receives 120 queries yearly.

Submissions
Query with writing samples. Accepts hard copy. SASE. Responds in 6–12 months.
Articles: 2,000–4,000 words. Informational, factual, self-help, and how-to articles; personal experience pieces; and humor. Topics include college life, careers, computers, current events, health, fitness, religion, science, technology, sports, and family.
Depts/columns: To 1,500 words. Commentary, campus news, book reviews, and alumni updates.
Artwork: 35mm color prints or transparencies.
Other: Word lengths vary. BYU trivia.

Sample Issue
64 pages (15% advertising): 4 articles; 7 depts/columns. Sample copy, free. Guidelines available.
- "Sunday at School." Article provides a glimpse of all the activities and happenings on BYU's campus on a typical Sunday.
- "Finding Answers." Article discusses why a search for spiritual answers must include seeking the companionship of the Holy Ghost.
- Sample dept/column: "Book Nook" reviews Latter-day Saint histories.

Rights and Payment
First North American serial rights. Articles, $.35 per word. Pays on publication. Provides 10 contributor's copies.

Editor's Comments
Your article ideas must have some connection to the University, and all of the issues you address must be consistent with the standards of our sponsoring church. Write for an educated audience.

Cadet Quest

Calvinist Cadet Corps
P.O. Box 7259
Grand Rapids, MI 49510

Editor: G. Richard Broene

Description and Interests
This magazine is designed specifically for boys who are members of the Calvinist Cadet Corps, a ministry of more than 650 boys' clubs throughout the U.S. and Canada. The goal of the Corps is to help boys grow more Christ-like in all areas of their lives.
• **Audience:** Boys, 9–14 years
• **Frequency:** 7 times each year
• **Circulation:** 8,000
• **Website:** www.calvinistcadets.org

Freelance Potential
58% written by nonstaff writers. Publishes 25 freelance submissions yearly; 3% by unpublished writers, 5% by authors who are new to the magazine. Receives 400 unsolicited mss yearly.

Submissions
Send complete ms. Accepts hard copy, email submissions to submissions@calvinistcadets.org (no attachments), and simultaneous submissions if identified. SASE. Responds in 1 month.
Articles: 400–1,000 words. Informational and factual articles; profiles; and interviews. Topics include religion and spirituality, camping skills, crafts, hobbies, sports, the environment, stewardship, and serving God.
Depts/columns: Word lengths vary. Bible lessons and Cadet Corps news.
Other: Puzzles and cartoons.

Sample Issue
22 pages (2% advertising): 3 articles; 1 story; 2 depts/columns; 3 activities; 1 comic. Sample copy, free with 9x12 SASE ($1.01 postage). Guidelines and theme list available with SASE or at website.
• "Bad Calls." Story features a hockey player who can't keep his temper in check.
• "Howls of Thunder." Article presents facts about howler monkeys.
• "Not Just Another Pretty Shape." Article explains the value of arches in architecture.

Rights and Payment
First and second serial rights. Written material, $.04–$.05 per word. Other material, payment rates vary. Pays on acceptance. Provides 1 author's copy.

Editor's Comments
We'd like to see fiction from a Christian perspective that will appeal to our readers. Articles about real Christian role models are also welcome.

Calliope

Cobblestone Publishing
30 Grove Street, Suite C
Peterborough, NH 03458

Editors: Rosalie F. Baker and Charles F. Baker

Description and Interests
This magazine features themed issues on world history. Subjects are presented in a lively and entertaining way, while accuracy of content is maintained.
• **Audience:** 9–14 years
• **Frequency:** 9 times each year
• **Circulation:** 12,000
• **Website:** www.cobblestonepub.com

Freelance Potential
95% written by nonstaff writers. Publishes 75 freelance submissions yearly; 25% by unpublished writers, 30–40% by authors who are new to the magazine. Receives 300 queries yearly.

Submissions
Query with outline, bibliography, and clips or writing samples. All material must relate to upcoming themes. Responds in 4 months.
Articles: Features, 700–800 words. Sidebars, 300–600 words. Informational articles and profiles. Topics include Western and Eastern world history.
Fiction: To 800 words. Genres include historical and biographical fiction, adventure, and historical plays.
Depts/columns: 300–600 words. Current events, archaeology, languages, and book reviews.
Artwork: B/W or color prints or slides. B/W or color line art.
Other: Puzzles, games, activities, crafts, and recipes, to 700 words.

Sample Issue
50 pages (no advertising): 16 articles; 6 depts/columns; 4 activities. Sample copy, $4.95 with 9x12 SASE ($2 postage). Guidelines and theme list available.
• "The Legend of the Horse-Head Fiddle." Story retells the Mongolian legend about the beautiful musical instrument inspired by a horse.
• Sample dept/column: "Activity" shows readers how to build their own silk road instruments.

Rights and Payment
All rights. Articles and fiction, $.20–$.25 per word. Other material, payment rates vary. Pays on publication. Provides 2 contributor's copies.

Editor's Comments
We are looking for writing that goes beyond what most textbooks can offer. Submissions must be educational, entertaining, and engaging. We want readers to get excited about world history.

Camping Magazine

American Camp Association
5000 State Road 67 North
Martinsville, IN 46151-7902

Editor-in-Chief: Harriet Gamble

Description and Interests
This magazine from the American Camp Association is filled with ideas for running innovative recreational camps for children. Read by both camp managers and staff, it reports on news and trends while also providing youth development information.
• **Audience:** Camp managers and educators
• **Frequency:** 6 times each year
• **Circulation:** 7,500
• **Website:** www.ACAcamps.org

Freelance Potential
98% written by nonstaff writers. Publishes 20 freelance submissions yearly; 50% by unpublished writers, 50% by authors who are new to the magazine. Receives 96 queries yearly.

Submissions
Query with outline. Prefers email queries to magazine@acacamps.org. Will accept hard copy. SASE. Response time varies.
Articles: 1,500–4,000 words. Informational and how-to articles. Topics include camp management, special education, social issues, careers, health, recreation, crafts, and hobbies.
Depts/columns: 800–1,000 words. News, opinion pieces, risk management, and building and construction information.
Artwork: B/W or color prints or slides.

Sample Issue
52 pages (20% advertising): 5 articles; 10 depts/columns. Sample copy, $4.50 with 9x12 SASE. Guidelines and editorial calendar available.
• "Camp Shriver." Article describes a day camp program that offers a model for including children with intellectual disabilities.
• "Getting It, Learning It, Laughing at It." Article offers advice for helping campers with chronic conditions, such as Type I Diabetes, adjust and thrive.
• Sample dept/column: "Risk Management" tells how to minimize risks when working with volunteers.

Rights and Payment
All rights. No payment. Provides 3 author's copies.

Editor's Comments
We want to see well-written, well-researched material that gives our readers new programming and management strategies and ideas. Most of our authors have hands-on experience in this field.

Canadian Children's Literature

Department of English, University of Winnipeg
515 Portage Avenue
Winnipeg, Manitoba R3B 2E9
Canada

Editor: Perry Nodelman

Description and Interests
This bilingual academic journal publishes theoretically informed articles about all aspects of Canadian children's literature and other media.
• **Audience:** Educators, scholars, and librarians
• **Frequency:** Twice each year
• **Circulation:** 400
• **Website:** http://ccl.uwinnipeg.ca

Freelance Potential
99% written by nonstaff writers. Publishes 25–30 freelance submissions yearly; 10% by unpublished writers, 40% by authors who are new to the magazine. Receives 120 unsolicited mss yearly.

Submissions
Query with summary; or send 3 copies of complete ms. Accepts hard copy and email submissions to ccl@uwinnipeg.ca (Microsoft Word or RTF attachments). SAE/IRC. Responds to queries in 6 weeks, to mss in 6 months.
Articles: 2,000–6,000 words. Informational articles; reviews; profiles; and interviews. Topics include children's literature; film, video, and drama for children; and children's authors.

Sample Issue
178 pages (2% advertising): 9 articles. Sample copy, $10. Guidelines and theme list available at website.
• "'The World is Our Classroom': Developing Global Awareness in Adolescents by Teaching Deborah Ellis's Breadwinner Trilogy." Article suggests lessons that can be taught from these books about girls struggling to survive in Taliban-era Afghanistan.
• "Shared Characteristics of Boys and Men in Recent Canadian Children's Fiction." Article reviews what English-language books for Canadian boys reveal together as a genre of texts.

Rights and Payment
First serial rights. No payment. Provides 1 contributor's copy.

Editor's Comments
We seek articles from specialists in English and/or French literature; theater and drama; media studies; literary theory; education; information science; childhood and cultural studies; and related disciplines. We also seek articles that explore the practical implications of the research we publish for librarians, teachers, and other practitioners who work with child readers.

Canadian Guider

Girl Guides of Canada
50 Merton Street
Toronto, Ontario M4S 1A3
Canada

Editor: Sharon Pruner

Description and Interests
This official publication of the Girl Guides of Canada embraces global issues as well as the basics of scouting life, such as community service, fundraising, and outdoor programs.
- **Audience:** Girl Guide leaders
- **Frequency:** 3 times each year
- **Circulation:** 40,000
- **Website:** www.girlguides.ca

Freelance Potential
5% written by nonstaff writers. Publishes 2 freelance submissions yearly; 50% by unpublished writers, 50% by authors who are new to the magazine. Receives 1 query monthly.

Submissions
Query with résumé for articles; send complete ms for depts/columns. Availability of artwork improves chance of acceptance. SAE/IRC. Responds in 1 month.
Articles: To 200 words. Informational and how-to articles; profiles; interviews; and personal experience pieces. Topics include leadership and life skills, health and fitness, camping, adventure, nature, the arts, social issues, and contemporary concerns.
Depts/columns: 50–100 words. "Innovators" features leadership profiles. "Ideas to Go" offers program-related crafts and activities.
Artwork: B/W and color prints. Digital images at 300 dpi.

Sample Issue
54 pages (12% advertising): 15 articles; 9 depts/columns. Sample copy, $3 with 9x12 SAE/IRC. Guidelines and editorial calendar available at website.
- "Investing in Each Other." Article provides an overview of the new Girl Guide Mentoring Program.
- "Diversity and You." Article explains the national bias awareness/equity training module for Girl Guides of Canada leaders.
- Sample dept/column: "Ideas to Go" includes a recipe for mock sushi made from candy and cereal.

Rights and Payment
All rights. No payment. Provides 2 author's copies.

Editor's Comments
Content must be written directly to Guiders. All material must have national significance with local relevance, and must be communicated responsibly, offering practical support and proactive resolution of challenges.

Capper's

1503 SW 42nd Street
Topeka, KS 66609

Editor-in-Chief: Katherine Compton

Description and Interests
Though it is distributed nationwide, this monthly tabloid is mainly read by residents of the rural Midwest. It features a wide variety of material that emphasizes traditional family values.
- **Audience:** Families
- **Frequency:** Monthly
- **Circulation:** 200,000
- **Website:** www.cappers.com

Freelance Potential
90% written by nonstaff writers. Publishes 40–50 freelance submissions yearly; 50% by unpublished writers, 70% by authors who are new to the magazine. Receives 480 unsolicited mss yearly.

Submissions
Send complete ms with photos for articles; query for fiction. Accepts hard copy. SASE. Responds to queries in 1 month, to mss in 3–4 months.
Articles: 700 words. General interest, historical, inspirational, and nostalgic articles. Topics include family life, travel, hobbies, and occupations.
Fiction: To 25,000 words. Serializes novels.
Depts/columns: 300 words. Personal experience pieces, humor, and essays.
Artwork: 35mm color slides, transparencies, or prints.
Other: Jokes; 5–6 per submission.

Sample Issue
48 pages (3% advertising): 24 articles; 1 serialized novel; 5 poems; 12 depts/columns. Sample copy, $1.95. Guidelines available.
- "Folks Still Go Bananas Over Sock Monkeys." Article reveals the story behind the development and popularity of these adorable dolls.
- "Class Allows Humans, Pets to Team Up for Relaxing Exercises." Article relates the experiences of people who participate in yoga classes with their pets.

Rights and Payment
Standard rights. Articles, $2.50 per column inch; serialized novels, $75–$300. Pays on publication for nonfiction, on acceptance for fiction. Provides up to 5 contributor's copies.

Editor's Comments
Our readership expects to find positive and wholesome material that every member of the family—young and old alike—can enjoy.

Careers and Colleges

2 LAN Drive, Suite 100
Westford, MA 01886

Editor: Anne Kandra

Description and Interests
High school students read *Careers and Colleges* for well-written and researched articles on higher education choices and career planning and opportunities. It also offers inspiring profiles of successful students.
• **Audience:** 15–18 years
• **Frequency:** 3 times each year
• **Circulation:** 752,000
• **Website:** www.careersandcolleges.com

Freelance Potential
80% written by nonstaff writers. Publishes 6 freelance submissions yearly; 10% by authors who are new to the magazine. Receives 96 queries yearly.

Submissions
Query with clips or writing samples. No unsolicited mss. Accepts hard copy. SASE. Responds in 2 months.
Articles: 800–2,400 words. Informational and how-to articles; profiles; interviews; and personal experience pieces. Topics include career choices, post-secondary education, independent living, social issues, and personal growth.
Depts/columns: Staff written.

Sample Issue
32 pages (29% advertising): 8 articles; 4 depts/columns. Sample copy, $6.95 with 10x13 SASE ($1.75 postage). Guidelines available.
• "Teens Most Likely to Succeed." Article profiles five talented and successful teens who have made a real difference in the lives of others.
• "The Truth About Summer Jobs." Article explains how working a summer job adds great value to a student's college application.
• "Finding the Right School." Article offers practical advice for choosing a suitable college.

Rights and Payment
First North American serial and electronic rights. Articles, $300–$800. Pays 2 months after acceptance. Provides 2 contributor's copies.

Editor's Comments
We are looking for a fresh approach to the topics related to college and career planning. In addition to well-researched material and fluent writing, every submitted article should include additional relevant resources to help students get more information about the topic.

Carolina Parent

5716 Fayetteville Road, Suite 201
Durham, NC 27713

Editor: Crickett Gibbons

Description and Interests
Parents living in North Carolina's Research Triangle area read this regional tabloid for family-related news and events coverage. Each issue centers around a theme.
• **Audience:** Parents
• **Frequency:** Monthly
• **Circulation:** 58,000
• **Website:** www.carolinaparent.com

Freelance Potential
50% written by nonstaff writers. Publishes 40 freelance submissions yearly; 20% by unpublished writers, 30% by authors who are new to the magazine.

Submissions
Query with outline and writing samples. New writers, send complete ms. Accepts hard copy and email submissions to editorial@carolinaparent.com (Microsoft Word attachments). SASE. Response time varies.
Articles: 500–1,200 words. Informational, self-help, and how-to articles; profiles; and personal experience pieces. Topics include college, careers, computers, crafts, hobbies, gifted education, health, fitness, humor, music, nature, the environment, recreation, regional news, science, technology, social issues, sports, and travel.
Depts/columns: Word lengths vary. Family finances, family issues, news, events, and health.

Sample Issue
92 pages: 7 articles; 17 depts/columns; 1 special insert. Guidelines and editorial calendar available.
• "Birthday Bashes on a Budget." Article offers 10 ways to save money and still throw a great party.
• "A Survival Guide to Camp—For Parents." Article presents a list of practical suggestions that go beyond the standard packing list.
• Sample dept/column: "Where Did All My Hair Go?" discusses postpartum hair loss and offers reassuring information about the three cycles of hair growth.

Rights and Payment
First and electronic rights. Written material, $50–$75. Pays on publication.

Editor's Comments
Features require thorough research (citing a minimum of three reliable sources), knowledge of our audience, and concise interviewing and writing skills. We prefer articles and essays with local relevancy; submissions should be exclusive within our region.

Catholic Digest

1 Montauk Avenue, Suite 200
New London, CT 06320

Associate Editor: Kerry Weber

Description and Interests
Catholic Digest celebrates the everyday miracles of life, and seeks to show that the solutions to life's problems can be found in faith, hope, and love. It is filled with inspiring stories about real people.
- **Audience:** Adults
- **Frequency:** Monthly
- **Circulation:** 350,000
- **Website:** www.catholicdigest.com

Freelance Potential
44% written by nonstaff writers. Publishes 100–200 freelance submissions yearly; 12% by new authors. Receives 4,800 unsolicited mss yearly.

Submissions
Send complete ms. Accepts hard copy, disk submissions, and email submissions to cdsubmissions@bayard-inc.com. No simultaneous submissions. SASE. Responds in 6–8 weeks.
Articles: 1,000–3,500 words. Informational articles; profiles; and personal experience pieces. Topics include religion, prayer, spirituality, relationships, family issues, history, science, and nostalgia.
Depts/columns: 50–500 words. True stories about faith, spotlights on community organizations, and profiles of volunteers.
Other: Filler, to 500 words.

Sample Issue
128 pages (13% advertising): 10 articles; 17 depts/columns. Sample copy, free with 6x9 SASE ($1 postage). Guidelines available.
- "Does Religious Life Have a Future?" Article describes the changes that have occurred in religious communities since the 1950s.
- "What My Dad Taught Me." Article tells about the many things a daughter can learn from her dad.
- Sample dept/column: "Be Well" offers advice on dealing with Parkinson's disease.

Rights and Payment
One-time rights. Articles, $100–$400. Depts/columns, $2 per published line. Pays on publication. Provides 2 contributor's copies.

Editor's Comments
We favor the anecdotal approach. That said, every submission must be strongly focused on a definitive topic, and must be true-to-life. Read an issue to become familiar with our tone and style.

Catholic Forester

P.O. Box 3012
335 Shuman Boulevard
Naperville, IL 60566-7012

Associate Editor: Patricia Baron

Description and Interests
This publication of the Catholic Order of Foresters includes news about the organization and its members, and strives to inform, educate, and entertain. Its readership includes a wide range of ages, from teens to senior citizens.
- **Audience:** Catholic Forester members
- **Frequency:** Quarterly
- **Circulation:** 100,000
- **Website:** www.catholicforester.com

Freelance Potential
20% written by nonstaff writers. Publishes 4–8 freelance submissions yearly; 5% by unpublished writers, 20% by authors who are new to the magazine. Receives 240 unsolicited mss yearly.

Submissions
Send complete ms. Accepts hard copy. SASE. Responds in 3–4 months.
Articles: 1,000 words. Informational and inspirational articles. Topics include money management, fitness, health, family life, investing, senior issues, careers, parenting, and nostalgia.
Fiction: 1,000 words. Inspirational, humorous, and light fiction.

Sample Issue
40 pages (no advertising): 6 articles; 2 activities; 5 depts/columns. Sample copy, free with 9x12 SASE (3 first-class stamps). Guidelines available.
- "Journey of Hope." Article recounts the cross-country bicycle trip taken by a member of the organization and his four-man team, and what the experience meant to the participants.
- "Type 2 Diabetes: Your Choices Can Make a Difference." Article describes five ways to live a healthier life in order to prevent diabetes in adults and children.

Rights and Payment
First North American serial rights. Written material, $.30 per word. Reprints, $50. Pays on acceptance. Provides 3 contributor's copies.

Editor's Comments
We are especially interested in articles on health and fitness, money management and investing, and parenting. Writers should try to include personal experiences and what they learned about the subject in order to help our readers. We also are looking for humorous pieces and light fiction.

Catholic Library World

100 North Street, Suite 224
Pittsfield, MA 01201-5109

Editor: Mary E. Gallagher, SSJ

Description and Interests
This official publication of the Catholic Library Association is filled with book and media reviews, informative articles on library science and librarianship, information for Catholic researchers, and news about the Catholic Library Association.
- **Audience:** Adults
- **Frequency:** Quarterly
- **Circulation:** 1,100
- **Website:** www.cathla.org

Freelance Potential
25% written by nonstaff writers. Publishes 12 freelance submissions yearly. Receives 12 queries and unsolicited mss yearly.

Submissions
Query or send complete ms. Accepts hard copy and email submissions to cla@cathla.org (Microsoft Word attachments). SASE.
Articles: Word lengths vary. Informational articles and reviews. Topics include books, reading, library science, and Catholic Library Association news.
Reviews: 150–300 words. Topics include theology, spirituality, pastoral issues, church history, education, history, literature, library science, philosophy, and reference; children's and young adult topics include biography, fiction, multicultural issues, picture books, reference, science, social studies, and values.
Artwork: B/W and color prints and transparencies. Line art.

Sample Issue
186 pages (2% advertising): 4 articles; 154 book reviews; 1 media review; 4 depts/columns. Sample copy, $15. Reviewers' guidelines available.
- "Models of Outstanding Leadership in Libraries." Article explains the value of taking a participative leadership approach.
- "The Latest Books to Come My Way and Perhaps Your Way Too?" Article provides recommendations and brief synopses of over three dozen books.

Rights and Payment
Rights vary. No payment. Provides 1 author's copy.

Editor's Comments
We are interested in well-researched articles on topics related to all types of libraries. Please follow our guidelines for book reviews to the letter. Do not submit reviews of adult fiction.

Celebrate

2923 Troost Avenue
Kansas City, MO 64109

Submissions: Abigail L. Takala

Description and Interests
Celebrate is a take-home Sunday school paper for children in preschool and kindergarten. It appeals to its audience with bright, colorful activities, Bible stories, songs, and poems that connect Christian principles to everyday life. Each issue covers a theme.
- **Audience:** 3–6 years
- **Frequency:** Weekly
- **Circulation:** 40,000
- **Website:** www.wordaction.com

Freelance Potential
90% written by nonstaff writers. Publishes 100 freelance submissions yearly; 30% by unpublished writers, 35% by authors who are new to the magazine. Receives 200 queries yearly.

Submissions
Query. Accepts hard copy and email queries to alt@wordaction.com (Microsoft Word attachments). SASE. Responds in 2–4 weeks.
Other: Poetry, 4–8 lines. Bible stories, songs, finger plays, action rhymes, crafts, activities, and recipes.

Sample Issue
4 pages (no advertising): 1 Bible story; 1 poem; 1 finger play; 1 activity. Sample copy, free with #10 SASE (1 first-class stamp). Guidelines and theme list available.
- "Stickers to Share." Activity provides instructions for making stickers at home using construction paper, wax paper, and glue.
- "Church Friends Share." Bible story tells how Jesus's disciples shared the good news about his life and teachings and tells how members of the early church cared for each other and shared their belongings.
- "Church Friends." Poem tells how God loves us through our friends.

Rights and Payment
Rights, payment rates, and payment policy vary.

Editor's Comments
Prospective writers should send for a theme list. We would like to see more hands-on activities that relate to our weekly Bible stories. Please don't send poems that are not theme related. Remember to use language that is appropriate for children ages three through six. Submissions should show character-building or life application of spiritual truths.

Central Penn Parent

101 North Second Street, 2nd Floor
Harrisburg, PA 17101

Editor: Karren Johnson

Description and Interests
Parents in central Pennsylvania read this tabloid for regional family activities and resources, as well as expert advice on raising children.
- **Audience:** Parents
- **Frequency:** Monthly
- **Circulation:** 35,000
- **Website:** www.centralpennparent.com

Freelance Potential
50% written by nonstaff writers. Publishes 10 freelance submissions yearly; 20% by unpublished writers, 10% by authors who are new to the magazine. Receives 96 queries yearly.

Submissions
All articles are assigned to local writers. Query for reprints only. Accepts email queries to karrenj@ journalpub.com. Availability of artwork improves chance of acceptance. SASE. Responds in 2 weeks.
Articles: 1,200–1,500 words. Informational articles and reviews. Topics include local family events and activities, health, nutrition, discipline, education, home life, technology, literature, parenting, and travel.
Depts/columns: 700 words. Family finances, health, infant issues, news, and education.
Artwork: Color prints and transparencies. Line art.
Other: Submit seasonal material at least 2 months in advance.

Sample Issue
48 pages (50% advertising): 1 article; 15 depts/ columns; 1 special section. Sample copy, free. Guidelines available.
- "Two, Three, Four and More." Article includes profiles of local families with twins, triplets, quadruplets, and sextuplets.
- "A Party for Charity." Article provides guidelines for asking birthday party guests to make a charitable contribution in lieu of bringing a gift for your child.
- Sample dept/column: "News You Can Use" encourages outdoor recreation for families.

Rights and Payment
All rights. Reprints, $35–$50. Pays on publication. Provides contributor's copies upon request.

Editor's Comments
We prefer to work with writers from Cumberland, Dauphin, Lancaster, and York counties in Pennsylvania. Our audience is parents of newborns to teens.

Characters

P.O. Box 708
Newport, NH 03773

Editor: Cindy Davis

Description and Interests
This self-professed "kids' short story outlet" favors fiction by children and teens, though it does accept work from authors of all ages.
- **Audience:** 8–18 years
- **Frequency:** Four times during the school year
- **Circulation:** Unavailable
- **Website:** www.cdavisnh.net

Freelance Potential
100% written by nonstaff writers. Publishes 44 freelance submissions yearly; 75% by unpublished writers, 50% by authors who are new to the magazine. Receives 500 unsolicited mss yearly.

Submissions
Send complete ms with short biography. Accepts hard copy, email to hotdog@nhvt.net (no attachments), and simultaneous submissions if identified. SASE. Responds in 2–4 weeks.
Fiction: To 2,000 words. Genres include mystery, contemporary and historical fiction, humor, fantasy, adventure, science fiction, romance, and stories with nature themes.

Sample Issue
43 pages (no advertising): 7 stories. Sample copy, $5.75. Guidelines available.
- "The Message." Story tells how one interaction with a new teacher changes a girl's viewpoint.
- "Breakfast for a Dragon." Story depicts a girl's attempt to rescue her prince from a dragon.
- "The Case of the Stone Shoes." Story follows a brother and sister as they solve a mystery.
- "Barbara's Trip." Story describes a disabled girl's life-affirming dream and its aftermath.

Rights and Payment
One-time and electronic rights. Written material, $5. Pays on publication. Provides 1 contributor's copy.

Editor's Comments
We see too many stories featuring talking animals or parents as the main characters. Stories must be written from a child's point of view. We want to see a child who, when confronted with a problem, finds a way to solve it with little intervention from adults. Please also note that all submissions must be typed and double-spaced, with name, address, and word count on the title page. We are no longer accepting poetry submissions.

Charlotte Parent

2125 Southend Drive, Suite 253
Charlotte, NC 28230

Editor: Eve White

Description and Interests

For more than 20 years, *Charlotte Parent* has been filling its pages with a mix of general parenting articles, product reviews, family activity ideas, and event listings. In addition to parents, it reaches teachers, childcare providers, and child advocates.
- **Audience:** Parents
- **Frequency:** Monthly
- **Circulation:** 55,000
- **Website:** www.charlotteparent.com

Freelance Potential

50% written by nonstaff writers. Publishes 45 freelance submissions yearly; 15% by unpublished writers, 25% by authors who are new to the magazine. Receives 1,000 queries, 800 unsolicited mss yearly.

Submissions

Query or send complete ms with résumé and bibliography. Prefers email to editor@charlotteparent.com. Will accept hard copy, Macintosh disk submissions, and simultaneous submissions if identified. SASE. Responds if interested.
Articles: 500–1,000 words. Informational and how-to articles. Topics include parenting, family life, finances, education, health, fitness, vacations, entertainment, regional activities, and the environment.
Depts/columns: Word lengths vary. Child development information, restaurant and media reviews, and children's health.
Artwork: High-density Macintosh-format artwork.
Other: Activities. Submit seasonal material 2–3 months in advance.

Sample Issue

72 pages (35% advertising): 7 articles; 11 depts/columns; 1 calendar. Sample copy, free with 9x12 SASE (5 first-class stamps). Guidelines and editorial calendar available.
- "Taking On the Outdoors." Article tells how parents can make outdoor play a priority.
- "Creative Care Packages for Campers." Article offers fun ideas for sending goodies to your child.

Rights and Payment

First and Internet rights. Written material, payment rates vary. Pays on publication. Provides 1 copy.

Editor's Comments

Most issues revolve around a theme, so check the editorial calendar before sending your idea.

ChemMatters

American Chemical Society
1155 16th Street NW
Washington, DC 20036

Editor: Carl Heltzel

Description and Interests

Targeted to high school students taking introductory chemistry classes, this magazine covers chemistry topics in a way that sparks students' interests.
- **Audience:** 14–18 years
- **Frequency:** 5 times each year
- **Circulation:** 40,000
- **Website:** www.acs.org/education/chemmatters.html

Freelance Potential

90% written by nonstaff writers. Publishes 20 freelance submissions yearly; 80% by unpublished writers. Receives 30–40 queries yearly.

Submissions

Query with abstract, outline, or related material that conveys the scientific content, and a writing sample. Prefers email queries to chemmatters@acs.org. Accepts hard copy. SASE. Responds in 5 days.
Articles: 1,400–2,100 words. Informational articles. Topics include chemistry, the human body, current events, food, and history.
Depts/columns: 1,400–2,100 words. "ChemSumer," reports on new products for teens and explains their chemistry. "Mystery Matters" explains how forensic chemistry solves crimes.
Artwork: JPEG or GIF line art.
Other: Chemistry-oriented puzzles, activities.

Sample Issue

20 pages (no advertising): 3 articles; 3 depts/columns. Sample copy available at website. Writers' guidelines and theme list available by email to chemmatters@acs.org.
- "Chemistry on the Fast Track." Article examines all the chemical products and reactions that are involved in NASCAR racing.
- Sample dept/column: "ChemHistory" details the life work of a young chemist who helped to cure leprosy.

Rights and Payment

All rights. Articles, $500–$1,000. Pays on acceptance. Provides 5 contributor's copies.

Editor's Comments

Our mission is to demystify everyday chemistry and show that chemistry is interesting—even exciting. Our readership relies on us for informative and accurate material. Successful articles appeal to both teens and teachers. Forensic chemistry pieces are particularly popular.

Chesapeake Family

929 West Street, Suite 307
Annapolis, MD 21401

Editor: Cathy Ashby

Description and Interests
Written primarily for parents of school-age children, this magazine covers educational issues, fun family activities and travel, children's health and development, and regional news. It is distributed to families living in Annapolis, Maryland, and the surrounding Chesapeake Bay communities.
• **Audience:** Parents
• **Frequency:** Monthly
• **Circulation:** 40,000
• **Website:** www.chesapeakefamily.com

Freelance Potential
80% written by nonstaff writers. Publishes 20 freelance submissions yearly; 20% by authors who are new to the magazine. Receives 120 mss yearly.

Submissions
Send complete ms. Accepts hard copy. SASE. Response time varies.
Articles: 1,000–1,200 words. Informational and how-to articles; and profiles. Topics include parenting, the environment, music, regional news, current events, education, entertainment, health, and family travel destinations.
Fiction: "Just for Kids" features stories and poems by local 4- to 12-year-old children.
Depts/columns: 700–900 words. Health, education, and child development.
Other: Submit seasonal material 3–6 months in advance.

Sample Issue
68 pages (45% advertising): 5 articles; 9 depts/columns; 1 events calendar. Guidelines and editorial calendar available.
• "College Prep at Summer Camp." Article discusses programs offered by colleges and universities to help high schoolers prepare for higher education.
• Sample dept/column: "Understanding Children" tells why negative words can have such harmful effects on children.

Rights and Payment
Geographic print rights; electronic rights negotiable. Features, $75–$110. Depts/columns, $50. Reprints, $35. Payment policy varies.

Editor's Comments
We want writers with good interviewing and research skills. Being local has a distinct advantage.

Chess Life

P.O. Box 3967
Crossville, TN 38557-3967

Editor: Daniel Lucas

Description and Interests
Self-proclaimed as "the world's most widely read chess magazine," *Chess Life* covers all facets of the classic game, from strategies and analysis to tournaments and festivals. It also profiles chess masters.
• **Audience:** YA–Adult
• **Frequency:** Monthly
• **Circulation:** 80,000
• **Website:** www.uschess.org

Freelance Potential
75% written by nonstaff writers. Publishes 30 freelance submissions yearly; 30% by unpublished writers. Receives 180–420 queries yearly.

Submissions
Query with clips or writing samples. Accepts hard copy, IBM disk submissions (ASCII), and email to dlucas@uschess.org. SASE. Responds in 1–3 months.
Articles: 800–3,000 words. Informational, how-to, and historical articles; personal experience and opinion pieces; profiles; and humor. Topics include chess games and strategies, tournaments and events, and personalities.
Depts/columns: To 1,000 words. Book and product reviews; short how-to's; and player profiles.
Artwork: B/W and color prints.
Other: Chess-oriented cartoons, contests, and games.

Sample Issue
80 pages (16% advertising): 9 articles; 13 depts/columns. Sample copy, free with 9x12 SASE. Guidelines available at website.
• "IM Jesse Kraai Joins the Elite." Article presents an interview with the first American to make Grand Master in 10 years.
• "All-Girls' National Again a Success." Article deconstructs the 2007 Annual All-Girls Open National Championships in Chicago.
• Sample dept/column: "Looks at Books" includes a full-length review of the new edition of John Nunn's *Secrets of Practical Chess*.

Rights and Payment
All rights. Written material, $100 per page. Artwork, $15–$100. Kill fee, 30%. Pays on publication. Provides 2 contributor's copies.

Editor's Comments
There is only one all-encompassing injunction: The game of chess must be central to every submission.

Chess Life for Kids

P.O. Box 3967
Crossville, TN 38577

Editor: Glenn Petersen

Description and Interests
This magazine for the scholastic members of the U.S. Chess Federation emphasizes instruction and tournament participation. It also features articles on chess camps, upcoming tournaments, and other Federation-related matters.
- **Audience:** 12 years and under
- **Frequency:** 6 times each year
- **Circulation:** 22,700
- **Website:** www.uschess.org

Freelance Potential
75% written by nonstaff writers. Publishes 18 freelance submissions yearly; 10% by unpublished writers, 20% by authors who are new to the magazine. Receives 20–30 queries and unsolicited mss yearly.

Submissions
Query or send complete ms. Accepts email submissions to gpetersen@uschess.org and simultaneous submissions if identified. Responds in 2 weeks.
Articles: To 1,000 words. Informational and instructional articles; and profiles. Topics include chess instruction, game tips, tournaments, chess camps, and chess lessons.

Sample Issue
24 pages: 8 articles.
- "How to Read and Write Chess." Article describes in detail the algebraic notation method of writing chess moves.
- "The Best Way to Improve." Article reveals the three most important areas of the game on which to focus.
- "Wishing Doesn't Make It So." Article gives a move-by-move description of an amazing game between two 10-year-old players.

Rights and Payment
First North American serial rights. Written material, $75 per page. Pays on publication.

Editor's Comments
We are read by children ages 12 and under who really know how to play chess well but still read at the elementary school level. Therefore, write in a way that will appeal to both boys and girls in this age group while still imparting detailed information, instructions, and advice. We strongly urge you to read a recent issue of *Chess Life for Kids* to get a clear understanding of the writing style we prefer.

Chicago Parent

141 South Oak Park Avenue
Chicago, IL 60302

Editor: Tamara O'Shaughnessy

Description and Interests
This free tabloid offers lively, informative articles and listings for parents in the greater Chicago area.
- **Audience:** Parents
- **Frequency:** Monthly
- **Circulation:** 138,000
- **Website:** www.chicagoparent.com

Freelance Potential
85% written by nonstaff writers. Publishes 50+ freelance submissions yearly; 20% by unpublished writers, 20% by authors who are new to the magazine. Receives 480–540 queries yearly.

Submissions
Query with résumé and clips. Accepts email queries to chiparent@chicagoparent.com. Responds in 6 weeks.
Articles: 1,500–2,500 words. Informational articles; profiles; personal experience pieces; and humor. Topics include pregnancy, childbirth, parenting, grandparenting, foster care, adoption, day care, child development, health, education, and family issues.
Depts/columns: 850 words. Crafts and activities; book, video, music, and stage reviews; health; travel; family finances; and regional events.
Other: Cartoons for parents. Submit seasonal material at least 2 months in advance.

Sample Issue
108 pages (60% advertising): 11 articles; 15 depts/columns. Sample copy, $3.95. Guidelines and editorial calendar available.
- "The Up Side of Simple Chores." Article suggests several simple chores kids can be in charge of that will make everyday life easier and the kids more responsible.
- "Sometimes It's More Than the Wiggles." Article discusses sensory processing disorder, formerly known as sensory integration dysfunction.
- Sample dept/column: "Healthy Matters" details the dangers of lawn mowers.

Rights and Payment
One-time and Illinois exclusive rights. Articles, $125–$350. Depts/columns, $25–$100. Kill fee, 10%. Pays on publication. Provides author's copies upon request.

Editor's Comments
Please send holiday and special-event queries well in advance of the issue's deadline; consult our editorial calendar for cut-off dates.

Childhood Education

Association for Childhood Education International
17904 Georgia Avenue, Suite 215
Olney, MA 20832

Editor: Anne W. Bauer

Description and Interests
Childhood Education is the voice of the Association for Childhood Education International (ACEI) and a professional medium for those concerned with the education and well-being of children from infancy through early adolescence.
• **Audience:** Educators, parents, and child-care workers
• **Frequency:** 6 times each year
• **Circulation:** 10,000
• **Website: www.acei.org**

Freelance Potential
98% written by nonstaff writers. Publishes 40 freelance submissions yearly; 75% by authors who are new to the magazine. Receives 120 unsolicited mss yearly.

Submissions
Send 4 copies of complete ms. Accepts hard copy and Macintosh or IBM disk submissions. SASE. Responds in 3 months.
Articles: 1,400–3,500 words. Informational articles. Topics include innovative teaching strategies, the teaching profession, research findings, parenting and family issues, communities, drug education, and safe environments for children.
Depts/columns: 1,000 words. "Review of Research," "Issues in Education," "For Parents Particularly," "Books for Children," "Professional Books," "Spanish Books," "Among the Periodicals," and media reviews.

Sample Issue
194 pages: 5 articles; 8 depts/columns. Sample copy, free with 9x12 SASE (3 first-class stamps). Guidelines and editorial calendar available.
• "Health and Safety in the Early Childhood Classroom." Article provides guidelines for curriculum development in these subject areas.
• "9/11 to the Iraq War." Article discusses using books to help children understand troubled times.
• Sample dept/column: "Issues in Education" identifies bad advice given to bilingual families.

Rights and Payment
All rights. No payment. Provides 5 author's copies.

Editor's Comments
Unsolicited manuscripts on focus topics outlined in our editorial calendar are encouraged. These may include accounts of innovative practices in the classroom; reviews of research; discussion of timely issues; human interest stories; and bits of humor or satire.

Children and Families

1651 Prince Street
Alexandria, VA 22310

Editor: Julie Antoniou

Description and Interests
Issues of concern to early childhood professionals are addressed in *Children and Families*, a publication of the National Head Start Association. Readers turn to each issue to find informative pieces on early childhood development, parent involvement, and classroom management strategies.
• **Audience:** Early childhood professionals
• **Frequency:** Quarterly
• **Circulation:** 12,000
• **Website: www.nhsa.org**

Freelance Potential
90% written by nonstaff writers. Publishes 25 freelance submissions yearly; 70% by unpublished writers, 70% by authors who are new to the magazine. Receives 24 queries yearly.

Submissions
Query with outline and possible sidebar information. Accepts email queries to julie@nhsa.org. Responds in 1–12 weeks.
Articles: 1,600–4,000 words. Informational and how-to articles. Topics include computers, gifted and special education, health, fitness, mathematics, multicultural issues, music, science, and technology.
Depts/columns: Word lengths vary. News, science lessons, learning styles, and development.
Artwork: Color prints or transparencies.
Other: Jokes about young children. Submit seasonal material 4 months in advance.

Sample Issue
76 pages (20% advertising): 5 articles; 10 depts/columns. Writers' guidelines available and theme list available.
• "Children's Self-Regulation and School Readiness." Article analyzes behavioral issues in relation to transitioning into kindergarten.
• "Flustered in the Classroom." Article tells how to handle sexual play in the preschool setting.
• Sample dept/column: "Men and Children" talks about helping fathers deal with ADHD.

Rights and Payment
First rights. No payment. Provides 2+ author's copies.

Editor's Comments
We encourage our readers to share their knowledge, experiences, and successes with other early childhood professionals.

Children's Digest

Children's Better Health Institute
1100 Waterway Boulevard
Indianapolis, IN 46202

Editor: Danny Lee

Description and Interests
One of a number of magazines for kids from the Children's Better Health Institute, *Children's Digest* covers science, fitness, and safety topics in a fun, colorful way that appeals to pre-teens. It also includes book reviews, puzzles, and activities.
• **Audience:** 10–12 years
• **Frequency:** 6 times each year
• **Circulation:** 60,000
• **Website:** www.childrensdigestmag.org

Freelance Potential
10% written by nonstaff writers. Publishes 15 freelance submissions yearly; 70% by unpublished writers. Receives 1,200 queries yearly.

Submissions
Query only. No unsolicited ms. Accepts hard copy and email queries to d.lee@chdi.org. SASE. Responds in 3 months.
Articles: To 1,200 words. Informational and how-to articles; profiles; interviews; and personal experience pieces. Topics include health, exercise, safety, hygiene, drug education, and nutrition.
Fiction: To 1,500 words. Genres include multicultural and ethnic fiction, science fiction, fantasy, adventure, mystery, humor, and stories about animals and sports.
Depts/columns: To 1,200 words. Reviews, recipes, and health Q&As.
Other: Puzzles, games, and activities. Poetry, to 25 lines. Submit seasonal material 8 months in advance.

Sample Issue
36 pages (6% advertising): 3 articles; 1 story; 2 depts/columns; 4 activities; 5 reviews. Sample copy, $1.25 with 9x12 SASE. Guidelines available.
• "The Recycled Bike." Story tells how a boy deals with his disappointment over not having a new bike for a bike race.
• "Metric—Measure for Measure." Article tells how metric measurements are used in sporting events.

Rights and Payment
All rights. Written material, $.12 per word. Pays prior to publication. Provides 10 contributor's copies.

Editor's Comments
We need more stories that reflect our changing times but at the same time communicate good, wholesome values. Sports and fitness are our primary focus.

Children's Ministry

1515 Cascade Avenue
Loveland, CO 80539

Associate Editor: Carmen Kamrath

Description and Interests
Self-described as "the leading resource for people who serve children in the church," this magazine is filled with ideas, strategies, and inspirational articles for Christian children's ministry.
• **Audience:** Children's ministry leaders; volunteers
• **Frequency:** 6 times each year
• **Circulation:** 65,000
• **Website:** www.childrensministry.com

Freelance Potential
50% written by nonstaff writers. Publishes 50 freelance submissions yearly; 60% by unpublished writers, 60% by authors who are new to the magazine. Receives 2,400 queries and unsolicited mss yearly.

Submissions
Query or send complete ms. Prefers email submissions to ckamrath@cmmag.com. Accepts hard copy. SASE. Responds in 2–3 months.
Articles: 500–1,700 words. Informational and how-to articles; and personal experience pieces. Topics include Christian education, family issues, child development, and faith.
Depts/columns: 50–300 words. Educational issues, activities, devotionals, family ministry, parenting, crafts, and resources.
Other: Activities, games, and tips. Submit seasonal material 6–8 months in advance.

Sample Issue
138 pages (50% advertising): 8 articles; 16 depts/columns. Sample copy, $2 with 9x12 SASE. Writers' guidelines available.
• "Intensive Care." Article discusses ways to minister to kids who are in crisis.
• "Kids Rule!" Article offers ideas for elevating your church's view of children's ministry from a pastor based in Sydney, Australia.
• Sample dept/column: "Leading Volunteers" offers ideas for motivating and inspiring volunteers.

Rights and Payment
All rights. Articles, $25–$300. Depts/columns, $40–$75. Pays on acceptance. Provides 1 author's copy.

Editor's Comments
Well-written articles that talk about communicating with children about faith, morals, money, friends, grades, and choices are always considered. We also accept submissions for our ideas columns.

Children's Playmate

Children's Better Health Institute
1100 Waterway Boulevard
P.O. Box 567
Indianapolis, IN 46206–0567

Editor: Terry Harshman

Description and Interests
This magazine lives up to its name with entertaining stories, puzzles, recipes, and activities written specifically for children, including rebus fiction that encourages early reading. The artwork and poetry of youngsters is also featured.
- **Audience:** 6–8 years
- **Frequency:** 6 times each year
- **Circulation:** 80,000
- **Website:** www.childrensplaymatemag.org

Freelance Potential
25% written by nonstaff writers. Publishes 30 freelance submissions yearly; 10% by unpublished writers, 50% by authors who are new to the magazine. Receives 900 unsolicited mss yearly.

Submissions
Send complete ms. Accepts hard copy. SASE. Responds in 2–3 months.
Articles: To 500 words. Humorous and how-to articles. Topics include health, fitness, nature, the environment, science, hobbies, crafts, multicultural and ethnic subjects, and sports.
Fiction: To 100 words. Humor and rebus stories.
Other: Puzzles, activities, games, and recipes. Poetry, to 20 lines. Submit seasonal material about unusual holidays 8 months in advance.

Sample Issue
36 pages (no advertising): 1 story; 1 rebus; 7 poems; 3 depts/columns; 10 activities; 1 recipe. Sample copy, $1.75 with 9x12 SASE. Guidelines available.
- "Old Snore." Story tells about a lazy dog who is forced into action by a nasty cat.
- "The Birthday Wish." Rebus tells of a little boy who longs to go to the circus.
- Sample dept/column: "Fun Science" provides step-by-step instructions for making a spinning color wheel that demonstrates white light.

Rights and Payment
All rights; returns book rights upon request. Written material, $.17 per word. Pays on publication. Provides up to 10 contributor's copies.

Editor's Comments
In keeping with our mission at the Children's Better Health Institute, all of our content promotes a healthy lifestyle, whether it be good nutrition, regular exercise, sun protection, or safety.

Children's Voice

2345 Crystal Drive, Suite 250
Arlington, VA 22202

Managing Editor: Jennifer Michael

Description and Interests
This publication from the Child Welfare League of America features articles directed at workers in the child welfare field, including front-line workers, educators, pediatricians, law enforcement, foster care, welfare agency employees, and many more.
- **Audience:** Child welfare professionals
- **Frequency:** 6 times each year
- **Circulation:** 25,000
- **Website:** www.cwla.org/voice

Freelance Potential
30% written by nonstaff writers. Publishes 5 freelance submissions yearly; 50% by unpublished writers, 50% by authors who are new to the magazine. Receives 10 queries yearly.

Submissions
Query. Accepts email queries to voice@cwla.org (text only). Availability of artwork improves chance of acceptance. Responds in 1 month.
Articles: 1,500–3,000 words. Informational and how-to articles; personal experience pieces; profiles; and interviews. Topics include child welfare issues and events, and agency programs.
Depts/columns: 200–500 words. Legislative updates; agency and organizational news.

Sample Issue
40 pages (20% advertising): 4 articles; 9 depts/columns. Sample copy, $10. Guidelines available at website.
- "Change Agents." Article examines the impact parent educators have in helping parents play a greater role in their child's development.
- "Fighting Meth, Healing Families: Seven Promising Solutions." Article offers ways families and communities can work to cure methamphetamine addiction.
- Sample dept/column: "HealthBeat" details issues related to the mental and physical health of growing children and youth.

Rights and Payment
All rights. No payment. Provides contributor's copies and a 1-year subscription.

Editor's Comments
We seek child welfare experts to submit articles that provide in-depth treatment of issues and events that affect children, youth, and families and those who work with them or for them.

Children's Writer

Institute of Children's Literature
95 Long Ridge Road
West Redding, CT 06896-1124

Editor: Susan Tierney

Description and Interests
This newsletter provides an in-depth exploration of the current market for children's writing, while also offering informative articles about the writing process, writing techniques, and research. It is read by both experienced and aspiring writers.
- **Audience:** Children's writers
- **Frequency:** Monthly
- **Circulation:** 14,000
- **Website: www.childrenswriter.com**

Freelance Potential
100% written by nonstaff writers. Publishes 75 freelance submissions yearly; 10% by unpublished writers, 15% by authors who are new to the magazine. Receives 60+ queries yearly.

Submissions
Query with outline, synopsis, and résumé. Prefers email submissions through website. Accepts hard copy and disk submissions. SASE. Responds in 2 months.
Articles: 1,500–2,000 words. Reports on children's book and magazine publishing trends that feature interviews with editors and writers. Topics include industry trends, new markets, and publishers. Also publishes features on writing technique, research, motivation, and business issues.
Depts/columns: To 750 words, plus 125-word sidebar. Practical pieces about writing technique and careers, inside tips, and children's publishing.

Sample Issue
12 pages (no advertising): 5 articles; 2 depts/columns. Sample copy, free with #10 SASE (1 first-class stamp). Writers' guidelines available with SASE and at website.
- "Striking Character Types." Article describes character-development techniques that help writers create real people—not stereotypes—for their stories.
- Sample dept/column: "Profession" offers ideas for selling yourself and your skills to new markets.

Rights and Payment
First North American serial rights. Articles, $135–$350. Pays on acceptance.

Editor's Comments
Our goal is to help writers sell their work, so we're always interested in helpful writing technique articles and market analysis pieces.

Child Welfare Report

1439 Church Hill Street, Unit 302
Crystal Plaza
Waupaca, IL 54981

Editor: Mike Jacquart

Description and Interests
This newsletter contains timely information for professionals working with children and teenagers. Each issue also includes three inserts: "Parent Talk," "Teen Connections," and "Mental Health Matters."
- **Audience:** Child welfare professionals
- **Frequency:** Monthly
- **Circulation:** 500
- **Website: www.impact-publications.com**

Freelance Potential
40% written by nonstaff writers. Publishes 30 freelance submissions yearly; 75% by authors who are new to the magazine. Receives 150 queries yearly.

Submissions
Query with outline. Accepts hard copy and IBM disk submissions (Microsoft Word). Availability of artwork improves chance of acceptance. SASE. Responds in 1 month.
Articles: Word lengths vary. Informational and how-to articles; personal experience and opinion pieces; interviews; and new product information. Topics include gifted and special education, disabilities, government programs and legislation, foster care, adoption, career choices, family life, parenting, psychology, mentoring, and multicultural and ethnic issues.

Sample Issue
8 pages (no advertising): 4 articles; 1 book review; 3 inserts. Sample copy, $6.95 with #10 SASE (1 first-class stamp). Guidelines available.
- "Adoption Q&A." Article includes an interview with adoption experts, and answers key questions about the Hague Convention on Intercountry Adoption.
- "Start School Days with Special Time." Article explains the importance of one-on-one time with a child, free from all interruptions, in order to express approval, improve parent-child communication, and decrease stress.

Rights and Payment
First rights. No payment.

Editor's Comments
We often receive submissions on topics that are too generic or too overdone, for example, general well-being and childhood obesity. Instead we need expert opinion pieces on children in the courts, teen mental health, and specific child welfare policies (other than No Child Left Behind).

Christian Home & School

3350 East Paris Avenue SE
Grand Rapids, MI 48512-3054

Senior Editor: Roger Schmurr

Description and Interests
Published by Christian Schools International, this magazine is for parents who send their children to Christian schools. Its focus is on Christian education and parenting issues.
- **Audience:** Parents
- **Frequency:** Quarterly
- **Circulation:** 66,000
- **Website: www.csionline.org**

Freelance Potential
75% written by nonstaff writers. Publishes 25–30 free-lance submissions yearly; 10% by unpublished writers, 30% by authors who are new to the magazine. Receives 60 queries, 300 unsolicited mss yearly.

Submissions
Query or send complete ms. Accepts hard copy, email submissions to rogers@csionline.org, and simultaneous submissions. SASE. Responds in 7–10 days.
Articles: 1,000–2,000 words. Informational and how-to articles; and self-help and personal experience pieces. Topics include education, parenting, life skills, decision-making, self-control, discipline, family travel, faith, marriage, and social issues.
Fiction: Word lengths vary. Publishes stories with Christian themes and Christmas stories.
Depts/columns: "Parentstuff," 100–250 words. Reviews and parenting tips, word lengths vary.

Sample Issue
36 pages (15% advertising): 4 articles; 10 depts/columns. Sample copy, free with 9x12 SASE ($1.11 postage). Guidelines available.
- "Battling Bullying." Article provides parents with tools for recognizing and reacting to bullying, whether their child is the victim or the perpetrator.
- "Winning Financial Strategies." Article encourages couples to fight off materialistic impulses in order to curb debt and pay down bills.

Rights and Payment
First rights. Written material, $175–$250. "Parent-stuff," $25–$40. Pays on publication. Provides 5 contributor's copies.

Editor's Comments
We are interested in issues that affect Christian parents, including Christian schooling and the relationship of parents to Christian schools. Articles should reflect a biblical perspective.

The Christian Science Monitor

1 Norway Street
Boston, MA 02115

Home Forum Editor: Judy Lowe

Description and Interests
Each Tuesday, this daily newspaper devotes its "Home Forum" section entirely to "Kidspace," which features articles aimed at children. Regular "Home Forum" fare includes personal essays on parenting.
- **Audience:** Adults; children, 7–12 years
- **Frequency:** Daily; "Kidspace," weekly
- **Circulation:** 80,000
- **Website: www.csmonitor.com**

Freelance Potential
99% written by nonstaff writers. Publishes 1,000 free-lance submissions yearly; 10% by unpublished writers, 40% by authors who are new to the magazine. Receives 7,500 queries and unsolicited mss yearly.

Submissions
Query with résumé and clips for "Kidspace." Send complete ms for "Home Forum." Accepts email submissions to homeforum@csmonitor.com. Responds in 3 weeks.
Articles: "Kidspace," 700–900 words, plus sidebars. Informational articles; profiles; and interviews. Topics include occupations and everyday science. "Home Forum" essays, 300–1,000 words. Personal experience pieces and humor. Topics include home, family, and parenting.
Other: Short bits of information of interest to kids, 150–400 words. Poetry, to 20 lines. Submit seasonal material 1 month in advance.

Sample Issue
20 pages (15% advertising): 14 articles; 14 depts/columns. Guidelines available.
- "Fresh Ravioli Wins Out." Article describes a woman's experience creating homemade pasta, and includes a recipe for Italian Egg Pasta.
- "A Reluctant Skier Takes the Slow Path." Essay describes a woman's first cross-country skiing experience.

Rights and Payment
Exclusive rights. Kidspace, $230+. Essays, $75–$160. Poetry, $20–$40 per poem. Short bits, $70. Pays on publication. Provides 1 contributor's copy.

Editor's Comments
We're looking for stories on high-interest topics that will engage, empower, entertain, and educate kids ages six to twelve. You should stand as close to your subject as possible.

Christian Work at Home Moms

14607 Willow Creek Drive
Omaha, NE 68138

Editor: Jill Hart

Description and Interests
The mission of this website is to help mothers find a great work-at-home career, and to help current work-at-home moms market their businesses. It features articles written from a Christian perspective that offer support and encouragement.
• **Audience:** Parents
• **Frequency:** Weekly
• **Hits per month:** 1 million
• **Website: www.cwahm.com**

Freelance Potential
99% written by nonstaff writers. Publishes 130 freelance submissions yearly; 75% by unpublished writers. Receives 200 mss yearly.

Submissions
Send complete ms. Accepts submissions through website only. Response time varies.
Articles: Word lengths vary. Informational and how-to articles; personal experience pieces; profiles; and interviews. Topics include telecommuting, home businesses, website management and graphic design, search engine optimization, copywriting, money management, blogging, marriage, parenting, spiritual growth, and homeschooling.

Sample Issue
Sample copy and guidelines available at website.
• "The Valentine's Day Challenge." Personal experience piece tells how one couple had the best Valentine's Day ever by spending $10 or less.
• "How to Survive a Road Trip with the Kids." Article explains how to turn a lengthy road trip into an adventure rather than an ordeal.
• "Why I Love Homeschooling." Article profiles a mother who both homeschools her children and works from home.

Rights and Payment
Electronic rights. No payment.

Editor's Comments
We are always looking for columnists and regular contributors to *Christian Work at Home Moms*. Inspirational and uplifting articles, articles on spiritual growth, and material on homeschooling are needed. Personal success stories are also always of interest. We offer no compensation, but you will be listed in our "About the Author" section.

Church Educator

165 Plaza Drive
Prescott, AZ 86303

Editor: Linda Davidson

Description and Interests
Christian educators working in mainline Protestant churches subscribe to this magazine for its practical and creative teaching ideas and program descriptions. Each issue is divided into sections on children's ministry, youth ministry, adult ministry, worship, and leadership. It caters to both large and small churches.
• **Audience:** Christian educators
• **Frequency:** Monthly
• **Circulation:** 1,500
• **Website: www.eduationalministries.com**

Freelance Potential
90% written by nonstaff writers. Publishes 85 freelance submissions yearly; 10% by unpublished writers, 5% by authors who are new to the magazine. Receives 300 unsolicited mss yearly.

Submissions
Send complete ms. Accepts hard copy. SASE. Responds in 1 month.
Articles: 500–1,500 words. How-to articles. Topics include faith education, teaching ideas, successful church programs and events, spirituality, and religion.
Depts/columns: Staff written.
Artwork: B/W prints and illustrations.
Other: Submit seasonal material about Advent, Christmas, Lent, Easter, and Pentecost 4 months in advance.

Sample Issue
40 pages (no advertising): 11 articles; 7 depts/columns. Sample copy, free with 9x12 SASE ($.83 postage). Guidelines and theme list available.
• "Keeping Volunteers Happy." Article maintains that volunteers need support and recognition.
• "Sharing Sacred Stories with Other Faiths." Article details an activity that brings people from different faiths and cultures together.
• "Summer Worship Alternatives." Article offers ideas for adding some flexibility to summer programs.

Rights and Payment
One-time rights. Written material, $.03 per word. Pays on publication. Provides 2 contributor's copies.

Editor's Comments
Children's ministry ideas are always welcome from new writers. Lesson plans, learning center activities, craft projects, prayers, and liturgies will all be considered for publication.

Cicada

70 East Lake Street, Suite 300
Chicago, IL 60601

Submissions Editor: Jenny Gillespie

Description and Interests
This literary magazine is filled with original short stories, poetry, and essays. It also features a section called "Expressions," which presents reader opinion and commentary on the social and cultural issues that teens and young adults face today. *Cicada* is currently undergoing changes to its editorial focus.
• **Audience:** 14–21 years
• **Frequency:** 6 times each year
• **Circulation:** 18,500
• **Website:** www.cricketmag.com

Freelance Potential
98% written by nonstaff writers. Publishes 100 freelance submissions yearly; 40% by unpublished writers, 60% by new authors. Receives 2,000 unsolicited mss yearly.

Submissions
Not currently accepting new material. Check website for updates to this policy.
Articles: To 5,000 words. Essays and personal experience pieces.
Fiction: To 5,000 words. Genres include adventure; fantasy; humor; and historical, contemporary, and science fiction. Also features plays and stories presented in sophisticated cartoon format. Novellas, to 15,000 words.
Depts/columns: 300–500 words. Book reviews. "Expressions," 350–1,000 words.
Other: Cartoons. Poetry, to 25 lines.

Sample Issue
128 pages (no advertising): 7 stories; 4 poems; 4 depts/columns. Sample copy, $8.50. Writers' guidelines available.
• "Part of This Good Green Earth." Story is a historical fantasy set in the Midwest during the Dust Bowl years.
• "This Little Pig." Story revolves around a classic car, a 1952 MG-TD, and how it affects the characters' lives.

Rights and Payment
All rights. Pays on publication. Fiction and articles, to $.25 per word. Poetry, to $3 per line.

Editor's Comments
We are currently re-examining the focus, scope, and format of *Cicada*. We are not currently accepting submissions. Please check our website for updates to this policy. As we evolve with the growing interests and tastes of teenagers, we will again accept material.

Circle K

Circle K International
3636 Woodview Trace
Indianapolis, IN 46268-3196

Executive Editor: Kasey Jackson

Description and Interests
Described as "a magazine for student leaders," this publication was created specifically for members of Circle K International, a collegiate community service organization. Its articles focus on school and community leadership and career development.
• **Audience:** YA–Adult
• **Frequency:** 6 times each year
• **Circulation:** 10,000
• **Website:** www.circlek.org

Freelance Potential
50% written by nonstaff writers. Publishes 12 freelance submissions yearly; 50% by unpublished writers, 50% by authors who are new to the magazine. Receives 48+ unsolicited mss yearly.

Submissions
Prefers query with clips or writing samples; will accept complete ms. Accepts hard copy. SASE. Responds in 2 weeks.
Articles: 1,500–2,000 words. Informational and self-help articles. Topics include social issues, collegiate trends, community involvement, leadership, and career development.
Depts/columns: Word lengths vary. News and information about Circle K activities.
Artwork: 5x7 or 8x10 glossy prints; TIFF or JPEG files at 300 dpi or higher.

Sample Issue
20 pages (no advertising): 6 articles; 5 depts/columns. Sample copy, $.75 with 9x12 SASE ($.75 postage). Guidelines available.
• "Making It Work." Article profiles clubs that don't have a huge membership, but are making a huge impact on their communities.
• "Killer Résumé." Article emphasizes the importance of a résumé that will stand out from the rest.
• Sample dept/column: "Spotlight" features short articles about Circle K chapter events.

Rights and Payment
First North American serial rights. Written material, $150–$400. Artwork, payment rates vary. Pays on acceptance. Provides 3 contributor's copies.

Editor's Comments
We're planning a magazine redesign that will include more "Chapter Spotlight" and "In Action" stories. Most organizational news will move to our website.

City Parent

467 Speers Road
Oakville, Ontario L6K 3S4
Canada

Editor: Jane Muller

Description and Interests
This free, tabloid-format publication provides advice and activities for busy families in the cities of Toronto, York, Peel, Halton, Hamilton, Durham, and Ottawa.
- **Audience:** Parents
- **Frequency:** Monthly
- **Circulation:** 70,000
- **Website:** www.cityparent.com

Freelance Potential
50% written by nonstaff writers. Publishes 24–30 freelance submissions yearly; 10% by authors who are new to the magazine. Receives 300+ unsolicited submissions yearly.

Submissions
Send complete ms. Accepts email submissions to cityparent@haltonsearch.com. Availability of artwork improves chance of acceptance. Responds immediately if interested.
Articles: 500–1,000 words. Informational articles. Topics include arts and entertainment, health, fitness, multicultural and ethnic issues, recreation, self-help, social issues, travel, and crafts for children.
Depts/columns: Word lengths vary. Child-development stages, education tips, environmental issues, teen issues, and reviews of parenting and children's books.
Artwork: Color prints or transparencies.
Other: Events calendar.

Sample Issue
48 pages (65% advertising): 8 articles; 7 depts/columns. Editorial calendar available.
- "What a Ride." Article provides advice for choosing an equestrian program at summer camp.
- "Pirates, Piranhas and People." Article recommends activities and destinations for families traveling to the Bahamas.
- Sample dept/column: "The Virtuous Consumer" gives tips for green living.

Rights and Payment
First rights. Written material, $50–$100. Pays on publication. Provides 1 contributor's copy.

Editor's Comments
Each month we publish stories along a particular theme in addition to our regular departments and our local arts coverage. Please request an editorial calendar and submit articles at least three months in advance.

The Claremont Review

4980 Wesley Road
Victoria, British Columbia V8Y 1Y9
Canada

The Editors

Description and Interests
Showcasing the works of young adult Canadian writers for the past 15 years, this literary journal features poetry, short stories, short plays, artwork, and author interviews. It prefers work that reveals something about the human condition.
- **Audience:** 13–19 years
- **Frequency:** Twice each year
- **Circulation:** 800
- **Website:** www.theclaremontreview.ca

Freelance Potential
99% written by nonstaff writers. Publishes 150 freelance submissions yearly; 90% by unpublished writers, 90% by authors who are new to the magazine. Receives 540 unsolicited mss each year.

Submissions
Send complete ms with biography. Accepts hard copy. SAE/IRC. Responds in 1 month.
Articles: Word lengths vary. Interviews with contemporary authors and editors.
Fiction: To 5,000 words. Traditional, literary, experimental, and contemporary fiction.
Artwork: B/W or color prints or transparencies.
Other: Poetry, no line limit.

Sample Issue
116 pages (2% advertising): 16 stories; 30 poems. Sample copy, $10 with 9x12 SAE/IRC. Guidelines available at website.
- "Hooked." Story shares a grandmother's love of hula dancing and her memories of Hawaii.
- "Alzheimer's." Story details a boy's memories of his grandfather's progression with Alzheimer's disease.
- "Breakfast with Dad." Story recounts the narrator's memories of spending time with her father and how she later resented him.

Rights and Payment
Rights vary. Written material, payment rates and policy vary. Provides 1 contributor's copy.

Editor's Comments
We welcome submissions from 13- to 19-year-old writers from the English-speaking world. If you would like a written comment on your work, include an SAE/IRC along with your submission. While we are interested in receiving literary pieces, please note that we are not interested in fantasy, romance, or science fiction.

The Clearing House

Heldref Publications
1319 18th Street
Washington, DC 20036

Managing Editor: Melanie Bonsall

Description and Interests
Middle-grade and high school educators and administrators read this magazine for its timely articles on teaching strategies, educational innovations, research findings, and experiments.
• **Audience:** Educators
• **Frequency:** 6 times each year
• **Circulation:** 1,500
• **Website: www.heldref.org/tch.php**

Freelance Potential
100% written by nonstaff writers. Publishes 25 freelance submissions yearly; 60% by authors who are new to the magazine. Receives 121 unsolicited mss yearly.

Submissions
Send complete ms. Accepts online submissions at http://mc.manuscriptcentral.com/tch. Responds in 3–4 months.
Articles: To 2,500 words. Informational and how-to articles. Topics include educational trends and philosophy, pre-service and in-service education, curriculum, learning styles, discipline, guidance and counseling, gifted and special education, teaching techniques, educational testing and measurement, and technology.
Depts/columns: Word lengths vary. Educational news and opinion pieces.

Sample Issue
38 pages (no advertising): 6 articles. Sample copy, $19. Guidelines available in each issue.
• "Developing an Effective Transition Program for Students Entering Middle School or High School." Article examines how schools can ease the pressures experienced by students as they transition to middle school or high school.
• "Secondary Teachers as Cultural Mediators for Language Minority Students." Article argues that secondary teachers need to work as cultural mediators for the success of their language minority students.

Rights and Payment
All rights. No payment. Provides 2 contributor's copies.

Editor's Comments
Consideration is given to articles dealing with educational trends and philosophy; pre-service and in-service education; effective schools; curriculum; learning styles; discipline; community involvement; and gifted and talented programs.

Cleveland Family

35475 Vine Street, Suite 224
Eastlake, OH 44095-3147

Editor: Julie Hanahan

Description and Interests
This regional magazine provides parents with exhaustive resources for raising children from "tots to teens." In addition to advice on health, discipline, and child development, *Cleveland Family* offers timely information on area events and activities.
• **Audience:** Parents
• **Frequency:** Monthly
• **Circulation:** 70,000
• **Website: www.neohiofamily.com**

Freelance Potential
50% written by nonstaff writers. Publishes 40–50 freelance submissions yearly; 33% by authors who are new to the magazine. Receives 9,000+ queries yearly.

Submissions
Query. Accepts email to editor@tntpublications.com. Responds only if interested.
Articles: 500+ words. Informational, self-help, and how-to articles; profiles; and reviews. Topics include the arts, animals, computers, crafts, health, fitness, education, popular culture, sports, the environment, religion, family travel, and regional issues.
Depts/columns: Word lengths vary. News, advice, education, teen issues, humor, stepfamilies.
Artwork: High resolution JPEG and TIFF files.

Sample Issue
46 pages (50% advertising): 7 articles; 11 depts/columns. Editorial calendar available.
• "Diagnostic Imaging Is More Than X-Rays." Article describes different forms of diagnostic radiology, including MRI, CT scan, ultrasound, and X-ray.
• "Tooth Tips: How to Keep Kids Cavity-Free." Article provides guidelines for good dental hygiene.
• Sample dept/column: "Mommy Matters" is a humorous essay by a woman whose 6-year-old son says he wants to make license plates when he grows up.

Rights and Payment
Exclusive rights. Written material, payment rates vary. Pays on publication. Provides 1 contributor's copy.

Editor's Comments
We prefer factual articles written by authors who are intimately familiar with life in northeastern Ohio. Please keep in mind that our readers are mainly young, married, professional, well-educated parents who are looking for useful information that helps make their family happy and healthy.

Click

Carus Publishing
70 E. Lake Street, Suite 300
Chicago, IL 60601

Editor

Description and Interests
This nonfiction magazine allows young children to explore the world around them. Each thematic issue includes easy-to-read articles, colorful pictures, and fun activities on topics such as science, the arts, math, technology, and history.
• **Audience:** 3–7 years
• **Frequency:** 9 times each year
• **Circulation:** 62,000
• **Website:** www.cricketmag.com

Freelance Potential
80% written by nonstaff writers. Of the freelance submissions published yearly, 10% are by authors who are new to the magazine. Receives 48–60 queries yearly.

Submissions
Send résumé and clips. All material is commissioned from experienced authors.
Articles: To 1,000 words. Informational articles; interviews; and photo-essays. Topics include the natural, physical, and social sciences; the arts; technology; math; and history.
Other: Poetry, cartoons, and activities.

Sample Issue
34 pages (no advertising): 3 articles; 2 stories; 2 cartoons; 2 activities. Sample copy available for ordering at website.
• "Our Colorful World." Article takes a look at the colors of the world and how different the world would be without them.
• "Brown Bats and Blue Frogs." Article spotlights several birds and animals that see the world in color.
• "Green Eggs and Sam." Story tells of a mom who explains to her son how mixing primary colors makes new colors.

Rights and Payment
Rights vary. Written material, payment rates vary. Payment policy varies.

Editor's Comments
We strive to provide engaging and interesting stories and pictures to help children have fun while learning and to encourage them to question, observe, and explore the world around them. We would like to publish articles and stories from as many authors as possible, but we will only accept material of the highest quality. Be sure your writing is clear and age-appropriate, and that it covers one topic.

Cobblestone

Cobblestone Publishing
30 Grove Street, Suite C
Peterborough, NH 03458

Editor: Meg Chorlian

Description and Interests
Cobblestone aims to help kids "discover American history" through lively articles and stories related to a particular theme that changes with each issue.
• **Audience:** 8–14 years
• **Frequency:** 9 times each year
• **Circulation:** 27,000
• **Website:** www.cobblestonepub.com

Freelance Potential
85% written by nonstaff writers. Publishes 180 freelance submissions yearly; 20% by unpublished writers, 25% by authors who are new to the magazine. Receives 350 queries yearly.

Submissions
Query with outline, bibliography, and clips or writing samples. All queries must relate to upcoming themes. Accepts hard copy. SASE. Responds in 5 months.
Articles: Features, 700–800 words. Sidebars, 300–600 words. Informational articles; profiles; and interviews. Topics include American history and historical figures.
Fiction: To 800 words. Genres include historical, multicultural, and biographical fiction; adventure; and retold legends.
Artwork: Color prints or slides. Line art.
Other: Puzzles, activities, and games. Poetry.

Sample Issue
50 pages (no advertising): 10 articles; 10 depts/columns, 1 activity. Sample copy, $5.95 with 9x12 SASE ($1.24 postage). Guidelines and theme list available.
• "From Stage to Screen." Article chronicles the birth of motion pictures.
• "Walt Disney: Animation Pioneer." Profile tells how the man behind Mickey Mouse established a new genre of film.
• Sample dept/column: "The Past Is Present" tells how far movie special effects have come.

Rights and Payment
All rights. Written material, $.20–$.25 per word. Artwork, payment rates vary. Pays on publication. Provides 2 contributor's copies.

Editor's Comments
You may send as many queries for one issue as you wish, but each query must have a separate cover letter, outline, bibliography, and SASE. Telephone and email queries are not accepted.

College Outlook

20 East Gregory Boulevard
Kansas City, MO 64114-1145

Editor: Brooke Pearl

Description and Interests
High school students preparing for college turn to this magazine for information on college applications, how colleges select their incoming freshman class, and career planning and profiles.
• **Audience:** College-bound students
• **Frequency:** Twice each year
• **Circulation:** Spring, 440,000; fall, 710,000
• **Website: www.collegeoutlook.net**

Freelance Potential
85% written by nonstaff writers. Publishes 5–10 free-lance submissions yearly; 40% by unpublished writers, 60% by authors who are new to the magazine. Receives 96 queries and unsolicited mss yearly.

Submissions
Query with clips or writing samples; or send complete ms. Accepts hard copy. SASE. Responds in 1 month.
Articles: To 1,500 words. Informational and how-to articles; personal experience pieces; and humor. Topics include school selection, financial aid, scholar-ships, student life, extracurricular activities, money management, and college admissions procedures.
Artwork: 5x7 B/W and color transparencies.
Other: Gazette items on campus subjects, including fads, politics, classroom news, current events, leisure activities, and careers.

Sample Issue
48 pages (15% advertising): 15 articles. Sample copy, free. Guidelines available.
• "Why Study Abroad?" Article provides important questions to ask yourself when selecting a study abroad program.
• "17 Things I Wish I Knew . . ." Article provides incoming college freshmen with 17 helpful tips about starting school.

Rights and Payment
All rights. All material, payment rates vary. Provides contributor's copies.

Editor's Comments
It is our goal to provide college-bound students with the resources they need for choosing a college. We welcome submissions that are entertaining, easy-to-read, straightforward, and informative. We expect authors to be well-versed in their subject matter and non-biased toward any particular school or program.

Columbus Parent

5300 Crosswind Drive
Columbus, OH 43228

Editor: Donna Willis

Description and Interests
This free, tabloid-sized magazine is a valuable source of information for parents in the Columbus area. It delivers local news and in-depth features of interest to the region's families.
• **Audience:** Parents
• **Frequency:** Monthly
• **Circulation:** 125,000
• **Website: www.columbusparent.com**

Freelance Potential
80% written by nonstaff writers. Publishes 40 freelance submissions yearly; 25% by authors who are new to the magazine. Receives 100 queries yearly.

Submissions
Query. Accepts email queries to dwillis@ thisweeknews.com. Response time varies.
Articles: 700 words. Informational, self-help, and how-to articles; profiles; interviews; and reviews. Topics include current events, health, humor, music, recreation, and travel.
Fiction: 300 words. Humorous stories.
Depts/columns: 300 words. Local events and people; food; health; book reviews; and travel.
Artwork: Color prints and transparencies.
Other: Submit seasonal material 2 months in advance.

Sample Issue
48 pages (50% advertising): 4 articles; 16 depts/columns. Sample copy, free at local newsstands. Guidelines and theme list available.
• "Write On!" Article offers advice on ways to foster writing skills in children of all ages.
• "Not a Piece of Cake." Article describes the new, more sophisticated generation of home economics, called family and consumer science.
• Sample dept/column: "Feeding Hungry Minds and Bodies" gives some good ideas for indoor and out-door wintertime activities for families.

Rights and Payment
Rights vary. Written material, $.10 per word. Pays on publication.

Editor's Comments
We seek well-researched submissions that offer practical advice, reveal new or underreported information, or have a unique approach to a familiar topic. Children's stories, poetry, and cartoons are rarely accepted, and we have enough personal stories and essays on hand.

Complete Woman

875 North Michigan Avenue, Suite 3434
Chicago, IL 60611-1901

Executive Editor: Lora Wintz

Description and Interests
Targeting today's woman, this magazine focuses on self-help, relationships, and entertainment. It includes articles on exercise, love, fashion, diet, nutrition, fitness, and careers; profiles of popular celebrities; and erotic, humorous, and romance fiction.
• **Audience:** Adults
• **Frequency:** 6 times each year
• **Circulation:** 875,000
• **Website:** www.asspub.vflex.com

Freelance Potential
90% written by nonstaff writers. Publishes 75 freelance submissions yearly; 20% by unpublished writers, 30% by authors who are new to the magazine. Receives 720 queries yearly.

Submissions
Query or send complete ms with clips and résumé. Accepts hard copy and simultaneous submissions if identified. SASE. Responds in 3 months.
Articles: 800–1,200 words. Self-help articles; confession and personal experience pieces; humor; profiles; and interviews. Topics include health, exercise, beauty, skin care, fashion, food and dining, relationships, romance, business, sex, and self-improvement.
Depts/columns: Word lengths vary. Careers, new products, beauty, and news.

Sample Issue
106 pages (15% advertising): 36 articles; 7 depts/columns. Sample copy, $3.99 at newsstands.
• "Relationship Tune-Up." Article discusses setting goals in relationships and assessing them to determine if they are being met.
• "16 Foods That Fight Fat." Article takes a look at smart food choices that speed up metabolism for a healthy body.
• Sample dept/column: "Beauty Buzz" offers information on violet makeup shades, a book about cosmetic dentistry, and rich hair hues.

Rights and Payment
Rights vary. Written material, payment rates vary. Pays on publication. Provides 1 contributor's copy.

Editor's Comments
We are looking for articles on topics such as exercise, health, nutrition, celebrities, sex, and horoscopes, and would prefer writers to have a grasp of what we are all about. Please read an issue before submitting.

Conceive Magazine

622 East Washington Street, Suite 440
Orlando, FL 32801

Editor: Beth Weinhouse

Description and Interests
This magazine was created for any woman who is contemplating or actively trying to start or expand a family—through either natural conception, fertility treatments, or adoption. The focus is on general reproductive health and fertility.
• **Audience:** Women
• **Frequency:** Quarterly
• **Circulation:** 200,000
• **Website:** www.conceiveonline.com

Freelance Potential
75% written by nonstaff writers. Publishes 60 freelance submissions yearly; few by unpublished writers, few by authors who are new to the magazine.

Submissions
Query with résumé and clips. Accepts hard copy and email queries to bethweinhouse@ conceivemagazine.com. SASE. Response time varies.
Articles: Word lengths vary. Informational articles; profiles; and interviews. Topics include family planning, adoption, infertility issues, and baby products.
Depts/columns: Word lengths vary. Topics include fitness, health, medical updates, beauty, advice from counselors, and personal experiences.

Sample Issue
96 pages: 4 articles; 12 depts/columns. Sample copy, $4.99 at newsstands. Guidelines available at website.
• "A Baby for Trista and Ryan." Article profiles the star of the television program *The Bachelorette* and her husband, and chronicles their path to a successful pregnancy.
• "Drug Deals." Article offers advice for saving money on fertility medications.
• Sample dept/column: "A Fit Conception" features three types of Asian bodywork techniques that bring the body into balance.

Rights and Payment
All or first rights. Written material, $.50–$1 per word. Kill fee, varies. Pays on publication.

Editor's Comments
Please note that we are not a pregnancy or parenting magazine. We do some editorial coverage of very early, first trimester pregnancy, but we run almost nothing on childbirth or infant care. Most of our contributors are professionals who have experience writing about women's health issues.

Connect for Kids

1625 K Street
Washington, DC 20006

Editor: Caitlin Johnson

Description and Interests

Connect for Kids serves as an online forum for parents and anyone who is concerned about family and children's issues, including early childhood professionals and child advocates. It covers everything from health and development to current news and trends that have an impact on youth.
• **Audience:** Parents and others who work with children
• **Frequency:** Biweekly
• **Hits per month:** 50,000+
• **Website:** www.connectforkids.org

Freelance Potential

40% written by nonstaff writers. Publishes 24 freelance submissions yearly; 25% by authors who are new to the magazine. Receives 150 queries yearly.

Submissions

Query. Accepts hard copy and email queries to caitlingjohnson@gmail.com. SASE. Response time varies.
Articles: 900–1,500 words. Informational articles; profiles; reviews; and photo-essays. Topics include adoption, foster care, the arts, child abuse and neglect, health, education, child care and early development, kids and politics, community building, learning disabilities, crime and violence prevention, parent involvement in education, out-of-school time, diversity and awareness, education, family income, volunteering, and mentoring.

Sample Issue

Sample issue and guidelines available at website.
• "'Stop the Silence' to End Child Abuse: A Small Nonprofit Takes on a Big Issue." Article offers the author's personal experiences in finding funds for child abuse prevention and treatment programs.
• "Youth Movement: The Extreme Version." Article profiles a program that helps troubled teens train for marathon races.

Rights and Payment

All rights. No payment.

Editor's Comments

We like to see pieces that describe and offer solutions to the critical issues that are affecting children in this country today. Youth activism is another topic of interest. As of now, we offer no payment; please check our website for changes to this policy.

Connecticut Parent

420 East Main Street, Suite 18
Branford, CT 06405

Editor & Publisher: Joel MacClaren

Description and Interests

Connecticut parents look to this free publication for information about family events and activities, including travel, fitness, education, and the arts.
• **Audience:** Parents
• **Frequency:** Monthly
• **Circulation:** 60,000
• **Website:** www.ctparent.com

Freelance Potential

20% written by nonstaff writers. Publishes 50 freelance submissions yearly; 10% by authors who are new to the magazine. Receives 1,000+ unsolicited mss yearly.

Submissions

Send complete ms. Prefers email to ctparent@aol.com. Will accept hard copy. SASE. Response time varies.
Articles: 500–1,000 words. Informational, self-help, and how-to articles; profiles; and interviews. Topics include maternity and childbirth issues, parenting, regional news, family relationships, social issues, education, special education, health, fitness, nutrition, safety, entertainment, and travel.
Depts/columns: 600 words. Family news, new product information, and media reviews.

Sample Issue

66 pages (60% advertising): 7 articles; 2 depts/columns. Sample copy, $5 with 9x12 SASE. Guidelines available.
• "For New Moms." Article gives advice for coping with physical, emotional, and relationship changes in the first months of motherhood.
• "Children's Bookshelf." Article suggests winter reading for children.
• Sample dept/column: "Small Talk" briefs readers about a skating show and a motocross competition.

Rights and Payment

One-time rights. Written material, payment rates vary. Pays on publication. Provides 1 tearsheet.

Editor's Comments

We are currently not seeking articles about family travel, or anything that reads like a press release. We are interested in providing our readers with useful and important information that helps them become better parents and fosters a sense of community. Please keep in mind that articles must have a Connecticut focus.

Connecticut's County Kids

1175 Post Road East
Westport, CT 06880

Editor: Linda Greco

Description and Interests
This magazine is full of practical information on topics of interest to parents residing in Fairfield and New Haven counties in Connecticut. It includes articles covering topics such as child development, health, education, finances, and parenting issues.
- **Audience:** Parents
- **Frequency:** Monthly
- **Circulation:** 32,000
- **Website:** www.countykids.com

Freelance Potential
95% written by nonstaff writers. Publishes 60 freelance submissions yearly; 2% by unpublished writers, 2% by authors who are new to the magazine. Receives 600 queries and unsolicited mss yearly.

Submissions
Query or send complete ms. Prefers email submissions to countykids@ctcentral.com. Will accept hard copy. SASE. Responds only if interested.
Articles: 600–1,200 words. Informational articles; profiles; and personal experience pieces. Topics include nature, animals, crafts, ethnic subjects, and sports.
Depts/columns: 500–800 words. Parenting, pediatric health issues, growth and development, and family issues.

Sample Issue
46 pages (50% advertising): 17 articles; 15 depts/columns; 1 directory. Sample copy, free with 10x13 SASE. Guidelines and editorial calendar available.
- "Flying with Kids." Article discusses how to keep children entertained and in their seats when traveling by air.
- "Choosing the Right Swimming Program." Article offers advice on how to select the right swimming lessons for children.
- Sample dept/column: "Take Care of Earth" provides fun activities to celebrate Earth Day.

Rights and Payment
First rights. All material, payment rates vary. Pays on publication. Provides 2 contributor's copies.

Editor's Comments
We continue to be interested in articles on parenting topics and how-to family activities. Please note we are not interested in articles on ADHD or obesity, as we have enough of these.

Cousteau Kids

Weekly Reader
1 Reader's Digest Road
Pleasantville, NY 10570

Editor: Melissa Norkin

Description and Interests
This publication from Weekly Reader was created to educate children about oceans, marine biology, and the global water system. In addition to offering fun and factual articles and activities, it portrays kids who are active in caring for the planet.
- **Audience:** 8–12 years
- **Frequency:** 6 times each year
- **Circulation:** 80,000
- **Website:** www.cousteaukids.org

Freelance Potential
10% written by nonstaff writers. Publishes 4 freelance submissions yearly; 50% by authors who are new to the magazine. Receives 48 queries yearly.

Submissions
Query. Accepts hard copy and simultaneous submissions if identified. SASE. Responds only if interested.
Articles: 400–600 words. Shorter pieces, to 250 words. Informational articles. Topics include aquatic organisms, underwater habitats, ocean phenomena, the environment, and the physical properties of water.
Depts/columns: Staff written.
Artwork: Color slides.
Other: Games based on scientific fact, original science experiments, and art projects related to an ocean theme.

Sample Issue
24 pages (no advertising): 5 articles; 4 depts/columns; 2 activity pages. Sample copy, $2.50 with 9x12 SASE (3 first-class stamps). Guidelines available.
- "Butterflies of the Sea." Article provides photos and facts about the different types of butterfly fish.
- "Meet Cousteau Photographer Roberto Rinaldi." Article interviews a photographer about the challenges of filming underwater.
- Sample dept/column: "The Maritimes" features short updates about the environment.

Rights and Payment
One-time reprint rights; worldwide translation rights for use in Cousteau Society publications. Articles, $100–$350. Shorter pieces, $15–$100. Pays on publication. Provides 3 contributor's copies.

Editor's Comments
We want to delight, instruct, and instill in children an environmental ethic, including an understanding of the interconnectedness of living organisms.

Creative Kids

Prufrock Press
P.O. Box 8813
Waco, TX 76714

Editor: Lacy Elwood

Description and Interests

Creative Kids is filled with high-quality original writing and artwork by and for kids. No adult work is published in its pages.
- **Audience:** 8–16 years
- **Frequency:** Quarterly
- **Circulation:** 3,600
- **Website:** www.prufrock.com

Freelance Potential

98% written by nonstaff writers. Publishes 150 freelance submissions yearly; 90% by unpublished writers, 80% by authors who are new to the magazine. Receives 6,500 mss yearly.

Submissions

Send complete ms. Accepts hard copy. Availability of artwork improves chance of acceptance. SASE. Must include age of author/artist. Responds in 4–6 weeks.
Articles: 800–900 words. Informational, self-help, and how-to articles; humor; photo-essays; and personal experience pieces. Topics include animals, pets, sports, social issues, travel, and gifted education.
Fiction: 800–900 words. Genres include real-life and problem-solving stories; inspirational, historical, and multicultural fiction; mystery; suspense; folktales; humor; sports; and animals.
Artwork: B/W and color prints and transparencies. Line art on 8½ x11 white paper.
Other: Poetry, songs, word puzzles, games, and cartoons. Submit seasonal material 1 year in advance.

Sample Issue

34 pages (no advertising): 4 articles; 6 stories; 11 poems; 2 cartoons; 7 activities; 1 editorial. Writers' guidelines available.
- "When My Grandma Was Twelve." Article tells of the refugee life of the author's grandmother.
- "The Changer." Story relates a Native American legend about why leaves change color.

Rights and Payment

Rights vary. No payment. Provides 3–4 copies.

Editor's Comments

All work must be original and written by children ages 8 through 16. We need more boy-oriented stories and poems, as well as articles on trends among kids and teens. We have seen too much formulaic and seasonal poetry. Please refrain from overly violent and graphic themes, including natural disasters.

Cricket

Carus Publishing
70 East Lake Street, Suite 300
Chicago, IL 60601

Submissions Editor

Description and Interests

Through its outstanding collection of fantasy stories, adventures, humor, folktales, poems, and crafts, this literary magazine for children inspires older kids to read.
- **Audience:** 9–14 years
- **Frequency:** Monthly
- **Circulation:** 70,000
- **Website:** www.cricketmag.com

Freelance Potential

100% written by nonstaff writers. Publishes 150 freelance submissions yearly; 30% by unpublished writers, 50% by authors who are new to the magazine. Receives 12,000 mss yearly.

Submissions

Send complete ms; include bibliography for nonfiction. Accepts hard copy and simultaneous submissions. SASE. Responds in 4–6 months.
Articles: 200–1,500 words. Informational and how-to articles; biographies; and profiles. Topics include science, technology, history, architecture, geography, foreign culture, adventure, and sports.
Fiction: 200–2,000 words. Genres include humor, mystery, fantasy, science fiction, folktales, fairy tales, mythology, and historical and contemporary fiction.
Depts/columns: Staff written.
Other: Poetry, to 25 lines. Puzzles, games, crafts, recipes, and science experiments, word lengths vary.

Sample Issue

60 pages (no advertising): 2 articles; 7 stories; 4 poems; 1 activity. Sample copy, $5 with 9x12 SASE. Guidelines available.
- "Winter of the Snowshoe Hare." Story follows a snowshoe hare's struggle for survival.
- "Breakfast for Mrs. Roosevelt." Story tells of a young girl during the Great Depression and the morning she makes breakfast for the President's wife.

Rights and Payment

Rights vary. Articles and fiction, to $.25 per word. Poetry, to $3 per line. Pays on publication. Provides 6 contributor's copies.

Editor's Comments

We want only the best authors for our magazine. We encourage new writers to send us their best contemporary fiction, fantasy, science fiction, and adventure stories for young readers.

Crinkles

3401 Stockwell Street
Lincoln, NE 68506

Managing Editor: Deborah Levitov

Description and Interests
Sparking children's curiosity about people, places, things, and events—both real and imaginary—is the purpose of this magazine. It targets children ages seven through twelve with its informative articles and hands-on activities.
- **Audience:** 7–12 years
- **Frequency:** 6 times each year
- **Circulation:** 6,000
- **Website:** www.crinkles.com

Freelance Potential
70% written by nonstaff writers. Publishes 2–3 freelance submissions yearly; 10% by unpublished writers, 50% by authors who are new to the magazine. Receives 36 queries yearly.

Submissions
Query with résumé. Accepts email queries only to deborah.levitov@lu.com. Responds in 1 month.
Articles: Word lengths vary. Informational, factual, and how-to articles. Topics include history, culture, multicultural and ethnic subjects, social issues, science, animals, nature, the arts, and sports.

Sample Issue
50 pages (no advertising): 17 articles; 18 activities. Guidelines available.
- "Ranasinghe Premadasa." Article features a biography of the president of Sri Lanka and includes a timeline of his life.
- "Following the Stars: A Buddhist Tradition." Article provides information about astrology and explains that many people of Sri Lanka celebrate rituals and festivals on days calculated according to astrology.
- "Marvelous Masks." Activity includes instructions for masks made out of paper plates that are similar to those made in Sri Lanka.

Rights and Payment
All rights. Written material, $150. Payment policy varies. Provides contributor's copies upon request.

Editor's Comments
Please be aware that we solicit most of the articles that appear in our publication. Those articles are researched and written by leaders in the field of education to develop children's skills in critical thinking, independent research, and study habits. Most articles are accompanied by hands-on activities that sharpen problem-solving skills.

Curious Parents

301 North Church Street
Moorestown, NJ 08057

Editor: Matt Stringer

Description and Interests
Targeting mothers living in Philadelphia, the Delaware Valley, southern and central New Jersey, and the Lehigh Valley, this publication focuses on parenting, health, events, and fashion. It features articles, tips, and information on events in the region.
- **Audience:** Parents
- **Frequency:** Monthly
- **Circulation:** 265,000
- **Website:** www.curiousparents.com

Freelance Potential
60% written by nonstaff writers. Publishes 70–100 freelance submissions yearly; many by unpublished writers and authors who are new to the magazine.

Submissions
Send complete ms. Accepts email submissions to editor@curiousparents.com. Response time varies.
Articles: Word lengths vary. Informational, how-to, and self-help articles. Topics include crafts, hobbies, current events, recreation, special education, safety, health, entertainment, networking, parenting, and travel.
Depts/columns: Word lengths vary. Health, book reviews, automobiles.

Sample Issue
40 pages: 12 articles; 3 depts/columns.
- "Dinner Is Served." Humorous essay describes a mom's difficult time trying to meet everyone's needs at dinner time.
- "The Merry-Go-Round of Motherhood." Article compares motherhood to riding a merry-go-round with its ups and downs.
- Sample dept/column: "Curious Corner" includes information on a cell phone, water blaster, and a travel guide.

Rights and Payment
All rights. Written material, to $50. Pays on publication.

Editor's Comments
Our voice is a fun and informative one that broaches topics from celebrity journalism and fashion and beauty to serious issues, such as Iraq and autism. Material must be regional and target our audience of mothers ages 25 to 54. Please note that we do not accept previously published material. Writers must know the region well.

Current Health 1

Weekly Reader Corporation
1 Reader's Digest Road
Pleasantville, NY 10570

Editor: Jennifer Magid

Description and Interests
Distributed exclusively through schools, this member of the Weekly Reader family covers nutrition, fitness, disease prevention, drugs, alcohol, and emotional well-being for middle-grade students. Each issue is accompanied by a teacher's guide.
• **Audience:** Grades 4–7
• **Frequency:** 8 times each year
• **Circulation:** 163,973
• **Website: www.weeklyreader.com/ch1**

Freelance Potential
50% written by nonstaff writers. Publishes 50 freelance submissions yearly; 30% by authors who are new to the magazine.

Submissions
All articles are assigned. No unsolicited mss. Query with letter of introduction, areas of expertise, publishing credits, and clips. Accepts email queries to currenthealth@weeklyreader.com. Responds in 1–4 months.
Articles: 850–2,000 words. Informational articles. Topics include nutrition, fitness, disease prevention, drugs, alcohol, emotional well-being, and first aid.
Depts/columns: Word lengths vary. Physical activities; health news and advice; safety tips; and summaries of medical research.

Sample Issue
32 pages (no advertising): 5 articles; 8 depts/columns. Sample copy available. Guidelines provided upon agreement.
• "Pssst! Pass It On." Article tells how to discern harmless gossip from hurtful gossip.
• "Wad of Trouble." Article discusses the dangers of chewing tobacco.
• "Earth Day Your Way." Article profiles the environmental protection efforts of three teenagers from various parts of the country.
• Sample dept/column: "Safety Zone" provides tips for staying safe at large events, such as concerts.

Rights and Payment
All rights. Articles, $150+. Provides 2 author's copies.

Editor's Comments
Our products have been connecting students to the world for more than 100 years. We seek to illuminate current ideas, events, and issues that impact young people, but might otherwise escape their attention.

Current Health 2

Weekly Reader Corporation
1 Reader's Digest Road
Pleasantville, NY 10570

Editor: Meredith Matthews

Description and Interests
Provided as a curriculum resource for middle school through high school health courses, this magazine targets pre-teens and teens. It focuses on general health issues, including nutrition, fitness, psychology, relationships, substance abuse, and human sexuality.
• **Audience:** Grades 7–12
• **Frequency:** 8 times each year
• **Circulation:** 195,000
• **Website: www.weeklyreader.com/ch2**

Freelance Potential
80% written by nonstaff writers. Publishes 50 freelance submissions yearly; 5% by unpublished writers, 40% by authors who are new to the magazine. Receives 30 queries yearly.

Submissions
Query with letter of introduction listing areas of expertise, publishing credits, and clips. Accepts email queries to currenthealth@weeklyreader.com. No unsolicited mss. Responds in 1–4 months.
Articles: 800–1,000 words. Informational articles on subjects related to middle school and high school curricula. Topics include fitness, exercise, nutrition, disease, psychology, first aid, safety, human sexuality, drug education, risk-taking behavior, relationships, and public health.
Depts/columns: Word lengths vary. Health news, safety issues, and Q&As.

Sample Issue
32 pages (1% advertising): 6 articles; 6 depts/columns. Sample copy available. Guidelines and editorial calendar available.
• "Maybe We Should See Other People." Article provides advice on how to manage a good break-up with your significant other.
• "Gut Feeling." Article helps teens understand some serious stomach ailments.
• Sample dept/column: "Safety Zone" offers information on how to stay prepared for any emergency.

Rights and Payment
All rights. Articles, $.50 per word. Pays on publication. Provides 2 contributor's copies.

Editor's Comments
Some of our upcoming themes include summer health dangers, the emotional benefits of volunteering, and health effects of war.

The Dabbling Mum

508 West Main Street
Beresford, SD 57004

Editor & Owner: Alyice Edrich

Description and Interests
The Dabbling Mum website was launched in 1999 with the purpose of helping parents of both genders pursue their dreams—whether those dreams are to stay at home, to climb the corporate ladder, or to grow successful, profitable businesses.
• **Audience:** Parents
• **Frequency:** Monthly
• **Hits per month:** 40,000
• **Website: www.thedabblingmum.com**

Freelance Potential
99% written by nonstaff writers. Publishes 100 freelance submissions yearly; 40% by unpublished writers, 60% by authors who are new to the magazine. Receives 200–300 queries yearly.

Submissions
Query with writing samples. Accepts online submissions only. Responds in 4–8 weeks.
Articles: 500–1,500 words. Informational and how-to articles and personal experience pieces. Topics include family life, parenting, women's issues, home businesses, sales and marketing, Christian living, marriage, entertainment, education, child development, teen issues, and contemporary social concerns.

Sample Issue
Sample copy and writers' guidelines, available at website.
• "Connecting Through Badminton." Article tells how one family gets fit and has fun together by playing badminton in their backyard.
• "Home Portraits." Article offers tips for taking professional-quality photographs of your children at home.
• "A Seed Once Planted." First-person article tells how the author's mother instilled in him a love of words by playing Scrabble®.

Rights and Payment
One-month exclusive online rights; indefinite archival rights. Written material, $20–$40; reprints, $5. Pays on acceptance.

Editor's Comments
We want our website to be a place where moms and dads of all ages can learn and grow and dream. We want our readers to stop asking themselves "what if?" and start saying "why not?" We would like to see more articles on home business, direct sales, and effectively advertising and marketing small businesses.

Dallas Child

Lauren Publications
4275 Kellway Circle, Suite 146
Addison, TX 75001

Editorial Director: Shelley Hawes Pate

Description and Interests
This parenting magazine addresses the concerns and needs of families residing in the Dallas area. It focuses on children from prenatal through adolescence and includes educational and entertaining articles.
• **Audience:** Parents
• **Frequency:** Monthly
• **Circulation:** 80,000
• **Website: www.dallaschild.com**

Freelance Potential
30% written by nonstaff writers. Publishes 10–20 freelance submissions yearly; 5–10% by authors who are new to the magazine. Receives 396 queries yearly.

Submissions
Query with résumé. Accepts hard copy and simultaneous submissions if identified. SASE. Responds in 2–3 months.
Articles: 1,000–2,000 words. Informational and how-to articles; personal experience and self-help pieces; profiles; interviews; and humor. Topics include parenting, education, child development, family travel, regional news, recreation, entertainment, current events, social issues, multicultural and ethnic subjects, health, fitness, and crafts.
Depts/columns: 800 words. Local events, travel, and health news.

Sample Issue
94 pages (14% advertising): 2 articles; 13 depts/columns. Sample copy, free with 9x12 SASE. Guidelines available.
• "We Live On the Autism Spectrum." Essay shares a mom's journey of denial, discovery, and determination in dealing with her son's autism.
• "Moms We Admire." Article takes a look at five fabulous moms who are devoted to their families and communities.
• Sample dept/column: "Back Talk" describes one mom's patience in raising her son, who has several learning disorders.

Rights and Payment
First rights. Written material, payment rates vary. Pays on publication. Provides author's copies upon request.

Editor's Comments
We look for articles covering issues affecting families from writers from the Metroplex region. Material should inform, educate, and entertain our readers.

Dance Magazine

110 William Street, 23rd Floor
New York, NY 10038

Editor-in-Chief: Wendy Perron

Description and Interests
Dance Magazine is read by dancers, choreographers, instructors, and others interested in all types of dance. It offers how-to articles, profiles of dancers and dance companies, and show reviews.
- **Audience:** YA–Adult
- **Frequency:** Monthly
- **Circulation:** 50,000
- **Website: www.dancemagazine.com**

Freelance Potential
65% written by nonstaff writers. Publishes few freelance submissions yearly; 20% by unpublished writers, 5% by authors who are new to the magazine. Receives many queries yearly.

Submissions
Query. Accepts hard copy and email queries to wperron@dancemagazine.com. SASE. Response time varies.
Articles: Word lengths vary. Informational articles; profiles; and interviews. Topics include dance, dance instruction, choreography, the arts, family, and health concerns.
Fiction: To 4,000 words. Ethnic and multicultural fiction related to dance.
Depts/columns: Word lengths vary. New product information, reviews, dance news, and instruction.

Sample Issue
90 pages (33% advertising): 5 articles; 12 depts/columns. Sample copy, $4.95 with 9x12 SASE. Guidelines available.
- "In the Joffrey Tradition." Article describes the influence of the famous choreographer on other dance company directors.
- "All in the Family." Article profiles the up-and-coming tap dancing brother and sister team of Josette and Joseph Wiggan.
- Sample dept/column: "Mind Your Body" explains that yoga can help restore a ballet dancer's balance and help prevent injuries.

Rights and Payment
Rights negotiable. Written material, $.30 per word. Pays on publication.

Editor's Comments
We are interested in submissions from dance experts only. Our scope includes all types of dance, and covers all aspects of dancing.

Dance Teacher

110 William Street, Floor 23
New York, NY 10038

Managing Editor: Jeni Tu

Description and Interests
This sister publication of *Dance Magazine* provides practical information and business tips to professional dance teachers.
- **Audience:** Dance teachers and students
- **Frequency:** Monthly
- **Circulation:** 25,000
- **Website: www.dance-teacher.com**

Freelance Potential
67% written by nonstaff writers. Publishes 100–120 freelance submissions yearly; 10% by unpublished writers, 10–15% by authors who are new to the magazine. Receives 100 queries yearly.

Submissions
Query. Accepts hard copy and email to jtu@dancemedia.com. SASE. Responds in 2 months.
Articles: 1,000–2,000 words. Informational and how-to articles; and personal experience pieces. Topics include dance education, business, nutrition, health, injuries, performance production, competition, and personalities.
Depts/columns: 700–1,200 words. Fashion, teaching, competition, dance history, media and product reviews, and industry news.

Sample Issue
88 pages (50% advertising): 5 articles; 13 depts/columns; 1 special section. Sample copy, free with 9x12 SASE ($1.37 postage). Guidelines and theme list available.
- "The Family Business." Article profiles mother-daughter team Olga and Heather Berest, who run a dance studio together in New York.
- "When Disaster Strikes." Article shares the stories of four dance teachers who overcame flood, fire, hurricane, and accident damage to their studios.
- Sample dept/column: "History" examines the legacy of Fred Astaire and Ginger Rogers.

Rights and Payment
All rights. Articles, $200–$300. Depts/columns, $150–$200. Pays on publication. Provides 1 contributor's copy.

Editor's Comments
Please note that we discourage profiles of teachers and studios, as we simply receive too many of them. Also, we do not accept submissions of poetry, photographs, or fiction.

Daughters

34 East Superior Street, Suite 200
Duluth, MN 55802

Editor: Helen Cordes

Description and Interests
This newsletter features research, resources, and ideas for parents and other adults who care for and influence girls between the ages of 9 and 16. It includes self-help articles, essays, profiles, and interviews that are written to foster communication between adults and adolescent girls.
- **Audience:** Parents
- **Frequency:** 6 times each year
- **Circulation:** 25,000
- **Website:** www.daughters.com

Freelance Potential
65% written by nonstaff writers. Publishes 10 freelance submissions yearly; 25% by unpublished writers, 25% by authors who are new to the magazine. Receives 24–36 queries yearly.

Submissions
Query. Send complete ms for "Mothering Journey" and "Fathering Journey" only. Accepts email to editor@daughters.com (Microsoft Word attachments). Responds in 1–2 months.
Articles: 700 words. Informational and self-help articles; personal experience pieces; profiles; and interviews. Topics include adolescent girls, health, fitness, social issues, body image, sexuality, education, communication, and parenting.
Depts/columns: "Mothering/Fathering Journey," first-person pieces that describe the emotional journey of parenting daughters; 650 words. "Let's Talk," essays that discuss improving communication.

Sample Issue
16 pages (15% advertising): 7 articles; 1 dept/column. Sample copy and writers' guidelines available at website.
- "Too Young for a Boyfriend?" Article offers advice on guiding girls toward healthy choices as they learn to navigate romantic urges.
- "Boy-Bashing Doesn't Help Our Girls." Article tells why boy bashing slogans hurt everyone.

Rights and Payment
All rights. Written material, $.10–$.25 per word. Artwork, payment rates vary. Pays on publication. Provides 3 contributor's copies.

Editor's Comments
Departments offer the best way for freelancers to get started with us. Most are about 700 words.

Davey and Goliath
Devotions for Families on the Go

Augsburg Fortress Publishers
P.O. Box 1209
Minneapolis, MN 55440-1209

Senior Editor: Dawn Rundman

Description and Interests
Written for families who have children in elementary school, *Davey and Goliath* is a devotional publication that features Bible stories, activities, and prayers. All material is written from a Lutheran/mainline Protestant theological orientation.
- **Audience:** Families
- **Frequency:** Quarterly
- **Circulation:** 50,000
- **Website:** www.augsburgfortress.org/dg/ devotions

Freelance Potential
100% written by nonstaff writers. Publishes 2 freelance submissions yearly; 25% by unpublished writers, 50% by authors who are new to the magazine. Receives 15 queries yearly.

Submissions
Query with 6x9 SASE (2 first-class stamps). All work is assigned on a contract basis. Accepts email queries to dg@augsburgfortress.org. Responds in 1 month.
Articles: 100–125 words. Bible stories and how-to articles on sharing and celebrating the Word of God.
Depts/columns: 500 words. Bible facts, prayers, and activities.
Other: Puzzles, games, and mazes.

Sample Issue
64 pages (15% advertising): 26 devotionals; 13 activities. Sample copy and guidelines provided free to prospective writers.
- "Who Is My Neighbor?" Devotional explains the story of the good Samaritan and includes a prayer, Bible fact, and cultural activity.
- "A Helpful Dream." Devotional tells the story of how Joseph was visited in a dream by an angel who warned him about King Herod.
- "Daniel Keeps Praying." Devotional recounts the story of Daniel and stresses the importance of prayer.

Rights and Payment
All rights. Written material, payment rates vary. Pays on acceptance. Provides 2 contributor's copies.

Editor's Comments
Our devotionals consist of a Bible story and activities and prayers that support families as they share faith together. All material is assigned on a contract basis; we brief our writers very specifically about content.

Delmarva Youth Magazine

1226 North Division Street
Salisbury, MD 21801

Editor: Maria Cook

Description and Interests
This magazine is distributed free throughout a number of counties on the Delmarva Peninsula of Maryland. It addresses a variety of parenting issues, with an emphasis on how and where to find family-oriented goods and services.
- **Audience:** Parents
- **Frequency:** 6 times each year
- **Circulation:** 18,000
- **Website:** www.delmarvayouth.com

Freelance Potential
80% written by nonstaff writers. Publishes 60 freelance submissions yearly; 15% by unpublished writers, 20% by authors who are new to the magazine.

Submissions
Query or send complete ms. Prefers email submissions to delmarvayouth@hotmail.com (Microsoft Word attachments). Will accept hard copy. SASE. Response time varies.
Articles: 500–3,000 words. Informational and how-to articles; and interviews. Topics include parenting, family life, family events and activities, travel, education, health, music, sports, and family finance.
Depts/columns: Word lengths vary. School and camp news; family health and fitness; and the arts.

Sample Issue
56 pages (15% advertising): 8 articles; 5 depts/columns; 1 calendar. Sample copy, $2.50. Guidelines available at website.
- "Introducing Children to Classical Music." Article explores ways to bring the joys of classical music into your home.
- "Practical Approaches to Connecting with Your Kids This Summer." Article focuses on the importance of family meals and time spent together.
- Sample dept/column: "Family Health and Fitness" describes situations when 911 should be dialed.

Rights and Payment
First print and electronic rights. Articles, $25–$150. Pays on publication. Provides 1 contributor's copy.

Editor's Comments
We'll consider nonfiction pieces about surviving the newborn, preschool, school age, and adolescent years, as well as descriptions of places to go and things to do on the Eastern Shore. We also like to highlight successful youth in our region.

Devozine

1908 Grand Avenue
P.O. Box 340004
Nashville, TN 37203-0004

Editor: Sandy Miller

Description and Interests
Each issue of this hip, glossy, devotional magazine written for teens by teens contains meditations and articles on nine weekly themes, as well as media and product reviews.
- **Audience:** YA
- **Frequency:** 6 times each year
- **Circulation:** 90,000
- **Website:** www.devozine.org

Freelance Potential
100% written by nonstaff writers. Publishes 325 freelance submissions yearly; 50% by authors who are new to the magazine.

Submissions
Query. Accepts hard copy and email queries to devozine@upperroom.org. SASE. Responds in 4 months.
Articles: 150–500 words. Informational articles; personal experience pieces; profiles; and reviews. Topics include Christian faith, mentoring, independence, courage, teen parenting, creativity, social issues, and relationships.
Fiction: 150–250 words. Genres include contemporary and inspirational fiction.
Depts/columns: 75–100 words. Reviews of music, books, movies, websites, and products.
Other: Daily meditations, 150–250 words. Prayers and poetry, 10–20 lines. Submit seasonal material 6–8 months in advance.

Sample Issue
80 pages (no advertising): 8 articles, 53 meditations, 6 reviews. Writers' guidelines and theme list available at website.
- "The Day Jessie Daniels Was Bullied." Article shares what a girl learned from being beat up in eighth grade.
- Sample dept/column: "Are You Seeing Red?" details a marketing campaign to benefit African AIDS patients.

Rights and Payment
First and second rights. Features, $100. Meditations, $25. Pays on acceptance.

Editor's Comments
In a sense, this is a pilgrim journal. The stories of hope and of struggle that our readers recount in our pages give us a glimpse of their journey of faith—and the assurance that God is alive and at work in our lives.

Dig

Cobblestone Publishing
30 Grove Street, Suite C
Peterborough, NH 03458

Editor: Rosalie F. Baker

Description and Interests
Published in partnership with *Archaeology* magazine, *Dig* unearths the wonders of archaeology for middle-grade readers. Themed issues are filled with photos, fun facts, and activities.
- **Audience:** 9–14 years
- **Frequency:** 9 times each year
- **Circulation:** 19,000
- **Website:** www.cobblestonepub.com; www.digonsite.com

Freelance Potential
80% written by nonstaff writers. Publishes 40 freelance submissions yearly; 40% by unpublished writers, 60% by new authors. Receives 96+ queries yearly.

Submissions
Submissions must relate to an upcoming theme. Query with outline, bibliography, and clips or writing samples. SASE. Responds in 4 months.
Articles: Word lengths vary. Informational articles and photo-essays. Topics include nature, animals, science, and technology.
Articles: Word lengths vary. Stories related to the theme of the issue.
Depts/columns: Word lengths vary. Art, archaeology facts, quizzes, and projects.

Sample Issue
34 pages (no advertising): 9 articles; 7 depts/columns. Sample copy, $5.95 at newsstands. Guidelines available.
- "Before Cookbooks." Article describes the cooking methods of prehistoric humans, and includes several recipes to try at home.
- "Nectar of the Gods." Article reveals some interesting uses for honey throughout history.
- Sample dept/column: "Updates" tells readers about the headless mummy found in Huaca Pucllana, the oldest mummy ever uncovered in Lima, Peru.

Rights and Payment
All rights. Written material, $.20–$.25 per word. Pays on publication. Provides 2 contributor's copies.

Editor's Comments
We urge writers to obtain a theme list because all issues center around a main topic. Writers with a background in archaeology, paleontology, and related fields are encouraged to submit ideas based on our themes. Our readers have a keen interest in the subject and we want them to have fun while they learn.

Dimensions

1908 Association Drive
Reston, VA 20191

Editor: Lyn Fiscus

Description and Interests
Dimensions is written for high school students who are interested in business management, marketing, and leadership development and are members of DECA. The material it publishes is designed to correspond to the high school marketing curriculum.
- **Audience:** 14–18 years
- **Frequency:** Quarterly
- **Circulation:** 180,000
- **Website:** www.deca.org

Freelance Potential
60% written by nonstaff writers. Publishes 9 freelance submissions yearly; 50% by unpublished writers, 50% by authors who are new to the magazine.

Submissions
Query or send complete ms with short author biography. Accepts hard copy, Macintosh disk submissions (RTF files), email to leadershiplogistics@gmail.com, and simultaneous submissions if identified. SASE. Response time varies.
Articles: 800–1,200 words. Informational and how-to articles; profiles; interviews; and personal experience pieces. Topics include business issues, domestic and international management, marketing trends, sales, leadership development, franchising, personal finance, advertising, and business technology.
Depts/columns: 400–600 words. DECA chapter news, opinion pieces, and short news items.

Sample Issue
32 pages (45% advertising): 13 articles; 5 depts/columns. Sample copy, free with 9x12 SASE. Guidelines available.
- "Tackling Charity Fatigue with Teamwork." Article describes how an Ohio school created a unique fundraiser to help two local charities.
- "PR Campaign Exposes Drug Problem." Article tells how one DECA chapter heightened awareness of the methamphetamine problem.

Rights and Payment
First North American serial rights. Written material, payment rates vary. Pays on publication. Provides 2 contributor's copies.

Editor's Comments
We are an educational journal with a young yet sophisticated audience. We look for articles of substance written in a direct, conversational style.

Dimensions of Early Childhood

Southern Early Childhood Association
P.O. Box 55930
Little Rock, AR 72215-5930

Dimensions Manager: Jennifer Bean

Description and Interests

Everything that appears in *Dimensions of Early Childhood* supports high-quality experiences for young children. Its readers include teachers of young children, family and group child care providers, teacher educators, social workers, and education policy makers.
• **Audience:** Early childhood professionals
• **Frequency:** 3 times each year
• **Circulation:** 19,000
• **Website:** www.southernearlychildhood.org

Freelance Potential

99% written by nonstaff writers. Publishes 40 freelance submissions yearly; 90% by unpublished writers, 80% by authors who are new to the magazine. Receives 84 mss yearly.

Submissions

Send complete ms. Accepts email submissions to editor@southernearlychildhood.org. Responds in 3–4 months.
Articles: Word lengths vary. Informational articles. Topics include emergent curriculum for children, effective classroom practices, theory and research, program administration, family relationships, and resource systems.
Depts/columns: Word lengths vary. Book reviews.

Sample Issue

40 pages (20% advertising): 5 articles; 1 dept/column. Sample copy, $5. Guidelines available.
• "Evaluate Children with Disabilities; Recommendations for Early Childhood Educators." Article rethinks the way children with disabilities are assessed and suggests ways to plan individualized learning experiences.
• "Family Fun Day: Make a Difference in Your Community." Article features tips on how to plan a celebration of young children.
• "Creative Play." Article presents ideas teachers can use to build connections with children who are learning English.

Rights and Payment

All rights. No payment. Provides 2 author's copies.

Editor's Comments

Keep in mind that this is a refereed journal. The articles we publish address both the continuing interests of early childhood professionals and emerging issues in the field. Current research and theory must be cited as a basis for making recommendations for practice.

Dogs for Kids

BowTie, Inc.
P.O. Box 6050
Mission Viejo, CA 92690-6050

Editor: Jackie Franza

Description and Interests

This offspring of *Dog Fancy* fosters responsible dog ownership in children by presenting informative yet entertaining articles in a vivid and easy-to-read format.
• **Audience:** 8–13 years
• **Frequency:** 6 times each year
• **Circulation:** 300,000
• **Website:** www.dogsforkids.com

Freelance Potential

50% written by nonstaff writers. Publishes 25 freelance submissions yearly; 20% by authors who are new to the magazine. Receives 500 queries yearly.

Submissions

Query with writing samples. Accepts hard copy and email queries to dogsforkids@bowtieinc.com. SASE. Responds in 8–10 weeks.
Articles: 1,200 words. Informational and how-to articles; profiles; photo-essays; and personal experience pieces. Topics include pet care and dog-related activities and careers.
Depts/columns: To 650 words. Tips on dog behavior, health, and nutrition; canine news; and new products.
Other: Puzzles, activities, games, and quizzes.

Sample Issue

65 pages (10% advertising): 5 articles; 8 depts/columns; 8 activities. Sample copy, $2.99 with 9x12 SASE. Guidelines available.
• "Coco the Love Dog." Article profiles a therapy dog and her owner.
• "Getting Fido Fixed." Article lists five reasons to spay or neuter a dog.
• Sample dept/column: "Kids Can Do It" describes how one dog inspired a 10-year-old girl to become an author and dog trainer.

Rights and Payment

First rights. Articles, $300. Depts/columns, payment rates vary. Pays on publication. Provides 2 copies.

Editor's Comments

We would like to receive more personal stories about kids making a difference with dogs or for dogs, and fewer breed profiles and general-care pieces. All features should include at least one short sidebar to complement the main story, which should be organized in easy-to-handle chunks. Text should be positive, lively, motivational, and direct: Use the second-person—"you"—rather than "young dog owners" or "children."

Dovetail

A Journal By and For Jewish/Christian Families

775 Simon Greenwell Lane
Boston, KY 40107

Editor: Mary Rosenbaum

Description and Interests
Now published exclusively online, *Dovetail* tackles issues and concerns related to raising children in interfaith families. It also covers aspects of interfaith marriages and broader issues of interfaith family life.
- **Audience:** Interfaith families
- **Frequency:** Quarterly
- **Hits per month:** Unavailable
- **Website:** www.dovetailinstitute.org

Freelance Potential
95% written by nonstaff writers. Publishes 10 freelance submissions yearly; 90% by unpublished writers, 90% by authors who are new to the magazine. Receives 192 queries and unsolicited mss yearly.

Submissions
Query or send complete ms. Accepts hard copy, Macintosh and text file submissions, email submissions to DLIFE@Bardstown.com, and simultaneous submissions if identified. SASE. Responds in 1–2 months.
Articles: 800–1,000 words. Informational articles; profiles; interviews; reviews; and personal experience pieces. Topics include the interfaith community, parenting, anti-semitism, gender roles, religious holidays, family issues, social concerns, and education.
Other: Poetry, lengths vary.

Sample Issue
14 pages: 5 articles. Sample issue, guidelines, and theme list available at website.
- "A Marriage of Differences Enriches the Holidays." Article takes an uplifting and humorous look at a family Hanukkah dinner attended by the author's Christian husband.
- "The Shores of Galilee." Article tells how religion became the turning point in one couple's relationship.

Rights and Payment
One-time rights. Articles, $25. Reviews, $15. Pays on publication. Provides download access to copies.

Editor's Comments
Please note that we have no denominational affiliation or agenda. We accept articles that reflect a variety of approaches and strategies, but nothing you submit should have a proselytizing or negative tone. Personal experiences are welcome, but avoid trite observations or broad generalizations. Potential writers should familiarize themselves with our publication and review our theme list prior to submitting their work.

Dramatics

Educational Theatre Association
2343 Auburn Avenue
Cincinnati, OH 45219

Editor: Donald Corathers

Description and Interests
Dramatics provides tools and information to help high school drama students and their teachers produce better theater. It also covers other areas of the performing arts, including film, video, and dance.
- **Audience:** High school students and teachers
- **Frequency:** 9 times each year
- **Circulation:** 37,000
- **Website:** www.edta.org

Freelance Potential
80% written by nonstaff writers. Publishes 41 freelance submissions yearly; 25% by unpublished writers, 50% by authors who are new to the magazine. Receives 480 mss yearly.

Submissions
Send complete ms. Accepts hard copy and email submissions to dcorathers@edta.org. SASE. Responds in 2–4 months.
Articles: 750–4,000 words. Informational articles; book reviews; and interviews. Topics include playwriting, musical theater, acting, auditions, stage makeup, set design, and theater production.
Fiction: 500–3,500 words. Full-length and one-act plays suitable for high school audiences.
Artwork: 5x7 or larger B/W prints or 35mm or larger color transparencies. B/W line art. High resolution JPGs or TIFFs.

Sample Issue
48 pages (40% advertising): 4 articles; 4 depts/columns; 1 comic; 1 calendar. Sample copy, $3 with 9x12 SASE. Guidelines available.
- "Architects of the Stage." Article explores the world of the scenic designer and discusses the need to balance aesthetic and structural concerns when designing sets.
- "Character Is Action." Article is the first of three pieces about how to use the tools of acting.

Rights and Payment
First rights. Written material, $50–$400. Pays on publication. Provides 5 contributor's copies.

Editor's Comments
In addition to information about theatrical skills and techniques, we present resource information to help high school students make an informed decision about whether to pursue a career in theater, and about how to do so.

Earlychildhood News

2 Lower Ragsdale, Suite 125
Monterey, CA 93940

Managing Editor: Barbara Atkinson

Description and Interests

This online magazine is a resource for teachers and parents and provides articles about child development, health and safety, behavior, and assessment, among other topics.
- **Audience:** Early childhood professionals and parents
- **Frequency:** Monthly
- **Circulation:** 50,000
- **Website: www.earlychildhoodnews.com**

Freelance Potential

90% written by nonstaff writers. Publishes 10 freelance submissions yearly; 5% by unpublished writers, 15% by authors who are new to the magazine. Receives 96 queries and mss yearly.

Submissions

Query with clips and writing samples; or send complete ms. Accepts email submissions to batkinson@excelligencemail.com. Responds in 2 months.
Articles: 600–1,200 words. Informational and self-help articles; success stories; and interviews. Topics include early childhood education; health and safety; advocacy; testing; multicultural subjects; family, social, and emotional issues; and professional development.
Depts/columns: 500 words. Brief news items.

Sample Issue

Sample copy, guidelines, and editorial calendar available at website.
- "Meeting the Challenge of Second Language Learners." Article examines the challenges facing childcare providers who must teach children who don't speak English.
- "Using Assessment Results to Plan Your Curriculum." Article offers guidance to early childhood educators in assessing and following set guidelines.
- Sample dept/column: "Activity" offers ways of combining education, creativity, and dramatic play for young children.

Rights and Payment

All rights. Written material, $75–$300. Depts/columns, payment rates vary. Pays on acceptance.

Editor's Comments

We are always in need of craft and activity writers who can tie their projects to clear educational goals. We do not publish first-person essays, poetry, or fiction.

Early Childhood Today

Scholastic Inc.
557 Broadway
New York, NY 10012-3999

Editor-in-Chief: Diane Ohanesian

Description and Interests

This Scholastic publication is written specifically for professionals in the field of early childhood education. It offers information on child development and behavior, hands-on activities, resources, and leadership advice for teachers and center directors.
- **Audience:** Early childhood professionals
- **Frequency:** 8 times each year
- **Circulation:** 55,000
- **Website: www.scholastic.com/ect**

Freelance Potential

100% written by nonstaff writers. Publishes 5 freelance submissions yearly; 10% by unpublished writers, 5% by authors who are new to the magazine. Receives 10–15 queries yearly.

Submissions

Query. No unsolicited mss. Accepts hard copy. SASE. Responds in 1 month.
Articles: Word lengths vary. Informational, educational, and how-to articles. Topics include child advocacy, child development, special needs, communication, physical development, family issues, health, technology, and cultural issues.
Depts/columns: Word lengths vary. News, teacher tips, health, and age-appropriate activities.

Sample Issue

64 pages (15% advertising): 10 articles; 4 depts/columns. Sample copy available.
- "Helping Children Protect and Explore Our Planet." Article presents examples of ways to teach young children about conservation and recycling.
- "When a Child Is Unkind to Others." Article explores ways to find out about the source of a behavioral issue and correct the problem.
- "How Young Children Learn Language." Article tells how acquiring language is the result of active, repetitive, and complex learning.

Rights and Payment

All rights. Written material, payment rates vary. Pays on acceptance. Provides 3 contributor's copies.

Editor's Comments

We're looking for writers who can present practical information that our readers can put to use in their classrooms. We especially like pieces that show how to involve children in developmentally appropriate experiences and encourage teacher/child interaction.

East of the Web

361 Manhattan Building
Fairfield Road
London E32UL
England

Editor: Alex Patterson

Description and Interests
East of the Web offers fiction writers an opportunity to have their work seen and read in a high-quality, respected setting. It publishes short stories for children and adults in a number of genres, such as science fiction, horror, humor, and romance. This website presents work by both new voices and experienced authors.
• **Audience:** All ages
• **Frequency:** Unavailable
• **Hits per month:** 40,000+
• **Website: www.eastoftheweb.com**

Freelance Potential
96% written by nonstaff writers. Publishes 150 freelance submissions yearly; 50% by unpublished writers, 85% by authors who are new to the magazine. Receives 6,000 unsolicited mss yearly.

Submissions
Send complete ms. Accepts email submissions to submissions@eastoftheweb.com (Microsoft Word or TEXT file attachments). The subject line must consist only of the words "EoTW Submission" or "Short Story for EoTW." Responds in 3–4 months.
Fiction: Word lengths vary. Short stories for children and adults. Genres include contemporary fiction, mystery, folktales, fairy tales, humor, science fiction, and stories about animals.

Sample Issue
Sample copy and guidelines available at website.
• "Letter from the Understudy." Short story in letter form describes the feelings of an actor who has been temporarily banished from the theater.
• "Squirrel." Story revolves around a business meeting at which one of the businessmen wears a glove puppet of a squirrel.
• "Three Letters." Story focuses on a woman's reflections on the people of her past.

Rights and Payment
Non-exclusive rights. No payment.

Editor's Comments
Note that our editorial standards are high, and while we read all the submissions we receive, we do not publish them all. Our purpose is to provide exposure to writers, and our site receives attention from agents, the press, filmmakers, schools, universities, and other publishers.

Educational Horizons

Pi Lambda Theta
P.O. Box 6626
4101 East Third Street
Bloomington, IN 47407-6626

Managing Editor

Description and Interests
This scholarly, professional journal for educators offers articles that analyze and assess current educational problems and trends, both in the U.S. and around the world.
• **Audience:** Pi Lambda Theta members
• **Frequency:** Quarterly
• **Circulation:** 17,000
• **Website: www.pilambda.org**

Freelance Potential
95% written by nonstaff writers. Publishes 10–15 freelance submissions yearly; 75% by authors who are new to the magazine. Receives 60 queries, 12 unsolicited mss yearly.

Submissions
Query with outline/synopsis; or send complete ms with biography. Accepts hard copy and disk submissions. Availability of artwork improves chance of acceptance. SASE. Responds to queries in 1 month, to mss in 3–4 months.
Articles: 3,500–5,000 words. Informational articles; research reports; and scholarly essays. Topics include educational, social, and cultural issues.
Depts/columns: 500–750 words. Education topics in the news; multicultural education; legal issues; and book reviews.
Artwork: B/W prints and camera-ready illustrations.

Sample Issue
60 pages (4% advertising): 3 articles; 3 depts/columns. Sample copy, $5 with 9x12 SASE ($.87 postage). Writers' guidelines and theme list available at website.
• "Late to Class: Social Class and Schooling in the New Economy." Article discusses the many ways social class affects life in the classroom.
• Sample dept/column: "From the Trenches" discusses why educators often have to trade off "sacred" values in the face of competing demands.

Rights and Payment
First rights. No payment. Provides 5 author's copies.

Editor's Comments
Our publication was founded in the spirit of academic excellence to provide leadership in addressing educational, social, and cultural issues. Most articles relate to the issue's specific theme, although book reviews are not necessarily theme related.

Educational Leadership

1703 North Beauregard Street
Alexandria, VA 22311-1714

Editor: Marge Scherer

Description and Interests
This flagship journal of the Association for Supervision and Curriculum Development (ASCD) contains articles by leading educators; reports of effective programs and practices; and interpretations of research in the education field. Each issue centers around a theme.
- **Audience:** Educators
- **Frequency:** 8 times each year
- **Circulation:** 170,000
- **Website:** www.ascd.org

Freelance Potential
95% written by nonstaff writers. Publishes 130 freelance submissions yearly; 50% by unpublished writers, 50% by authors who are new to the magazine. Receives 1,000 unsolicited mss yearly.

Submissions
Send 2 copies of complete ms. Accepts hard copy. Does not return mss. Responds in 2 months.
Articles: 1,500–2,500 words. How-to articles and personal experience pieces. Topics include reading, assessment, instructional strategies, student achievement, gifted and special education, science, technology, and multicultural and ethnic subjects.
Depts/columns: Word lengths vary. Education news; opinion pieces; and policy and website reviews.
Artwork: B/W and color prints or slides; digital images at 300 dpi. Line art. Send only upon request.

Sample Issue
96 pages (25% advertising): 15 articles; 9 depts/columns. Sample copy, $7. Writers' guidelines and theme list available.
- "Balance in the Balance." Article discusses the need for school accountability systems that focus on more than basic skills.
- "How We Treat One Another in School." Article summarizes a survey of middle-school students' experiences with bullying.
- Sample dept/column: "The Principal Connection" gives one educator's account of how he uses summer vacation to enhance professional growth.

Rights and Payment
All or first rights. No payment. Provides 5 copies.

Editor's Comments
Please note that we no longer publish book reviews. We prefer articles in which the writer speaks directly to the reader in an informal, conversational style.

Education Forum

60 Mobile Drive
Toronto, Ontario M4A 2P3
Canada

Managing Editor: Marianne Clayton

Description and Interests
Articles on topics of interest to educators in the province of Ontario are featured in this magazine. Each issue includes teaching strategies, trends, issues, reviews, profiles, and travel pieces.
- **Audience:** Teachers
- **Frequency:** 3 times each year
- **Circulation:** 50,000
- **Website:** www.osstf.on.ca

Freelance Potential
90% written by nonstaff writers. Publishes 35 freelance submissions yearly; 20% by unpublished writers, 80% by authors who are new to the magazine. Receives 48 queries and unsolicited mss yearly.

Submissions
Query with clips or writing samples; or send complete ms. Accepts hard copy. No simultaneous submissions. SAE/IRC. Responds in 1–2 months.
Articles: To 2,500 words. How-to and practical application articles on education trends; discussions of controversial issues; and teaching techniques for use in secondary school classrooms.
Depts/columns: "Openers" features news and opinion pieces; to 300 words. "Forum Picks" uses media and software reviews.
Artwork: B/W prints and line art. Color prints and transparencies.
Other: Classroom activities, puzzles, and games. Submit seasonal material 8 months in advance.

Sample Issue
46 pages (18% advertising): 4 articles; 8 depts/columns. Sample copy, free with 9x12 SAE/IRC. Guidelines available.
- "Making Our Vote Count." Article explores the benefits of having proportional representation in the voting system.
- Sample dept/column: "Their Story" discusses the importance of being an organ donor.

Rights and Payment
First North American serial rights. No payment. Provides 5 contributor's copies.

Editor's Comments
We welcome submissions from new writers and are interested in well-written and researched articles covering trends in education, and profiles of successful trend-setting educational workers in public education.

Education Week

6935 Arlington Road, Suite 100
Bethesda, MD 20814-5233

Executive Editor: Greg Chronister

Description and Interests
Celebrating 25 years in print, this informative news-paper for education professionals covers the latest in curriculum trends, events and programs, laws and rules, and their effects on educators, as well as other educational issues.
• **Audience:** Educators
• **Frequency:** 44 times each year
• **Circulation:** 50,000
• **Website: www.edweek.org**

Freelance Potential
8% written by nonstaff writers. Publishes 125 free-lance submissions yearly; 80% by unpublished writers, 75% by authors who are new to the magazine. Receives 600 unsolicited mss yearly.

Submissions
Send complete ms. Accepts IBM disk submissions (WordPerfect or Microsoft Word) and Macintosh disk submissions (plain text). SASE. Responds in 6–8 weeks.
Articles: 1,200–1,500 words. Essays about child development and education related to grades K–12 for use in "Commentary" section.
Depts/columns: Staff written.

Sample Issue
40 pages (25% advertising): 7 articles; 1 story; 8 depts/columns. Sample copy, $3 with 9x12 SASE ($1 postage). Guidelines available.
• "In Buffalo, Opening Doors for the Overlooked." Article describes a program that seeks out talented students and offers them scholarships and support.
• "Cheap Laptops Getting Tryouts in Small Pilot Project." Article reports on a plan to give laptops to students in poor countries.
• "Headache Night." Article discusses the issues princi-pals deal with when trying to balance fun with safety on prom night.

Rights and Payment
First rights. "Commentary," $200. Pays on publication. Provides 2 contributor's copies.

Editor's Comments
While the majority of our material is written by staff, our "Commentary" section, which features opinion essays about child development and education, is open to free-lancers. Our content is geared toward elementary and secondary education, both public and private.

EduGuide

Partnership for Learning
321 North Pine
Lansing, MI 48933

Editor

Description and Interests
Published in four editions (elementary school, middle school, high school, and college), these journals from the Partnership for Learning are dedicated to helping students achieve.
• **Audience:** Parents and teens
• **Frequency:** 3 times each year
• **Circulation:** 600,000
• **Website: www.partnershipforlearning.org**

Freelance Potential
40% written by nonstaff writers. Publishes 25–30 free-lance submissions yearly; 10% by unpublished writers, 60% by authors who are new to the magazine. Receives 48 unsolicited mss yearly.

Submissions
Send complete ms. Accepts hard copy and email sub-missions to jan@partnershipforlearning.org. SASE. Responds in 4–6 weeks.
Articles: 500–1,000 words. Informational and how-to articles; profiles; interviews; and personal experience pieces. Topics include the arts, college, careers, com-puters, gifted education, health, fitness, history, humor, mathematics, music, science, technology, special education, and issues related to elementary and secondary education.
Depts/columns: Staff written.
Artwork: Color prints and transparencies. Line art.
Other: Submit seasonal material 3 months in advance.

Sample Issue
18 pages: 5 articles; 1 dept/column. Sample copy, $3 with 9x12 SASE ($1 postage). Guidelines and theme list/editorial calendar available.
• "Getting Settled." Article discusses the transition from high school to college.
• "Getting Involved." Article stresses the importance of building a social network in college.
• "Getting By." Article discusses financial aid and money management for college students.

Rights and Payment
First or second rights. All material, payment rates vary. Pays on acceptance. Provides 5 author's copies.

Editor's Comments
Partnership for Learning annually equips more than one million families, educators, and leaders to work together in new ways to lift student achievement.

Edutopia

P.O. Box 3494
San Rafael, CA 94912

Executive Editor: Jennifer Sweeney

Description and Interests
Published by the George Lucas Educational Foundation, which was founded by the *Star Wars* creator to celebrate and encourage innovation in schools, this upbeat magazine offers timely articles on issues affecting today's students.
- **Audience:** Educators; parents; policy makers
- **Frequency:** 8 times each year
- **Circulation:** 100,000
- **Website: www.edutopia.org**

Freelance Potential
70% written by nonstaff writers. Publishes 20 freelance submissions yearly; 30% by authors who are new to the magazine. Receives 36–60 queries yearly.

Submissions
Query with résumé and clips. Accepts email queries to edit@edutopia.org. Response time varies.
Articles: 300–2,500 words. Informational and how-to articles; and personal experience pieces. Topics include computers, education, current events, health and fitness, nature, the environment, popular culture, recreation, science, technology, social issues, and travel.
Depts/columns: 700 words. Health; education; and ethnic and multicultural issues.

Sample Issue
56 pages (35% advertising): 3 articles; 15 depts/columns. Sample copy, $4.95. Guidelines available.
- "Learning Curves." Article shares the personal stories of seven highly successful people, including Donald Trump and Christiane Amanpour.
- "Get on the Bus." Article spotlights the Topsy-Turvy Bus, a protest against federal budget priorities invented by Ben & Jerry's co-founder, Ben Cohen.
- Sample dept/column: "Sage Advice" offers teachers' suggestions for relating to students in this technology-driven age.

Rights and Payment
First North American serial rights. Written material, payment rates vary. Pays on acceptance. Provides 2 contributor's copies.

Editor's Comments
We publish stories of innovative teaching and learning at all grade levels of public schools. Our aim is to reach teachers as people as well as professionals through witty, sharp writing.

Elementary School Writer

Writer Publications
P.O. Box 718
Grand Rapids, MI 55744-0718

Editor: Emily Benes

Description and Interests
For more than 22 years, this newspaper has provided a national audience for writers who are elementary school students. Each issue showcases a number of stories, articles, essays, and poems submitted by students of subscribing teachers. It is primarily used as a teaching tool.
- **Audience:** Elementary school students
- **Frequency:** 6 times each year
- **Circulation:** Unavailable
- **Website: www.writerpublications.com**

Freelance Potential
100% written by nonstaff writers. Publishes 300 freelance submissions yearly; 95% by unpublished writers, 75% by authors who are new to the magazine. Receives 36,000 unsolicited mss yearly.

Submissions
Accepts submissions from students of subscribing teachers in elementary schools only. Accepts hard copy, email submissions to writer@mx3.com (ASCII text only), and simultaneous submissions if identified. SASE. Response time varies.
Articles: To 1,000 words. Informational and how-to articles; profiles; humor; and personal experience pieces. Topics include current events, multicultural and ethnic issues, nature, the environment, popular culture, creation, sports, and travel.
Fiction: To 1,000 words. Genres include humor, science fiction, and stories about nature, the environment, and sports.
Other: Poetry, no line limits. Seasonal material.

Sample Issue
8 pages (no advertising): 10 articles and essays; 14 stories; 17 poems. Guidelines available in each issue.
- "One Summer Day." Story features a town that goes into a tizzy when its gravity starts to change.
- "A Magical Backyard." Essay describes the author's favorite place to stretch her imagination.
- "Swimming at Negative Twenty Degrees." Article recounts a family trip to Chena Hot Springs.

Rights and Payment
One-time rights. No payment.

Editor's Comments
Please note that all submissions must be fewer than 1,000 words and must be respectful, exceeding the customary standards of decency.

Ellery Queen's Mystery Magazine

475 Park Avenue South, 11th Floor
New York, NY 10016

Editor: Janet Hutchings

Description and Interests
As the "world's leading mystery magazine," this publication features crime and detective stories written in the tradition of two mystery writers who pen-named themselves Ellery Queen.
- **Audience:** YA–Adult
- **Frequency:** 10 times each year
- **Circulation:** 180,780
- **Website:** www.themysteryplace.com/eqmm

Freelance Potential
100% written by nonstaff writers. Publishes 125 freelance submissions yearly; 7% by unpublished writers, 25% by authors who are new to the magazine. Receives 2,600 unsolicited mss yearly.

Submissions
Send complete ms. Accepts hard copy and simultaneous submissions if identified. SASE. Responds in 3 months.
Fiction: Feature length, 2,000–12,000 words. Minute mysteries, 250 words. Novellas by established authors, to 20,000 words. Genres include contemporary and historical crime fiction, psychological thrillers, mystery, suspense, and detective and private-eye stories.
Other: Poetry, line lengths vary.

Sample Issue
144 pages (6% advertising): 11 stories; 2 book reviews; 4 depts/columns. Sample copy, $3.99. Guidelines available.
- "The World Behind." Memoir-style mystery revolves around a young girl's disappearance as told by the boy who rescued her.
- "The Winning Ticket." Story features a hard-boiled detective who makes deductions based on visual cues and catches both his target and another criminal.

Rights and Payment
First and anthology rights. Written material, $.05–$.08 per word. Pays on acceptance. Provides 3 contributor's copies.

Editor's Comments
We continue to search for classic whodunits and hard-boiled detective stories. These types of stories are popular with our readers. We like to encourage unpublished authors trying to enter the mystery field. First-story submissions should be addressed to our Department of First Stories.

Exceptional Parent

416 Main Street
Johnstown, PA 15901

Editor-in-Chief: Dr. Rick Rader

Description and Interests
This magazine addresses the full spectrum of special needs, from infancy to old age. Its readers include parents and caregivers. Each issue addresses topics such as health, finances, education, technology, politics, and social issues.
- **Audience:** Parents, teachers, and professionals
- **Frequency:** Monthly
- **Circulation:** 70,000
- **Website:** www.eparent.com

Freelance Potential
95% written by nonstaff writers. Publishes 50–60 freelance submissions yearly; 50% by unpublished writers, 50% by authors who are new to the magazine. Receives 96+ queries yearly.

Submissions
Query. Accepts hard copy. SASE. Responds in 3–4 weeks.
Articles: To 2,500 words. Informational articles; profiles; interviews; and personal experience pieces. Topics include the social, psychological, legal, political, technological, financial, and educational concerns of individuals with disabilities.
Depts/columns: Word lengths vary. Opinion and personal experience pieces, news items, new product information, and media reviews.

Sample Issue
100 pages (50% advertising): 17 articles; 16 depts/columns. Sample copy, $4.99 with 9x12 SASE ($2 postage). Guidelines and editorial calendar available.
- "Seizures and Teens: Maximizing Health and Safety." Article explores factors that may affect a teen's safety during a seizure, and ways to lessen the risks.
- "Surfer's Healing." Article describes how a surfer started a traveling surfing day camp in California for autistic children.
- Sample dept/column: "Organizational Spotlight" takes a look at The Council of Parent Attorneys and Advocates, Inc. (COPAA).

Rights and Payment
First North American serial rights. No payment. Provides 2 contributor's copies.

Editor's Comments
We're looking for upbeat articles that offer practical information and advice for the special needs community. Please avoid technical jargon.

Exchange

Faces

P.O. Box 3249
Redmond, WA 98073-3249

Editor: Bonnie Neugebauer

Description and Interests
Formerly known as *Child Care Information Exchange*, this magazine serves child-care professionals with articles on staff and curriculum development, parenting, and the latest research in early childhood development.
• **Audience:** Child-care professionals
• **Frequency:** 6 times each year
• **Circulation:** 26,000
• **Website: www.childcareexchange.com**

Freelance Potential
65–75% written by nonstaff writers. Publishes 75 freelance submissions yearly; 50% by unpublished writers, 60% by authors who are new to the magazine.

Submissions
Send complete ms with current, high-res digital photo of author, brief author biography, Social Security number, contact information, and article references. Requires hard copy in addition to email submissions to bonnien@childcareexchange.com (Microsoft Word attachments or text). Availability of artwork improves chance of acceptance. SASE. Response time varies.
Articles: 1,800 words. Informational, how-to, and self-help articles. Topics include child development; education; and social, multicultural and ethnic issues.
Depts/columns: Word lengths vary. Staff development and training; parent perspectives.
Artwork: Color prints. Line art.

Sample Issue
96 pages: 15 articles; 6 depts/columns. Sample copy, $8. Guidelines and theme list available.
• "Early Childhood Trends Around the World." Article summarizes global developments in early education.
• "Imaginary Soup, Homemade Books, and Tattered Blankets." Article discusses the importance of creative thinking in early childhood.
• Sample dept/column: "From a Parent's Perspective" discusses when to say "no" and when to let go.

Rights and Payment
All rights. Articles, $300. Other material, payment rates vary. Pays on publication. Provides 2 copies.

Editor's Comments
We are committed to supporting early childhood professionals worldwide in their efforts to craft environments that foster friendship, curiosity, self-esteem, joy, and respect, where the talents of all are fully challenged and justly rewarded.

Cobblestone Publishing
30 Grove Street, Suite C
Peterborough, NH 03458

Editor: Elizabeth Carpentiere

Description and Interests
Each issue of this multicultural magazine for children is dedicated to a specific country, person, or world topic.
• **Audience:** 9–14 years
• **Frequency:** 9 times each year
• **Circulation:** 15,000
• **Website: www.cobblestonepub.com**

Freelance Potential
70% written by nonstaff writers. Publishes 80–90 freelance submissions yearly; 25% by unpublished writers, 15% by new authors. Receives 450 queries yearly.

Submissions
Query with outline, bibliography, and clips or writing samples. Accepts email queries to facesmag@ yahoo.com. Responds in 5 months.
Articles: 800 words. Sidebars, 300–600 words. Informational articles and personal experience pieces related to the theme of each issue. Topics include culture, geography, the environment, cuisine, special events, travel, history, and social issues.
Fiction: To 800 words. Stories, legends, and folktales from countries around the world—all related to the theme of each issue.
Depts/columns: Staff written.
Artwork: Color prints and transparencies.
Other: Games, crafts, puzzles, and activities, to 700 words. Poetry, to 100 lines.

Sample Issue
50 pages (no advertising): 14 articles; 1 play; 10 depts/columns; 3 activities. Sample copy, $5.95 with 9x12 SASE ($2 postage). Guidelines and theme list available at website.
• "Honduras: Facing Challenges Together." Article provides an overview of the country.
• "Playing Games Honduras-Style." Article describes activities popular among Honduran children.
• "The First People." Play retells a Mayan myth.

Rights and Payment
All rights. Articles and fiction, $.20–$.25 per word. Pays on publication. Provides 2 contributor's copies.

Editor's Comments
We welcome contributions of fun activities, word puzzles, and logic puzzles (other than crossword puzzles or word searches). Since our magazine deals with the contemporary aspects of a culture, we are not interested in historical articles.

Face Up

Faith & Family

75 Orwell Road
Rathgar, Dublin 6
Ireland

Editor: Gerard Moloney

432 Washington Avenue
North Haven, CT 06473

Editorial Director: Tom & April Hoopes

Description and Interests
This magazine for Irish teens provides in-depth coverage of the issues that concern today's youth. A Christian publication, *Face Up* conveys the values found in the Gospel while providing discussion and analysis of contemporary life challenges.
- **Audience:** 14–18 years
- **Frequency:** 10 times each year
- **Circulation:** 12,000
- **Website:** www.faceup.ie

Freelance Potential
100% written by nonstaff writers. Publishes 60 freelance submissions yearly; 30% by unpublished writers, 70% by authors who are new to the magazine. Receives 500 unsolicited mss yearly.

Submissions
Send complete ms. Accepts email submissions to info@faceup.ie. Availability of artwork improves chance of acceptance. Responds in 1 month.
Articles: 900 words. Informational and how-to articles; profiles; interviews; and personal experience pieces. Topics include college, careers, current events, relationships, health, fitness, music, popular culture, and sports.
Depts/columns: 500 words. Opinion pieces, advice, health issues, the Internet, and reviews.
Artwork: Color prints and transparencies.
Other: Submit seasonal material on Christmas, Easter, and final exams 3 months in advance.

Sample Issue
38 pages (5% advertising): 6 articles; 12 depts/columns. Sample copy, guidelines, and theme list/editorial calendar available.
- "Addicted, Me? . . . Never!" Article talks about how addictions can come in many forms, including shopping, eating, and the Internet.
- "I Make It Very Hard for Guys to Win My Heart." Article interviews superstar Natasha Bedingfield.

Rights and Payment
Rights vary. All material, payment rates vary. Pays on publication. Provides 2 contributor's copies.

Editor's Comments
We're interested in thoughtful and provocative articles that tackle the issues that interest today's teens. Send us articles that are direct, to the point, and written in an active voice.

Description and Interests
This magazine targets "real-world" committed Catholic moms. Each issue includes articles covering child raising, education, social and political issues, and other topics related to Catholic family life.
- **Audience:** Catholic families
- **Frequency:** Quarterly
- **Circulation:** 35,000
- **Website:** www.faithandfamilymag.com

Freelance Potential
75% written by nonstaff writers. Publishes 35 freelance submissions yearly; 15% by unpublished writers, 10% by authors who are new to the magazine. Receives 300 queries yearly.

Submissions
Query. Accepts email queries to editor@faithandfamilymag.com. Responds in 2–3 months.
Articles: 600–2,000 words. Informational, how-to and self-help articles; profiles; interviews; personal experience pieces; and media reviews. Topics include family life, parenting, marriage, religion, and social and political issues.
Depts/columns: Word lengths vary. Tips for home, garden, and food; entertainment reviews; spirituality.
Artwork: Prefers color prints or slides.

Sample Issue
96 pages (30% advertising): 7 articles; 15 depts/columns. Sample copy, $4.50. Writers' guidelines available.
- "Moms Who Never Gave Up Hope." Article shares the stories of three moms-to-be who, after being told their babies would die shortly after birth, stood up for life against the odds.
- "An Abundant Life." Article offers tips on how to start a vegetable garden and keep it thriving all year long.
- Sample dept/column: "Faith & Culture" maintains that patriotism is a Christian virtue.

Rights and Payment
First North American serial rights. Written material, $.33 per word. Pays on publication.

Editor's Comments
As obvious as it may seem, it is often easy to lose sight of one's purpose in writing for us, so remember the most important guideline of all: Write for the glory of God and the service of your reader!

Families on the Go

Life Media
P.O. Box 55445
St. Petersburg, FL 33732

Editor: Barbara Doyle

Description and Interests
This magazine, available online and in print, is distributed free throughout Pinellas and Hillsborough counties in Florida. It features articles on a variety of topics of interest to parents of busy families, such as health, education, and recreation. It also includes shopping guides, education resources, and camp directories.
• **Audience:** Families
• **Frequency:** 6 times each year
• **Circulation:** 120,000
• **Website: www.familiesonthego.org**

Freelance Potential
80% written by nonstaff writers. Publishes 50 freelance submissions yearly; 25% by unpublished writers, 20% by authors who are new to the magazine.

Submissions
Query or send ms. Accepts hard copy and email submissions to editor@familiesonthego.org (Microsoft Word attachments). SASE. Responds only if interested.
Articles: 350–750 words. Informational articles. Topics include health and wellness, parenting, education, family relationships, home, garden, the arts, travel, and entertainment.
Depts/columns: Word lengths vary. Community news.

Sample Issue
Sample copy, free with 9x12 SASE (4 first-class stamps); also available at website.
• "Remember Single Mothers." Article explains the challenges of being a single mother, and suggests ways for individuals to help them.
• "Dangers of Cell Phones on Our Children." Article reveals the mounting evidence of health risks for children using cell and cordless telephones, and offers tips on how to protect these youngsters.
• Sample dept/column: "Health & Wellness" discusses the bites and stings of common Florida insects.

Rights and Payment
Exclusive regional rights. Written material, payment rates vary. Pays on publication. Provides 2 contributor's copies.

Editor's Comments
We target an active and affluent readership interested in up-to-date information about their community. To that end, we seek practical, not theoretical, material that will appeal to busy, on-the-go families.

Family Circle

Meredith Corporation
375 Lexington Avenue, 9th Floor
New York, NY 10017

Senior Editor: Jonna Gallo

Description and Interests
Sold at newsstands and grocery stores across the country, this women's magazine is filled with articles and departments that cover home and family life, health, style, and food. *Family Circle* looks for practical pieces that help women manage their work, families, and homes.
• **Audience:** Families
• **Frequency:** 15 times each year
• **Circulation:** 3.8 million
• **Website: www.familycircle.com**

Freelance Potential
80% written by nonstaff writers. Publishes 50 freelance submissions yearly; 50% by unpublished writers, 20% by authors who are new to the magazine. Receives 300 queries yearly.

Submissions
Query with résumé, outline, and 5 clips. No simultaneous submissions. Accepts hard copy. SASE. Responds in 6–8 weeks.
Articles: 2,000–2,500 words. Profiles of women who make a difference; reports on contemporary family issues; and real-life inspirational pieces. Also offers informational articles on health, food, decorating, fashion, and cooking.
Depts/columns: 750–1,500 words. Beauty, fitness, legal issues, parenting, and relationships.

Sample Issue
188 pages (48% advertising): 21 articles; 10 depts/columns. Sample copy, $1.99 at newsstands. Guidelines available.
• "Crash-Proof Your Teen." Article explains how parents can help keep teens safe when they first get their drivers' licenses.
• "Summer Rash Rx." Article tells how to protect your family from summer skin irritants.
• Sample dept/column: "Family Time" features short news items on family activities and products.

Rights and Payment
Rights negotiable. Written material, $1 per word. Kill fee, 10%. Pays on acceptance. Provides 1 contributor's copy.

Editor's Comments
Most of our articles are written by freelancers and we welcome new contributors. We like stories about women who make a difference in their communities.

The Family Digest

P.O. Box 40137
Fort Wayne, IN 46804

Manuscript Editor: Corine B. Erlandson

Description and Interests
Dedicated to serving the needs of Catholic families, this magazine provides articles on family life, parish life, spiritual life, church traditions, saints' lives, and prayers.
• **Audience:** Catholic families
• **Circulation:** 150,000
• **Frequency:** 6 times each year

Freelance Potential
95% written by nonstaff writers. Publishes 60 freelance submissions yearly; 30% by authors who are new to the magazine. Receives 400 unsolicited mss yearly.

Submissions
Send complete ms. Accepts hard copy and disk submissions. No simultaneous submissions; previously published material will be considered. SASE. Responds in 1–2 months.
Articles: 700–1,300 words. Informational, self-help, how-to, and inspirational articles; and personal experience pieces. Topics include family and parish life, spiritual living, church traditions, prayer, saints' lives, and seasonal material.
Depts/columns: Staff written.
Other: Humorous anecdotes, 25–100 words. Cartoons. Submit seasonal material 7 months in advance.

Sample Issue
48 pages (no advertising): 11 articles; 5 depts/columns. Sample copy, free with 6x9 SASE (2 first-class stamps). Guidelines available.
• "Mary: A Woman for Our Time." Article recounts the life of Mary, the mother of Jesus, and how her story inspires people today.
• "Loving Katy." Article examines the author's joy and her unconditional love for a grandchild who is not yet born.
• "A Young Mother's Grief." Article details a young woman's journey back to God after suffering several miscarriages.

Rights and Payment
First North American serial rights. Articles, $40–$60. Anecdotes, $25. Pays 1–2 months after acceptance. Provides 2 contributor's copies.

Editor's Comments
We are looking for upbeat articles that affirm the simple ways in which the Catholic faith is expressed in everyday life.

FamilyFun

47 Pleasant Street
Northampton, MA 01060

Features Editor

Description and Interests
Parents looking for creative, imaginative ways to keep their children active and engaged in family life subscribe to *FamilyFun*. In addition to crafts, cooking, and travel ideas, it presents features on parenting and family relationships.
• **Audience:** Parents
• **Frequency:** 10 times each year
• **Circulation:** 2 million
• **Website:** www.familyfun.com

Freelance Potential
50% written by nonstaff writers. Publishes 100+ freelance submissions yearly; 1% by unpublished writers, 2% by authors who are new to the magazine. Receives thousands of queries yearly.

Submissions
Query with clips or writing samples. Accepts hard copy. SASE. Responds 2–3 months.
Articles: 750–3,000 words. Informational and how-to articles. Topics include cooking, games, crafts, activities, educational projects, sports, holiday parties, and creative solutions to household problems.
Depts/columns: 50–1,500 words. News items about family travel, media reviews, and inspirational or humorous pieces focusing on family life.
Other: Submit seasonal material 6 months in advance.

Sample Issue
112 pages (47% advertising): 7 articles; 9 depts/columns. Sample copy, $3.95 at newsstands. Guidelines available at website.
• "Ways to Make Your Backyard More Fun." Article features ideas for outdoor fun, including plans for making a stage, an art studio, and a star chart.
• "Cousin Fun." Article explores ways to strengthen family relationships among cousins.
• Sample dept/column: "Creative Solutions" explains a reward system that builds good behavior.

Rights and Payment
All rights. Articles, $1.25 per word. Other material, payment rates vary. Pays on acceptance.

Editor's Comments
Please remember that our focus is on fun, affordable activities that are easy for families to do together. We receive many, many queries, so your idea must really stand out.

Family Magazine/ La Familia

P.O. Box 2818
Bonita Springs, FL 34133

Editor: Rick Gutierrez

Description and Interests
Family Magazine/La Familia is the only bilingual publication serving the families of southwest Florida. It offers articles of interest to residents and guests alike, and also features a calendar of events, community news items, and dining guide.
- **Audience:** Families
- **Frequency:** Monthly
- **Circulation:** 15,000
- **Website: www.familymagazine.us; www.lafamiliamagcin.us**

Freelance Potential
50% written by nonstaff writers. Of the freelance submissions published yearly, 25% are by unpublished writers, 25% are by authors who are new to the magazine.

Submissions
Query or send complete ms. Accepts hard copy and email submissions to rick@leecountyfamily.com. SASE. Response time varies.
Articles: Word lengths vary. Informational articles. Topics include parenting, family life, education, finances, recreation, health, and social responsibility.
Depts/columns: Word lengths vary. Community calendar of events, community news, dining guide, and multimedia reviews.

Sample Issue
18 pages: 4 articles; 8 depts/columns.
- "Little Ways to Become a Better Health Model." Article suggests ways for parents to model good health habits for their children, and ultimately improve their own health.
- "Infants Are Active Members of Our Community." Article describes the basic Montessori principles and primary goals of the infant environment at the Renaissance School.
- Sample dept/column: "Multimedia" offers tips and tricks for improving composition of photographs.

Rights and Payment
Rights vary. Articles, $75. Depts/columns, payment rates vary. Payment policy varies.

Editor's Comments
We tend to be flexible with writers, and we offer no formal writers' guidelines. Our goal is to provide our English- and Spanish-speaking readership with the information they need to nurture and improve family life.

Family Works Magazine

4 Joseph Court
San Rafael, CA 94903

Editor: Lew Tremaine

Description and Interests
Subtitled "Strengthening Families . . . For a Lifetime," this publication includes regional information of specific interest to San Francisco area families, while also featuring helpful articles on education, health, and general parenting topics.
- **Audience:** Parents, caregivers, and professionals
- **Frequency:** Monthly
- **Circulation:** 30,000
- **Website: www.familyworks.org**

Freelance Potential
80% written by nonstaff writers. Publishes 75 freelance submissions yearly; 25% by unpublished writers, 25% by authors who are new to the magazine. Receives 100+ unsolicited mss yearly.

Submissions
Send complete ms. Accepts hard copy, disk submissions, and email submissions to familynews@ familyworks.org. Availability of artwork improves chance of acceptance. SASE. Responds in 1 month.
Articles: 1,000 words. Informational articles; profiles; and interviews. Topics include parenting, family issues, recreation, education, finance, crafts, hobbies, sports, health, fitness, nature, and the environment.
Depts/columns: Word lengths vary. Community news, reviews, and recipes.
Artwork: B/W and color prints.

Sample Issue
24 pages (46% advertising): 7 articles; 2 depts/ columns. Sample copy, free. Guidelines available.
- "Parenting with Emotional Intelligence." Article offers advice about ways to teach emotional intelligence to children as part of everyday life.
- "All Mothers Work." Personal experience piece reveals the realities of maternity leave.
- "The Secret to 'Likeability.'" Article analyzes the qualities of likeable people and tells why likeability is important in work and in life.

Rights and Payment
One-time rights. No payment. Provides 3 contributor's copies.

Editor's Comments
We continue to look for articles that discuss the complicated issues associated with adolescence and the teenage years. We're willing to work with both experienced and new writers.

Fandangle Magazine

14 Schult Street
Keene, NH 03431

Editor: Nancy A. Cavanaugh

Description and Interests
Fandangle Magazine is a secular, free online publication that features nonfiction, short stories, poetry, crafts, and learning activities. It is suitable for use in classrooms and homeschool settings.
• **Audience:** 6–10 years
• **Frequency:** Monthly
• **Hits per month:** 2,000
• **Website:** www.fandanglemagazine.com

Freelance Potential
98% written by nonstaff writers. Publishes 240 freelance submissions yearly; 70% by unpublished writers, 85% by authors who are new to the magazine.

Submissions
Query with synopsis, word count, and description of writing experience. Accepts hard copy and email queries to submissions@fandanglemagazine.com. SASE. Response time varies.
Articles: To 700 words. Informational articles. Topics include history, nature, animals and pets, the environment, science, and technology.
Fiction: To 700 words. Genres include fantasy, folktales, and folklore. Also offers stories about animals.
Other: Poetry, to 250 words. Filler, to 250 words. Crafts, to 700 words.

Sample Issue
26 pages (no advertising): 6 articles; 3 stories; 7 poems; 8 activities; 4 book reviews. Guidelines available at website.
• "It's a Grand Ole Flag." Article offers a brief history of the American flag.
• "Sybil Ludington—War Hero." Article reveals the lesser-known story of the teenage Revolutionary War hero who alerted colonists in a late-night ride.
• "The Mouse Catcher." Story tells of a pet snake who rids a kitchen of a mouse and thus becomes a welcome weekend guest.

Rights and Payment
First rights. No payment.

Editor's Comments
We seek submissions of fiction and nonfiction items that teach lessons in an entertaining way so that children don't feel as if they are being taught. We look forward to working with new and developing writers, and offer many resources to support them. Submissions without a proper query letter will be discarded.

Faze

4936 Yonge Street, Suite 2400
Toronto, Ontario M2N 6S3
Canada

Editorial Director: Denise Wild

Description and Interests
Described as "Canada's Teen Read," *Faze* mixes articles on popular culture with substantive, fact-filled pieces about health, social issues, and contemporary topics.
• **Audience:** 13–18 years
• **Frequency:** 5 times each year
• **Circulation:** 150,000
• **Website:** www.faze.ca

Freelance Potential
75% written by nonstaff writers. Publishes 10 freelance submissions yearly; 10% by unpublished writers, 40% by authors who are new to the magazine. Receives 100 queries yearly.

Submissions
Query. Accepts email queries to editor@fazeteen.com. Response time varies.
Articles: Word lengths vary. Informational and factual articles; profiles; interviews; and personal experience pieces. Topics include current affairs, real-life and social issues, famous people, entertainment, science, travel, business, technology, and health.
Depts/columns: Word lengths vary. Short profiles; career descriptions; new products.

Sample Issue
66 pages (30% advertising): 12 articles; 12 depts/columns. Sample copy, $3.50 Canadian. Guidelines available at website.
• "Rock Star." Article interviews Amy Lee of Evanescence about her group, her life, and breaking free.
• "Sex Gets Serious." Article warns about the dangers of irresponsible sex and provides facts about sexually transmitted diseases.
• Sample dept/column: "Headlines" features short, off-beat, and unusual news items of interest to teens.

Rights and Payment
All rights. Written material, $50–$150. Payment policy varies. Provides 1 contributor's copy.

Editor's Comments
We are currently trying to enhance our online presence. Because we want material that appeals to teens, we tend to favor writers who are younger, such as college journalism majors. The editorial content is determined by a teen panel. We would love to receive more articles about travel and some humor pieces. Right now, we are inundated with submissions about music.

Fertility Today

P.O. Box 117
Laurel, MD 20725

Editor: Diana Broomfield, M.D.

Description and Interests
Fertility Today provides expert medical opinions and personal experience pieces on issues surrounding infertility, including treatment, nutrition, emotional health, and long-awaited pregnancy.
- **Audience:** Adults
- **Frequency:** Quarterly
- **Circulation:** 150,000
- **Website: www.fertilitytoday.org**

Freelance Potential
75% written by nonstaff writers. Publishes 150 freelance submissions yearly; 15% by authors who are new to the magazine, 90% by experts. Receives 144 queries yearly.

Submissions
Query. Accepts email queries to dbroomfield@fertilitytoday.org. Responds in 2 months.
Articles: 1,800 words. Informational articles; opinion pieces; profiles; and interviews. Topics include fertility issues and treatments, and male and female reproductive health issues.
Depts/columns: 1,800 words. Fertility preservation, tubal infertility, reproductive genetics, contraception, alternative medicine, assistive reproductive technology, recurrent pregnancy loss, disease and fertility, law and ethics, nutrition, and fertility-related book reviews.

Sample Issue
96 pages (25% advertising): 1 article; 30 depts/columns. Sample copy, $6.95. Guidelines and editorial calendar available at website.
- "A Woman on a Crusade." Article profiles soap opera actress Amy Gibson, who founded a company that makes high-end wigs for cancer survivors.
- Sample dept/column: "Complementary and Alternative Medicine" discusses the use of Chinese acupuncture as a treatment for infertility.
- Sample dept/column: "Cancer and Fertility" looks at breast cancer risk factors, detection, and treatments.

Rights and Payment
All rights. Written material, $.50 per word. Kill fee, $100. Pays on acceptance. Provides 3 author's copies.

Editor's Comments
New writers have the best chance of being published if they submit a cover story or a personal essay to our "My Story" column. Other departments are written primarily by fertility specialists.

FitPregnancy

21100 Erwin Street
Woodland Hills, CA 91367

Executive Editor: Sharon Cohen

Description and Interests
Prenatal fitness and nutrition are covered in this magazine, as well as psychological and health issues related to pregnancy. It also addresses postpartum topics and offers tips for parenting children up to the age of two.
- **Audience:** Adults
- **Frequency:** 6 times each year
- **Circulation:** 500,000
- **Website: www.fitpregnancy.com**

Freelance Potential
40% written by nonstaff writers. Publishes 50 freelance submissions yearly; 30% by authors who are new to the magazine. Receives 360 queries yearly.

Submissions
Query with clips. Prefers email queries to scohen@fitpregnancy.com. Responds in 1 month.
Articles: 1,200–2,400 words. Informational articles and personal experience pieces. Topics include health, fitness, family issues, psychology, postpartum issues, and breastfeeding.
Fiction: Word lengths vary. Humorous stories.
Depts/columns: 600 words. Fatherhood, family issues, infant health, labor and delivery, and nutrition. Also publishes short personal essays.

Sample Issue
128 pages (42% advertising): 5 articles; 12 depts/columns. Sample copy, $4.95 at newsstands. Guidelines available.
- "What's Up with Your Post-Baby Body?" Article addresses seven common new-mom complaints and includes an ab workout.
- "Barriers to Breastfeeding." Article analyzes the cultural and lifestyle obstacles that prevent some women from breastfeeding.
- Sample dept/column: "Time Out" features a personal essay by a new mom.

Rights and Payment
Rights vary. Written material, payment rates vary. Pays on publication. Provides 2 contributor's copies.

Editor's Comments
Queries should be no more than one page in length. Tell us why your idea is important to our readers. Include information about experts you might interview and any expertise you might have in this area. Be specific about whether you are submitting an idea for a feature or a column.

FLW Outdoors

30 Gamble Lane
Benton, KY 42054

Managing Editor: Will Brantley

Description and Interests
Published by one of the world's largest fishing tournament organizations, this magazine targets anglers of all ages. It focuses on bass, walleye, redfish, kingfish, and striper fishing, and includes a special section just for kids.
- **Audience:** Adults; children, 5–12 years
- **Frequency:** 8 times each year
- **Circulation:** 50,000
- **Website: www.flwoutdoors.com**

Freelance Potential
50% written by nonstaff writers. Of the freelance submissions published yearly, 20% are by authors who are new to the magazine. Receives 300 queries each year.

Submissions
Query or submit writing sample. Accepts email submissions to wbrantley@flwoutdoors.com. Responds in 1 week.
Articles: 200 words. Factual, informational, and how-to articles; humor; and profiles. Topics include nature, the environment, and fishing.
Fiction: To 500 words. Genres include adventure fiction and nature stories.
Depts/columns: Word lengths vary. Tournaments, boat technology, fishing destinations, product reviews, and environmental issues.
Other: Puzzles.

Sample Issue
88 pages: 5 articles; 15 depts/columns; 1 special section for kids. Sample copy, $3.95 at newsstands. Guidelines available.
- "Deep Cranking with David Wright." Article profiles a man who has an obsession with the bass fishing technique of deep cranking.
- "Lure Profile." Article talks about circle hooks and slip-bogger rigs.
- Sample dept/column: "Species Profile" provides information for kids about bullheads.

Rights and Payment
First North American serial rights. Written material, $200–$500. Payment policy varies.

Editor's Comments
We're always interested in fishing adventure stories for kids and short, simple articles designed for readers ages five through twelve.

Focus on the Family Clubhouse

8605 Explorer Drive
Colorado Springs, CO 80902

Associate Editor: Suzanne Hadley

Description and Interests
Clubhouse, the middle-grade magazine in Focus on the Family's line of Christian publications, imparts value lessons through stories, factual articles, personal anecdotes, puzzles, and games.
- **Audience:** 8–12 years
- **Frequency:** Monthly
- **Circulation:** 90,000
- **Website: www.clubhousemagazine.com**

Freelance Potential
20% written by nonstaff writers. Publishes 12–15 freelance submissions yearly; 50% by unpublished writers, 5% by authors who are new to the magazine. Receives 1,140 unsolicited mss yearly.

Submissions
Send complete ms. Accepts hard copy. SASE. Responds in 4–6 weeks.
Articles: 800–1,000 words. Informational, how-to, and factual articles; interviews; personal experience pieces; and humor. Topics include sports, nature, travel, history, fantasy, religion, current events, and multicultural issues.
Fiction: 500–1,500 words. Genres include historical, contemporary, and religious fiction; parables; humor; and mystery.
Depts/columns: Word lengths vary. Personal anecdotes; archaeology and biblical history; and humor.
Other: Activities and comic strips. Submit Christian holiday material 7 months in advance.

Sample Issue
22 pages (5% advertising): 2 articles; 3 stories; 7 depts/columns. Sample copy, $1.50 with 9x12 SASE (2 first-class stamps). Guidelines available.
- "Jasmine's Big Problem." Story describes how a Filipino-American girl learns to appreciate her close-knit extended family.
- Sample dept/column: "Truth Seeker: The Greatest Book" discusses the transcription and accuracy of the Bible.

Rights and Payment
First rights. Written material, to $150. Pays on acceptance. Provides 5 contributor's copies.

Editor's Comments
We encourage submissions to our new "Truth Seeker" column, which helps kids to understand why they can rely on the Bible.

Focus on the Family Clubhouse Jr.

8605 Explorer Drive
Colorado Springs, CO 80902

Associate Editor: Suzanne Hadley

Description and Interests
Clubhouse Jr. uses stories, articles, and activities to teach young children Judeo-Christian values.
- **Audience:** 4–8 years
- **Frequency:** Monthly
- **Circulation:** 65,000
- **Website:** www.clubhousemagazine.com

Freelance Potential
20% written by nonstaff writers. Publishes 6–12 freelance submissions yearly; 1% by unpublished writers, 5% by authors who are new to the magazine. Receives 720 unsolicited mss yearly.

Submissions
Send complete ms. Accepts hard copy. No simultaneous submissions. SASE. Responds in 4–6 weeks.
Articles: To 600 words. Informational articles. Topics include Christian entertainment, recreation, fitness, health, nature, the environment, hobbies, and multicultural issues.
Fiction: 250–1,000 words. Genres include Bible stories; humor; folktales; and religious, contemporary, and historical fiction.
Depts/columns: Word lengths vary. Personal anecdotes; crafts and activities; comic strips; and humor.
Other: Poetry with biblical themes. Submit seasonal material 6 months in advance.

Sample Issue
22 pages (no advertising): 2 articles; 2 stories; 6 depts/columns. Sample copy, $1.50 with 9x12 SASE (2 first-class stamps). Guidelines available.
- "P.R.A.Y." Article by Christian entertainment troupe Go Fish teaches children to praise God, repent, ask God for things, and yield to God.
- "Penelope Pepper, Put on Your Patient Pants!" Story shows how a girl learns to turn a bad day into a good one.
- Sample dept/column: "You Said It" features drawings and descriptions of readers' favorite outdoor places and activities.

Rights and Payment
First North American serial rights. Written material, to $150. Pays on acceptance. Provides 2 author's copies.

Editor's Comments
Submissions should be written for or from a child's perspective, and should implicitly impart biblical lessons.

Fort Myers & SW Florida Magazine

15880 Summerlin Road, Suite 189
Fort Myers, FL 33908

Publisher: Andrew Elias

Description and Interests
This tabloid covers regional arts, living, and cultural topics for southwest Florida.
- **Audience:** Adults
- **Frequency:** 6 times each year
- **Circulation:** 20,000
- **Website:** www.ftmyersmagazine.com

Freelance Potential
90% written by nonstaff writers. Publishes 15–30 freelance submissions yearly; 30% by unpublished writers, 60% by authors who are new to the magazine. Receives 2,400–3,000 queries and unsolicited mss each year.

Submissions
Query or send complete ms. Accepts hard copy, Macintosh disk submissions, and email submissions to ftmyers@optonline.net. SASE. Responds in 1–6 weeks.
Articles: 500–2,000 words. Informational articles; profiles; interviews; reviews; and local news. Topics include the arts, media, entertainment, travel, computers, crafts, current events, health and fitness, history, popular culture, recreation, social and environmental issues, and parenting.
Depts/columns: Word lengths vary. Sports, recreation, and book reviews.
Artwork: JPG, TIFF, or PDF images.

Sample Issue
30 pages (40% advertising): 2 articles; 2 reviews; 1 dept/column; 1 calendar. Sample copy, $3 with 9x12 SASE ($.77 postage). Guidelines and editorial calendar available at website.
- "Finding the Yoga for You." Article summarizes the various types of yoga offered in classes.
- "Paradise at the End of the Earth." Article describes visiting beautiful Los Cabos in Mexico.
- "Tomorrow's Techno-Terrorism." Article reviews *Breakpoint*, by Richard Clarke.

Rights and Payment
One-time rights. Pays 30 days from publication. Written material, $.10 per word. Provides 2 contributor's copies.

Editor's Comments
We seek pieces on environmental, cultural, and historical issues and events that are important to our active, well-educated, successful, and creative readers, who are 20 to 75 years old.

Fort Worth Child

Lauren Publications
4275 Kellway Circle, Suite 146
Addison, TX 75001

Editorial Director: Shelley Hawes Pate

Description and Interests
This self-described "ultimate city guide for parents" covers family events and activities in the greater Fort Worth area, including Arlington and the mid-cities. It also includes articles on parenting and childhood.
• **Audience:** Parents
• **Frequency:** Monthly
• **Circulation:** 40,000
• **Website:** www.fortworthchild.com

Freelance Potential
25% written by nonstaff writers. Publishes 12–15 freelance submissions yearly; 20% by authors who are new to the magazine. Receives 240 queries yearly.

Submissions
Query with résumé. Accepts hard copy, email queries to editorial@dallaschild.com, and simultaneous submissions if identified. SASE. Response time varies.
Articles: 1,000–2,500 words. Informational, self-help, and how-to articles; humor; profiles; and personal experience pieces. Topics include parenting, education, health, nutrition, fitness, travel, recreation, crafts, hobbies, and regional news.
Depts/columns: 800 words. Family activities; health and safety; legislation and advocacy; news and trends; education and development; humor; and reviews.

Sample Issue
62 pages (14% advertising): 5 articles; 14 depts/columns. Sample copy, free with 9x12 SASE. Guidelines available at website.
• "The Dad Next Door." Article profiles a local father who is also a restaurateur, author, TV personality, and ADHD advocate.
• "Video Game Addiction." Article discusses how some kids become so obsessed with online activities that their grades drop and their social lives falter.
• Sample dept/column: "BackTalk" is a humorous look at engaging fathers in diaper-changing.

Rights and Payment
First rights. Written material, payment rates vary. Pays on publication. Provides contributor's copies upon request.

Editor's Comments
We strive to include fresh voices, ideas, and perspectives in our magazine. We emphasize stories with a local focus and prefer to work with writers from the Metroplex area.

Fostering Families Today

541 East Garden Drive, Unit N
Windsor, CO 80550

Editor: Richard Fischer

Description and Interests
This is a resource magazine for adoptive and fostering families as well as child-welfare professionals. Articles cover the emotional, legal, and health aspects of foster-parenting.
• **Audience:** Parents
• **Frequency:** 6 times each year
• **Circulation:** 26,000
• **Website:** www.fosteringfamiliestoday.com

Freelance Potential
80% written by nonstaff writers. Publishes 40 freelance submissions yearly; 20% by unpublished writers, 50% by authors who are new to the magazine. Receives 80 unsolicited mss yearly.

Submissions
Send complete ms. Accepts hard copy, IBM disk submissions, and email submissions to louis@adoptinfo.net. SASE. Response time varies.
Articles: 500–1,200 words. Informational and how-to articles; profiles; and personal experience pieces. Topics include adoption, foster parenting, child development, research, health, education, and legal issues.
Depts/columns: Word lengths vary. News, opinion pieces, advice, profiles, legislation, book reviews, advocacy.
Other: Poetry.

Sample Issue
62 pages (no advertising): 14 articles; 8 depts/columns. Guidelines available.
• "Don't Be Left in the Waiting Room." Article stresses the importance of including foster parents in their children's therapy sessions.
• "Attachment: It Takes Two, At Least." Article describes why some children have trouble bonding to their new families, and explores ways to avoid this problem.
• Sample dept/column: "Fostering Reading" looks at ways to encourage boys to read, and includes a selection of books known for their boy-appeal.

Rights and Payment
One-time rights. No payment. Provides 2 contributor's copies and a 1-year subscription.

Editor's Comments
We would like to see more articles that offer foster-parenting tips, as well as how-to articles about the challenges of parenting difficult children.

The Friend

The Church of Jesus Christ of Latter-day Saints
50 East North Temple, 24th Floor
Salt Lake City, UT 84150

Managing Editor: Vivian Paulsen

Description and Interests
Published by the Mormon church for children under the age of twelve, *The Friend* features stories, articles, poetry, and comics that help readers apply the principles of the Gospel to their everyday lives.
- **Audience:** 3–11 years
- **Frequency:** Monthly
- **Circulation:** 252,000
- **Website:** www.lds.org

Freelance Potential
60% written by nonstaff writers.

Submissions
Send complete ms. Accepts hard copy. SASE. Responds in 2 months.
Articles: To 1,200 words. Informational and factual articles; personal experience pieces; profiles; and true stories. Topics include spirituality, the Mormon church, personal faith, and conflict resolution.
Depts/columns: Word lengths vary. Profiles of children from different countries.
Other: Poetry, word lengths vary. Puzzles, activities, crafts, and cartoons. Submit seasonal material 8 months in advance

Sample Issue
50 pages (no advertising): 4 articles; 7 true stories; 4 depts/columns; 1 poem; 5 activities; 2 comics. Sample copy, $1.50 with 9x12 SASE (4 first-class stamps). Guidelines available.
- "Sustaining Bishop Sheets." True story shows how a girl learns from the example of her church's new bishop.
- "The Creation." Article and activity emphasize that we should show reverence and gratitude for God's creation.
- "Jacob's Testimony." True story features a boy who is preparing for baptism.

Rights and Payment
First rights. Written material, $100–$250. Poetry, $30. Activities, $20. Pays on acceptance. Provides 2 contributor's copies.

Editor's Comments
Stories must be based on true incidents. Names, dialogue, and details may be fictionalized to shape the story, but the main events must be factual. Stories should feature real children discovering or applying Gospel truths in overcoming real-life temptations and conflicts. Follow the rule of "show, don't tell."

Fuel

401 Richmond Street West, Suite 245
Toronto, Ontario M5V 1X3
Canada

Editorial Assistant: Nick Aveling

Description and Interests
Created specifically for Canada's teens, *Fuel* focuses on music, technology, computers, fashion, and cars. It also presents discussions of relationships and social and personal issues in a way that appeals to young adults. Published by Youth Culture Group, it is distributed through schools.
- **Audience:** 14–18 years
- **Frequency:** Monthly
- **Circulation:** 100,000
- **Website:** www.fuelpowered.com

Freelance Potential
75% written by nonstaff writers. Publishes 10 freelance submissions yearly; 100% by authors who are new to the magazine. Receives 55 queries yearly.

Submissions
Query. Accepts hard copy and email queries to nick@youthculture.com. SAE/IRC. Response time varies.
Articles: 1,200–2,000 words. Informational and how-to articles; profiles; interviews; personal experience pieces; and reviews. Topics include health and fitness, college and career, social and personal issues, gaming, sports, and technology.
Depts/columns: Word lengths vary. Film, music, health, cars, relationships, and fashion.

Sample Issue
22 pages: 5 articles; 5 depts/columns. Sample copy available at website. Guidelines available.
- "Work for It." Article suggests ways to find the perfect summer job, including tips on networking, interviewing, and volunteering to build experience.
- "We Want Your Bra!" Article interviews members of a Canadian band that has an unusual name.
- "Indie Inspiration." Article reports on the kind of independent music that can be found on college radio stations.

Rights and Payment
Rights vary. Written material, payment rates vary. Pays on publication.

Editor's Comments
Our readers are teens with a keen awareness of the most current trends in popular culture—so you must understand their world to write for us. Well-written, innovative pieces on music, film, social issues, and relationships will be considered.

Fun For Kidz

P.O. Box 227
Bluffton, OH 48517-0227

Editor: Marilyn Edwards

Description and Interests
This activity magazine is created for boys and girls. It looks for articles, poems, games, jokes, and activities that encourage children to think and to read.
- **Audience:** 5–14 years
- **Frequency:** 6 times each year
- **Circulation:** 7,000
- **Website:** www.funforkidz.com

Freelance Potential
90% written by nonstaff writers. Publishes 100–150 freelance submissions yearly; 60% by unpublished writers, 40% by authors who are new to the magazine. Receives 2,000–3,000 unsolicited mss yearly.

Submissions
Send complete ms. Accepts hard copy and simultaneous submissions if identified. Availability of artwork improves chance of acceptance. SASE. Responds in 4–6 weeks.
Articles: 500 words. Informational and how-to articles. Topics include nature, animals, pets, careers, cooking, and sports.
Fiction: 500 words. Animal stories, humorous fiction, and adventure.
Depts/columns: Word lengths vary. Puzzles, science, and collecting.
Artwork: B/W and color prints or transparencies. Line art.
Other: Activities, filler, games, jokes, and puzzles. Submit seasonal material 6–12 months in advance.

Sample Issue
50 pages (no advertising): 1 article; 3 jokes; 1 story; 3 cartoons; 2 activities; 2 poems; 8 puzzles; 5 depts/columns. Sample copy, $6. Guidelines and theme list available.
- "Loads of Laughs: Pantomime." Article explains what pantomime is and how it is done.
- Sample dept/column: "Science" provides a simple science experiment that can be done with household items.

Rights and Payment
First or reprint rights. Written material, $.05 per word. Artwork, payment rates vary. Pays on publication. Provides 1 contributor's copy.

Editor's Comments
We need more submissions of nonfiction stories accompanied by photographic images.

Games

6198 Butler Pike, Suite 200
Blue Bell, PA 19422-2600

Editor-in-Chief: R. Wayne Schmittberger

Description and Interests
This unusual magazine caters to young adults and adults who enjoy the mental challenges of all styles of games, including visual and verbal puzzles, and quizzes. It also includes game reviews and contests.
- **Audience:** YA–Adult
- **Frequency:** 10 times each year
- **Circulation:** 75,000
- **Website:** www.gamesmagazine-online.com

Freelance Potential
86% written by nonstaff writers. Publishes 200+ freelance submissions yearly; 10% by unpublished writers, 20% by authors who are new to the magazine. Receives 960 queries and unsolicited mss each year.

Submissions
Query with outline for articles. Send complete ms for longer pieces. Accepts hard copy. SASE. Responds in 6–8 weeks.
Articles: 1,500–3,000 words. Informational articles; profiles; and humor. Topics include game-related events and people, wordplay, and human ingenuity. Game reviews by assignment only.
Depts/columns: Staff written, except for "Gamebits."
Other: Visual and verbal puzzles, quizzes, contests, two-play games, and adventures.

Sample Issue
82 pages (8% advertising): 1 article; 5 depts/columns; 25 puzzles and games. Sample copy, $4.50 with 9x12 SASE ($1.24 postage). Guidelines available.
- "The Box Wizard." Article looks at the expert craftsmanship and brilliant design of Kagen Schaefer's puzzle boxes.
- "Lay On!" Article examines the Belegrath Medieval Combat Society and the sport of medieval-style fighting with foam weapons.

Rights and Payment
All North American serial rights. Articles, $500–$1,200. "Gamebits," $100–$250. Pays on publication. Provides 1 contributor's copy.

Editor's Comments
Our readers enjoy exercising their minds in new and playful ways. Feature articles can cover almost any subject—game- or puzzle-related events, people, mysteries, wordplay, and humor.

Genesee Valley Parent

GeoParent

1 Grove Street, Suite 204
Pittsford, NY 14534

Managing Editor: Margo Perine

Description and Interests
Filled with the latest news and resources of interest to parents in the greater Rochester, New York, area, *Genesee Valley Parent* has been distributed free for more than 14 years. It includes a calendar that lists family activities and support group meetings, as well as party planning and camp guides.
- **Audience:** Parents
- **Frequency:** Monthly
- **Circulation:** 37,000
- **Website:** www.gvparent.com

Freelance Potential
75% written by nonstaff writers. Publishes 50 free-lance submissions yearly; 5% by authors who are new to the magazine. Receives 240 queries yearly.

Submissions
Query with clips or writing samples. Accepts hard copy and simultaneous submissions if identified. SASE. Responds in 1–3 months.
Articles: 700–1,200 words. Informational and how-to articles; personal experience pieces; interviews; reviews; and humor. Topics include regional family events and concerns, special and gifted education, social issues, family problems, health and fitness, and parenting issues.
Depts/columns: 500–600 words. Family health, teen issues, toddler issues, and short news items.
Other: Submit seasonal material 4 months in advance.

Sample Issue
46 pages (50% advertising): 4 articles; 7 depts/columns; 2 calendars. Guidelines and editorial calendar available.
- "Choosing the Best Camp for Your Child." Article offers expert advice on selecting a high-quality summer program for your child.
- "The Angry Child: At School and Home." Article discusses how to deal with behavior problems.
- Sample dept/column: "Short Takes" features short regional news items of interest to families.

Rights and Payment
Second rights. Articles, $30–$45. Depts/columns, $25–$30. Pays on publication. Provides 1 tearsheet.

Editor's Comments
Accuracy and thorough research are a must if you wish to write for us.

7944 East Beck Lane
Scottsdale, AZ 85260

Editor: Betsy Bailey & Nancy Price

Description and Interests
This online magazine tackles a myriad of issues of concern to parents and families—everything from nutrition and child development to family travel and how to talk to kids about current events. Catering to families with children of all ages, it offers interactive tools and practical resources, as well as accurate, informative articles.
- **Audience:** Parents
- **Frequency:** Weekly
- **Hits per month:** Unavailable
- **Website:** www.geoparent.com

Freelance Potential
90% written by nonstaff writers. Publishes 50 free-lance submissions yearly. Receives 50 queries and unsolicited mss yearly.

Submissions
Prefers query. Will accept complete ms. Accepts hard copy, email submissions to content@coincide.com, and submissions through website. SASE. Response time varies.
Articles: 500–2,500 words. Informational articles and advice. Topics include parenting, child development, family issues, pregnancy and childbirth, infancy, child care, nutrition, health, education, and gifted and special education.
Depts/columns: Word lengths vary. Parenting advice.

Sample Issue
Sample copy and guidelines available at website.
- "Where Did All the Bunnies Go?" Article describes the difficulties that occur when pets, such as bunnies and chicks at Easter, are an impulse buy rather than an educated decision.
- "Toddlers and Meal Time." Article offers tips for keeping toddlers occupied while you fix dinner.
- "Family Cruise Proves to Be All Wet." Article offers first-hand advice for families who are planning to take a cruise.

Rights and Payment
Rights vary. Written material, $25–$50; $10 for reprints. Pays on publication.

Editor's Comments
If you're interested in writing for us, keep in mind that we're looking for well-researched articles based on interviews with experts. The writing style should be personal and friendly.

Georgia Family Magazine

523 Sioux Drive
Macon, GA 31210

Publisher: Olya Fessard

Description and Interests
Families in Georgia read this magazine for well-written and insightful articles on educational issues and health. Also featured is a monthly regional arts and events calendar.
- **Audience:** Families
- **Frequency:** Monthly
- **Circulation:** 20,000
- **Website:** www.georgiafamily.com

Freelance Potential
60% written by nonstaff writers. Publishes 100–125 freelance submissions yearly.

Submissions
Send complete ms. Accepts email submissions to publisher@georgiafamily.com. Response time varies.
Articles: Word lengths vary. Informational articles. Topics include parenting, family issues, education, gifted and special education, health, and fitness.
Depts/columns: Word lengths vary. Financial and money matters, science and technology, travel, the arts, etiquette, home and garden, media and new product reviews.

Sample Issue
64 pages: 4 articles; 14 depts/columns.
- "Answers to Tough Baby Product Questions." Article uses a Q&A format to highlight important features to look for when shopping for baby items.
- "Introducing Baby—Preventing Sibling Rivalry." Article offers advice on how to welcome new babies into the family so that siblings don't feel threatened.
- Sample dept/column: "Money Matters" discusses the statute of limitations on debts, and offers suggestions for dealing with debt collectors.

Rights and Payment
One-time, reprint, and electronic rights. Written material, payment rates vary. Payment policy varies.

Editor's Comments
We welcome submissions from new writers. Since most topics have been covered many times before, we are seeking fresh voices and new approaches. Our particular areas of interest at this time include special education, finances, decorating, children's or women's health, and fun activities for families. We have no need for any more articles on self-esteem or behavioral issues (unless your article features a brand-new slant), or for craft projects.

Gifted Education Press Quarterly

10201 Yuma Court
P.O. Box 1586
Manassas, VA 20109

Editor & Publisher: Maurice D. Fisher

Description and Interests
For more than 20 years, this newsletter—now also available online—has been publishing scholarly articles and personal essays about the education of gifted children, with a special emphasis on minority students.
- **Audience:** Educators, administrators, and parents
- **Frequency:** Quarterly
- **Circulation:** 13,000
- **Website:** www.giftedpress.com

Freelance Potential
90% written by nonstaff writers. Publishes 15 freelance submissions yearly; 20% by unpublished writers, 80% by authors who are new to the magazine. Receives 30 queries yearly.

Submissions
Query. Accepts hard copy. SASE. Responds in 2 weeks.
Articles: 3,000–5,000 words. Informational and how-to articles; personal experience pieces; profiles; and interviews. Topics include gifted education, homeschooling, multiple intelligence, parent advocates, social issues, science, history, the environment, and popular culture.

Sample Issue
16 pages (no advertising): 5 articles. Sample copy, $4 with 9x12 SASE.
- "Gifted English Language Learners." Article discusses strategies for teaching gifted students whose primary language is not English.
- "A Thinking Strategy for Tomorrow's Gifted Leaders: Six Thinking Hats." Article details a curriculum designed to improve reading comprehension, decision-making, and problem-solving.
- "Gifted Students Left Behind: A Student's Perspective." Article posits that the No Child Left Behind Act unfairly leaves behind more talented students because it focuses on proficiency levels as opposed to excellence.

Rights and Payment
All rights. No payment. Provides 5 author's copies.

Editor's Comments
We currently need articles on teaching gifted children about literature, and we're always interested in material about gifted inner-city students. As our core readership of educators and parents continues to grow, we look forward to another decade of publishing articles by knowledgeable and creative authors.

Girls' Life

4529 Harford Road
Baltimore, MD 21214

Associate Editor: Mandy Forr

Description and Interests

This is a lively read for pre-teen and early-teen girls that focuses on their interests, from fashion to friendship, beauty to boys.
- **Audience:** 10–14 years
- **Frequency:** 6 times each year
- **Circulation:** 400,000
- **Website:** www.girlslife.com

Freelance Potential

50% written by nonstaff writers. Publishes 100+ freelance submissions yearly; 10% by unpublished writers, 20% by authors who are new to the magazine. Receives 1,000 queries yearly.

Submissions

Query with outline. Accepts hard copy and email queries to mandy@girlslife.com. SASE. Responds in 3 months.
Articles: 1,200–2,500 words. Informational, service-oriented articles. Topics include self-esteem, health, friendship, relationships, sibling rivalry, school issues, facing challenges, and setting goals.
Fiction: 2,000–2,500 words. Stories about girls.
Depts/columns: 300–800 words. Celebrity spotlights; profiles of real girls; advice about friendship, beauty, and dating; fashion trends; decorating tips; cooking; crafts; and media reviews.
Other: Quizzes; fashion spreads.

Sample Issue

80 pages (30% advertising): 8 articles; 17 depts/columns; 1 story; 1 quiz. Sample copy, $5. Guidelines and editorial calendar available at website.
- "Who Says Three's a Crowd?" Article profiles the multimedia group, The Cheetah Girls.
- "The GL Guide to Getting the Guy of Your Dreams." Article provides step-by-step instructions for landing a crush.
- Sample dept/column: "GL Guys: Forget Him . . . Fast!" tells how to get over a breakup quickly.

Rights and Payment

All or first rights. Written material, payment rates vary. Pays on publication. Provides 1 contributor's copy.

Editor's Comments

We would like to receive more pitches pertaining to friendship. If material accompanied by an SASE is not returned in due time, it has been placed in a file for possible future consideration.

Green Teacher

95 Robert Street
Toronto, Ontario M5S 2K5
Canada

Co-Editor: Tim Grant

Description and Interests

Subtitled "Education for Planet Earth," this magazine is designed to help teachers foster environmental and global awareness among students in kindergarten through twelfth grade.
- **Audience:** Teachers, grades K–12
- **Frequency:** Quarterly
- **Circulation:** 7,500
- **Website:** www.greenteacher.com

Freelance Potential

60% written by nonstaff writers. Publishes 30 freelance submissions yearly; 80% by unpublished writers. Receives 120 unsolicited mss each year.

Submissions

Prefers query with summary or outline. Accepts hard copy, disk submissions with hard copy, fax submissions to 416-925-3474, and email to tim@greenteacher.com. Availability of artwork improves chance of acceptance. SAE/IRC. Responds in 2 months.
Articles: 1,500–3,000 words. Informational and how-to articles. Topics include the environment, science, education, and mathematics.
Depts/columns: Word lengths vary. Resources, reviews, and announcements.
Artwork: B/W or color prints or transparencies. Line art.
Other: Submit material for Earth Day 6 months in advance.

Sample Issue

48 pages (12% advertising): 7 articles; 2 depts/columns. Sample copy, $7. Writer's guidelines available at website.
- "The Start of Something Big: Environmental Education in China." Article examines the challenges that environmental educators face in China as the country's economy grows.
- "Getting Fresh with Farm-to-School Programs." Article explores how connections between farms and schools lead to healthier food choices for schoolchildren.

Rights and Payment

Rights negotiable. No payment. Provides 5 contributor's copies and a free subscription.

Editor's Comments

We publish everything from practical activities for the classroom, to discussions of the role of environmental education in the curriculum. Both teachers and freelancers write for us.

Grit

1503 SW 42nd Street
Topeka, KS 66609-1265

Editor-in-Chief: K. C. Compton

Description and Interests
Celebrating country and rural lifestyles, *Grit* presents articles the whole family can enjoy. Practical pieces about gardening and farming appear along with personal experiences and observations that promote the importance of community.
- **Audience:** Families
- **Frequency:** 6 times each year
- **Circulation:** 150,000
- **Website:** www.grit.com

Freelance Potential
90% written by nonstaff writers. Publishes 80–90 freelance submissions yearly; 50% by unpublished writers, 50% by authors who are new to the magazine. Receives 2,400 queries yearly.

Submissions
Query. No unsolicited mss. Prefers email queries to grit@grit.com (include "Query" in subject line). Accepts hard copy. SASE. Response time varies.
Articles: 800–1,500 words. Factual and how-to articles; profiles; and personal experience pieces. Topics include American history, family lifestyles, parenting, pets, crafts, community involvement, and antiques.
Depts/columns: 500–1,500 words. Topics include farm economics, comfort food, technology, equipment, and medical advice.
Artwork: Color slides. B/W prints for nostalgia pieces.

Sample Issue
96 pages (50% advertising): 4 articles; 11 depts/columns. Sample copy, $4. Guidelines and editorial calendar available.
- "Keeping 'em Down on the Farm." Personal experience piece talks about what to do with bored teenagers on the farm in the summer.
- Sample dept/column: "In the Shop" provides step-by-step plans for building a dog house.

Rights and Payment
Shared rights. All material, payment rates vary. Pays on publication. Provides 1 contributor's copy.

Editor's Comments
Our magazine emphasizes the importance of community and stewardship. We'll entertain ideas on a broad range of topics that appeal to those already living in the country and those who aspire to get there. Our readers are well educated and successful.

Group

Group Publishing, Inc.
P.O. Box 481
Loveland, CO 80539-0481

Associate Editor: Scott Firestone

Description and Interests
This magazine strives to equip Christian youth leaders with the resources they need to perform outreach and disciple teenagers while promoting spiritual and professional growth.
- **Audience:** Adults
- **Frequency:** 6 times each year
- **Circulation:** 55,000
- **Website:** www.groupmag.com

Freelance Potential
60% written by nonstaff writers. Publishes 200 freelance submissions yearly; 50% by unpublished writers, 80% by authors who are new to the magazine. Receives 300 queries yearly.

Submissions
Query with outline/synopsis and clips or writing samples. Accepts hard copy. State if artwork is available. SASE. Responds in 8–10 weeks.
Articles: 500–1,700 words. Informational and how-to articles. Topics include youth ministry strategies, recruiting and training adult leaders, understanding youth culture, professionalism, time management, leadership skills, and the professional and spiritual growth of youth ministers.
Depts/columns: "Try This One," to 300 words. "Hands-On Help," to 175 words.
Artwork: B/W or color illustration samples; submit to art department. No prints.

Sample Issue
82 pages (30% advertising): 3 articles; 23 depts/columns. Sample copy, $2 with 9x12 SASE. Guidelines available.
- "Built to Last." Article offers advice from youth pastors about maintaining relationships with teens.
- "Recruiting Leaders the Jesus Way." Article takes a look at Jesus' volunteer recruiting methods and offers ideas and strategies for starting a ministry.
- Sample dept/column: "Hands on Help" takes a look at custom luggage tags made by a youth group.

Rights and Payment
All rights. Articles, $125–$225. Depts/columns, $40. Pays on acceptance.

Editor's Comments
We need fresh ideas for recruiting, training, and keeping adult leaders; youth-led ministry ideas; fun and experiential programming ideas; and outreach ideas.

Guide

Review and Herald Publishing Association
55 West Oak Ridge Drive
Hagerstown, MD 21740

Editor: Randy Fishell

Description and Interests
This publication of the Seventh-day Adventist Church contains inspirational, true stories "pointing to Jesus" and aimed at young people. Some content is published in both English and Spanish.
- **Audience:** 10–14 years
- **Frequency:** Weekly
- **Circulation:** 29,000
- **Website:** www.guidemagazine.org

Freelance Potential
100% written by nonstaff writers. Publishes 175 freelance submissions yearly; 15% by unpublished writers, 20% by authors who are new to the magazine. Receives 420 unsolicited mss yearly.

Submissions
Send complete ms. Prefers email submissions to guide@rhpa.org. Will accept hard copy and simultaneous submissions if identified. SASE. Responds in 4–6 weeks.
Articles: To 1,200 words. True stories with inspirational and personal-growth themes; true adventure pieces; and humor. Nature articles with a religious emphasis, 750 words.
Other: Puzzles, activities, games, trivia, and Bible lessons. Submit seasonal material about Thanksgiving, Christmas, Mother's Day, and Father's Day 8 months in advance.

Sample Issue
30 pages: 4 stories; 1 dept/column; 3 activities; 2 Bible lessons. Sample copy, free with 9x12 SASE (2 first-class stamps). Guidelines available.
- "Preaching with Pride." Story depicts the consequences of a 13-year-old boy's overconfidence during a sermon competition.
- "Heaping Coals on Kelsey Payne." Story tells how a girl turns an enemy into a friend.
- "Born Lucky." Bilingual story illustrates a girl's special relationship with her grandfather.

Rights and Payment
First and reprint rights. Written material, $.06–$.12 per word. Pays on acceptance. Provides 3 contributor's copies.

Editor's Comments
Before writing any story for us, we encourage you to ask for the Holy Spirit's involvement. Think true, and keep your protagonists ages 10 to 14.

Gumbo Teen Magazine

1818 North Dr. Martin Luther King Drive
Milwaukee, WI 53212

Managing Editor: Carrie Trousil

Description and Interests
"Teen" is the middle name of this award-winning magazine, which is written by teenagers for teenagers and covers everything from light entertainment to weighty social issues.
- **Audience:** 13–19 years
- **Frequency:** 6 times each year
- **Circulation:** 25,000
- **Website:** www.gumboteenmagazine.com

Freelance Potential
15% written by nonstaff writers. Publishes 20 freelance submissions yearly; 90% by unpublished writers, 50% by new authors. Receives 50 queries yearly.

Submissions
Query. Accepts email queries to carrie@mygumbo.com. Responds in 6 weeks.
Articles: 500–1,000 words. Informational articles; personal experience pieces; profiles; and interviews. Topics include entertainment, popular culture, current events, health, and multicultural and social issues.
Depts/columns: Word lengths vary. Fashion, travel, African American history, careers, Q&A, living legends, school, health, book and music reviews, current events, sports, and technology.
Other: Poetry, to 500 words. Submit seasonal material 6 months in advance.

Sample Issue
58 pages (30% advertising): 3 articles; 20 depts/columns; 1 poem. Sample copy, $3 with 8x10 SASE ($1.23 postage). Guidelines available.
- "Tavis Smiley: Attitude Determines Altitude." Interview with the noted journalist focuses on his advice to African American youth.
- "Rush into AJ & Aly." Profile of teen sister-celebrities Amanda Joy and Alyson Michalka examines their multimedia success.
- Sample dept/column: "One World: Brazil" details a young woman's life-changing mission to a rural, poverty-stricken part of the country.

Rights and Payment
One-time rights. Written material, $25. Pays on publication. Provides 10 contributor's copies.

Editor's Comments
We only accept queries from writers ages 13 to 19 years of age. We are looking for more articles about political and teen social issues, and fewer entertainment pieces.

Gwinnett Parents Magazine

3651 Peachtree Parkway, Suite 325
Suwanee, GA 30024

Editor: Terrie Porter

Description and Interests
This digest-sized "guide to family living in and around Gwinnett County" in Georgia contains parenting articles as well as self-help tips for Mom and Dad.
- **Audience:** Parents
- **Frequency:** Monthly
- **Circulation:** Unavailable
- **Website:** www.gwinnettparents.com

Freelance Potential
40% written by nonstaff writers. Publishes several freelance submissions yearly.

Submissions
Query or send complete ms. Accepts email submissions only to editor@gwinnettparents.com (include "Editorial Submission" in subject line). Responds in 3–4 weeks.
Articles: 500–1,000 words. Informational and self-help articles; profiles; and personal experience pieces. Topics include education, recreation, sports, health, working parents, and family finances.
Depts/columns: Word lengths vary. Parenting advice; health, education, and community news; recipes; restaurant, media, and product reviews; pet care; and "Dad's 2 Cents."

Sample Issue
60 pages (50% advertising): 5 articles; 15 depts/columns. Sample copy, $4 with 9x12 SASE ($.77 postage). Guidelines available.
- "Nintendo Wii + Wii Sports = Good for Fitness in Children?" Article gives an overview of a video-game system that requires players to actually move.
- "The Importance of Toddler Routines." Article stresses the benefits of keeping young children on a regular schedule and provides tips for doing so.
- Sample dept/column: "Show & Tell" includes book and product recommendations.

Rights and Payment
First and non-exclusive online archival rights. Articles, $75. Depts/columns, $50. Pays on publication.

Editor's Comments
Accuracy is extremely important. If statistics, figures, or "facts" are used, the source must be cited. Always provide contact information for sources. Topics with a "local flair" are preferable to those citing sources or incidents outside of Gwinnett County. If a subject is global or national in nature, find a way to localize it.

Happiness

P.O. Box 388
Portland, TN 37148

Editor: Sue Fuller

Description and Interests
At the heart of *Happiness* is a television guide, but surrounding it are upbeat, family-oriented articles and children's stories, plus puzzles and poems.
- **Audience:** Families
- **Frequency:** Weekly
- **Circulation:** 150,000
- **Website:** www.happiness.com

Freelance Potential
75% written by nonstaff writers. Of the freelance submissions published yearly, 25% are by unpublished writers, 25% by authors who are new to the magazine.

Submissions
Send complete ms. Accepts hard copy. Availability of artwork improves chance of acceptance. SASE. Responds in 3 months.
Articles: 500 words. Informational, self-help, and how-to articles; humor; and personal experience pieces. Topics include careers, education, health, fitness, crafts, hobbies, animals, pets, nature, the environment, recreation, and travel.
Depts/columns: 25–75 words. Crafts, cooking, health, humor, and tips from readers.
Artwork: Color prints.
Other: Puzzles, games, and poetry. Submit seasonal material 4 months in advance.

Sample Issue
32 pages (no advertising): 3 articles; 7 depts/columns; 6 activities. Guidelines available.
- "Bringing Out the Best in Yourself." Article encourages readers to tap into their ultimate potential to achieve success.
- "Leave Loving Memories." Article tells how to leave a legacy of giving.
- Sample dept/column: "We Love Our Pets" is a collection of reader-contributed photos and anecdotes about silly things their animals do.

Rights and Payment
First rights. All material, payment rates vary. Pays on publication.

Editor's Comments
We do not accept religious material with a specific doctrinal slant, nor do we accept wording that points to evolution, mythology, or mystical powers. We seek only positive reading material, especially personal, true-to-life stories with good morals.

High Adventure

General Council of the Assemblies of God
1445 North Boonville Avenue
Springfield, MO 65802-1894

Editor: John Hicks

Description and Interests
This magazine is the official publication of the National Royal Rangers Ministries of the General Council of the Assemblies of God. Its purpose is to foster the spirit of the Royal Rangers.
• **Audience:** Boys, grades K–12
• **Frequency:** Quarterly
• **Circulation:** 87,000
• **Website: www.royalrangers.ag.org**

Freelance Potential
40% written by nonstaff writers. Publishes 6–10 freelance submissions yearly. Receives 150–200 unsolicited mss yearly.

Submissions
Send complete ms. Accepts hard copy, IBM disk submissions, email submissions to ranger@ag.org, and simultaneous submissions if identified. SASE. Responds in 1–2 weeks.
Articles: 1,000 words. Informational, self-help, and how-to articles. Topics include nature and wildlife themes, Christian youth issues, and salvation. Also publishes adventure pieces, historical biographies, and personal testimonies.
Depts/columns: Word lengths vary. News.
Artwork: Color prints.
Other: Puzzles, games, activities, and jokes. Submit seasonal material 6 months in advance.

Sample Issue
16 pages (no advertising): 3 articles; 3 depts/columns; 1 comic. Sample copy, free with 9x12 SASE. Guidelines available.
• "Essential Backpacking Equipment." Article details items every camper must have to be properly prepared.
• Sample dept/column: "Feature Creature" describes the coyote's physical and behavioral characteristics.

Rights and Payment
First or all rights. All material, payment rates vary. Pays on publication. Provides 2 contributor's copies.

Editor's Comments
We're interested only in material that adheres to clear biblical standards of conduct and morality. All items must promote the mental, physical, spiritual, and social growth of boys. We especially need well-researched, informative articles on nature and wildlife, accompanied by a bibliography or other documentation.

Higher Things
Dare To Be Lutheran

Good Shepherd Lutheran Church
5009 Cassia Street
Boise, ID 83705

Managing Editor: Julie Stiegemeyer

Description and Interests
The mission of this magazine is to assist parents, pastors, and congregations in cultivating a Lutheran identity among youth.
• **Audience:** 13–19 years
• **Frequency:** Quarterly
• **Circulation:** Unavailable
• **Website: www.higherthings.org**

Freelance Potential
25% written by nonstaff writers. Publishes 20 freelance submissions yearly.

Submissions
Query or send complete ms. Accepts hard copy and email submissions to submissions@higherthings.org. SASE. Response time varies.
Articles: 500–800 words. Informational and how-to articles; profiles; interviews; and personal experience pieces. Topics include religion, current events, recreation, social issues, and travel.
Depts/columns: Staff written.

Sample Issue
32 pages (10% advertising): 6 articles; 5 depts/columns. Sample copy, $3. Guidelines available.
• "Jesus Comes to You." Article profiles a pastor who builds Lutheran congregations in the African jungle.
• "What I Didn't Say in the Confessional." Article reveals the author's thoughts on receiving Holy Absolution.
• "The Five Greatest Movies Never Made." Article features the author speaking as Martin Luther, who describes fictitious Christian films that he believes should be in theaters.

Rights and Payment
Rights vary. Articles, $50–$100. Pays on publication. Kill fee, $25. Provides 12 contributor's copies.

Editor's Comments
As you write, consider your audience carefully. Write to the 14-year-old confirmand who loves to rollerblade on her quiet cul-de-sac, or to the 17-year-old track star who's experimenting with sex and cigarettes. Your writing should be fresh and lively, and consideration should be made regarding vocabulary, readability, and subject matter. Please provide one or two layout or art suggestions for your article, as well as several Bible study questions.

Highlights for Children

803 Church Street
Honesdale, PA 18431

Manuscript Submissions

Description and Interests
Since 1946, this magazine has been using a wholesome approach to teaching young children basic skills, creativity, and sensitivity to others. It features stories, articles, poems, crafts, puzzles, and activities.
• **Audience:** 2–12 years
• **Frequency:** Monthly
• **Circulation:** 2.5 million
• **Website:** www.highlights.com

Freelance Potential
99% written by nonstaff writers. Publishes 200 freelance submissions yearly; 40% by unpublished writers, 60% by authors who are new to the magazine. Receives 6,500 mss yearly.

Submissions
Send complete ms for fiction; query or send complete ms for nonfiction. Accepts hard copy. SASE. Responds to queries in 2–4 weeks, to mss in 4–6 weeks.
Articles: To 400 words for 3–7 years; to 800 words for 8–12 years. Informational articles; interviews; personal experience pieces; and profiles. Topics include nature, animals, science, crafts, hobbies, world culture, history, arts, and sports.
Fiction: To 400 words for 3–7 years; to 800 words for 8–12 years. Rebuses, to 120 words. Genres include mystery, adventure, and multicultural fiction. Also features sports stories and retellings of traditional stories.
Depts/columns: Word lengths vary. Science and crafts.
Other: Puzzles and games. Poetry, to 10 lines.

Sample Issue
44 pages (no advertising): 4 articles; 11 stories; 1 rebus; 12 activities; 6 depts/columns. Sample copy, free with 9x12 SASE (4 first-class stamps). Guidelines available.
• "When Do Monkeys Talk?" Article describes how and when monkeys talk to one another.
• "My Sister Snores." Story of two sisters who try sleeping in separate rooms but find they miss each other.

Rights and Payment
All rights. Written material, payment rates vary. Pays on acceptance. Provides 2 contributor's copies.

Editor's Comments
We are looking for more fiction and nonfiction pieces that emphasize our global community.

High School Writer

Junior High Edition

Writer Publications
P.O. Box 718
Grand Rapids, MN 55744-0718

Editor: Emily Benes

Description and Interests
This newspaper has been featuring articles, essays, stories, and poems by junior high school students across the country for 23 years. Writing must be submitted through teachers who subscribe to the publication.
• **Audience:** Junior high school students
• **Frequency:** 6 times each year
• **Circulation:** 44,000
• **Website:** www.writerpublications.com

Freelance Potential
100% written by nonstaff writers. Publishes 1,000 freelance submissions yearly; 1% by unpublished writers, 99% by new authors. Receives 36,000 unsolicited mss each year.

Submissions
Accepts submissions from students of subscribing teachers in junior high school only. Send complete ms. Accepts hard copy and simultaneous submissions if identified. SASE. Response time varies.
Articles: To 2,000 words. Informational and how-to articles; personal experience pieces; and profiles. Topics include family, religion, health, social issues, careers, college, multicultural issues, travel, nature, the environment, science, and computers.
Fiction: To 2,000 words. Genres include historical and contemporary fiction, science fiction, drama, adventure, suspense, mystery, humor, fantasy, and stories about sports and nature.
Other: Poetry, no line limit.

Sample Issue
8 pages (no advertising): 17 stories; 9 articles; 6 poems. Sample copy, free. Guidelines available in each issue.
• "Christmas Traditions." Personal experience piece features the author's remembrances of Christmas with her family.
• "Out in the Oil Field." Story tells how a midget working in an oil field causes an accident.
• "The Hockey Day." Essay shares the author's memories of a hockey game.

Rights and Payment
One-time rights. No payment. Provides 2 copies.

Editor's Comments
We are looking for stories that encourage students toward greater academic or literary achievement. No school-age romance, please.

Home Education Magazine

P.O. Box 1083
Tonasket, WA 98855

Editor: Carol Narigon

Description and Interests
This award-winning magazine for homeschooling families focuses on "unschooling" and takes an active political stance for empowering its readership.
- **Audience:** Parents
- **Frequency:** 6 times each year
- **Circulation:** 110,000
- **Website:** www.homeedmag.com

Freelance Potential
40% written by nonstaff writers. Publishes 40 freelance submissions yearly; 25% by unpublished writers, 40% by authors who are new to the magazine. Receives 720+ queries yearly.

Submissions
Query. Prefers email queries to articles@homeedmag.com. Will accept hard copy. SASE. Responds in 1–2 months.
Articles: 900–1,700 words. Informational, how-to, and personal experience pieces; interviews; and profiles. Topics include homeschooling, activism, lessons, and parenting.
Depts/columns: Staff written.
Artwork: B/W and color prints. Digital images at 200 dpi; 300 dpi for cover images.
Other: Poetry.

Sample Issue
58 pages (13% advertising): 8 articles; 12 depts/columns. Sample copy, $6.50. Guidelines available at website.
- "Don't Quake—Conjugate!" Article explains how to take the fear out of learning a foreign language.
- "Full-Time Work, Full-Time Homeschooling." Article describes how one family continued homeschooling after their mother was forced back to work.
- "Keep It Clean." Article provides tips for juggling housekeeping and kids.

Rights and Payment
First North American serial and electronic rights. Articles, $50–$100. Artwork, $12.50; $100 for cover art. Pays on acceptance. Provides 1+ author's copies.

Editor's Comments
Please feel free to submit an article on any topic at any time, and we will schedule it appropriately. We do not publish or conform to an editorial calendar, preferring to select the best articles submitted at any given time.

Home Educator's Family Times

P.O. Box 6442
Brunswick, ME 04011

Editor: Jane R. Boswell

Description and Interests
This newspaper for homeschooling families and others who are interested in the education of children appears both in print and online. It offers general articles on homeschooling as well as curriculum ideas.
- **Audience:** Parents
- **Frequency:** 6 times each year
- **Circulation:** 25,000
- **Hits per month:** 400,000
- **Website:** www.homeeducatorsfamilytimes.com

Freelance Potential
96% written by nonstaff writers. Publishes 75 freelance submissions yearly, many from authors who are new to the publication.

Submissions
Send complete ms with brief biography, byline, and permission statement from guidelines. Accepts email submissions to famtimes@blazenetme.net (no attachments). Response time varies.
Articles: 1,000–1,500 words. Informational and how-to articles; opinion and personal experience pieces. Topics include homeschooling methods and lessons, family life, parenting, pets, reading, art, science, and creative writing.
Depts/columns: Staff written.

Sample Issue
24 pages (41% advertising): 14 articles; 2 depts/columns. Sample copy and guidelines available at website.
- "Dogs Have Been a Big Part of My Curriculum." Personal essay tells what a girl has learned from training and competing with Belgian sheepdogs.
- "Beyond the ABCs: Nurturing the Love of Reading." Article gives tips for teaching reading comprehension to children.
- "Studying the Masters: Winslow Homer." Article describes the life and work of the famous painter.

Rights and Payment
First, reprint, and electronic rights. No payment.

Editor's Comments
Please note that we do not usually compensate authors for published articles. The majority of authors have submitted their work without a fee, seeking instead to bring attention to their product or service. If you are seeking monetary reimbursement, the average fee paid for an accepted article is $20.

Homeschooling Today

P.O. Box 244
Abingdon, VA 24212

Editor-in-Chief: Jim Bob Howard

Description and Interests
The mission of this magazine is to encourage the reformation of the family through homeschooling. It offers lesson plans, ready-to-use study units, advice, and tips for parents, with an emphasis on teaching literature, history, fine arts, and Christian living.
- **Audience:** Parents
- **Frequency:** Subscription; newsstand
- **Circulation:** 11,500
- **Website:** www.homeschooltoday.com

Freelance Potential
85% written by nonstaff writers. Publishes 50 freelance submissions yearly; 20% by unpublished writers, 35% by authors who are new to the magazine. Receives 60–120 unsolicited mss yearly.

Submissions
Send ms. Accepts hard copy and email submissions to editor@homeschooltoday.com (Microsoft Word or RTF attachments). SASE. Responds in 3–6 months.
Articles: 1,000–2,500 words. Informational, self-help, and how-to articles; profiles; interviews; and personal experience pieces. Topics include education, music, technology, special education, the arts, history, mathematics, and science.
Depts/columns: Word lengths vary. Reviews, new product information, the arts, music, and literature.

Sample Issue
84 pages: 5 articles; 14 depts/columns. Sample copy, $5.95. Guidelines and theme list available at website.
- "28 Ways to Teach Beginning Math Without Textbooks." Article explains how to use ordinary household items to teach math skills to young children.
- "First Things First: Suggestions for Working with Preschoolers." Article explains ways to build a foundation for learning within a family framework.
- "Drawing Out the Illustrator in Your Child." Article discusses the value of illustrating stories and other drawing exercises.

Rights and Payment
First rights. Written material, $.08 per word. Pays on publication. Provides 1 contributor's copy.

Editor's Comments
We strongly suggest that authors browse the theme lists posted at our website for ideas and inspiration. Remember that we look for material that promotes a Christian worldview.

Hopscotch

P.O. Box 164
Bluffton, OH 45817-0164

Editor: Marilyn Edwards

Description and Interests
This magazine is an alternative to the publications for young girls that emphasize dating, fashion, and the other trappings of adulthood. *Hopscotch* is instead filled with wholesome, creative fiction and high-quality articles and activities.
- **Audience:** 5–14 years
- **Frequency:** 6 times each year
- **Circulation:** 16,000
- **Website:** www.hopscotchmagazine.com

Freelance Potential
90% written by nonstaff writers. Publishes 100–250 freelance submissions yearly; 60% by unpublished writers, 40% by authors who are new to the magazine. Receives 2,000–3,000 queries and unsolicited mss yearly.

Submissions
Query or send complete ms. Include artwork with nonfiction. Accepts hard copy and simultaneous submissions if identified. SASE. Responds to queries in 1–2 weeks, to mss in 2–3 months.
Articles: To 500 words. Informational articles; profiles; and personal experience pieces. Topics include crafts and hobbies, games, sports, pets, nature, careers, and cooking.
Fiction: To 1,000 words. Genres include mystery, adventure, historical fiction, and multicultural fiction.
Depts/columns: 500 words. Crafts and cooking.
Artwork: Prefers B/W prints; will accept color.
Other: Puzzles, activities, and poetry.

Sample Issue
50 pages (no advertising): 8 articles; 2 stories; 6 depts/columns; 2 poems; 1 comic. Sample copy, $5 with 9x12 SASE. Guidelines and theme list available.
- "The Sandwich: The Original Fast Food." Article details the history and some interesting facts about this "quick and easy portable meal."
- Sample dept/column: "Science" explores the differences between salt and sugar crystals.

Rights and Payment
First and second rights. Written material, $.05 per word. Artwork, payment rates vary. Pays on publication. Provides 1 contributor's copy.

Editor's Comments
We don't need fiction just now, but we do need clearly written and illustrated crafts and activities, and innovative but simple recipes to go with an open theme.

The Horn Book Magazine

56 Roland Street, Suite 200
Boston, MA 02129

Editor-in-Chief: Roger Sutton

Description and Interests
Children's literature is the focus of *The Horn Book Magazine*. For more than 80 years, it has published reviews of children's books along with articles and essays that offer criticism and analysis of interest to adults who care about children's writing.
- **Audience:** Parents, teachers, librarians
- **Frequency:** 6 times each year
- **Circulation:** 16,000
- **Website: www.hbook.com**

Freelance Potential
70% written by nonstaff writers. Publishes 12–15 freelance submissions yearly; 10% by unpublished writers, 30% by authors who are new to the magazine. Receives 240 queries, 120 unsolicited mss yearly.

Submissions
Query or send complete ms. Accepts hard copy. SASE. Responds in 4 months.
Articles: To 2,800 words. Interviews with children's authors, illustrators, and editors; critical articles about children's and young adult literature; and book reviews.
Depts/columns: Word lengths vary. Perspectives from illustrators; children's publishing updates; and special columns.

Sample Issue
94 pages (20% advertising): 2 articles; 4 depts/columns; 70 reviews. Sample copy, free with 9x12 SASE. Guidelines and editorial calendar available.
- "Problems, Paperbacks, and the Printz: Forty Years of YA Books." Article examines the evolution of books written primarily for teen readers.
- "Missing from the Meadow: Philippa Pearce, 1920–2006." Article expresses an appreciation for the author of *Tom's Midnight Garden* and other works for children.
- Sample dept/column: "Featured Review" looks at a biography of Beatrix Potter.

Rights and Payment
All rights. Written material, payment rates vary. Pays on publication. Provides 1 contributor's copy.

Editor's Comments
Write for an audience that is knowledgeable about children's literature: teachers, librarians, writers, publishers, booksellers, and parents. We look for pieces that celebrate the best and expose the worst.

Horsemen's Yankee Pedlar

83 Leicester Street
North Oxford, MA 01537

Editor: Molly Johns

Description and Interests
This hefty magazine is written for Northeastern equestrians interested in "all breeds and all disciplines"—from Arabians to Quarter Horses, English to Western, driven dressage to barrel racing. It includes regional and national equine news.
- **Audience:** YA–Adult
- **Frequency:** Monthly
- **Circulation:** 50,000
- **Website: www.pedlar.com**

Freelance Potential
50% written by nonstaff writers. Publishes 40 freelance submissions yearly; 5% by authors who are new to the magazine. Receives 360 queries, 240 mss yearly.

Submissions
Query or send complete ms. Accepts hard copy and simultaneous submissions if identified. SASE. Responds to queries in 1–2 weeks, to mss in 2–3 months.
Articles: 500–800 words. Informational and how-to articles; personal experience pieces; interviews; and reviews. Topics include horse breeds, disciplines, training, health care, and equestrian equipment.
Depts/columns: Word lengths vary. News, book reviews, business issues, nutrition, and legal issues.
Artwork: B/W and color prints.

Sample Issue
226 pages (75% advertising): 39 articles; 15 depts/columns. Sample copy, $3.99 with 9x12 SASE (7 first-class stamps). Guidelines available.
- "Reining Strategies for Non-Pros." Article provides tips from a champion trainer.
- "Uncovering the Mystery of the Mustang." Article gives an overview of the breed that is seen as a symbol of American freedom.
- Sample dept/column: "Trail Talk" tells how to condition a horse for trail riding.

Rights and Payment
First North American serial rights. Written material, $2 per published column inch. Show coverage, $75 per day. Pays 30 days after publication. Provides 1 tearsheet.

Editor's Comments
We provide an essential resource for horsemen who want timely, cutting-edge news and industry updates from the equine industry in the northeastern U.S.

Horsepower

P.O. Box 670
Aurora, Ontario L4G 4J9
Canada

Managing Editor: Susan Stafford

Description and Interests
Subtitled "The Magazine for Young Horse Lovers," this publication features articles designed to educate and entertain readers. The content focuses on horse care, stable skills, equine health, and training with an emphasis on safety.
- **Audience:** 9–15 years
- **Frequency:** 6 times each year
- **Circulation:** 10,000
- **Website:** www.horse-canada.com

Freelance Potential
20% written by nonstaff writers. Publishes 8–10 freelance submissions yearly; 10% by unpublished writers, 10% by authors who are new to the magazine. Receives 30 unsolicited mss yearly.

Submissions
Query with outline or synopsis; or send complete ms with résumé. Accepts hard copy, IBM disk submissions (ASCII or WordPerfect), and email submissions to info@horse-canada.com. SAE/IRC. Responds to queries in 1–2 weeks, to mss in 2–3 months.
Articles: 500–1,000 words. Informational and how-to articles; profiles; and humor. Topics include breeds, training, stable skills, equine health, and tack.
Fiction: 500 words. Adventure, humorous stories, and sports stories related to horses.
Depts/columns: Staff written.
Artwork: B/W and color prints.
Other: Horse-themed activities, games, and puzzles.

Sample Issue
14 pages (20% advertising): 3 articles; 5 depts/columns; 2 puzzles; 2 activities; 1 poster. Sample copy, $3.95. Guidelines and theme list available.
- "Celebs and Their Horses." Article talks about and provides pictures of celebrities who own horses.
- "Breed Profile: The Nokota Horse." Article reports on a horse that descended from wild herds in the badlands of North Dakota.

Rights and Payment
First North American serial rights. Written material, $50–$90. Artwork, $10–$75. Pays on publication. Provides 1 contributor's copy.

Editor's Comments
Please note that we can no longer accept more than one or two articles written by non-Canadian contributors each year due to Canadian content regulations.

Hudson Valley Parent

174 South Street
Newburgh, NY 12550

Editor: Leah Black

Description and Interests
This free publication is distributed to parents living in the mid-Hudson Valley of New York. It is a resource guide on parenting children from infants to age 14.
- **Audience:** Parents
- **Frequency:** Monthly
- **Circulation:** 35,000
- **Website:** www.excitingread.com

Freelance Potential
95% written by nonstaff writers. Publishes 130 freelance submissions yearly; 13% by unpublished writers, 26% by authors who are new to the magazine. Receives 96 queries, 240 unsolicited mss yearly.

Submissions
Query with writing samples; or send complete ms. Prefers email queries to editor@excitingread.com. Accepts hard copy. SASE. Responds in 3–6 weeks.
Articles: 700–1,200 words. Informational and how-to articles; and practical application pieces. Topics include parenting, grandparenting, computers, technology, recreation, health, fitness, sports, hobbies, and the home.
Depts/columns: 700 words. Health, education, and adolescent issues.
Other: Submit seasonal material 6 months in advance. "Vida y Familia Hispana," Spanish section.

Sample Issue
62 pages (50% advertising): 8 articles; 4 depts/columns. Sample copy, free with 9x12 SASE. Guidelines and editorial calendar available.
- "A Sleepover Survival Guide." Article outlines rules for planning a fun, problem-free birthday party.
- "Supervising or Snooping?" Article gives parents advice on judicious use of computer surveillance software to "chaperone" their children's online activities.
- Sample dept/column: "Kid-Friendly Kitchen" offers quick, easy recipes and time-saving kitchen tips for busy parents.

Rights and Payment
One-time rights. Written material, $25–$70. Pays on publication. Provides contributor's copies.

Editor's Comments
We prefer first-person accounts. Submit manuscripts or query with ideas you can sell us on. Describe your research and list other sources you'll consult.

Humpty Dumpty's Magazine

Children's Better Health Institute
1100 Waterway Boulevard
P.O. Box 567
Indianapolis, IN 46206-0567

Editor: Phyllis Lybarger

Description and Interests
This member of the Children's Better Health Institute family of magazines targets emergent readers with articles, stories, recipes, and games that encourage a healthy, active lifestyle.
- **Audience:** 4–6 years
- **Frequency:** 6 times each year
- **Circulation:** 236,000
- **Website:** www.humptydumptymag.org

Freelance Potential
10% written by nonstaff writers. Publishes 10–12 freelance submissions yearly; 5% by unpublished writers, 12% by authors who are new to the magazine.

Submissions
Send complete ms. Accepts hard copy. SASE. Responds in 10–12 weeks.
Articles: To 250 words. Informational and how-to articles. Topics include health, fitness, sports, science, nature, animals, crafts, and hobbies.
Fiction: To 300 words. Genres include early reader contemporary and multicultural fiction; stories about sports; fantasy; folktales; mystery; drama; and humor.
Depts/columns: Word lengths vary. Recipes, health advice, and book excerpts.
Other: Puzzles, activities, and games. Poetry. Submit seasonal material 8 months in advance.

Sample Issue
36 pages (2% advertising): 2 articles; 2 stories; 3 depts/columns; 1 poem; 7 activities. Sample copy, $1.25. Guidelines available.
- "Just Jerry." Story tells about a young girl's relationship with an anthropomorphic rope.
- "Let's Play Ball!" Article provides tips for becoming a great baseball fielder.
- Sample dept/column: "Mix & Fix" offers a recipe for honey fruit crisps.

Rights and Payment
All rights. Written material, $.22 per word. Pays on publication. Provides 10 contributor's copies.

Editor's Comments
Our magazine is designed to be read aloud to children who are not yet reading independently; therefore, we look for submissions with a good "read-aloud" quality. Games and crafts should require a minimum of adult guidance, have clear instructions, and use readily available materials.

Ignite Your Faith

Christianity Today
465 Gunderson Drive
Carol Stream, IL 60188

Editor: Chris Lutes

Description and Interests
Christian teens in high school and the early college years find writing that deepens their faith in this magazine. Published by Christianity Today, it ties spirituality and biblical principles to the experiences young adults face in today's world.
- **Audience:** 13–19 years
- **Frequency:** 9 times each year
- **Circulation:** 100,000
- **Website:** www.igniteyourfaith.com

Freelance Potential
60% written by nonstaff writers. Publishes 15–20 freelance submissions yearly; 10% by unpublished writers, 20% by authors who are new to the magazine. Receives 300 queries yearly.

Submissions
Query with 1-page synopsis. No unsolicited mss. Accepts hard copy and simultaneous submissions if identified. SASE. Responds in 3–6 weeks.
Articles: 700–1,500 words. Personal experience pieces; and humor. Topics include Christian values, beliefs, and Christian education.
Fiction: 1,000–1,500 words. Genres include contemporary fiction with religious themes.
Depts/columns: Staff written.

Sample Issue
56 pages (30% advertising): 4 articles; 24 depts/columns. Sample copy, $3 with 9x12 SASE (3 first-class stamps). Guidelines available.
- "If God Were a Talent Show Judge." Article discusses why it is important to please God, not perform for Him.
- "I Survived Hell." True story tells of a child in Uganda who was kidnapped and forced to become a soldier.
- "Old Story, New Script." Article examines how the life of Christ has inspired some of our favorite movies.

Rights and Payment
First rights. Written material, $.20–$.25 per word. Pays on acceptance. Provides 2 contributor's copies.

Editor's Comments
For the coming year, we would like to see more fiction from new sources. Stories should offer a tie to the life experiences of teenagers. Avoid simplistic religious answers and a preachy tone. We're also publishing more columns.

The Illuminata

5624 Fairway Drive
Zachary, LA 70791

Editor-in-Chief: Bret Funk

Description and Interests
This online magazine about the science fiction and fantasy genres, produced by book publisher Tyrannosaurus Press, targets would-be authors. In addition to writing tips and reviews, it publishes original works of fiction.
- **Audience:** YA–Adult
- **Frequency:** Monthly
- **Hits per month:** 400
- **Website:** www.tyrannosauruspress.com

Freelance Potential
25% written by nonstaff writers. Publishes 10–15 freelance submissions yearly; 95% by unpublished writers, 90% by authors who are new to the magazine. Receives 10 queries yearly.

Submissions
Query following detailed guidelines at website. Accepts email queries to submissions@ tyrannosauruspress.com (no attachments). Responds in 1–3 months.
Articles: 1–2 pages in length. Informational articles about writing science fiction, fantasy, and horror.
Fiction: Word lengths vary. Genres include science fiction, fantasy, and horror.
Depts/columns: "Reviews," 500–1,000 words. Reviews of science fiction and fantasy books and stories.

Sample Issue
25 pages (no advertising): 2 articles; 4 depts/columns; 1 story. Sample copy and guidelines available at website.
- "University of SF." Article spotlights an author, who reviews his journey through science fiction.
- "The 4th Dimension and Time." Article debates quantum physics.
- Sample dept/column: "The Writer's Block: Rest in Peace, Short Story!" discusses the demise of the short-story format.

Rights and Payment
Rights vary. No payment.

Editor's Comments
While to many it may seem common knowledge to include contact information in emails, more than a few submissions have arrived without it. Submitting an email does not mean you can be less professional. Email queries *must* contain full contact information for the author: address, phone number, and email address.

Indy's Child

1901 Broad Ripple Avenue
Indianapolis, IN 46220

Assistant Editor: Lynette Rowland

Description and Interests
This tabloid serves parents in central Indiana with information on family activities and events as well as health and child-rearing advice.
- **Audience:** Parents
- **Frequency:** Monthly
- **Circulation:** 50,000
- **Website:** www.indyschild.com

Freelance Potential
95% written by nonstaff writers. Publishes 240+ freelance submissions yearly; 50% by authors who are new to the magazine. Receives 1,200+ unsolicited mss yearly.

Submissions
Send complete ms with artwork, author bio and photo, and contract from website. No queries. Accepts email submissions to editorial@ indyschild.com; include "Manuscript: Topic of Article" in subject line. Responds only if interested.
Articles: 800–1,500 words. Informational and how-to articles; and profiles. Topics include parenting and child development, hobbies and talents, safety, sports and recreation, home improvement, entertainment, travel, and social issues.
Depts/columns: To 1,000 words. Media and product reviews; women's health; museum notes; "Tweens and Teens"; college information; and local profiles.
Artwork: Color digital images.
Other: Submit seasonal material 3 months in advance.

Sample Issue
48 pages (50% advertising): 6 articles; 13 depts/columns. Sample copy, guidelines, and editorial calendar available at website.
- "Beaches and Theme Parks and Fairs—Oh My!" Article provides tips for keeping kids safe in public places.
- Sample dept/column: "Tweens and Teens" contrasts technical skills with emotional coping skills.

Rights and Payment
First or second rights. Written material, $100–$250. Reprints, $25–$50. Pays on publication.

Editor's Comments
We are in need of articles directed toward parents of teens in particular. We prefer topical articles using Indiana references. We do not accept first-person stories or simultaneous submissions within Indiana.

InQuest Gamer

151 Wells Avenue
Congers, NY 10920

Editor: Brent Fischdaugh

Description and Interests
For more than 10 years, teens and adults who love to play electronic and other types of games have been reading *InQuest Gamer*. In addition to offering game-playing strategies and tips, it provides information about new products and industry news. Video games, computer games, collectible card games, role playing games, and board games are all covered.
- **Audience:** YA–Adult
- **Frequency:** Monthly
- **Circulation:** Unavailable
- **Website: www.wizardworld.com**

Freelance Potential
50% written by nonstaff writers. Publishes many freelance submissions yearly.

Submissions
Query or send complete ms. Accepts email submissions to bfischdaugh@wizarduniverse.com. Response time varies.
Articles: Word lengths vary. Informational articles; new product reviews; opinion pieces; and media reviews. Topics include audio, video, software, computers, entertainment, and games.
Depts/columns: Word lengths vary. Game updates, news, notes, previews, and computer information.

Sample Issue
88 pages: 8 articles; 11 depts/columns; 1 comic. Sample copy, $4 with 9x12 SASE ($.77 postage). Guidelines available.
- "The Winds of Change." Article interviews Mark Rosewater, the head designer of *Magic: The Gathering,* about a future expansion of the game.
- "'Portal' Combat." Article offers a guide to preventing your own fatality in the World of Warcraft tournament scene in Mortal Kombat.
- Sample dept/column: "Game Plan" takes a look at new collectible models.

Rights and Payment
Rights vary. Written material, payment rates and payment policy vary.

Editor's Comments
We're always interested in detailed articles that provide gaming strategies, as well as cutting-edge news about the gaming world. Send us something that will spark an interest in gaming enthusiasts and keep them coming back for more.

Inside Out

United Pentecostal Church International
8855 Dunn Road
Hazelwood, MO 63042-2299

Submissions: T. Schultz

Description and Interests
Published by the United Pentecostal Church International, this magazine, formerly known as *The Conqueror*, aims to foster spiritual growth and nurture faith in God in its young adult readers.
- **Audience:** 12–18 years
- **Frequency:** 6 times each year
- **Circulation:** 5,200
- **Website: http://pentecostalyouth.org**

Freelance Potential
80% written by nonstaff writers. Publishes 24 freelance submissions yearly; 25% by unpublished writers, 20% by authors who are new to the magazine. Receives 150–200 unsolicited mss yearly.

Submissions
Send complete ms. Accepts email submissions to tschultz@upci.org and simultaneous submissions if identified. Responds in 3 months.
Articles: Features, 1,200-1,800 words. Shorter articles, 600–800 words. Personal experience pieces and profiles. Topics include religion, missionary-related subjects, spiritual growth, social issues, and current events.
Fiction: 600–900 words. Real-life fiction with Christian themes. Genres include humor and romance.
Depts/columns: Word lengths vary. Book and music reviews; opinion and first-person pieces by teens; and reports on church events.

Sample Issue
16 pages (11% advertising): 4 articles; 1 story; 2 depts/columns. Sample copy, free with 9x12 SASE (2 first-class stamps). Guidelines available.
- "Divine Math." Article tells how to make Jesus a "smart addition" to your life.
- "Living Victoriously." Feature uses story of Travis, a teenager faced with peer pressure, to illustrate the satisfaction of resisting temptation to sin.
- Sample dept/column: "Heart of Love" tells what the writer learned during a Latvian mission trip.

Rights and Payment
All rights. Articles, $.07 per word. Filler, $5–$10. Pays on publication. Provides 1 contributor's copy.

Editor's Comments
We aim to inspire our youth readers to live victoriously through their faith in God with articles on trends, culture, and community awareness.

Insight

55 West Oak Ridge Drive
Hagerstown, MD 21740-7390

Editor: Dwain Neilson Esmond

Description and Interests

Published by the Seventh-day Adventist Church, *Insight* offers teens inspirational true stories and profiles that are written to help them navigate the challenges of contemporary life.
- **Audience:** 14–21 years
- **Frequency:** Weekly
- **Circulation:** 21,000
- **Website:** www.insightmagazine.org

Freelance Potential

99% written by nonstaff writers. Publishes 150+ freelance submissions yearly; 50% by unpublished writers, 70% by authors who are new to the magazine. Receives 996 unsolicited mss yearly.

Submissions

Send complete ms. Accepts hard copy, disk submissions (Microsoft Word), and email submissions to insight@rhpa.org. SASE. Responds in 1–3 months.
Articles: 500–1,500 words. Informational articles; profiles; biographies; reports on volunteer and mission trips; and humor. Topics include social issues, religion, music, and careers.
Depts/columns: Word lengths vary. True-to-life stories and personal experience pieces.
Other: Submit material about Christmas, Easter, Mother's Day, Father's Day, and Valentine's Day 6 months in advance.

Sample Issue

24 pages (2% advertising): 3 articles; 4 depts/columns. Sample copy, $2 with 9x12 SASE (2 first-class stamps). Guidelines available.
- "Got God?" Article recounts how one man's search for God was complete after he began listening to a radio preacher named Ravi Zacharias.
- "Thorn in My Back." First-person story tells how one teen coped with constant pain after a car accident.
- Sample dept/column: "Life Skills" discusses the damage that lying can do.

Rights and Payment

First rights. Written material, $50–$125. Pays on acceptance. Provides 3 contributor's copies.

Editor's Comments

We're always interested in true stories with a spiritual message, as well as profiles of Christian celebrities and outstanding Seventh-day Adventist youth. Keep in mind that our readership is diverse.

InSite

P.O. Box 62189
Colorado Springs, CO 80962-2189

Editor: Alison Philips

Description and Interests

InSite is a publication of Christian Camping International/USA. The magazine provides in-depth how-to and inspirational articles for adults involved with Christian camping and conferences.
- **Audience:** Adults
- **Frequency:** 6 times each year
- **Circulation:** 8,500
- **Website:** www.ccca.org

Freelance Potential

90% written by nonstaff writers. Publishes 80 freelance submissions yearly, 15% by unpublished writers, 22% by authors who are new to the magazine. Receives 12 queries yearly.

Submissions

Query with résumé and writing samples. Accepts email queries to editor@cca.org. Availability of artwork may improve chance of acceptance. Responds in 1 month.
Articles: 800–1,500 words. Informational and how-to articles; profiles; and interviews. Topics include biography, crafts, hobbies, health and fitness, multicultural and ethnic issues, nature, popular culture, recreation, religion, social issues, and sports.
Depts/columns: Staff written.
Artwork: B/W and color prints and transparencies.
Other: Submit seasonal material 6 months in advance.

Sample Issue

42 pages (25% advertising): 7 articles; 8 depts/columns. Sample copy, $4.95 with 9x12 SASE ($1.40 postage). Writers' guidelines and theme list available at website.
- "Weathering Summer Storms." Article discusses the importance of safety plans and lists resources.
- "Tough Kids." Article offers advice on handling incidents and establishing effective rules to avoid problems.

Rights and Payment

First rights. Written material, $.16 per word. Artwork, $25–$250. Pays on publication. Provides 1 copy.

Editor's Comments

Freelancers will be most successful with profiles and interviews—articles showing God's work in Christian camping and conferences. We highly recommend looking at a sample copy before querying.

Instructor

Scholastic Inc.
557 Broadway
New York, NY 10016

Features Editor

Description and Interests
This magazine for elementary and middle school teachers covers workplace issues and offers curriculum ideas in a reader-friendly format.
- **Audience:** Teachers, grades K–8
- **Frequency:** 6 times each year
- **Circulation:** 225,000
- **Website:** www.scholastic.com/instructor

Freelance Potential
60% written by nonstaff writers. Publishes 10 freelance submissions yearly; 20% by unpublished writers, 70% by authors who are new to the magazine. Receives 100 queries yearly.

Submissions
Query. Accepts hard copy. Availability of artwork improves chance of acceptance. SASE. Responds in 3–4 months.
Articles: 1,200 words. Informational and how-to articles; and personal experience pieces. Topics include workplace issues, technology, learning issues, literacy, book reviews, and teaching of such subjects as reading, writing, mathematics, science, and social studies.
Depts/columns: News items, Q&As, technology, and "Teachers' Picks," word lengths vary. Classroom activities, to 250 words. Humorous or poignant personal essays, to 400 words.

Sample Issue
72 pages (40% advertising): 7 articles; 6 activities; 6 depts/columns. Sample copy, $3 with 9x12 SASE ($.77 postage). Guidelines and theme list available at website.
- "Best Easy Summer-Learning Ideas." Article suggests summer activities to share with parents.
- "Not Getting Along?" Article discusses how strained relations between faculty and principals can affect student success.
- Sample dept/column: "Teachers' Lounge" talks about battling childhood obesity in schools, and robots that help immune-deficient students attend school from home.

Rights and Payment
All rights. Articles, $600. Depts/columns, $250–$300. Pays on publication. Provides 2 contributor's copies.

Editor's Comments
We are looking for articles on child development and special-needs topics for our audience of teachers.

InTeen

P.O. Box 436987
Chicago, IL 60643

Editor: Aja Carr

Description and Interests
Distributed through inner-city religious education classes, this magazine includes Bible study guides and Bible lessons that help teens connect Christian principles to their everyday lives. It is published by Urban Ministries, an African American Christian publishing company.
- **Audience:** 15–17 years
- **Frequency:** Quarterly
- **Circulation:** 75,000
- **Website:** www.urbanministries.com

Freelance Potential
95% written by nonstaff writers. Publishes 52 freelance submissions yearly; 60% by unpublished writers, 50% by authors who are new to the magazine. Receives 360 queries yearly.

Submissions
Send résumé with writing samples. All material is written on assignment. SASE. Responds in 3–6 months.
Articles: Word lengths vary. Bible study guides and Bible lessons; how-to articles; profiles; interviews; and reviews. Topics include religion, biography, college, careers, black history, music, social issues, and multicultural and ethnic topics.
Fiction: Word lengths vary. Stories are sometimes included as part of study plans. Genres include inspirational, multicultural, and ethnic fiction; real-life stories; and problem-solving stories.
Other: Puzzles, activities, and poetry. Submit seasonal material 1 year in advance.

Sample Issue
48 pages (no advertising): 8 articles; 1 story; 1 poem; 1 Bible verse; 13 Bible study guides. Writers' guidelines available.
- "Serving Your City." Article examines the volunteer work conducted by Hands On Atlanta.
- "Faithful Teamwork." Bible study based on 1 Corinthians 3:1 focuses on the need to collaborate with other Christians.

Rights and Payment
All rights. All material, payment rates vary. Pays 2 months after acceptance. Provides 2 author's copies.

Editor's Comments
We encourage you to send a writing sample that reflects your ability to write in a way that appeals to urban, African American teens.

InTeen Teacher

P.O. Box 436987
Chicago, IL 60643

Editor: Aja Carr

Description and Interests
Published by Urban Ministries, an African American owned and operated Christian media company, *InTeen Teacher* includes teaching plans and Bible study guides that are designed to be used with the lessons provided in *InTeen*. All of the material it publishes supports teachers as they help their students follow Jesus Christ and face life's challenges.
• **Audience:** Religious educators
• **Frequency:** Quarterly
• **Circulation:** 75,000
• **Website:** www.urbanministries.com

Freelance Potential
95% written by nonstaff writers. Publishes 52 freelance submissions yearly; 60% by unpublished writers, 50% by authors who are new to the magazine. Receives 360 queries yearly.

Submissions
All material is written on assignment. Send résumé with writing samples. SASE. Responds in 3–6 months.
Articles: Word lengths vary. Publishes Bible study plans and guides for teaching Christian values to African American teens.
Fiction: Word lengths vary. Stories are sometimes included as part of study plans. Genres include inspirational, multicultural, and ethnic fiction. Also publishes real-life and problem-solving stories.
Other: Puzzles, activities, and poetry. Submit seasonal material 1 year in advance.

Sample Issue
80 pages (no advertising): 3 articles; 13 teaching plans; 13 Bible study guides. Guidelines available.
• "Called to Share Your Gifts." Bible lesson teaches that God gives each of us spiritual gifts that are meant to be shared with the church community.
• "Servants of Unity." Bible study based on 1 Corinthians 1:10–17 teaches that God requires us to be united in Jesus Christ.

Rights and Payment
All rights. Written material, payment rates vary. Pays 2 months after acceptance. Provides 2 copies.

Editor's Comments
Our products are developed by seasoned Christian educators who have experienced the African or the African American worldview. If this sounds like you, send us a résumé.

International Gymnast

P.O. Box 721020
Norman, OK 73070

Editor: Dwight Normile

Description and Interests
Comprehensive coverage of the sport of gymnastics is found in this magazine, in publication for more than 50 years. It offers a mix of competition reports, athlete profiles, and training tips and techniques for gymnasts in their pre-teen and teen years.
• **Audience:** 10–16 years
• **Frequency:** 10 times each year
• **Circulation:** 17,000
• **Website:** www.intlgymnast.com

Freelance Potential
10% written by nonstaff writers. Publishes 5 freelance submissions yearly; 50% by unpublished writers, 50% by authors who are new to the magazine. Receives fewer than 12 unsolicited mss yearly.

Submissions
Send complete ms. Accepts hard copy and simultaneous submissions if identified. SASE. Responds in 1 month.
Articles: 1,000–2,250 words. Informational articles; profiles; and interviews. Topics include gymnastics competitions, coaching, and personalities involved in the sport around the world.
Fiction: To 1,500 words. Stories about gymnastics.
Depts/columns: 700–1,000 words. News, training tips, and opinion pieces.
Artwork: B/W prints. 35mm color slides for cover.

Sample Issue
46 pages (14% advertising): 4 articles; 9 depts/columns. Sample copy, $5 with 9x12 SASE. Guidelines available.
• "Italian Ice." Article reports on the winners of the French International.
• "Gene Wettstone." Article profiles a Penn State coaching legend who was as good at running tournaments as he was at winning them.
• Sample dept/column: "All Around the World" presents global gymnastics news.

Rights and Payment
All rights. Written material, $15–$25. Artwork, $5–$50. Pays on publication. Provides 1 author's copy.

Editor's Comments
We continue to look for well-written articles and interviews that focus on the top figures in artistic/rhythmic gymnastics and sports gymnastics. Include interesting facts; tell us something we don't already know.

Jack And Jill

Children's Better Health Institute
1100 Waterway Boulevard
P.O. Box 567
Indianapolis, IN 46206-0567

Editor: Daniel Lee

Description and Interests
Principles of good health and nutrition are at the heart of all the materials found in *Jack And Jill*. Its articles, stories, puzzles, and activities are designed to appeal to children in second and third grades.
- **Audience:** 7–10 years
- **Frequency:** 6 times each year
- **Circulation:** 200,000
- **Website: www.jackandjillmag.org**

Freelance Potential
10% written by nonstaff writers. Publishes 10 freelance submissions yearly; 70% by authors who are new to the magazine. Receives 1,200 unsolicited mss yearly.

Submissions
Send complete ms. Accepts hard copy. SASE. Responds in 3 months.
Articles: 500–600 words. Informational and how-to articles; humor; profiles; and biographies. Topics include sports, health, exercise, safety, nutrition, and hygiene.
Fiction: 500–900 words. Genres include mystery, fantasy, folktales, humor, science fiction, and stories about sports and animals.
Artwork: Submit sketches to Andrea O'Shea, art director; photos to Daniel Lee, editor.
Other: Poetry, games, puzzles, activities, and cartoons. Submit seasonal material 8 months in advance.

Sample Issue
36 pages (4% advertising): 4 articles; 1 story; 7 activities; 1 cartoon; 2 poems. Sample copy, $6.50 ($2 postage). Guidelines available.
- "Nature's Magician." Article presents fun scientific facts about water and the mechanics of how things float.
- "The Milky Way." Article explains the differences between goat's milk and cow's milk.
- "The Kids and the Wolf." Funny story features wolves that get hooked on video games.

Rights and Payment
All rights. Articles and fiction, $.17 per word. Other material, payment rates vary. Pays on publication. Provides 10 contributor's copies.

Editor's Comments
Humorous stories are especially needed. Nonfiction may deal with sports, science, nature—even historical and biographical topics—and should touch on health and fitness.

JAKES Magazine

P.O. Box 530
Edgefield, SC 29824

Editor: Matt Lindler

Description and Interests
This is the membership magazine of the National Wild Turkey Federation's youth club, Juniors Acquiring Knowledge, Ethics and Sportsmanship (JAKES). Its content teaches readers the importance of wildlife conservation and the stewardship of natural resources. The magazine includes a special section for teens, *Xtreme JAKES*.
- **Audience:** 10–17 years
- **Frequency:** Quarterly
- **Circulation:** 200,000
- **Website: www.nwtf.org/jakes**

Freelance Potential
50% written by nonstaff writers. Publishes 30 freelance submissions yearly; 10% by unpublished writers, 50% by authors who are new to the magazine. Receives 150–200 queries and unsolicited mss yearly.

Submissions
Query or send complete ms. Accepts material between May and December only. Accepts hard copy, email to MLindler@nwtf.org, and simultaneous submissions if identified. SASE. Response time varies.
Articles: 600–1,200 words. Informational articles; profiles; and personal experience pieces. Topics include nature, the environment, animals, pets, hunting, fishing, and other outdoor sports.
Fiction: 800–1,200 words. Historical fiction.

Sample Issue
32 pages: 6 articles; 1 story; 11 depts/columns. Guidelines available at website.
- "Watch Your Step." Article explains that new species of animals are still being discovered.
- "An Appreciation for Ditches." Article tells how duck hunters can sometimes find their prey in irrigation ditches.
- Sample dept/column: "Super JAKES" profiles a young hunter.

Rights and Payment
Rights vary. Written material, $100–$300. Pays on publication. Provides 2 contributor's copies.

Editor's Comments
We are interested in submissions for all sections of our magazine. We need fun stories that will hold the interest of our younger readers, as well as seasonal articles on extreme sports for our teen section, *Xtreme JAKES*.

Journal of Adolescent & Adult Literacy

International Reading Association
800 Barksdale Road, P.O. Box 8139
Newark, DE 19714-8139

Editorial Assistant: Cynthia Sawaya

Description and Interests
This magazine offers articles and resources for educators to assist them in motivating children to embrace the written word. It includes information on research and practices for teaching reading and current theories.
- **Audience:** Reading education professionals
- **Frequency:** 8 times each year
- **Circulation:** 16,000
- **Website: www.reading.org**

Freelance Potential
95% written by nonstaff writers. Publishes 50 freelance submissions yearly; 30% by unpublished writers, 50% by authors who are new to the magazine. Receives 300 unsolicited mss yearly.

Submissions
Send complete ms. Accepts electronic submissions through http://mc.manuscripts.com/ira/jaal. Responds in 2–3 months.
Articles: 1,000–6,000 words. Informational and how-to articles; and personal experience pieces. Topics include reading theory, research, and practice; and trends in teaching literacy.
Depts/columns: Word lengths vary. Opinion pieces, reviews, and technology information.

Sample Issue
94 pages (7% advertising): 5 articles; 5 depts/columns. Sample copy, $10.
- "Monstrous Acts: Problematizing Violence in Young Adult Literature." Article presents an analysis of eight novels and offers ideas and resources for engaging students in discussion.
- "Multicultural Literature and Young Adolescents: A Kaleidoscope of Opportunity." Article discusses why it is beneficial for teachers to incorporate multicultural literature into their curriculum.
- Sample dept/column: "First Person" looks at a reading strategy of a middle school reading teacher.

Rights and Payment
All rights. No payment. Provides 5 contributor's copies for articles; 2 copies for depts/columns.

Editor's Comments
Articles that detail classroom strategies are needed at this time. Research studies should be presented as well-written articles with statistics incorporated into the text. Please avoid stereotyping on the basis of age, sex, or race.

Journal of Adventist Education

12501 Old Columbia Pike
Silver Spring, MD 20904-6600

Editor: Beverly J. Rumble

Description and Interests
Educators who nurture and foster the principles of the Seventh-day Adventist faith subscribe to this magazine. It looks for innovative, effective, and inspirational teaching strategies that can be used at the elementary, secondary, and college levels.
- **Audience:** Educators, school board members
- **Frequency:** 5 times each year
- **Circulation:** 15,000
- **Website: http://education.gc.adventist.org/JAE**

Freelance Potential
90% written by nonstaff writers. Publishes 30 freelance submissions yearly. Receives 24–48 queries each year.

Submissions
Query. Accepts hard copy. Availability of artwork improves chance of acceptance. SASE. Responds in 3 weeks.
Articles: To 2,000 words. Informational and how-to articles. Topics include parochial, gifted, and special education; new teaching methods and educational approaches; school administration and supervision; classroom management; religion; mathematics; science; and technology.
Artwork: B/W and color prints and transparencies. Line art.

Sample Issue
46 pages (5% advertising): 7 articles. Sample copy, $3.50 with 9x12 SASE ($.68 postage). Writers' guidelines available.
- "What Adventist Colleges Are Looking for in Academy Graduates." Article argues for the need to begin a collaborative conversation about expectations and standards at all levels of Adventist education.
- "Families Go Back to School." Article details a pilot program at an Adventist school that promotes parent involvement in education.

Rights and Payment
First North American serial rights. Articles, to $100. Artwork, payment rates vary. Pays on publication. Provides 2 contributor's copies.

Editor's Comments
Good quality photographs play an important role in whether or not your article will be accepted. Color images are preferred. We also tend to favor articles that are more practical than theoretical.

Journal of School Health

American School Health Association
7263 State Route 43
P.O. Box 708
Kent, OH 44240-0708

Editor: James H. Price

Description and Interests
For 78 years, this official journal of the American School Health Association has kept health care professionals up to date with information pertaining to the health of children. It features educational articles and research papers.
• **Audience:** School health professionals
• **Frequency:** 10 times each year
• **Circulation:** 5,000
• **Website:** www.ashaweb.org

Freelance Potential
95% written by nonstaff writers. Publishes 60 freelance submissions yearly; 90% by authors who are new to the magazine. Receives 120 queries yearly.

Submissions
Query or send complete ms. Accepts email only through www.manuscriptcentral.com/josh. Responds to queries in 2 weeks, to mss in 3–4 months.
Articles: 2,500 words. Informational articles; research papers; commentaries; and practical application pieces. Topics include teaching techniques, health services in the school system, nursing, medicine, substance abuse, nutrition, counseling, and ADD/ADHD.

Sample Issue
58 pages (no advertising): 3 articles; 4 research papers; 1 commentary. Sample copy, $8.50 with 9x12 SASE. Guidelines available at website.
• "Fetal Alcohol Spectrum Disorders." Article addresses diagnostic issues related to fetal alcohol syndrome (FAS) and other alcohol-related disabilities, discusses features and behaviors, and introduces interventions to support children with FASD.
• "Food Fight: The Battle Over Redefining Competitive Foods." Article focuses on the school lunch environment and examines the key legal and policy factors that affect the value of competitive foods in schools and legislation on redefining it.

Rights and Payment
All rights. No payment. Provides 2 author's copies.

Editor's Comments
We are open to articles, research papers, commentaries, teaching techniques, and health service applications on topics related to safeguarding the health of school-aged children. Writers should be professionals in the health care field, and must submit in accordance with our specific guidelines.

JUCO Review

1755 Telstar Drive, Suite 103
Colorado Springs, CO 80920

Executive Director: Wayne Baker

Description and Interests
As the official publication of the National Junior College Athletic Association, this magazine provides its members with news about the association, coaches, athletes, and junior colleges.
• **Audience:** YA–Adult
• **Frequency:** 10 times each year
• **Circulation:** 2,850
• **Website:** www.njcaa.com

Freelance Potential
30–40% written by nonstaff writers. Publishes 5–7 freelance submissions yearly. Receives up to 12 unsolicited mss yearly.

Submissions
Send complete ms. Accepts hard copy. Availability of artwork improves chance of acceptance. SASE. Responds in 2 months.
Articles: 1,500–2,000 words. Informational articles. Topics include sports, college, careers, health, fitness, and NJCAA news.
Artwork: B/W prints and transparencies.

Sample Issue
24 pages (25% advertising): 7 articles. Sample copy, $4 for current issue; $3 for back issue with 9x12 SASE. Editorial calendar available.
• "Bismarck State College." Article profiles the athletic program at this North Dakota school.
• "Anoka-Ramsey's Women's Basketball Team Captures College's Sixth Title." News story summarizes this Minnesota junior college's championship game.
• "2006-07 NJCAA Division II Men's Basketball National Championship." Article summarizes the tournament and mentions key players.

Rights and Payment
One-time rights. No payment. Provides 3 copies.

Editor's Comments
Coverage of the sports programs, players, and coaches of member schools is the predominant focus of the magazine. On occasion, we will publish general interest articles about nutrition, health, and fitness targeted to both male and female athletes at the junior college level. Writers with ties to junior college basketball, ice hockey, bowling, wrestling, track and field, or swimming and diving are welcome to submit a piece for our review.

Junior Baseball

P.O. Box 9099
Canoga Park, CA 91309

Editor/Publisher: Dave Destler

Description and Interests
"America's youth baseball magazine" offers technical tips and other information in articles written for specific age groups, including parents and coaches.
• **Audience:** 7–17 years; parents and coaches
• **Frequency:** 6 times each year
• **Circulation:** 32,000
• **Website:** www.juniorbaseball.com

Freelance Potential
50% written by nonstaff writers. Publishes 20 freelance submissions yearly; 10% by unpublished writers, 20% by authors who are new to the magazine. Receives 50 queries and unsolicited mss yearly.

Submissions
Query with writing samples; or send complete ms with color photos. Prefers email submissions to dave@ juniorbaseball.com (Microsoft Word attachments or text). Availability of artwork improves chance of acceptance. SASE. Responds in 1–2 weeks.
Articles: 1,000–2,000 words. Informational and how-to articles; profiles; and interviews. Topics include playing tips, teams and leagues, and player safety.
Depts/columns: "Player's Story," 500 words. "In the Spotlight" news and reviews, 50–100 words. "Hot Prospects," 500–1,000 words. "Coaches' Clinic," 100–1,000 words.
Artwork: 4x5, 5x7 and 8x10 color prints. Color digital images at 300 dpi.

Sample Issue
34 pages (30% advertising): 5 articles; 12 depts/ columns. Sample copy, $3.95 with 9x12 SASE ($1.35 postage). Guidelines available.
• "When I Was a Kid." Article features an interview with Major League pitcher Andy Pettitte.
• "The Myth of the Level Swing." Article explains why a great swing is actually not level at all.
• Sample dept/column: "Player's Story" is an essay by a young boy about playing in a championship.

Rights and Payment
All rights. Articles, $.20 per word. Depts/columns, $25–$100. Artwork, $50–$150. Pays on publication. Provides 1 contributor's copy.

Editor's Comments
Writers interested in contributing must be well-versed in the subject matter, as our readers are intelligent and know their sport!

JuniorWay

P.O. Box 436987
Chicago, IL 60643

Editor: Katherine Steward

Description and Interests
Distributed to urban children through Sunday school programs, *JuniorWay* offers fun activities and stories centering on a different theme each issue. Its content expresses and explores Christian values through hip, child-friendly language.
• **Audience:** 9–11 years
• **Frequency:** Quarterly
• **Circulation:** 75,000
• **Website:** www.urbanministries.com

Freelance Potential
95% written by nonstaff writers. Publishes 52 freelance submissions yearly. Receives 240 queries yearly.

Submissions
Query with résumé and writing samples. All material is written on assignment. Response time varies.
Articles: Word lengths vary. Bible lessons, personal experience pieces, and humor. Topics include religion, relationships, social issues, hobbies, crafts, sports, recreation, and multicultural subjects.
Fiction: Word lengths vary. Inspirational stories with multicultural or ethnic themes, adventure stories, humor, and folktales.
Artwork: B/W and color prints and transparencies.
Other: Puzzles, activities, games, and jokes. Poetry. Seasonal material about Vacation Bible School.

Sample Issue
34 pages (no advertising): 1 article; 13 Bible lessons; 4 activities; 1 poem; 4 jokes. Sample copy, free. Guidelines and theme list available.
• "Pathfinders." Article profiles the Fisk Jubilee Singers, who introduced and popularized Negro spirituals in the 1800s.
• "With This Ring." Story and Bible lesson describe a girl's pledge of chastity until marriage.
• Sample dept/column: "Phat Phun" includes silly jokes submitted by readers.

Rights and Payment
All rights. All material, payment rates vary. Pays on publication.

Editor's Comments
Since 1970, we have been developing quality Sunday school lessons especially designed to empower African American children for successful Christian living. We give teachers the tools to inspire these children while they learn about and follow Jesus Christ.

Justine Magazine

6263 Poplar Avenue, Suite 1154
Memphis, TN 38119

Editorial Director/Publisher: Jana Petty

Description and Interests

Justine Magazine seeks to set itself apart from other teen celebrity and beauty magazines by offering wholesome, tasteful articles that appeal to adolescent girls. Its features focus on building self-confidence and healthy relationships while also presenting nutrition, exercise, fashion, beauty, and makeup advice. It also includes updates on books, movies, and entertainment for teens.
- **Audience:** 13–18 years
- **Frequency:** 6 times each year
- **Circulation:** 250,000
- **Website:** www.justinemagazine.com

Freelance Potential

20% written by nonstaff writers. Publishes 25 freelance submissions yearly; 25% by unpublished writers, 90% by authors who are new to the magazine. Receives 100 queries yearly.

Submissions

Query with résumé and clips. Accepts hard copy. SASE. Response time varies.
Articles: Word lengths vary. Informational articles; profiles; and personal experience pieces. Topics include room decorating, beauty, health, nutrition, family issues, recreation, travel, and fashion.
Depts/columns: Word lengths vary. Media and book reviews, entertainment, exercise, and community service activities.

Sample Issue

96 pages: 5 articles; 32 depts/columns; 1 quiz. Sample copy, $2.99 at newsstands.
- "Rooney Rules." Article profiles a five-piece rock/pop band from California that is currently touring with superstar Fergie.
- "High Mile(y)age." Article visits with Miley Stewart, the star of *Hannah Montana.*
- Sample dept/column: "Just' Beauty" offers tips for revamping your makeup before school starts.

Rights and Payment

Rights vary. Written material, payment rates vary. Pays 30 days after publication.

Editor's Comments

Our purpose is to provide up-to-the-minute reports on fashion, beauty, popular culture, and entertainment while keeping our content wholesome. Contact us if you feel your writing will fit in with our mission.

Kaboose.com

505 University Avenue
Toronto, Ontario M5G 1X3
Canada

Editor: Leigh Felesky

Description and Interests

Moms turn to this online magazine for information, ideas, and inspiration that will help them plan a better life for their family. Most readers have children between the ages of four and fourteen.
- **Audience:** Mothers
- **Frequency:** Unavailable
- **Hits per month:** Unavailable
- **Website:** www.kaboose.com

Freelance Potential

95% written by nonstaff writers. Publishes 30 freelance submissions yearly; 10% by unpublished writers, 30% by authors who are new to the magazine. Receives 150 queries yearly.

Submissions

Query with outline. Accepts email queries to leigh.felesky@kaboose.com. SASE. Responds in 6 weeks.
Articles: 2,000 words. Informational and how-to articles. Topics include health, fitness, food, kids' activities, celebrity updates, style, home and garden, crafts, hobbies, and pets.
Depts/columns: 500 words. Advice, travel, entertainment, recipes, parties, and holidays.
Other: Accepts material on Christmas, Easter, Thanksgiving, and other events that bring families together 6 months in advance.

Sample Issue

Sample copy, writers' guidelines, and theme list available at website.
- "Share Memories: 9 Tips for Scrapbooking with Your Daughter." Article tells how to make the most of quality time with your daughter by creating a scrapbook together.
- "Immune Boosters for the Whole Family." Article features expert advice for staying healthy over the winter.
- Sample dept/column: "Crafts" provides instructions for making a sparkly snowflake mobile.

Rights and Payment

Rights vary. Written material, $.85 per word. Pays on acceptance. Contributor's copies available at website.

Editor's Comments

We're looking for concise, accessible articles written in the active voice. New writers have the best chance if they submit material on health, food, and style. Please don't send first-hand stories with a narrow focus.

Kaleidoscope

Exploring the Experience of Disability through Literature & Fine Arts

701 South Main Street
Akron, OH 44311-1019

Editor-in-Chief: Gail Willmott

Description and Interests
The experience of disability is examined through the lens of fine arts and literature in *Kaleidoscope*. Its articles are written from the perspectives of individuals, families, and healthcare professionals.
- **Audience:** YA–Adult
- **Frequency:** Twice each year
- **Circulation:** 1,000
- **Website:** www.udsakron.org

Freelance Potential
90% written by nonstaff writers. Publishes 50 freelance submissions yearly; 10% by unpublished writers, 90% by authors who are new to the magazine. Receives 300–400 queries and unsolicited mss yearly.

Submissions
Query or send complete ms with author bio. Accepts hard copy and email submissions to mshiplett@udsakron.org (Microsoft Word attachments). SASE. Responds to queries in 2 weeks, to mss in 6 months.
Articles: 5,000 words. Informational articles; personal experience pieces; profiles; interviews; reviews; and humor. Topics include art, literature, biography, multicultural and social issues, and disabilities.
Fiction: 5,000 words. Genres include folktales, humor, and multicultural and problem-solving fiction.
Other: Poetry.

Sample Issue
64 pages (no advertising): 8 articles; 4 stories; 11 poems; 1 comic. Sample copy, $6 with 9x12 SASE. Guidelines and editorial calendar available.
- "Inner Strength Revealed by Being Torn Apart." Article showcases the work of an artist who suffers from fibromyalgia.
- "A Sign and a Prayer." Story features a woman who signs for the deaf at a church service.

Rights and Payment
First rights. Written material, $25–$100. Poetry, $10. Pays on publication. Provides 2 contributor's copies.

Editor's Comments
To be published in our magazine, you must avoid stereotypical, patronizing, and sentimental attitudes about disability. The criteria of good writing apply: effective technique and thought-provoking subject matter. We are interested in reviewing more humorous pieces.

Kansas School Naturalist

Department of Biological Sciences
Emporia State University
1200 Commercial Street
Emporia, KS 66801-5087

Editor: John Richard Schrock

Description and Interests
Each issue of *Kansas School Naturalist* provides an in-depth investigation of a topic relating to the state's natural ecology. Wildlife, birds, insects, natural resources, and natural history are among the subjects covered. Published collaboratively by Emporia State University and the Kansas Department of Wildlife and Parks, it is used as a teaching tool in schools, universities, and nature-education programs.
- **Audience:** Teachers; librarians; conservationists
- **Frequency:** Irregular
- **Circulation:** 9,800
- **Website:** www.emporia.edu/ksn

Freelance Potential
75% written by nonstaff writers. Of the freelance submissions published yearly, 20% are by unpublished writers and 75% are by authors who are new to the magazine.

Submissions
Query or send complete ms. Accepts hard copy and IBM disk submissions. SASE. Response time varies.
Articles: Word lengths vary. Informational and how-to articles. Topics include natural history, nature, science, technology, animals, health, and education—all with a Kansas focus.
Artwork: B/W and color prints and transparencies.
Other: Seasonal material.

Sample Issue
16 pages (no advertising): 1 article. Sample copy, free.
- "Life History of Kansas Freshwater Mussels." Article reviews the life cycle of freshwater mussels and explains that they are one of the most imperiled animals in North America, with seven species now state-listed as endangered in Kansas and five species gone from the state.

Rights and Payment
All rights. No payment. Provides contributor's copies.

Editor's Comments
All of the material we publish is scientifically and technically accurate, but the writing style of the articles is approachable rather than overly academic. You must have scientific qualifications to write about the subject you are addressing, and your article must in some way address the nature, wildlife, or natural history of Kansas.

Keeping Family First Online Magazine

P.O. Box 36594
Detroit, MI 48236

Executive Editor: Anita S. Lane

Description and Interests
Keeping Family First is an online community of moms and dads who are dedicated to building strong families. The first of its kind on the Web, it offers solutions-oriented articles; inspirational interviews; resources for the family; and home, work, and leisure ideas to today's busy mom and dad.
• **Audience:** Parents
• **Frequency:** 6 times each year
• **Hits per month:** 40,000
• **Website:** www.KeepingFamilyFirst.org

Freelance Potential
100% written by nonstaff writers. Publishes 70 freelance submissions yearly; 56% by unpublished writers, 10% by authors who are new to the magazine.

Submissions
Query. Accepts email queries with online query form at www.keepingfamilyfirst.org/submissions.html. Response time varies.
Articles: Word lengths vary. Informational articles; profiles; and personal experience pieces. Topics include parenting, health, spirituality, education, recreation, home, leisure, entertainment.
Depts/columns: Word lengths vary. Parenting tips, family issues, travel, and recreation.

Sample Issue
8 articles; 13 depts/columns. Guidelines available at website.
• "Sweet Contentment!" Article discusses the importance of being satisfied with yourself before searching for a soul mate.
• "Naturally Cool." Article describes the benefits of wearing cotton during the summer months.
• Sample dept/column: "HomeSpot" explores the importance of families having a paper management plan in place.

Rights and Payment
Rights vary. No payment.

Editor's Comments
We're catching on and spreading like wildfire among families, and are always on the lookout for well-written articles from freelance writers. Articles of interest to us include practical solutions and advice for time-stretched, busy moms and dads; inspirational pieces on the challenges parents face; and articles covering home, leisure, and entertainment topics.

Keynoter

Key Club International
3636 Woodview Trace
Indianapolis, IN 46268-3196

Executive Editor: Shanna Mooney

Description and Interests
Keynoter is published for high school students who are involved in their local Key Clubs. In addition to reports on club activities and events, it prints articles of general interest to teens on academics, community service, and social issues.
• **Audience:** 14–18 years
• **Frequency:** 8 times each year
• **Circulation:** 240,000
• **Website:** www.keyclub.org/magazine

Freelance Potential
40% written by nonstaff writers. Publishes 16 freelance submissions yearly; 10% by unpublished writers, 30% by authors who are new to the magazine. Receives 100 queries yearly.

Submissions
Query with outline/synopsis and clips or writing samples. Accepts hard copy, email queries to keynoter@kiwanis.org, and simultaneous submissions if identified. SASE. Responds in 1 month.
Articles: 1,000–1,500 words. Informational, self-help, and service-related articles. Topics include education, teen concerns, community service, leadership, school activities, social issues, and careers.
Depts/columns: Staff written.
Artwork: Color prints and illustrations.
Other: Submit seasonal material about back to school, college, and summer activities 3–7 months in advance.

Sample Issue
18 pages (5% advertising): 3 articles; 3 depts/columns. Sample copy, free with 9x12 SASE ($.83 postage). Guidelines available.
• "Etiquette Makes a Comeback." Article addresses the nuances of dressing appropriately, properly introducing people, and writing thank you notes.
• Sample dept/column: "Spotlight" reports on how a number of clubs in Arizona worked together on a suicide prevention project.

Rights and Payment
First North American serial rights. All material, $150–$350. Pays on acceptance. Provides 3 copies.

Editor's Comments
We continue to look for articles that offer a high school student's perspective on contemporary social and cultural issues.

Keys for Kids

P.O. Box 1001
Grand Rapids, MI 49510

Editor: Hazel Merett

Description and Interests
This Christian publication targets children in grade school and middle school. Each digest-sized issue of *Keys for Kids* is filled with devotionals based on Scripture passages that include key Bible verses and key thoughts.
• **Audience:** 6–12 years
• **Frequency:** 6 times each year
• **Circulation:** 70,000
• **Website:** www.keysforkids.org

Freelance Potential
99% written by nonstaff writers. Publishes 50–60 freelance submissions yearly; 50% by authors who are new to the magazine. Receives 144 unsolicited mss yearly.

Submissions
Send complete ms. Accepts hard copy and email submissions to hazel@cbhministries.org. SASE. Responds in 2 months.
Articles: 400 words. Devotionals with related Scripture passages and a key thought. Topics include contemporary social issues, family life, trust, friendship, salvation, witnessing, prayer, marriage, and faith.

Sample Issue
72 pages: 61 devotionals. Sample copy, free with 9x12 SASE. Guidelines available.
• "All-the-Time Friend." Devotional features a girl whose friend is only her friend when she needs something.
• "The Free Tickets." Devotional explores what it takes to get into heaven through a story about buying tickets to a baseball game.
• "The Ticking Watch." Devotional addresses issues associated with grief and the loss of a loved one.

Rights and Payment
First, second, and reprint rights. Written material, $25. Pays on acceptance. Provides 1 contributor's copy.

Editor's Comments
The devotionals you submit should include an illustration of the lesson being taught—an everyday happening or object that illustrates a spiritual or biblical truth. The kids in the stories should be normal, ordinary kids, not "goody-goodies." You should always include some action—not conversation only. We are willing to address controversial subjects as long as they are handled carefully and clearly.

The Kids Hall of Fame® News

3 Ibsen Court
Dix Hills, NY 11746

Publisher: Dr. Victoria Nesnick

Description and Interests
This online magazine profiles young people with extraordinary talents or achievements, from a 2-year-old political whiz to an 18-year-old award-winning violinist.
• **Audience:** All ages
• **Frequency:** Unavailable
• **Hits per month:** 8,000
• **Website:** www.thekidshalloffame.com

Freelance Potential
40% written by nonstaff writers. Publishes 300 freelance submissions yearly; 10% by unpublished writers, 20% by authors who are new to the magazine. Receives 1,200 unsolicited mss yearly.

Submissions
Send complete ms with nomination form, photos, and optional supporting material. Accepts hard copy. SASE. Responds in 1–2 months.
Articles: 1,000–2,000 words. Profiles and personal experience pieces about extraordinary youngsters, grouped by age and category.
Artwork: 4x6, 5x7, or 8x10 color prints. Photos should depict significant aspects of the achievement.

Sample Issue
Sample copy and guidelines available at website.
• "Mayalee Hogan." Article profiles a 2-year-old jigsaw puzzle expert and geography whiz.
• "Richard Foster." Article profiles a 7-year-old carpenter and entrepreneur who went on to tape a television show, acquire patents for innovative wooden clocks, and start his own company by age 14.
• "Andrew Dunckelman." Article profiles a 15-year-old boy who founded Operation Cover-Up, a nonprofit organization that educates inner-city parents and children about the risks of sun exposure.

Rights and Payment
Rights vary. Payment rates vary. Pays on acceptance.

Editor's Comments
Please see our website for categories and nomination forms. The nominee's story should focus on one specific age and explain the significance of the achievement; who or what provided inspiration; trade-offs or sacrifices; obstacles surmounted; support team; and advice to peers. Additional supporting material, such as newspaper and magazine clippings, is optional. Include as many photos as you'd like.

Kids Life

1426 22nd Avenue
Tuscaloosa, AL 35401

Publisher: Mary Jane Turner

Description and Interests
A regional parenting publication, *Kids Life* caters to families who reside in western Alabama and the Tuscaloosa area. Its articles and departments focus on general parenting topics, pediatric health, education, family activities, and regional resources.
- **Audience:** Parents
- **Frequency:** 6 times each year
- **Circulation:** 30,000
- **Website:** www.kidslifemagazine.com

Freelance Potential
75% written by nonstaff writers. Publishes 20 freelance submissions yearly; 50% by unpublished writers, 10% by authors who are new to the magazine. Receives 100 unsolicited mss each year.

Submissions
Query or send complete ms. Accepts hard copy and email submissions to kidslife@comcast.net. SASE. Responds to email in 2 weeks.
Articles: 1,000 words. Informational articles; reviews; and personal experience pieces. Topics include parenting, education, child care, religion, cooking, crafts, health, and current events.
Artwork: Color prints or transparencies. Line art.
Other: Puzzles and games. Poetry, to 100 lines.

Sample Issue
40 pages (60% advertising): 6 articles; 4 depts/columns; 1 calendar. Sample copy, free.
- "Communicating with Tweens: Are You Listening to Me?" Article explains how to keep the lines of communication open with children during those pre-teen years.
- "Homeschooling in Tuscaloosa: A Portrait of Family and Faith." Article chronicles the typical day of a homeschooling family.
- Sample dept/column: "Time Keeps on Slipping" is an essay about teaching kids kindness in a self-absorbed world.

Rights and Payment
Rights vary. Written material, to $30. Pays on publication. Provides 1 contributor's copy.

Editor's Comments
This year, we would like to see more write-ups that deal with parenting teens and tweens. Regional child-related events and family activities are also always welcome. Remember, our readers are busy moms and dads.

Kids' Ministry Ideas

55 West Oak Ridge Drive
Hagerstown, MD 21740

Editor

Description and Interests
Published by the Seventh-day Adventists, this magazine provides information and support to adults who work with children in local churches. Each issue contains programming and teaching ideas while affirming the importance of teachers and leaders in the spiritual growth of children.
- **Audience:** Teachers; youth leaders; parents
- **Frequency:** Quarterly
- **Circulation:** 4,500
- **Website:** www.reviewandherald.org

Freelance Potential
100% written by nonstaff writers. Publishes 60 freelance submissions yearly.

Submissions
Send complete ms. Accepts hard copy and email submissions to kidsmin@rhpa.org. SASE. Response time varies.
Articles: 300–800 words. Informational articles. Topics include religious program ideas, resources, youth ministry, family, Vacation Bible School, spirituality, faith, and prayer.
Depts/columns: Word lengths vary. Leadership and teaching ideas, crafts.

Sample Issue
32 pages: 4 articles; 8 depts/columns. Sample copy and guidelines available.
- "The Only Jesus." Article reflects on why it's important to continue to teach Sabbath School despite the challenges, and offers tips for keeping a classroom running smoothly.
- "Sidewalk Kids' Hour." Article describes an innovative, mobile children's program being piloted in the Portland, Oregon, area.
- Sample dept/column: "Capturing Curiosity" tells why we should be thankful for the gifts our pets give us.

Rights and Payment
First North American serial rights. Written material, $20–$100. Pays 5–6 weeks after acceptance. Provides 1 contributor's copy.

Editor's Comments
We are dedicated to strengthening children's outreach plans, and keeping kids eager and growing. We want material that will help put a sparkle into the weekly programs offered for children. All articles should use quotes and cite sources.

Kids VT

10½ Alfred Street
Burlington, VT 05401

Editor: Susan Holson

Description and Interests
Subtitled "Vermont's Family Newspaper," this free tabloid targets parents with helpful articles on everything from pregnancy to primary school. It also provides a guide to regional happenings.
- **Audience:** Parents
- **Frequency:** 10 times each year
- **Circulation:** 25,000
- **Website:** www.kidsvt.com

Freelance Potential
50% written by nonstaff writers. Publishes 25–30 freelance submissions yearly; 30% by authors who are new to the magazine. Receives 480–960 unsolicited mss yearly.

Submissions
Send complete ms. Prefers email to editorial@kidsvt.com (no attachments). Will accept hard copy, disk submissions (Microsoft Word), and simultaneous submissions if identified. SASE. Responds only if interested.
Articles: 500–1,500 words. Informational articles; profiles; interviews; and humor. Topics include the arts, education, recreation, nature, the environment, music, camps, pregnancy, and infancy.
Depts/columns: Word lengths vary. News and media reviews.
Other: Activities and games. Submit seasonal material 2 months in advance.

Sample Issue
40 pages (50% advertising): 11 articles; 11 depts/columns. Guidelines and editorial calendar available at website.
- "A Different Kind of Baby Gift." Article discusses the European tradition of giving wine from a child's birth year to keep until adulthood.
- "Ending the Cycle." Article talks about the effects of parental depression on children.
- Sample dept/column: "Just for Fun" details the Vermont Balloon and Music Festival.

Rights and Payment
Exclusive Vermont rights. Written material, payment rates vary. Pays 30 days after publication. Provides 1–2 contributor's copies.

Editor's Comments
A well-written local piece is preferred. We also like to print local sidebars to general articles.

Kid Zone

801 W. Norton Avenue, Suite 200
Muskegon, MI 49441

Editor: Anne Huizenga

Description and Interests
This magazine offers a great way for kids to have fun reading, creating, learning, and exploring. Each issue is chock full of informational articles on topics such as animals, science, and history, as well as games, recipes, trivia, puzzles, and crafts.
- **Audience:** 4–12 years
- **Frequency:** 6 times each year
- **Circulation:** 65,000
- **Website:** www.scottpublications.com

Freelance Potential
90% written by nonstaff writers. Publishes 20–30 freelance submissions yearly; 25% by authors who are new to the magazine. Receives 60–100 queries and unsolicited mss yearly.

Submissions
Query or send complete ms. Accepts hard copy and email to ahuizenga@scottpublications.com. Availability of artwork improves chance of acceptance. SASE. Responds to queries in 1 month, to mss in 1 year.
Articles: 500 words. Factual and informational articles. Topics include animals, food, culture, holiday and seasonal topics, science, and safety.
Artwork: Color prints or transparencies.
Other: Submit seasonal material 4–6 months in advance. See guidelines for specifics.

Sample Issue
50 pages (no advertising): 7 articles; 3 depts/columns; 10 puzzles and activities. Sample copy, $4.99 with 9x12 SASE. Guidelines and theme list available.
- "Grits." Article explores the history of grits and offers several recipes for making grits dishes.
- "Purple Gallinule." Article describes the characteristics of this dark green and purple bird.
- "The Diary." Story tells how animals learn about privacy when they read a friend's diary.

Rights and Payment
World rights. All material, payment rates vary. Pays on publication. Provides 2 contributor's copies.

Editor's Comments
We look for writing using "kid slang." We are interested in articles for our "Zones," including "Culture Zone," "Chop Zone," "Fun Zone," and "Critter Zone." You don't need to provide everything for the feature, you may provide just the information, but extras (games, projects, etc.) will increase your chances of acceptance.

Know

The Science Magazine for Curious Kids

501-3960 Quadra Street
Victoria, British Columbia V8X 4A3
Canada

Managing Editor: Adrienne Mason

Description and Interests
This Canadian magazine strives to engage readers and foster an interest in and appreciation of science. It includes short news items, hands-on activities, theme-related articles, and fiction.
- **Audience:** 6–9 years
- **Frequency:** 6 times each year
- **Circulation:** 9,000
- **Website:** www.knowmag.ca

Freelance Potential
60% written by nonstaff writers. Publishes 20 freelance submissions yearly; 5% by unpublished writers, 20% by new authors. Receives 150 queries yearly.

Submissions
Query with résumé and clips. Send complete ms for poetry and fiction. Accepts hard copy and email submissions to adrienne@knowmag.ca. Include an email address instead of SASE. Responds to queries in 1 month, to mss in 3 months.
Articles: 250 words. Informational and how-to articles. Topics include science, technology, computers, math, nature, the environment, animals, pets, biography, and history of science.
Fiction: 400 words. Theme-related stories.
Depts/columns: 200–250 words. Science news and book and product reviews.
Other: Games, jokes, riddles, poetry, and science experiments.

Sample Issue
32 pages (6% advertising): 5 articles; 9 depts/columns. Sample copy, $3.95 Canadian. Guidelines and theme list available.
- "Science in Action." Article offers a profile of a professor/author who loves dogs.
- "Great Moments in Science." Article spotlights Dorothy Harrison Eustis, a woman who started training schools for guide dogs.
- Sample dept/column: "Digging Dinos" takes a look at a duckbilled dinosaur, the Parasaurolophus.

Rights and Payment
First North American serial rights. Written material, $.40 per word. Pays on publication. Provides 2 contributor's copies.

Editor's Comments
We are looking for material covering science news. Use simple text aimed at curious kids.

Know Your World Extra

Weekly Reader Corporation
1 Reader's Digest Road
Pleasantville, NY 10570

Associate Editor: Jessica Livingston

Description and Interests
This lively magazine aims to inspire reading and expand language skills in students who are struggling to keep up in these areas. Articles are written at a fourth-grade reading level.
- **Audience:** 10–18 years
- **Frequency:** Monthly
- **Circulation:** 97,000
- **Website:** www.weeklyreader.com/kyw

Freelance Potential
5% written by nonstaff writers. Publishes 2–3 freelance submissions yearly; 30% by unpublished writers, 5% by new authors. Receives 10+ queries yearly.

Submissions
Query with writing samples. Accepts hard copy. SASE. Response time varies.
Articles: 350–500 words. Informational and how-to articles; plays; profiles; and interviews. Topics include animals, current events, health, fitness, history, humor, music, popular culture, science, and sports.
Depts/columns: 150–200 words. Current events, health, animals, and sports.
Other: Crosswords, riddles, and puzzles.

Sample Issue
16 pages (no advertising): 3 articles; 1 play; 2 depts/columns. Sample copy, free with 9x12 SASE. Writers' guidelines available.
- "Going to the Dogs." Article profiles a seventh-grade girl who trains puppies to be guide dogs.
- "You're Never Too Old." Play tells the story of a brother and sister whose volunteer work is disrupted by a cartoon ferret.
- Sample dept/column: "Hot Topics" includes a Q&A with drummer Shannon Leto along with technology and food briefs.

Rights and Payment
One-time rights. Written material, payment rates vary. Pays on acceptance. Provides 5 contributor's copies.

Editor's Comments
We aim to catch student interest with timely stories about topics that interest them. Our readers like celebrities, music, and movies, but they are also interested in real-life stories about their peers. Stories about teens overcoming adversity or facing down a perilous situation are popular with our readers. Avoid material that reads like a textbook article or term paper.

Ladies' Home Journal

Meredith Corporation
375 Lexington Avenue, 9th Floor
New York, NY 10017

Deputy Editor: Margot Gilman

Description and Interests
Family life and women's issues are at the core of this widely read magazine. In addition to health, fashion, and beauty features, it includes articles on home management and relationships.
• **Audience:** Women
• **Frequency:** Monthly
• **Circulation:** 4.1 million
• **Website:** www.lhj.com

Freelance Potential
85% written by nonstaff writers. Publishes 25 freelance submissions yearly; 1% by unpublished writers, 5% by authors who are new to the magazine. Receives 2,400 queries yearly.

Submissions
Query with résumé, outline, and clips or writing samples for nonfiction. Accepts fiction through literary agents only. SASE. Responds in 1–3 months.
Articles: 1,500–2,000 words. Informational, how-to, and personal experience articles. Topics include family issues, parenting, social concerns, fashion, beauty, and women's health.
Fiction: Word lengths vary. Accepts agented submissions only.
Depts/columns: Word lengths vary. Parenting and marriage issues; fashion and beauty advice; short lifestyle items.

Sample Issue
156 pages (15% advertising): 13 articles; 7 depts/columns. Sample copy, $2.49 at newsstands.
• "What's Your Stress Weak Spot?" Article explores how stress can affect your body and how to treat the pain that it triggers.
• "Crime and Punishment." Article features a parent's perspective on why discipline is an important factor in shaping a child's character.
• Sample dept/column: "Health Journal" explains why normal sadness is different from depression.

Rights and Payment
All rights. All material, payment rates vary. Pays on publication. Provides 2 contributor's copies.

Editor's Comments
Newsworthy health updates that are of interest to a broad audience are always welcome. We also use dramatic, first-person accounts of challenges faced by parents and families.

Ladybug
The Magazine for Young Children

70 East Lake Street, Suite 300
Chicago, IL 60601

Submissions Editor: Jenny Gillespie

Description and Interests
Ladybug is filled with beautifully illustrated stories, poems, and activities created to delight and enlighten very young children.
• **Audience:** 2–6 years
• **Frequency:** Monthly
• **Circulation:** 125,000
• **Website:** www.cricketmag.com

Freelance Potential
100% written by nonstaff writers. Publishes 100 freelance submissions yearly. Receives 2,400 unsolicited mss yearly.

Submissions
Send complete ms with exact word count. Accepts hard copy and simultaneous submissions. SASE. Responds in 6 months.
Articles: To 400 words. Informational, humorous, and how-to articles. Topics include nature, family, animals, the environment, and other age-appropriate topics.
Fiction: To 800 words. Read-aloud, early reader, picture, and rebus stories. Genres include adventure, humor, fantasy, folktales, and contemporary fiction.
Other: Puzzles, learning activities, games, crafts, finger plays, action rhymes, and songs. Poetry, to 20 lines.

Sample Issue
36 pages (no advertising): 4 stories; 3 poems; 1 song; 1 finger play. Sample copy, $5. Guidelines available at website.
• "Princess Clarabelle." Story tells how a frustrated young princess and her sympathetic mother rewrite the rules for princesses.
• "Midnight and the Night Watchman." Story follows a night watchman as he discovers a special little kitten.
• "Making Music." Four-part finger play teaches about instruments and their sounds.

Rights and Payment
Rights vary. Stories and articles, $.25 per word; $25 minimum. Poems, $3 per line; $25 minimum. Other material, payment rates vary. Pays on publication. Provides 6 contributor's copies.

Editor's Comments
We are geared toward the very young, so every submission must reflect the innocence and wonder of this age group. Poetry and short stories from a child's point of view, as well as fantasy and folktales, are particularly sought at this time.

The Lamp-Post

1106 West 16th Street
Santa Ana, CA 92706

Senior Editor: David G. Clark

Description and Interests
This digest-sized publication is devoted exclusively to the life and works of C. S. Lewis. Published by the C. S. Lewis Society of Southern California, it includes reviews, essays, and articles about this author's writings, as well as stories written in a style similar to his.
- **Audience:** Adults
- **Frequency:** Quarterly
- **Circulation:** 100

Freelance Potential
90% written by nonstaff writers. Publishes 12 freelance submissions yearly; 20% by unpublished writers, 60% by authors who are new to the magazine. Receives 15 unsolicited mss yearly.

Submissions
Send complete ms. Accepts hard copy and email to dgclark@adelphia.net (Microsoft Word or RTF attachments). No simultaneous submissions. SASE. Responds in 2 days.
Articles: 2,000 words. Informational articles and essays. Topics include C. S. Lewis, his works, and the mythopoeic tradition to which Lewis and J. R. R. Tolkien have contributed.
Fiction: Word lengths vary. Stories in the style of the works of C. S. Lewis.
Depts/columns: Word lengths vary. Book reviews.
Other: Poetry, word lengths vary.

Sample Issue
40 pages (15% advertising): 5 articles; 2 poems; 2 depts/columns. Sample copy, $4. Guidelines available in each issue.
- "The Light in the Room: Reflections on Kathryn." Article offers a tribute to a founding member of the C. S. Lewis Society.
- "Poetry." Article examines the history of poetry and why people both love and hate it.

Rights and Payment
Rights vary. No payment. Provides 2 contributor's copies.

Editor's Comments
We always welcome contributions for future issues. While we do accept some fiction, we especially seek thoughtful articles (scholarly or informal), book reviews, and poems that help our readers understand, appreciate, and experience the person and works of C. S. Lewis and his circle of influence.

Language Arts

Ohio State University
333 Arps Hall
1945 North High Street
Columbus, OH 43210

Language Arts Editorial Team

Description and Interests
Published by the National Council of Teachers of English, this journal presents articles about language arts learning and teaching—particularly issues concerning children from preschool through eighth grade.
- **Audience:** Teachers and teacher-educators
- **Frequency:** 6 times each year
- **Circulation:** 22,000
- **Website: www.ncte.org/pubs/journals/la**

Freelance Potential
90% written by nonstaff writers. Publishes 60 freelance submissions yearly; 15% by unpublished writers, 30% by authors who are new to the magazine. Receives 200 unsolicited mss yearly.

Submissions
Send 6 copies of complete ms; include Microsoft Word file on disk or CD. Accepts hard copy and IBM or Macintosh disk submissions. SASE. Responds in 3–12 months.
Articles: 2,500–6,500 words. Research articles; position papers; personal experience pieces; and opinion pieces. Topics include language arts, linguistics, and literacy.
Depts/columns: Word lengths vary. Profiles of children's authors and illustrators; reviews of children's trade books and professional resources; and theme-related research papers.

Sample Issue
87 pages (8% advertising): 4 articles; 6 depts/columns. Sample copy, $12.50 sent to NCTE, 1111 W. Kenyon Rd., Urbana, IL 61801-1096. Guidelines and theme list available from langarts@osu.edu.
- "Santa Stories." Article describes how to handle children's questions about race during picture book read-alouds.
- "Proceed with Caution." Author offers advice on selecting children's books that present Native Americans realistically and accurately.
- Sample dept/column: "Profiles & Perspectives" offers an interview with poet Nikki Grimes.

Rights and Payment
All rights. No payment. Provides 2 author's copies.

Editor's Comments
Personal reflections should be set within a solid research frame. We are not looking for lesson plans or for work that does not challenge the status quo.

170

L.A. Parent

443 East Irving Drive, Suite A
Burbank, CA 91504

Editor: Carolyn Graham

Description and Interests
This award-winning publication provides Southern California's parents with timely information on child rearing, health, education, and social issues, while also keeping its readers up to date on regional family events and activities.
- **Audience:** Parents
- **Frequency:** Monthly
- **Circulation:** 120,000
- **Website:** www.laparent.com

Freelance Potential
70% written by nonstaff writers. Publishes 20 free-lance submissions yearly; 5% by unpublished writers, 10% by authors who are new to the magazine. Receives 120 queries yearly.

Submissions
Query with clips. Accepts hard copy. SASE. Responds in 6 months.
Articles: 400–1,500 words. Practical application and how-to articles; profiles; and interviews. Topics include parenting and family issues, health, fitness, social issues, travel, and gifted and special education.
Depts/columns: 1,000 words. Family life, technology, travel destinations, and crafts.
Artwork: B/W and color prints and transparencies.

Sample Issue
106 pages (60% advertising): 4 articles; 17 depts/columns; 1 calendar. Sample copy, $3. Guidelines and theme list available.
- "Billboard Busters." Article reports that a group of parents fought for the removal of a gruesome bill-board and tells why some outdoor advertising can be a nightmare for parents.
- "Harboring Water Fears." Article talks about ways to prepare children for swimming lessons.
- Sample dept/column: "Ages & Stages" features tips for making sure your child is safe in another family's home.

Rights and Payment
First serial rights. Written material, payment rates vary. Pays on publication. Provides contributor's copies.

Editor's Comments
We are currently looking for articles on education topics, as well as outing-oriented submissions that focus on local places and events. Our tone is friendly, informal, and informative.

Launch Pad

Teen Missions International
885 East Hall Road
Merritt Island, FL 32953

Editor: Linda Maher

Description and Interests
This tabloid publication from Teen Missions International profiles the teen missions and evangelical work done by young Christians around the world. It includes articles about members, alumni news, and personal accounts.
- **Audience:** YA–Adult
- **Frequency:** Once each year
- **Circulation:** Unavailable
- **Website:** www.teenmissions.org

Freelance Potential
10% written by nonstaff writers. Publishes 10 freelance submissions yearly; 15% by unpublished writers, 10% by authors who are new to the magazine. Receives 12–24 queries yearly.

Submissions
Query. Accepts hard copy. SASE. Response time varies.
Articles: Word lengths vary. Informational and factual articles; personal experience pieces; profiles; interviews; and photo-essays. Topics include mission work and teen evangelism in different countries.
Fiction: Word lengths vary. Inspirational, ethnic, and multicultural fiction.
Depts/columns: Word lengths vary. Alumni news and teen mission opportunities.

Sample Issue
8 pages (5% advertising): 3 articles; 3 depts/columns. Sample copy available.
- "New Motorcycle Sunday School Ministry." Article details a new ministry to bring spiritual education and Sunday school classes to remote areas where there are no religious institutions.
- "Highlight on the Petersens." Article tells of the work of a married couple in Zambia and their need for a suitable house to conduct their work.
- Sample dept/column: "Teen Missions Bible Schools Around the World" highlights the Bible, Missionary & Work Training Program around the world.

Rights and Payment
Rights policy varies. No payment.

Editor's Comments
We strive to shine a light on the positive, uplifting work being done by teenagers at our missions around the world. We are in need of testimonials that illustrate the impact teens are making as a result of their short-term mission experiences.

Leadership for Student Activities

National Association of Secondary School Principals
1904 Association Drive
Reston, VA 20191-1537

Editor: Mary E. Johnson

Description and Interests
This magazine serves students, activity advisors, and administrators in secondary schools nationwide and in more than 70 countries internationally. It focuses on activity ideas for honor societies, student councils, and other student volunteer organizations.
- **Audience:** Student leaders and advisors
- **Frequency:** 9 times each year
- **Circulation:** 30,000
- **Website: www.nasc.us**

Freelance Potential
67% written by nonstaff writers. Publishes 18–25 freelance submissions yearly; 75% by unpublished writers, 50% by authors who are new to the magazine. Receives 12–24 queries, 48 unsolicited mss yearly.

Submissions
Query with clips; or send complete ms. Accepts hard copy and email submissions to L4SA@att.net. SASE. Responds to queries in 2 weeks, to mss in 1 month.
Articles: 1,200–1,700 words. Informational and how-to articles; profiles; and interviews. Topics include student activities, leadership development, and careers.
Depts/columns: Reports on special events; 100–350 words. Advice for and by activity advisors; 1,000–1,500 words. National and regional news, leadership plans, and opinion pieces; word lengths vary.
Artwork: B/W and color prints or transparencies.
Other: Submit seasonal material 4 months in advance.

Sample Issue
44 pages (21% advertising): 5 articles; 11 depts/columns. Sample copy, free with 9x12 SASE ($1.24 postage). Guidelines and theme list available.
- "Setting a Standard for Service." Article visits students in Missouri who learned the importance of having a positive impact on the community.
- Sample dept/column: "Project Showcase" describes an event held in a school cafeteria to promote membership in the student council.

Rights and Payment
All rights. Written material, payment rates vary. Payment policy varies. Provides 5 contributor's copies.

Editor's Comments
We want manuscripts that provide practical information for student advisors and student leaders.

Leading Edge

4064 JFSB
Provo, UT 84602

Fiction Director

Description and Interests
Leading Edge publishes science fiction and fantasy short stories, with a focus on new authors. It also offers poetry, articles, book reviews, and interviews related to the science fiction and fantasy genres.
- **Audience:** YA–Adult
- **Frequency:** Twice each year
- **Circulation:** 500
- **Website: www.leadingedgemagazine.com**

Freelance Potential
90% written by nonstaff writers. Publishes 12 freelance submissions yearly; 90% by unpublished writers, 90% by authors who are new to the magazine. Receives 500 unsolicited mss yearly.

Submissions
Send complete ms. Accepts hard copy. No simultaneous submissions. SASE. Responds in 2–3 months.
Articles: 1,000–10,000 words. Informational articles; interviews; and book reviews. Topics include science fiction, fantasy, science, mythology, and speculative anthropology.
Fiction: To 17,000 words. Genres include science fiction and fantasy.
Depts/columns: Staff written.
Other: Poetry, no line limit.

Sample Issue
148 pages (no advertising): 5 stories; 3 poems; 4 depts/columns. Sample copy, $4.95. Writers' guidelines available.
- "Handel's Duelist." Story intertwines the power of computer technology, music, romance, and espionage in a futuristic setting.
- "The Dreamweaver's Dispute." Story features gnomes and other underground dwellers who seek the powers of a dreamweaver.
- "Sleepers, Sleep No More." Story tells of ageless, nomadic space voyagers hiding from death.

Rights and Payment
First North American serial rights. Written material, $.01 per word. Pays on publication. Provides 2 contributor's copies.

Editor's Comments
We are interested in submissions of creative, exciting science fiction and fantasy short stories from new authors. Our editors will supply writers with a critique of their work upon request.

Learning and Leading with Technology

International Society for Technology in Education
175 West Broadway, Suite 300
Eugene, OR 97401-3003

Managing Editor: Davis N. Smith

Description and Interests
Practical ideas for integrating technology into kindergarten through twelfth-grade classrooms are showcased in this publication. It is read by teachers and administrators who are interested in innovative curriculum development ideas.
- **Audience:** Educators, grades K–12
- **Frequency:** 8 times each year
- **Circulation:** 25,000
- **Website:** www.iste.org/LL

Freelance Potential
90% written by nonstaff writers. Publishes 75 freelance submissions yearly; 50% by unpublished writers, 75% by authors who are new to the magazine. Receives 75 queries yearly.

Submissions
Query. Accepts email queries to submissions@ iste.org and simultaneous submissions if identified. Response time varies.
Articles: 600–2,000 words. Informational and how-to articles; and personal experience pieces. Topics include computers and computer science, software, technology, media applications, teaching methods, and telecommunications.
Depts/columns: Word lengths vary. Research, software reviews, and curriculum ideas.
Artwork: B/W prints. Line art.

Sample Issue
48 pages (20% advertising): 7 articles; 9 depts/columns. Sample copy, free with 9x12 SASE (3 first-class stamps). Guidelines and editorial calendar available at website.
- "Real-Life Migrants on the MUVE." Article explains how one teacher incorporated a multi-user virtual environment into her curriculum.
- "Online Professional Development That Works." Article tells how the author created an online course on the science of sound.
- Sample dept/column: "Media Matters" explains how to refine Google searches.

Rights and Payment
All rights; returns limited rights to author upon request. No payment. Provides 3 contributor's copies.

Editor's Comments
We look for articles that focus on the how-to aspects of integrating technology into classrooms.

Lexington Family Magazine

138 East Reynolds Road, Suite 201
Lexington, KY 40517

Publisher: Dana Tackett

Description and Interests
Lexington Family Magazine covers a range of issues of interest to parents living in central Kentucky. Information on local resources appears along with general parenting articles on health, education, and travel.
- **Audience:** Parents
- **Frequency:** Monthly
- **Circulation:** 30,000
- **Website:** www.lexingtonfamily.com

Freelance Potential
50% written by nonstaff writers. Publishes 36 freelance submissions yearly; 40% by authors who are new to the magazine. Receives 250 unsolicited mss yearly.

Submissions
Query or send complete ms. Accepts hard copy. SASE. Response time varies.
Articles: 500–1,500 words. Informational and how-to articles. Topics include the arts, hobbies, current events, education, health, fitness, regional history, multicultural issues, popular culture, recreation, science, technology, family travel, and women's issues.
Depts/columns: 800 words. Child development, medical issues, and news for families.
Artwork: B/W and color prints. Line art.
Other: Puzzles, activities, and poetry.

Sample Issue
28 pages (50% advertising): 10 articles; 6 depts/columns; 1 calendar. Sample copy, free with 9x12 SASE ($1.50 postage). Writers' guidelines and theme list available.
- "Learn What's Missing from Your Diet." Article explains the importance of incorporating Vitamin D into your family's diet.
- Sample dept/column: "Children's Health" provides information about the new cervical cancer vaccine for girls.

Rights and Payment
All rights. Written material, payment rates vary. Pays on publication. Provides 2 contributor's copies.

Editor's Comments
We currently need more articles on travel, women's issues, health, and education. Material of interest to teachers is also needed. We are coming out with two new ancillary publications: one is a teacher resource guide, the other a guide to aging successfully.

Library Media Connection

3650 Olentangy River Road, Suite 250
Columbus, OH 43214

Editor: Carol Simpson

Description and Interests
Now celebrating its 25th year, *Library Media Connection* provides essential information for school media and technology specialists. It mixes reports on up-to-date research with practical programming ideas and book and media reviews.
• **Audience:** School librarians and media specialists
• **Frequency:** 7 times each year
• **Circulation:** 14,000
• **Website:** www.linworth.com

Freelance Potential
100% written by nonstaff writers. Publishes 215 freelance submissions yearly; 50% by unpublished writers, 50% by authors who are new to the magazine. Receives 144 queries, 144 unsolicited mss yearly.

Submissions
Query or send complete ms with résumé. Accepts hard copy, disk submissions (Microsoft Word or ASCII), and email submissions to linworth@ linworthpublishing.com. SASE. Responds in 2 weeks.
Articles: Word lengths vary. Informational and how-to articles; and personal experience and opinion pieces. Topics include library science, research, technology, education, computers, and media services.
Depts/columns: Word lengths vary. New product information, reviews, and teaching tips.
Other: Submit seasonal material 6 months in advance.

Sample Issue
98 pages (15% advertising): 10 articles; 8 depts/ columns. Sample copy, $11 with 9x12 SASE. Guidelines and theme list available at website.
• "Teen Chick Lit." Article tells how this genre of fiction is getting girls out of the malls and back into the library.
• "How to Host a School Visit." Article features tips for running a successful author event.
• Sample dept/column: "Author Profile" examines the multi-faceted life of Helen Frost.

Rights and Payment
All rights. Written material, payment rates vary. Pays on publication. Provides 4 contributor's copies.

Editor's Comments
We want practical material that readers can use in their libraries and media centers. Please check our website for upcoming themes.

LibrarySparks

W5527 State Road 106
P.O. Box 800
Fort Atkinson, WI 53580

Managing Editor: Michelle McCardell

Description and Interests
Elementary educators use the activities and lesson ideas featured in *LibrarySparks* to encourage a love of reading and literature in their students. Both teachers and librarians subscribe to this publication.
• **Audience:** Librarians and teachers
• **Frequency:** 9 times each year
• **Circulation:** Unavailable
• **Website:** www.librarysparks.com

Freelance Potential
95% written by nonstaff writers. Publishes 5 freelance submissions yearly; 25% by unpublished writers, 25% by authors who are new to the magazine. Receives 20 queries and mss yearly.

Submissions
Query or send complete ms. Accepts hard copy and email submissions to librarysparks@highsmith.com. SASE. Response time varies.
Articles: Word lengths vary. Informational articles and profiles. Topics include connecting literature to the curriculum, lesson plans for librarians, library skills, children's authors and illustrators, and ideas and activities for motivating students to read.
Depts/columns: Word lengths vary. New resources, author profiles, storytelling activities, booktalks, and ready-made lessons.
Other: Reproducible games; activities and crafts.

Sample Issue
56 pages (no advertising): 1 article; 12 depts/ columns. Sample copy available at website. Guidelines and editorial calendar available.
• "Bountiful Biographies!" Article discusses the value of using biographies with elementary students and features a list of suggested titles.
• Sample dept/column: "In the Spotlight" makes literature and curriculum connections to the life of Gregor Mendel.

Rights and Payment
Rights vary. Written material, payment rates vary. Pays on publication. Provides 1 contributor's copy.

Editor's Comments
Our purpose is to provide fun and engaging programming ideas for elementary students. Send us something that is practical and ready to use. We also always need short helpful hints and five-minute fillers.

Lifted Magazine

14781 Memorial Drive, Suite 1747
Houston, TX 77079

Editor: Tiffany Simpson

Description and Interests
Lifted Magazine is an online Christian lifestyle magazine for young adults. It contains articles on faith as well as travel, the outdoors, food, relationships, college, careers, and entertainment.
• **Audience:** 18–34 years
• **Frequency:** 6 times each year
• **Hits per month:** 2,000
• **Website:** www.liftedmagazine.com

Freelance Potential
90% written by nonstaff writers. Publishes 100 freelance submissions yearly; 50% by unpublished writers, 50% by authors who are new to the magazine.

Submissions
Send complete ms. Accepts email submissions to articles@liftedmag.com (Microsoft Word or text attachments). Response time varies.
Articles: Word lengths vary. Informational articles and personal experience pieces. Topics include faith, Scripture, dating and relationships, college, careers, travel, and cooking.
Fiction: 1,000+ words. Inspirational and contemporary fiction.
Depts/columns: 250–1,000 words. Devotions; product and media reviews; special events; and concerts.
Other: Poetry.

Sample Issue
Sample copy, guidelines, and editorial calendar available at website.
• "I Want to Be . . ." Essay describes the struggles and joys of being a young wife, mother, and student.
• "Student Loans? Don't Bother Me. I'm Eccentric." Essay discusses a young man's deliberate choice to be different from his peers.
• "Helping Volunteers Volunteer." Article profiles an organization that makes it easy to donate time.

Rights and Payment
Rights vary. No payment.

Editor's Comments
We are constantly looking for new writers to provide content targeted at Generations X and Y with a Christian bias. We are always looking for those with a positive outlook and fresh ideas to share. We rarely insist on what should be covered by writers, but instead let them write about what interests them at the moment.

The Lion

Lions Club International
300 West 22nd Street
Oak Brook, IL 60523-8842

Senior Editor: Jay Copp

Description and Interests
The service projects and activities of Lions Clubs are showcased in this magazine, first published in 1918. It covers local, national, and international Lions Club work, as well as club news. Member profiles also appear regularly.
• **Audience:** Members of the Lions Club
• **Frequency:** 10 times each year
• **Circulation:** 490,000
• **Website:** www.lionsclub.org

Freelance Potential
20% written by nonstaff writers. Publishes 20 freelance submissions yearly; 30% by new authors. Receives 100 queries and unsolicited mss yearly.

Submissions
Prefers query; accepts complete ms. Accepts hard copy. SASE. Responds to queries in 10 days, to mss in 2 months.
Articles: 300–2,000 words. Informational articles; humor; and family-oriented photo-essays. Topics include Lions Club service projects, disabilities, social issues, and special education.
Depts/columns: Staff written.
Artwork: 5x7 glossy prints, slides, and digital images.

Sample Issue
56 pages (6% advertising): 15 articles; 11 depts/columns. Sample copy, free. Guidelines available.
• "Lions World Sight Day Events Held in Mali." Article describes efforts by the Lions Club to eradicate preventable blindness in West Africa.
• "Family Comes Naturally for Michigan Lions Club." Article tells how a club in White Cloud, Michigan, includes mothers, fathers, sons, and daughters in its activities.
• Sample dept/column: "Membership Matters" explains why teamwork is the key to recruiting new members.

Rights and Payment
All rights. Written material, $100–$700. Pays on acceptance. Provides 4–10 contributor's copies.

Editor's Comments
In addition to pieces that cover Lions Clubs projects, we also accept general interest articles that reflect the humanitarian, community betterment, and service activism ideals of our worldwide association. We want stories that really "sizzle," accompanied by high-quality photographs.

Listen Magazine

55 West Oak Ridge Drive
Hagerstown, MD 21740

Editor: Céleste Perrino-Walker

Description and Interests
High schools around the country use this magazine in their classrooms because it encourages teenagers to embrace a healthy lifestyle that includes abstaining from tobacco, alcohol, and drugs.
- **Audience:** 12–18 years
- **Frequency:** 9 times each year
- **Circulation:** 40,000
- **Website:** www.listenmagazine.org

Freelance Potential
60% written by nonstaff writers. Publishes 90+ freelance submissions yearly; 15% by unpublished writers, 20% by authors who are new to the magazine. Receives 500 mss yearly.

Submissions
Query or send complete ms. Accepts hard copy, email submissions to editor@listenmagazine.org, and simultaneous submissions if identified. SASE. Responds as soon as possible.
Articles: 800 words. Informational articles; self-help pieces; and profiles. Topics include peer pressure, decision making, family conflict, suicide, self-esteem, self-discipline, and hobbies.
Depts/columns: 800 words. Opinion pieces and short pieces on social issues. Columns are staff written.

Sample Issue
32 pages (no advertising): 11 articles; 6 depts/columns. Sample copy, $2 with 9x12 SASE (2 first class stamps). Guidelines and editorial calendar available.
- "Joey Cheek: Heart of Olympic Gold." Article profiles the gold medal speed skater and his dedication to making the world a better place.
- "Down a Dangerous Road: Matt's Story." Article tells how a smart high schooler became addicted to inhaling chemicals and the price he paid.
- Sample dept/column: "Good For You" provides helpful health information for teenagers.

Rights and Payment
All rights. Written material, $.05–$.10 per word. Pays on acceptance. Provides 3 contributor's copies.

Editor's Comments
We would like to see more true stories about teenagers' experiences and about young people making positive choices in their lives. We do not accept fiction, and would like to see less on cutting and overcoming addiction.

Live

General Council of the Assemblies of God
1445 North Boonville Avenue
Springfield, MO 65802-1894

Editor: Richard Bennett

Description and Interests
This take-home story paper is distributed weekly in young adult and adult Sunday school classes. It includes realistic fiction and true stories that inspire readers to live according to God's will, and to look for guidance in the Bible.
- **Audience:** 18+ years
- **Frequency:** Quarterly, in weekly sections
- **Circulation:** 50,000

Freelance Potential
100% written by nonstaff writers. Publishes 110 freelance submissions yearly; 20% by unpublished writers, 20% by authors who are new to the magazine. Receives 1,500 queries and unsolicited mss yearly.

Submissions
Query or send complete ms. Accepts hard copy, email submissions to rl-live@gph.org, and simultaneous submissions if identified. SASE. Responds in 6 weeks.
Articles: 800–1,200 words. Informational articles; humor; and personal experience pieces. Topics include family issues, parenting, child care, and religious history.
Fiction: 800–1,200 words. Inspirational and historical fiction, adventure, and stories about family celebrations and traditions.
Other: Poetry, 12–25 lines. Filler, 200–600 words. Submit seasonal material 1 year in advance.

Sample Issue
8 pages (no advertising): 1 article; 2 stories. Sample copy, free with #10 SASE ($.39 postage). Writers' guidelines available.
- "Confession from a Pastor's Wife." Story relates the author's guilt about not reading the Bible, and how her promise to God gave her peace.
- "Birthday Surprise." Story tells how heartfelt words and forgiveness mended the rift between a grown woman and her mother.

Rights and Payment
First and second rights. Written material, $.10 per word for first rights; $.07 per word for second rights. Pays on acceptance. Provides 2 contributor's copies.

Editor's Comments
We need more true stories, particularly about pastor appreciation. Also sought are holiday-themed articles about Valentine's Day and Independence Day.

Living

1251 Virginia Avenue
Harrisonburg, VA 22802

Editor: Melodie Davis

Description and Interests
This family-oriented magazine strives to encourage
readers to lead a healthy life by providing positive and
inspiring articles. All material is written with a
Christian slant.
• **Audience:** Families
• **Frequency:** Quarterly
• **Circulation:** 150,000
• **Website: www.churchoutreach.com**

Freelance Potential
85% written by nonstaff writers. Publishes 55 freelance
submissions yearly; 5% by unpublished writers, 30%
by authors who are new to the magazine. Receives
600 unsolicited mss yearly.

Submissions
Send complete ms. Accepts hard copy, simultaneous
submissions if identified, and email submissions to
melodiemd@msn.com (include name of magazine and
title of article in the subject line; include your email
address in the body of the email). SASE. Responds in
3–4 months.
Articles: 500–1,000 words. Informational and how-to
articles; opinion and personal experience pieces. Topics
include health, fitness, recreation, religion, social issues,
education, and multicultural and ethnic issues.
Depts/columns: Staff written.

Sample Issue
32 pages (20% advertising): 13 articles; 5 depts/
columns. Sample copy, free with 9x12 SASE (4 first-
class stamps). Guidelines available at website.
• "Dude, Where's My Son?" Essay details a mother's
  view of the changes in her son during adolescence.
• "My Sister's Gamble." Personal experience piece
  tells how a woman forgives her true love for leaving
  her after he returns, and how her sister is not
  as forgiving.
• "Crop Circles." Humorous essay follows a mother's
  crazy morning.

Rights and Payment
One-time and second rights. Articles, $30–$60. Pays
on publication. Provides 2 contributor's copies.

Editor's Comments
We look for great reading material that the whole family can enjoy and are open to a wide variety of topics
that people face in the home and workplace. Writing
must be upbeat.

Living Safety

Canada Safety Council
1020 Thomas Spratt Place
Ottawa, Ontario K1G 5L5
Canada

President: Jack Smith

Description and Interests
Written to appeal to families, *Living Safety* stresses
safety awareness in the home, in the car, and in recre-
ational environments. It is intended primarily for a
Canadian audience.
• **Audience:** All ages
• **Frequency:** Quarterly
• **Circulation:** 80,000
• **Website: www.safety-council.org**

Freelance Potential
75% written by nonstaff writers. Publishes 25 freelance submissions yearly; 65% by unpublished
writers, 10% by authors who are new to the magazine.
Receives 12 queries yearly.

Submissions
Query with résumé and clips or writing samples.
Accepts hard copy. SAE/IRC. Responds in 2 weeks.
Articles: 1,500–2,500 words. Informational articles.
Topics include recreational, home, traffic, and school
safety; and health issues.
Depts/columns: Word lengths vary. Safety news,
research findings, opinions, and product recalls.
Other: Children's activities.

Sample Issue
30 pages (no advertising): 4 articles; 3 depts/
columns; 1 kids' page. Sample copy, free with 9x12
SAE/IRC. Guidelines available.
• "Riding on Air." Article states that the proper maintenance of tires is critical to the safe operation of your
  car and will also improve fuel economy and vehicle
  handling.
• "Germs: Myths vs. Facts." Article describes the
  places where germs collect in our home and work
  environments.
• Sample dept/column: "Safety First" features tips for
  safe gardening and for using batteries properly.

Rights and Payment
All rights. Articles, to $500. Depts/columns, payment
rates vary. Pays on acceptance. Provides 1–5 contributor's copies.

Editor's Comments
Our publication serves as a key consumer safety magazine, covering timely public safety topics relating to
home, traffic, and recreational settings. We look for
writers who can use a non-preaching tone to get the
prevention message across to readers.

Living with Teenagers

One LifeWay Plaza
Nashville, TN 37234-0174

Editor: Bob Bunn

Description and Interests
This Christian magazine specifically addresses the needs and concerns of parents who have children in the teen years. It offers inspiring, biblically-based solutions to common problems and discussions of ways to strengthen family life.
- **Audience:** Parents
- **Frequency:** Monthly
- **Circulation:** 42,000
- **Website:** www.lifeway.com

Freelance Potential
90% written by nonstaff writers.

Submissions
All work is done on assignment. No queries or unsolicited mss. Submit writing samples if you wish to be considered for an assignment. SASE.
Articles: 600–2,000 words. Informational, self-help, and how-to articles; profiles; interviews; and reviews. Topics include parenting, family life, education, planning for college, health, fitness, recreation, religion, and social, spiritual, multicultural, and ethnic issues.
Depts/columns: Staff written.

Sample Issue
34 pages (no advertising): 5 articles; 10 depts/columns. Sample copy, free.
- "Tracing the Past." Article explains that the idea of teenagers is a relatively new one, tells how the distinction fell into place, and why it still matters in contemporary culture.
- "Follow the Leader." Article analyzes the parental role in creating teenage leaders who have integrity and trustworthiness.
- "The Family That Plays Together." Article describes how having fun together can strengthen family bonds and communication.

Rights and Payment
All rights with non-exclusive license to the writer. Articles, $100–$300. Pays on acceptance. Provides 3 contributor's copies.

Editor's Comments
Our purpose is to encourage and equip parents with biblical solutions to transform families. We're looking for trained, highly-qualified Christian writers who can work closely with us to develop ideas and craft articles that our readers will find useful. Connect to our website and follow the prompts for writer interest.

Long Island Woman

P.O. Box 176
Malverne, NY 11565

Publisher: Arie Nadboy

Description and Interests
This free, tabloid-sized magazine distributed throughout Long Island includes articles on parenting and family among its women-centered content.
- **Audience:** Women, 35–65 years
- **Frequency:** Monthly
- **Circulation:** 40,000
- **Website:** www.liwomanonline.com

Freelance Potential
100% written by nonstaff writers. Publishes 25 freelance submissions yearly. Receives 1,000 unsolicited mss yearly.

Submissions
Send complete ms. Accepts email submissions to editor@liwomanonline.com. Availability of artwork improves chance of acceptance. Responds in 8–10 weeks.
Articles: 350–2,000 words. Informational and how-to articles; profiles; and interviews. Topics include regional news, lifestyles, family, health, sports, fitness, nutrition, dining, fashion, beauty, business, finance, decorating, gardening, entertainment, media, travel, and celebrities.
Depts/columns: 500–1,000 words. Book reviews, health advice, personal essays, profiles.
Artwork: Electronic B/W and color prints. Line art.
Other: Submit seasonal material 90 days in advance.

Sample Issue
41 pages (60% advertising): 3 articles; 6 depts/columns. Sample copy, $5. Guidelines available.
- "Suzanne Somers." Interview with the actress/author/entrepreneur focuses on her health and vitality.
- "Mirror, Mirror on the Wall." Article describes economical ways to transform a home.
- Sample dept/column: "Book Corner" provides an overview of holiday cookbooks.

Rights and Payment
One-time and electronic rights. Written material, $70–$200. Kill fee, 20%. Pays on publication. Provides 1 tearsheet.

Editor's Comments
We are seeking more articles on fashion and home design, and fewer personal essays and diet stories. Please keep in mind that issues are planned four to five months in advance of their publication date.

Look-Look Magazine

732 North Highland Avenue
Los Angeles, CA 90038

Editor

Description and Interests
Launched in 2003, *Look-Look Magazine* was created by and for artists, photographers, writers, and poets between the ages of 12 and 30. It publishes photojournalism, fiction, creative nonfiction, essays, and other forms of artistic expression.
• **Audience:** 12–30 years
• **Frequency:** Twice each year
• **Circulation:** 55,000
• **Website:** www.look-lookmagazine.com

Freelance Potential
95% written by nonstaff writers. Publishes 120 freelance submissions yearly; 100% by unpublished writers, 100% by authors who are new to the magazine. Receives 8,000 queries yearly.

Submissions
Query. Accepts queries through website only. Response time varies.
Articles: To 2,000 words. How-to articles; profiles; interviews; and personal experience pieces. Topics include the arts and popular culture.
Fiction: To 2,000 words. Genres include contemporary and multicultural fiction and humor.
Artwork: B/W and color prints and transparencies; digital images at 300 dpi. Line art.
Other: Poetry. Submit seasonal material 4 months in advance.

Sample Issue
96 pages (5% advertising): 2 articles; 3 essays, 10 poems; 6 photo collections. Sample copy, $5.95 with 9x12 SASE ($.77 postage). Guidelines and editorial calendar available at website.
• "Mind's Eye." Article features a discussion and photos of the Exotic World Museum in Las Vegas.
• "Possessed." Personal experience piece describes the life of an amateur mystic.
• "People I Like." Article interviews the owner of an unusual ice cream truck.

Rights and Payment
All rights. No payment. Provides 2 contributor's copies.

Editor's Comments
To submit to us, you must be someone between the ages of 12 and 30 who does not get paid for your work. Please don't send any more poems about relationship break-ups.

Loud Magazine

P.O. Box 50547
Palo Alto, CA 94303

Editor-in-Chief: Anne Schukat

Description and Interests
Subtitled "News of the Next Generation," this magazine focuses on youth leadership and activism. It fills its pages with reporting and analysis of the pivotal issues facing young people today, while also offering information on careers and education in a format that is appealing to teens.
• **Audience:** 12–16 years
• **Frequency:** Quarterly
• **Circulation:** Unavailable
• **Website:** www.loudmagazine.com

Freelance Potential
30% written by nonstaff writers. Publishes 30 freelance submissions yearly.

Submissions
Query with clips. Prefers email queries to submissions@loudmagazine.com. Will accept hard copy. SASE. Response time varies.
Articles: Word lengths vary. Informational and how-to articles and profiles. Topics include youth rights, entrepreneurs, activists, politics, entertainment, technology, science, marketing, careers, and fashion.
Depts/columns: Word lengths vary. Music, science, education, travel, sports, technology, health, news items, and reviews.

Sample Issue
70 pages: 12 articles; 18 depts/columns; 1 quiz. Sample copy, $3.95. Guidelines available.
• "Should Intelligent Design Be Taught in Schools?" Article covers the controversy over whether the idea that life was created by an intelligent being should be incorporated into the school curriculum.
• "A (Very) Short History of Youth Rights." Article assesses the status of youth rights in this country since the 1940s.
• "Making the Band 3." Article interviews teens who auditioned for a reality show.

Rights and Payment
Rights vary. No payment for first-time authors; will pay for additional articles. Written material, payment rates vary. Pays on publication. Provides 1 author's copy.

Editor's Comments
When sending your pitch, please include a couple of writing samples (ideally published clips). We continue to focus on teen rights, teen entrepreneurs, and entertainment.

The Magazine

643 Queen Street East
Toronto, Ontario M4M 1G4
Canada

Editor: Karen Wong

Description and Interests

The Magazine is an entertainment digest for tweens and teens that covers everything pop cultural—from television to movies, music to books, video games to the Internet. It also includes a smattering of nutrition and fitness information and a dash of science and nature.

- **Audience:** 10–18 years
- **Frequency:** Monthly
- **Circulation:** 89,000
- **Website:** www.themagazine.ca

Freelance Potential

60% written by nonstaff writers. Publishes 100 freelance submissions yearly; 50% by unpublished writers, 50% by authors who are new to the magazine.

Submissions

Query or send complete ms. Accepts hard copy. SAE/IRC. Response time varies.
Articles: Word lengths vary. Informational articles; profiles; interviews; humor; and reviews. Topics include popular culture and entertainment, including television, movies, video games, books, music, and lifestyles.
Depts/columns: Word lengths vary. Entertainment updates and gossip; nutrition briefs; nature briefs; and reviews of CDs, DVDs, books, video games, e-zines, and websites.

Sample Issue

96 pages: 6 articles; 25 depts/columns; 5 posters. Sample copy, $3.95. Guidelines available with SAE/IRC or via email request to work@themagazine.ca.

- "Nancy Drew: Super Sleuth." Article previews the new Nancy Drew movie, starring Emma Roberts in the title role.
- "Carving the Asphalt." Article provides readers with an overview of the "longboarding" trend, which features giant skateboards.
- Sample dept/column: "Rumour Mill" shares gossip about which actors and directors will be working on upcoming films.

Rights and Payment

All rights. Written material, payment rates and payment policy vary.

Editor's Comments

We negotiate payment based on content and length. Submissions must be exclusive to us. We reserve the right to reprint articles without written permission.

Magazine of Fantasy & Science Fiction

P.O. Box 3447
Hoboken, NJ 07030

Editor: Gordon Van Gelder

Description and Interests

This digest-sized collection of short stories, novellas, and novelettes also contains staff-written reviews and essays about the fantasy and science fiction genres. The magazine has been in print for nearly 60 years.

- **Audience:** YA–Adult
- **Frequency:** Monthly
- **Circulation:** 45,000
- **Website:** www.sfsite.com/fsf

Freelance Potential

100% written by nonstaff writers. Publishes 60–90 freelance submissions yearly; 5–10% by unpublished writers, 10–15% by authors who are new to the magazine. Receives 500–700 unsolicited mss yearly.

Submissions

Send complete ms. Accepts hard copy. No simultaneous submissions. SASE. Responds in 1 month.
Fiction: 1,000–25,000 words. Short stories, novellas, and novelettes. Genres include science fiction, fantasy, and humor.
Depts/columns: Staff-written.

Sample Issue

162 pages (1% advertising): 3 novelettes; 3 short stories; 5 depts/columns. Sample copy, $5. Guidelines available.

- "Bye the Rules." Novelette follows the continuing adventures of noöonaut Guth Bandar.
- "The Christmas Witch." Novelette tells the dark tale of a little girl who stumbles into sorcery.
- "Dazzle the Pundit." Short story chronicles the adventures of Dazzle the dog as he accepts a guest professorship at a Berlin university.
- "John Uskglass and the Cumbrian Charcoal Burner." Short story retells a popular Northern English folktale about the Raven King.

Rights and Payment

First world rights with option of anthology rights. Written material, $.06–$.09 per word. Pays on acceptance. Provides 2 contributor's copies.

Editor's Comments

Please do not send us stories about virus outbreaks! We receive too many of them. Please *do* send us original, speculative, character-driven science fiction stories. The science fiction element may be slight, but it should be present. We receive a lot of high fantasy fiction, but never enough science fiction or humor.

Mahoning Valley Parent

100 DeBartolo Place, Suite 210
Youngstown, OH 44512

Editor & Publisher: Amy Leigh Wilson

Description and Interests
Northeastern Ohio parents turn to this regional publication for news about family activities and entertainment, as well as advice from fellow parents and teachers.
• **Audience:** Parents
• **Frequency:** Monthly
• **Circulation:** 50,000
• **Website: www.forparentsonline.com**

Freelance Potential
99% written by nonstaff writers. Publishes 100 freelance submissions yearly; 5% by unpublished writers, 20% by authors who are new to the magazine. Receives 500 unsolicited mss yearly.

Submissions
Send complete ms. Accepts hard copy and email submissions to editor@mvparentmagazine.com. Retains all material on file for possible use; does not respond until publication. Include SASE if retaining ms is not acceptable.
Articles: 1,000–1,800 words. Informational and how-to articles; profiles; and reviews. Topics include regional news, current events, parenting, the environment, nature, health, crafts, travel, recreation, hobbies, and ethnic and multicultural subjects.
Depts/columns: Word lengths vary. Parenting issues, book reviews, events for kids.
Artwork: B/W and color prints.
Other: Submit seasonal material 3 months in advance.

Sample Issue
42 pages (70% advertising): 4 articles; 5 depts/columns. Sample copy, free with 9x12 SASE. Guidelines and editorial calendar available.
• "Adoption Brings a New Friend to Sesame Street." Article talks about the addition of a new character to the popular children's program.
• Sample dept/column: "Special Parents, Special Kids" provides guidance to families on dealing with unexpected issues and learning from them.

Rights and Payment
One-time rights. Articles, $20–$50. Pays on publication. Provides tearsheets.

Editor's Comments
We encourage writers to send articles and reprints on speculation—but know that we will respond only if interested and hold all articles for one year. We are not interested in first-person essays.

The Majellan: Champion of the Family

P.O. Box 43
Brighton, Victoria 3186
Australia

Editor: Father Paul Bird

Description and Interests
This Catholic publication, distributed in Australia and New Zealand, aims to help its readers build stronger relationships. Published by the Redemptorists, it also regularly features short lessons in the Catholic faith.
• **Audience:** Parents
• **Frequency:** Quarterly
• **Circulation:** 23,000
• **Website: www.majellan.org.au**

Freelance Potential
60% written by nonstaff writers. Publishes 10 freelance submissions yearly; 10% by unpublished writers, 20% by authors who are new to the magazine. Receives 30 unsolicited mss yearly.

Submissions
Send complete ms. Accepts hard copy and email submissions to editor@majellan.org.au (Microsoft Word or RTF attachments). SAE/IRC. Response time varies.
Articles: 750–1,500 words. Informational articles and personal experience pieces about marriage and family life.
Depts/columns: Staff written.
Other: Filler; prayers and photos from readers.

Sample Issue
48 pages (15% advertising): 9 articles; 4 depts/columns.
• "The Young Generation." Article discusses the results of an Australia-wide survey of young people, who ranked relationships with family and friends as most important to them.
• "An Impossible Dream?" Article profiles a woman who overcame hearing loss and became a doctor.
• "Mothers and Adolescent Daughters." Article helps parents understand and respond to the behavior of teenage girls.

Rights and Payment
Rights vary. Written material, $50–$80 Australian. Pays on acceptance.

Editor's Comments
We seek articles that promote the sanctity of marriage and foster Christian family life, including those that tackle controversial yet pertinent issues from a Catholic point of view. Parenting articles comprise much of our content, particularly those that offer advice and guidance on parenting teens.

Maryland Family

10750 Little Patuxent Parkway
Columbia, MD 21044

Editor: Betsy Stein

Description and Interests
Baltimore-area parents looking for resources and family activity ideas turn to the information and calendars that fill the pages of *Maryland Family*. It also offers features on general child-raising topics, media reviews, and expert advice columns.
- **Audience:** Maryland families
- **Frequency:** Monthly
- **Circulation:** 50,000
- **Website: www.marylandfamilymagazine.com**

Freelance Potential
75% written by nonstaff writers. Publishes 50 freelance submissions yearly; 10% by unpublished writers, 10% by authors who are new to the magazine. Receives 360–600 queries yearly.

Submissions
Query with description of your experience in proposed subject. Accepts hard copy. SASE. Responds in 1 month.
Articles: 800–1,000 words. Practical application pieces; how-to articles; and profiles. Topics include family issues, parenting, summer camp, and local angles on national trends that affect families.
Depts/columns: Word lengths vary. News briefs on timely, local subjects and readers' photos. "Family Matters," 100–400 words.
Artwork: Color prints and transparencies.
Other: Submit seasonal material about holidays and events 2–3 months in advance.

Sample Issue
46 pages (50% advertising): 7 articles; 2 depts/columns; 1 calendar; 1 kids' activity page. Sample copy, free with 9x12 SASE.
- "Mayhem." Article offers one parent's perspective on how to survive the month of May, which is often the busiest time of year for families.
- "What Your Daycare Provider Wants You to Know." Article presents six rules that will ensure harmony with your childcare provider.

Rights and Payment
First and electronic rights. Written material, payment rates vary. Pays on publication. Provides 1 contributor's copy.

Editor's Comments
Articles that offer a local angle are most likely to be accepted for publication.

Massive Online Gamer

15850 Dallas Parkway
Dallas, TX 75248

Editor: Douglas Kale

Description and Interests
Young adults and adults who enjoy playing MMO (massively multiplayer online) games read this publication for articles covering the biggest multiplayer online games to the smallest. It includes game descriptions, strategies, and techniques and features MMO games that focus on science fiction, adventure, fantasy, pirates, war, and automobiles.
- **Audience:** YA–Adult
- **Frequency:** 6 times each year
- **Circulation:** 75,000
- **Website: www.beckettmog.com**

Freelance Potential
50% written by nonstaff writers. Publishes 60 freelance submissions yearly; 50% by unpublished writers, 90% by authors who are new to the magazine.

Submissions
Query with writing sample and list of MMO experience. Accepts hard copy. SASE. Response time varies.
Articles: Word lengths vary. Informational and how-to articles; personal experience pieces; and interviews. Topics include MMO game descriptions, strategies, and techniques.
Depts/columns: Word lengths vary. MMO etiquette, technology, contests, and news.

Sample Issue
88 pages: 24 articles; 10 depts/columns. Guidelines available upon email request to mog@beckett.com.
- "Magic Online." Article describes the Wizards of the Coast's online version of the famous and beloved fantasy-based card game.
- "Gamers in the Military." Article discusses the rapidly expanding segment of the MMO community composed of members of various armed services around the world.
- Sample dept/column: "New Tech" takes a look at different flat panel monitors for gaming.

Rights and Payment
All rights. Written material, $25–$150. Pays 45 days after publication.

Editor's Comments
In order to write for us, you must be an experienced MMO gamer with extensive knowledge. Send us articles that cover the latest games and news in the MMO industry. Keep in mind our audience includes both experienced gamers and those new to MMO gaming.

Metro Parent Magazine

22041 Woodward Avenue
Ferndale, MI 48220

Managing Editor: Julia Elliott

Description and Interests
Distributed free throughout the metropolitan Detroit area, this magazine features current, cutting-edge information on parenting issues, child development, and education, with an emphasis on topics of specific interest to Michigan families.
• **Audience:** Parents
• **Frequency:** Monthly
• **Circulation:** 80,000
• **Website: www.metroparent.com**

Freelance Potential
75% written by nonstaff writers. Publishes 250 freelance submissions yearly; 5% by unpublished writers, 35% by authors who are new to the magazine. Receives 960+ unsolicited mss yearly.

Submissions
Send complete ms. Accepts email submissions to jelliott@metroparent.com. Responds in 1–2 days.
Articles: 1,500–2,500 words. Informational, self-help, and how-to articles; personal experience pieces; and interviews. Topics include parenting and family life, childbirth, education, social issues, child development, crafts, vacation travel, personal finance, fitness, health, and nature.
Depts/columns: 850–900 words. Women's health, family fun, new product information, media reviews, crafts, and computers.

Sample Issue
69 pages (60% advertising): 6 articles; 12 depts/columns. Sample copy, free. Guidelines available.
• "The Birds and the Bees . . . and a Thing Called Love." Article discusses the importance of talking to your kids about sex in a meaningful way in today's provocative times.
• "From Wrecked to Rockin'." Article describes ways to create a magical room for your child.
• Sample dept/column: "Ages & Stages" presents 10 tips for toddler-proofing your home.

Rights and Payment
First rights. Articles, $150–$300. Depts/columns, $50–$100. Pays on publication. Provides 1 contributor's copy.

Editor's Comments
We're especially interested in up-to-date information on family health and fun family activities. You must have solid reporting and writing skills to work with us.

Midwifery Today

P.O. Box 2672
Eugene, OR 97402

Managing Editor: Cheryl K. Smith

Description and Interests
Midwives, doulas, birth educators, and doctors read this publication for its well-researched, expert information on childbirth education, the birthing process, and breastfeeding.
• **Audience:** Childbirth practitioners
• **Frequency:** Quarterly
• **Circulation:** 4,000
• **Website: www.midwiferytoday.com**

Freelance Potential
90% written by nonstaff writers. Publishes 80–100 freelance submissions yearly; 35% by unpublished writers, 50% by new authors. Receives 150–200 queries yearly.

Submissions
Query with author background; or send ms. Accepts email submissions to editorial@midwiferytoday.com (Microsoft Word or RTF attachments). No simultaneous submissions. SASE. Responds in 1 month.
Articles: 800–1,500 words. Informational and instructional articles; profiles; interviews; personal experience pieces; and media reviews. Topics include feminism, health, fitness, medical care and services, diet, nutrition, and multicultural and ethnic issues related to childbirth.
Artwork: B/W and color prints.

Sample Issue
72 pages (10% advertising): 19 articles; 10 depts/columns. Sample copy, $12.50. Guidelines and editorial calendar available.
• "Epidurals: Risks and Concerns for Mother and Baby." Article makes the case for childbirth without epidurals and other spinal injections because of the risks to both the mother and the baby.
• "Nine Web Site Strategies to Generate More Clients." Article gives advice on proven ways to use the World Wide Web to start, build, and improve your childbirth-related business.

Rights and Payment
Joint rights. No payment. Provides 2 author's copies and a 1-year subscription for articles over 800 words.

Editor's Comments
We are seeking more articles on the role of fathers during the birth process; the clinical and technical issues of childbirth; as well as philosophical and personal pieces. Birth-related art, humor, and poetry are always welcome.

Minnesota Conservation Volunteer

500 Lafayette Road
St. Paul, MN 55155

Development Officer: Susan Omoto

Description and Interests
People who appreciate, and wish to preserve, Minnesota's natural resources read this publication. Its features showcase the state's wildlife and its opportunities for anglers, hunters, and paddlers. The "Young Naturalist" section appeals to children.
- **Audience:** Children, 10–14 years; and adults
- **Frequency:** Monthly
- **Circulation:** 150,000
- **Website: www.dnr.state.mn.us/magazine**

Freelance Potential
50% written by nonstaff writers. Receives 40 queries each year.

Submissions
Query with synopsis. Accepts hard copy and email queries to cathy.mix@dnr.state.mn.us. SASE. Response time varies.
Articles: 1,200–1,800 words. Informational articles and essays. Topics include natural resources, conservation, nature, the environment, fishing, hiking, state parks, and outdoor recreation.
Depts/columns: Word lengths vary. "Young Naturalist" features information on Minnesota natural resources and outdoor recreation for ages 10 to 14. "Field Notes," 200–500 words.

Sample Issue
64 pages: 7 articles; 4 depts/columns. Sample copy, free. Guidelines available at website.
- "The Wolves of Camp Ripley." Article tells how the radio collars carried by gray wolves on a military base offer a glimpse into the lives of these creatures.
- "On Thinner Ice." Article chronicles the work of Will Steger, a polar explorer, who is traveling the world to tell the story of thinning ice.
- "Nature's Calendar." Article teaches young naturalists the phenomenon of phenology.

Rights and Payment
First North American serial rights. Written material, $.50 per word and $100 for electronic rights. Payment policy varies.

Editor's Comments
We are very interested in features for our Young Naturalist section. Please log on to our website for specific information about this section and to learn more about our style, tone, and approach, as well as to find out what topics we have covered recently.

Mission

223 Main Street
Ottawa, Ontario K1S 1C4
Canada

Editor: Peter Pandimakil

Description and Interests
Read by young adults and adults, *Mission* is a Canadian publication that focuses on intercultural and interreligious issues while promoting faith-based communities and values.
- **Audience:** 14 years–Adult
- **Frequency:** Twice each year
- **Circulation:** 400
- **Website: www.ustpaul.ca**

Freelance Potential
95% written by nonstaff writers. Publishes 8–10 freelance submissions yearly; 25% by unpublished writers, 40% by authors who are new to the magazine. Receives 10–15 unsolicited mss yearly.

Submissions
Send complete ms with résumé. Accepts disk submissions (RTF files), email submissions to ppandimakil@ustpaul.ca, and simultaneous submissions if identified. SAE/IRC. Responds in 1–2 months.
Articles: 8,000–10,000 words. Bilingual articles; reviews; and personal experience pieces. Topics include current events; history; religion; and multicultural, ethnic, and social issues.
Fiction: Word lengths vary. Historical, multicultural, ethnic, and problem-solving stories.
Artwork: 8x10 B/W and color prints.

Sample Issue
200 pages (no advertising): 8 articles; 13 book reviews. Sample copy, $12 U.S. with 8x6 SAE/IRC. Guidelines available.
- "A Social Justice Perspective on The Lord's Prayer." Article explores how The Lord's Prayer relates to the social justice teachings of the church.
- "Can the African Christian 'Problem' Ever Be Resolved?" Article analyzes the tensions between African Traditional Religion and Christianity.
- "War and Peace in Monotheistic Religions." Article discusses the punishment theory of war and peace in monotheistic religions.

Rights and Payment
Rights vary. No payment. Provides 3 contributor's copies.

Editor's Comments
We are interested in reviewing pieces that explore globalization, village communities, and cross cultural issues. We see too many historical pieces.

Momentum

National Catholic Educational Association
1077 30th Street NW, Suite 100
Washington, DC 20007-3852

Editor: Brian Gray

Description and Interests
Teachers and administrators working in Catholic schools turn to this magazine for articles on education for preschool through college-age students. It also includes topics that are of interest to religious education teachers.
• **Audience:** Teachers, school administrators, parents
• **Frequency:** Quarterly
• **Circulation:** 23,000
• **Website:** www.ncea.org

Freelance Potential
95% written by nonstaff writers. Publishes 90 freelance submissions yearly; 25% by unpublished writers, 80% by authors who are new to the magazine. Receives 125 unsolicited mss yearly.

Submissions
Send complete ms with résumé and bibliography. Accepts hard copy, disk submissions (Microsoft Word), and email to momentum@nea.org. SASE. Responds in 1–3 months.
Articles: 1,000–1,500 words. Informational and scholarly articles on education. Topics include teacher and in-service education, educational trends, technology, research, management, and public relations—all as they relate to Catholic education and schools.
Depts/columns: Book reviews, 300 words. "Trends in Technology," 900 words. "From the Field," 700 words.

Sample Issue
94 pages (20% advertising): 17 articles; 8 depts/columns. Sample copy, free with 9x12 SASE ($1.05 postage). Guidelines and editorial calendar available.
• "Catholic High Schools Surmounting Crises." Article looks at how these schools re-emerged in the aftermath of Hurricane Katrina.
• "Envisioning the Future of Catholic Early Childhood Education." Article explores the role schools play in providing a quality learning experience for marginalized children.

Rights and Payment
First rights. Articles, $75. Depts/columns, $50. Pays on publication. Provides 2 contributor's copies.

Editor's Comments
We need articles that focus on ideas, trends, and successes found in Catholic elementary schools. We do not use "inspirational" material.

MOM Magazine

2397 NW Kings Boulevard, #105
Corvallis, OR 97330

Editors: Raeann Van Arsdall & Barb Thompson

Description and Interests
Targeted to moms with children under the age of 12 living in the Pacific Northwest, this magazine has a subscription base that is growing to include readers nationwide and worldwide. It appears in a glossy, full-color format.
• **Audience:** Mothers
• **Frequency:** 6 times each year
• **Circulation:** 20,000
• **Website:** www.mommag.com

Freelance Potential
80% written by nonstaff writers. Publishes 60 freelance submissions yearly; 80% by unpublished writers, 50% by authors who are new to the magazine.

Submissions
Query or send complete ms. Accepts email submissions to editor@mommag.com (Microsoft Word attachments). Availability of artwork improves chance of acceptance. Response time varies.
Articles: 500 words. Informational articles; personal experience pieces; and profiles. Topics include parenting, family life, recreation and activities, pets, health, and fitness.
Depts/columns: Word lengths vary. Family travel, fatherhood issues, book reviews.
Artwork: 5x7 JPEG or TIF images at 300 dpi; include photo releases.
Other: Call-outs, 25–50 words (statistics, recipes).

Sample Issue
32 pages: 11 articles; 6 depts/columns. Guidelines available at website.
• "Being Mom and More." Article stresses the importance of taking time to cultivate friendships that are not focused on the kids.
• "Trading Places for Tiny Faces." Personal experience piece tells how a mother traded in a glamorous job to stay at home with her children.
• Sample dept/column: "Book It" reviews books for children and adults.

Rights and Payment
Reprint rights. No payment.

Editor's Comments
The goal of our magazine is to remind readers that we're all in this together. We're creating an interactive community where moms can share fun stories, ideas, and more than a few laughs.

MomSense

2370 South Trenton Way
Denver, CO 80231-3822

Editor: Mary Darr

Description and Interests
The purpose of this magazine is to network and nurture mothers of preschoolers from a Christian perspective with articles that inform and inspire on issues relating to being a mother and a woman.
- **Audience:** Mothers
- **Frequency:** 6 times each year
- **Circulation:** 120,000
- **Website:** www.MomSense.com

Freelance Potential
70% written by nonstaff writers. Publishes 100 freelance submissions yearly; 20% by unpublished writers, 20% by authors who are new to the magazine. Receives 60 queries, 250 unsolicited mss yearly.

Submissions
Query or send ms. Prefers email submissions to MOMSense@mops.org (Microsoft Word attachments). Will accept hard copy. Availability of artwork improves chance of acceptance. SASE. Response time varies.
Articles: 500–1,000 words. Informational articles; profiles; and personal experience pieces. Topics include parenting, religion, and humor.
Depts/columns: Word lengths vary. Parenting and family life articles.
Artwork: B/W and color prints or transparencies.
Other: Accepts seasonal material 6–12 months in advance.

Sample Issue
32 pages (no advertising): 10 articles; 6 depts/columns. Sample copy, free. Guidelines available.
- "Who Ya Gonna Call?" Article shares the story of a mom who turns a stressful day into a manageable one.
- "Mom Care." Article offers ideas on personal care and eating to stay healthy.
- Sample dept/column: "Mentor Mom" suggests that it is okay for moms to cry in front of their children sometimes.

Rights and Payment
First rights. Written material, $.15–$.25 per word. Payment policy varies. Provides contributor's copies.

Editor's Comments
We look for articles written from a biblical perspective that meet the needs of moms with different lifestyles who share a similar desire to be the very best moms that they can be.

MomsVoice.com

27909 NE 26th Street
Redmond, WA 98053

Editor: Krista Sweeney

Description and Interests
This online magazine for mothers of all stripes—working moms, stay-at-home moms, new moms, adoptive moms, older moms, single moms, step-moms, and moms-to-be—publishes personal and professional pieces designed to help women balance their lives and care for their children.
- **Audience:** Mothers
- **Frequency:** Monthly
- **Hits per month:** 10,000
- **Website:** www.momsvoice.com

Freelance Potential
100% written by nonstaff writers. Publishes 100 freelance submissions yearly; 10% by unpublished writers, 20% by authors who are new to the magazine. Receives 120 queries yearly.

Submissions
Query with writing samples; or send complete ms. Accepts email to writers@momsvoice.com (Microsoft Word attachments). Responds in 1 week.
Articles: 2,500 words. Informational and how-to articles; profiles; personal experience pieces; and reviews. Topics include pregnancy, childbirth, parenting, health, fitness, spirituality, finance, food, hobbies and crafts, social issues, education, gifted and special education, family travel, and regional news.
Fiction: 2,500 words. Genres include real-life and inspirational fiction and humor.
Depts/columns: 2,500 words. Crafts, cooking, parenting tips, and book reviews.

Sample Issue
Sample copy and guidelines available at website.
- "Work and Childcare Don't Have to Be Polar Opposites." Personal essay recounts a woman's search for the right day-care center.
- "Trust Your Gut." Article relates one woman's experience with sensory integration dysfunction.
- "Nine Ways to Ease Your Child's Transition from Elementary to Middle School." Article suggests ways to ease the anxiety that often accompanies this period.

Rights and Payment
First rights for 2 months. No payment.

Editor's Comments
We review articles on all topics. Originality is the preferred source, but we also accept reprints. Sidebars that emphasize related information are welcome.

Mom Writer's Literary Magazine

1006 Black Oak Drive
Liberty, MO 64068

Editor-in-Chief: Samantha Gianulis

Description and Interests
This magazine, subtitled "Moms with Something to Say," was founded with the belief that the art of motherhood deserves literary attention. Its creative nonfiction essays, poetry, and profiles are written by moms, for moms.
• **Audience:** Mothers
• **Frequency:** Quarterly
• **Circulation:** 10,000
• **Website: www.momwriterslitmag.com**

Freelance Potential
90% written by nonstaff writers. Publishes 64 freelance submissions yearly; 90% by unpublished writers, 95% by authors who are new to the magazine. Receives 600–1,200 queries and unsolicited mss each year.

Submissions
Query or send complete ms. Accepts email submissions to editor@momwriterslitmag.com (no attachments) and simultaneous submissions if identified. Responds in 2–4 weeks.
Articles: 600–3,000 words. Creative nonfiction essays written by mothers—biological, adoptive, foster, step—and grandmothers. Topics include motherhood, writing, and mom writers.
Depts/columns: Staff written.
Other: Poetry, line lengths vary. Book reviews, 700–1,000 words. Profiles, 800–2,500 words.

Sample Issue
52 pages: 8 essays; 4 profiles; 2 stories (contest winners); 6 poems; 3 reviews; 4 depts/columns. Guidelines available at website.
• "Butterfly." Essay relates a brief but poignant encounter between a mother of the bride and a little girl in a bridal shop.
• "Good Night Sweet Princess." Essay recounts the author's thoughts and feelings when she reads a bedtime story to her young daughter.
• "An Interview with Lisa Collier Cool." Article relates the writer's experiences and advice.

Rights and Payment
One-time electronic rights. No payment.

Editor's Comments
We are looking for writing that is down-to-earth, vivid, sincere, complex, and practical. Creative nonfiction essays should read like fiction.

Montessori Life

281 Park Avenue South
New York, NY 10010

Editor

Description and Interests
This publication of the American Montessori Society covers research, curricula, and other issues in education for Montessori teachers and parents.
• **Audience:** Educators and parents
• **Frequency:** Quarterly
• **Circulation:** 10,500
• **Website: www.amshq.org**

Freelance Potential
90% written by nonstaff writers. Publishes 40 freelance submissions yearly; 30% by unpublished writers, 30% by authors who are new to the magazine. Receives 120–240 unsolicited mss yearly.

Submissions
Send complete ms. Accepts email submissions to edmontessorilife@aol.com. Responds in 3 months.
Articles: 1,000–4,000 words. Informational, academic, and how-to articles; profiles; interviews; and humor. Topics include education trends, social issues, gifted and special education, and family life—all as they pertain to Montessori education.
Fiction: 1,000–1,500 words. Allegorical fiction.
Depts/columns: 500–1,000 words. Montessori community news and events, media reviews, and humor. Teachers and parents sections, and peace section.

Sample Issue
66 pages (25% advertising): 7 articles; 10 depts/columns. Sample copy, $5 with 9x12 SASE.
Guidelines and editorial calendar available at website.
• "Life without Scissors and Tape." Article summarizes a classroom research project that observed what students did when these basic tools were removed.
• "Widening the Circle." Article discusses how to teach adolescent students compassion and service.
• Sample dept/column: "Heads" features an essay by the head of a Montessori school in Illinois about the benefits of technology in the classroom.

Rights and Payment
All rights. Written material, payment rates vary. Pays on publication. Provides 1–5 contributor's copies.

Editor's Comments
Have you ever wanted to write for us, but our themes didn't fit your interests, expertise, or schedule? If so, 2008 is the year for you. For these four issues, we are going themeless! Now is your chance to write what you want, when you want to write it.

Moo-Cow Fan Club

P.O. Box 165
Peterborough, NH 03458

Editor: Becky Ances

Description and Interests
This children's magazine, described as both "funny and smart," is currently being reorganized as an e-zine and will no longer be available in print. Each online edition of the magazine will continue to explore the unique aspects of a certain topic, covering it in a way that it may not be covered in school.
• **Audience:** 6–12 years
• **Frequency:** Quarterly
• **Circulation:** 3,000
• **Website:** www.moocowfanclub.com

Freelance Potential
20% written by nonstaff writers. Publishes 8 freelance submissions yearly; 60% by unpublished writers, 90% by new authors. Receives 100+ queries yearly.

Submissions
Not accepting material until later in 2008. Query with sample article. Accepts hard copy and email queries to editor@moocowfanclub.com (no attachments). SASE. Responds in 3 weeks.
Articles: 300–550 words. Informational and how-to articles; profiles; and interviews. Topics include nature, animals, science, sports, and travel.
Fiction: 300–550 words. Genres include folktales and folklore.
Depts/columns: Staff written.

Sample Issue
48 pages (no advertising): 5 articles; 1 story; 3 depts/columns; 4 activities; and 2 comics. Sample copy, guidelines, and theme list available at website.
• "Clouds." Article explains how to tell the difference between the types of clouds and how clouds are formed.
• "Ye Gods!" Article talks about the role the weather played in ancient mythology.
• "Weird Weather." Article describes strange events caused by tornados throughout history, including a frog storm and a fish storm.

Rights and Payment
All rights. Written material, $50. Pays on publication. Provides 3 contributor's copies.

Editor's Comments
We will be open to receiving queries again later in 2008, when our period of reorganization is complete. Check the website for updates to our content and submission policy.

Mothering

P.O. Box 1690
Santa Fe, NM 87504

Articles Editor: Candace Walsh

Description and Interests
This magazine strives to provide empowering articles to help parents make the right choices for natural family living. It includes practical and inspirational articles on pregnancy, childbirth, and parenting.
• **Audience:** Parents
• **Frequency:** 6 times each year
• **Circulation:** 25,000
• **Website:** www.mothering.com

Freelance Potential
90% written by nonstaff writers. Publishes 60 freelance submissions yearly; 20% by unpublished writers, 70% by new authors. Receives 108 queries yearly.

Submissions
Query with outline/synopsis. Accepts hard copy. SASE. Responds in 2–4 weeks.
Articles: 2,000 words. Informational and factual articles; profiles; and personal experience pieces. Topics include pregnancy, childbirth, midwifery, health, homeopathy, teen issues, and organic issues.
Depts/columns: Word lengths vary. Cooking, book and product reviews, health news, parenting updates, and inspirational pieces.
Artwork: 5x7 B/W and color prints.
Other: Children's activities and arts and crafts. Poetry about motherhood and families. Submit seasonal material 6–8 months in advance.

Sample Issue
88 pages (35% advertising): 3 articles; 9 depts/columns. Sample copy, $5.95 with 9x12 SASE. Guidelines available at website.
• "Bang! Bang! You're Dead." Article explores ways to teach nonviolence and respect for weapons and encourage imaginative play.
• "Welcome to the World, Sister!" Personal experience piece tells of a mom's decision to invite her children to their sibling's birth.
• Sample dept/column: "Way of Learning" discusses the benefits of teaching children chess.

Rights and Payment
First rights. Written material, $100+. Artwork, payment rates vary. Pays on publication. Provides 2 copies and a 1-year subscription.

Editor's Comments
We seek articles that help parents make informed choices as they create a healthy family environment.

Mr. Marquis' Museletter

Box 29556
Maple Ridge, British Columbia V2X 2V0
Canada

Editor: Kalen Marquis

Description and Interests
Short, reflective autobiographical works, fictional stories of "gentle truth and beauty," and short pieces of creative nonfiction fill each issue of this literary newsletter.
• **Audience:** 2–21 years
• **Frequency:** Quarterly
• **Circulation:** 150

Freelance Potential
90% written by nonstaff writers. Publishes 40 freelance submissions yearly; 90% by unpublished writers, 90% by authors who are new to the magazine. Receives 200 queries and unsolicited mss yearly.

Submissions
Query with writing samples; or send complete ms. Accepts hard copy, email to kwilville@shaw.ca, and simultaneous submissions if identified. SAE/IRC. Responds in 4 months.
Articles: 300 words. Informational articles; opinion and personal experience pieces; profiles; interviews; and book reviews. Topics include nature, the arts, current events, history, multicultural and ethnic issues, music, and popular culture. Also publishes biographies of painters, writers, and inventors.
Fiction: 300 words. Genres include adventure; contemporary, historical, multicultural, and inspirational fiction; and problem-solving stories.
Artwork: Line art.
Other: Poetry, 4–16 lines. Accepts seasonal material 6 months in advance.

Sample Issue
10 pages (no advertising): 1 article; 2 stories; 10 poems. Sample copy, $2 with #10 SAE/IRC. Guidelines available.
• "Kelly and the Crystal Cup." Story tells how a child learns to get her own cup of water at bedtime.
• "Mr. Marquis Went to Paris!" Article describes a Christmas in Paris.

Rights and Payment
One-time rights. No payment. Provides 1 copy.

Editor's Comments
Trust that your thoughts, feelings, and experiences are worthy of expression and that your craft will improve over time. We are currently emphasizing inspirational literature, biographies, and personal tributes to mentors.

M: The Magazine for Montessori Families

3 Werner Way
Lebanon, NJ 08833

Editor-in-Chief

Description and Interests
The goal of this magazine is to provide a variety of informative and entertaining features about the underlying principles of Montessori education.
• **Audience:** Parents
• **Frequency:** Quarterly
• **Circulation:** Unavailable
• **Website:** www.mthemagazine.com

Freelance Potential
25% written by nonstaff writers. Publishes 20 freelance submissions yearly.

Submissions
Query with writing sample. Accepts hard copy. SASE. Response time varies.
Articles: Word lengths vary. Informational articles; profiles; personal experience pieces; interviews; and reviews. Topics include Montessori teaching methods and benefits, history of Montessori, family issues, parenting, and student motivation.
Depts/columns: Word lengths vary. Ethical issues, parenting advice, cooking with children, news, and reading resources.

Sample Issue
40 pages: 7 articles; 6 depts/columns. Sample copy, $8.50.
• "Maria Montessori and the Great War, 1914–1919." Article explores the origins and development of the Montessori peace philosophy.
• "Finding the Flow in Montessori." Article reviews research that has found Montessori students to be more intrinsically motivated than their traditionally educated counterparts.
• "Training to Become a Montessori Teacher." Article explains why parents often become Montessori teachers in mid-career.
• Sample dept/column: "First Person Singular" is a personal essay about taking the lead as a parent.

Rights and Payment
First North American serial rights. Written material, payment rates vary. Pays on publication.

Editor's Comments
We recognize that Montessori is a philosophy of life whose principles apply to everyone, not just the children who attend its schools. Our mission is to help parents apply these principles at home, and to support their children as well as their children's education.

MultiCultural Review

194 Lenox Avenue
Albany, NY 12208

Editor: Lyn Miller-Lachmann

Description and Interests
The ethnic, racial, and religious diversity in the U.S. is examined and celebrated in this journal. Its feature articles and book reviews are targeted to teachers and librarians working at all educational levels.
- **Audience:** Teachers and librarians
- **Frequency:** Quarterly
- **Circulation:** 3,500+
- **Website:** www.mcreview.com

Freelance Potential
80% written by nonstaff writers. Publishes 8 freelance submissions yearly; 10% by unpublished writers, 20% by authors who are new to the magazine. Receives 80 unsolicited mss yearly.

Submissions
Send complete ms. Accepts hard copy and disk submissions. SASE. Responds in 3–4 months.
Articles: 2,000–6,000 words. Informational and how-to articles; profiles; and opinion pieces. Topics include the arts, education, writing, and social, multicultural, and ethnic issues.
Depts/columns: 1,500–2,000 words. News, reports on new book releases.
Other: Book and media reviews, 200–300 words.

Sample Issue
114 pages (10% advertising): 4 articles; 5 depts/columns; 149 book reviews. Sample copy, $15. Guidelines and theme list available.
- "Mother Goose Teaches on the Wild Side." Article describes ways to use a multicultural curriculum to motivate at-risk Mexican and Chicano students.
- "Al-Razi and Cumpleaños Feliz: Recent Children's Books in Spanish." Article provides an overview of a broad spectrum of children's literature now available in Spanish.

Rights and Payment
First serial rights. Articles, $50–$100. Depts/columns, $50. Reviews, no payment. Pays on publication. Provides 2 contributor's copies.

Editor's Comments
We need topical biographies, especially for grades nine through twelve. Book reviews in all subject areas are also always needed. In addition, we use discussions of current issues related to multiculturalism, ethnographic articles on specific groups, and articles on nonprofit resources that present diverse cultures.

MultiMedia & Internet Schools

14508 NE 20th Avenue, Suite 102
Vancouver, WA 98646

Editor: David Hoffman

Description and Interests
This magazine examines the numerous ways in which technology is being used to advance learning in kindergarten through twelfth-grade classrooms. It covers the educational uses of the Internet, computers, and other technology tools.
- **Audience:** Librarians, teachers, and technology coordinators
- **Frequency:** 6 times each year
- **Circulation:** 12,000
- **Website:** www.mmischools.com

Freelance Potential
90% written by nonstaff writers. Publishes 20–24 freelance submissions yearly; 20% by unpublished writers, 20% by authors who are new to the magazine. Receives 60 queries yearly.

Submissions
Query or send complete ms. Accepts email submissions to hoffmand@infotoday. Artwork improves chance of acceptance. Responds in 6–8 weeks.
Articles: 1,500 words. Informational and how-to articles. Topics include K–12 education, the Internet, multimedia and electronic resources, technology-based tools, and curriculum integration.
Depts/columns: Word lengths vary. Product news and reviews and ideas from educators.
Artwork: TIFF images at 300 dpi.

Sample Issue
48 pages (15% advertising): 8 articles; 5 depts/columns. Sample copy and guidelines, $7.95 with 9x12 SASE.
- "Healthy Choices." Article features ideas for using technology and websites to integrate health topics into the school curriculum.
- "E-Scheduling." Article details the different types of online calendars that are available to teachers and media specialists.
- Sample dept/column: "Product Reviews" reports on middle and high school software and websites.

Rights and Payment
First rights. Written material, $300–$500. Artwork, payment rates vary. Pays on publication. Provides 2 contributor's copies.

Editor's Comments
We tend to seek out experts on the topics we want covered, but we are open to article suggestions.

Muse

Carus Publishing
70 East Lake Street, Suite 300
Chicago, IL 60603

Editor: Virginia Edwards

Description and Interests
Muse was created as a collaboration between the Cricket Magazine Group and *Smithsonian* magazine. Designed to appeal to teens and pre-teens, it addresses everything from science and technology to history and art. All of its material is intended to stimulate thinking in young readers.
• **Audience:** 10+ years
• **Frequency:** 9 times each year
• **Circulation:** 51,000
• **Website: www.cricketmag.com**

Freelance Potential
100% written by nonstaff writers. Of the freelance submissions published yearly, 20% are by authors who are new to the magazine.

Submissions
All material is commissioned from experienced authors. Send résumé and clips. Response time varies.
Articles: To 1,500 words. Informational articles; interviews; and photo-essays. Topics include science, the environment, nature, computers, technology, history, math, and the arts.
Depts/columns: Word lengths vary. News items, Q&As, and activities.

Sample Issue
48 pages (no advertising): 6 articles; 5 depts/columns; 1 contest; 1 comic. Sample copy and guidelines available at website.
• "The Beast in the Middle." Article discusses black holes, how they occur, and how scientists discovered their existence.
• "Tenrec Tales." Article features photos and facts describing an unusual animal from Madagascar.
• "Rampaging Reptiles." Article examines the mythology surrounding dragons and why such legends became so popular in the Middle Ages.

Rights and Payment
Rights vary. Written material, payment rates vary. Payment policy varies.

Editor's Comments
We're primarily interested in first-person accounts written by working scientists, historians, artists, or other professionals. We want to see both your scholarly and journalistic credentials. You should be able to write for a magazine, not just textbooks.

Music Educators Journal

Music Educators National Conference
1806 Robert Fulton Drive
Reston, VA 20191

Managing Editor: Dorothy Wagener

Description and Interests
Music education is the focus of this magazine, with an emphasis on current teaching methods, practical instruction techniques, and professional philosophy.
• **Audience:** Music teachers
• **Frequency:** 5 times each year
• **Circulation:** 80,000
• **Website: www.menc.org**

Freelance Potential
85% written by nonstaff writers. Publishes 30 freelance submissions yearly; 25% by unpublished writers. Receives 100 mss yearly.

Submissions
Send 6 copies of complete ms. Accepts hard copy. SASE. Responds in 3 months.
Articles: 1,800–3,000 words. Instructional and informational articles; and historical studies of music education. Topics include teaching methods, professional philosophy, and current issues in music teaching and learning.
Depts/columns: Word lengths vary. Video reviews, teaching ideas, technology updates, and MENC news.
Other: Submit seasonal material 8–12 months in advance.

Sample Issue
74 pages (40% advertising): 6 articles; 6 depts/columns. Sample copy, $6 with 9x12 SASE ($2 postage). Guidelines available.
• "Every Child a Singer." Article describes techniques for assisting developing singers.
• "Effective Time Management in Ensemble Rehearsals." Article stresses the importance of teachers setting the pace during rehearsals for school performances.
• Sample dept/column: "For Your Library" features short reviews of books about music and music education.

Rights and Payment
All rights. No payment. Provides 2 copies.

Editor's Comments
Thousands of music educators read our magazine, and we want articles that will appeal to this broad cross-section of teachers. Articles should be written in a straightforward, conversational style that avoids unnecessary jargon, quotations, and footnotes. The ideas you present should be based on solid research; avoid personal asides that aren't relevant to the topic.

My Family Doctor

The Magazine That Makes House Calls

P.O. Box 38790
Colorado Springs, CO 80906

Managing Editor: Leigh Ann Hubbard

Description and Interests
Health-care professionals are the principal authors of this magazine that provides upbeat, practical, and reliable information and advice to individuals dedicated to keeping themselves healthy and happy.
• **Audience:** Adults
• **Frequency:** Quarterly
• **Circulation:** 60,000
• **Website:** www.myfamilydoctormag.com

Freelance Potential
100% written by nonstaff writers. Of the freelance submissions published yearly, 35% are by new authors.

Submissions
Query with writing samples. Prefers email queries to managingeditor@familydoctormag.com. Response time varies.
Articles: 400–1,200 words. Informational articles. Topics include health, fitness, nutrition, and preventive medicine.
Depts/columns: 200–400 words. Medical studies and breakthroughs.
Other: Filler, 200–400 words.

Sample Issue
68 pages (2% advertising): 10 articles; 16 depts/columns. Sample copy, $4.95 at newsstands. Guidelines available.
• "Naturally Healthy." Article provides answers from medical experts and health professionals on weight loss, exercise, and nutrition.
• "Like a Dream." Article explores the importance of sleep and answers common questions about sleep-related issues.
• Sample dept/column: "First Aid" provides helpful information for surviving an emergency, including the supplies to have on hand.

Rights and Payment
First North American serial, exclusive syndication for one year, and non-exclusive rights. Written material, $.25–$.30 per word. Pays on publication.

Editor's Comments
We are looking for submissions that present preventive health information in a creative, fun, new approach that is still evidence-based. We are receiving too many pieces on alternative medicine without scientific support. We are interested in these subjects, but only from an evidence-based, non-biased point of view.

Nashville Parent Magazine

2270 Metro Center Boulevard
Nashville, TN 37228

Editor: Susan B. Day

Description and Interests
An award-winning parenting resource publication, *Nashville Parent Magazine* was created primarily for families with young children. It reports on regional events while also offering discussions of contemporary issues relating to family life.
• **Audience:** Parents
• **Frequency:** Monthly
• **Circulation:** 85,000
• **Website:** www.parentworld.com

Freelance Potential
15–20% written by nonstaff writers. Publishes 400 freelance submissions yearly; 40% by authors who are new to the magazine. Receives 1,200 unsolicited mss yearly.

Submissions
Send complete ms. Accepts hard copy, Macintosh disk submissions with hard copy, and email submissions to npinfo@nashvilleparent.com. Availability of artwork improves chance of acceptance. SASE. Response time varies.
Articles: 800–1,000 words. Informational and how-to articles; profiles; interviews; photo-essays; and personal experience pieces. Topics include parenting, family issues, current events, social issues, health, music, travel, recreation, religion, the arts, crafts, computers, and multicultural and ethnic issues.
Depts/columns: Staff written.
Artwork: B/W color prints.
Other: Submit seasonal material related to Christmas, Easter, and Halloween 2 months in advance.

Sample Issue
116 pages (50% advertising): 7 articles; 9 depts/columns. Sample copy, free with 9x12 SASE. Guidelines available.
• "Heart to Heart: Talking to Your Kids About Death." Article advises parents on how and when to handle this sensitive subject.
• "Weighing In." Article discusses the best approaches to preventing obesity in children.

Rights and Payment
One-time rights. Written material, $35. Pays on publication. Provides 3 contributor's copies on request.

Editor's Comments
Write in a style that's easily accessible to busy parents and cite local sources.

NASSP Bulletin

Sage Publications
2455 Teller Road
Thousand Oaks, CA 91320

Editor: Len Foster

Description and Interests
This peer-reviewed journal of the National Association of Secondary School Principals contains scholarly and research-based articles that advance the vision and performance of middle-level and high school principals.
- **Audience:** Secondary school principals
- **Frequency:** Quarterly
- **Circulation:** Unavailable
- **Website:** http://bulletin.sagepub.com

Freelance Potential
100% written by nonstaff writers. Publishes 20–25 freelance submissions yearly; 15% by unpublished writers, 30% by authors who are new to the magazine. Receives 192 unsolicited mss yearly.

Submissions
Send complete ms (written in American Psychological Association style) with abstract and letter of intent. Prefers email submissions to lenf@wsu.edu (Microsoft Word attachments). Will accept hard copy with CD. SASE. Responds in 4–6 weeks.
Articles: 4,000 words. Informational articles. Topics include disadvantaged students, accountability in the classroom, family and community partnerships, funding and equity, legal issues in education, safe schools, literacy in secondary schools, organizational learning, instructional leadership, professional development and research-based best practices, and school reform.
Depts/columns: Word lengths vary. "Resource Review" features book and product reviews.

Sample Issue
180 pages: 5 articles; 1 dept/column. Sample copy, free with 8x10 SASE. Guidelines available at website.
- "Making Meaning of Educational Leaders." Article explores how future educational leaders make meaning of the principalship through metaphor.
- "Implementation of Learning Community Principles." Article tracks the efforts of educators at six high schools to develop learning communities.

Rights and Payment
All rights. No payment. Provides 2 author's copies.

Editor's Comments
We publish a wide range of articles that promote student learning and achievement; provide insight for strategic planning and decision-making in schools; and provide research and contemporary perspectives on educational reform and policies.

National Geographic Kids

National Geographic Society
1145 17th Street NW
Washington, DC 20036-4688

Editor: Julie Agnone

Description and Interests
This children's version of the well-known geography and natural science publication strives to teach kids about the world around them through fun, entertaining articles, activities, games, and puzzles. Like its counterpart, it is filled with high-quality color photos.
- **Audience:** 6–14 years
- **Frequency:** 10 times each year
- **Circulation:** 1.3 million
- **Website:** http://kids.nationalgeographic.com

Freelance Potential
85% written by nonstaff writers. Publishes 20–25 freelance submissions yearly; 1% by unpublished writers, 30% by authors who are new to the magazine. Receives 360 queries yearly.

Submissions
Query with clips. No unsolicited mss. SASE. Response time varies.
Articles: Word lengths vary. Informational articles. Topics include geography, archaeology, paleontology, history, entertainment, and the environment.
Depts/columns: Word lengths vary. News and trends, amazing animals, and fun facts.
Other: Original games and jokes.

Sample Issue
42 pages (20% advertising): 5 articles; 15 depts/columns. Sample copy, $3.95. Guidelines available.
- "Wolf Speak." Article describes how wolves use their voices, body language, and even body odor to communicate.
- "Gorilla Rescue." Article tells the true story of how an endangered gorilla baby found a new family.
- Sample dept/column: "Inside Scoop" explains how scientists were able to re-create how George Washington looked at various times in his life.

Rights and Payment
All rights. Written material, payment rates vary. Artwork, $100–$600. Pays on acceptance. Provides 3–5 contributor's copies.

Editor's Comments
We're delighted to hear about stories that have kid appeal. Geography and archaeology story ideas must answer the question: "What's fun about that?" We always need animals to feature in our "Amazing Animals" section.

National Geographic Little Kids

National Geographic Society
1145 17th Street NW
Washington, DC 20036

Executive Editor: Julie Agnone

Description and Interests
This cheerful new magazine from the publishers of *National Geographic Kids* (and its venerable parent publication) brings animals, nature, science, and just plain fun to the littlest learners with brief articles, rebus stories, and lots of puzzles and games.
• **Audience:** 3–6 years
• **Frequency:** 6 times each year
• **Circulation:** Unavailable
• **Website:** http://littlekids.nationalgeographic.com

Freelance Potential
10% written by nonstaff writers. Publishes 5 freelance submissions yearly.

Submissions
Query with résumé. Accepts hard copy. SASE. Response time varies.
Articles: Word lengths vary. Informational articles. Topics include nature, animals, science, geography, history, and multicultural subjects.
Fiction: Word lengths vary. Rebus stories about animals and other cultures.
Other: Puzzles, activities, games, and jokes.

Sample Issue
24 pages (no advertising): 4 articles; 1 rebus story; 7 activities.
• "Life as a Tree Frog." Article describes the life-cycle of a red-eyed tree frog in the rainforest.
• "Meet the Matis." Article introduces children to a tribe of people who live in the Brazilian rainforest.
• "Making Colors." Article provides step-by-step instructions for making a color wheel.
• "Explore with Mama Mirabelle." Rebus tells about a mother elephant who lives in Africa.

Rights and Payment
All rights. Written material, payment rates vary. Pays on acceptance. Provides 3–5 contributor's copies.

Editor's Comments
Everything parents need to help their preschooler become a bright, curious explorer can be found in our pages. Captivating animal stories develop pre-reading and reading skills while answering questions about kids' favorite creatures. Features about different cultures bring the world to children and inspire a sense of understanding. Interactive experiments introduce simple science, and fun puzzles and games teach skills such as logic and counting.

Nature Friend Magazine

4253 Woodcock Lane
Dayton, VA 22821

Editor: Kevin Shauk

Description and Interests
Produced by a conservative Christian publisher, *Nature Friend Magazine* celebrates God's creation and the natural world through factual articles, stories, and activities.
• **Audience:** 6–12 years
• **Frequency:** Monthly
• **Circulation:** 12,000
• **Website:** www.naturefriendmagazine.com

Freelance Potential
90% written by nonstaff writers. Publishes 36 freelance submissions yearly; 5% by unpublished writers, 10% by authors who are new to the magazine. Receives 480–720 unsolicited mss yearly.

Submissions
Send complete ms. Accepts hard copy. SASE. Response time varies.
Articles: 300–900 words. Informational and how-to articles. Topics include science, nature, and wildlife.
Fiction: 300–900 words. Genres include adventure stories and stories about the outdoors, wildlife, nature, and the environment.
Artwork: 4x6 or larger prints.
Other: Puzzles and projects related to nature or science.

Sample Issue
24 pages (no advertising): 6 articles; 1 story; 2 depts/columns; 3 activities. Sample copy and guidelines, $8.
• "An Engineering Marvel: The Garden Spider's Web." Story recounts how a young girl and her mother explored the intricacies of design and creation in a spider's web.
• "Why Does Salt Melt Ice?" Article includes an experiment that investigates the freezing point of a solution.
• "Busy Little Creators." Article tells how two species of insects have special God-given talents and knowledge.

Rights and Payment
One-time rights. Written material, $.05 per word; pays on publication. Artwork, payment policy and rates vary. Provides 1 tearsheet.

Editor's Comments
Our mission is to increase children's awareness of God and an appreciation for His works and gifts. We like to show how instinctive virtues, such as wisdom, love, and loyalty, can be found in various creatures.

N.E.W. & Fox Valley Kids

P.O. Box 11737
Green Bay, WI 54307

Publisher: Dr. Brookh Lyonns

Description and Interests

This parenting magazine keeps families in the greater Green Bay area informed of the latest news, activities, and events in the region. It also includes articles on topics such as parenting, health, and education.
• **Audience:** Parents
• **Frequency:** Monthly
• **Circulation:** 40,000
• **Website:** www.newandfoxvalleykids.com

Freelance Potential

100% written by nonstaff writers. Publishes many freelance submissions yearly; 5% by unpublished writers, 10% by new authors. Receives 204 queries, 36 unsolicited mss yearly.

Submissions

Query or send complete ms. Accepts hard copy and disk submissions (RTF files). SASE. Response time varies.
Articles: To 750 words. Informational articles and humorous pieces. Topics include parenting, family issues, education, gifted and special education, regional and national news, crafts, hobbies, music, the arts, health, fitness, sports, animals, pets, travel, popular culture, and multicultural and ethnic issues.
Depts/columns: To 750 words. Women's and children's health, school news, and essays.
Other: Submit seasonal material 4 months in advance.

Sample Issue

12 pages (50% advertising): 5 articles; 7 depts/columns. Sample copy, free with 9x12 SASE. Guidelines and editorial calendar available.
• "Around the World in a Week." Article describes how to have fun and explore the world without leaving the neighborhood.
• "The Colors of Health." Article tells how to have fun with your kids and keep them healthy by eating colorful fruit and vegetables.
• Sample dept/column: "Women's Health Today" discusses how planning ahead will make a doctor's visit an easier experience.

Rights and Payment

Rights negotiable. All material, payment rates vary. Pays on publication. Provides 2 author's copies.

Editor's Comments

We are looking for articles covering proactive health topics, organics, and positive humor.

New Expression

Youth Communications
Columbia College
619 South Wabash, Suite 207
Chicago, IL 60605

Program Manager: Lurlene Brown

Description and Interests

Written "by, for, and about teens," this Chicago-area tabloid gives young people a vehicle through which to voice their ideas. It is published by Youth Communications at Columbia College with the support of numerous educational and journalistic foundations.
• **Audience:** YA
• **Frequency:** 9 times each year
• **Circulation:** 45,000
• **Website:** www.newexpression.org

Freelance Potential

10% written by nonstaff writers. Publishes 40–50 freelance submissions yearly; 50% by unpublished writers, 50% by authors who are new to the magazine. Receives 36–48 unsolicited mss yearly.

Submissions

Send complete ms. Accepts hard copy and email submissions to lurlene@youthcommunications.org. Availability of artwork improves chance of acceptance. SASE. Response time varies.
Articles: No word limit. Informational articles; reviews; and personal experience pieces. Topics include current events, music, popular culture, and social issues.
Depts/columns: Word lengths vary. News briefs; media reviews; opinions; teen business; school issues; and sports.
Artwork: B/W JPEG images.
Other: Poetry.

Sample Issue

28 pages (10% advertising): 16 articles; 22 depts/columns; 6 poems. Sample copy, $1. Guidelines and editorial calendar available.
• "More CPS Graduates Going to College." Article reviews Chicago Public Schools statistics.
• "Windy Mixx Talent Search." Article previews a local music and spoken-word competition.
• Sample dept/column: "Sports" includes a profile of NBA player Luol Deng.

Rights and Payment

All rights. No payment.

Editor's Comments

We believe that youth must be heard and understood. The expression and sharing of their experiences, concerns, and solutions are critical to their ability to shape their present and future worlds.

New Jersey Suburban Parent

Middlesex Publications
850 Route 1
North Brunswick, NJ 08902

Editor: Melodie Dhondt

Description and Interests
This regional tabloid, printed in three geographical editions, keeps New Jersey parents apprised of area news and events. It also publishes general articles on such topics as child development, education, health, recreation, and travel.
• **Audience:** Parents
• **Frequency:** Monthly
• **Circulation:** 78,000
• **Website:** www.njparentweb.com

Freelance Potential
80% written by nonstaff writers. Publishes 12 freelance submissions yearly; 20% by unpublished writers, 40% by authors who are new to the magazine. Receives 1,440 queries yearly.

Submissions
Query with writing samples. Accepts hard copy and simultaneous submissions if identified. SASE. Responds in 2–8 weeks.
Articles: 700–1,000 words. Informational and how-to articles. Topics include parenting, pregnancy, childbirth, family issues, health, education, summer camp, recreation, sports, travel, cultural events, finance, careers, and entertainment.
Depts/columns: Staff written.
Artwork: B/W and color prints.
Other: Submit seasonal material 4 months in advance.

Sample Issue
24 pages (60% advertising): 9 articles; 4 depts/columns. Sample copy, free with 9x12 SASE. Guidelines and editorial calendar available.
• "Graduation Season Brings Risk and Reward." Article gives advice on transforming the parent-teen relationship as the child heads into adulthood.
• "Healthy Kids & Family Trips." Article provides tips for safe summer travel.
• "Get Every Mile Out of Your Gas Tank." Article discusses how to conserve fuel.

Rights and Payment
Rights vary. Articles, $30. Artwork, payment rates vary. Pays on acceptance. Provides 1+ contributor's copies.

Editor's Comments
Many of our topics recur year after year. Even if your subject was assigned to another writer, your article may be held for future use.

New Moon

2 West First Street, Suite 101
Duluth, MN 55802

Editorial Department

Description and Interests
New Moon is written and edited by and for girls who want their voices heard and their dreams taken seriously. Its goal is to empower and support girls as they grow into women.
• **Audience:** Girls, 8-14 years
• **Frequency:** 6 times each year
• **Circulation:** 25,000
• **Website: www.newmoon.org**

Freelance Potential
90% written by nonstaff writers. Publishes 50 freelance submissions yearly; 85% by unpublished writers, 20% by authors who are new to the magazine. Receives 720 queries and unsolicited mss yearly.

Submissions
Female authors only. Query or send complete ms. Prefers email submissions to girl@newmoon.org; also accepts hard copy and simultaneous submissions if identified. Does not return mss. Responds in 4–6 months.
Articles: 300–1,200 words. Profiles and interviews. Topics include careers, fitness, recreation, science, technology, and social issues.
Fiction: 900–1,600 words. Genres include contemporary, inspirational, multicultural, and ethnic fiction.
Depts/columns: Word lengths vary. Health advice, profiles, and historical pieces.
Other: Poetry from girls ages 8–14 only.

Sample Issue
48 pages (no advertising): 4 articles; 1 story; 15 depts/columns; 2 poems. Sample copy, $7. Guidelines available.
• "Horses In My Heart." Article describes a 12-year-old girl's animal activism.
• "Save the Internet!" Article explains the importance of network neutrality.
• Sample dept/column: "Body Language" discusses what is considered "normal" health.

Rights and Payment
All rights. Written material, $.06–$.10 per word. Pays on publication. Provides 3 contributor's copies.

Editor's Comments
All material should be pro-girl and focus on girls, women, or female issues. An editorial board of girls ages 8 to 14 makes final decisions on all material appearing in the magazine, and submissions from children and teens take precedence.

New York Family

63 West 38th Street, Suite 206
New York, NY 10018

Editor: Eric Messinger

Description and Interests
Tips, essays, and articles on topics of interest to parents living in New York City appear in this useful magazine. Distributed free throughout the area, it also includes local resources and up-to-date information on family-friendly places and events.
• **Audience:** Parents
• **Frequency:** Monthly
• **Circulation:** 25,000
• **Website:** www.manhattanmedia.com

Freelance Potential
50% written by nonstaff writers. Publishes 40 freelance submissions yearly; 40% by authors who are new to the magazine. Receives 600 queries yearly.

Submissions
Query with clips. Accepts hard copy. SASE. Response time varies.
Articles: 800–1,200 words. Informational articles; profiles; interviews; photo-essays; and personal experience pieces. Topics include gifted education, music, recreation, regional news, social issues, special education, travel, and women's issues.
Depts/columns: 400–800 words. News and reviews.

Sample Issue
80 pages: 4 articles; 18 depts/columns. Sample copy, free with 9x12 SASE. Guidelines available.
• "Summer Sweep." Article offers tips on how to have an organized home, including eliminating clutter and making cleaning a family fun event.
• "KidHampton." Article offers a summer guide filled with things to do and see while enjoying family life in the Hamptons.
• Sample dept/column: "Adults Only" discusses the problems with child-centered marriages, including the negative impact on children's attitudes.

Rights and Payment
First rights. Written material, $25–$300. Pays on publication. Provides 3 contributor's copies.

Editor's Comments
We are currently interested in seeing more personal essays on topics of interest to New York City parents. In addition, we are looking for features about local issues, education, financial planning, family-friendly destinations, and authoritative articles with national scope and local relevance. Material should be thought-provoking and family-oriented.

New York Times Upfront

Scholastic Inc.
555 Broadway
New York, NY 10012-3999

Editor

Description and Interests
Published collaboratively by *The New York Times* and Scholastic Inc., this online publication is directed at high school students. Its purpose is to update teens on news and current affairs while also providing connections to the school social studies curriculum.
• **Audience:** 14–18 years
• **Frequency:** 18 times each year
• **Hits per month:** 250,000
• **Website:** www.upfrontmagazine.com

Freelance Potential
10% written by nonstaff writers. Publishes 2 freelance submissions yearly; 10% by authors who are new to the magazine. Receives 144 queries yearly.

Submissions
Query with résumé and published clips. Accepts hard copy. Availability of artwork improves chance of acceptance. SASE. Responds in 2–4 weeks only if interested.
Articles: 500–1,200 words. Informational articles; profiles; and interviews. Topics include popular culture, current events, social issues, history, careers, college, the arts, the environment, technology, science, politics, government, business, and multicultural and ethnic issues.
Depts/columns: Word lengths vary. First-person accounts from teens, news, and trends.
Artwork: High-resolution color prints or transparencies.

Sample Issue
Sample copy available at website. Guidelines available.
• "Is Multitasking a Crime?" Article reports on legislative proposals that would outlaw such activities as eating and interacting with pets while driving, or listening to an iPod while crossing at a crosswalk.
• "American Idols." Article lists the 100 most influential Americans according to 10 prominent historians and a well-respected magazine.

Rights and Payment
All rights. All material, payment rates vary. Pays on publication.

Editor's Comments
If you wish to contribute to our website, you must be able to write in a way that will appeal to savvy, smart teens who are in touch with their world. Send us something that's timely and engaging that correlates with the high school curriculum.

The Next Step Magazine

86 West Main Street
Victor, NY 14564

Editor-in-Chief: Laura Jeanne Hammond

Description and Interests
The Next Step Magazine is distributed in high schools all across the U.S. It offers high school and college students unbiased advice on college and career planning. Articles on life skills, such as managing personal finances, are also featured.
• **Audience:** 14–21 years
• **Frequency:** 5 times each year
• **Circulation:** 900,000
• **Website: www.nextSTEPmag.com**

Freelance Potential
90% written by nonstaff writers. Publishes 40 freelance submissions yearly.

Submissions
Query. Accepts email queries to laura@ nextSTEPmag.com. Response time varies.
Articles: 700–1,000 words. Informational, self-help, and how-to articles; profiles; interviews; personal experience and opinion pieces; humor; and essays. Topics include college planning, financial aid, campus tours, choosing a career, life skills, résumé writing, public speaking, personal finances, computers, multicultural and ethnic issues, sports, and special education.

Sample Issue
54 pages; 11 articles. Sample copy available at website. Guidelines available.
• "Creativity Pays." Article outlines careers in the arts, and gives advice on how to assemble and submit portfolios.
• "What Community College Can Do for You." Article busts the many myths readers may have heard about the value of a community college education.
• "Are You Religiously Affiliated College Material?" Article includes a quiz to determine whether a college with religious affiliation is right for the reader.

Rights and Payment
All rights. Articles, payment rates vary. Pays within 30 days of acceptance.

Editor's Comments
We are always looking for up-to-date information on what is available for students who are planning their next move, whether it's college or a career. Currently we are seeking articles written for high school counselors covering some aspect of college or career planning. Articles should be tightly written and well researched.

No Crime

Young People's Press
374 Fraser Street
North Bay, Ontario P1B 3W7
Canada

President and CEO: Don Curry

Description and Interests
This online magazine from Young People's Press seeks to reduce youth crime by advocating a safe and secure environment; modeling positive behavior; providing encouragement and support; and showing young people that adults care about them. Its content is written both by youths themselves and by professionals who work with them.
• **Audience:** YA–Adult
• **Frequency:** 6 times each year
• **Hits per month:** 24,000
• **Website: www.nocrimetime.net**

Freelance Potential
100% written by nonstaff writers. Publishes 150–200 freelance submissions yearly; 70% by unpublished writers, 75% by authors who are new to the magazine.

Submissions
Send complete ms. Accepts email submissions to media@ypp.net. Responds immediately.
Articles: 500–1,000 words. Informational articles and personal experience pieces. Topics include youth justice, youth crime, and community-based programs in crime prevention.
Depts/Columns: "True Life" personal essay, 400–800 words. Opinion pieces, 500–800 words. "PopMachine" entertainment pieces, 500–1,000 words. Media reviews, 80–120 words.

Sample Issue
9 articles. Sample copy and writers' guidelines available at website.
• "Fighting Back." Article profiles the work of a police officer who started a boxing program for young people in conflict with the law.
• "Recycling Lives." Article describes Kans 4 Kids, a recycling program in Calgary, Alberta, that provides at-risk youth with work skills and self-esteem.
• "Understanding the Legal System." Article discusses the Ontario Justice Education Network, which teaches young people how the legal system works.

Rights and Payment
Non-exclusive rights. Written material, payment rates vary. Payment policy varies.

Editor's Comments
This e-zine is part of a larger project that includes articles about youth crime prevention written by young people as well as by professional staff writers.

Northern Michigan Family Magazine

P.O. Box 579
Indian River, MI 49749

Editor: L. Scott Swanson

Description and Interests
Parents residing in Northern Michigan turn to this publication for its articles on topics such as family life, parenting, education, current events, recreation, and social issues. In addition, it provides regional resources and information on events.
- **Audience:** Parents
- **Frequency:** 6 times each year
- **Circulation:** 6,000

Freelance Potential
20% written by nonstaff writers. Publishes 12 freelance submissions yearly. Receives 100 queries and unsolicited mss yearly.

Submissions
Query or send complete ms. Accepts hard copy, email to editor@resorter.com, and simultaneous submissions if identified. Availability of artwork improves chance of acceptance. SASE. Response time varies.
Articles: 200–1,500 words. Informational, self-help, and how-to articles; profiles; interviews; and personal experience pieces. Topics include parenting, family life, gifted and special education, current events, music, nature, the environment, regional news, recreation, and social issues.
Depts/columns: Word lengths vary. Family news and resources, health information, area events, and perspectives from parents.

Sample Issue
22 pages: 3 articles; 10 depts/columns. Sample copy, free with 9x12 SASE. Guidelines available.
- "The History of Little League Baseball." Article takes a look at the roots of Little League baseball and the the Little League World Series.
- "Heart Gallery on Display in Petoskey." Article describes an exhibit which includes portraits of Michigan foster children waiting for adoption.
- Sample dept/column: "Musings From Mom" discusses the pressures parents face regarding putting kids in activities.

Rights and Payment
All rights. Unsolicited articles and reprints, $10–$25; assigned articles, $25–$100. Payment policy varies.

Editor's Comments
Editorial contributions are welcome. Topics such as children's health issues, safety, and recreation continue to be of interest to us. Craft ideas are also a hit.

The Northland

P.O. Box 841
Schumacher, Ontario P0N 1G0
Canada

Submissions Editor

Description and Interests
Members of the Diocese of Moosonee of the Anglican Church of Canada read this small family magazine for church news, sermons, prayers, and other inspirational content.
- **Audience:** Adults
- **Frequency:** Quarterly
- **Circulation:** 500

Freelance Potential
100% written by nonstaff writers. Publishes several freelance submissions yearly. Receives few unsolicited mss yearly.

Submissions
Send complete ms. Accepts hard copy. SASE. Response time varies.
Articles: Word lengths vary. Informational and inspirational articles. Topics include the Anglican Church, ministry, faith, prayer, church rites, sacraments, worship, and sermon ideas.
Depts/columns: Word lengths vary. Local church news and events.

Sample Issue
24 pages (no advertising): 8 articles; 2 depts/columns. Sample copy available.
- "The Best Kept Secret." Article explains the little-known function of the Provincial Synod and Executive Council of the Anglican Church.
- "48 Hours in Kashechewan." Article chronicles the archbishop's annual visit to a small parish that recently suffered widespread flood damage.
- "Reflecting on the Environment: Christian Perspectives." Article discusses the work of a church-based social justice group that has taken on such ecological concerns as water and energy.
- Sample dept/column: "Moose Notes" provides updates from various parishes within the diocese.

Rights and Payment
Rights vary. No payment.

Editor's Comments
As a small, local church publication, we are interested in what is happening throughout the parishes that comprise our diocese, whether it be articles on religious celebrations or first-person essays about living a spiritual life. All of our content must be consistent with Anglican Church values and relevant to our readership here in northern Canada.

North Star Family Matters ☆

689 East Promontory Road
Shelton, WA 98584

Editor-in-Chief: Wendy Garrido

Description and Interests
The goal of this magazine, distributed free throughout Washington's Puget Sound area, is to inspire conscious parenting and empower kids. Articles for adults provide concrete tools for raising children positively, while kid-friendly features and activities teach children how to express themselves and achieve their goals.
• **Audience:** Parents; children ages 1–15
• **Frequency:** Monthly
• **Circulation:** 32,000
• **Website: www.northstarfamilymatters.com**

Freelance Potential
60% written by nonstaff writers. Publishes 48 freelance submissions yearly; 20% by unpublished writers, 35% by authors who are new to the magazine.

Submissions
Query. Accepts email queries to submit@ northstarfamilymatters.com. Response time varies.
Articles: 300–1,500 words. Informational and how-to articles; personal experience pieces; and book excerpts. Topics include communication, empowerment, discipline, conflict resolution, anger management, emotional support, attention, and reading.
Depts/columns: Staff written.
Other: Puzzles, games, and activities.

Sample Issue
30 pages: 9 articles; 2 depts/columns; 13 activities. Guidelines available.
• "CJ and the CODE." Article written for children tells how a boy uses empathy to disarm and befriend an angry classmate.
• "It's Never Too Late to Empower Your Teen." Personal essay by an 18-year-old girl recounts how her mother's trust changed their relationship; sidebar gives the mother's perspective.
• "Conscious Parenting Principles: Emotional Support." Article discusses the importance of empathy.

Rights and Payment
First and electronic rights. Articles, to $150. Payment policy varies. Provides 1 contributor's copy.

Editor's Comments
All articles should be in line with the "Our Beliefs" page of our magazine and website, and must clearly emphasize how the subject matter will have a meaningful and positive impact on empowering children and inspiring conscious parenting.

Northwest Baby & Child

4395 Rollinghill Road
Clinton, WA 98236

Editor: Betty Freeman

Description and Interests
This free monthly newspaper provides information, resources, support, and inspiration to expectant and new parents in the Puget Sound area of Washington.
• **Audience:** Parents
• **Frequency:** Monthly
• **Circulation:** 35,000
• **Website: www.nwbaby.com**

Freelance Potential
50% written by nonstaff writers. Publishes 50 freelance submissions yearly; 10% by unpublished writers, 30% by authors who are new to the magazine.

Submissions
Send ms. Accepts email to editor@nwbaby.com (no attachments). Responds in 2–3 months if interested.
Articles: 250–750 words. Informational and how-to articles; personal experience pieces; and interviews. Topics include pregnancy, childbirth, motherhood, early education, party ideas, family life, travel, traditions, and the environment.
Depts/columns: 250–750 words. Health, parenting tips, activities, and regional resources.
Artwork: B/W and color TIFF or PDF images. No JPEGs.
Other: Poetry.

Sample Issue
12 pages (15% advertising): 5 articles; 7 depts/ columns. Guidelines and editorial calendar available at website.
• "Motherhood: Finding Your Balance." Article provides advice on staying centered amid the difficulties and distractions of parenting.
• "Team Mom." Personal essay sings the praises of fellow mothers who have supported the author in her parenting experiences.
• Sample dept/column: "Family Fun" suggests taking an "eco-vacation" with the kids.

Rights and Payment
First rights. Articles and depts/columns, $40. Poetry and artwork, $10. Pays on publication. Provides 1–2 contributor's copies.

Editor's Comments
We have a theme for each issue, and the articles throughout the paper reflect our theme. Please download our editorial calendar, which may be found under Writers' Resources at our website.

OC Family

The News Magazine for Parents

1451 Quail Street, Suite 201
Newport Beach, CA 92660

Executive Editor: Craig Reem

Description and Interests
Catering to parents who live in Orange County, California, this glossy magazine offers party planning and camp guides, as well as information for parents of children of all ages about health, education, family activities, and child development.
• **Audience:** Families
• **Frequency:** Monthly
• **Circulation:** 70,000
• **Website:** www.ocfamily.com

Freelance Potential
82% written by nonstaff writers. Publishes 50 freelance submissions yearly; 1% by unpublished writers, 1% by authors who are new to the magazine. Receives 144 queries yearly.

Submissions
Query. Accepts hard copy and email queries to creem@churmmedia.com. SASE. Responds in 1 month.
Articles: 800–2,500 words. Informational articles and profiles. Topics include education, the Internet, family activities, fine arts, regional food and dining, consumer interest, and grandparenting.
Depts/columns: Word lengths vary. Family life, personal finances, book and software reviews, and women's health.
Artwork: B/W and color prints.

Sample Issue
204 pages (60% advertising): 3 articles; 20 depts/columns; 2 directories. Sample copy, free. Editorial calendar available.
• "Scale Down: Is Your Preschooler Overweight?" Article talks about ways parents may unwittingly teach children to overeat and ignore their body's cues.
• "Sizzling Summer." Article lists 50 ways to spend the day with your family in Orange County.
• "Five Young Sports Stars." Article profiles young rising stars in local athletics.

Rights and Payment
One-time rights. Articles, $100–$500. Artwork, $90. Kill fee, $50. Pays 45 days after publication. Provides 3 contributor's copies.

Editor's Comments
We want to see newsy stories of interest to families that have a local twist. Always include local resources and references.

Odyssey

Carus Publishing
30 Grove Street, Suite C
Peterborough, NH 03458

Senior Editor: Elizabeth E. Lindstrom

Description and Interests
Inventive, lively articles about science, math, and technology for students in middle school and high school are found in *Odyssey*. It also publishes some science fiction.
• **Audience:** 10–16 years
• **Frequency:** 9 times each year
• **Circulation:** 25,000
• **Website:** www.odysseymagazine.com

Freelance Potential
75% written by nonstaff writers. Publishes 50 freelance submissions yearly; 2% by unpublished writers, 25% by new authors. Receives 180 queries yearly.

Submissions
Query with outline, biography, and clips or writing samples. Accepts hard copy. Availability of artwork improves chance of acceptance. Responds in 5 months only if interested.
Articles: 750–1,000 words. Informational articles; biographies; and interviews. Topics include mathematics, science, and technology.
Fiction: To 1,000 words. Science fiction and science-related stories.
Depts/columns: Word lengths vary. Astronomy, animals, profiles, and short science news items.
Other: Activities, to 500 words. Seasonal material about notable space or astronomy events.

Sample Issue
48 pages (no advertising): 8 articles; 1 story; 6 depts/columns; 2 activities. Sample copy, $4.50 with 9x12 SASE (4 first-class stamps). Writers' guidelines and theme list available.
• "Bird Flu: Pandemic of Fear?" Article describes how viruses spread and the history of flu outbreaks around the world.
• Sample dept/column: "People to Discover" profiles an epidemiologist with the Centers for Disease Control.

Rights and Payment
All rights. Written material, $.20–$.25 per word. Artwork, payment rates vary. Pays on publication. Provides 2 contributor's copies.

Editor's Comments
Please note that all material must relate to an upcoming theme in order to be considered. We would like to review more submissions of activities, interviews, and science or science-related fiction.

The Old Schoolhouse

P.O. Box 8426
Gray, TN 37615

Editors: Paul & Gena Suarez

Description and Interests
The Old Schoolhouse addresses the variety of issues of interest to parents who are homeschooling their children. Written with a Christian slant, it publishes practical and inspirational articles about teaching and learning styles, curricula, and current trends in the home education field.
- **Audience:** Homeschool families
- **Frequency:** Quarterly
- **Circulation:** 100,000
- **Website:** www.thehomeschoolmagazine.com

Freelance Potential
98% written by nonstaff writers. Publishes 160 freelance submissions yearly; 30% by unpublished writers, 50% by authors who are new to the magazine. Receives 192 queries yearly.

Submissions
Query with outline, sample paragraphs, and brief author bio. Accepts queries submitted electronically using forms provided at the website. Users of Homeschoolblogger.com should note their user name on their query. No simultaneous submissions. Responds in 4–6 weeks.
Articles: 1,000–2,000 words. Informational and how-to articles and personal experience pieces. Topics include homeschooling, education, family life, art, music, spirituality, literature, child development, teen issues, science, history, and mathematics.
Depts/columns: Word lengths vary. Short news items, teaching styles, opinion pieces, children with special needs, and humor.

Sample Issue
200 pages (40% advertising): 3 articles; 21 depts/columns. Sample copy available. Guidelines available at website.
- "The Evidence Is So Positive." Article presents the latest research about homeschooled students.
- Sample dept/column: "HisStory" offers ideas for teaching military geography.

Rights and Payment
First rights (6-month exclusive). Written material, payment rates vary. Pays on publication. Provides 2 contributor's copies.

Editor's Comments
We want to work with writers who can present homeschooling solutions with wit and insight.

Once Upon a Time

553 Winston Court
St. Paul, MN 55118

Editor/Publisher: Audrey B. Baird

Description and Interests
Once Upon a Time is a support publication for children's writers and illustrators. It uses first-person pieces and how-to articles that help writers and artists improve their work and get it published.
- **Audience:** Children's writers and illustrators
- **Frequency:** Quarterly
- **Circulation:** 1,000
- **Website:** www.onceuponatimemag.com

Freelance Potential
66% written by nonstaff writers. Publishes 160 freelance submissions yearly; 30% by unpublished writers. Receives 80–100 mss yearly.

Submissions
Send complete ms. No queries. Accepts hard copy. SASE. Responds in 2 months.
Articles: To 900 words. Informational, self-help, and how-to articles; and personal experience pieces. Topics include writing and illustrating for children.
Depts/columns: Staff written.
Artwork: B/W line art.
Other: Poetry for adults about writing.

Sample Issue
32 pages (2% advertising): 11 articles; 10 depts/columns. Sample copy, $5. Guidelines available.
- "Journal: A Writer Prays." Article describes the author's personal experience with a 27-day bout of writer's block.
- "Finding Joy Again." Article recounts a successful writer's early days and how she regained her love of writing.
- "The Nasty Writing Teacher Trick." Humorous article tells how a writing instructor helped to develop a novel's protagonist.

Rights and Payment
One-time rights. No payment. Provides 2 contributor's copies.

Editor's Comments
We have an ongoing need for instructional, informative, supportive, and entertaining articles on writing for children. We would particularly like to see more humor and how-to articles. Give our readers a glimpse into the writer's life by sharing news of how you work, keep up the learning process, and connect with others in the field. Don't send articles about rejection or comparing writing to giving birth!

On Course

General Council of the Assemblies of God
1445 North Boonville Avenue
Springfield, MO 65802-1894

Editor

Description and Interests
Written specifically for Christian teens, On Course covers contemporary issues and the problems teens face on a daily basis. All of the articles present a biblical approach to overcoming life's challenges. It also covers popular culture and entertainment from a Christian viewpoint.
• **Audience:** 12–18 years
• **Frequency:** Quarterly
• **Circulation:** 160,000
• **Website:** www.oncourse.ag.org

Freelance Potential
95% written by nonstaff writers. Publishes 32 freelance submissions yearly; 30% by unpublished writers, 40% by authors who are new to the magazine.

Submissions
Send résumé with clips or writing samples. All work is done on assignment only.
Articles: To 1,000 words. How-to articles; profiles; interviews; humor; and personal experience pieces. Topics include social issues, music, health, religion, sports, careers, college, and multicultural subjects.
Depts/columns: Word lengths vary. Profiles and brief news items.

Sample Issue
32 pages (33% advertising): 4 articles; 6 depts/columns. Sample copy, free. Guidelines available.
• "Secrets." Article chronicles the story of a girl who was sexually abused by her uncle, and tells how she found help with The Seven Project.
• "Confessions of an Internet Porn Addict: Steps to Recovery." Article interviews a troubled youth who got help for his addiction.
• "Youth Ministry: In the Aftermath of Katrina." Personal experience piece describes a youth pastor's life in New Orleans after the hurricane.

Rights and Payment
First and electronic rights. Articles, $30 for a single-page feature; $60 for a double-page feature; $15 for reviews and sidebars. No payment for online reprints. Payment policy varies. Provides 5 author's copies.

Editor's Comments
All of our material is assigned, but we welcome résumés and writing samples from both new and established writers. We're not afraid of hard-hitting issues, but we also cover the lighter subjects.

Organic Family Magazine

P.O. Box 1614
Wallingford, CT 06492-1214

Editor: Catherine Wong

Description and Interests
This magazine encourages families to live an organic, natural lifestyle through its articles on organic gardening, natural products, the environment, and progressive politics. It even publishes stories and poems that have nature and environmental themes.
• **Audience:** Families
• **Frequency:** Twice each year
• **Circulation:** 200
• **Website:** www.organicfamilymagazine.com

Freelance Potential
90% written by nonstaff writers. Publishes 40 freelance submissions yearly.

Submissions
Query or send complete ms. Prefers email submissions to sciencelibrarian@hotmail.com. Will accept hard copy. SASE. Response time varies.
Articles: Word lengths vary. Informational articles; interviews; and personal experience pieces. Topics include nature, organic agriculture, conservation, parenting, natural pet care, herbs, gardening, nutrition, progressive politics, health, wellness, and environmental issues.
Fiction: Word lengths vary. Stories about nature and the environment.
Depts/columns: Word lengths vary. New product reviews; recipes; profiles of conservation organizations; and book, movie, and website reviews.
Other: Poetry.

Sample Issue
28 pages: 8 articles; 1 story; 11 depts/columns; 1 poem. Guidelines available at website.
• "Our Top Transition Tips: How Mom and Her 10-Year-Old Son Went Organic." Article provides a true account of how one family made the transition to organic living.
• "Waste Not, Want Not." Article written by a soldier in Iraq describes how people survive and thrive on American garbage in that country.

Rights and Payment
One-time rights. No payment. Provides 1 copy.

Editor's Comments
Practical information, how-to articles, and tips that help families live the organic lifestyle are always welcome. We also publish progressive political commentary. New writers are encouraged to submit.

Our Children

National PTA
541 North Fairbanks Court, Suite 1300
Chicago, IL 60611-3396

Editor: Marilyn Ferdinand

Description and Interests
As the magazine of the National PTA, *Our Children* carries articles about running effective local PTA chapters, as well as more general articles about parent involvement in education and educational health and safety issues.
- **Audience:** Parents, educators, school administrators
- **Frequency:** 5 times each year
- **Circulation:** 31,000
- **Website: www.pta.org**

Freelance Potential
50% written by nonstaff writers. Publishes 20–25 freelance submissions yearly; 75% by authors who are new to the magazine. Receives 180–240 queries and unsolicited mss yearly.

Submissions
Query or send complete ms. Accepts email submissions to mferdinand@pta.org. No simultaneous submissions. Accepted mss must be sent on disk. Responds in 2 months.
Articles: 1,200–1,800 words. Informational and how-to articles. Topics include running local PTA chapters, child welfare, education, and family life.
Depts/columns: Word lengths vary. Short updates on parenting and education issues and member advice.
Artwork: 3x5 or larger color prints and slides.
Other: Submit seasonal material 3 months in advance.

Sample Issue
24 pages (no advertising): 5 articles; 9 depts/columns. Sample copy, $2.50 with 9x12 SASE ($1 postage). Guidelines and theme list available.
- "The Social Networking Faceoff." Article explains how to set rules on Internet socializing to protect your children.
- "Boost Your Child's Money Smarts." Article provides age-specific advice for teaching kids about money.
- Sample dept/column: "Child Advocacy" explores issues associated with No Child Left Behind.

Rights and Payment
First rights. No payment. Provides 3 author's copies.

Editor's Comments
We're always interested in ideas for running successful PTA programs. We will also consider more general articles about educational issues, written in a conversational style.

Pack-O-Fun

2400 Devon, Suite 292
Des Plaines, IL 60018-4618

Editor: Annie Niemiec

Description and Interests
This magazine is chock-full of fun, easy-to-make crafts using everyday household materials, as well as activities that build self-esteem and group-friendly projects. It targets teachers, parents, and group leaders.
- **Audience:** 6–12 years
- **Frequency:** 6 times each year
- **Circulation:** 130,000
- **Website: www.pack-o-fun.com**

Freelance Potential
100% written by nonstaff writers. Receives 504 unsolicited mss yearly.

Submissions
Query or send complete ms with instructions and sketches if appropriate. Accepts hard copy. SASE. Responds in 4–6 weeks.
Articles: To 200 words. How-to's, craft projects, and party ideas.
Depts/columns: Word lengths vary. Art ideas; projects for children and adults to do together; ideas for vacation Bible school programs; and pictures of projects from readers.
Artwork: B/W and line art.
Other: Puzzles, activities, games, and skits. Poetry.

Sample Issue
66 pages (10% advertising): 10 crafts and activities; 4 depts/columns. Sample copy, $4,99 with 9x12 SASE (2 first-class stamps). Guidelines available.
- "Wrapping Paper Kite." Article offers step-by-step instructions for making a simple kite.
- "Summer Journals." Article provides directions for making fun journals for daily summer writing.
- Sample dept/column: "Art Smarts" discusses how to get kids involved in taking pictures of nature.

Rights and Payment
All rights. Written material, $10–$15. Artwork, payment rates vary. Pays 30 days after signed contract. Provides 3 contributor's copies.

Editor's Comments
Our interests currently include Halloween costume submissions. Include all patterns and suggest any illustrations you feel necessary to make things clear. Keep in mind that we look for fun, inexpensive projects, from simple to complex. We are receiving a lot of articles that recycle the same ideas. Send us something fresh we haven't seen before.

Pageantry Magazine

P.O. Box 160307
Alamonte Springs, FL 32716

Editor: Frank Abel

Description and Interests
Pageantry Magazine has been covering the world of beauty competitions for more than 25 years. Each issue includes features on fitness, modeling, and interviewing techniques, as well as reports on competitions and success stories. It also includes articles for parents of children who want to enter pageants.
• **Audience:** YA–Adult
• **Frequency:** Quarterly
• **Circulation:** Unavailable
• **Website: www.pageantrymagazine.com**

Freelance Potential
10% written by nonstaff writers. Publishes 5 freelance submissions yearly.

Submissions
Query. Accepts hard copy and email queries to editor@pageantrymagazine.com. SASE. Response time varies.
Articles: Word lengths vary. Informational articles; profiles; interviews; and personal experience pieces. Topics include beauty pageants for children and adults, fitness, breaking into show business, modeling, pageant coverage, makeup tips, interviewing techniques, dance, winning psychology, judges' perspectives, pageant etiquette, coaching, celebrities, talent competitions, and fashion.
Depts/columns: Word lengths vary. Hair styling, body shaping, and jewelry.

Sample Issue
144 pages: 5 articles; 10 depts/columns. Sample copy, $4.95.
• "Fashion Forecast: Queen Beads." Article showcases the deeper, warmer colors and the glitzy, glamorous beading found in fall's formal fashions.
• "Goodie Bag." Article depicts the latest necessities for the savvy shopper.
• Sample dept/column: "Fitness" outlines exercises for shaping your upper and lower back.

Rights and Payment
First North American serial rights. Written material, payment rates vary. Payment policy varies. Provides 1 contributor's copy.

Editor's Comments
We want writers who can cover both national and international events or who have expertise in beauty, fitness, fashion, or children's pageants.

Parent and Preschooler Newsletter

North Shore Child & Family Guidance Center
480 Old Westbury Road
Roslyn Heights, NY 11577-2215

Editor: Neala S. Schwartzberg, Ph.D.

Description and Interests
Child development and family-life issues are the focus of this international resource for parents, librarians, educators, and other child-care professionals. English and Spanish editions are published.
• **Audience:** Parents, caregivers, and early childhood professionals
• **Frequency:** 6 times each year
• **Website: www.northshorechildguidance.org**

Freelance Potential
90% written by nonstaff writers. Publishes 10 freelance submissions yearly; 50% by authors who are new to the magazine. Receives 72 queries yearly.

Submissions
Query with outline. Accepts email queries to nealas@panix.com. SASE. Responds in 1 week.
Articles: 2,000 words. Practical information and how-to articles. Topics include education, self-esteem, discipline, children's health, parenting skills, fostering cooperation through play, and coping with death.
Depts/columns: Staff written.

Sample Issue
8 pages (no advertising): 3 articles; 2 depts/ columns. Sample copy, $3 with #10 SASE (1 first-class stamp). Guidelines and editorial calendar available.
• "Question Reality." Article suggests that quantum physics should be taught to preschoolers.
• "Helping Our Kids Learn to Love Learning." Article discusses the importance of encouraging real exploration and intellectual questioning in young children.
• "Learning Through Bathtub Toys." Article explains what a 1992 cargo spill can teach children about ocean currents today.

Rights and Payment
First world rights. Articles, $200. Pays on publication. Provides 10 contributor's copies.

Editor's Comments
If there's a theme that runs through our newsletter, it's that children are joyful little folks who respond to love and enthusiasm. Keep in mind our international readership as you prepare your query for us, and please remember that we concentrate on universal concerns related to child care and development.

Parentguide News

419 Park Avenue South, 13th Floor
New York, NY 10016

Editor: Jenna Greditor

Description and Interests
This free tabloid serves parents in the New York metropolitan area with information on local events and family issues.
- **Audience:** Parents
- **Frequency:** Monthly
- **Circulation:** 280,000
- **Website: www.parentguidenews.com**

Freelance Potential
85% written by nonstaff writers. Publishes 45 freelance submissions yearly; 20% by unpublished writers, 80% by authors who are new to the magazine. Receives 12 queries and unsolicited mss yearly.

Submissions
Query or send complete ms with résumé. Accepts hard copy. SASE. Responds in 3–4 weeks.
Articles: 750–1,500 words. Informational and self-help articles; humor; and personal experience pieces. Topics include parenting, family life, education, social issues, current events, regional issues, popular culture, health, careers, computers, and science.
Depts/columns: 500 words. Local news and events; health; travel; and reviews.

Sample Issue
70 pages (39% advertising): 13 articles; 8 depts/columns; 3 directories. Sample copy, free with 10x13 SASE. Guidelines available.
- "Being a Dad." Personal essay reflects on one father's first few days as a parent.
- "The Most Common Nutritional Mistakes Parents Make." Article provides facts and advice about the nutritional needs of children.
- "A Fresh Start." Article provides tips for mothers on organizing life with their children.
- Sample dept/column: "Update" offers reviews of baby products, toys, clothing, and books.

Rights and Payment
Rights negotiable. No payment. Provides 1+ contributor's copies.

Editor's Comments
Parentguide caters to the needs of parents who have children under 12 years of age with monthly columns and feature articles that address both national and local parenting issues, such as health, education, child-rearing, and recreation. Every issue is jam-packed with pertinent information.

Parenting

135 West 50th Street, 3rd Floor
New York, NY 10026

Submissions Editor

Description and Interests
This well-known magazine is filled with useful parenting advice, information on child development and health, articles on relationships, and personal experience pieces from parents. It also offers product and media reviews.
- **Audience:** Parents
- **Frequency:** 11 times each year
- **Circulation:** 2 million+
- **Website: www.parenting.com**

Freelance Potential
80% written by nonstaff writers. Publishes 10–15 freelance submissions yearly; 5% by unpublished writers, 10% by authors who are new to the magazine. Receives 1,000 queries yearly.

Submissions
Query with clips. Accepts hard copy. SASE. Responds in 1–2 months.
Articles: 1,000–2,500 words. Informational, how-to, and self-help articles; profiles; and personal experience pieces. Topics include child development, behavior, health, pregnancy, and family activities.
Depts/columns: 100–1,000 words. Parenting tips and advice, child development by age range, work and family, and health and beauty advice for moms.

Sample Issue
170 pages (50% advertising): 10 articles; 15 depts/columns. Sample copy, $5.95 (mark envelope Attn: Back Issues). Guidelines available.
- "Making Family Dinners Fun." Article explains the realities of mealtime with young children, and how to deal with them.
- "8 Things No One Tells You About Being a Mom." Article lists the challenges along with the blessings of raising children.
- Sample dept/column: "Work & Family" offers advice on talking to kids about parents' salaries.

Rights and Payment
First world rights with 2 months' exclusivity. Written material, payment rates vary. Pays on acceptance. Provides 1 contributor's copy.

Editor's Comments
Our readers count on us to deliver the latest and best parenting information, reality-tested advice, and quick tips. We're always looking for a fresh approach to the usual topics of interest to new and expectant parents.

Parenting New Hampshire

P.O. Box 1291
Nashua, NH 03061-1291

Editor: Beth Quarm Todgham

Description and Interests
This publication provides information, tips, and resources for families throughout New Hampshire. It covers topics such as childbirth, education, child development, health, and other topics of interest to parents.
- **Audience:** Parents
- **Frequency:** 100% controlled
- **Circulation:** 27,500
- **Website:** www.parentingnh.com

Freelance Potential
90% written by nonstaff writers. Publishes 24–30 freelance submissions yearly; 20% by unpublished writers, 50% by authors who are new to the magazine. Receives 700+ queries and unsolicited mss yearly.

Submissions
Query or send complete ms. Accepts hard copy, disk submissions, and email submissions to news@parentingnh.com. SASE. Response time varies.
Articles: Word lengths vary. Informational and how-to articles; profiles; and interviews. Topics include parenting, education, maternity, childbirth, special needs, gifted education, fathering, child development, summer fun, birthday parties, holidays, back to school, and health.
Depts/columns: Word lengths vary. Child development, parenting issues, and medicine.
Other: Submit seasonal material 2 months in advance.

Sample Issue
48 pages (42% advertising): 2 articles; 11 depts/columns. Sample copy, free. Guidelines available.
- "Pre-Teen Physicals." Article discusses the changes in health care needs for children experiencing the onset of puberty.
- "Working from Home." Article explores ways to work at home and keep your baby happy at the same time.
- Sample dept/column: "Dad on Board" discusses the insanity with kids and organized sports.

Rights and Payment
All rights. Articles, $30. Other material, payment rates vary. Pays on acceptance. Provides 3 author's copies.

Editor's Comments
We would like to see more parenting articles written from a father's perspective.

ParentingUniverse.com

Best Parenting Resources, LLC
546 Charing Cross Drive
Marietta, GA 30066

Editor: Alicia Hagan

Description and Interests
In addition to advice on topics such as pregnancy, child development, education, health, and nutrition, this online newsletter presents ideas for family activities and crafts. It is read by both experienced and expectant mothers.
- **Audience:** Women, 23–56 years
- **Frequency:** Daily
- **Circulation:** 2+ million
- **Website:** www.parentinguniverse.com

Freelance Potential
90% written by nonstaff writers. Publishes 500+ freelance submissions yearly. Receives 5,000+ queries, 144 unsolicited mss yearly.

Submissions
Query or send complete ms. Prefers online submissions through website. Will accept hard copy and email submissions to alicia@parentinguniverse.com. SASE. Response time varies.
Articles: Word lengths vary. Informational, how-to, and self-help articles; profiles; reviews; interviews; and personal experience pieces. Topics include education, gifted and special education, parenting, pregnancy, health, fitness, recreation, crafts, and family activities.
Depts/columns: Word lengths vary. Parenting tips and guides.

Sample Issue
Sample issue and guidelines available at website.
- "The Challenges of Single Parenting." Article explains why single parents have to play the roles of both nurturer and protector.
- "Awareness of Autism." Article discusses the importance of teaching others about the symptoms and behaviors of autism.
- "8 Steps to Financially Intelligent Parenting." Article talks about everyday "money moments" that can be used to teach children about finances.

Rights and Payment
Electronic rights. Written material, payment rates vary. Pays on publication. Provides 2 contributor's copies.

Editor's Comments
We are interested in well-written, engaging articles on all aspects of parenting. Parenting tips and fun activities are also needed. We don't use articles on any type of business issue.

Parent Life

One LifeWay Plaza
Nashville, TN 37234-0172

Editor: Jodi Skulley

Description and Interests
This magazine from LifeWay Christian Resources focuses on families with children under the age of twelve. Most of its readers are Evangelical Christian parents, with mothers making up the majority of its audience.
• **Audience:** Parents
• **Frequency:** Monthly
• **Circulation:** 78,000
• **Website:** www.lifeway.com/magazines

Freelance Potential
90% written by nonstaff writers. Publishes 12 freelance submissions yearly; 5% by unpublished writers, 5% by authors who are new to the magazine. Receives 240 queries and mss yearly.

Submissions
Query or send complete ms. Accepts hard copy and email submissions to jodi.skully@ lifeway.com. SASE. Response time varies.
Articles: 500–1,500 words. Informational and how-to articles and personal experience pieces. Topics include family issues, religion, education, health, and hobbies.
Depts/columns: 500 words. Age-appropriate advice, fathers' perspectives, medical advice.
Artwork: Color prints or transparencies.
Other: Accepts seasonal material for Christmas and Thanksgiving.

Sample Issue
50 pages: 8 articles; 11 depts/columns. Sample copy, $2.95 with 10x13 SASE. Writers' guidelines available.
• "How Racism Impacts Your Family." Article offers perspectives from four missionaries of different ethnic and cultural backgrounds.
• "Preparing Your Child for a Hospital Visit." Article shows parents the best ways to reduce family stress before a child's hospitalization.
• Sample dept/column: "Dad's Life" urges fathers to focus on people, not results.

Rights and Payment
Non-exclusive rights. All material, payment rates vary. Pays on publication. Provides 1 contributor's copy.

Editor's Comments
Writers must now go through the LifeWay Church Resources' writer approval process. You must provide a statement of faith, writing sample, and references. We're looking for material that offers biblical solutions that transform families.

Parents & Kids

2727 Old Canton Road, Suite 294
Jackson, MS 39216

Editor: Gretchen Cook

Description and Interests
This magazine provides activities and advice for parents in the Jackson, Mississippi, area.
• **Audience:** Parents
• **Frequency:** 9 times each year
• **Circulation:** 35,000
• **Website:** www.parents-kids.com

Freelance Potential
80% written by nonstaff writers. Publishes 80 freelance submissions yearly; 50% by unpublished writers. Receives 396 unsolicited mss yearly.

Submissions
Send complete ms. Accepts email submissions to magazine@parents-kids.com (in text of message and as Microsoft Word attachment). Responds in 6 weeks.
Articles: 700 words. Informational, self-help, and how-to articles. Topics include the arts; computers; crafts and hobbies; health and fitness; multicultural and ethnic issues; recreation; regional news; social issues; special education; sports; and travel.
Depts/columns: 500 words. Travel, cooking, and computers.
Artwork: B/W prints or transparencies. Line art. Prefers electronic files; contact publisher for specifics.
Other: Submit seasonal material 3–6 months in advance.

Sample Issue
50 pages (54% advertising): 5 articles; 6 depts/columns. Sample copy, free with 9x12 SASE ($1.06 postage). Guidelines available at website.
• "Move Over, Apple." Article describes the physical and emotional benefits of outdoor play.
• "Birthday Party Brainstorm." Article provides easy ideas for fabulous birthday celebrations.
• Sample dept/column: "Parent Points" gives suggestions for a safe and enjoyable family trip to a water park.

Rights and Payment
One-time rights. Articles and depts/columns, $25. Pays on publication. Provides tearsheet.

Editor's Comments
We welcome submissions from freelance writers, photographers, and artists. Reprints or articles written for publications outside of Mississippi are also considered. We prefer articles with local information using local sources and quotes.

Parents' Press

1564 Sixth Street
Berkeley, CA 94710

Editor: Dixie M. Jordan

Description and Interests
This regional magazine is for parents of young children in the San Francisco Bay area. It features research-based articles on topics such as child development, education, safety, health, and other parenting issues. It also includes local resources and events.
• **Audience:** Parents
• **Frequency:** Monthly
• **Circulation:** 75,000
• **Website:** www.parentspress.com

Freelance Potential
30–40% written by nonstaff writers. Publishes 60 freelance submissions yearly; 15% by authors who are new to the magazine. Receives 720 unsolicited mss yearly.

Submissions
Send complete ms. Accepts hard copy and email submissions to parentsprs@aol.com. SASE. Responds in 2 months.
Articles: To 1,500 words. Informational and how-to articles. Topics include child development, education, health, safety, party planning, and regional family events and activities.
Depts/columns: Staff written.
Artwork: B/W prints and transparencies. Line art.
Other: Submit seasonal material 2 months in advance.

Sample Issue
32 pages (63% advertising): 3 articles; 5 depts/columns; 1 directory; 1 calendar. Sample copy, $3 with 9x12 SASE ($1.93 postage). Guidelines available at website.
• "Digital Sanity." Article takes a look at ways parents can balance the responsibilities and interests in their lives and their children's lives.
• "Weaning Your Baby." Article discusses how to know when a baby is ready to stop nursing and offers advice for weaning.

Rights and Payment
All or second rights. Articles, $50–$500. Pays 45 days after publication.

Editor's Comments
Our primary need is for local San Francisco Bay area material. We require thorough research and excellent quality of writing. We're not interested in didactic "how to raise your kids" pieces, materials researched primarily on the Web, or personal experience stories.

Parent:Wise Austin

55501-A Balcones Drive, Suite 102
Austin, TX 78731

Editor/Publisher: Kim Pleticha

Description and Interests
This publication seeks to inform and educate central Texas parents with children up to the age of 17. In addition to news and feature stories, it offers book and music reviews and an extensive event calendar that includes storytimes, classes, and support groups.
• **Audience:** Parents
• **Frequency:** Monthly
• **Circulation:** 32,000
• **Website:** www.parentwiseaustin.com

Freelance Potential
25% written by nonstaff writers. Publishes 6 freelance submissions yearly; 33% by authors who are new to the magazine.

Submissions
Query with 4 clips for articles. Send complete ms for "Essays" and "My Life as a Parent" (monthly humor article). Accepts email submissions to storyideas@ parentwiseaustin.com. Response time varies.
Articles: 2,000–2,500 words for cover stories; to 1,000 words for news articles. Informational articles and profiles. Topics include parenting, family life, education, regional news, and people in the Austin community who work to make life better for others.
Depts/columns: Word lengths vary. Restaurant and music reviews, humor about parenting and family life, and medical advice.
Other: Poetry about parenting, children, or families; line lengths vary.

Sample Issue
40 pages: 3 articles; 7 depts/columns; 4 calendars. Sample copy and guidelines available at website.
• "Operation Special Delivery." Article describes one woman's experiences with a labor support doula.
• "Cool or Crummy?" Article reviews good—and not so good—products for parents.
• Sample dept/column: "My Life as a Parent" describes a funny event at an indoor play space.

Rights and Payment
First North American serial and Internet rights. Cover stories, $200. Other written material, payment rates vary. Payment policy varies.

Editor's Comments
We prefer local writers but will consider writers from other areas of the country if they have demonstrated experience writing for our type of publication.

Partners

Christian Light Publications
P.O. Box 1212
Harrisonburg, VA 22803-1212

Editor: Etta Martin

Description and Interests
Partners is a Sunday school take-home story paper that promotes the beliefs of the Mennonite faith community. Printed in four parts, each issue offers Bible-centered lessons in the form of articles, short stories, and poems.
- **Audience:** 9–14 years
- **Frequency:** Monthly
- **Circulation:** 6,519
- **Website:** www.clp.org

Freelance Potential
98% written by nonstaff writers. Publishes 200–500 freelance submissions yearly; 5% by unpublished writers, 5% by authors who were new to the magazine. Receives 60–80 unsolicited mss yearly.

Submissions
Send complete ms. Prefers email submissions to partners@clp.org. Will accept hard copy, disk submissions, and simultaneous submissions if identified. SASE. Responds in 6 weeks.
Articles: 200–800 words. Informational articles. Topics include nature, customs, history, and teachings.
Fiction: 400–1,600 words. Stories emphasizing Mennonite beliefs and biblical interpretations.
Other: Puzzles and activities with Christian themes. Poetry, no line limits. Submit seasonal material 6 months in advance.

Sample Issue
16 pages (no advertising): 4 articles; 4 stories; 8 activities; 4 poems. Sample copy, free with 9x12 SASE ($.87 postage). Guidelines and theme list available.
- "The Zebra's Fingerprints." Article concludes that only God knows why zebras have stripes.
- "Too Many Dishes?" Story tells how a grandfather's reminiscences help his grandson learn to work with a grateful heart.
- Sample poem: "The Might of Right." Poem explains the meaning of true courage.

Rights and Payment
First, reprint, or multiple use rights. Articles and stories, $.03–$.05 per word. Poetry, $.35–$.75 per line. Other material, payment rates vary. Pays on acceptance. Provides 1 author's copy.

Editor's Comments
We are committed to printing only material that adheres to Bible teachings, fosters reverence for God, and reflects the joy of serving Christ.

Passport

WordAction Publishing
2923 Troost Avenue
Kansas City, MO 64109

Assistant Editor: Kimberly Adams

Description and Interests
This full-color weekly story paper corresponds with the WordAction Sunday School program. In addition to curriculum-related materials, it covers cutting-edge topics that have spiritual applications for its readers.
- **Audience:** 11–12 years
- **Frequency:** Weekly
- **Circulation:** 55,000
- **Website:** www.wordaction.com

Freelance Potential
90% written by nonstaff writers. Publishes 30 freelance submissions yearly; 20% by unpublished writers, 20% by authors who are new to the magazine. Receives 240 queries and unsolicited mss yearly.

Submissions
Query with author information; or send complete ms. Accepts hard copy. SASE. Responds in 4–6 weeks.
Articles: Word lengths vary. Uses Scripture-related lessons.
Depts/columns: "Survival Guide" uses "hot topics" that have spiritual applications, 400–500 words. "Curiosity Island" covers hobbies, fun activities, clever tips, and unique career ideas.

Sample Issue
8 pages (no advertising): 2 articles; 1 dept/column; 1 puzzle page; 1 Scripture activity. Sample copy, free with 5x7 SASE. Guidelines available.
- "Trashing and Smashing." Article talks about how to deal with anger and why it is sometimes appropriate to be angry.
- "Voyage to the Past: Do You Eat Bread?" Article explains how bread was made and stored in ancient Israel.
- Sample dept/column: "Curiosity Island" presents fun facts about panda bears.

Rights and Payment
Rights vary. Written material, $15–$25. Pays on publication. Provides 2 contributor's copies.

Editor's Comments
We need submissions for our "Survival Guide" section. These must have spiritual applications, but do not have to be related directly to the curriculum lesson of the day. We look for material written in a casual style that holds short attention spans. Always remember to write for an international audience—avoid extensive cultural or holiday references.

Pediatrics for Parents

120 Western Avenue
Gloucester, MA 01930

Editor: Richard J. Sagall, M.D.

Description and Interests
This newsletter for "people who care for children," focuses on pediatric health care, with an emphasis on prevention. Its articles take a common-sense approach.
• **Audience:** Parents
• **Frequency:** Monthly
• **Circulation:** 60,000
• **Website: www.pedsforparents.com**

Freelance Potential
50% written by nonstaff writers. Publishes 30 freelance submissions yearly; 50% by unpublished writers, 50% by authors who are new to the magazine. Receives 50 queries and unsolicited mss yearly.

Submissions
Query or send complete ms. Accepts hard copy and email submissions to articles@pedsforparents.com. SASE. Response time varies.
Articles: 750–1,500 words. Informational articles. Topics include prevention, fitness, medical advancements, new treatments, wellness, and pregnancy.
Depts/columns: Word lengths vary. New product information and article reprints.

Sample Issue
12 pages (no advertising): 11 articles; 2 depts/columns. Sample copy, $3. Writers' guidelines available.
• "Childhood Obsessive-Compulsive Disorder: Guide to Effective Treatment." Article presents information on cognitive-behavioral therapy and pharmacotherapy, as well as tips for parents and practitioners.
• "Is My Baby Tongue-Tied?" Article describes problems associated with having a short or tight frenulum.
• "Hoarseness in Children: What Every Parent Should Know." Articles examines the causes of hoarseness and when it should be evaluated and treated.

Rights and Payment
First rights. Written material, to $25. Pays on publication. Provides 3 contributor's copies and a 1-year subscription.

Editor's Comments
If you're not a medical professional, your article must be thoroughly researched, accurate, and original. We cover topics related to the health of newborns to children in their early teens.

Piedmont Parent

P.O. Box 11740
Winston-Salem, NC 27116

Editor

Description and Interests
Launched in 1995, this magazine serves families living in the North Carolina "triad" cities of Greensboro, Winston-Salem, and High Point. It covers all issues associated with family life, from pregnancy through parenting teens.
• **Audience:** Parents
• **Frequency:** Monthly
• **Circulation:** 39,000
• **Website: www.piedmontparent.com**

Freelance Potential
50% written by nonstaff writers. Publishes 36–40 freelance submissions yearly; 25% by unpublished writers, 50% by authors who are new to the magazine. Receives 1,000+ queries and unsolicited mss yearly.

Submissions
Query or send complete ms. Accepts email submissions to editor@piedmontparent.com (Microsoft Word attachments) and simultaneous submissions if identified. Responds in 1–2 months.
Articles: 500–1,200 words. Informational and how-to articles; and interviews. Topics include child development, day care, summer camps, gifted and special education, local and regional news, science, social issues, sports, popular culture, health, and travel.
Depts/columns: 600–900 words. Family health and parenting news.
Other: Family games and activities.

Sample Issue
40 pages (47% advertising): 8 articles; 5 depts/columns; 1 calendar. Sample copy, free with 9x12 SASE ($1.50 postage). Writers' guidelines and theme list available.
• "Learning About Labor and Delivery Rooms." Article provides a primer on the equipment and technology used to deliver babies.
• "Move Over Apple." Article stresses the importance of outdoor play.
• Sample dept/column: "Is My Kid OK?" answers a question about picky eaters.

Rights and Payment
One-time rights. Written material, payment rates vary. Pays on publication. Provides 1 tearsheet.

Editor's Comments
All feature articles must demonstrate thorough research and include at least three sources.

Pikes Peak Parent

30 South Prospect Street
Colorado Springs, CO 80903

Editor: Lisa Carpenter

Description and Interests
This regional tabloid offers information about events and resources in the Colorado Springs area. It also features articles on parenting issues, as well as profiles of local people and places.
- **Audience:** Parents
- **Frequency:** Monthly
- **Circulation:** 30,000
- **Website: www.pikespeakparent.com**

Freelance Potential
5% written by nonstaff writers. Publishes 4 freelance submissions yearly; 2% by authors who are new to the publishing house. Receives 60 queries each year.

Submissions
Query with writing samples. Accepts hard copy and email queries to parent@gazette.com. SASE. Response time varies.
Articles: 800–1,500 words. Informational and how-to articles. Topics include regional news, local resources, parenting, family life, travel, health, sports, social issues, and recreation.
Depts/columns: Word lengths vary. News, health, family issues, profiles, and events.

Sample Issue
30 pages (50% advertising): 5 articles; 12 depts/columns. Sample copy, free with 9x12 SASE.
- "Money Matters." Article suggests ways parents can teach their children about money.
- "Hiding Out." Article provides some clever ideas for keeping kids entertained by building forts indoors.
- Sample dept/column: "Ask a Teacher" tackles the question: "How do I keep my middle school-aged child excited about learning?"

Rights and Payment
All rights on original content for assigned pieces, and second rights. Written material, payment rates vary. Pays on publication. Provides 1 contributor's copy.

Editor's Comments
We are primarily interested in material specific to the Colorado Springs area. Our readers are seeking reliable information on nearby places to explore with their families, and all descriptions should be accurate and honest. We do not need any more personal essays on parenting at this time. We do need more stories about child care that are well written and carefully researched.

Pittsburgh Parent

P.O. Box 374
Bakerstown, PA 15007

Editor: Pat Poshard

Description and Interests
The tone is informative and upbeat in this parenting magazine that targets Pittsburgh-area families with children of all ages. In addition to general parenting advice, it includes media reviews and updates on local events and activities.
- **Audience:** Parents
- **Frequency:** Monthly
- **Circulation:** 50,000+
- **Website: www.pittsburghparent.com**

Freelance Potential
100% written by nonstaff writers. Publishes 150 freelance submissions yearly; 20% by authors who are new to the magazine. Receives 1,500 queries and unsolicited mss yearly.

Submissions
Query or send complete ms. Accepts hard copy, email submissions to editor@pittsburghparent.com, and simultaneous submissions if identified. SASE. Response time varies.
Articles: Cover story; 2,500–2,750 words. Other material; 400–900 words. Informational articles; profiles; and interviews. Topics include family issues, parenting, education, science, fitness, health, nature, college, computers, and multicultural subjects.
Fiction: 1,000 words. Genres include mystery, adventure, and historical and multicultural fiction.
Depts/columns: Word lengths vary. Education issues; book reviews; teen issues; and humor.
Other: Submit seasonal material 3 months in advance.

Sample Issue
44 pages (65% advertising): 10 articles; 5 depts/columns. Sample copy, free. Guidelines and editorial calendar available.
- "Language Lessons in the Kitchen." Article describes everyday activities that boost language skills.
- Sample dept/column: "Humor" takes a light look at the special role dads play in kids' lives.

Rights and Payment
First serial rights. All material, payment rates vary. Pays 45 days after publication. Provides 1 tearsheet.

Editor's Comments
A local angle is a must if you wish to write for us; always include information about local resources. We also accept personal stories from parents.

Plays
The Drama Magazine for Young People

P.O. Box 600160
Newton, MA 02460

Editor: Elizabeth Preston

Description and Interests
As the subtitle suggests, this magazine publishes one-act plays that are appropriate for performance by students of various ages.
- **Audience:** 6–17 years
- **Frequency:** 7 times each school year
- **Circulation:** 5,300
- **Website:** www.playsmag.com

Freelance Potential
100% written by nonstaff writers. Publishes 75 freelance submissions yearly; 25% by unpublished writers, 50% by authors who are new to the magazine. Receives 250 queries and unsolicited mss yearly.

Submissions
Query for adaptations of classics and folktales. Send complete ms for other material. Accepts hard copy. SASE. Responds to queries in 2 weeks, to mss in 1 month.
Fiction: One-act plays for high school, to 5,000 words; for middle school, to 3,750 words; for elementary school, to 2,500 words. Also publishes skits, monologues, puppet plays, and dramatized classics. Genres include patriotic, historical, and biographical drama; mystery; melodrama; fairy tales and folktales; comedy; and farce.
Other: Submit seasonal material 4 months in advance.

Sample Issue
64 pages (5% advertising): 5 plays; 1 dramatized classic; 1 skit. Sample copy, free with 6x9 SASE ($.87 postage). Guidelines available.
- "Everybody's Got a Cell." Play for upper-grade students deals with popularity, honesty, and integrity.
- "The King's Creampuffs." Play for the middle grades tells about a witch who steals a royal recipe.
- "A Mother Goose Makeover." Skit for the lower and middle grades takes a cue from reality TV to give nursery rhyme characters new looks.

Rights and Payment
All rights. Written material, payment rates vary. Pays on acceptance. Provides 1 contributor's copy.

Editor's Comments
Plays must be simple to produce, with minimum requirements for costumes, stage sets, and lighting. One setting is preferred.

Pockets

The Upper Room
1908 Grand Avenue
P.O. Box 340004
Nashville, TN 37203-0004

Editor: Lynn W. Gilliam

Description and Interests
This magazine for children in the elementary grades uses articles, stories, poems, and activities to teach children that God loves them and that God's grace calls us to community. Each issue covers a specific theme.
- **Audience:** 6–11 years
- **Frequency:** 11 times each year
- **Circulation:** 98,000
- **Website:** www.pockets.org

Freelance Potential
98% written by nonstaff writers. Publishes 220 freelance submissions yearly; 40% by unpublished writers, 20% by authors who are new to the magazine. Receives 2,000 mss yearly.

Submissions
Send complete ms. Accepts hard copy. SASE. Responds in 6 weeks.
Articles: 400–1,000 words. Informational articles; profiles; and personal experience pieces. Topics include multicultural and community issues, and persons whose lives reflect their Christian commitment.
Fiction: 600–1,400. Stories that demonstrate Christian values.
Depts/columns: Word lengths vary. Scripture readings and recipes.
Artwork: 3x5 color prints; digital images at 300 dpi.
Other: Puzzles, activities, games, and poetry.

Sample Issue
48 pages (no advertising): 1 article; 6 stories; 6 depts/columns; 7 activities; 4 poems. Sample copy, free with 9x12 SASE (4 first-class stamps). Guidelines and theme list available at website.
- "Happy New Year Pepito Burrito." Story features a boy whose guinea pig is having trouble adjusting to the family's new home.
- "Packed with Love." Article describes how one fourth-grade girl helped send filled backpacks to children affected by Hurricane Katrina.

Rights and Payment
First and second rights. Written material, $.14 per word. Games, $25–$50. Pays on acceptance. Provides 3–5 contributor's copies.

Editor's Comments
We want articles about real children involved in environmental efforts, peacemaking, and helping others. We also use one theme-based story in each issue.

Pocono Parent Magazine

P.O. Box 291
Analomink, PA 18320

Editor: Teri O'Brien

Description and Interests
In addition to specific how-to and where-to pieces, *Pocono Parent Magazine* features articles that address universal parenting concerns, such as health, education, and child development. It targets families living in Monroe County, Pennsylvania.
- **Audience:** Parents
- **Frequency:** 6 times each year
- **Circulation:** 10,000
- **Website:** www.poconoparent.com

Freelance Potential
25% written by nonstaff writers. Publishes 20 freelance submissions yearly.

Submissions
Send complete ms. Accepts email submissions to editor@poconoparent.com (no attachments). Response time varies.
Articles: 750–1,000 words. Informational and how-to articles; profiles; interviews; reviews; photo-essays; and personal experience pieces. Topics include parenting, family issues, education, social issues, current events, health, fitness, nature, the environment, recreation, and regional news.
Depts/columns: Word lengths vary. Family finances, teen and "tween" issues, restaurant reviews, pets, and family fitness.

Sample Issue
38 pages: 4 articles; 13 depts/columns. Sample copy and guidelines available at website.
- "Calling All Dads: Do You Know Where Your Children Are Physically?" Article discusses the rise of childhood obesity and diabetes, and stresses the importance of monitoring the amount of time children spend being physically active.
- Sample dept/column: "The Playroom" talks about the benefits of setting a family meeting time to keep up with each other's busy lives.

Rights and Payment
Rights vary. Written material, payment rates vary. Payment policy varies. Provides 2 contributor's copies.

Editor's Comments
Our mission is to help Monroe County parents. The focus of every article should be: Here are the facts, and here's what you can do with your child to prevent/promote/help the situation. We like articles that are both practical and creative at the same time.

Pointe

110 William Street, 23rd Floor
New York, NY 10038

Managing Editor: Jocelyn Anderson

Description and Interests
Subtitled "Ballet at Its Best," this magazine is written for ballet students, instructors, and fans. It profiles dancers and ballet companies while also publishing news and event coverage.
- **Audience:** 10–18 years
- **Frequency:** 6 times each year
- **Circulation:** 40,000
- **Website:** www.pointemagazine.com

Freelance Potential
75% written by nonstaff writers. Publishes 5 freelance submissions yearly; 10% by unpublished writers, 25% by authors who are new to the magazine. Receives 24 queries yearly.

Submissions
Query. Accepts hard copy. SASE. Responds in 2 months.
Articles: 1,200 words. Informational articles; profiles; interviews; personal experience pieces; and photo-essays. Topics include ballet news, events, places, people, and trends.
Depts/columns: 800–1,000 words. Happenings, premieres, opinion pieces, performance information, equipment, and costumes.
Artwork: B/W and color prints and transparencies. Digital photos. Line art.

Sample Issue
72 pages (50% advertising): 4 articles; 16 depts/columns. Sample copy available.
- "Intimate Stories." Article looks at the life and work of Hamburg Ballet director and choreographer John Neumeier and his focus on the human condition.
- "A Prima in Her Prime." Article examines the career of international ballerina Alessandra Ferri.
- Sample dept/column: "Company Life" talks about the benefits of making a career in the corps de ballet of a major company.

Rights and Payment
All rights. Written material, payment rates vary. Pays on acceptance. Provides 2 contributor's copies.

Editor's Comments
We'll consider all types of editorial content that covers the world of ballet—news, events, trends, and personalities. Short company profiles are always in demand, and probably offer the best opportunity for writers who are new to us.

Popcorn Magazine for Children

8320 Brookfield Road
Richmond, VA 23227

Editor: Charlene Warner Coleman

Description and Interests
Popcorn Magazine for Children has been re-launched in the form of a hard copy magazine, a website, and as the "Popcorn Magazine" television program. All versions of this creative and innovative approach offer writers the chance to have their work presented to a wider audience.
- **Audience:** 5–13 years
- **Frequency:** 6 times each year
- **Circulation:** 250,000
- **Website: www.popcornmagazine.us**

Freelance Potential
75% written by nonstaff writers. Publishes 500+ freelance submissions yearly.

Submissions
Send complete ms. Accepts hard copy and email submissions to cwcoleman1@comcast.net. SASE. Response time varies.
Articles: Word lengths vary. Informational and how-to articles; and profiles. Topics include sports, art, science, travel, fashion, cooking, technology, nature, and animals.
Fiction: Word lengths vary. Genres include humor, fantasy, and adventure.
Depts/columns: 500 words. Arts and crafts, fashion, cooking, building projects, product reviews, and book and movie reviews.
Other: Puzzles and games. Poetry.

Sample Issue
30 pages: 4 articles; 3 stories; 6 depts/columns; 2 poems. Guidelines available.
- "Dead as a Dodo." Article discusses the natural history of the dodo bird and concludes that man's actions were the main reason for its extinction.
- "Ask Shaq's Mom." Article relates an interview with basketball great Shaquille O'Neal's mother.
- Sample dept/column: "What's Cooking?" features an easy recipe for delicious banana oatmeal cookies.

Rights and Payment
Rights vary. No payment.

Editor's Comments
Our goal is to encourage young readers. Because we are active in more than one medium, we are seeking submissions in all subject areas. Creativity, a fresh voice, and high-interest subjects are necessary ingredients for a submission to be considered by us.

Potluck Children's Literary Magazine

P.O. Box 546
Deerfield, IL 60015-0546

Editor-in-Chief: Susan Napoli Picchietti

Description and Interests
Celebrating 10 years in print, this journal for children features short stories, poems, book reviews, and artwork by children. In addition, it includes informational articles to strengthen writing skills.
- **Audience:** All ages
- **Frequency:** Quarterly
- **Circulation:** Unavailable
- **Website: www.potluckmagazine.org**

Freelance Potential
99% written by nonstaff writers. Publishes 2,400 freelance submissions yearly; 95% by unpublished writers, 95% by authors who are new to the magazine. Receives 2,400 unsolicited mss each year.

Submissions
Send complete ms. Accepts hard copy and email submissions to submissions@potluckmagazine.org. SASE. Response time varies.
Articles: Word lengths vary. Informational and how-to articles. Topics include writing, grammar, and character and story development.
Fiction: To 2,500 words. Genres include contemporary and science fiction, mystery, folktales, and fantasy.
Artwork: 8½ x 11 color photocopies.

Other: Book reviews, to 250 words. Poetry, to 30 lines.

Sample Issue
48 pages (no advertising): 8 stories; 18 poems. Sample copy, $5.80. Guidelines available with SASE, at website, and in each issue.
- "A False Find." Story tells of a girl who finds a message in a bottle that contains a riddle.
- "Alone in the Dark." Story features a girl who, after walking home late one night, thinks she is being stalked by a murderer.
- "With One Dollar Left." Story follows an old rich man who gives away all his money to one of his maids.

Rights and Payment
First rights. No payment. Provides 1 contributor's copy.

Editor's Comments
We provide an encouraging environment for young writers and artists to share their creativity. Please note we do not publish "I am" poems, "color" poems, or "name" poems.

Prehistoric Times

145 Bayline Circle
Folsom, CA 95630-8077

Editor: Mike Fredericks

Description and Interests
Prehistoric Times is read by teens and adults who are fascinated by prehistoric animals. It is lavishly illustrated, and includes scientific articles as well as information about related art and collectibles.
- **Audience:** YA–Adult
- **Frequency:** Quarterly
- **Circulation:** Unavailable
- **Website: www.prehistorictimes.com**

Freelance Potential
40% written by nonstaff writers. Publishes 12 freelance submissions yearly; 60% by unpublished writers, 40% by new authors. Receives 24+ unsolicited mss yearly.

Submissions
Send complete ms. Accepts email submissions to pretimes@comcast.net (attach file). Response time varies.
Articles: 1,500–2,000 words. Informational articles. Topics include dinosaurs, paleontology, prehistoric life, drawing dinosaurs, and dinosaur-related collectibles.
Depts/columns: Word lengths vary. Field news, dinosaur models, media reviews, interviews, and in-depth descriptions of dinosaurs and other prehistoric species.

Sample Issue
58 pages (30% advertising): 12 articles; 6 depts/columns. Sample copy, $7. Guidelines available via email to pretimes@comcast.net.
- "The PT Interview: Argentine Paleoartist Gabriel Lio." Article presents an interview with the renowned artist.
- "The Reptile Test." Article explains the methods used to perform the first-ever complete test on the traditional family tree of the Reptilia.
- Sample dept/column: "Non-Extinct Dinosaur" reviews books, DVDs, artwork, and other items pertaining to dinosaurs.

Rights and Payment
All rights. Written material, payment rates and policy vary. Provides contributor's copies.

Editor's Comments
Our readers are serious about their study and love of dinosaurs and prehistoric animals, so we are constantly seeking to provide them with the latest information in the field. We continue to need interviews with scientists, artists, and makers and collectors of dinosaur models.

Prep Traveler

621 Plainfield Road, Suite 406
Willowbrook, IL 60527

Editorial Coordinator: Kelley Thompson

Description and Interests
Designed specifically to assist youth sports and performance travel groups, this publication includes informative articles and tips on destinations, traveling, performance facilities, entertainment, lodging, and many other issues of interest to youth group leaders and coordinators.
- **Audience:** Youth travel planners
- **Frequency:** Twice each year
- **Circulation:** 26,000
- **Website: www.preptraveler.com**

Freelance Potential
10% written by nonstaff writers. Publishes 2–3 freelance submissions yearly; 50% by unpublished writers. Receives 50 queries yearly.

Submissions
Query with résumé and field experience. Accepts email queries to kelley@ptmgroups.com (no attachments). Responds in 1 week.
Articles: Word lengths vary. Informational and how-to articles; and profiles. Topics include travel destinations, music, health, and fitness.
Depts/columns: 700–2,000 words. Information related to youth travel planning.

Sample Issue
62 pages (40% advertising): 2 articles; 7 depts/columns. Guidelines and theme list available.
- "Go Someplace Else." Article discusses why so many student tours limit their selection of travel destinations.
- "Budgeting for Sports Events." Article describes how to develop an event budget and outlines income generating opportunities.
- Sample dept/column: "New & Noteworthy" offers information on places for students and groups to visit in New England.

Rights and Payment
All rights. Written material, payment rates vary. Pays on publication. Provides contributor's copies.

Editor's Comments
We need articles covering major student market destinations from writers who are experts on student sports and performance markets. Writing should be direct, with not much filler. Please note that while our features are not open to new writers, we are always looking for editorial from experts for our columns.

Preschool Playhouse

Urban Ministries
1551 Regency Court
Calumet City, IL 60409

Senior Editor: Dr. Judith St. Clair Hull

Description and Interests
This story paper conveys Christian values to young children living in urban areas. Each issue of *Preschool Playhouse* features a Bible story and a life-action story that encourages its audience to follow Jesus. Urban Ministries also publishes a teacher's guide to accompany the story papers.
- **Audience:** Preschool children
- **Frequency:** Quarterly, with weekly take-home sections
- **Circulation:** 50,000
- **Website: www.urbanministries.com**

Freelance Potential
25% written by nonstaff writers. Publishes 12 freelance submissions yearly; 10% by unpublished writers, 25% by authors who are new to the magazine. Receives 50+ unsolicited mss yearly.

Submissions
Send résumé with clips or writing samples. All material is written on assignment. Response time varies.
Articles: Word lengths vary. Informational articles; how-to and personal experience pieces; photo-essays; and Bible stories. Topics include crafts, animals, hobbies, African American history, multicultural and social issues, nature, the environment, and religion.
Depts/columns: Word lengths vary. Games, puzzles, and filler.
Artwork: B/W or color prints or transparencies.

Sample Issue
4 pages: 1 Bible story; 1 contemporary story; 1 activity; 1 dept/column; 2 memory verses. Sample copy, free. Guidelines available.
- "Love One Another." Article tells how John wrote three letters, included in the Bible, that tell us that Jesus wanted us to love one another.
- "Knowing." Activity depicts the different ways Jesus showed love in the Bible.

Rights and Payment
All rights. Written material, payment rates vary. Pays on publication. Provides 1 contributor's copy.

Editor's Comments
Although all of the material that appears in our publication is written on assignment, we encourage you to contact us with your credentials if you have the ability to present Bible concepts and stories in age-appropriate ways.

PresenTense Magazine

214 Sullivan Street, Suite 2A
New York, NY 10012

Editor: Ariel Beery

Description and Interests
PresenTense Magazine highlights new personalities, ideas, and projects in the Jewish community—especially those led and developed by youth.
- **Audience:** YA–Adult
- **Frequency:** Twice each year
- **Circulation:** 30,000
- **Website: www.presentensemagazine.org**

Freelance Potential
80% written by nonstaff writers. Publishes 40 freelance submissions yearly; 40% by unpublished writers, 70% by authors who are new to the magazine.

Submissions
Query or send complete ms. Accepts email submissions to editor@presentensemagazine.org (attach document) and simultaneous submissions if identified. Responds to queries in 2 weeks, to mss in 2 months.
Articles: Features, 800–1,200 words. Sidebars, 50–150 words. Informational articles and profiles. Topics include the environment, agriculture, activism, technology, Israel, the Diaspora, religion, and ethnic issues.
Fiction: Word lengths vary.
Depts/columns: "Here and Now," 600–800 words. Reviews, 800–1,000 words. "Paradigm Shift," 1,200–2,000 words. Jewish culture and contributions; the arts; food; and reviews.
Other: Photo-essays.

Sample Issue
64 pages: 8 articles; 28 depts/columns. Guidelines available at website.
- "Ebb and Flow." Article talks about the political and economic importance of Israel's expertise in water management and conservation.
- "The Death of Eco-Kosher." Article describes efforts to encourage the Jewish community to think more deeply and broadly about what it means to keep kosher.
- Sample dept/column: "Paradigm Shift" discusses the significance of spending a year in service.

Rights and Payment
Rights vary. No payment. Provides 3 author's copies.

Editor's Comments
We seek to invigorate Hebrew culture by providing a nurturing environment where Jewish youth can explore and enrich their Jewish identity.

Primary Street

Urban Ministries
1551 Regency Court
Calumet City, IL 60409

Senior Editor: Dr. Judith St. Clair Hull

Description and Interests
Primary school students who take religious education classes in urban areas are the target of this take-home story paper. It provides weekly Scripture lessons, Bible stories, and activities that promote Christian values. A teacher's guide is included with every issue.
• **Audience:** 6–8 years
• **Frequency:** Quarterly
• **Circulation:** 50,000
• **Website: www.urbanministries.com**

Freelance Potential
25% written by nonstaff writers. Publishes 15 free-lance submissions yearly; 25% by unpublished writers, 25% by authors who are new to the magazine. Receives 180 queries yearly.

Submissions
Query with résumé and writing samples. All work is assigned. Response time varies.
Articles: Word lengths vary. Informational and how-to articles; personal experience pieces; photo-essays; and Bible stories. Topics include nature, the environment, animals, pets, crafts, hobbies, African history, multicultural and ethnic subjects, regional news, and social issues and concerns.
Depts/columns: Word lengths vary. Bible verses and activities.
Artwork: B/W and color prints and transparencies.
Other: Puzzles, games, activities, and jokes.

Sample Issue
4 pages (no advertising): 1 article; 1 Bible lesson; 1 activity; 2 depts/columns. Sample copy, free. Guidelines available.
• "What Do You Like About Easter?" Article talks about all the good things associated with Easter.
• "Jesus Is Alive!" Bible story tells how Mary found Jesus's empty tomb.
• Sample dept/column: "Good Attitude" offers activities that show how Jesus is with us.

Rights and Payment
All rights. Written material, payment rates vary. Pays on publication. Provides 1 contributor's copy.

Editor's Comments
We look for writers who can provide us with regular material that appeals to young children and helps them follow the teachings of Christ.

Primary Treasure

Pacific Press Publishing
P.O. Box 5353
Nampa, ID 83653-5353

Editor: Aileen Andres Sox

Description and Interests
Elementary students attending Sabbath school are the target audience of this take-home paper. Published by the Seventh-day Adventist Church, it features stories based on Christian beliefs and practices, as well as Bible lessons.
• **Audience:** 6–9 years
• **Frequency:** Weekly
• **Circulation:** 250,000
• **Website: www.primarytreasure.com**

Freelance Potential
10% written by nonstaff writers. Publishes 52 freelance submissions yearly; 10% by unpublished writers, 30% by new authors. Receives 240 unsolicited mss yearly.

Submissions
Query for serials. Send complete ms for other submissions. Accepts hard copy, email submissions to ailsox@pacificpress.com, and simultaneous submissions if identified. SASE. Responds in 4 months.
Articles: 600–1,000 words. Features true stories about children in Christian settings and true, problem-solving pieces that help children learn about themselves in relation to God and others. All material must be consistent with Seventh-day Adventist beliefs and practices.
Other: Submit seasonal material 7 months in advance.

Sample Issue
16 pages (no advertising): 4 articles; 1 Bible lesson; 1 puzzle. Sample copy, free with 9x12 SASE (2 first-class stamps). Guidelines available.
• "The Kittens and the Thief." Story features a girl who finds out who is stealing her father's grain while she is looking for new kittens.
• "A Monument to Morsel." Story tells how a boy's grandfather consoles him after his pet mouse dies.
• "Maria's Wild Animals." Story features a teen who learns a lesson about rules when she volunteers to help babysit.

Rights and Payment
One-time rights. Written material, $25–$50. Pays on acceptance. Provides 3 contributor's copies.

Editor's Comments
We look for stories that will help foster a relationship with God. Keep words simple, sentences uncomplicated, and description minimal.

Principal

1615 Duke Street
Alexandria, VA 22314

Editor: Lee Greene

Description and Interests
This magazine published by the National Association of Elementary School Principals (NAESP) offers conversational articles dealing with various aspects of school administration.
- **Audience:** K–8 school administrators
- **Frequency:** 5 times each year
- **Circulation:** 36,000
- **Website:** www.naesp.org

Freelance Potential
90% written by nonstaff writers. Publishes 20 freelance submissions yearly; 80% by authors who are new to the magazine. Receives 84 unsolicited mss yearly.

Submissions
Send complete ms. Accepts hard copy, PC-compatible disk submissions, and email submissions to publications@naesp.org. No simultaneous submissions. SASE. Responds in 6 weeks.
Articles: 1,000–2,500 words. Informational and instructional articles; profiles; and opinion and personal experience pieces. Topics include elementary education; gifted and special education; parenting; mentoring; and technology.
Depts/columns: 750–1,500 words. "Parents & Schools," "Urban Connections," "It's the Law," "Practitioner's Corner," and "Tech Support."

Sample Issue
64 pages (25% advertising): 9 articles; 10 depts/columns. Sample copy, $8. Writers' guidelines and theme list available.
- "Mission Possible." Article describes a school's success with teaching through technology.
- "How Effective Principals Encourage Their Teachers." Article gives tips for effective interaction between principals and teachers.
- Sample dept/column: "Ten to Teen" details the work of the National Runaway Switchboard.

Rights and Payment
All North American serial rights. No payment. Provides 3 contributor's copies.

Editor's Comments
Principal is a magazine, not a scholarly journal. Our articles are generally shorter, less structured, and more subjective than scholarly papers. Please write in plain English, avoid jargon, and clarify technical terms.

Queens Parent

350 Fifth Avenue, Suite 2420
New York, NY 10118

Executive Editor: Helen Freedman

Description and Interests
This tabloid offers parents and families in Queens, New York, coverage of the latest local news, trends, and events. It also features articles on parenting and family issues.
- **Audience:** Parents
- **Frequency:** Monthly
- **Circulation:** 68,000
- **Website:** www.parentsknow.com

Freelance Potential
10% written by nonstaff writers. Publishes 20 freelance submissions yearly; 25% by authors who are new to the magazine. Receives 300 queries yearly.

Submissions
Query or send complete ms. Accepts hard copy. Prefers email to hellonwheels@parentsknow.com. SASE. Responds to queries in 1 week.
Articles: 800–1,000 words. Informational and how-to articles; personal experience pieces; profiles; interviews; and humor. Topics include family issues, health, fitness, nature, current events, gifted and special education, nutrition, crafts, and regional news.
Depts/columns: 750 words. News and reviews.
Other: Submit seasonal material 4 months in advance.

Sample Issue
62 pages (60% advertising): 3 articles; 7 depts/columns; 1 camp guide; 1 calendar of events. Sample copy, free. Guidelines available.
- "Are Your Kids Making You Eat More?" Article reports on a study that shows that adults who live with children eat more fat than those who don't have children living at home.
- Sample dept/column: "Family Travel" covers the many opportunities for family fun on the Hawaiian islands of Kauai and Maui.

Rights and Payment
First New York area rights. No payment.

Editor's Comments
We are seeking the latest news of interest to families living in Queens, with a concentration on New York City events. Articles must be well researched and have a fresh and lively approach. Subject matter should be timely and pertinent to our readership. Due to a backlog of travel, humor, and general child-raising pieces, we are no longer reading submissions on those topics.

Rainbow Kids

P.O. Box 202
Harvey, LA 70059

Editor: Martha Osborne

Description and Interests
Rainbow Kids has been online since 1996, offering inspiring true-life stories of adoptive families. It is the leading e-zine dedicated to informing and supporting individuals and families before, during, and after adoption. Each monthly issue is updated weekly.
- **Audience:** Adoptive families
- **Frequency:** Monthly
- **Hits per month:** 1.5 million
- **Website: www.rainbowkids.com**

Freelance Potential
80% written by nonstaff writers. Publishes 40 free-lance submissions yearly; 50% by authors who are new to the magazine.

Submissions
Query or send complete ms. Accepts hard copy and email submissions to martha@rainbowkids.com (attachment files). Availability of artwork improves chance of acceptance. SASE. Responds in 2–3 days.
Articles: Word lengths vary. Informational articles and personal experience pieces. Topics include all matters related to adoption and adoptive families, both domestic and foreign. Also publishes adoption guidelines, adoption events, and photo listings.

Sample Issue
Sample issue available at website.
- "My Unique Family." Article describes the experience of a single mom who adopted two older children: a daughter from Russia and a son from Kazakhstan.
- "Birth Parents." Article looks at all sides of the issue of adopted children seeking information about their birth families.
- "The Benefits of Birth Family Connections." Article explores the changing face of international adoption regarding gathering information about birth families.

Rights and Payment
Electronic rights. No payment.

Editor's Comments
We want to hear your stories, and we encourage you to share your insights about the adoption process and your own experiences. We are interested in submissions concerning adoptions of older children, adoptive parent support groups, financial considerations, special needs adoption, transracial issues, domestic adoptions, and adoptive parents of color. We welcome suggestions for other topic ideas.

Ranger Rick

National Wildlife Federation
1100 Wildlife Center Drive
Reston, VA 20190-5362

Editor: Mary Dalheim

Description and Interests
Children and young adults enjoy discovering nature and learning about wildlife conservation through the stories, articles, and activities in this magazine published by the National Wildlife Federation.
- **Audience:** 7–12 years
- **Frequency:** Monthly
- **Circulation:** 560,000
- **Website: www.nwf.org/gowild**

Freelance Potential
10% written by nonstaff writers. Publishes 1–2 freelance submissions yearly; 1% by authors who are new to the magazine. Receives 1,200 queries yearly.

Submissions
Query with outline and sample paragraph. Accepts hard copy. SASE. Response time varies.
Articles: 900 words. Informational articles. Topics include nature, animals, crafts, the environment, outdoor adventure, dinosaurs, oceanography, and insects.
Fiction: 900 words. Genres include mystery, adventure, fantasy, fables, and nature stories.
Depts/columns: Staff written.
Other: Puzzles on topics related to nature. Submit seasonal material 1 month in advance.

Sample Issue
40 pages (no advertising): 4 articles; 2 stories; 10 activities. Guidelines available.
- "Slime Time." Article explores the world of snails, including how they move, eat, sleep, see, and reproduce.
- "Mystery in the Treetops." Article follows a scientist as she travels to New Guinea to study tree kangaroos.
- "Handimals." Article examines how an artist creates lifelike portraits of animals on human hands.

Rights and Payment
Rights vary. All material, payment rates vary. Pays on acceptance. Provides 2 contributor's copies.

Editor's Comments
We primarily use staff writers and contracted free-lancers, but we are always interested in reading a great story told in a unique fashion that will appeal to young people. We pride ourselves in providing exciting nonfiction articles that motivate even reluctant readers. If you're up to the challenge, send us your submission.

The Reading Teacher

International Reading Association
800 Barksdale Road
P.O. Box 8139
Newark, DE 19714-8139

Assistant Editor: Cynthia Sawaya

Description and Interests
Professionals committed to improving literacy instruction for children through age 12 turn to this peer-reviewed journal for its articles covering reading research, effective classroom techniques, and advances in educational technology in teaching literacy.
• **Audience:** Educators
• **Frequency:** 8 times each year
• **Circulation:** 57,500
• **Website:** www.reading.org

Freelance Potential
95% written by nonstaff writers. Publishes 50 freelance submissions yearly; 20% by unpublished writers, 30% by new authors. Receives 300 unsolicited mss yearly.

Submissions
Submit manuscripts online by creating an account at http://mc.manuscriptscentral.com/ira. Responds in 1–2 months.
Articles: To 6,000 words. Informational and how-to articles; profiles; and personal experience pieces. Topics include literacy, reading education, instructional techniques, classroom strategies, reading research, and educational technology.
Depts/columns: 1,500–2,500 words. Reviews of children's books, teaching tips, and material on cultural diversity.

Sample Issue
98 pages (17% advertising): 6 articles; 5 depts/columns. Sample copy, $10. Guidelines available.
• "Engaging in Retrospective Reflection." Article takes a look at the benefits of audiotaping book club discussions for later reflection.
• "The Family Stories Project: Using Funds of Knowledge for Writing." Article describes a literacy project with fourth-grade Latino students in a bilingual classroom.
• Sample dept/column: "Teaching Tips" outlines the process for creating a student-involved classroom library.

Rights and Payment
All rights. No payment. Provides 5 contributor's copies for articles, 2 copies for depts/columns.

Editor's Comments
We are interested in articles covering classroom strategies. Writing must be descriptive and clear. Graphic material may accompany the article.

Reading Today

International Reading Association (IRA)
800 Barksdale Road
P.O. Box 8139
Newark, DE 19714-8139

Editor-in-Chief: John Micklos, Jr.

Description and Interests
This tabloid for reading educators includes everything from interviews with children's book authors to articles about innovative reading programs.
• **Audience:** IRA members
• **Frequency:** 6 times each year
• **Circulation:** 88,000
• **Website:** www.reading.org

Freelance Potential
35% written by nonstaff writers. Publishes 30 freelance submissions yearly; 10% by unpublished writers, 25% by authors who are new to the magazine. Receives 200 queries and unsolicited mss yearly.

Submissions
Prefers query; accepts complete ms. Prefers email submissions to readingtoday@reading.org. Accepts hard copy and simultaneous submissions if identified. SASE. Responds in 1 month.
Articles: 500–1,500 words. Informational and factual articles and interviews. Topics include reading and reading education, community programs, staffing, assessment, program funding, and censorship.
Depts/columns: To 750 words. News, book reviews, education policy information, ideas for administrators.
Artwork: B/W and color prints. Line art.

Sample Issue
48 pages (30% advertising): 20 articles; 11 depts/columns. Sample copy, $6. Guidelines available.
• "The Power of Poetry." Article showcases a unique program that matches graduate students and long-term care residents to explore the poetry writing process.
• Sample dept/column: "Forum" features commentary from two lifelong teacher educators.

Rights and Payment
All rights. Written material, $.20–$.30 per word. Pays on acceptance. Provides 3 contributor's copies.

Editor's Comments
For the coming year, we are particularly interested in features about innovative reading activities in schools and communities. Please remember that this is a newspaper, not a journal. Potential writers should familiarize themselves with our publication prior to submitting. The shorter the article, the greater chance there is we can use it.

Research in Middle Level Education

College of Education
Southwest Missouri State University
Springfield, MO 65804

Editor: Micki M. Caskey

Description and Interests

Research in Middle Level Education is an online journal that publishes the latest research pertaining to education in the middle grades. Its contents include research papers, case studies, interpretations of research literature, and data-based quantitative and qualitative studies. A peer-reviewed journal, it is endorsed by the Middle Level Education Research Special Interest Group of the American Educational Research Association.
• **Audience:** Educators
• **Frequency:** Twice each year
• **Hits per month:** 30,000
• **Website:** www.nmsa.org

Freelance Potential

95% written by nonstaff writers. Publishes 10 freelance submissions yearly; 90% by unpublished writers, 50% by authors who are new to the magazine. Receives 72 unsolicited mss yearly.

Submissions

Send 5 full-binded copies of complete ms including title page and 150- to 200-word abstract. Accepts hard copy and email submissions to caskeym@pdx.edu (Microsoft Word attachments). SASE. Responds in 1 week.
Articles: 7,000–12,000 words. Informational articles on education issues; research syntheses; integrative reviews; and case studies—all related to the education of students in the middle grades.

Sample Issue

Sample copy and guidelines available at website.
• "Research on Same-Gender Grouping in Eighth Grade Science Classrooms." Article describes the results of a study to determine whether student achievement and classroom atmosphere were better in same-gender science classrooms.
• "Middle Level Teacher Certification in South Carolina: A Case Study in Educational Policy Development." Article documents the process through which the state enacted legislation to certify teachers.

Rights and Payment

All rights. No payment. Provides 1 contributor's copy.

Editor's Comments

Prospective writers must have a thorough knowledge of the field in order to successfully navigate the peer-review process that each submission undergoes.

Reunions Magazine

P.O. Box 11727
Milwaukee, WI 53211-0727

Editor: Edith Wagner

Description and Interests

Ideas, advice, and inspiration for people who plan reunions are found in this magazine. It addresses issues associated with family, school, military, and other types of reunions.
• **Audience:** Adults
• **Frequency:** 6 times each year
• **Circulation:** 20,000
• **Website: www.reunionsmag.com**

Freelance Potential

75% written by nonstaff writers. Publishes 100 freelance submissions yearly; 60% by unpublished writers, 80% by authors who are new to the magazine. Receives 20–30 queries and unsolicited mss yearly.

Submissions

Query with outline; or send complete ms. Accepts hard copy and email submissions to reunions@execpc.com. SASE. Responds in 12–18 months.
Articles: Word lengths vary. Informational, factual, and how-to articles; personal experience pieces; and profiles. Topics include organizing reunions, choosing locations, entertainment, activities, and genealogy.
Depts/columns: 250–1,000 words. Opinion pieces, resource information, and news.
Artwork: Color prints. JPEG, TIF, or PDF files.
Other: Recipes, cartoons, and filler.

Sample Issue

60 pages (45% advertising): 8 articles; 5 depts/columns. Sample copy, $3. Guidelines and editorial calendar available.
• "Our Family Quilt." Article describes in detail how one family planned a reunion in Tennessee with quilts as the theme.
• "Almost Like Coming Home." Article recounts how a mother and daughter planned a family reunion, despite the mother's terminal illness.
• Sample dept/column: "Scrapbook" reports on reunion news from around the country.

Rights and Payment

One-time rights. Payment rates and policy vary. Provides 2 contributor's copies.

Editor's Comments

Our readers want concrete articles about organizing successful reunions. We want to see smashingly fresh ideas. Right now, we need more on committees and budgeting. We also need reunion games, activities, and surprises.

Parents
onthly

5511 Staples Mill Road, Suite 103
Richmond, VA 23228

Editor: Angela Lehman-Rios

Description and Interests

Parents in the Richmond area of Virginia turn to this tabloid for the latest news on childcare and issues of concern to parents, as well as for information about local entertainment and summer camps.
- **Audience:** Parents
- **Frequency:** Monthly
- **Circulation:** 30,000
- **Website:** www.richmondparents.com

Freelance Potential

90% written by nonstaff writers. Publishes 70–90 freelance submissions yearly; 5% by authors who are new to the magazine. Receives 600 queries yearly.

Submissions

Query. Accepts email submissions to mail@richmondpublishing.com. Availability of artwork improves chance of acceptance. Responds in 1–3 weeks.

Articles: 600–1,000 words. Informational and self-help articles. Topics include the arts, camps for children, pets, home and garden, birthday parties, school, education, children's health, and holidays.

Depts/columns: Word lengths vary. Family-related news, media reviews, technology.

Artwork: Color prints and transparencies.

Sample Issue

52 pages (15% advertising): 5 articles; 9 depts/columns; 1 calendar; 1 contest. Sample copy, free. Guidelines and editorial calendar available.
- "Passion in Their Blood." Article describes how some talented residents in the Richmond area have inspired their children due to their passion for their art.
- "School-Based Community Service Programs." Article explains what parents need to know about these programs, and how to encourage their children to make a difference.

Rights and Payment

One-time rights. Written material, $52–$295 based on page length. Pays on publication.

Editor's Comments

Although we primarily work with local writers, we will consider submissions from authors outside our area as long as they demonstrate a keen knowledge about our region and the families who live here. We're primarily interested in articles about education and schools.

Sacramento Parent

457 Grass Valley Highway, Suite 5
Auburn, CA 95603

Editor-in-Chief: Shelly Bokman

Description and Interests

This magazine provides articles of interest to families with children and grandchildren of all ages and with a variety of lifestyles and beliefs.
- **Audience:** Parents and grandparents
- **Frequency:** Monthly
- **Circulation:** 50,000
- **Website:** www.sacramentoparent.com

Freelance Potential

75% written by nonstaff writers. Publishes 50 freelance submissions yearly; 10% by unpublished writers, 25% by authors who are new to the magazine. Receives 780 queries yearly.

Submissions

Query with list of topics and writing samples. Accepts email queries to ssparent@pacbell.net. Response time varies.

Articles: 700–1,000 words. Informational and how-to articles; personal experience pieces; and humor. Topics include fitness, family finance, alternative education, family travel, learning disabilities, grandparenting, sports, adoption, and regional news.

Depts/columns: 400–500 words. Child development, opinions, and hometown highlights.

Sample Issue

50 pages (50% advertising): 4 articles; 12 depts/columns. Sample copy, free with 9x12 SASE ($1.29 postage). Guidelines and theme list available.
- "Sharing the Gift of Motherhood." Article shares the views of three surrogate mothers.
- "Batteries Not Included." Article discusses why some summer camps are not allowing children to bring along their electronic equipment.
- Sample dept/column: "Brain Power" offers ideas for making a dress-up box for children.

Rights and Payment

Second rights. Articles, $50. Depts/columns, $25–$40. Pays on publication. Provides author's copies.

Editor's Comments

We strive to share information and experiences with others while remaining respectful of differing family values. We are interested in articles that promote a developmentally appropriate, healthy, and peaceful environment for children. Our publication is dedicated to encouraging the powerful bond of "family" through our editorial content.

St. Louis Parent

P.O. Box 300218
St. Louis, MO 63130

Editor: Barb MacRobie

Description and Interests

Parents residing in the St. Louis area read this newsletter for articles and tips covering parenting topics, health, education, finances, and child development. It also lists local resources and events.

- **Audience:** Parents
- **Frequency:** 10 times each year
- **Circulation:** 45,000
- **Website:** www.stlouisparent.com

Freelance Potential

90% written by nonstaff writers. Publishes 30–50 freelance submissions yearly; 5% by unpublished writers, 25% by authors who are new to the magazine. Receives 60 queries yearly.

Submissions

Query with résumé, outline/synopsis, and clips or writing samples. Accepts hard copy and simultaneous submissions if identified. SASE. Response time varies.
Articles: 700 words. Informational and how-to articles. Topics include education; family health; safety; nutrition; child care; personal finances; and regional resources, services, and events.
Other: Submit seasonal material 6 months in advance.

Sample Issue

18 pages (40% advertising): 5 articles; 1 directory. Sample copy, free with 9x12 SASE ($1 postage). Guidelines and editorial calendar available.

- "Why Teens Still Get Pregnant." Article discusses family communication about sexuality and the lack of sex education in many schools.
- "Cleaning Up a Potty Mouth." Article takes a look at why children may use bad words and offers ideas for cleaning up a child's potty mouth.
- Sample dept/column: "Educational Services" takes a look at rules to help children succeed in school.

Rights and Payment

All rights. Articles, $50. Other material, payment rates vary. Pays on acceptance. Provides 2 author's copies.

Editor's Comments

We are interested in fresh ideas for articles that are of interest to parents in the St. Louis region. Sidebars with information on resources and quotes from local experts are always a plus. Topics such as education, technology, and health issues continue to be of interest to us. Writers must know the region.

San Diego Family Magazine

P.O. Box 23960
San Diego, CA 92193

Publisher and Editor-in-Chief: Sharon Bay

Description and Interests

Read by parents living in the San Diego area, this magazine provides informative articles emphasizing the importance and joys of parenting. It focuses on the region's resources for parents and families.

- **Audience:** Parents
- **Frequency:** Monthly
- **Circulation:** 120,000
- **Website:** www.sandiegofamily.com

Freelance Potential

90% written by nonstaff writers. Publishes 50 freelance submissions yearly; 50% by unpublished writers. Receives 360–600 queries and unsolicited mss yearly.

Submissions

Query or send complete ms. Accepts hard copy. SASE. Responds in 1 month.
Articles: 750–1,000 words. Informational, self-help, and how-to articles. Topics include parenting, gifted and special education, family issues, travel, health, fitness, sports, and multicultural issues. Also publishes humorous articles.
Depts/columns: Word lengths vary. Book reviews, restaurant reviews, advice, health, and the home.
Artwork: 3x5 or 5x7 four-color glossy prints.

Sample Issue

154 pages (60% advertising): 17 articles; 19 depts/columns. Sample copy, $4.50 with 9x12 SASE ($1 postage). Guidelines available at website.

- "How to Keep the Whole Family Healthy." Article details the annual checkups, vaccinations, and tests that every member of the family should have in order to maintain basic physical health.
- Sample dept/column: "Grandparenting" explains the importance of a grandparent's influence in children's lives and describes some ways to get them more involved.

Rights and Payment

First or second and all regional rights. Written material, $1.25 per published column inch. Pays on publication. Provides 1 contributor's copy.

Editor's Comments

We are always looking for the positive and uplifting approach to family and parenting issues. We publish practical and factual how-to material as well as more subtle and insightful pieces. All submissions must be well written and timely.

Santa Barbara Family Life

P.O. Box 4867
Santa Barbara, CA 93140

Editor

Description and Interests
Now in its tenth year of publication, *Santa Barbara Family Life* keeps local residents informed of happenings in this California community. In addition to activity calendars and camp guides, it includes articles on health, education, and family recreation.
- **Audience:** Parents
- **Frequency:** Monthly
- **Circulation:** 60,000
- **Website:** www.sbfamilylife.com

Freelance Potential
25% written by nonstaff writers. Publishes 15–25 freelance submissions yearly.

Submissions
Query or send complete ms. Accepts hard copy. SASE. Response time varies.
Articles: Word lengths vary. Informational articles; profiles; interviews; photo-essays; and personal experience pieces. Topics include regional events and activities, parenting, family life, education, recreation, crafts, hobbies, and current events.
Depts/columns: Word lengths vary. Love and relationships, arts and entertainment, health issues, and inspirational pieces.

Sample Issue
32 pages: 4 articles; 5 depts/columns; 2 events calendars; 1 kids' section. Sample copy and guidelines available at website.
- "Butterflies Alive! Returns to Natural History Museum." Article reports on a museum exhibit that features 1,000 free-flying butterflies in their natural habitat.
- "Healing Horses." Article tells how horseback riding can help children with cognitive function.
- Sample dept/column: "Health Watch" looks at natural remedies for summertime bites, stings, and rashes.

Rights and Payment
Rights vary. Written material, payment rates vary. Payment policy varies.

Editor's Comments
We believe educational information that assists family members with creating happy, healthy relationships benefits us all. So we try to act as a resource that not only educates and entertains its readers, but connects families to other members, events, activities, and businesses within our communities.

Scholastic Choices

Scholastic Inc.
557 Broadway
New York, NY 10012-3999

Editor: Bob Hugel

Description and Interests
Used in middle school and high school classrooms, this magazine covers family and consumer science, health, and life skills. It is designed to promote discussions about the challenges faced by today's teens, including peer pressure and family issues.
- **Audience:** 12–18 years
- **Frequency:** 6 times each year
- **Circulation:** 200,000
- **Website:** www.scholastic.com

Freelance Potential
90% written by nonstaff writers. Publishes 30–40 freelance submissions yearly; 10% by unpublished writers. Receives 60 queries, 60 unsolicited mss yearly.

Submissions
Query or send complete ms. Accepts hard copy and email submissions to choicesmag@scholastic.com. SASE. Responds to queries in 2 months, to mss in 3 months.
Articles: 500–1,000 words. Informational and self-help articles and personal experience pieces. Topics include health, fitness, sports, personal development, relationships, safety, social issues, consumer and resource management, careers, the environment, nature, popular culture, nutrition, and substance abuse prevention.
Depts/columns: Staff written.

Sample Issue
32 pages (20% advertising): 10 articles; 1 dept/column; 1 recipe; 1 quiz. Sample copy, free with 9x12 SASE. Guidelines and editorial calendar available.
- "Driven to Be Thin." Article explains that many boys have begun to suffer from eating disorders.
- "Generation RX." Article explores the growing problem of abuse of prescription drugs among teens.
- "Safe Surfing." Article tells teens how to protect themselves from online predators.

Rights and Payment
All rights. Written material, payment rates vary. Pays on publication. Provides 10 contributor's copies.

Editor's Comments
We're interested in detailed, well-written articles about nutrition, health, relationships, decision-making, family life, and substance abuse. Our "Personal Responsibility" pieces feature real teens solving familiar, real-world problems.

Scholastic DynaMath

Scholastic Inc.
557 Broadway, Room 4052
New York, NY 10012-3999

Editor: Matt Friedman

Description and Interests

DynaMath uses a lively format to teach math to students in grades three through six. Each issue includes features, skills pages, games, puzzles, and math activities, as well as a teacher's edition that includes lesson plans and reproducibles.
- **Audience:** 8–11 years
- **Frequency:** 8 times each year
- **Circulation:** 200,000
- **Website:** www.scholastic.com/dynamath

Freelance Potential

10% written by nonstaff writers. Publishes 5 freelance submissions yearly; 25% by unpublished writers, 25% by authors who are new to the magazine. Receives 48 queries and unsolicited mss yearly.

Submissions

Query with outline or synopsis; or send complete ms. Accepts hard copy and simultaneous submissions if identified. SASE. Responds in 1–2 months.
Articles: To 600 words. Informational articles about math skills. Topics include critical thinking, chart and graph reading, measurement, addition, subtraction, fractions, division, decimals, problem solving, interdisciplinary issues, popular culture, sports, consumer awareness, geography, nature, and the media.
Other: Filler, puzzles, games, and jokes. Submit holiday material 4–6 months in advance.

Sample Issue

16 pages (15% advertising): 5 articles; 11 activities. Sample copy, $4 with 9x12 SASE. Guidelines and editorial calendar available.
- "The Suite Logic of Yack and Coldy." Read-aloud play features two twins who learn how to fix a mess using logic.
- "'Byte' into Place Value." Article shows the importance of place value in determining storage space on electronic gadgets.
- "Doc on the Clock." Article uses a doctor's schedule to help kids learn to count minutes and hours.

Rights and Payment

All rights. Articles, $250–$400. Puzzles, $25–$50. Pays on acceptance. Provides 3 contributor's copies.

Editor's Comments

We look for activities that make math fun and relevant through the use of real-life applications. Our new "Word Wise" department helps to build math literacy.

Scholastic Math Magazine

Scholastic Inc.
557 Broadway
New York, NY 10012-3999

Editor: Jack Silbert

Description and Interests

This Scholastic publication strives to put a new spin on teaching math to students in grades six through nine. A take-home paper distributed in classrooms, it focuses on real-world and consumer math that can be taught using connections to teen issues, sports, TV, movies, and music.
- **Audience:** 11–14 years
- **Frequency:** 26 times each year
- **Circulation:** 200,000
- **Website:** www.scholastic.com/classmags

Freelance Potential

30% written by nonstaff writers. Publishes 10 freelance submissions yearly; 10% by unpublished writers. Receives 24 queries yearly.

Submissions

Query. Accepts hard copy. SASE. Responds in 2–3 months.
Articles: 600 words. Articles about real-world math, consumer math, and math-related news. Topics include teen issues, sports, celebrities, TV, music, movies, and current events—all with a connection to math.
Depts/columns: 140 words. Skill-building exercises, quizzes, and practice tests.
Other: Puzzles, activities, comic strips, Q&As, and mystery photos.

Sample Issue

16 pages (no advertising): 6 articles; 1 dept/column, 1 comic. Sample copy, free with 9x12 SASE (3 first-class stamps). Writers' guidelines and editorial calendar available.
- "Hallie's Working Wages." Article focuses on teen star Hallie Kate Eisenberg and how she calculates babysitting wages by the hour.
- "Turn Down the Tunes!" Article uses a bar graph to show how long teens can safely listen to loud music through iPods and at rock concerts.

Rights and Payment

All rights. Articles, $300+. Depts/columns, $35. Pays on publication.

Editor's Comments

Fun career stories that have a math connection will always get a second look. We try to publish material that answers the question: "When will I need to use this again?"

...astic Parent & Child

Scholastic Inc.
557 Broadway
New York, NY 10012-3999

Assistant Editor: Samantha Brody

Description and Interests
This magazine serves as a link between home and school for parents of preschool and kindergarten students. With the help of teachers and experts, it gives parents insight into their children's education and provides ways to extend and enhance that learning outside of the classroom.
- **Audience:** Parents
- **Frequency:** 8 times each year
- **Circulation:** 1.2 million
- **Website:** www.parentandchildonline.com

Freelance Potential
90% written by nonstaff writers. Publishes 20 freelance submissions yearly; 90% by unpublished writers, 10% by authors who are new to the magazine. Receives 144 queries and unsolicited mss yearly.

Submissions
Query or send complete ms. Accepts hard copy. SASE. Responds to queries in 3 months, to mss in 2 months.
Articles: 500–1,000 words. Informational articles and interviews. Topics include child development and education.
Depts/columns: Word lengths vary. Literacy; health; parent/teacher relationships; arts and crafts; child development; product recommendations; travel; cooking; and family issues.

Sample Issue
72 pages (33% advertising): 4 articles; 12 depts/columns. Guidelines available.
- "Can Homework Backfire?" Q&A with author Alfie Kohn discusses his theory that too much homework is bad for kids.
- "Raising Happy Kids." Article explains how to bring out lifelong joy in children.
- Sample dept/column: "Inspiring Words" features a brief interview with Jamie Lee Curtis about raising kids who care.

Rights and Payment
All rights. Written material, payment rates vary. Pays on publication. Provides contributor's copies.

Editor's Comments
We offer expert advice, tips, and activities to help parents make the most of this early learning stage of their children's development. We are looking for cutting-edge techniques, strategies, and activities from educators with substantial expertise in early childhood development.

Scholastic Scope

Scholastic Inc.
557 Broadway
New York, NY 10012-3999

Associate Editor: Lisa Feder-Feitel

Description and Interests
Classic and contemporary literature, as well as timely teen-oriented fiction, appear in this magazine for students in grades six through ten. It also publishes classroom plays based on current movies, and "No-Sweat Test Prep" materials that give students strategies for taking standardized tests.
- **Audience:** 12–18 years
- **Frequency:** 17 times each year
- **Circulation:** 550,000
- **Website:** www.scholastic.com/scope

Freelance Potential
30% written by nonstaff writers. Publishes few freelance submissions yearly; 2% by unpublished writers, 10% by authors who are new to the magazine. Receives 200–300 queries yearly.

Submissions
Query with résumé, outline/synopsis, and clips. Accepts hard copy. SASE. Response time varies.
Articles: 1,000 words. News and features that appeal to teens and profiles of young adults who have overcome obstacles, performed heroic acts, or had interesting experiences.
Fiction: 1,500 words. Realistic stories about relationships and family problems, school issues, and other teen concerns. Also accepts science fiction.
Depts/columns: Staff written.
Other: Crossword puzzles and word activities. Submit seasonal material 4 months in advance.

Sample Issue
22 pages (8% advertising): 4 articles; 1 play; 2 activities. Sample copy, $1.75 with 9x12 SASE (2 first-class stamps).
- "Meet a Video Game Designer." Article details the different skills required if students wish to pursue this career choice.
- "Voices from the Storm." Article portrays the lives of students in New Orleans one year after Hurricane Katrina.

Rights and Payment
Rights negotiable. Written material, $100+. Pays on acceptance. Provides contributor's copies on request.

Editor's Comments
High-quality, engaging articles and stories that help teens build literacy skills are always in demand here. Write for a sixth- through eighth-grade reading level.

SchoolArts

Davis Publications
2223 Parkside Drive
Denton, TX 76201

Editor: Nancy Walkup

Description and Interests
This publication is filled with ideas and information for art educators. Creative classroom activities, innovative lessons, and proven teaching strategies have made SchoolArts a valuable resource for over a century.
- **Audience:** Teachers, grades K–12
- **Frequency:** 9 times each year
- **Circulation:** 20,000
- **Website:** www.davisart.com

Freelance Potential
90% written by nonstaff writers. Publishes 200 freelance submissions yearly; 60% by unpublished writers, 60% by authors who are new to the magazine. Receives 300 unsolicited mss yearly.

Submissions
Send complete ms with artwork. Accepts hard copy. SASE. Responds in 6 weeks.
Articles: 300–800 words. Informational, self-help, and how-to articles. Topics include teaching art; techniques; art history; projects and activities; curriculum development; and art programs for the gifted, handicapped, and learning-disabled student.
Depts/columns: 500–1,200 words. Crafts, cooking, and accessibility issues.
Artwork: B/W prints or 35mm color slides. B/W line art. Fine-quality digital images.

Sample Issue
64 pages (40% advertising): 12 articles; 7 depts/columns; 5 ready-to-use resources. Sample copy, $5. Guidelines and editorial calendar available.
- "Architectural Adventures in Your Community." Article reveals ways to introduce elementary art students to the fascinating forms of architecture.
- Sample dept/column: "Visual Culture" tells how the author's doll collection aids her in teaching students about women artists.

Rights and Payment
First serial rights. Written material, $25–$150. Other material, payment rates vary. Pays on publication. Provides 2 contributor's copies.

Editor's Comments
We are always interested in giving art educators new ideas, information, and inspiration. We have enough material for elementary teachers, but need more for middle and high school level instructors.

The School Librarian's Workshop

1 Deerfield Court
Basking Ridge, NJ 07920

Editor: Ruth Toor

Description and Interests
This newsletter for school media specialists and librarians fills its pages with book reviews, literacy units, bulletin board ideas, reports on new research, and other materials of interest to professionals working in this field.
- **Audience:** School librarians
- **Frequency:** 6 times each year
- **Circulation:** 7,000
- **Website:** www.school-librarians-workshop.com

Freelance Potential
10% written by nonstaff writers. Publishes 20 freelance submissions yearly; 5–10% by unpublished writers. Receives 24 unsolicited mss yearly.

Submissions
Send 2 copies of complete ms. Prefers disk submissions (Microsoft Word); accepts hard copy. SASE. Responds in 3 weeks.
Articles: To 1,000 words. Informational, how-to, and practical application articles; profiles; and interviews. Topics include librarianship, literature, special education, ethnic studies, computers, technology, social and multicultural issues, and the environment.
Artwork: Line art.
Other: Submit seasonal material 8 months in advance.

Sample Issue
24 pages (no advertising): 15 articles. Sample copy, free with 9x12 SASE. Guidelines and theme list available.
- "Teaching Together." Article describes a collaborative activity for middle-school world language teachers and librarians.
- "Noteworthy Nonfiction." Article provides an overview of new books about animals.
- "More for Your Media Center." Article tells how to lure reluctant readers with a well-liked book by Gary Paulsen.

Rights and Payment
First rights. No payment. Provides 3 contributor's copies.

Editor's Comments
We encourage you to share your experiences and ideas with our readers. Submissions should be practical and easy to understand. We would like to see more articles about graphic novels and more on professional learning communities. Please keep the material you submit jargon-free.

School Library Journal

360 Park Avenue South
New York, NY 10010

News & Features Editor: Rick Margolis

Description and Interests
School librarians read this magazine for information on the latest technology and trends in their field. The hefty volume includes articles on specific library programs as well as comprehensive multimedia reviews.
- **Audience:** School librarians
- **Frequency:** Monthly
- **Circulation:** 34,500
- **Website: www.slj.com**

Freelance Potential
80% written by nonstaff writers. Publishes 25 freelance submissions yearly; 60% by unpublished writers, 60% by authors who are new to the magazine. Receives 48–72 unsolicited mss yearly.

Submissions
Query or send complete ms. Accepts disk submissions (ASCII or Microsoft Word) and email submissions to rmargolis@reedbusiness.com. SASE. Responds to queries in 1 month, to mss in 3 months.
Articles: 1,500–2,500 words. Informational articles and interviews. Topics include children's and young adult literature, school library management, and library careers.
Depts/columns: 1,500–2,500 words. Book and media reviews; descriptions of successful library programs; and opinion pieces.
Artwork: Color prints, tables, charts, and cartoons.

Sample Issue
188 pages (25% advertising): 5 articles; 15 depts/columns; 3 review sections. Sample copy, $6.75. Guidelines available at website.
- "The Great Cover-Up." Article discusses how students are influenced by the covers of books.
- "Yo, Hamlet!" Article tells how one teacher uses hip-hop to get his students interested in the classics.
- Sample dept/column: "Teenage Riot" provides advice on compiling young adult libraries that include controversial material.

Rights and Payment
First rights. Articles, $400. Depts/columns, $100–$200. Pays on publication. Provides 4 contributor's copies.

Editor's Comments
We give librarians up-to-date information needed to integrate libraries into the school curriculum; become leaders in the areas of technology, reading, and information literacy; and create high-quality collections for children and young adults.

School Library Media Activities Monthly

3401 Stockwell Street
Lincoln, NE 68506

Managing Editor: Deborah Levitov

Description and Interests
School library media specialists read this magazine for the latest updates in technology, instructional materials, and research tools. They also find ideas for activities and ways to introduce literature to students.
- **Audience:** School library and media specialists, grades K–8
- **Frequency:** 10 times each year
- **Circulation:** 12,000
- **Website: www.schoollibrarymedia.com**

Freelance Potential
80% written by nonstaff writers. Publishes 25 freelance submissions yearly; 15% by unpublished writers, 50% by authors who are new to the magazine. Receives 50 queries and mss yearly.

Submissions
Query or send complete ms. Accepts email submissions to deborah.levitov@lu.com. SASE. Responds in 2 months.
Articles: 1,000–1,500 words. Informational and factual articles. Topics include media education, information technology, integrating curriculum materials, and library management.
Depts/columns: "Into the Curriculum" uses lesson plans. Also publishes media reviews and short articles on media production.

Sample Issue
58 pages (no advertising): 3 articles; 14 depts/columns. Guidelines available.
- "Assessing Information Fluency: Gathering Evidence of Student Learning." Article provides methods, including checklists, to measure how students apply learned skills.
- "Look in Their Eyes: Eye Tracking, Usability, and Children." Article explains how to determine what children's eyes really see when they are viewing websites.
- Sample dept/column: "Sharing Skills" shows how a teacher's travel experiences can be used as a classroom lesson.

Rights and Payment
All rights. Written material, payment rates vary. Pays on publication. Provides 3+ contributor's copies.

Editor's Comments
We are seeking material that strengthens and adds to the skills needed by school library media specialists. Lesson plans and activities should be classroom-tested.

The School Magazine

P.O. Box 1928
Macquarie Centre, NSW 2113
Australia

Editor: Suzanne Eggins

Description and Interests
Although most of the children who read this literary magazine receive their copies in the classroom, this Australian publication is also available to individual subscribers. It includes a set of four magazines in each issue, each one targeting a different reading and comprehension level.
- **Audience:** 8–12 years
- **Frequency:** 10 times each year
- **Circulation:** 150,000
- **Website:** www.schools.nsw.edu.au.school.libraries/schoolmagazine

Freelance Potential
85% written by nonstaff writers. Publishes 100 freelance submissions yearly; 20% by unpublished writers, 30% by authors who are new to the magazine.

Submissions
Query for nonfiction. Send complete ms for fiction. Accepts hard copy. SAE/IRC. Responds in 6–8 weeks.
Articles: 800–2,000 words. Informational and factual articles. Topics include nature, pets, the environment, history, biography, science, technology, and multicultural and ethnic issues.
Fiction: 800–2,000 words. Adventure; humor; fantasy; science fiction; horror; mystery; folktales; problem-solving and real-life stories; and contemporary, multicultural, and historical fiction.
Depts/columns: Staff written.

Sample Issue
36 pages (no advertising): 5 stories; 5 poems; 4 depts/columns. Sample copy, free with IRC ($2 postage). Guidelines available at website.
- "Tony Paganini's Violin." Story tells of a man who learns to put his feelings into his music.
- "What Granddad Says." Story features a young girl whose grandfather teaches her not to be afraid of her tooth falling out.

Rights and Payment
One-time serial rights. Written material, $226 (Australian) per 1,000 words. Poetry, payment rates vary. Pays on acceptance. Provides 2 contributor's copies.

Editor's Comments
We welcome nonfiction articles at any of the reading levels in our magazine. We prefer that authors include a note detailing the sources or research material they consulted.

Science Activities

Heldref Publications
1319 18th Street NW
Washington, DC 20036-1802

Managing Editor: Min Shepherd

Description and Interests
This peer-reviewed journal provides teachers with creative, classroom-tested projects, experiments, and curricula that help make science relevant to students.
- **Audience:** Teachers, grades K–12
- **Frequency:** Quarterly
- **Circulation:** 1,286
- **Website:** www.heldref.org

Freelance Potential
80% written by nonstaff writers. Publishes 25 freelance submissions yearly; 25% by unpublished writers, 75% by authors who are new to the magazine. Receives 60 queries and unsolicited mss yearly.

Submissions
Query or send complete ms. Accepts email to SA@heldref.org. Responds in 3 months.
Articles: Word lengths vary. Informational and how-to articles. Topics include biological, physical, environmental, chemical, Earth, behavioral, and technological science.
Depts/columns: Word lengths vary. "News Notes," "Computer News," "Classroom Aids," and book reviews.
Artwork: B/W prints, and slides. Line art and diagrams.

Sample Issue
48 pages (1% advertising): 5 articles; 4 depts/columns. Sample copy, $6 with 9x12 SASE. Guidelines available.
- "The Case for Forensic Toxicology." Investigative laboratory exercise uses food-based case studies to promote critical thinking and improve students' understanding of science and technology.
- "Can You Hear Them Now?" Article presents a five-step lesson in investigating radio waves.
- Sample dept/column: "News Notes" announces scholarships, teacher awards, and projects.

Rights and Payment
All rights. No payment. Provides 2 author's copies.

Editor's Comments
We are currently seeking articles about science education, environmental philosophy, humanities, and the Internet. All activities should contain most of the following: a materials list; step-by-step procedures; related background information; cross-curricular applications; and appropriate assessment suggestions or developed rubrics.

...ie and Children

National Science Teachers Association
1840 Wilson Boulevard
Arlington, VA 22201-3000

Managing Editor: Monica Zerry

Description and Interests
The purpose of this publication is to allow elementary school science teachers to share information with their colleagues across the country. It fills its pages with original, creative activities, descriptions of successful programs, and discussions of current issues in science education.
- **Audience:** Science teachers, preK–grade 8
- **Frequency:** 9 times each year
- **Circulation:** 18,000
- **Website:** www.nsta.org/elementaryschool

Freelance Potential
99% written by nonstaff writers. Publishes 25 freelance submissions yearly; 95% by unpublished writers, 50% by authors who are new to the magazine. Receives 360 unsolicited mss yearly.

Submissions
Accepts submissions from practicing educators only. Send complete ms. Accepts email submissions to msrs.nsta.org. Responds in 6 months.
Articles: To 1,500 words. Informational and how-to articles; profiles; interviews; personal experience pieces; and reviews. Topics include science education, teacher training and techniques, staff development, classroom activities, astronomy, biology, chemistry, physics, and Earth science.
Depts/columns: To 1,500 words. "Helpful Hints" and "In the Schools," to 500 words.
Other: Submit seasonal material 1 year in advance.

Sample Issue
76 pages (2% advertising): 7 articles; 8 depts/columns; 2 calendars. Sample copy, free. Guidelines available at website.
- "A Drop Through Time." Article provides a lesson plan for teaching students about the water cycle.
- "Perspectives: Cultural Diversity in the Classroom." Article addresses how students' cultural heritages, religious beliefs, and family backgrounds affect science teaching and learning.

Rights and Payment
All rights. No payment. Provides 5 author's copies.

Editor's Comments
Our content reflects the needs of teachers, science supervisors and administrators, teacher educators, and parents. In your article, share the complete experience of your teaching activity.

The Science Teacher

National Science Teachers Association
1840 Wilson Boulevard
Arlington, VA 22201-3000

Managing Editor: Jennifer Henderson

Description and Interests
The purpose of this magazine is to allow high school science teachers to exchange ideas. It looks for original, creative inquiry activities, descriptions of successful programs, and discussions of current issues in science education.
- **Audience:** Science educators, grades 7–12
- **Frequency:** 9 times each year
- **Circulation:** 29,000
- **Website:** www.nsta.org/highschool

Freelance Potential
100% written by nonstaff writers. Of the freelance submissions published yearly, 70% are by unpublished writers and 50% are by authors who are new to the magazine. Receives 360 unsolicited mss yearly.

Submissions
Send complete ms. Accepts email submissions to jhenderson@nsta.org. Responds in 1 month.
Articles: 2,000 words. Informational articles; classroom projects; and experiments. Topics include science education, biology, Earth science, computers, social issues, space, technology, and sports medicine.
Depts/columns: 500 words. Science updates, association news, and science careers.
Artwork: 5x7 or larger B/W glossy prints. Tables, diagrams, and line art.

Sample Issue
84 pages (40% advertising): 6 articles; 6 depts/columns. Sample copy, $4.25. Guidelines available.
- "Mentoring New Science Teachers." Article presents a checklist that can help mentor teachers assess the teaching skills of new science teachers.
- "Floating Boats." Article offers a scientific exploration of floating, sinking, and density.
- Sample dept/column: "Career of the Month" profiles an ethnobotanist.

Rights and Payment
First rights. No payment. Provides author's copies.

Editor's Comments
Please check the "Call for Papers" section in our most recent issue to see the topics we're interested in. In your manuscript, share the complete experience, including what you did, what worked, and what didn't. When describing a teaching activity, identify its place in the curriculum, the appropriate grade level, assessment techniques, and any safety considerations.

Science Weekly

2141 Industrial Parkway, Suite 202
Silver Spring, MD 20904

Publisher: Dr. Claude Mayberry

Description and Interests
This magazine provides hands-on learning activities through exciting and informative experiments for children, which combine writing skills, scientific thinking, and problem-solving. It is published in six reading levels for students in kindergarten through grade six.
- **Audience:** Grades K–6
- **Frequency:** 14 times each year
- **Circulation:** 200,000
- **Website:** www.scienceweekly.com

Freelance Potential
100% written by nonstaff writers. Of the freelance submissions published yearly, 20% are by unpublished writers and 20% are by authors who are new to the magazine.

Submissions
Query with résumé only. All work is assigned to writers in the District of Columbia, Maryland, or Virginia. SASE. Response time varies.
Articles: Word lengths vary. Informational articles. Topics include space exploration, ecology, the environment, nature, biology, the human body, meteorology, ocean science, navigation, nutrition, photography, physical science, and secret codes.
Other: Theme-related puzzles, games, activities.

Sample Issue
4 pages (no advertising): 1 article; 6 activities. Sample copy and theme list available.
- "Rain." Short article explains rain, where it comes from, and what makes rain; includes a short vocabulary list.
- "Weekly Lab." At-home activity teaches children how to recreate a water cycle in a bowl.
- "Writing in Science." Activity asks children to write the autobiography of a raindrop.

Rights and Payment
All rights. Written material, payment rates vary. Pays on publication.

Editor's Comments
We develop an annual theme list, then assign topics from this list to contributing writers who reside in the Washington, DC, area. Our objective is to publish a magazine that will expose students to a variety of interesting scientific topics, and combine them with activities that develop writing and problem-solving skills.

Scouting

Boy Scouts of America
1325 West Walnut Hill Lane
P.O. Box 152079
Irving, TX 75015-2079

Editor: Jon C. Halter

Description and Interests
This guide for Boy Scout leaders features successful activities programs, winning leadership techniques, and first-person accounts of scouting's positive impact.
- **Audience:** Scout leaders and parents
- **Frequency:** 6 times each year
- **Circulation:** 1 million
- **Website:** www.scoutingmagazine.org

Freelance Potential
80% written by nonstaff writers. Publishes 4–6 freelance submissions yearly; 5–10% by authors who are new to the magazine. Receives 150 queries yearly.

Submissions
Query with outline. Accepts hard copy. SASE. Responds in 3 weeks.
Articles: 500–1,200 words. Informational and how-to articles; personal experience pieces; profiles; interviews; and humor. Topics include scout programs; leadership; volunteering; nature; social issues and trends; and history.
Depts/columns: 500–700 words. "News Briefs," "Family Talk," "Front Line Stuff," and "Outdoor Smarts."
Other: Quizzes, puzzles, and games.

Sample Issue
50 pages (33% advertising): 6 articles; 6 depts/columns. Sample copy, $2.50 with 9x12 SASE. Guidelines available.
- "What It Means to Be an Eagle Scout." Article discusses a book that highlights the lasting significance of scouting on a diverse group of men.
- "Staying Alive in Avalanche Country." Article follows scouts in northern Nevada as they learn the basics of avalanche safety.
- Sample dept/column: "Family Talk" offers tips for keeping children safe on the Internet.

Rights and Payment
First North American serial rights. Written material, $300–$800. Pays on acceptance. Provides 2 copies.

Editor's Comments
We need well-written, concise profiles of urban Scout leaders or troops, and those from minority communities (including Native American Scouts) and underrepresented religious groups (i.e., Islamic and Hindu). We see too many articles about outstanding individual Eagle Scout projects.

Seattle's Child

511 Second Avenue West
Seattle, WA 98119

Publisher: Ann Bergman

Description and Interests
This free publication keeps parents in the greater Seattle area informed with articles on family health, education, recreation, and other activities, with an emphasis on local resources.
- **Audience:** Parents
- **Frequency:** Monthly
- **Circulation:** 80,000
- **Website:** www.seattleschild.com

Freelance Potential
80% written by nonstaff writers. Publishes 30 freelance submissions yearly; 10% by unpublished writers, 25% by authors who are new to the magazine. Receives 120+ queries yearly.

Submissions
Query with outline. Accepts hard copy, email queries to editor@seattleschild.com, and simultaneous submissions if identified. SASE. Responds in 1 month.
Articles: Word lengths vary. Informational and how-to articles; and personal experience pieces. Topics include family and parenting issues, health, fitness, regional news, travel, and social issues.
Depts/columns: Word lengths vary. Profiles, cooking, and media reviews.

Sample Issue
50 pages (30% advertising): 3 articles; 3 depts/columns. Sample copy, $3. Guidelines and theme list available.
- "Taking the Long View: Thirty Years of Parenting." Article features the perspectives of four parenting experts on how parenting has changed over the past three decades.
- "Channeling Nancy Drew and Other Book Diversions from Nancy Pearl." Article includes book recommendations from Seattle's world-renowned librarian.
- Sample dept/column: "Our Schools" features an opinion piece on why the upcoming Seattle School Board races are important.

Rights and Payment
Rights vary. Written material, $100–$450. Pays on acceptance. Provides 2 contributor's copies.

Editor's Comments
We are not in the market for national stories; we prefer to publish well-written articles that approach parenting topics from a local angle. Writers do not need to be from Seattle, but must know the region.

Seek

Standard Publishing Company
8805 Governor's Hill Drive, Suite 400
Cincinnati, OH 45249

Editor: Margaret K. Williams

Description and Interests
Subtitled "The Abundant Life," *Seek* provides Christian guidance to young adults and adults to help them face the challenges of contemporary life. A Sunday school pamphlet, it offers both inspirational fiction and nonfiction, as well as weekly Bible readings.
- **Audience:** YA–Adult
- **Frequency:** Weekly
- **Circulation:** 27,000
- **Website:** www.standardpub.com

Freelance Potential
85% written by nonstaff writers. Publishes 150–200 freelance submissions yearly; 80% by authors who are new to the magazine.

Submissions
Send complete ms that relates to an upcoming theme. Prefers email to seek@standardpub.com. Will accept hard copy. No simultaneous submissions. SASE. Responds in 3–6 months.
Articles: 500–1,200 words. Inspirational, devotional, and personal experience pieces. Topics include religious and contemporary issues, Christian living, coping with moral and ethical dilemmas, and controversial subjects.
Fiction: 500–1,200 words. Stories about Christian living, moral and ethical problems, controversial topics, and dealing with contemporary life challenges.
Other: Submit seasonal material 1 year in advance.

Sample Issue
8 pages (no advertising): 3 articles; 1 Bible lesson. Sample copy, free with 6x9 SASE. Guidelines and theme list available.
- "Doing the Right Thing." Article explores the complexities of human justice and the rights and duties of those living in communities.
- "Judgment, Justice, and Joy." Article compares the justice practiced by men here on Earth to the ultimate justice of God.

Rights and Payment
First and second rights. Written material, $.05–$.07 per word. Artwork, $50. Pays on acceptance. Provides 5 contributor's copies.

Editor's Comments
If you're interested in writing for us, log on to our website and check the theme list. Then send something relevant and well-written on one of the topics.

Seventeen

300 West 57th Street
New York, NY 10019

Submissions: Zandile Blay

Description and Interests
A typical issue of this popular magazine for teenage girls would include the latest fashion, beauty, fitness, and celebrity updates, as well as more in-depth discussions of relationships, families, and current social issues.
- **Audience:** 13–21 years
- **Frequency:** Monthly
- **Circulation:** 2 million
- **Website:** www.seventeen.com

Freelance Potential
20% written by nonstaff writers. Publishes 20 freelance submissions yearly; 5% by unpublished writers, 40% by authors who are new to the magazine. Receives 46 queries, 200 unsolicited mss yearly.

Submissions
Query with outline and clips or writing samples for nonfiction. Send complete ms for fiction. Accepts hard copy and simultaneous submissions if identified. SASE. Response time varies.
Articles: 650–3,000 words. Informational and self-help articles; profiles; and personal experience pieces. Topics include relationships, dating, family issues, current events, social concerns, friendship, and popular culture.
Fiction: 1,000–3,000 words. Stories that feature female teenage experiences.
Depts/columns: 500–1,000 words. Fashion, beauty, health, and fitness.
Other: Submit seasonal material 6 months in advance.

Sample Issue
166 pages (50% advertising): 7 articles; 24 depts/columns. Sample copy, $2.99 at newsstands. Guidelines available.
- "Online Dating Tips." Article tells how to meet guys safely—and successfully—on the Internet.
- Sample dept/column: "Health" details health risks that even well-educated girls may not be aware of.

Rights and Payment
First rights. Written material, $1–$1.50 per word. Pays on acceptance.

Editor's Comments
Original pieces about real girls who have had to make difficult decisions are needed. We also want cutting-edge, "newsy" material that interests teens.

Sharing the Victory

Fellowship of Christian Athletes
8701 Leeds Road
Kansas City, MO 64129

Editorial Assistant: Ashley Burns

Description and Interests
This Christian magazine focuses on athletes, professional and otherwise, whose faith influences their lives on and off the playing field.
- **Audience:** Athletes and coaches, grades 7 and up
- **Frequency:** 9 times each year
- **Circulation:** 80,000
- **Website:** www.sharingthevictory.com

Freelance Potential
40% written by nonstaff writers. Publishes 20 freelance submissions yearly; 25% by unpublished writers, 10% by authors who are new to the magazine. Receives 48 queries and unsolicited mss yearly.

Submissions
Query with outline/synopsis and clips or writing samples; or send complete ms. Accepts hard copy and IBM disk submissions. SASE. Availability of artwork improves chance of acceptance. Response time varies.
Articles: To 1,200 words. Informational articles; profiles; interviews; and personal experience pieces. Topics include sports, competition, training, and Christian education.
Depts/columns: Staff written.
Artwork: Color prints.
Other: Submit seasonal material 3–4 months in advance.

Sample Issue
38 pages (30% advertising): 6 articles; 11 depts/columns. Sample copy, $1 with 9x12 SASE (3 first-class stamps. Guidelines available.
- "Hoosier to Hawkeye." Article gives an inside look at coach Steve Alford's journey of faith and basketball.
- "One-on-One with Kapua Torres." Article profiles one of the nation's top female wrestlers and describes how her faith keeps her going.

Rights and Payment
First serial rights. Articles, $150–$400. Pays on publication.

Editor's Comments
While we will continue to consider submissions pertaining to all Christian athletes, we are currently most interested in the inspiring stories about athletes with ties to the Fellowship of Christian Athletes. Our particular interests include the female athletes and coaches in the FCA.

Shine Brightly

P.O. Box 87334
Canton, MI 48187

Editor: Sara Lynne Hilton

Description and Interests
Shine Brightly is a Christian magazine for pre-teen and young teenage girls. Its articles and stories are written to help girls reach out and serve the needs of others in their homes, schools, communities, and across the world.
- **Audience:** 9–14 years
- **Frequency:** 9 times each year
- **Circulation:** 15,500
- **Website:** www.gemsgc.org

Freelance Potential
30% written by nonstaff writers. Publishes 20 freelance submissions yearly; 15% by unpublished writers, 90% by authors who are new to the magazine. Receives 500 unsolicited mss yearly.

Submissions
Send complete ms. Accepts hard copy and simultaneous submissions if identified. No email submissions. SASE. Responds in 1 month.
Articles: 50–500 words. Informational and how-to articles; personal experience pieces; profiles; and humor. Topics include community service, stewardship, contemporary social issues, family and friend relationships, and peer pressure.
Fiction: 400–900 words. Genres include contemporary fiction, romance, mystery, science fiction, and adventure. Also publishes stories about nature, animals, and sports.
Depts/columns: Staff written.
Artwork: 5x7 or larger B/W and color prints.
Other: Puzzles, activities, and cartoons.

Sample Issue
24 pages (no advertising): 1 article; 2 stories; 2 depts/columns. Sample copy, $1 with 9x12 SASE ($.75 postage). Guidelines available.
- "Fragments." Article talks about how girls from Zambia and America are learning and growing together.
- "Castle Courage." Story features a girl and her father who have entered a sand sculpture contest.

Rights and Payment
First, second, and simultaneous rights. Articles and fiction, $.02–$.05 per word. Other material, payment rates vary. Pays on publication. Provides 2 copies.

Editor's Comments
We try to equip, motivate, and engage girls in living out their faith in Jesus Christ.

Single Mother

National Organization of Single Mothers
P.O. Box 68
Midland, NC 28107-0068

Editor: Andrea Engber

Description and Interests
Now published exclusively online, this newsletter from the National Organization of Single Mothers provides advice, information, and support to women who are parenting by themselves. It covers everything from pregnancy and childbirth to family finances and child support.
- **Audience:** Single mothers
- **Frequency:** Quarterly
- **Circulation:** 3,000–5,000
- **Website:** www.singlemothers.org

Freelance Potential
10% written by nonstaff writers. Publishes 6 freelance submissions yearly. Receives 12–24 queries and unsolicited mss yearly.

Submissions
Query or send complete ms. Accepts hard copy. SASE. Response time varies.
Articles: Word lengths vary. Informational articles. Topics include parenting, money and time management, absent dads, dating, handling ex-families, death, pregnancy and childbirth, adoption, donor insemination, child support, paternity, custody, and visitation rights.
Depts/columns: Word lengths vary. News, book reviews, advice.

Sample Issue
Sample copy available at website.
- "Single Moms: Too Sexy for Minivans!" Article offers a humorous look at why minivans are *not* the right vehicle for attracting a man.
- "One of 'Those' Kids." Article offers the personal experiences of a woman who was raised by a divorced mother.
- "Seven Tips for Single Mom Success." Article reveals the secrets of happy, successful single mothers.

Rights and Payment
Rights vary. Written material, payment rates vary. Payment policy varies.

Editor's Comments
For more than 16 years, our organization has been dedicated to helping women who are single moms by choice or by chance meet the challenges of daily life with wisdom, wit, dignity, confidence, and courage. We want to hear from writers who can provide us with advice and information our readers will find useful.

Sisterhood Agenda

524 Ridge Street
Newark, NJ 07104

Editor: Angela D. Coleman

Description and Interests
The purpose of this new magazine is to empower girls and young women of African descent with self-knowledge, self-development, and self-esteem. Published both online and in print, *Sisterhood Agenda* is distributed free of charge through schools, libraries, hair salons, and bookstores.
- **Audience:** 13–32 years
- **Frequency:** Quarterly
- **Circulation:** 500,000
- **Website:** www.sisterhoodagenda.com

Freelance Potential
80% written by nonstaff writers. Publishes 40 freelance submissions yearly; 75% by unpublished writers, 90% by authors who are new to the magazine.

Submissions
Send complete ms. Accepts email submissions to acoleman@sisterhoodagenda.com (Microsoft Word attachments). Response time varies.
Articles: 1,500–1,800 words. Informational articles; profiles; interviews; and reviews. Topics include life skills, education, careers, health, music, heritage, community service, current events, and finances.
Depts/columns: First-person essays, 550 words. Book reviews, word lengths vary.
Other: Poetry, to 30 lines.

Sample Issue
50 pages: 12 articles; 3 depts/columns; 1 poem. Sample copy, guidelines, and editorial calendar available at website.
- "African American Female Writers." Article presents short biographies of writers, including Phillis Wheatley and Octavia Butler.
- "Tools for Survival." Article details strategies for creating work and life success.
- Sample dept/column: "Hype" features cultural news and public affairs items that affect women of African descent.

Rights and Payment
One-time rights. No payment.

Editor's Comments
We're always seeking vibrant, fresh, and exciting content that will uplift and aid in the self-development of women and girls of African descent. We have a unique distribution strategy that includes international as well as urban U.S. markets.

Skating

United States Figure Skating Association
20 First Street
Colorado Springs, CO 80906

Director of Publications

Description and Interests
Read by members of the U.S. Figure Skating Association—most of whom are girls under the age of 17—this magazine covers figure skating programs, personalities, events, and trends.
- **Audience:** 5 years–Adult
- **Frequency:** 10 times each year
- **Circulation:** 45,000
- **Website:** www.usfigureskating.org

Freelance Potential
70% written by nonstaff writers. Publishes 15 freelance submissions yearly; 10% by unpublished writers, 20% by authors who are new to the magazine. Receives 72 queries and unsolicited mss yearly.

Submissions
Query with résumé, clips or writing samples, and photo ideas; or send complete ms. Accepts hard copy, MacIntosh Zip disk submissions, and email to skating-magazine@usfigureskating.org. SASE. Responds in 1 month.
Articles: 750–2,000 words. Informational articles; profiles; and interviews. Topics include association news, competitions, techniques, personalities, and training.
Depts/columns: 600–800 words. Competition results; profiles of skaters and coaches; sports medicine; fitness; and technique tips.
Artwork: B/W and color prints, slides, or transparencies. Electronic images at 300 dpi.

Sample Issue
48 pages: 4 articles; 10 depts/columns. Sample copy, $3 with 9x12 SASE. Guidelines available.
- "Fantastic Finish." Article describes the Marshalls U.S. Figure Skating Showcase in Reading, Pennsylvania.
- "Two of a Kind." Article gives an overview of the U.S. Figure Skating National Pairs Camp and Tryouts in Colorado Springs.
- Sample dept/column: "Where Are They Now?" profiles former figure skating champion Randy Gardner.

Rights and Payment
First serial rights. Articles, $75–$150. Depts/columns, $75. Artwork, payment rates vary. Pays on publication. Provides 5–10 contributor's copies.

Editor's Comments
There are three main types of stories that we run: competition reviews; features on skaters, coaches, and judges; and our regular columns.

Skipping Stones

A Multicultural Magazine

P.O. Box 3939
Eugene, OR 97403-0939

Editor: Arun N. Toké

Description and Interests

This award-winning publication celebrates ecological awareness and cultural diversity with contributions from young people and adults.
- **Audience:** 7–17 years; teachers; parents
- **Frequency:** 5 times each year
- **Circulation:** 2,500
- **Website:** www.skippingstones.org

Freelance Potential

90% written by nonstaff writers. Publishes 175–200 freelance submissions yearly; 60% by unpublished writers, 75% by authors who are new to the magazine. Receives 2,400 unsolicited mss yearly.

Submissions

Send complete ms with bio. Accepts hard copy, Macintosh disk, and email submissions to editor@skippingstones.org. SASE. Responds in 3–4 months.
Articles: 750–1,000 words. Informational articles; photo-essays; personal experience pieces; profiles; and humor. Topics include cultural and religious celebrations, architecture, nature, parenting, and activism.
Fiction: To 1,000 words. Genres include multicultural fiction and folktales.
Depts/columns: 100–200 words. "What's on Your Mind?"; "Health Rocks!"; "Folktale!"; "Taking Action"; and "For Parents & Teachers."
Other: Puzzles and games. Poetry by children, to 30 lines. Submit seasonal material 3–4 months in advance.

Sample Issue

35 pages (no advertising): 10 articles; 5 stories; 18 poems; 1 photo-essay; 10 depts/columns. Sample copy, $5 with 9x12 SASE ($1 postage). Guidelines and editorial calendar available.
- "Good Morning! Breakfast Anybody?" Article lists typical morning meals from around the world.
- Sample dept/column: "Health Rocks!" provides lessons on winter cheer from Scandinavia.

Rights and Payment

First and nonexclusive reprint rights. No payment. Provides contributor's copies and discounts.

Editor's Comments

Our readers hail from diverse cultural and socioeconomic backgrounds. Writing should challenge them to think, learn, cooperate, and create.

Slap

High Speed Productions
1303 Underwood Avenue
San Francisco, CA 94124

Editor: Mark Whiteley

Description and Interests

"SLAP" stands for Skateboarding, Life, Art, and Progression, which sums up the content of this ultra hip magazine for young adults. The key word here is "skateboarding"—articles cover everything from techniques to terrain in a jargon-heavy, skater-dude style.
- **Audience:** YA
- **Frequency:** Monthly
- **Circulation:** 130,000
- **Website:** www.slapmagazine.com

Freelance Potential

40% written by nonstaff writers. Publishes 24 freelance submissions yearly; 20% by unpublished writers.

Submissions

Send complete ms. Accepts hard copy, IBM or Macintosh disk submissions, and simultaneous submissions if identified. Availability of artwork improves chance of acceptance. SASE. Responds in 2 months.
Articles: Word lengths vary. Informational and how-to articles; interviews; and personal experience pieces. Topics include skateboarding techniques and equipment, contest reports, music, art, and culture.
Depts/columns: Word lengths vary. Media reviews, interviews, gear, gossip, and skateboard tricks.
Artwork: 35mm B/W negatives; color prints and transparencies. B/W and color line art.
Other: Photo-essays, cartoons, and contests.

Sample Issue

168 pages (40% advertising): 7 articles; 9 depts/columns. Sample copy, free with 9x12 SASE ($1.95 postage). Guidelines and editorial calendar available.
- "Out of the Blue." Article gives an overview of the recent Nike SB Tour to Australia.
- "Portfolio: Ben Horton." Article profiles a skater/artist and includes several examples of his work.
- Sample dept/column: "Shorts" includes an interview with a skate photographer who recently made a video about fixed-gear bike riders.

Rights and Payment

First rights. All material, payment rates vary. Pays on publication. Provides 1 contributor's copy.

Editor's Comments

You must be a true skater or have an uncanny grasp of the skate scene to even think of writing for us. Our readers live and breathe skateboarding and music, and expect the same from our writers.

Social Studies and the Young Learner

303 Townsend Hall
University of Missouri–Columbia
Columbia, MO 65211-2400

Editor: Dr. Linda Bennett

Description and Interests
The goal of this publication is to ignite enthusiasm in elementary teachers across the country while providing relevant and useful information about the teaching of social studies to elementary students.
- **Audience:** Teachers, grades K–6
- **Frequency:** Quarterly
- **Circulation:** 10,000
- **Website:** www.socialstudies.org/publications/ssyl

Freelance Potential
100% written by nonstaff writers. Publishes 32 freelance submissions yearly; 30% by unpublished writers, 50% by authors who are new to the magazine. Receives 60 unsolicited mss yearly.

Submissions
Send complete ms. Accepts email submissions to ssyl@missouri.edu. Response time varies.
Articles: To 2,000 words. Informational articles; profiles; and personal experience pieces. Topics include current events, gifted and special education, multicultural issues, social issues, history, and the humanities.
Fiction: Word lengths vary. Genres include folktales; folklore; and multicultural, ethnic, and historical fiction.
Depts/columns: To 500 words. Classroom resources and perspectives on topics related to social studies.
Artwork: B/W and color prints and transparencies. Line art.
Other: Filler, puzzles, and activities. Submit articles based on themes 4 months in advance.

Sample Issue
32 pages: 6 articles; 3 depts/columns. Sample copy, $7.50. Guidelines and theme list/editorial calendar available at website.
- "Viewing American History Through Native Eyes." Article provides ideas for teaching American history from the perspective of Native Americans.
- Sample dept/column: "Teaching Resources" gives a curriculum for examining a Native American culture through hands-on museum artifacts.

Rights and Payment
All rights. No payment.

Editor's Comments
We especially encourage submissions of manuscripts authored by kindergarten through grade-five classroom teachers themselves, or co-authored by professors and classroom teachers.

Softball Youth

Dugout Media Inc.
P.O. Box 983
Morehead, KY 40351

President: Scott Hacker

Description and Interests
This lively new magazine seeks to provide young girls with the best source of everything for youth softball, including information on gear, training, tournaments, teams, and players. It also features craft projects and health and beauty tips.
- **Audience:** Girls
- **Frequency:** Quarterly
- **Circulation:** Unavailable
- **Website:** www.softballyouth.com

Freelance Potential
50% written by nonstaff writers. Publishes 10–20 freelance submissions yearly.

Submissions
Query or send ms. Accepts email submissions to mailbox@softballyouth.com. Response time varies.
Articles: Word lengths vary. Informational and how-to articles; profiles; interviews; and personal experience pieces. Topics include techniques, training, and softball personalities.
Depts/columns: Word lengths vary. Gear; health, beauty, and fitness; youth ballpark profiles; product reviews; college profiles.
Other: Contests, horoscopes, quizzes, puzzles, crafts, and activities.

Sample Issue
38 pages: 3 articles; 7 depts/columns. Writers' guidelines available.
- "Nobody Does It Better." Article profiles Olympic gold medalist and professional softball player Cat Osterman.
- "Keep Your Shoulders Strong." Article provides training tips to avoid rotator-cuff injuries.
- Sample dept/column: "College Profile" spotlights the University of Arizona Wildcats.

Rights and Payment
Exclusive rights. Written material, payment rates vary. Pays on publication.

Editor's Comments
We want readers to be inspired and motivated to play softball. We want to re-energize the sport with fun stories that cover youth softball all over the world, plus health, beauty, and fitness. Softball is obviously the main focus, but we know girls are into other things, and we want to make this a fun magazine for them to read and interact with.

South Florida Parenting

6501 Nob Hill Road
Tamarac, FL 33321

Managing Editor: Vicki McCash Brennan

Description and Interests
A wide range of parenting and family topics are covered in *South Florida Parenting*, a magazine distributed free in Miami-Dade, Broward, and Palm Beach counties. Parents pick it up for news on regional activities, as well as articles offering advice on raising children from birth through the teen years.
- **Audience:** Parents
- **Frequency:** Monthly
- **Circulation:** 110,000
- **Website:** www.sfparenting.com

Freelance Potential
85% written by nonstaff writers. Publishes 90 freelance submissions yearly; 10% by authors who are new to the magazine. Receives 996 unsolicited mss each year.

Submissions
Prefers complete ms; will accept queries. Accepts hard copy and email submissions to vmccash@sfparenting.com. SASE. Responds in 2–3 months.
Articles: 800–2,000 words. Informational and how-to articles; profiles; interviews; and personal experience pieces. Topics include family life, travel, parenting, education, leisure, music, health, and regional events and activities.
Depts/columns: To 750 words. Family finances, health, nutrition, advice on infants and pre-teens.

Sample Issue
142 pages (60% advertising): 3 articles; 13 depts/columns; 1 calendar; 1 support group listing. Guidelines available.
- "Stay Connected . . . Safely." Article explains how to raise a technologically savvy child in a sometimes scary world.
- "Back to School Rules—Made to Be Broken?" Article talks about how schools have to balance zero-tolerance policies with sound judgment.
- Sample dept/column: "Family Travel" describes day trips and longer family vacations.

Rights and Payment
One-time regional rights. Written material, $100–$300. Pays on publication. Provides contributor's copies upon request.

Editor's Comments
Most of the material we publish has a South Florida slant, but we also cover universal parenting themes.

South Jersey Mom

P.O. Box 2413
Vineland, NJ 08362-2413

Editor: Adrienne Richardson

Description and Interests
This local parenting publication targets moms with children ages 12 and under. It is full of inspiring stories, debates over hot parenting issues, and local opinions about national issues, as well as information on events and regional resources.
- **Audience:** Parents
- **Frequency:** Monthly
- **Circulation:** 35,000
- **Website:** www.southjerseymom.com

Freelance Potential
100% written by nonstaff writers. Publishes 200 freelance submissions yearly; 20% by unpublished writers, 60% by authors who are new to the magazine.

Submissions
Query with two writing samples. Accepts email queries to adrienne@southjerseymom.com. Response time varies.
Articles: Word lengths vary. Informational articles; profiles; and personal experience pieces. Topics include parenting issues, trend information, family issues, pregnancy, technology, education, exercise, safety, sports, and recreation.
Depts/columns: Word lengths vary. Health topics, gear, technology.

Sample Issue
10 articles; 8 depts/columns. Guidelines available at website.
- "The Great Cell Phone Debate." Article takes a look at why parents need to decide whether or not to get their pre-teen a cell phone.
- "Does Your Family Have an Emergency Plan?" Article discusses the importance of having a family action plan in place to be ready in emergencies.
- Sample dept/column: "Life Sentences" reports on skin cancer and protecting skin from the sun.

Rights and Payment
Rights vary. No payment.

Editor's Comments
We look for articles that are original must-reads. If you are assigned a story, please observe the following: include interviews with moms and local experts; advice and information from more than one expert; data on the latest trends; and detailed anecdotes to illustrate the issue. Remember to fact-check your article, and include a catchy title and byline.

Sparkle

P.O. Box 7259
Grand Rapids, MI 49510

Publications Coordinator: Sarah Vanderaa

Description and Interests

Sparkle is designed specifically for Christian girls in the first through third grades. Published by an international ministry that starts Bible-based, all-girl club programs in churches and other Christian organizations, its mission is to prepare girls for a life of living out their faith. Each issue revolves around a theme.
- **Audience:** Girls, 6–9 years
- **Frequency:** 6 times each year
- **Circulation:** 5,065
- **Website: www.gemsgc.org**

Freelance Potential

80% written by nonstaff writers. Publishes 20 freelance submissions yearly; 80% by unpublished writers, 90% by authors who are new to the magazine. Receives 100 mss yearly.

Submissions

Send ms. SASE. Responds in 4–6 weeks.
Articles: 100–400 words. Informational articles. Topics include animals, sports, music, musicians, famous people, interaction with family and friends, service projects, and dealing with school work.
Fiction: 100–400 words. Genres include adventure, mystery, and contemporary fiction. Also publishes stories about animals.
Other: Puzzles, games, recipes, party ideas, short humorous pieces, cartoons, and inexpensive craft ideas.

Sample Issue

14 pages (no advertising): 3 articles; 2 stories; 2 activities; 1 Bible lesson. Sample copy, $1 with 9x12 SASE. Guidelines and theme list available.
- "Spreading Joy." Story features a kind neighbor whose thankfulness to God brings joy to others and herself.
- "What's So Special About Camels?" Article includes fun facts about desert creatures.

Rights and Payment

Rights vary. Articles, $20. Other material, payment rates vary. Pays on publication. Provides 2 contributor's copies.

Editor's Comments

We need more articles and stories relating to animal themes. Articles about nature and fun fact pieces that talk about God's amazing creation are also especially welcome. Please check our theme list before submitting; we get too many "miscellaneous" submissions.

Spider

The Magazine for Children

Cricket Magazine Group
70 East Lake Street, Suite 300
Chicago, IL 60601

Submissions Editor

Description and Interests

Independent readers love this magazine for its stories, poetry, articles, colorful illustrations, and activities.
- **Audience:** 6–9 years
- **Frequency:** Monthly
- **Circulation:** 60,000
- **Website: www.cricketmag.com**

Freelance Potential

97% written by nonstaff writers. Publishes 50 freelance submissions yearly; 30% by unpublished writers, 50% by authors who are new to the magazine. Receives 3,600 mss yearly.

Submissions

Send complete ms; include bibliography for nonfiction. Accepts hard copy and simultaneous submissions if identified. Availability of artwork improves chance of acceptance. SASE. Responds in 6 months.
Articles: 300–800 words. Informational and how-to articles; profiles; and interviews. Topics include nature, animals, science, technology, history, multicultural issues, foreign cultures, and the environment.
Fiction: 300–1,000 words. Easy-to-read stories. Genres include humor; fantasy; fairy tales; folktales; and realistic, historical, and science fiction.
Other: Recipes, crafts, puzzles, games, brainteasers, and math and word activities. Poetry, to 20 lines.

Sample Issue

34 pages (no advertising): 1 article; 4 stories; 2 poems; 2 recipes; 2 activities. Sample copy, $5 with 9x12 SASE. Guidelines available at website.
- "Brrr: Growing Up in Antarctica." Article describes how a baby Emperor Penguin grows from birth to four years of age.
- "Snow Secrets." Story solves the mystery of who has been leaving a little girl gifts in the snow.
- "Howling Up the Moon." Story of an old wolf and an Eskimo girl incorporates words from the Eskimo language.

Rights and Payment

All rights. Articles and fiction, $.25 per word. Poetry, to $3 per line. Other material, payment rates vary. Pays on publication. Provides 2 contributor's copies.

Editor's Comments

Send us short stories and nonfiction pieces on humanities and the arts.

SportingKid

3650 Brookside Parkway, Suite 300
Alpharetta, GA 30022

Editor: Michael J. Pallerino

Description and Interests
Written for parents, *SportingKid* emphasizes the importance of keeping children physically active. It covers training, coaching, and fitness topics as they relate to a broad spectrum of sports, while also featuring player profiles.
- **Audience:** Parents
- **Frequency:** 6 times each year
- **Circulation:** 400,000
- **Website: www.sportingkid.com**

Freelance Potential
20–30% written by nonstaff writers. Publishes 10 freelance submissions yearly; 10% by authors who are new to the magazine. Receives 600 queries and unsolicited mss yearly.

Submissions
Query or send complete ms. Accepts email submissions to editor@sportingkid.com. Queries must be pasted into the email message; manuscripts must be attached as Microsoft Word documents. Responds in 1 month.
Articles: Word lengths vary. Informational and how-to articles and personal experience pieces. Topics include all sports played by children, as well as issues related to coaching and training for those sports.
Depts/columns: Word lengths vary. New product information, the culture of youth sports, profiles of prominent sports figures, and essays written from a parent's perspective.

Sample Issue
40 pages: 7 articles; 9 depts/columns. Sample copy and guidelines available at website.
- "Personal Fitness Lessons from the Olympics." Article looks at lessons that can be learned about fitness—and ways you can get motivated to exercise—by watching sports on television.
- "Healthy Eating: The Key to a Healthy Body Image." Article discusses how healthy eating and exercise habits can decrease the rates of obesity and eating disorders among children.

Rights and Payment
First and electronic rights. Written material, payment rates vary. Pays on publication.

Editor's Comments
We want to hear from people who have interesting stories of how youth sports affected their lives.

Sports Illustrated Kids

Time & Life Building
1271 Avenue of the Americas
New York, NY 10020

Managing Editor: Bob Der

Description and Interests
Young sports enthusiasts subscribe to this magazine to read the most up-to-date information on their favorite teams and players. It also features profiles of inspirational and up-and-coming athletes.
- **Audience:** 8–14 years
- **Frequency:** Monthly
- **Circulation:** 1.1 million
- **Website: www.sikids.com**

Freelance Potential
3–5% written by nonstaff writers. Publishes 3–5 freelance submissions yearly. Receives 204 queries each year.

Submissions
Query or send complete ms. Send for guidelines or check website to determine which department your material should be sent to. Accepts hard copy. SASE. Responds in 2 months.
Articles: Lead articles and profiles, 500–700 words. Short features, 500–600 words. Topics include professional and aspiring athletes, fitness, health, safety, sports tips, hobbies, science, technology, and multicultural issues.
Depts/columns: Word lengths vary. Events coverage, team profiles, and humor.
Other: Puzzles, games, and trivia. Poetry and drawings created by kids.

Sample Issue
60 pages (24% advertising): 7 articles; 9 depts/columns; 1 comic; 1 card page; 1 poster. Sample copy, $3.50 with 9x12 SASE to *Sports Illustrated Kids*, P.O. Box 830609, Birmingham, AL 35283. Guidelines available.
- "The Strongest Lynx." Article profiles Seimone Augustus of the Minnesota Lynx, last year's WNBA Rookie of the Year.
- "The Ultimate Athlete Challenge." Article looks at four top high school athletes and how they measure up using a new skills test.

Rights and Payment
All rights. Articles, $100–$1,500. Depts/columns, payment rates vary. Pays on acceptance. Provides copies.

Editor's Comments
Before contacting us, check our writers' guidelines to make sure your topic will be appropriate for the age range we target.

Stone Soup

The Magazine by Young Writers & Artists

P.O. Box 83
Santa Cruz, CA 95063

Editor: Gerry Mandel

Description and Interests

Stone Soup is written by and for young authors and artists. Each colorful issue features their short stories, book reviews, poetry, and artwork.
- **Audience:** 8–14 years
- **Frequency:** 6 times each year
- **Circulation:** 20,000
- **Website:** www.stonesoup.com

Freelance Potential

100% written by nonstaff writers. Publishes 65 freelance submissions yearly; 90% by unpublished writers, 90% by new authors. Receives 15,000 unsolicited mss yearly.

Submissions

Send complete ms. Accepts submissions by writers under 14 years of age only. Accepts hard copy. No simultaneous submissions. SASE. Responds in 6 weeks only if interested.
Fiction: To 2,500 words. Genres include multicultural, ethnic, and historical fiction; adventure; mystery; suspense; and science fiction.
Depts/columns: Book reviews, word lengths vary.
Other: Poetry, line lengths vary.

Sample Issue

48 pages (no advertising): 8 stories; 2 book reviews; 1 poem. Sample copy, $5.75. Writers' guidelines available at website.
- "They're Pigs!" Short story makes the reader wonder whether a young boy's family members really had turned into pigs.
- "Guess What, Rebecca Baits?" Story features the familiar theme of what it feels like to leave your friends behind and eventually make new friends, but with a surprising twist at the end.
- Sample dept/column: "Book Review" recommends a historical fiction book based on a real-life teenage abolitionist who risked his life during the Civil War.

Rights and Payment

All rights. Written material, $40. Artwork, $25. Pays on publication. Provides 2 contributor's copies.

Editor's Comments

We encourage prospective authors to visit our website to read examples of stories, poems, and book reviews that have appeared in *Stone Soup*. Detailed contributor guidelines also are available online, and should be consulted to ensure that your submission is received for consideration.

Story Mates

Christian Light Publications
P.O. Box 1212
Harrisonburg, VA 22803-1212

Editor: Crystal Shank

Description and Interests

Story Mates is used by Mennonite Sunday schools to help children appreciate God's plan of salvation, and understand how to live in a way pleasing to God. It offers stories, poems, and puzzles to these ends.
- **Audience:** 4–8 years
- **Frequency:** Monthly
- **Circulation:** 6,192
- **Website:** www.clp.org

Freelance Potential

90% written by nonstaff writers. Publishes 200 freelance submissions yearly. Receives 600 unsolicited mss yearly.

Submissions

Send complete ms. Accepts hard copy and email submissions to storymates@clp.org. SASE. Responds in 6 weeks.
Fiction: Stories related to Sunday school lessons and true-to-life stories; to 800 words. Picture stories; 120–150 words.
Other: Bible puzzles, crafts, and activities. Poetry, word lengths vary. Submit seasonal material 6 months in advance.

Sample Issue

20 pages (no advertising): 6 stories; 8 poems; 5 puzzles. Sample copy, free with 9x12 SASE ($.87 postage). Guidelines and theme list available.
- "Chewing Gum Lesson." Story tells of a little girl who learns a lesson about exaggerating from her mother.
- "Jesus Did Not Run Away." Story shows how a Bible parable helps a young girl understand the importance of spending time with her brothers.
- "Important Things First." Story shows how two young sisters learn to put obedience before having fun.

Rights and Payment

First, reprint, or multiple-use rights. Fiction, $.03–$.05 per word. Poetry, $.35–$.75 per line. Other material, payment rates vary. Pays on acceptance. Provides 1 contributor's copy.

Editor's Comments

We are interested in stories that show an important lesson rather than merely tell it through dialogue. Use only the King James Version of the Bible for all quotes. Avoid questionable language and references to popular culture. Our purpose is to foster reverence for God as Father and Creator.

Student Assistance Journal

1270 Rankin Drive, Suite F
Troy, MI 48083

Editor: Erin Bell

Description and Interests
As "the voice of student assistance programs," this magazine provides strategies and updates to professionals who counsel troubled students in such areas as substance abuse, body image, and bullying. It is published by the National Student Assistance Association.
- **Audience:** Student assistance personnel, K–12
- **Frequency:** Quarterly
- **Circulation:** 15,000
- **Website:** www.prponline.net

Freelance Potential
90% written by nonstaff writers. Publishes 12 freelance submissions yearly; 50% by unpublished writers. Receives 36 queries yearly.

Submissions
Query if outside the field. Professionals should send complete ms. Accepts hard copy, IBM disk submissions, and simultaneous submissions if identified. SASE. Responds only if interested.
Articles: 1,500 words. Informational and how-to articles; and personal experience pieces. Topics include high-risk students, special education, drug testing, substance-abuse prevention, school violence, legal issues, federal funding, and staff development.
Depts/columns: 750–800 words. Book reviews, events, commentaries, news briefs, legal issues, media resources, and related research.

Sample Issue
34 pages (20% advertising): 4 articles; 4 depts/columns. Sample copy, free. Guidelines available.
- "Model Behavior." Article provides ways to recognize and deal with body image dissatisfaction in diverse student populations.
- "Defusing and Disarming Out-of-Control Parents." Article discusses strategies for calming down angry parents of students.
- Sample dept/column: "NSAA News" discusses student assistance in Vermont schools.

Rights and Payment
First rights. No payment. Provides 5 author's copies.

Editor's Comments
We're looking for concise, instructional how-to articles. They should contain information that student assistance professionals or other youth workers can use to enhance their programs' effectiveness or their professional practice.

Student Leader

Oxendine Publishing
412 Northwest 16th Avenue
Gainesville, FL 32604-2097

Editor: Anna Campitelli

Description and Interests
Motivating and informing teens who are active in student government is the purpose of this magazine. Targeting high school and college students and their advisors, it focuses on leadership and organizational skills, as well as volunteer and fund-raising projects.
- **Audience:** High school and college students
- **Frequency:** 3 times each year
- **Circulation:** 130,000 .
- **Website:** www.studentleader.com

Freelance Potential
10% written by nonstaff writers. Publishes 10 freelance submissions yearly; 50% by unpublished writers, 80% by authors who are new to the magazine. Receives 60 queries yearly.

Submissions
Query. Accepts hard copy, email queries to info@studentleader.com, and simultaneous submissions if identified. Availability of artwork improves chance of acceptance. SASE. Responds in 6 weeks.
Articles: 1,000 words. Informational articles. Topics include organizational management, service projects, fund-raising, student motivation, interpersonal skills, promoting special events, editorial standards, communication, and volunteerism.
Depts/columns: 250 words. Updates from the American Student Government Association.
Artwork: Color prints and 35mm slides.

Sample Issue
14 pages (50% advertising): 4 articles; 1 dept/column. Sample copy, $3.50 with 9x12 SASE ($1.07 postage). Guidelines and editorial calendar available.
- "A Solid Foundation: Building Blocks for SGA Growth." Article uses Columbia College Chicago's new Student Government Association as an example of an effective and credible student group.
- "Gubernatorial Gurus." Article profiles participants in a Gubernatorial Fellowship program.

Rights and Payment
All rights. All material, payment rates vary. Pays on publication. Provides 1 contributor's copy.

Editor's Comments
We get our articles from a variety of sources: college advisors, experts in higher education, and professional freelancers. Just remember that the focus has to be on issues related to student government.

SuperScience

Scholastic Inc.
557 Broadway
New York, NY 10012-3999

Editor: Britt Norlander

Description and Interests
Distributed in elementary school classrooms, this magazine from Scholastic features fun and unusual science facts and news accompanied by photos and hands-on activities. Curriculum tie-ins appear in the teacher guides that come with each issue.
- **Audience:** Grades 3–6
- **Frequency:** 8 times each year
- **Circulation:** 200,000
- **Website:** www.scholastic.com/superscience

Freelance Potential
75% written by nonstaff writers. Publishes 20 freelance submissions yearly; 50% by authors who are new to the magazine. Receives 60–120 unsolicited mss yearly.

Submissions
Query with résumé and clips. No unsolicited mss. Accepts hard copy. SASE. Response time varies.
Articles: 300–1,000 words. Informational and how-to articles; profiles; interviews; and personal experience pieces. Topics include Earth, physical, and life science; health; technology; chemistry; nature; and the environment.
Depts/columns: Word lengths vary. Science news.
Artwork: 8x10 B/W and color prints. Line art.
Other: Puzzles and activities.

Sample Issue
16 pages (no advertising): 7 articles; 1 dept/column. Sample copy, free with 9x12 SASE. Guidelines and editorial calendar available.
- "Mythical Creatures Revealed." Article explores the science behind some ancient legends and magical creatures.
- "Perfect Pitch?" Article looks at the physics of a new baseball pitch called the "gyroball."
- Sample dept/column: "Newsblast" features short updates on a new type of boat and the use of snakes to predict earthquakes.

Rights and Payment
First rights. Articles, $75–$600. Other material, payment rates vary. Pays on acceptance. Provides 2 contributor's copies.

Editor's Comments
We're always interested in topics that excite young readers, but all of our material is written on assignment. Check our editorial calendar before you query.

SW Florida Parent & Child

2422 Dr. Martin Luther King Jr. Boulevard
Fort Myers, FL 33901

Editor: Pamela Smith Hayford

Description and Interests
SW Florida Parent & Child is a regional parenting magazine that strives to provide useful information on parenting topics, activities, and family-friendly destinations and events.
- **Audience:** Parents
- **Frequency:** Monthly
- **Circulation:** 25,000
- **Website:** www.gulfcoastmoms.com

Freelance Potential
75% written by nonstaff writers. Publishes 160 freelance submissions yearly; 5% by unpublished writers, 25% by authors who are new to the magazine. Receives 275 queries and unsolicited mss yearly.

Submissions
Query or send complete ms. Prefers email submissions to info@swflparentchild.com. Will accept hard copy. SASE. Response time varies.
Articles: To 500 words. Informational articles; profiles; and personal experience pieces. Topics include family issues, parenting, education, travel, sports, health, fitness, computers, and social and regional issues.
Depts/columns: To 500 words. Dining, travel, parenting, education, and nutrition.

Sample Issue
84 pages (50% advertising): 4 articles; 21 depts/columns. Guidelines available.
- "Cloth Diaper Making Comeback." Article discusses the new trend of using cloth diapers.
- "Summertime Chores Teach Responsibility." Article takes a look at how to introduce the concept of family chores to children.
- Sample dept/column: "Clever You" offers ideas for getting kids to eat vegetables.

Rights and Payment
All rights. Written material, $25–$200. Pays on publication.

Editor's Comments
Our readers turn to us to provide them with practical information on topics related to parenting, education, health, and family issues. Material should be informative, inspiring, and entertaining. We're also interested in parenting tips, as well as information on regional resources and events. Most of our freelance material is contributed by writers who are from the area.

Swimming World and Junior Swimmer

90 Bell Rock Plaza, Suite 200
Sedona, AZ 86351

Editor

Description and Interests
Competitive swimmers of all ages subscribe to this magazine to find out about the latest meet results and to get the most up-to-date information on training, nutrition, fitness, and health. Inspiring personal stories and profiles are also part of the mix.
- **Audience:** All ages
- **Frequency:** Monthly
- **Circulation:** 59,000
- **Website:** www.swimmingworldmagazine.com

Freelance Potential
60% written by nonstaff writers. Publishes 100 freelance submissions yearly; 5% by unpublished writers. Receives 192+ queries yearly.

Submissions
Query. Accepts hard copy and email queries to editorial@swimmingworldmagazine.com. SASE. Responds in 1 month.
Articles: 500–3,500 words. Informational and how-to articles; profiles; and personal experience pieces. Topics include swimming, training, competition, medical advice, swim drills, nutrition, dryland exercise, exercise physiology, and fitness.
Depts/columns: 500–750 words. Swimming news, new product reviews, and nutrition advice.
Artwork: Color prints and transparencies. Line art.
Other: Activities, games, and jokes. Submit seasonal material 1–2 months in advance.

Sample Issue
62 pages (30% advertising): 10 articles; 9 depts/columns. Sample copy, $4.50 with 9x12 SASE ($1.80 postage). Guidelines available.
- "Jessica Long: Elite Company." Article profiles a U.S. Paralympic swimmer who won the Sullivan Award.
- "The Dynasty Is Still Alive." Article reports on the NCAA Division II Championships.
- Sample dept/column: "Dryside Training" depicts individual medley exercises.

Rights and Payment
All rights. Written material, $.12 per word. Artwork, payment rates vary. Pays on publication. Provides 2–5 contributor's copies.

Editor's Comments
We look for well-written articles that will appeal to at least one of the major segments of our readership. Send something that informs, instructs, or inspires.

Synapse

25 Beacon Street
Boston, MA 02108

Editor

Description and Interests
Published by the Young Religious Unitarian Universalists, *Synapse* features articles, poetry, song lyrics, paintings, and drawings by teens. It also reports on youth group projects and the personal experiences of teens who attend UU conferences. It appears both online and in print.
- **Audience:** 14–21 years
- **Frequency:** 3 times yearly online; annually in print
- **Circulation:** 2,500
- **Website:** www.uua.org/yruu/synapse

Freelance Potential
85% written by nonstaff writers. Of the freelance submissions published yearly, 90% are by unpublished writers.

Submissions
Send complete ms with contact information. Accepts disk submissions (QuarkXPress) and email submissions to YRUU@uua.org. SASE. Responds in 1 month.
Articles: Word lengths vary. Informational articles; personal experience pieces; and opinion pieces. Topics include current events, social issues, popular culture, regional events, youth programs, history, and ethnic and multicultural issues.
Depts/columns: Word lengths vary. Social action news, readings by Unitarian Universalist youth, sermons, homilies, and religious and spiritual reflections.
Other: Puzzles, activities, games, jokes, and poetry related to Unitarian Universalism.

Sample Issue
40 pages (7% advertising): 7 articles; 10 depts/columns; 1 calendar of events. Sample copy and guidelines available at website.
- "Tell All." First-person essay explores racial and other issues from the perspective of a teen of African American and West African heritage.
- "Violence in Interpersonal Relationships: Toward an Understanding and a Faithful Response." Article examines the many forms of abuse and how they affect our contemporary society.

Rights and Payment
All rights. No payment.

Editor's Comments
We give teens a chance to exchange information and energy. Ideas for articles and essays that match our upcoming themes are found at our website.

Syracuse Parent

5910 Firestone Drive
Syracuse, NY 13206

Editor: Brittany Jared

Description and Interests

This free parenting tabloid keeps parents in central New York up to date on activities and events of interest to families. Regular columns, a calendar, and community updates are found alongside articles on general parenting topics, such as education and health.
• **Audience:** Parents
• **Frequency:** Monthly
• **Circulation:** 26,500
• **Website:** www.syracuseparent.com

Freelance Potential

40% written by nonstaff writers. Publishes 15 freelance submissions yearly; 25% by unpublished writers, 10% by authors who are new to the magazine. Receives 96 queries yearly.

Submissions

Query. Accepts hard copy. SASE. Responds in 4–6 weeks.
Articles: 800–1,000 words. Informational and how-to articles; personal experience and practical application pieces; profiles; interviews; and humor. Topics include parenting, family issues, animals, pets, education, health, current events, regional news, social issues, nature, the environment, computers, music, travel, and sports.
Depts/columns: Staff written.
Other: Submit seasonal material 3–4 months in advance.

Sample Issue

24 pages (50% advertising): 6 articles; 7 depts/columns; 1 calendar. Sample copy, guidelines, and editorial calendar, $1 with 9x12 SASE.
• "New Fitness Mats Target Sedentary Lifestyle." Article talks about new, versatile exercise mats that children find to be fun and exciting.
• "Library Walls Leap Alive with Art." Article provides an overview of the art exhibition and receptions being offered in Onandaga County libraries.

Rights and Payment

First rights. Articles, $25–$30. Pays on publication.

Editor's Comments

If you look through our publication, you'll see that almost all of our articles report on local events or activities or connect our readers with local resources. We also like to see parenting pieces that are written with a touch of humor.

Take Five Plus

The General Council of the Assemblies of God
1445 North Boonville Avenue
Springfield, MO 65802-1894

Director of Editorial Services: Paul Smith

Description and Interests

Take Five Plus is a youth devotional guide for teen and young adult members of the Assemblies of God Church. In addition to daily devotionals, inspirational poetry and artwork by teens are featured.
• **Audience:** 12–19 years
• **Frequency:** Quarterly
• **Circulation:** 20,000
• **Website:** www.gospelpublishing.com

Freelance Potential

98% written by nonstaff writers. Of the freelance submissions published yearly, 10% are by authors who are new to the magazine.

Submissions

All material is assigned. Send letter of introduction with résumé, church background, and clips or writing samples. Accepts hard copy. SASE. Responds in 3 months.
Articles: 200–235 words. Daily devotionals based on Scripture readings.
Artwork: Accepts material from teenagers only. 8x10 B/W prints and 35mm color slides. 8x10 or smaller color line art.
Other: Poetry by teenagers, to 20 lines.

Sample Issue

104 pages (no advertising): 90 devotionals; 1 poem. Guidelines and sample devotional available on request for sample assignment.
• "A Perfect Score." Devotional based on Joshua 21:43–45 reminds us that promises may be hard for us to keep, but God can be trusted to keep His promises 100 percent of the time.
• "Sadly Wealthy." Devotional based on Luke 18:18–30 explains that material possessions can come between a person and God.

Rights and Payment

First rights. Written material, $.05 per word. Artwork, payment rates vary. Pays on publication. Provides 2 contributor's copies.

Editor's Comments

We are looking for well-written and well-founded devotionals that explore the issues faced by young adults in today's society. Each piece must contain an anecdote that is relevant to a Scripture reading. Prospective writers should contact us for detailed guidelines before preparing a sample devotional for us.

TAP: The Autism Perspective

10153½ Riverside Drive, Suite 243
Toluca, CA 91602

Publisher: Nicki Fisher

Description and Interests
Written to help people who are on the autism spectrum and those who care for them, this magazine strives to be a comprehensive resource for information about services, options, and treatments. It also includes personal life stories about triumphs, struggles, and humanness.
• **Audience:** Adults
• **Frequency:** Quarterly
• **Circulation:** Unavailable
• **Website:** www.theautismperspective.org

Freelance Potential
100% written by nonstaff writers. Publishes 120–140 freelance submissions yearly. Receives 360 queries each year.

Submissions
Query. Accepts hard copy and email queries to submissions@theautismperspective.org. SASE. Response time varies.
Articles: 800–1,000 words. Informational articles and personal experience pieces. Topics include autism, Asperger's, PDD, or related developmental disabilities; treatments; therapies; intervention; and research.
Depts/columns: 1,200 words. Grandparent and sibling stories; reflections on living with autism.
Artwork: B/W or color prints. Line art; cartoons.

Sample Issue
76 pages: 11 articles; 4 depts/columns. Sample copy and guidelines available at website.
• "Dreams for Dean." Article provides one parent's perspective on her son's autism and how she found the proper treatments for it.
• "How to Select the Correct Program for a Child with Special Needs." Article explores ways to develop comprehensive treatment approaches.
• Sample dept/column: "Living with A.S.D." discusses public school versus homeschooling for children with Asperger's Syndrome.

Rights and Payment
All rights. All material, payment rates vary. Payment policy varies. Provides 1 contributor's copy.

Editor's Comments
Our purpose is to provide unbiased information and treatment options while educating our readership on the latest research and cutting-edge news. First-person stories are also welcome.

Tar Heel Junior Historian

North Carolina Museum of History
4650 Mail Service Center
Raleigh, NC 27699-4650

Editor: Lisa Coston Hall

Description and Interests
This scholarly publication of the North Carolina Museum of History complements the state's middle-school and high-school curricula.
• **Audience:** 9–18 years
• **Frequency:** Twice each year
• **Circulation:** 9,000
• **Website:** http://ncmuseumofhistory.org

Freelance Potential
50% written by nonstaff writers. Publishes 16 freelance submissions yearly; 20% by unpublished writers, 50% by authors who are new to the magazine.

Submissions
Query. Accepts hard copy. SASE. Response time varies.
Articles: 700–1,000 words. Informational articles; personal experience pieces; profiles; and interviews. Topics include regional history; geography; government; and social, multicultural, and ethnic issues.
Fiction: Word lengths vary. Genres include historical, ethnic, and multicultural fiction; folktales; and folklore.
Artwork: B/W and color prints or transparencies. Line art.
Other: Puzzles, activities, and word games.

Sample Issue
35 pages (no advertising): 17 articles; 3 activities. Sample copy, $4 with 9x12 SASE ($2 postage). Guidelines and theme list available.
• "The Man Who Helped the World Breathe Easier." Article profiles Lunsford Richardson II, inventor of Vicks VapoRub.
• "Solving Modern Problems in Agriculture." Article profiles a contemporary agricultural engineer.
• "The Box That Changed the World." Article describes the birth of the shipping container, which was invented by a native of North Carolina.

Rights and Payment
All rights. No payment. Provides 10 contributor's copies.

Editor's Comments
We solicit manuscripts from expert scholars for each issue. Articles are selected for publication by the editor in consultation with the conceptual editor and other experts. We reserve the right to make changes in accepted articles, but will consult the author should substantive questions arise.

Teacher Librarian

15200 NBN Way
Blue Ridge Summit, PA 17214

Managing Editor: Kim Tabor

Description and Interests
This journal is dedicated to improving student learning by providing school librarians with practical teaching ideas, book reviews, and information on all aspects of library services for children and young adults.
- **Audience:** School library professionals
- **Frequency:** 5 times each year
- **Circulation:** 10,000
- **Website:** www.teacherlibrarian.com

Freelance Potential
60% written by nonstaff writers. Publishes 10 freelance submissions yearly; 25% by unpublished writers. Receives 6 queries and unsolicited mss yearly.

Submissions
Query or send complete ms with résumé, abstract, or bibliography. Accepts hard copy, disk submissions, and email submissions to editor@teacherlibrarian.com. SASE. Responds in 2 months.
Articles: 2,000+ words. Informational and analytical articles; and profiles. Topics include library funding, technology, leadership, library management, audio/visual material, cooperative teaching, and young adult services.
Depts/columns: Staff written.

Sample Issue
76 pages (20% advertising): 6 articles; 19 depts/columns; 14 reviews. Guidelines and editorial calendar available.
- "If You Build It They Will Come: Creating a School Library that Embraces Students and Teachers." Article makes a strong case for the importance of creating a welcoming environment for teachers and students alike.
- "Teacher-Librarian as Literacy Leader." Article tells why the school library must be an integral part of a school's reading program.

Rights and Payment
All rights. Written material, $100. Pays on publication. Provides 2 contributor's copies.

Editor's Comments
We're seeking material that will contribute to excellence in school library programs. Of particular interest are submissions focusing on collaboration and technology in the twenty-first century school library. Drawings and cartoons are welcome.

Teachers & Writers

520 Eighth Avenue, Suite 2020
New York, NY 10018

Editor: Susan Karwoska

Description and Interests
English teachers and educators turn to this magazine for articles regarding new techniques and theories for teaching creative writing to students from kindergarten through college.
- **Audience:** Teachers
- **Frequency:** Quarterly
- **Circulation:** 3,000
- **Website:** www.twc.org

Freelance Potential
60% written by nonstaff writers. Publishes 8 freelance submissions yearly; 5% by unpublished writers, 50% by authors who are new to the magazine. Receives 50 unsolicited mss yearly.

Submissions
Send complete ms. Accepts hard copy and simultaneous submissions if identified. SASE. Response time varies.
Articles: 700–5,000 words. Practical and theoretical articles featuring innovative teaching ideas, and fresh approaches to familiar teaching methods. Topics include teaching writing in conjunction with the visual arts; teaching oral history; and teaching writing to senior citizens. Also publishes translations.
Depts/columns: Word lengths vary. Information on events; book reviews.
Other: Submit seasonal material 6 months in advance.

Sample Issue
42 pages (no advertising): 6 articles. Sample copy, $4. Guidelines available.
- "Start with Rhythm." Article is based on a new book that encourages children to explore jazz through poetry and images.
- "The Midnight Rabbit Jumps Through the Sky." Article examines the important role music can play in teaching children to compose poetry.

Rights and Payment
First serial rights. Written material, $20 per printed column. Pays on publication. Provides 10 copies.

Editor's Comments
We are always interested in submissions from writers who have a new and innovative approach to teaching writing. Our readers are educational professionals who are eager to improve their classroom skills and improve the learning capacity of their students.

Teacher Interaction

Concordia Publishing House
3358 South Jefferson Avenue
St. Louis, MO 63118-3698

Editor: Thomas A. Nummela

Description and Interests
In print for 47 years, this magazine for Sunday school educators and administrators features articles, teaching tips, and classroom strategies.
• **Audience:** Sunday school teachers
• **Frequency:** Quarterly
• **Circulation:** 12,000
• **Website:** www.cph.org

Freelance Potential
95% written by nonstaff writers. Publishes 20 freelance submissions yearly; 10% by unpublished writers, 20% by authors who are new to the magazine. Receives 48 unsolicited mss yearly.

Submissions
Query or send complete ms; include Social Security number. Prefers email submissions to tom.nummela@cph.org. Will accept hard copy. SASE. Responds in 3 months.
Articles: To 1,100 words. How-to articles and personal experience pieces. Topics include education, theology, teaching methods, and child development.
Depts/columns: 400 words. Humor, teaching tips, and classroom strategies.
Other: Submit seasonal material 10 months in advance.

Sample Issue
30 pages (no advertising): 3 articles; 10 depts/columns. Sample copy, $4.99. Writers' guidelines available.
• "Media Resources for the Sunday School." Article explores how visual classrooms have created an environment that engages students' senses.
• "The Virtual Classroom." Article discusses how today's technology is making the dreams of teachers and students a reality.
• Sample dept/column: "Teaching Young Children" takes a look at relationship skills.

Rights and Payment
All rights. Articles, $55–$110. "The Teachers Toolbox," $20–$40. Pays on publication. Provides 1 contributor's copy.

Editor's Comments
We use very few freelance materials these days. All authors must be members of the Lutheran Church–Missouri Synod, and have previous experience writing for us.

Teachers of Vision

227 North Magnolia Avenue, Suite 2
Anaheim, CA 92801

Managing Editor: Denise Trippett

Description and Interests
This magazine has been published since 1955 for Christians who serve in public and private education. Its articles promote excellence in education.
• **Audience:** Christian teachers
• **Frequency:** Quarterly
• **Circulation:** 8,000
• **Website:** www.ceai.org

Freelance Potential
75% written by nonstaff writers. Publishes 55–70 freelance submissions yearly; few by unpublished writers, 35–40% by authors who are new to the magazine. Receives 80–100 unsolicited mss yearly.

Submissions
Send complete ms with brief biography. Prefers email submissions to tov@ceai.org. Will accept hard copy. SASE. Responds in 2–3 months.
Articles: 400–1,000 words. How-to articles, personal experience pieces, and documented reports; 800–1,000 words. Topics include education issues, educational philosophy, and methodology. Interviews with noted Christian educators; 500–800 words. Teaching techniques, news, and special events; 400–500 words.
Depts/columns: 100–200 words. Reviews of books, videos, curricula, games, and other curricula resources for K–12 teachers.
Depts/columns: Submit seasonal material 4 months in advance.

Sample Issue
14 pages (1% advertising): 6 articles; 8 depts/columns. Sample copy, free with 9x12 SASE (5 first-class stamps). Guidelines available at website.
• "Learning to Be the Teacher." Article shares the experiences of a Latin teacher.
• "Its Write Hear on the Chester Drawers." Article shares an English teacher's classroom experiences with eighth-grade students.
• Sample dept/column: "Living by the Book" offers lessons in leadership.

Rights and Payment
First and electronic rights. Articles, $20–$40. Reviews, $5. Pays on publication. Provides 2 author's copies.

Editor's Comments
We are seeking well-written articles that are not "preaching" but faith-based.

Teaching Music

The National Association for Music Education
1806 Robert Fulton Drive
Reston, VA 20191

Managing Editor: Elizabeth Pontiff

Description and Interests
This magazine offers music educators a forum for the exchange of practical ideas that will help them become more effective teachers. Written in an easy-to-read style, it includes information to inform and inspire music teachers.
• **Audience:** Teachers
• **Frequency:** 5 times each year
• **Circulation:** 80,000
• **Website:** www.menc.org

Freelance Potential
80% written by nonstaff writers. Publishes 25 freelance submissions yearly; 50% by unpublished writers. Receives 75+ queries and unsolicited mss yearly.

Submissions
Query with proposal; or send complete ms. Accepts hard copy. No simultaneous submissions. SASE. Responds to queries in 6–8 weeks; to mss in 2–4 months.
Articles: 1,000–1,400 words. Informational and how-to articles on music education. Topics include general music, band, orchestra, chorus, technology, early childhood music education, advocacy, research, teacher education, and professional development.
Depts/columns: Word lengths vary. News, reviews, editorials, and commentaries.

Sample Issue
70 pages (30% advertising): 5 articles; 12 depts/columns. Sample copy, $6. Writers' guidelines and theme list available.
• "Starting a Community Youth Orchestra." Article examines the benefits of starting a youth orchestra to provide young musicians with more ensemble play time.
• "Building Shared Goals in the High School Music Department." Article explains the importance of music faculty staff working together to achieve department goals.

Rights and Payment
All rights. No payment.

Editor's Comments
We welcome manuscripts that describe effective and innovative instructional strategies or thoughtful solutions to problems faced by music educators. We prefer pieces written in a direct, conversational style. Footnotes or endnotes are not required.

Teaching PreK–8

40 Richards Avenue
Norwalk, CT 06854

Senior Editor: Katherine Pierpont

Description and Interests
This vibrant magazine, published by a subsidiary of the venerable Highlights for Children, Inc., focuses on classroom strategies and teacher development. Its website features additional media reviews.
• **Audience:** Teachers, preK–grade 8
• **Frequency:** 8 times each year
• **Circulation:** 130,000
• **Website: www.teachingk-8.com**

Freelance Potential
80% written by nonstaff writers. Publishes 24–30 freelance submissions yearly; 97–98% by unpublished writers, 95% by authors who are new to the magazine. Receives 2,000 unsolicited mss yearly.

Submissions
Send complete ms. Accepts hard copy. No simultaneous submissions. SASE. Responds in 1 month.
Articles: To 1,000 words. Informational and how-to articles; and personal experience pieces. Topics include curriculum development; classroom management; gifted and special education; character education; teaching methods; early childhood education; math; social studies; science; and language arts.
Depts/columns: Staff written.
Artwork: Color prints. No digital images.

Sample Issue
72 pages (50% advertising): 9 articles; 19 depts/columns. Sample copy, $4.50 with 9x12 SASE (10 first-class stamps). Guidelines and theme list available.
• "A School That's Really High Tech." Article describes a middle school's comprehensive approach to technology.
• "Esmé Raji Codell: First Lady of Read-Aloud." Article profiles a teacher and literacy expert.
• "Our Changing Climate." Article takes a look at one teacher's science experiments that demonstrate global warming.

Rights and Payment
All North American serial rights. Written material, $20–$50. Artwork, payment rates vary. Pays on publication. Provides 2 contributor's copies.

Editor's Comments
We would like to see more articles focusing on good practices for teachers, and less regurgitations of in-service pieces.

Teaching Theatre

2343 Auburn Avenue
Cincinnati, OH 45219

Editor: James Palmarini

Description and Interests
Published by a professional association for theatre educators and artists, this magazine presents models for theatre education, innovative ideas, and specific teaching methodologies. The focus is on theatre education in middle and high schools.
- **Audience:** Theatre teachers
- **Frequency:** Quarterly
- **Circulation:** 4,500
- **Website:** www.edta.org

Freelance Potential
70% written by nonstaff writers. Publishes 15 freelance submissions yearly; 30% by unpublished writers, 50% by authors who are new to the magazine. Receives 75 queries yearly.

Submissions
Query with outline. Accepts hard copy. SASE. Responds in 1 month.
Articles: 1,000–3,000 words. Informational articles and personal experience pieces. Topics include theatre education, the arts, and curriculum materials.
Depts/columns: Word lengths vary. "Promptbook" features classroom exercises, ideas, technical advice, and textbook or play suggestions.

Sample Issue
30 pages (3–5% advertising): 3 articles; 2 depts/columns. Sample copy, $2 with 9x12 SASE ($2 postage). Guidelines available.
- "Learning to Listen." Article describes how tape recorders can be used to sharpen drama students' scenework.
- "Welcome to Our Theatre." Article examines the various ways guest directors can bring new experiences to a theatre program.
- Sample dept/column: "News & Notes" reports on the possibility of new Advanced Placement exams in theatre and dance.

Rights and Payment
One-time rights. Written material, payment rates vary. Pays on publication. Provides 5 contributor's copies.

Editor's Comments
Our magazine offers an even blend of advocacy, how-to, and theory. Our readers are well educated and experienced, so we don't need essays on the value of educational theatre. We want instructional pieces, curriculum ideas, and profiles of exemplary programs.

Teach Kids!

P.O. Box 348
Warrenton, MO 63383-0348

Editor: Elsie Lippy

Description and Interests
Used by Sunday school, children's church, and Bible club teachers of children ages four to eleven, this magazine includes teacher aids, ideas, and resources.
- **Audience:** Christian educators
- **Frequency:** 6 times each year
- **Circulation:** 12,000
- **Website:** www.teachkidsmag.com

Freelance Potential
75% written by nonstaff writers. Publishes 50 freelance submissions yearly; 5% by unpublished writers, 20% by authors who are new to the magazine.

Submissions
Query with outline; or send complete ms. Accepts hard copy and email submissions to editor@teachkidsmag.com. SASE. Responds to queries in 1 month, to mss in 2 months.
Articles: 800–900 words. How-to, factual, and idea pieces. Topics include Christian education, religion, teaching techniques, and understanding children.
Fiction: 800–900 words for stories written at the third- and fourth-grade level. Features contemporary stories with scriptural solutions to problems faced by today's children.
Depts/columns: "Easy Ideas," 200–300 words, offers creative ideas teachers can use with children ages 4–11.

Sample Issue
64 pages (25% advertising): 4 articles; 5 depts/columns. Sample copy, $3. Guidelines available.
- "Keeping God's Word Front and Center." Article explains the importance of using the Bible as a visual aid in the Christian classroom.
- Sample dept/column: "Flexible Lesson" is a visualized lesson plan with related activities.

Rights and Payment
All, first, one-time, or electronic rights. Written material, payment rates vary. Pays within 60 days of acceptance. Provides 1 contributor's copy or clipping.

Editor's Comments
We value writers who can bring fresh ideas to the world of winning children to Christ. We are happy to work with new writers who have taken time to study our publication and writing style. We suggest that new writers get started by submitting short articles to our "Community" department or ideas for "Basic 6" cards.

Tech Directions

Prakken Publications
832 Phoenix Drive
P.O. Box 8623
Ann Arbor, MI 48107

Managing Editor: Susanne Peckham

Description and Interests
This magazine chronicles advancements in technical and industrial education, with an emphasis on vocational training.
- **Audience:** Teachers; administrators
- **Frequency:** 10 times each year
- **Circulation:** 43,000
- **Website:** www.techdirections.com

Freelance Potential
80% written by nonstaff writers. Publishes 40 freelance submissions yearly; 50% by unpublished writers, 50% by new authors. Receives 192 unsolicited mss yearly.

Submissions
Query or send complete ms. Accepts hard copy and email to susanne@techdirections.com. SASE. Availability of artwork improves chance of acceptance. Responds to queries in 1 week, to mss in 1 month.
Articles: To 3,000 words. Informational and how-to articles. Topics include teaching techniques and unusual projects in the fields of automotives, building trades, computers, drafting, electronics, graphics, hydraulics, lasers, manufacturing, radio and TV, robotics, software, welding, woodworking, and other vocational education.
Depts/columns: Word lengths vary. Legislative updates; technology news and history; media reviews; and new product information.
Artwork: Color prints, slides, and transparencies; B/W prints. B/W line art. CAD plots.
Other: Puzzles, games, and quizzes.

Sample Issue
32 pages (40% advertising): 6 articles; 7 depts/columns; 2 quizzes. Sample copy, $5 with 9x12 SASE (2 first-class stamps). Guidelines available.
- "The Battling 'Bots of Bloomsburg High." Article details an industrial technology class in robotics.
- Sample dept/column: "Technology's Past" gives a brief history of motion-picture projection.

Rights and Payment
All rights. Articles, $50+. Depts/columns, to $25. Pays on publication. Provides 3 contributor's copies.

Editor's Comments
Although subject content is the most critical element in a manuscript, such factors as correct spelling, clear and lucid writing, good photographs and drawings, and overall neatness contribute to a favorable evaluation.

Techniques

1410 King Street
Alexandria, VA 22314

Senior Director: Peter Magnuson

Description and Interests
This publication of the Association for Career and Technical Education keeps professionals in these fields apprised of industry news and equipped with the tools they need to teach job skills effectively.
- **Audience:** Educators
- **Frequency:** 8 times each year
- **Circulation:** 35,000
- **Website:** www.acteonline.org

Freelance Potential
50% written by nonstaff writers. Publishes 10–20 freelance submissions yearly; 15% by unpublished writers, 30% by authors who are new to the magazine. Receives 96 unsolicited mss yearly.

Submissions
Query or send complete ms. Prefers email submissions to pmagnuson@acteonline.org. Will accept hard copy and disk submissions (Microsoft Word). SASE. Responds in 4 months.
Articles: To 2,000 words. Informational and how-to articles; profiles; and reviews. Topics include careers, technology, education, college, current events, science, math, and social studies.
Depts/columns: 500–850 words. Leadership, classroom management, advocacy, news, research, hot jobs, product information, opinion pieces, and legislative updates.
Artwork: Color prints and transparencies. Line art.
Other: Submit material about the end of the school year in March.

Sample Issue
62 pages (30% advertising): 9 articles; 11 depts/columns. Writers' guidelines and theme list available at website.
- "Making a Great First Impression." Article discusses teaching the effects of appearance and attitude.
- "Realize the Full Potential of Your New Facility." Article tells how to maximize operations in a new building.
- Sample dept/column: "Classroom Connection" gives tips for remaining calm in the classroom.

Rights and Payment
All rights. No payment.

Editor's Comments
Our mission is to connect education and careers through conversational yet informative articles that inspire educators to excellence.

Technology & Learning

NewBay Media LLC
1111 Bayhill Drive, Suite 125
San Bruno, CA 94066

Managing Editor: Mark Smith

Description and Interests
This magazine publishes articles that encourage educators to think about new approaches to teaching and new ways to use technology in the classroom. It includes product and website reviews as well as practical tips.
- **Audience:** Teachers; school administrators; technology coordinators
- **Frequency:** Monthly
- **Circulation:** 85,000
- **Website:** www.techlearning.com

Freelance Potential
50% written by nonstaff writers. Publishes 50 freelance submissions yearly; 50% by unpublished writers, 50% by new authors. Receives 60–96 queries yearly.

Submissions
Query with outline and clips or writing samples. Accepts hard copy and email submissions to techlearning_editors@nbmedia.com. SASE. Responds in 3 months.
Articles: 1,200–2,500 words. Informational and how-to articles. Topics include technology, education, and research.
Depts/columns: To 600 words. Product reviews, news, trends, opinions, the Internet, funding, grants, and emerging technologies.
Other: Submit material about the end of the school year in March.

Sample Issue
32 pages (40% advertising): 2 articles; 8 depts/columns. Guidelines available.
- "Measuring Up in a Flat World." Cover story discusses how to prepare for the global digital workforce.
- "One-to-One in Texas." Article chronicles a school district's path to providing all of its students with equal access to technology.
- Sample dept/column: "How To" tells how to create and post a video blog.

Rights and Payment
First rights. Articles, $400–$600. Software reviews, $150. Depts/columns, payment rates vary. Pays on publication. Provides 1 contributor's copy.

Editor's Comments
Our articles appeal to a broad audience of educators, covering a range of grade levels and subject areas. We cover all aspects of educational technology: hardware, software, and the Web.

Teen

3000 Ocean Park Boulevard, Suite 3048
Santa Monica, CA 90405

Editor: Jane Fort

Description and Interests
Teen girls turn to this photo-filled magazine for its celebrity news, fashion and beauty advice, and quizzes that help them answer their questions about themselves, relationships, and other issues. Also featured are profiles and stories about real teens.
- **Audience:** 12–16 years
- **Frequency:** Quarterly
- **Circulation:** 650,000
- **Website:** www.teenmag.com

Freelance Potential
60% written by nonstaff writers. Of the freelance submissions published yearly, 5% are by authors who are new to the magazine. Receives 500 queries yearly.

Submissions
Query for nonfiction. Send complete ms for fiction. Accepts hard copy and simultaneous submissions if identified. SASE. Responds in 2 months.
Articles: 800 words. Informational and how-to articles; and personal experience pieces. Topics include relationships, beauty, fashion, music, popular culture, recreation, the arts, crafts, current events, and social issues.
Fiction: 1,000 words. Genres include romance and inspirational fiction.
Depts/columns: Word lengths vary. Advice.

Sample Issue
110 pages (10% advertising): 8 articles; 2 stories; 30 depts/columns; 2 quizzes. Sample copy, $3.99 at newsstands.
- "Best of Both Worlds." Article profiles Miley Cyrus and Emily Osment, best friends and teen stars of the TV show *Hannah Montana*, in interview format.
- "Top 25 Hair Tips." Article outlines 25 ways to improve the health and appearance of hair.
- Sample dept/column: "Who Said?" features selected quotes from celebrities.

Rights and Payment
All rights. Written material, payment rates vary. Pays on publication. Provides 2 contributor's copies.

Editor's Comments
Prospective writers need to be in-the-know about what teens who read this publication want to know: boyfriends, girlfriends, and the latest trends. Since most of the topics have been covered many times before, a fresh, new approach is a must.

Teenage Christian Magazine

915 E Market, Box 10750
Searcy, AR 72149

Managing Editor: Laura Kaiser

Description and Interests

This growing magazine's mission is to provide a positive, faith-based approach to the issues that today's Christian teens face. It features articles that inspire, inform, and entertain.
- **Audience:** 13–19 years
- **Frequency:** Quarterly
- **Circulation:** 7,000+
- **Website:** www.tcmagazine.org

Freelance Potential

35% written by nonstaff writers. Publishes 5–10 freelance submissions yearly; 20% by unpublished writers, 30% by authors who are new to the magazine. Receives 60 queries and unsolicited mss yearly.

Submissions

Query or send complete ms. Accepts email submissions to info@tcmagazine.org. Response time varies.
Articles: 450–700 words. Informational articles; profiles; interviews; photo-essays; and personal experience pieces. Topics include health, fitness, multicultural and ethnic issues, music, popular culture, religion, and social issues.
Depts/columns: Word lengths vary. Advice, sports, and music.

Sample Issue

48 pages: 7 articles; 7 depts/columns. Sample copy, $3.95. Guidelines available at website.
- "Giving Something Back." Article profiles *High School Musical* actor Corbin Bleu and highlights his volunteering activities.
- "A Goat, Volleyball, and Jesus." Article describes the creative fundraising and evangelizing efforts of a Ugandan youth group.
- Sample dept/column: "Entertain This" reviews current movies, music, books, and electronics for teens.

Rights and Payment

All rights. Written material, payment rates vary. Payment policy varies.

Editor's Comments

We encourage freelancers to become familiar with our style before submitting work. We're most interested in ideas from our readers, particularly about popular culture. Also, interviews with inspiring Christian teens are sought. We are not looking for articles with a preachy or condescending tone.

Teen Graffiti

P.O. Box 452721
Garland, TX 75045-2721

Publisher: Sharon Jones-Scaife

Description and Interests

Teen Graffiti seeks to write on the imaginary walls between teenagers and adults, and between teenagers and their peers, all that often goes unsaid: the concerns, opinions, and dreams of young people. It also publishes the advice of experts.
- **Audience:** 12–19 years
- **Frequency:** 6 times each year
- **Circulation:** 10,000
- **Website:** www.teengraffiti.com

Freelance Potential

70% written by nonstaff writers. Publishes 30–40 freelance submissions yearly.

Submissions

Query or send complete ms. Prefers email submissions to publish@teengraffiti.com. Accepts hard copy. SASE. Response time varies.
Articles: 250 words. Informational articles; personal experience and opinion pieces; and essays. Topics include college, careers, current events, popular culture, sex, health, and social issues.
Depts/columns: 100–200 words. Advice and resources from teachers; teen-to-teen advice; and book, movie, and music reviews.
Artwork: B/W and color prints from teens only.
Other: Poetry written by teens.

Sample Issue

30 pages (3% advertising): 4 articles; 9 depts/columns; 2 poems. Sample copy, $2.75. Guidelines included in each issue.
- "What Makes My Single Mom Special." Essay by a teenage girl describes her relationship with her mother, who raised her alone.
- "My Senior Year: Advice I Must Share." Article by a recent high school graduate tells students how to make the most of their senior year.
- Sample dept/column: "Advice" encourages teenagers not to be pressured into oral sex, and explains the health risks.

Rights and Payment

One-time rights. No payment.

Editor's Comments

Our mission is to be the voice of teenagers across the nation by providing a platform for the expression of their styles, concerns, ideas, talents, achievements, and community involvement.

Teen Tribute

71 Barber Greene Road
Dons Mills, Ontario M3C 2A2
Canada

Editor: Toni-Marie Ippolito

Description and Interests
Popular culture and entertainment are the focal points of this magazine for Canadian teens. It fills its pages with celebrity profiles and interviews, as well as news about the latest movie and music releases. Fashion and beauty tips also appear regularly.
- **Audience:** 14–18 years
- **Frequency:** Quarterly
- **Circulation:** 310,000
- **Website:** www.tribute.ca

Freelance Potential
10% written by nonstaff writers. Publishes 5–10 freelance submissions yearly; 1% by authors who are new to the magazine. Receives 24 queries yearly.

Submissions
Query with clips or writing samples. Accepts hard copy. Availability of artwork improves chance of acceptance. SAE/IRC. Responds in 1–2 months.
Articles: 400–500 words. Informational articles; profiles; interviews; and personal experience pieces. Topics include movies, the film industry, entertainment, the arts, music, popular culture, and social issues.
Depts/columns: Word lengths vary. Music, DVD, and game reviews.
Artwork: Color prints or transparencies.

Sample Issue
38 pages (50% advertising): 8 articles; 9 depts/columns. Sample copy, $1.95 Canadian with 9x12 SAE/IRC ($.86 Canadian postage).
- "Two Men, One Dream: Blades of Glory." Article talks about a new comedy film that stars Will Ferrell and Jon Heder, and provides biographical information about these two actors.
- "Musical Wonder." Article interviews Ashley Tisdale, star of *High School Musical*, about her new CD and her rising success.
- Sample dept/column: "Hot Flicks" updates readers about the latest movie releases.

Rights and Payment
First serial rights. Written material, $100–$400 Canadian. Artwork, payment rates vary. Pays on publication. Provides 1 contributor's copy.

Editor's Comments
We always need celebrity profiles, so we're looking for writers who have access to the stars and can provide inside information on the entertainment world.

Teen Voices

P.O. Box 120-027
Boston, MA 02112-0027

Editor-in-Chief: Ellyn Ruthstrom

Description and Interests
The mission of this multimedia publication is to further social and economic justice by empowering teenage and young adult women. It is written by, for, and about teenage girls.
- **Audience:** YA
- **Frequency:** Monthly online; twice yearly in print
- **Circulation:** 55,000
- **Website:** www.teenvoices.com

Freelance Potential
95% written by nonstaff writers. Publishes 100 freelance submissions yearly; 95% by unpublished writers, 95% by authors who are new to the magazine. Receives 2,000 unsolicited mss yearly.

Submissions
Accepts mss written by girls ages 13–19 only. Send complete ms. SASE. Response time varies.
Articles: Word lengths vary. Informational and self-help articles; interviews; and profiles. Topics include ethnic and religious traditions, the Internet, multicultural issues, surviving sexual assault, family relationships, teen motherhood, disability, health, nutrition, cooking, the arts, the media, and activism.
Fiction: Word lengths vary. Humorous, inspirational, contemporary, ethnic, and multicultural fiction.
Depts/columns: Word lengths vary. "Read It," "Hear It," "Watch It," "Girl Talk," "SHOUT! Notes," "Top 10."
Other: Poetry. Comic strips.

Sample Issue
57 pages (8% advertising): 7 articles; 5 depts/columns; 10 poems. Guidelines available.
- "Chick Pop That Won't Stop." Article profiles artist/musician Magdalen Hsu-Li.
- "From Girlhood to Womanhood: Are We There Yet?" Article details rites of passage.
- Sample dept/column: "Girl Talk" discusses young people advocating for equality and a new vaccine for HPV.

Rights and Payment
First or one-time rights. No payment. Provides 5 contributor's copies.

Editor's Comments
We are always looking for submissions! Don't be limited by our regular features—send us your essays, poems, or other writing on any topic.

Teenwire.com

434 West 33rd Street
New York, NY 10001

Editor: Amy Bryant

Description and Interests
For the past nine years, this e-zine has been providing teens with the straight facts about sexuality to aid them in making responsible choices. It includes fresh content about self-esteem, body image, drugs and alcohol, communication, and relationship advice.
• **Audience:** 13–21 years
• **Frequency:** Daily
• **Hits per month:** 15 million
• **Website: www.teenwire.com**

Freelance Potential
25% written by nonstaff writers. Publishes 100–156 freelance submissions yearly; 10% by unpublished writers, 25% by authors who are new to the magazine.

Submissions
Query with brief biography and clips or writing samples. Accepts email queries to twstaff@ppfa.org (include "Write for Teenwire" in subject line). Responds in 1 week.
Articles: 500 words. Informational and factual articles; profiles; interviews; and Spanish pieces. Topics include teen relationships, sexual health, birth control, pregnancy, sexually transmitted diseases, teen activism, international youth issues, the arts, colleges, careers, current events, music, popular culture, recreation, substance abuse, social concerns, and multicultural and ethnic issues.
Other: Puzzles, games, and quizzes.

Sample Issue
Sample copy and guidelines available at website.
• *"Teenwire.com Talks with Judy Blume."* Article features an interview with the famous author of young adult books.
• "Being Stephanie Daley." Article offers an interview with Amber Tamblyn, the star of the movie *Stephanie Daley*.
• "Crystal Meth Part Two: The Body Breakdown." Article explores this dangerous and addictive stimulant and its effects on the body.

Rights and Payment
All rights. Articles, $300. Pays on acceptance.

Editor's Comments
We are interested in receiving inquiries from freelance writers who can cover topics such as sexual health, sexuality, global issues, relationships, and teen activism.

Texas Child Care Quarterly

P.O. Box 162881
Austin, TX 78716-2881

Editor: Louise Parks

Description and Interests
Despite the word "Texas" in its name, this publication bills itself as "the quarterly journal for caregivers everywhere." It contains features on parenting, discipline, and child development alongside information on running a child-care business.
• **Audience:** Child-care workers and parents
• **Frequency:** Quarterly
• **Circulation:** 32,000
• **Website: www.childcarequarterly.com**

Freelance Potential
50% written by nonstaff writers. Publishes 12–15 freelance submissions yearly; 10% by unpublished writers, 50% by authors who are new to the magazine. Receives 24–36 unsolicited mss yearly.

Submissions
Send complete ms. Accepts email submissions to editor@childcarequarterly.com. Responds in 3 weeks.
Articles: 2,500 words. Informational articles. Topics include child care, education, program administration, infant care, professional development, and issues and activities relating to school-age children.
Depts/columns: Word lengths vary. Child-care news, child-care licensing, product information, early childhood intervention, business tips, study guides, and parenting news.
Other: Submit seasonal material 6 months in advance.

Sample Issue
44 pages (no advertising): 6 articles; 5 depts/columns, 1 special section. Sample copy, $6.25. Guidelines available at website.
• "Ouch! Biting Hurts." Article discusses why young children bite and how to prevent the behavior.
• "Manage the Mess." Article provides tips for keeping an early childhood classroom relatively organized.
• Sample dept/column: "Stuff & New Stuff" reviews activity guides for school-age children.

Rights and Payment
All rights. No payment. Provides 3 contributor's copies and a 1-year subscription.

Editor's Comments
We publish two types of articles: feature articles that focus on child development theory and professional development; and child-building articles that provide hands-on activities to do with children. Both types should support adults caring for children.

Thrasher

1303 Underwood Avenue
San Francisco, CA 94121

Managing Editor: Ryan Henry

Description and Interests
Thrasher is dedicated to covering the sports of skate-boarding and snowboarding. Read primarily by teen boys, it reports on equipment, competitions, and the music and culture surrounding these sports. Graphic language is part of this scene, and is often included in the magazine.
- **Audience:** Boys, 12–20 years
- **Frequency:** Monthly
- **Circulation:** 200,000
- **Website:** www.thrashermagazine.com

Freelance Potential
20% written by nonstaff writers. Publishes 20 free-lance submissions yearly; 100% by unpublished writers. Receives 72–120 unsolicited mss yearly.

Submissions
Send complete ms. Prefers email submissions to ryan@thrashermagazine.com (Macintosh compatible Microsoft Word attachments). Will accept hard copy, disk submissions, and simultaneous submissions if identified. Availability of artwork improves chance of acceptance. SASE. Responds in 1 month.
Articles: To 1,500 words. Informational articles; pro-files; and interviews. Topics include skateboarding, snowboarding, sports, and music.
Fiction: To 2,500 words. Stories with skateboarding and snowboarding themes.
Depts/columns: 750–1,000 words. News, tips.
Artwork: Color prints or transparencies; 35mm B/W negatives. B/W or color line art.

Sample Issue
236 pages (45% advertising): 12 articles; 8 depts/columns. Sample copy, $3.99. Guidelines available.
- "Torta Tour." Article recounts a 19-day trip across Vancouver visiting skateboarding sites and doing photo shoots of tricks.
- "Cody McEntire." Article profiles a well-known skateboarder.

Rights and Payment
First North American serial rights. Written material, $.15 per word. Artwork, payment rates vary. Pays on publication. Provides 2 contributor's copies.

Editor's Comments
You must be very familiar with the skateboarding culture in order to capture the kind of writing style that we're looking for.

Tiger Beat

330 North Brand
Glendale, CA 91203

Editor: Leesa Coble

Description and Interests
When tweens want the scoop on their favorite young stars, they turn to *Tiger Beat*. This celebrity-focused magazine uses a bright, busy, photo-heavy layout and brief text peppered with hip jargon to deliver interviews and tidbits to its young audience.
- **Audience:** 10–16 years
- **Frequency:** Monthly
- **Circulation:** 200,000
- **Website:** www.tigerbeatmag.com

Freelance Potential
1% written by nonstaff writers. Publishes 2 freelance submissions yearly; 50% by authors who are new to the magazine. Receives 20 queries yearly.

Submissions
Query with résumé and clips for celebrity angles only. Accepts hard copy and simultaneous submissions if identified. SASE. Responds in 3 months.
Articles: To 700 words. Interviews and profiles. Topics include young celebrities in the film, television, and recording industries.
Depts/columns: Staff written.
Artwork: Color digital images.
Other: Submit seasonal material 3 months in advance.

Sample Issue
82 pages (1% advertising): 14 articles; 10 quizzes; 13 depts/columns.
- "I Wish I Could Take It Back." Article features a dis-cussion with *Hannah Montana* star Miley Cyrus about her biggest mistake.
- "Is Life Really That Sweet?" Article spotlights the cast of *The Suite Life of Zack and Cody*.
- Sample dept/column: "Hear It!" presents an inter-view with Corbin Bleu.

Rights and Payment
All rights. Written material, payment rates vary. Pays on publication. Provides 2 contributor's copies.

Editor's Comments
We would like to see more celebrity interview tran-scripts and Hollywood event coverage. While our staff and regular contributors write the bulk of our copy, we are constantly on the lookout for new angles on young actors and recording artists. Our goal is to provide our readers with the best news, features, and pin-ups of their favorite stars.

Time for Kids

Time-Life Building
1271 Avenue of the Americas
New York, NY 10020

Editor: Martha Pickerill

Description and Interests
This children's version of the well-known news-magazine is distributed through schools to be used as a teaching tool with elementary and middle school students. *Time for Kids* provides news and discussions of current events in a format appealing to younger readers.
• **Audience:** 5–12 years
• **Frequency:** Weekly
• **Circulation:** 4.1 million
• **Website: www.timeforkids.com**

Freelance Potential
4% written by nonstaff writers. Publishes 4 freelance submissions yearly. Receives many queries and unsolicited mss yearly.

Submissions
Send résumé only. No unsolicited mss.
Articles: Word lengths vary. Informational and biographical articles. Topics include world news, current events, animals, education, health, fitness, science, technology, math, social studies, geography, multicultural and ethnic issues, music, popular culture, recreation, regional news, sports, travel, and social issues.
Depts/columns: Word lengths vary. Profiles and short news items.
Artwork: Color prints and transparencies.
Other: Theme-related activities.

Sample Issue
8 pages (no advertising): 3 articles; 4 depts/columns. Subscription, $3.95.
• "The Magic Moment." Article reports on the excitement surrounding the release of the last book in the Harry Potter series.
• "Hair-Raising High School Musical." Article interviews Tracy Turnblad and other members of the movie musical *Hairspray*.
• Sample dept/column: "World Report" offers facts about the 400th anniversary of Jamestown.

Rights and Payment
All rights. Written material, payment rates vary. Pays on publication.

Editor's Comments
Engaging, informative, and newsworthy pieces that kids find interesting are the mainstay of our magazine. If you wish to write for us you must submit a résumé describing your qualifications.

Today's Catholic Teacher

2621 Dryden Road, Suite 300
Dayton, OH 45439

Editor-in-Chief: Mary Noschang

Description and Interests
This magazine is written for educators concerned with private education in general and Catholic education in particular. Its articles provide practical information for classroom teachers, though it is also read by administrators, pastors, and parents.
• **Audience:** Teachers, grades K–8
• **Frequency:** 6 times each year
• **Circulation:** 50,000
• **Website: www.peterli.com**

Freelance Potential
95% written by nonstaff writers. Publishes 20 freelance submissions yearly; 50% by authors who are new to the magazine. Receives 190+ queries and unsolicited mss each year.

Submissions
Query or send complete ms. Accepts hard copy, disk submissions with hard copy, email submissions to mnoschang@peterli.com; and simultaneous submissions if identified. SASE. Responds to queries in 1 month, to mss in 3 months.
Articles: 600–1,500 words. Informational, self-help, and how-to articles. Topics include technology, fundraising, classroom management, curriculum development, administration, and educational issues and trends.
Depts/columns: Word lengths vary. Opinions, news, software, character development, curricula, teaching tools, and school profiles.
Artwork: 8x10 color prints, slides, or transparencies.
Other: Classroom-ready reproducible activity pages.

Sample Issue
66 pages (45% advertising): 5 articles; 8 depts/columns. Sample copy, $3. Guidelines available.
• "Books That Turn Boys into Readers." Article suggests ways to encourage boys to read.
• "Podcasting in Education." Article discusses the classroom benefits of this technology.
• Sample dept/column: "School of the Month" profiles a school's creative arts program.

Rights and Payment
All rights. Written material, $100–$250. Pays on publication. Provides contributor's copies.

Editor's Comments
We look for high-interest feature articles and special reports written in a direct yet informal style. Query letters are encouraged.

Today's Christian Woman

465 Gundersen Drive
Carol Stream, IL 60188

Associate Editor: Lisa Ann Cockrel

Description and Interests
Contemporary issues that affect the lives of women in their 20s, 30s, and 40s are addressed in *Today's Christian Woman*. It provides readers with articles covering family life, parenting, and relationships. All of its material offers Christian perspectives and solutions to everyday problems.
- **Audience:** Women
- **Frequency:** 6 times each year
- **Circulation:** 250,000
- **Website: www.todayschristianwoman.com**

Freelance Potential
85% written by nonstaff writers. Publishes 65 freelance submissions yearly; 5% by unpublished writers. Receives 1,200 queries yearly.

Submissions
Query with résumé and summary. Accepts hard copy. No simultaneous submissions. SASE. Responds in 2 months.
Articles: 1,000–2,000 words. Informational and self-help articles; personal experience pieces; and humor. Topics include parenting, family issues, relationships, spiritual living, contemporary women's concerns, and turning points in life.
Depts/columns: 100–300 words. First-person narratives, reviews, and pieces on parenting and faith.

Sample Issue
66 pages (25% advertising): 8 articles; 9 depts/columns. Sample copy, $5 with 9x12 SASE ($3.19 postage). Guidelines available.
- "The HPV Vaccine." Article provides facts about Gardisil and discusses the concerns many conservative parents have about the vaccine.
- "Whatever Happened to Family Meals?" Article offers one woman's perspective on "eating on the run."
- "From Tears to Joy." Article chronicles how a miscarriage led to a ministry to unwed mothers.

Rights and Payment
First rights. Written material, $.20 per word. Pays on publication. Provides 2 contributor's copies.

Editor's Comments
The most successful submissions contain both real-life anecdotes and quotes and advice from Christian professionals. Many of our readers are actively involved in a church and knowledgeable about the Bible, but others are new to the faith.

Today's Parent

1 Mount Pleasant Road, 8th Floor
Toronto, Ontario M4Y 2Y5
Canada

Managing Editor

Description and Interests
Today's Parent strives to fill its pages with positive, supportive articles that help its readers make good parenting decisions. Targeting Canadian parents of children up to the age of 14, it features both practical and philosophical articles.
- **Audience:** Parents
- **Frequency:** Monthly
- **Circulation:** 215,000
- **Website: www.todaysparent.com**

Freelance Potential
Of the freelance submissions published yearly, many are by unpublished writers and authors who are new to the magazine. Receives many queries yearly.

Submissions
Query with clips or writing samples; include information on article length. No unsolicited mss. Accepts hard copy. SAE/IRC. Response time varies.
Articles: 1,800–2,500 words. Informational, how-to, and self-help articles. Topics include parenting, family life, child development, health, nutrition, pregnancy, and childbirth.
Depts/columns: First-person forum for parents, 800 words; women's health and well-being, 1,200 words; education, 1,200–1,500 words; humor, 500 words.

Sample Issue
146 pages (15% advertising): 6 articles; 1 children's story; 13 depts/columns. Sample copy, $4.50 (Canadian) at newsstands. Guidelines available at website.
- "Know Your Place: Birth Order." Article analyzes how birth order can impact a child's personality and tells how to tailor your parenting style to the needs of oldest, middle, and youngest children.
- "Nature's Call." Article discusses the benefits of teaching kids to explore the great outdoors.
- "Top Wheels." Article offers a guide to the best new family vehicles.

Rights and Payment
All North American serial rights. Articles, $700–$1,500. Depts/columns, payment rates vary. Pays on publication. Provides 2 contributor's copies.

Editor's Comments
We know that mothers and fathers are "parenting experts" too, and we rely on their anecdotes and experiences as sources of wisdom in our articles. We try to balance the light-hearted with the investigative.

Today's Playground Magazine

360 B Street
Idaho Falls, ID 83402

Editor: Shannon Amy

Description and Interests
Described as "the world's authority on play structures, amenities, and industry trends," this magazine provides information to people who plan and manage playgrounds, such as parks and recreation directors, early childhood center directors, and school administrators. It covers water play equipment, climbing walls, and skate parks, as well as playgrounds.
- **Audience:** Adults
- **Frequency:** 7 times each year
- **Circulation:** 35,000
- **Website:** www.todaysplayground.com

Freelance Potential
40% written by nonstaff writers. Publishes 14–20 freelance submissions yearly; 30% by authors who are new to the magazine.

Submissions
Query or send complete ms. Accepts hard copy and email to shannon@todaysplayground.com. SASE. Responds in 1–2 months.
Articles: 800–1,200 words. Informational and how-to articles. Topics include all kinds of play structures, playground planning and design, water parks, skate parks, climbing walls, industry trends, and amenities.
Depts/columns: Word lengths vary. Legal issues, news, industry updates, landscaping, and design.

Sample Issue
62 pages: 8 articles; 8 depts/columns. Sample copy, $5. Guidelines available.
- "The Hottest in Cool Fun!" Article talks about ways kids in the inner city can have fun and cool off with water structures.
- "Cozy Spaces for Little People." Article describes small areas for young children that provide a perception of separation from adult interruptions.
- "Learn the 3 Cs of Outdoor Play." Article emphasizes the importance of getting kids outside, away from television and video games.

Rights and Payment
First serial rights. Articles, $100–$300. Depts/columns, $50–$175. Payment policy varies.

Editor's Comments
We would like to hear from individuals with experience in the playground industry and in early childhood development. Early childhood structures are of special interest.

Toledo Area Parent News

1120 Adams Street
Toledo, OH 43624

Managing Editor: Jason Webber

Description and Interests
A broad spectrum of parenting issues—from education to health, fitness, and family entertainment—is covered in this free tabloid for Toledo-area parents. All of its material has a local slant, with references to Toledo-area events and resources.
- **Audience:** Parents
- **Frequency:** Monthly
- **Circulation:** 81,000
- **Website:** www.toledoparent.com

Freelance Potential
75% written by nonstaff writers. Publishes 12 freelance submissions yearly; 10% by unpublished writers, 20% by authors who are new to the magazine. Receives 48 queries and unsolicited mss yearly.

Submissions
Query with clips; or send complete ms. Prefers email submissions to jwebber@toledoparent.com. Will accept hard copy. SASE. Responds in 1 month.
Articles: 700–2,000 words. Informational articles; profiles; and interviews. Topics include family issues, parenting, teen issues, education, social issues, health, and fitness.
Depts/columns: Word lengths vary. Restaurant reviews and brief news items related to family issues.

Sample Issue
40 pages (60% advertising): 1 article; 7 depts/columns; 1 calendar. Sample copy available via email request to kdevol@toledocitypaper.com. Writers' guidelines available.
- "That's Entertainment!" Article provides an overview of the best entertainers for children's parties in the Toledo area.
- Sample dept/column: "Parent Profile" looks at the work of an educator who gathers and reports on important data regarding teen drug use in Lucas and Wood counties.

Rights and Payment
All North American serial rights. Written material, $30–$200. Pays on publication.

Editor's Comments
While we're always interested in providing our readers with information on how to parent better, it is important to note that everything we publish has a local slant. We only want profiles of local parents and information about local resources and events.

Transitions Abroad

P.O. Box 745
Bennington, VT 05201

Editor/Publisher: Sherry Schwarz

Description and Interests
Anyone planning a cultural immersion trip should find this publication useful, as it provides practical guidance to educational travel.
- **Audience:** YA–Adult
- **Frequency:** 6 times each year
- **Circulation:** 12,000
- **Website: www.transitionsabroad.com**

Freelance Potential
90% written by nonstaff writers. Publishes 250 freelance submissions yearly; 70% by unpublished writers, 90% by new authors. Receives 300–420 mss yearly.

Submissions
Prefers query with outline. Will accept complete ms with bibliography. Prefers email submissions to editor@transitionsabroad.com. Will accept hard copy. Availability of artwork improves chance of acceptance. SASE. Responds in 1–2 months.
Articles: To 1,500 words. Informational and how-to articles. Topics include living, working, and studying abroad; immersion travel by region; and cultural travel trends.
Depts/columns: Word lengths vary. Budget travel, responsible travel, volunteer travel, adventure travel, and senior travel; interviews; food; music; and book reviews.
Artwork: Color prints or slides; JPEG or TIFF images.

Sample Issue
112 pages (50% advertising): 30 articles; 12 depts/columns. Sample copy, $4.95. Guidelines and editorial calendar available at website only.
- "Geocaching." Article describes the trend of global treasure hunts.
- "Trekking the Himalayas." Article provides information on gear, budget, weather, and terrain.
- Sample dept/column: "Travel to Eat" explores Malay cuisine and includes a recipe.

Rights and Payment
First rights. Written material, $2 per column inch; minimum $25. Artwork, payment rates vary. Pays on publication. Provides 2 contributor's copies.

Editor's Comments
We do not want sightseeing or destination pieces that focus on what to see rather than on the people and culture, nor do we want travelogues. Please submit practical information gained from first-hand experience.

Treasure Valley Family

13191 West Scotfield Street
Boise, ID 83713-0899

Publisher: Liz Buckingham

Description and Interests
This is a free, regional, family-focused magazine distributed in the state of Idaho. It provides resources, activities, and advice for local parents with children under the age of 12.
- **Audience:** Parents
- **Frequency:** 10 times each year
- **Circulation:** 20,000
- **Website: www.treasurevalleyfamily.com**

Freelance Potential
95% written by nonstaff writers. Publishes 20 freelance submissions yearly; 1–2% by authors who are new to the magazine. Receives 500 unsolicited mss yearly.

Submissions
Send complete ms with résumé and clips. Accepts hard copy and email submissions to magazine@treasurevalleyfamily.com. SASE. Responds in 2–3 months.
Articles: To 1,200 words. Informational and how-to articles. Topics include education, health, fitness, travel, crafts, hobbies, the arts, and recreation.
Depts/columns: 700–900 words. Resources, activities, book reviews, family interviews, community news, advice, age-specific games, and tips.

Sample Issue
58 pages (45% advertising): 3 articles; 10 depts/columns. Sample copy, free with 9x12 SASE ($1.50 postage). Guidelines available.
- "Hidden Sweets and Sweeteners in Kids' Diets." Article by a registered dietician details the nutritional pitfalls of common foods and beverages, and provides guidelines for recognizing them.
- "When to Take a Child to the ER." Article discusses the reasons for increased emergency-room visits and how to define urgent care.
- Sample dept/column: "Family Support" contains a brief profile of the Big Brothers–Big Sisters mentorship program.

Rights and Payment
First North American serial rights. All material, payment rates vary. Pays on publication. Provides 2 copies.

Editor's Comments
When submitting your work, please include word count, address, phone number, Social Security number, and a one-sentence byline. Include your fee or pricing.

True Girl

703 Michigan Avenue, Suite 2
LaPorte, IN 46350

Editor-in-Chief: Brandi Lee

Description and Interests
This magazine for Catholic teenage girls focuses on faith, life, and wholesome-yet-hip fashion. It seeks to provide practical advice on relationships, to help build real-world skills, and to promote community service and a positive self-image among its readership.
- **Audience:** Girls, 12–18 years
- **Frequency:** 6 times each year
- **Circulation:** 5,000+
- **Website:** www.truegirlonline.com

Freelance Potential
60% written by nonstaff writers. Publishes 25 freelance submissions yearly; 5% by unpublished writers, 50% by authors who are new to the magazine. Receives 25 queries and unsolicited mss yearly.

Submissions
Query or send complete ms. Accepts hard copy and email to brandi@truegirlonline.com. No simultaneous submissions. SASE. Responds in 4–6 weeks.
Articles: 800–1,200 words. Informational, self-help, and how-to articles; and personal experience and opinion pieces. Topics include faith, recreation, current events, and social issues.
Depts/columns: 150–1,200 words. Social-justice and teen issues; life skills; spirituality; education; book, movie, and music reviews; crafts; and interviews.
Other: Quizzes, 6 questions with answers and corresponding scoring.

Sample Issue
31 pages (no advertising): 2 articles; 10 depts/columns; 1 quiz. Guidelines available.
- "Post-Prom." Article provides guidelines for choosing responsible prom-night activities.
- "iCulture." Author discusses balancing self and others in accordance with Catholic teachings.
- Sample dept/column: "True Girl Saint" takes lessons from the life of Saint Hildegard.

Rights and Payment
First North American serial and electronic rights for 1 year. Written material, $.15–$.20 per word or flat fee. Pays on acceptance.

Editor's Comments
Our tone may range from lighthearted and fun to serious and introspective, depending on the subject matter. Articles should assume a certain level of education and maturity in our audience.

Tulsa Kids Magazine

1820 South Boulder Avenue, Suite 400
Tulsa, OK 74119-4409

Editor: Betty Casey

Description and Interests
Parents in Tulsa, Oklahoma, read this publication for enlightening articles on family matters, including health and education, as well as for coverage of regional travel, events, and activities.
- **Audience:** Families
- **Frequency:** Monthly
- **Circulation:** 20,000
- **Website:** www.tulsakids.com

Freelance Potential
99% written by nonstaff writers. Publishes 100+ freelance submissions yearly; 5% by unpublished writers, 1% by authors who are new to the magazine. Receives 1,200 unsolicited mss yearly.

Submissions
Send complete ms. Accepts hard copy, disk submissions, and simultaneous submissions if identified. SASE. Responds in 2–3 months.
Articles: 500–800 words. Informational articles; profiles; interviews; humor; and personal experience pieces. Topics include family life, education, parenting, recreation, entertainment, college, health, fitness, careers, crafts, and social issues.
Depts/columns: 100–300 words. News, book reviews, safety, and family cooking.

Sample Issue
52 pages (50% advertising): 2 articles; 11 depts/columns; 1 calendar of events. Sample copy, free with 10x13 SASE ($.75 postage). Guidelines available.
- "The Art of Summer: The Art of BBQ and More Fabulous Festivals, Events and Celebrations." Article describes an annual fundraising event that blends art and barbeque.
- "Family Travel." Article explores the family fun potential of six resort parks in the state.
- Sample dept/column: "Raising Responsible Children: Making a Difference When Your Child Is Different" profiles a mother who learned to be an advocate for her developmentally disabled son.

Rights and Payment
One-time rights. Written material, $25–$100. Payment policy varies. Provides 1 contributor's copy.

Editor's Comments
We do not want any more overly long articles or personal essays. Send concise travel articles and collections of four or five recipes instead.

Turtle

Children's Better Health Institute
1100 Waterway Boulevard
P.O. Box 567
Indianapolis, IN 46206–0567

Editor: Terry Harshman

Description and Interests
Like its sister publication, *Children's Playmate*, this magazine for preschoolers features health-focused stories, puzzles, and activities, including rebus fiction and extra-large type to aid emerging readers.
- **Audience:** 2–5 years
- **Frequency:** 6 times each year
- **Circulation:** 382,000
- **Website:** www.turtlemag.org

Freelance Potential
20% written by nonstaff writers. Publishes 20 freelance submissions yearly.

Submissions
Send complete ms. Accepts hard copy. SASE. Responds in 2–3 months.
Articles: To 500 words. Informational articles and book reviews. Topics include health, fitness, nutrition, nature, the environment, science, hobbies, and crafts.
Fiction: To 100 words for rebus stories. Genres include mystery; adventure; fantasy; humor; problem-solving stories; and contemporary, ethnic, and multicultural fiction.
Other: Puzzles, activities, and games. Poetry. Submit seasonal material 8 months in advance.

Sample Issue
34 pages (6% advertising): 1 story; 1 rebus; 3 poems; 4 depts/columns; 8 activities. Sample copy, $1.75 with 9x12 SASE. Guidelines available.
- "I'm a Hungry Apatosaurus." Story tells about a boy who pretends he is a plant-eating dinosaur and learns where his food comes from in the process.
- "The Ant's Breakfast." Rebus follows an insect on his quest to bring home breakfast.
- Sample dept/column: "Action Time" is a rhyme that encourages children to stomp around and roar like dinosaurs while someone reads it to them.

Rights and Payment
All rights. Articles and fiction, $.22 per word. Other material, payment rates vary. Pays on publication. Provides up to 10 contributor's copies.

Editor's Comments
We are committed to improving the health and well-being of children. Our purpose is to encourage children of all races and cultures to strive for excellence in the areas of academics, personal fitness, and science.

Twins

11211 East Arapahoe Road, Suite 101
Centennial, CO 80112

Editor-in-Chief: Susan Alt

Description and Interests
This consumer publication focuses on providing information and education to parents of twins, triplets, and higher order multiples. Child development, baby care, traveling with young children, and new products and supplies are the topics that are typically covered in each issue.
- **Audience:** Parents
- **Frequency:** 6 times each year
- **Circulation:** 40,000
- **Website:** www.twinsmagazine.com

Freelance Potential
80% written by nonstaff writers. Publishes 60 freelance submissions yearly; 25% by unpublished writers, 25% by authors who are new to the magazine. Receives 252 queries yearly.

Submissions
Query. Accepts email queries to editor@businessword.com. Responds in 3 months.
Articles: 800–1,300 words. Informational and how-to articles; profiles; and personal experience pieces. Topics include parenting, family life, health, fitness, education, music, the arts, house and home, nutrition, diet, sports, social issues, crafts, and hobbies.
Depts/columns: To 800 words. News, new product information, opinion pieces, and short items on child development.

Sample Issue
62 pages (30% advertising): 10 articles; 12 depts/columns. Sample copy, $5.50. Writers' guidelines available at website.
- "The Truth About Antibacterial Soaps." Article explains why plain old soap and water may be healthier for children than antibacterial soaps.
- "Best Friends for Life." Article details the unique connections that form between twins and explains how to nurture those bonds.
- Sample dept/column: "Twin Takes" discusses when to intervene in sibling squabbles.

Rights and Payment
All rights. Written material, payment rates vary. Pays on publication. Provides 2 contributor's copies.

Editor's Comments
Parents turn to our magazine for professional advice and reassurance. Contributors should use a friendly, conversational tone.

Twist

270 Sylvan Avenue
Englewood Cliffs, NJ 07632

Associate Editor: Ellen Collis

Description and Interests

This colorful, photo-packed magazine provides teens with intimate details about their favorite young celebrities in articles built around interview quotes and gossip. It also features "Star Style" fashion layouts, beauty tips, and romantic advice for its largely female readership.

- **Audience:** 14–19 years
- **Frequency:** 10 times each year
- **Circulation:** 230,000
- **Website: www.twistmagazine.com**

Freelance Potential

5% written by nonstaff writers. Publishes 10 freelance submissions yearly; 5% by unpublished writers, 5% by authors who are new to the magazine. Receives 240 queries yearly.

Submissions

Query. Accepts hard copy. SASE. Responds in 2–3 weeks.
Articles: Word lengths vary. Informational articles and humor. Topics include celebrities, popular culture, music, movies, fashion, beauty, health, fitness, nutrition, sex, and relationships.
Depts/columns: Word lengths vary. Advice, horoscopes, new fashion and beauty products, and embarrassing moments.
Other: Quizzes.

Sample Issue

86 pages (25% advertising): 11 articles; 26 depts/columns; 3 quizzes. Sample copy, $3.99 with 9x12 SASE. Guidelines available.

- "Flirt Fest: Summer Love Secrets." Article features quotes from teenage celebrities about their summer crushes.
- "Five Things You Didn't Know About Harry Potter." Article gives behind-the-scenes information about the latest Harry Potter film.
- Sample dept/column: "The Must List" features the latest movie and music releases.

Rights and Payment

First North American serial rights. Written material, payment rates vary. Pays on acceptance. Provides 2 contributor's copies.

Editor's Comments

We are always in need of original quizzes and celebrity interviews.

U Mag

United Services Automobile Association
9800 Fredericksburg Road
San Antonio, TX 78288-0264

Editor

Description and Interests

This is one of several publications that the United Services Automobile Association (USAA) sends for free to its members' children. Its goal is to develop a lifelong relationship with the next generation while helping them grow into responsible adults.

- **Audience:** 8–12 years
- **Frequency:** Quarterly
- **Circulation:** 600,000
- **Website: www.usaa.com**

Freelance Potential

90% written by nonstaff writers. Publishes 10 freelance submissions yearly; 1% by unpublished writers, 5% by authors who are new to the magazine. Receives 20 queries yearly.

Submissions

Query with résumé and clips. Accepts hard copy. SASE. Responds in 6–8 weeks.
Articles: Word lengths vary. Informational, self-help, and how-to articles; profiles; interviews; and personal experience pieces. Topics include hobbies, history, mathematics, music, popular culture, current events, science, technology, social issues, the environment, the arts, travel, finance, and safety issues.
Other: Puzzles, games, activities, and jokes.

Sample Issue

15 pages (no advertising): 4 articles; 3 activities. Sample copy, free with 9x12 SASE ($2 postage). Guidelines and theme list available.

- "Special Delivery." Article provides guidelines for sending care packages to deployed military service members.
- "A Breath of Fresh Air." Article profiles two young sisters who advocate for environmentally-friendly cement production.
- "Pet Math." Article covers the cost of keeping a pet.

Rights and Payment

All rights. Written material, payment rates vary. Pays on acceptance. Provides 3–5 contributor's copies.

Editor's Comments

We prefer that profile subjects be young USAA members and their families, but it is not mandatory. Profile subjects don't have to be super-kids. Instead, we aim to profile children that our readers—who are mostly current and former military dependents—can relate to.

The Universe in the Classroom

Astronomical Society of the Pacific
390 Ashton Avenue
San Francisco, CA 94112

Editor: Anna Hurst

Description and Interests
This free, online newsletter from the Astronomical Society of the Pacific is a great resource for teachers and parents who homeschool. Specifically geared toward elementary and secondary school students, it offers interesting and well-researched articles on astronomy, along with activities that bring lessons to life for students.
- **Audience:** Teachers
- **Frequency:** Quarterly
- **Hits per month:** 10,000
- **Website: www.astrosociety.org**

Freelance Potential
75% written by nonstaff writers. Publishes 8 freelance submissions yearly; 10% by unpublished writers, 75% by authors who are new to the magazine. Receives 12 queries yearly.

Submissions
Query with outline. Accepts hard copy. Availability of artwork improves chance of acceptance. SASE. Responds 1 month.
Articles: 3,000 words. Informational and factual articles. Topics include astronomy, teaching methods, and astrobiology.
Artwork: Color prints and transparencies.
Other: Classroom activities.

Sample Issue
Sample copy available at website.
- "Hubble Observations of Ceres and Pluto: A Closer Look at the 'Ugly Ducklings' of the Solar System." Article explores the history of how planets are defined, and the controversy surrounding Pluto's recent demotion to dwarf planet.
- "Egg Balancing at the Equinox: Good or Bad Astronomy?" Article explains the connection between the vernal equinox and the contention that eggs can be balanced only at this time.

Rights and Payment
One-time rights. No payment.

Editor's Comments
We expect authors to have expert knowledge about their topics, and to be able to convey that knowledge in a way that gets students excited about learning. We're interested in any astronomical topic. Send us your ideas, and include at least one hands-on activity related to the subject.

USA Gymnastics

Pan American Plaza
201 South Capitol Avenue, Suite 300
Indianapolis, IN 46225

Publication Director: Luan Peszek

Description and Interests
Young gymnastic athletes and enthusiasts find information about competitions, training, and up-and-coming stars in this magazine. It covers men's and women's gymnastics, rhythmic gymnastics, and trampoline tumbling.
- **Audience:** 10+ years
- **Frequency:** 6 times each year
- **Circulation:** 98,000
- **Website: www.usa-gymnastics.org**

Freelance Potential
5% written by nonstaff writers. Publishes 5–10 freelance submissions yearly; 5% by experts. Receives 6 queries and unsolicited mss yearly.

Submissions
Query or send complete ms. Accepts email submissions to lpeszek@usa-gymnastics.org. Responds in 1–2 months.
Articles: To 1,000 words. Informational articles; profiles; and personal experience pieces. Topics include all aspects of gymnastics, as well as sports psychology and nutrition.
Depts/columns: Word lengths vary. Event schedules and results, gym updates.

Sample Issue
50 pages (35% advertising): 3 articles; 4 depts/columns. Sample copy, $3.95. Guidelines available.
- "Worlds 2006." Article reports that the U.S. earned five silver medals at the World Championships in Aarhus, Denmark.
- "Junior Pan Am Championships." Article describes both the men's and women's results from a competition held every two years, and includes short profiles of star athletes.
- Sample dept/column: "Faces in the Gym" features photos and short write-ups about athletes who are making their mark on the sport of gymnastics.

Rights and Payment
All rights. Written material, payment rates vary. Pays on publication.

Editor's Comments
We try to present editorial content that will connect with gymnasts, parents, coaches, volunteers, clubs, and fans of this sport. We want to inspire and enable our readers to reach excellence. Most of our contributors are experts in this field.

U-Turn Magazine

United Services Automobile Association
9800 Fredericksburg Road
San Antonio, TX 78288-0264

U-Turn Editor

Description and Interests
This is one of several publications that the United Services Automobile Association (USAA) sends for free to its members' children, who are current and former military dependents. Its goal is to develop a lifelong relationship with the next generation while helping them grow into responsible adults.
- **Audience:** 13–17 years
- **Frequency:** Quarterly
- **Circulation:** 600,000
- **Website: www.usaa.com**

Freelance Potential
80% written by nonstaff writers. Publishes 5 freelance submissions yearly; 5% by unpublished writers, 10% by authors who are new to the magazine. Receives 20 queries yearly.

Submissions
Query with clips. Accepts hard copy and email submissions to uturn@usaa.com. SASE. Responds in 6–8 weeks.
Articles: Word lengths vary. Informational articles; profiles; interviews; and personal experience pieces. Topics include the arts, college, careers, hobbies, current events, history, music, popular culture, recreation, science, technology, social issues, sports, travel, teen driving, money, safety, and relationships.
Other: Puzzles, games, activities, jokes, and quizzes.

Sample Issue
31 pages (no advertising): 6 articles; 2 activities. Sample copy, free with 9x12 SASE ($2 postage). Guidelines and theme list available.
- "Speed Racer." Article profiles a 15-year-old USAA member who races sprint cars.
- "You're Getting Verrrrryyy Sleeeepy . . ." Article discusses sleep-deprivation in teenagers.
- "Who Wants to Be a Millionaire?" Article presents various plans for saving money.

Rights and Payment
All rights. Written material, payment rates vary. Pays on acceptance. Provides 3–5 contributor's copies.

Editor's Comments
Our readers react negatively to adult or parental tones, which may be construed as condescending. As such, we rely on and reinforce the importance of our readers' voices and ideas by publishing their submissions in each issue.

U.25

United Services Automobile Association
9800 Fredericksburg Road
San Antonio, TX 78288

Editor: Carol Barnes

Description and Interests
Teens and young adults who are members of the United Services Automobile Association (USAA) are the target audience for this magazine. Its purpose is to prepare readers for responsible adulthood by providing them with information on education, career choices, financial planning, driving, and lifestyle choices.
- **Audience:** 18–24 years
- **Frequency:** Quarterly
- **Circulation:** 500,000
- **Website: www.usaa.com**

Freelance Potential
90% written by nonstaff writers. Publishes 10–15 freelance submissions yearly. Receives 60 queries yearly.

Submissions
Query with résumé and clips for feature articles. Send complete ms for shorter pieces. Accepts hard copy. Mss are not returned. Responds in 6–8 weeks.
Articles: 1,000 words. Shorter pieces; 300 words. Informational and how-to articles; profiles; interviews; and personal experience pieces. Topics include college, careers, saving and investing money, driving, and lifestyle issues.
Depts/columns: Word lengths vary. News items, money advice, and career guidance.
Other: Activities, games.

Sample Issue
30 pages: 4 articles; 6 depts/columns. Sample copy, free with 9x12 SASE ($1.80 postage). Writers' guidelines available.
- "Military Cub to Football Lion." Article profiles Brian Calhoun, a 22-year-old running back who is beginning his career with the Detroit Lions.
- "Unplugged." Article chronicles 24 hours in the life of a young Silicon Valley techie.
- Sample dept/column: "Road Scholar" examines the different types of bike racks you can buy for your car and talks about the need for regular oil changes.

Rights and Payment
All rights. Feature articles, $500–$1,000. Other material, rates vary. Kill fee varies. Pays on acceptance.

Editor's Comments
We are very interested in hearing from freelancers who can write with a voice and style that appeal to young readers. Send ideas that will help our audience be successful in life and at work.

Vancouver Family Magazine

P.O. Box 820264
Vancouver, WA 98682

Editor: Nikki Klock

Description and Interests
Vancouver Family Magazine is a regional publication for families living in Clark County in Washington State. Articles cover family-related issues such as health and fitness, relationships, and recreation. This magazine also serves as a valuable resource for information about regional events, activities, and businesses.
- **Audience:** Families
- **Frequency:** Monthly
- **Circulation:** 7,000
- **Website:** www.vancouverfamilymagazine.com

Freelance Potential
75% written by nonstaff writers. Publishes 30–40 freelance submissions yearly; 50% by unpublished writers, 20% by authors who are new to the magazine.

Submissions
Query. Accepts hard copy. SASE. Response time varies.
Articles: Word lengths vary. Informational articles. Topics include parenting, family-related issues, health and fitness, relationships, and recreation.
Depts/columns: Word lengths vary. Parenting and family issues, local businesses, local news.

Sample Issue
30 pages (50% advertising): 4 articles; 5 depts/columns.
- "Downtown Vancouver Quiz." Article tests readers' knowledge of downtown Vancouver with questions about its past and present.
- "Go Out and Play." Article describes how children are removed from contact with nature, and what can be done to remedy the situation.
- Sample dept/column: "Parenting with a Purpose" tells how being "stuck" together during the summer months benefits families.

Rights and Payment
Rights vary. Assigned articles, $.15 per word. Payment policy varies.

Editor's Comments
As the only magazine dedicated exclusively to Vancouver area families, we are committed to providing the community with the information and resources necessary to raise healthy, well-adjusted children, and to helping to ensure that our community is a great one. To that end, we are interested in well-researched and thoughtfully presented submissions, and we prefer to work with local writers.

Vegetarian Baby & Child

47565 323rd Avenue
Cass Lake, MN 56633

Editor: Melanie Wilson

Description and Interests
Vegetarian and vegan families read this online magazine for informative articles, personal experience pieces, and original recipes. The magazine also serves as a networking and support resource.
- **Audience:** Parents
- **Frequency:** Quarterly
- **Hits per month:** 90,000
- **Website:** www.vegetarianbaby.com

Freelance Potential
95% written by nonstaff writers. Publishes 25 freelance submissions yearly. Receives 24 queries, 12–24 unsolicited mss yearly.

Submissions
Query or send complete ms. Accepts hard copy and email submissions to melanie@vegetarianbaby.com (Microsoft Word attachments). SASE. Response time varies.
Articles: 350–1,500 words. Informational and how-to articles; profiles; interviews; and personal experience pieces. Topics include general nutrition, vegetarian pregnancy, dealing with friends and family, living with nonvegetarians, health, child care, activism, and vegetarian support networks.
Depts/columns: Word lengths vary. Q&As, recipes, and book and new product reviews.
Other: Activities, games, and crafts for children.

Sample Issue
Sample copy and guidelines available at website.
- "Oh, Deer!" Article describes the author's mixed feelings about a teen who hunts and also eats the meatless food she prepares for him.
- "All About Chocolate." Article recounts the history of chocolate, and provides some interesting facts and figures regarding its popularity.
- "Alternative Outfitters." Article relays an interview with food scientists who have started a business selling fashionable, cruelty-free products.

Rights and Payment
First rights. Articles, $15. Pays on publication.

Editor's Comments
We are always interested in "healthy kid" stories of 400 to 800 words, or any articles about vegetarianism for children and families. All health benefit claims must be verifiable. Check out the current categories on our website to see if your work fits our needs.

Vegetarianteen.com

47565 323rd Avenue
Cass Lake, MN 56633

Editor: Melanie Wilson

Description and Interests
This e-zine is written by and for teens seeking information about the vegetarian or vegan lifestyle. It offers informative articles and personal experience pieces on healthy, cruelty-free, and environmentally conscientious living.
• **Audience:** YA–Adult
• **Frequency:** Quarterly
• **Hits per month:** Unavailable
• **Website: www.vegetarianteen.com**

Freelance Potential
95% written by nonstaff writers. Publishes 10 freelance submissions yearly; 50% by authors who are new to the magazine. Receives 12–60 queries, 12–24 unsolicited mss yearly.

Submissions
Query or send complete ms. Accepts hard copy and email submissions to melanie@vegetarianbaby.com (Microsoft Word attachments). SASE. Response time varies.
Articles: 350–1,200 words. Informational and how-to articles; profiles; interviews; and personal experience pieces. Topics include health, food, fitness, family issues, animal activism, and nutrition.
Depts/columns: Word lengths vary. Recipes, book and product reviews.

Sample Issue
Sample copy and guidelines available at website.
• "Cruel Fur." Article states some facts and figures regarding the fur coat industry, and explains why wearing fur is cruel and bad for the environment.
• "A Letter to Iams on Animal Testing." Article relays the email sent to the pet food company CEO, and the response to it, regarding animal testing performed at one of its independent research facilities.
• "Mushroom Sandwiches and Silk." Article details the author's journey from meat-eater to vegetarian, and describes some of the challenges of vegetarianism.

Rights and Payment
Rights vary. No payment.

Editor's Comments
We are always looking for "how I went vegetarian/vegan" stories from teens and young adults. However, minor children must have parental consent to submit. Also sought are media and product reviews, and your creative, original vegetarian/vegan recipes.

VegFamily

9436 Deer Lodge Lane
Las Vegas, NV 89129

Editor: Erin Pavlina

Description and Interests
VegFamily is an online magazine for vegan parenting, veganism, and natural family living. Read primarily by mothers, it includes articles, vegan recipes, profiles, and cooking tips.
• **Audience:** YA–Adult
• **Frequency:** Monthly
• **Hits per month:** 150,000
• **Website: www.vegfamily.com**

Freelance Potential
90% written by nonstaff writers. Publishes 150+ freelance submissions yearly; 90% by unpublished writers, 50% by authors who are new to the magazine. Receives 60 queries yearly.

Submissions
Query. Accepts email queries to contact@ vegfamily.com. Responds in 2 weeks.
Articles: 1,000 words. Informational, self-help, and how-to articles; profiles; and personal experience pieces. Topics include vegan pregnancy, babies and toddlers, vegan children and teens, health, nutrition, cooking, and parenting.
Fiction: 1,000 words. Genres include inspirational fiction, animal stories, and stories with nature and environmental themes.
Depts/columns: Word lengths vary. Recipes and book and product reviews.
Artwork: JPEG and GIF files.
Other: Activities. Submit seasonal material 2 months in advance.

Sample Issue
Sample copy and guidelines available at website.
• "One Mother at a Time." Article describes how a mother introduced baby slings to her community.
• "My Husband the Meat Eater." Essay tells how a woman faces the challenges of living with a non-vegan partner.
• Sample dept/column: "Health and Fitness" offers tips for making blended fruit smoothies and discusses their nutritional value.

Rights and Payment
All electronic rights. Articles, $20. Pays on publication.

Editor's Comments
We are interested in articles that provide our readers with advice on vegan parenting. Information should be presented in a friendly, conversational tone.

Ventura County Parent Magazine

45 West Easy Street, Suite 24
Simi Valley, CA 93065

Editor & Publisher: Jean Sutton

Description and Interests

In print since 1997, this resourceful magazine keeps parents living in Ventura County, California, abreast of local news, events, educational issues, and new products. It also includes articles on topics related to raising a family.
- **Audience:** Parents
- **Frequency:** Monthly
- **Circulation:** 42,000
- **Website:** www.vcparent.com

Freelance Potential

50% written by nonstaff writers. Publishes 50 freelance submissions yearly; 10% by unpublished writers, 10% by authors who are new to the magazine. Receives 100+ queries, 50–75 unsolicited mss yearly.

Submissions

Query with sample paragraph; or send complete ms. Accepts Macintosh disk submissions and email submissions to info@vcparent.com. SASE. Responds to queries in 2 months, to mss in 6 weeks.
Articles: 1,000–1,500 words. Informational articles and personal experience pieces. Topics include animals, crafts, hobbies, pets, the arts, computers, current events, education, health, fitness, social issues, popular culture, and news.
Fiction: 1,000–1,500 words. Publishes real-life and problem-solving fiction.
Depts/columns: 600 words. Health and safety news, media reviews, and Internet tips.
Artwork: B/W or color prints. Line art.
Other: Activities and filler on local topics.

Sample Issue

40 pages (44% advertising): 3 articles; 11 depts/columns. Sample copy, free with 12x14 SASE. Guidelines and theme list available.
- "Be a Yard Working Family." Article discusses how to get the whole family involved in doing yard work.
- Sample dept/column: "Healthwise" reports on asthma, a lighted nail clipper, and eye problems.

Rights and Payment

Exclusive regional rights. Written material, $35–$100. Artwork, payment rates vary. Pays on publication. Provides 1 contributor's copy.

Editor's Comments

We are interested in articles covering education, parenting, health, and the Internet.

VerveGirl

401 Richmond Street West, Suite 245
Toronto, Ontario M5V 1X5
Canada

Editor-in-Chief: Sara Graham

Description and Interests

This magazine for teen girls covers fashion, beauty, celebrities, and entertainment, while also offering features on more serious topics, such as education, social issues, careers, and the environment. It is published by Canada's Youth Culture Group in both English and French.
- **Audience:** Girls, 14–18 years
- **Frequency:** 8 times each year
- **Circulation:** 150,000 English; 30,000 French
- **Website:** www.vervegirl.com

Freelance Potential

75% written by nonstaff writers. Publishes 10–20 freelance submissions yearly. Receives 200 queries each year.

Submissions

Query. Accepts hard copy. SASE. Response time varies.
Articles: Word lengths vary. Informational and self-help articles; profiles; interviews; and personal experience pieces. Topics include health, nutrition, fashion, beauty, social issues, current events, the environment, education, careers, and music.
Depts/columns: Word lengths vary. Entertainment, nutrition, fashion tips, and health advice.

Sample Issue

50 pages: 5 articles; 5 depts/columns. Sample copy available at website.
- "Green Machine." Article discusses the importance of environmental awareness and offers advice to readers who want to get involved in the green movement and reduce their impact on the Earth.
- "Argentina's Invisible Children." Article visits this South American country and details the problems that have led many children to live in poverty.
- Sample dept/column: "Beauty Boot Camp" presents a four-week beauty plan for getting ready for the prom, including workout and weight loss ideas.

Rights and Payment

Rights vary. Written material, payment rates vary. Pays on publication.

Editor's Comments

While we do offer the kinds of fashion and beauty features that teen girls look for, we also keep our readers up to date on the current social and cultural issues that affect their world.

Voice of Youth Advocates

4501 Forbes Boulevard, Suite 200
Lanham, MD 20706

Editor-in-Chief: Cathi Dunn MacRae

Description and Interests
Now in its thirtieth year, *Voice of Youth Advocates* focuses primarily on literature and media for young adults. Its subscribers include librarians, educators, and professional youth workers. Book reviews, profiles of authors, and writing by teens are regularly found in its pages.
• **Audience:** Professionals who work with youth
• **Frequency:** 6 times each year
• **Circulation:** 6,500
• **Website: www.voya.com**

Freelance Potential
95% written by nonstaff writers. Publishes 50 free-lance submissions yearly; 5% by unpublished writers, 60% by authors who are new to the magazine. Receives 60 queries yearly.

Submissions
Query with résumé, synopsis, and market analysis. Accepts hard copy and email queries to cmacrae@voya.com. Availability of artwork improves chance of acceptance. SASE. Responds in 2–4 months.
Articles: 800–3,000 words. Informational and how-to articles; book reviews; and book lists. Topics include young adult literature, contemporary authors, and library programs.
Other: Submit seasonal material 1 year in advance.

Sample Issue
94 pages (20% advertising): 3 articles; 8 depts/columns; 6 contributions from teen writers; 166 reviews. Sample copy, free with 9x12 SASE. Guidelines available with SASE or at website.
• "Mormons." Article presents resources that can help teens gain a better understanding of the Church of Jesus Christ of Latter-day Saints.
• "Best Science Fiction, Fantasy & Horror." Article provides short descriptions of the year's best books in these genres.
• Sample dept/column: "Teen Screen" reviews films about art that are of interest to teens.

Rights and Payment
All rights. Written material, $50–$125. Pays on publication. Provides 3 contributor's copies.

Editor's Comments
Please note that we are not a teen magazine, although we do offer opportunities for teen writers. We primarily want non-scholarly writing about teen literature.

Voices from the Middle

University of Texas at San Antonio
Dept. of Interdisciplinary Learning & Teaching
One UTSA Circle
San Antonio, TX 78249

Submissions

Description and Interests
Literacy and learning at the middle school level is studied in this journal from the National Council of Teachers of English. Each thematic issue features authentic classroom practices, reviews of adolescent literature, and information on resources for teachers.
• **Audience:** Teachers
• **Frequency:** Quarterly
• **Circulation:** 11,000
• **Website: www.ncte.org/pubs**

Freelance Potential
70% written by nonstaff writers. Publishes 20 freelance submissions yearly; 60% by unpublished writers, 85% by authors who are new to the magazine. Receives 150 unsolicited mss yearly.

Submissions
Send 3 copies of complete ms. Accepts hard copy and email to voices@utsa.edu (Microsoft Word attachments; include issue for which you are submitting in subject line). SASE. Responds in 3–5 months.
Articles: 2,500–4,000 words. Educational articles and personal experience pieces related to the issue's theme. Topics include middle school language arts and English instruction.
Depts/columns: Staff written.

Sample Issue
64 pages (9% advertising): 8 articles; 12 depts/columns. Sample copy, $6. Guidelines and theme list available at website.
• "Intervention All Day Long: New Hope for Struggling Readers." Article explores appropriate ways to provide intervention to struggling readers, both inside and outside the classroom.
• "Using a Writing Marathon to Create a College Culture Among At-Risk Sixth-Graders." Article endorses the idea of introducing a "college culture" at the middle school level as a way of promoting post-secondary education for all students.

Rights and Payment
First and second rights. No payment. Provides 2 contributor's copies.

Editor's Comments
Each of our issues is devoted to one topic or concept related to middle school literacy. Check the website or the journal for upcoming topics. We like articles that make connections between theory and practice.

Washington Family Magazine

485 Spring Park Place, Suite 550
Herndon, VA 20170

Managing Editor: Marae Leggs

Description and Interests

Family directories, school and camp guides, and resources for children of all ages are found in *Washington Family Magazine*, a publication for parents living in and around the nation's capital. It also offers informative articles on general parenting topics.
- **Audience:** Parents
- **Frequency:** Monthly
- **Circulation:** 100,000
- **Website:** www.washingtonfamily.com

Freelance Potential

75% written by nonstaff writers. Publishes 90 freelance submissions yearly; 50% by unpublished writers, 50% by authors who are new to the magazine. Receives 1,200 queries and unsolicited mss yearly.

Submissions

Query or send complete ms. Accepts Macintosh disk submissions and email submissions to editor@ thefamilymagazine.com. SASE. Response time varies.
Articles: 500–700 words. How-to and self-help articles; and personal experience pieces. Topics include parenting, family life, relationships, fitness, crafts, hobbies, the arts, gifted and special education, music, multicultural and ethnic issues, social issues, music, education, and travel.
Depts/columns: Word lengths vary. News of interest to families, family travel, and health.
Artwork: B/W prints or transparencies. Line art.
Other: Submit seasonal material 6 months in advance.

Sample Issue

126 pages (50% advertising): 14 articles; 9 depts/ columns; 5 family directories. Sample copy, $4 with 9x12 SASE. Writers' guidelines and editorial calendar available.
- "It's Not Fair." Article tells why it is impossible to be equal and fair to all your children all the time.
- "Estate Planning for Our Children." Article explores legal issues associated with estates and trusts.

Rights and Payment

Regional rights. Articles, $35–$50. Depts/columns, payment rates vary. Pays on publication. Provides 1 contributor's copy.

Editor's Comments

Adoption and pregnancy are issues that still interest us. We would also like to see more on fine arts.

Washington Parent

4701 Sangamore Road, Suite N720
Bethesda, MD 20186

Editor: Margaret Hut

Description and Interests

This tabloid for parents in the Washington, D.C., area describes fun family places to go and things to do, while also reporting the latest information on child development, health, and education. Parents are directed to local resources in its special sections.
- **Audience:** Families
- **Frequency:** Monthly
- **Circulation:** 75,000
- **Website:** www.washingtonparent.com

Freelance Potential

90% written by nonstaff writers. Publishes 20 freelance submissions yearly. Receives 1,200 queries and unsolicited mss yearly.

Submissions

Query. Accepts email queries to contactus@ washingtonparent.net (Microsoft Word or WordPerfect attachments). SASE. Response time varies.
Articles: 1,000–2,000 words. Informational and how-to articles. Topics include regional news and events, parenting, family issues, entertainment, gifted and special education, child development, health, fitness, the environment, and multicultural and ethnic issues.
Depts/columns: Word lengths vary. Family travel, book and media reviews, education, topics relating to children with special needs, and short news items.

Sample Issue

122 pages (63% advertising): 12 articles; 7 depts/ columns; 5 special resource sections. Sample copy, guidelines, and editorial calendar available.
- "Nurturing the Budding Gardener." Article presents ideas for introducing young children to gardening.
- "Five Steps to Raising a Compassionate Child." Article tells how to teach children about empathy, humility, courage, understanding, and compassion.
- Sample dept/column: "Washington Parent 911" talks about ways to instill confidence in children.

Rights and Payment

First rights. Written material, payment rates vary. Provides 3 contributor's copies.

Editor's Comments

We'll consider any idea that will help us inform and support parents living in our area. In addition to reports on current events in the region, we welcome articles that address child-care issues, health, and education.

Weatherwise

1319 Eighteenth Street NW
Washington, DC 20036

Managing Editor: Margaret Benner

Description and Interests
Avid weather enthusiasts, from teens through adults, turn to this magazine for up-to-date information on the latest meteorological discoveries and events.
- **Audience:** YA–Adult
- **Frequency:** 6 times each year
- **Circulation:** 5,800
- **Website:** www.weatherwise.org

Freelance Potential
50% written by nonstaff writers. Publishes 36 freelance submissions yearly; 30% by authors who are new to the magazine. Receives 100 queries yearly.

Submissions
Query with résumé and clips. Accepts email queries to mbenner@heldref.org. Availability of artwork improves chance of acceptance. Responds in 2 months.
Articles: Word lengths vary. Informational articles; photo-essays; and reviews. Topics include storms, storm tracking, safety issues, and other topics related to the weather—all with a scientific basis.
Depts/columns: Word lengths vary. Weather Q&As; book reviews; weather highlights; forecasts; and history.
Artwork: Color prints or transparencies.

Sample Issue
82 pages: 6 articles; 9 depts/columns. Writers' guidelines available.
- "California Washed Away." Article recounts the events surrounding the Great Flood of 1862, and compares them to events in 2005–2006.
- "Up in Smoke." Article examines the role weather played in Ontario's 2006 fire season.
- Sample dept/column: "Weatherfront" features short news items related to meteorological science and weather events.

Rights and Payment
All rights. All material, payment rates vary. Pays on publication.

Editor's Comments
We are interested in receiving more hard science articles and more pieces that cover advanced meteorology. We see too many queries for articles on global warming. All material must be accurate, authoritative, and easily understood by a large, non-technical audience that includes teachers and students.

Wee Ones

P.O. Box 226
Darlington, MD 21034

Editor: Jennifer Reed

Description and Interests
Wee Ones is an online magazine for children and their parents featuring stories, articles, and activities centered on age-appropriate subjects.
- **Audience:** 5–10 years
- **Frequency:** 6 times each year
- **Hits per month:** 40,000+
- **Website:** www.weeonesmag.com

Freelance Potential
100% written by nonstaff writers. Publishes 200 freelance submissions yearly; 50% by unpublished writers, 50% by authors who are new to the magazine. Receives 960 unsolicited mss yearly.

Submissions
Send complete ms. Accepts email submissions only to submissions@weeonesmag.com (attach artwork). Responds in 1–4 weeks.
Articles: 500 words. Informational and how-to articles. Topics include animals, nature, arts and crafts, hobbies, current events, health, fitness, history, music, multicultural and ethnic issues, sports, travel, and recreation. Also publishes biographical articles.
Fiction: 500 words. Genres include contemporary, historical, and multicultural fiction; adventure; mystery; and suspense. Also publishes humor, sports stories, and read-along stories.
Artwork: Line art.
Other: Submit seasonal material 6 months in advance.

Sample Issue
Sample copy and guidelines available at website.
- "I Want to Be a Hero!" Story depicts a little boy's quest to help someone.
- "Habitats for Odonates." Article gives an overview of dragonflies and damselflies, and tells how to build a pond to attract them.
- "Pick Me Polly." Story tells about a girl who always wants to be the center of attention.

Rights and Payment
Non-exclusive worldwide, electronic, and reprint rights. Written material, $.05 per word. Pays on publication.

Editor's Comments
We are the first online children's magazine providing original stories and articles to readers. Submissions should be written in the active voice, with short, lively sentences. We are not interested in stories depicting homosexuality, violence, drug use, or overt religion.

Westchester Family

7 Purdy Street, Suite 201
Harrison, NY 10528

Editor: Jean Sheff

Description and Interests
This regional magazine is read by parents living in Westchester County, New York. It offers parenting and family-related articles on a variety of topics, including education, recreation, and health. Dining, entertainment, and shopping tips round out each issue.
- **Audience:** Parents
- **Frequency:** Monthly
- **Circulation:** 59,000
- **Website:** www.westchesterfamily.com

Freelance Potential
80% written by nonstaff writers. Publishes 40 freelance submissions yearly; 10% by unpublished writers, 30% by authors who are new to the magazine. Receives 600 queries yearly.

Submissions
Query with clips. Accepts hard copy. SASE. Response time varies.
Articles: 800–1,200 words. Informational articles; humor; profiles; interviews; photo-essays; and personal experience pieces. Topics include gifted education, music, recreation, regional news, social issues, special education, travel, and women's issues.
Depts/columns: 400–800 words. News and reviews.

Sample Issue
74 pages (52% advertising): 2 articles; 13 depts/columns. Sample copy, free with 9x12 SASE. Guidelines available.
- "Family Favorites." Article lists and describes a wide variety of places for families to visit, from nature centers to shopping malls.
- "Hip Parenting." Article profiles several parents who try to balance their commitment to their children with their own edgy pursuits.
- Sample dept/column: "Good Stuff" reviews products that make travel easier for families.

Rights and Payment
First rights. Written material, $25–$200. Pays on publication. Provides 1 contributor's copy.

Editor's Comments
Most family and parenting issues have been covered in the pages of our magazine, so we are looking for a fresh perspective on these topics. Whether the approach is light or serious, writers should know their subjects and be able to connect them to parents and families living in Westchester County.

Westchester Parent

350 Fifth Avenue, Suite 2420
New York, NY 10118

Editor: Christine Adler

Description and Interests
This tabloid caters to parents and families living in New York's Westchester and Rockland Counties, as well as in the towns of Greenwich and Stamford in Connecticut. It covers the latest local news, trends, and events while featuring articles on parenting and family issues.
- **Audience:** Parents
- **Frequency:** Monthly
- **Circulation:** 66,000
- **Website:** www.parentsknow.com

Freelance Potential
10% written by nonstaff writers. Publishes 20 freelance submissions yearly; 5% by unpublished writers, 20% by authors who are new to the magazine. Receives 300 queries and unsolicited mss yearly.

Submissions
Query or send complete ms. Accepts hard copy and email submissions to christinewp@gmail.com. SASE. Response time varies.
Articles: 800–1,000 words. Informational, self-help, and how-to articles; profiles; interviews; and personal experience pieces. Topics include parenting, family life, child development, animals, pets, the arts, computers, crafts, hobbies, current events, gifted and special education, health, nutrition, fitness, recreation, regional news, and travel.
Depts/columns: 750 words. Short news items, family travel pieces, and media reviews.
Other: Submit seasonal material 4 months in advance.

Sample Issue
94 pages: 15 articles; 11 depts/columns; 1 camp guide; 2 resource guides. Sample copy, free with 10x13 SASE. Guidelines available via email request.
- "Learning About Good Eating From the Ground Up." Article discusses ways to cultivate appreciation for healthy food choices.
- Sample dept/column: "Family Health" helps parents recognize Oppositional Defiant Disorder in children.

Rights and Payment
First New York area rights. No payment.

Editor's Comments
We are always looking for well-written and carefully researched articles. Keep in mind that we never publish fiction, memoir, or poetry.

West Coast Families

13988 Maycrest Way, Unit 140
Richmond, British Columbia V6V 3C3
Canada

Editor: Michelle Froese

Description and Interests
This free regional magazine distributed throughout British Columbia covers parenting issues and family events and activities.
- **Audience:** Families
- **Frequency:** 8 times each year
- **Circulation:** 50,000
- **Website:** www.westcoastfamilies.com

Freelance Potential
75% written by nonstaff writers. Publishes 40 freelance submissions yearly; 25% by authors who are new to the magazine. Receives 300 queries yearly.

Submissions
Query. Accepts hard copy and email to editor@ westcoastfamilies.com. SAE/IRC. Response time varies.
Articles: 600–800 words. Informational, self-help, and how-to articles; personal experience pieces; profiles; and interviews. Topics include family life, parenting, recreation, travel, religion, current events, health, fitness, education, sports, hobbies, science, technology, nature, and animals.
Depts/columns: Staff written.
Other: Puzzles, activities, jokes, and games. Submit seasonal material 3 months in advance.

Sample Issue
42 pages (8% advertising): 5 articles; 13 depts/columns. Sample copy, free with 9x12 SASE ($1.45 Canadian postage). Writers' guidelines and editorial calendar available.
- "Making It Big." Article features an interview with local music star and new mother, Kelly Brock.
- "Women & Cars: The New Dealer in Town." Article describes the new trend of female-focused car dealerships.
- "Defining Self." Profile tells how one mother quit her job to pursue photography.

Rights and Payment
One-time and electronic rights. Written material, payment rates vary. Pays on publication. Provides contributor's copies upon request.

Editor's Comments
We are greater Vancouver's guide to family fun and facts. Our audience consists of parents and kids, mostly women with children in the home. Local relevancy is important to our publication; U.S. references or angles are not acceptable.

Western New York Family

3147 Delaware Avenue, Suite B
Buffalo, NY 14217

Editor: Michele Miller

Description and Interests
Parents in the greater Buffalo area read this free publication for information on family issues and events.
- **Audience:** Parents
- **Frequency:** Monthly
- **Circulation:** 24,500
- **Website:** www.wnyfamilymagazine.com

Freelance Potential
70% written by nonstaff writers. Publishes 125–150 freelance submissions yearly; 30% by unpublished writers, 30% by authors who are new to the magazine. Receives 2,000 mss yearly.

Submissions
Send ms with brief biography. Accepts email to michele@wnyfamilymagazine.com (no attachments).
Articles: Main-theme articles, 2,500–3,000 words. Shorter pieces, 750–1,500 words. Informational, self-help, and how-to articles; creative nonfiction; humor; and personal experience pieces. Topics include family, parenting, health, fitness, education, and travel.
Depts/columns: Word lengths vary. "Tips & Tidbits," "What's New in the Kid Biz," and "Single Parenting."
Other: Submit seasonal material 3 months in advance.

Sample Issue
64 pages (40% advertising): 15 articles; 12 depts/columns. Sample copy, $2.50 with 9x12 SASE ($1.79 postage). Guidelines and editorial calendar available at website.
- "Traditions That Keep Your Family Close." Article discusses family rituals.
- "How To Choose the Right Pet for You." Article provides tips for picking a family pet.
- Sample dept/column: "Single Parenting" discusses whether kids need counseling after their parents have divorced.

Rights and Payment
First or second rights. Articles, $40–$150. Pays on publication. Provides 1 contributor's copy.

Editor's Comments
We are seeking articles that help parents deal with today's technology—cell phones, computer use, the online community—as it affects our children's development, positively or negatively. Local writers receive preference.

What If?

19 Lynwood Place
Guelph, Ontario N1G 2V9
Canada

Managing Editor: Mike Leslie

Description and Interests
This magazine features quality fiction, poetry, opinion pieces, photography, and artwork created by and for young Canadians.
- **Audience:** 12–19 years
- **Frequency:** Quarterly
- **Circulation:** 3,000
- **Website:** www.whatifmagazine.com

Freelance Potential
95% written by nonstaff writers. Publishes 100 freelance submissions yearly; 90% by unpublished writers, 90% by authors who are new to the magazine. Receives 3,000 unsolicited mss yearly.

Submissions
Send complete ms with résumé. Accepts hard copy, email submissions to editor@whatifmagazine.com (Microsoft Word attachments), and simultaneous submissions if identified. Availability of artwork improves chance of acceptance. SAE/IRC. Responds in 3 months.
Articles: To 1,000 words. Opinion pieces and editorials.
Fiction: To 3,000 words. Genres include mystery; suspense; fantasy; humor; science fiction; and contemporary, real-life, and inspirational fiction.
Artwork: Full-color prints. Line art.
Other: Poetry, to 20 lines.

Sample Issue
48 pages (3% advertising): 4 articles; 7 stories; 8 poems; 3 opinion pieces. Sample copy, $8 with 9x12 SAE. Guidelines available.
- "Write Angles: Write What You Know---Sort Of." Article gives writers advice on determining what it is they do know, understanding what it means, and then turning it into a great story.
- "Park Bench." Story relates the narrator's chance meeting with a crying stranger, and how it changed, for the better, the direction his life had been taking.

Rights and Payment
First rights. No payment. Provides 3 contributor's copies.

Editor's Comments
While we are always looking for high-quality fiction, we have seen too many drug and suicide themed stories. We would like to receive more issue-oriented nonfiction, especially well-thought-out opinion pieces from young Canadian writers.

What's Up Kids Family Magazine

496 Metler Road
Ridgeville, Ontario L0S 1M0
Canada

Editor-in-Chief: Paul Baswick

Description and Interests
This cheerful, family-friendly magazine features content for both parents and children. It is divided into two sections: one featuring articles on practical issues like vacation planning and baby showers; the other a colorful "kids' fun section" of puzzles, picture games, and upbeat stories.
- **Audience:** Families
- **Frequency:** 6 times each year
- **Circulation:** 200,000
- **Website:** www.whatsupkids.com

Freelance Potential
80% written by nonstaff writers. Publishes 30 freelance submissions yearly; 60% by authors who are new to the magazine. Receives 348 queries yearly.

Submissions
Canadian authors only. Query. Accepts email queries only to paul@whatsupkids.com. Response time varies.
Articles: Word lengths vary. Informational articles; profiles; and interviews. Topics include education, family issues, travel, fitness, nutrition, health, the arts, and entertainment.
Depts/columns: Word lengths vary. "Mom Time," "Health Matters," "Family Fit," "Family Tips," "Family Finances," "Baby Steps," "From the Kitchen," "Learning Curves," "Family Travel," "What's Up with Dad?" "Kids' Space," "Kid 2 Kid," "Cool Careers," "Kid Craft," and other children's activities.

Sample Issue
98 pages (15% advertising): 5 articles; 18 depts/columns; 5 activities.
- "Parties That Really Cook." Article describes the newest craze in baby showers—freezer parties.
- "Shrek the Third." Article previewing the new film features an interview with cast member Julie Andrews.
- Sample dept/column: "Baby Steps" provides sun-safety tips for babies.

Rights and Payment
All rights. Written material, payment rates and payment policy vary. Provides contributor's copies.

Editor's Comments
We are looking for hard-hitting news of interest to families as well as fun features and celebrity profiles. We are also in need of educational yet entertaining activities for children up to age 13. Preference is given to Canadian authors.

Winner

55 West Oak Ridge Drive
Hagerstown, MD 21740

Editor: Jan Schleifer

Description and Interests
Winner targets an audience of sixth- through ninth-grade students with its drug education and life skills articles. Its goal is to help kids say "no" to drugs and "yes" to life.
- **Audience:** 9–13 years
- **Frequency:** 9 times each year
- **Circulation:** 4,500
- **Website:** www.winnermagazine.org

Freelance Potential
25% written by nonstaff writers. Publishes 10–15 freelance submissions yearly; 5% by unpublished writers, 20% by authors who are new to the magazine. Receives 100 unsolicited mss yearly.

Submissions
Send complete ms. Accepts email submissions to jschleifer@rhpa.org. Responds in 4–6 weeks.
Articles: 625–650 words. Informational, self-help, and how-to articles; and profiles. Topics include family issues; sports; peer pressure; the dangers of alcohol use; life skills; social issues; and personal relationships.
Fiction: 625–650 words. True-life and problem-solving stories that focus on positive lifestyles.
Artwork: Color prints and transparencies. Line art.

Sample Issue
16 pages (no advertising): 2 articles; 3 stories; 1 comic; 2 activities. Sample copy, $2 with 9x12 SASE (3 first-class stamps). Guidelines available at website.
- "When Words Aren't Enough." Story features twins who are struggling to deal with the death of their best friend's father.
- "Climb Brainiac Mountain." Article features facts about the dangers of cocaine use and includes a quiz.
- "Kimmie Meissner: Triple Triumph." Article profiles a world champion ice skater.

Rights and Payment
First rights. Articles, $80. Pays on acceptance. Provides 3 contributor's copies.

Editor's Comments
Because of the age group of our readers, we like writers to use what we call a story-article form, in which the facts are presented within the framework of a story. We also like profiles of young, well-known personalities who don't use alcohol, tobacco, or drugs. Most pieces are accompanied by three thought questions and a pencil activity.

Wire Tap Magazine

c/o Independent Media Institute
77 Federal Road
San Francisco, CA 94107

Associate Editor: Kristina Rizga

Description and Interests
Teens and young adults who wish to express their opinions about politics, social issues, current events, and contemporary culture find a voice in *Wire Tap Magazine*. Published online exclusively, it presents reader-written articles, editorials, and poetry.
- **Audience:** 18–30 years
- **Frequency:** Daily
- **Hits per month:** 60,000
- **Website:** www.wiretapmag.org

Freelance Potential
95% written by nonstaff writers. Publishes 120 freelance submissions yearly. Receives 300 queries each year.

Submissions
Query. Accepts email queries to submissions@ wiretapmag.org (no attachments). Response time varies.
Articles: Word lengths vary. Informational articles; profiles; interviews; and personal experience pieces. Topics include social issues, politics, contemporary culture, and current events.
Depts/columns: Word lengths vary. Reviews, politics, and news.
Other: Poetry.

Sample Issue
Sample copy and guidelines available at website.
- "Darfur: Actions Against Atrocities." Article reports that students across the United States are leading efforts to address the crisis in Western Sudan, even though governments are slow to take action.
- "Hip-Hop Dogmatism and Potential Problems for Political Organizing." Article discusses whether hip-hoppers are avoiding internal issues, such as patriarchy and sexism, which may affect their ability to fight for social justice.
- "Schooling Bill Gates." Article offers ideas for fixing schools from the bottom up.

Rights and Payment
Electronic rights. Written material, $50–$400 for assigned pieces. No payment for unsolicited submissions. Payment policy varies.

Editor's Comments
Most of the articles we post have an activist slant that asks the question: "What are you going to DO about it?" We always want to hear from new writers.

Wondertime

47 Pleasant Street
Northampton, MA 01060

Editor: Lisa Stiepock

Description and Interests
Wondertime strives to go beyond typical parenting topics—such as potty training, colic, and tantrums—to focus on the amazing things kids learn and do every day. It emphasizes the joys of child raising while offering insight into the ways children develop.
- **Audience:** Parents
- **Frequency:** 6 times each year
- **Circulation:** 400,000
- **Website:** www.wondertime.com

Freelance Potential
90% written by nonstaff writers. Publishes many freelance submissions yearly; 100% by authors who are new to the magazine.

Submissions
Query with clips. Accepts email queries to wondertime.editors@disney.com. Response time varies.
Articles: Word lengths vary. Informational articles. Topics include the social, physical, intellectual, creative, and emotional aspects of child development; parenting; family issues; and family activities.
Depts/columns: Word lengths vary. New product information, food, book reviews, outdoor activities.

Sample Issue
144 pages: 7 articles; 8 depts/columns. Sample copy, $4.95 at newsstands. Guidelines available at website.
- "Giant Steps." Article relates the personal experiences of a lifelong football fan who takes his son to their first game together.
- "Fantasy Island." Article visits a tiny, rocky island off the southeast coast of Maine that is home to fairy dwellings created by children.
- Sample dept/column: "The Long View" offers one parent's perspective on her children's strong sibling relationships.

Rights and Payment
Exclusive worldwide first periodical rights. Written material, $1+ per word. Payment policy varies.

Editor's Comments
Bear in mind that our content is geared to parents of children from birth through kindergarten and first grade. The articles we publish help our readers see the world through the eyes of their children. We want to hear from smart, funny, inquisitive writers who are also parents.

Writers' Journal

P.O. Box 394
Perham, MN 56573

Editor: Leon Ogroske

Description and Interests
This is a magazine for writers of all stripes. Its goal is to provide its readers with the skills necessary for successful writing careers, from the mechanics of writing to the business side of freelancing.
- **Audience:** YA–Adult
- **Frequency:** 6 times each year
- **Circulation:** 23,000
- **Website:** www.writersjournal.com

Freelance Potential
50% written by nonstaff writers. Publishes 40 freelance submissions yearly; 20% by unpublished writers, 80% by authors who are new to the magazine. Receives 200 queries and unsolicited mss yearly.

Submissions
Query with clips; or send complete ms. Accepts hard copy. SASE. Responds in 2–6 months.
Articles: 1,000–2,200 words. Informational and how-to articles; profiles; and interviews. Topics include fiction writing, travel writing, technical writing, business writing, writing skills, interviewing techniques, research, record keeping, income venues, and finances.
Depts/columns: Software reviews, 500–700 words. Marketing ideas and photography tips, 1,200–2,000 words.
Other: Poetry, to 15 lines.

Sample Issue
65 pages (10% advertising): 8 articles; 14 depts/columns. Guidelines available.
- "Six Clues to Potential Markets." Article shares a seasoned writer's secrets for getting published.
- "Becoming a Travel Writer." Article answers frequently asked questions about travel writing.
- Sample dept/column: "Photography Techniques" is a step-by-step lesson in digital photo manipulation.

Rights and Payment
One-time rights. Written material, $30 plus a 1-year subscription. Pays on publication. Provides 2 contributor's copies upon request.

Editor's Comments
We want to see highly informative articles of an advisory nature that feature a positive and practical approach to the topic being covered. We particularly like to see a narrow focus, and the subject covered well in a tightly written style.

Yes Mag

501-3960 Quadra Street
Victoria, British Columbia V8X 4A3
Canada

Managing Editor: Jude Isabella

Description and Interests
Subtitled "The Science Magazine for Adventurous Minds," this award-winning Canadian publication aims to make science, technology, engineering, and mathematics exciting and fun for kids. Each issue focuses on a particular theme.
- **Audience:** 9–14 years
- **Frequency:** 6 times each year
- **Circulation:** 23,000
- **Website:** www.yesmag.ca

Freelance Potential
70% written by nonstaff writers. Publishes 30 freelance submissions yearly; 5% by unpublished writers, 15% by authors who are new to the magazine. Receives 300 queries yearly.

Submissions
Query. Accepts email queries to editor@yesmag.ca. Response time varies.
Articles: Features, 300–800 words. Short, theme-related articles, 300–600 words. Informational articles, 250 words. Topics include astronomy, engineering, math, science, technology, plants, animals, and the environment.
Depts/columns: 250 words. Science and technology news; entomology; world records; environmental updates; book and product reviews; and experiments to try at home.

Sample Issue
30 pages (no advertising): 5 articles; 7 depts/columns. Sample copy, $4.50 with SAE/IRC. Guidelines and theme list available.
- "Science So Cool, It's Frigid." Article gives an overview of the North and South Poles and the studies currently being conducted there.
- "Polar Scientists: What Do They Do?" Article profiles two scientists studying climate change in the Arctic and pollution in the Antarctic.
- Sample dept/column: "Kids, Try This at Home" is an experiment in the freezing points of different foods.

Rights and Payment
First rights. Written material, $.20 per word. Other material, payment rates vary. Pays on publication. Provides 1 contributor's copy.

Editor's Comments
We focus on Canadian content throughout our magazine. Canadian science and scientists are highlighted.

Young Adult Today

P.O. Box 436987
Chicago, IL 60643-6987

Editor: Aja Carr

Description and Interests
Young Adult Today offers African American youth, who are enrolled in Urban Ministries' education programs, devotionals and weekly Bible study guides with lessons that can be applied to everyday life.
- **Audience:** 18–24 years
- **Frequency:** Quarterly
- **Circulation:** 25,000
- **Website: www.urbanministries.com**

Freelance Potential
95% written by nonstaff writers. Publishes 52 freelance submissions yearly; 50% by unpublished writers, 50% by authors who are new to the magazine. Receives 240 queries yearly.

Submissions
Query with résumé. No unsolicited mss. All articles and Bible lessons are assigned. SASE. Responds in 2 months.
Articles: To 400 words. Lessons consist of discussion pieces, questions, devotional readings, and Bible study guides that explain how to apply the lessons learned from Scripture to modern life.

Sample Issue
80 pages (4% advertising): 1 article; 13 discussion pieces; 13 corresponding Bible study guides; 1 poem. Sample copy, $2.25 with 9x12 SASE ($.87 postage). Guidelines provided on assignment.
- "Spiritual Community." Article describes how to recognize the three kinds of people that can be found in any spiritual community.
- "The Light of Love." Bible study teaches that true love means looking out for the best interests of others without expecting anything in return.
- "Loving the Unlovable." Discussion piece explains that while it's hard to love people who cause you pain, it is possible to do so with Jesus in your life.

Rights and Payment
Rights negotiable. Written material, $150 per lesson. Pays on publication.

Editor's Comments
We are interested in hearing from writers who want to join our ministry to provide urban African American young adults with lessons in Christian living. Become familiar with our publication; then if you have an idea for a devotional, query us with the Bible Scripture, planned discussion piece, and your résumé.

Young Adult Today Leader

P.O. Box 436987
Chicago, IL 60643-6987

Editor: Aja Carr

Description and Interests
This companion publication to Urban Ministries' *Young Adult Today* is for the religious education teachers of the ministry. Each issue contains the teachers' corresponding lesson plans for the discussion pieces read by the students. Urban Ministries' religious education program is specifically targeted toward young African American adults.
• **Audience:** Teachers
• **Frequency:** Quarterly
• **Circulation:** 15,000
• **Website:** www.urbanministries.com

Freelance Potential
95% written by nonstaff writers. Publishes 52 freelance submissions yearly; 50% by unpublished writers, 50% by authors who are new to the magazine. Receives 240 queries yearly.

Submissions
Query with résumé. All work is done on assignment. No unsolicited mss. SASE. Responds in 2 months.
Articles: Devotionals, 400 words. Topics include current events and social issues as they relate to Christianity and the Bible.

Sample Issue
80 pages (no advertising): 1 article; 13 teaching plans; 13 Bible study guides; 1 poem. Sample copy, $2.25 with 9x12 SASE ($.87 postage). Writers' guidelines available.
• "Believing the Impossible." Teaching plan offers guidance for helping students understand that believing in God can be difficult at times.
• "The Test of Love." Bible study summarizes how Christ taught us to relate to one another, and how to apply this lesson in daily life.
• "Doing the Love You Talk About." Lesson plan helps teachers explain to their students that love includes both words and deeds.

Rights and Payment
Rights negotiable. Written material, $150. Pays on publication.

Editor's Comments
We are interested in hearing from Christian educators and youth leaders who understand and can communicate the African American experience. We encourage prospective writers to read at least one issue of each publication before sending us a query.

Young People's Press

374 Fraser Street
North Bay, Ontario P1B 2W7
Canada

Chief Executive Officer: Don Curry

Description and Interests
The purpose of this website is to provide a forum for youth and young adult writers who are seeking a voice in the mainstream media. It accepts contributions by teen writers about current events, the arts, culture, and social issues. Its articles have appeared in newspapers and Internet sites throughout the U.S. and Canada.
• **Audience:** 14–24 years
• **Frequency:** Updated on an ongoing basis
• **Hits per month:** 4,000
• **Website:** www.ypp.net

Freelance Potential
80% written by nonstaff writers. Publishes 100 freelance submissions yearly; 70% by unpublished writers, 70% by authors who are new to the magazine. Receives 600 queries, 600 unsolicited mss yearly.

Submissions
Prefers complete ms with contact information. Will accept query. Accepts email submissions to doncurry@ontera.net (Microsoft Word attachments). Availability of artwork improves chance of acceptance. Responds in 1 week.
Articles: 400–1,000 words. Informational and self-help articles; profiles; reviews; and personal experience pieces. Topics include music, the arts, current events, multicultural and social issues, and popular culture.
Depts/columns: Word lengths vary. Media reviews.
Artwork: Electronic images only.
Other: Submit seasonal material 1 month in advance.

Sample Issue
Sample copy and guidelines available at website.
• "Are Obesity Standards Realistic?" Article questions the definition of obesity set by national agencies and the body mass index.
• "I Miss You, Friendly Lion." Essay recounts a range of emotions felt after a pet's death.
• "Our Fingerprints Linger with Katrina Victim Families." Personal experience piece describes one teen's trip to New Orleans.

Rights and Payment
Rights vary. No payment.

Editor's Comments
We want original writing by teens, but please don't send in your homework assignments.

Young Rider

P.O. Box 8237
Lexington, KY 40533

Editor: Lesley Ward

Description and Interests
Subtitled "The Magazine for Horse and Pony Lovers," this publication for young equestrians features practical articles about riding and horse care, while also focusing on the fun and excitement of this sport.
- **Audience:** 6–14 years
- **Frequency:** 6 times each year
- **Circulation:** 92,000
- **Website: www.youngrider.com**

Freelance Potential
20% written by nonstaff writers. Publishes 20 freelance submissions yearly; 10% by unpublished writers, 10% by authors who are new to the magazine. Receives 60 queries yearly.

Submissions
Query. Prefers email queries to yreditor@bowtieinc.com (Microsoft Word attachments). Responds in 2 weeks.
Articles: Word lengths vary. Informational and how-to articles and profiles. Topics include horseback riding, training, techniques, careers, and general horse grooming and care.
Fiction: 1,200 words. Stories that feature horses and youth themes.
Artwork: Color prints or transparencies; high-resolution digital images.

Sample Issue
64 pages (28% advertising): 7 articles; 1 story; 6 depts/columns; 1 special camp section. Sample copy, $3.99 with 9x12 SASE ($1 postage). Guidelines and editorial calendar available.
- "Cute & Clever." Article provides fun and factual information about the American miniature horse.
- "Searching for a Lesson Barn." Article stresses the importance of doing research before choosing riding lessons.
- Sample dept/column: "My Horsey Life" is a first-person piece about fox hunting.

Rights and Payment
First serial rights. Written material, $.10 per word. Artwork, payment rates vary. Pays on publication. Provides 2 contributor's copies.

Editor's Comments
Good short fiction with horse themes is always needed. We also use "horsey interest" articles from freelance writers. The practical riding tips and horse care articles are written in-house by our own staff.

Young Salvationist

The Salvation Army
615 Slaters Lane
Alexandria, VA 22314

Editor: Major Curtiss A. Hartley

Description and Interests
Teens read this magazine from the Salvation Army for a Christian perspective on contemporary life and social issues. It also helps readers develop and mature in their faith and find out about opportunities for personal ministry.
- **Audience:** 13–21 years
- **Frequency:** 10 times each year
- **Circulation:** 43,000

Freelance Potential
95% written by nonstaff writers. Publishes 60 freelance submissions yearly; 5% by unpublished writers, 10% by authors who are new to the magazine. Receives 480 unsolicited mss yearly.

Submissions
Send complete ms. Accepts hard copy, email submissions to ys@usn.salvationarmy.org, and simultaneous submissions if identified. SASE. Responds in 2 months.
Articles: 1,000–1,500 words. How-to, inspirational, and personal experience articles; profiles; interviews; and humor. Topics include religion and issues of relevance to teens.
Fiction: 500–1,200 words. Genres include adventure, fantasy, romance, humor, and religious and science fiction—all written from a Christian perspective.
Other: Submit seasonal material 6 months in advance.

Sample Issue
24 pages (no advertising): 8 articles; 1 story. Sample copy, free with 9x12 SASE (3 first-class stamps). Guidelines and theme list available with #10 SASE.
- "She Stole More Than My Money." Personal experience piece tells how the author's friend was stealing from her family.
- "Choose Life!" Article presents three reasons why suicide should never be an option.

Rights and Payment
First and second rights. Written material, $.15 per word for reprint rights. Pays on acceptance. Provides 4 contributor's copies.

Editor's Comments
If you're interested in writing for us, try submitting a short article that creatively conveys the Gospel. It always works best to draw from everyday examples, rather than abstract theology. Write with a real 16-year-old in mind.

Youth & Christian Education Leadership

1080 Montgomery Avenue
Cleveland, TN 37311

Editor: Wanda Griffith

Description and Interests
This magazine serves a broad audience of adults working with Christian youth—including Sunday school teachers, youth pastors, and children's church leaders. It features informative articles, personal experience pieces, and profiles that are both practical and inspirational.
- **Audience:** Adults
- **Frequency:** Quarterly
- **Circulation:** 10,000
- **Website:** www.pathwaypress.org

Freelance Potential
10% written by nonstaff writers. Publishes 10 freelance submissions yearly; 90% by unpublished writers, 10% by authors who are new to the magazine. Receives 30–35 queries, 20–25 mss yearly.

Submissions
Prefers complete ms with author biography. Will accept query. Accepts disk submissions (Microsoft Word or WordPerfect) and email to Wanda_Griffith@ pathwayspress.org. SASE. Responds in 3 weeks.
Articles: 500–1,000 words. Informational and how-to articles; profiles; interviews; humor; and personal experience pieces. Topics include current events, music, religion, social issues, psychology, parenting, and multicultural and ethnic subjects.
Depts/columns: Staff written.

Sample Issue
30 pages (2% advertising): 10 articles; 8 depts/ columns. Sample copy, $1 with 9x12 SASE (2 first-class stamps). Guidelines available at website.
- "Solving the Leadership Puzzle." Article explains that allowing others to lead can widen the circle of involvement for accomplishing ministry.
- "Breaking Out of the Prison of Disordered Eating." Article offers ideas for using spirituality to treat unhealthy eating patterns.

Rights and Payment
First rights. Written material, $25–$50. Kill fee, 50%. Pays on publication. Provides 1–10 author's copies.

Editor's Comments
We always like articles that highlight successful Christian education ministries. We also want to hear about individuals or groups who are advancing Christian education through distinctive ministries. Use real-life examples and quote experts when possible.

Youth Today

1200 17th Street NW, 4th Floor
Washington, DC 20036

Editor: Patrick Boyle

Description and Interests
Published by the American Youth Work Center, this newspaper addresses issues of concern to professionals who serve children and adolescents through public and private agencies. It covers topics such as after-school programs, child welfare, civic engagement, program management, and funding.
- **Audience:** Youth workers
- **Frequency:** 10 times each year
- **Circulation:** 12,000
- **Website:** www.youthtoday.org

Freelance Potential
50% written by nonstaff writers. Publishes 25 freelance submissions yearly; 10% by authors who are new to the magazine. Receives 36 queries yearly.

Submissions
Query with résumé and clips. Responds in 3 months.
Articles: 1,000–2,500 words. Informational articles; news and research reports; profiles of youth workers and youth programs; and business features. Topics include foster care, child abuse, youth program management, violence, adolescent health, juvenile justice, job training, school-to-work programs, after-school programs, mentoring, and other social issues related to youth development.
Depts/columns: Book and video reviews; news briefs; opinion pieces; and people in the news.

Sample Issue
36 pages (50% advertising): 48 articles; 8 depts/ columns. Sample copy, $5. Guidelines available.
- "Abstinence Ed's Nightmare." Article reports reactions to a federal study that says abstinence education isn't working.
- "Restraints That Kill." Article talks about a tragedy at a Maryland youth agency.
- Sample dept/column: "Promising Practices" describes the many benefits of providing mentors to foster parents.

Rights and Payment
First and Internet rights. Written material, $.50–$.75 per word. Pays on acceptance. Provides 2 copies.

Editor's Comments
First-hand descriptions of successful and effective youth programs are welcome. We'll also consider articles about valuable resources that are available to youth workers.

YouthWorker Journal

104 Woodmont Boulevard, Suite 300
Nashville, TN 37205

Editor: Steve Rabey

Description and Interests
YouthWorker Journal serves those who minister to young people by providing resources that help them grow spiritually and professionally so they can increase their effectiveness and deepen their impact.
- **Audience:** Adults who work with youth
- **Frequency:** 6 times each year
- **Circulation:** 15,000
- **Website: www.youthworker.com**

Freelance Potential
95% written by nonstaff writers. Publishes 50+ freelance submissions yearly; 15% by unpublished writers, 25% by authors who are new to the magazine. Receives 720 queries yearly.

Submissions
Query with short biography. Prefers email queries to steve@youthworker.com (include "Query" in subject line). Accepts hard copy and faxes to 615-385-4412. SASE. Responds in 6–8 weeks.
Articles: Word lengths vary. Informational and practical application articles; personal experience pieces; and reviews. Topics include youth ministry, theology, helping youth, spreading the word of Christ, student worship, family ministry, education, family issues, popular culture, the media, and volunteering.
Depts/columns: Word lengths vary. National and regional trends; quotes from youth workers.

Sample Issue
64 pages (30% advertising): 5 articles; 11 depts/columns. Sample copy, $8. Guidelines and theme list available at website.
- "The Teacher's Journey." Article features an interview with a highly respected teacher, writer, and activist.
- "Beyond Teaching to Learning." Article provides research and recommendations on teaching.
- Sample dept/column: "The Urban Take" features an essay by an inner-city pastor on how to reach urban youth with the message of Jesus Christ.

Rights and Payment
All rights. Written material, $15–$300. Pays on publication. Provides 1 contributor's copy.

Editor's Comments
Submissions should address one or more of these five crucial needs: theological understanding; knowledge of today's kids; cultural literacy; faith, witness, and action; and soul care.

Zamoof!

644 Spruceview Place South
Kelowna, British Columbia V1V 2P7
Canada

Editor/Publisher: TeLeni Koochin

Description and Interests
This new publication offers fun and entertaining material from Canadian authors, along with educational editorial designed to prepare young people for the difficult teen years ahead. It provides a platform for children to share their thoughts and creativity.
- **Audience:** 6–12 years
- **Frequency:** 6 times each year
- **Circulation:** 4,000–7,000
- **Website: www.zamoofmag.com**

Freelance Potential
90% written by nonstaff writers. Publishes several freelance submissions yearly; 80% by unpublished writers, 100% by authors who are new to the magazine.

Submissions
Accepts material from Canadian residents only. Query or send complete ms with résumé and clips. Accepts hard copy. SASE. Responds in 2–3 weeks.
Articles: Staff written.
Fiction: 1,675–1,700 words. Genres include adventure; folktales; mystery; fantasy; horror; multicultural, inspirational, and science fiction; and stories about sports.
Other: Submit seasonal material 3–4 months in advance.

Sample Issue
82 pages: 8 articles; 5 stories; 4 comics; 7 games; 2 interviews. Sample copy, $3.49 (U.S.), $4.25 (Canadian). Guidelines available.
- "Gareth, the Unusual Duck-Billed Platypus." Story follows the journey of a duck-billed platypus through the rainforests of Tasmania.
- "Me As a Maple Tree." First-person story describes how a maple tree changes through the seasons.
- "Should've Learned the First Time." Story details the aftermath of Little Red Riding Hood.

Rights and Payment
Rights vary. Written material, $.25 per word. Pays on acceptance. Provides 2 contributor's copies.

Editor's Comments
At this time we are only accepting short stories from Canadian writers. While we will consider material on a wide range of topics and themes, we will not publish stories that involve violence or death unless they are handled in a constructive way.

Additional Listings

We have selected the following magazines to offer you additional publishing opportunities. These magazines range from general-interest publications to women's magazines to craft and hobby magazines. While children, young adults, parents, or teachers are not their primary target audience, these publications do publish a limited amount of children's-related material.

As you review the listings that follow, use the Description and Readership section as your guide to the particular needs of each magazine. This section offers general information about the magazine and its readers' interests, as well as the type of material it usually publishes. The Freelance Potential section will provide information about the publication's receptivity to freelance manuscripts.

After you survey the listings to determine if your work meets the magazine's specifications, be sure to read a recent sample copy and the current writers' guidelines before submitting your material.

Action Pursuit Games

P.O. Box 417
Licking, MO 65542

Editor: Daniel Reeves

Description and Interests
This monthly targets young adults and adults who enjoy the sport of paintball. Technique articles, reviews of new products, and contemporary fiction involving paintball make up the majority of its content. Circ: 80,000.
Website: www.actionpursuitgames.com

Freelance Potential
60% written by nonstaff writers. Publishes 150+ freelance submissions yearly; 20% by unpublished writers, 30% by new authors. Receives 1,200+ unsolicited mss yearly.
Submissions and Payment: Sample copy, $4.99 with 9x12 SASE (15 first-class stamps). Send complete ms with TIF images. Accepts disk submissions and email submissions to editor@actionpursuitgames.com. SASE. Responds in 1 month. All rights. Articles, 300–2,000 words. Fiction, 300–600 words. Depts/columns, 300–500 words. Written material, payment rates vary. Pays on publication. Provides 1 contributor's copy.

Adventures

2923 Troost Avenue
Kansas City, MO 64109

Submissions: Abigail L. Takala

Description and Interests
Designed to connect Sunday school learning with daily experiences and growth, this take-home paper includes character-building stories and activities for children ages six to eight. It is interested in adventures that show children dealing with issues related to a Bible story. Characters and events must be realistic. Circ: Unavailable.
Website: www.wordaction.com

Freelance Potential
75% written by nonstaff writers. Publishes 15 freelance submissions yearly; 10% by unpublished writers, 10% by new authors. Receives 300 queries yearly.
Submissions and Payment: Guidelines and theme list available. Query. Accepts hard copy. SASE. Responds in 4–6 weeks. First North American serial rights. Articles, word lengths and payment rates vary. Pays on acceptance. Provides 1 contributor's copy.

The ALAN Review

College of Liberal Arts & Sciences
Department of English
Arizona State University
P.O. Box 870302
Tempe, AZ 85287

Editor: Dr. James Blasingame

Description and Interests
This magazine provides members of the National Council of Teachers of English with articles on young adult literature, interviews with authors, and reviews. It appears three times each year. Circ: 2,500.
Website: www.alan.ya.org

Freelance Potential
84% written by nonstaff writers. Publishes 38 freelance submissions yearly; 5% by unpublished writers, 65% by new authors. Receives 90 unsolicited mss yearly.
Submissions and Payment: Guidelines available in magazine. Sample copy, free. Send 3 copies of complete ms with disk (ASCII or Microsoft Word 5.1 or higher). Accepts simultaneous submissions if identified. Availability of artwork improves chance of acceptance. SASE. Responds in 2 months. All rights. Articles, to 3,000 words. Depts/columns, word lengths vary. No payment. Provides 2 contributor's copies.

Amazing Kids!

3224 East Yorba Linda Boulevard, #442
Fullerton, CA 92831

Editor: Alyse Rome

Description and Interests
This e-zine is part of the Amazing Kids! website. A non-profit educational organization, it is dedicated to fostering excellence in children by encouraging them to live up to their full potential. The organization is looking for adult volunteers to write profiles for the e-zine's Kids of the Month section. Hits per month: 640,000.
Website: www.amazing-kids.org

Freelance Potential
40% written by nonstaff writers. Publishes 70 freelance submissions yearly; 90% by unpublished writers, 70% by authors who are new to the magazine. Receives 3,000 queries and unsolicited mss yearly.
Submissions and Payment: Sample copy available at website. Query or send complete ms. Accepts email submissions to info@amazing-kids.org. Response time varies. All rights. Articles, word lengths vary. No payment.

All About Kids
Parenting Magazine

1071 Celestial Street, Suite 1104
Cincinnati, OH 45202

Editor: Tom Wynne

Description and Interests
Appearing monthly, this magazine targets parents living in the greater Cincinnati area. Each issue features articles on health, education, and other parenting and family related topics. In addition, it includes local news and information on regional events and resources. Since it is entirely freelance written, it depends on quality writers to stock its pages. Circ: 120,000.
Website: www.aakmagazine.com

Freelance Potential
100% written by nonstaff writers. Publishes 30 freelance submissions yearly.
Submissions and Payment: Guidelines available at website. Send complete ms. Accepts hard copy and disk submissions (text files only). SASE. Response time varies. Rights vary. Articles and depts/columns, word lengths and payment rates vary. Payment policy varies. Provides 1 contributor's copy.

American History

Weider History Magazine Group
741 Miller Drive SE, Suite D2
Leesburg, VA 20175

Editorial Director: Roger Vance

Description and Interests
Six times each year, *American History* magazine delivers well-researched and high-interest articles on the people and events that have shaped U.S. history. It covers important topics in a highly readable style that appeals to history buffs and the general public alike. Circ: 100,000.
Website: www.thehistorynet.com/ahi

Freelance Potential
80% written by nonstaff writers. Publishes 30 freelance submissions yearly; 50% by authors who are new to the magazine. Receives 1,200 queries yearly.
Submissions and Payment: Sample copy and guidelines, $6 with return label. Query with 1–2 page proposal. Accepts hard copy. SASE. Responds in 10 weeks. All rights. Articles, 2,000–4,000 words; $.20 per word. Depts/columns, word lengths vary; $75. Pays on acceptance. Provides 5 contributor's copies.

American School Board Journal

1680 Duke Street
Alexandria, VA 22314

Editor-in-Chief: Glenn Cook

Description and Interests

This publication strives to provide the best, most comprehensive accounts of emerging education trends and solutions available. Targeting teachers, school board members, and other professionals in the field, it appears monthly, and explores topics such as management, leadership, and social issues. Circ: 50,200.
Website: www.asbj.com

Freelance Potential

50% written by nonstaff writers. Publishes 35 freelance submissions yearly. Receives 360 queries yearly.
Submissions and Payment: Sample copy, $5. Query with clips. Accepts hard copy. SASE. Responds in 2 months. All rights. Articles, 2,200–2,500 words. Depts/columns, 1,000–1,200 words. Solicited articles, $800. Unsolicited articles and depts/columns, no payment. Pays on publication. Provides 3 contributor's copies.

AMomsLove.com

1032 Duss Avenue
Ambridge, PA 15003

Editor: Caroline G. Shaw

Description and Interests

Stay-at-home, work-from-home, and working mothers enjoy this monthly online magazine for its insightful and inspirational articles on parenting, cooking, finance, organizing the home, gardening, and beauty. It provides a place for women to grow and learn from each other. Hits per month: 30,000.
Website: www.amomslove.com

Freelance Potential

75% written by nonstaff writers. Publishes 60 freelance submissions yearly; 20% by authors who are new to the magazine.
Submissions and Payment: Sample copy available at website. Send complete ms with short bio. Accepts email submissions to mom@amomslove.com (prefers HTML attachments; will accept Microsoft Word attachments). Response time varies. First rights. Articles, 700–1,100 words. No payment.

AppleSeeds

Cobblestone Publishing Company
30 Grove Street
Peterborough, NH 03458

Editor: Susan Buckley

Description and Interests

This multidisciplinary, nonfiction social studies magazine targets children in grades three and four. Appearing nine times each year, it features articles, stories, and activities. It seeks historically accurate articles that are lively and exhibit an original approach to a theme. All queries must be theme-related. Circ: 10,000.
Website: www.cobblestonepub.com

Freelance Potential

90% written by nonstaff writers. Publishes 90–100 freelance submissions yearly; 20% by unpublished writers, 35% by new authors. Receives 600+ queries yearly.
Submissions and Payment: Guidelines and theme list available at website. Query. Prefers email queries to swbuc@aol.com. Will accept hard copy. SASE. Responds in 2–3 months if interested. All rights. Written material, $50 per page. Pays on publication. Provides 2 contributor's copies.

The Apprentice Writer

Susquehanna University, Box GG
Selinsgrove, PA 17870-1001

Writers' Institute Director: Gary Fincke

Description and Interests

The pages of this publication are filled with top-notch work by high school students from across the U.S. Published annually, it includes fiction, essays, plays, photographs, and artwork. Circ: 10,500.
Website: www.susqu.edu/writers (click on High School Students)

Freelance Potential

100% written by nonstaff writers. Publishes 80 freelance submissions yearly; 95% by unpublished writers, 95% by authors who are new to the magazine. Receives 5,000 unsolicited mss yearly.
Submissions and Payment: Sample copy, $3 with 9x12 SASE ($1.17 postage). Send complete ms. Accepts hard copy and simultaneous submissions if identified. SASE. Responds during the month of May. First rights. Articles and fiction, 7,000 words. Poetry, no line limits. No payment. Provides 2 author's copies.

Arizona Parenting

2432 West Peoria Avenue, Suite 1206
Phoenix, AZ 85029

Editor: Lyn Wolford

Description and Interests
Distributed free to parents living in Arizona, this resourceful magazine features articles and useful tips on parenting topics, as well as information on regional events. It appears monthly. Circ: 80,000.
Website: www.azparenting.com

Freelance Potential
50% written by nonstaff writers. Publishes 20 freelance submissions yearly; 5% by unpublished writers, 25% by new authors. Receives 520 queries, 300 mss yearly.
Submissions and Payment: Sample copy and editorial calendar, free with 9x12 SASE ($2 postage). Query or send complete ms. Prefers email to lyn.wolford@azparenting.com. Will accept hard copy. SASE. Responds in 2–3 months. First North American serial and electronic rights. Articles, 850–2,400 words. Depts/columns, 400–850 words. All material, payment rates vary. Pays on publication. Provides 2–3 author's copies.

Athens Parent

P.O. Box 1251
Athens, GA 30603

Editor-in-Chief: Shannon Walsh Howell

Description and Interests
Families in the Athens region of Georgia find informative and entertaining articles in this magazine. Published eight times each year, *Athens Parent* offers articles on family life, parenting, pregnancy, health and fitness, regional travel and recreation, education, careers, and regional subjects. It also features personal experience pieces, news, profiles, and interviews. Circ: Unavailable.
Website: www.athensparent.com

Freelance Potential
85% written by nonstaff writers. Publishes 40 freelance submissions yearly. Receives 500 queries yearly.
Submissions and Payment: Query. Accepts hard copy and email queries to mail@metromags.com. SASE. Response time varies. First rights. Articles and depts/columns, word lengths and payment rates vary. Payment policy varies.

Art Jewelry

21027 Crossroads Circle
Waukesha, WI 53187

Editorial Assistant: Katie Streeter

Description and Interests
Published six times each year, this magazine features jewelry-making projects of all difficulty levels. It continues to seek submissions for its "Beyond Jewelry" department. Circ: 40,000.
Website: www.artjewelrymag.com

Freelance Potential
50% written by nonstaff writers. Publishes 54 freelance submissions yearly; 30% by unpublished writers, 50% by authors who are new to the magazine. Receives 350 queries yearly.
Submissions and Payment: Guidelines available. Sample copy, $5.95. Query with jewelry samples or photos. Accepts hard copy and email queries with JPEG images to editor@jewelrymag.com. SASE. Responds in 1–2 months. All rights. Written material, word lengths and payment rates vary. Pays on acceptance. Provides 2 contributor's copies.

Austin Family

P.O. Box 7559
Round Rock, TX 78683-7559

Editor: Barbara Cooper

Description and Interests
This award-winning monthly magazine provides families living in the Austin area with articles covering a wide variety of topics on current parenting issues, tips and trends, and events. Circ: 35,000.
Website: www.austinfamily.com

Freelance Potential
70% written by nonstaff writers. Publishes 18 freelance submissions yearly; 10% by unpublished writers, 50% by new authors. Receives 1,200 queries and mss yearly.
Submissions and Payment: Sample copy, free. Query or send ms. Accepts email to 2003@austinfamily.com and simultaneous submissions. Availability of sidebars, pull quotes, and/or artwork improves chance of acceptance. Responds in 3–6 months. First and second serial rights. Articles, 800–1,200 words. Depts/columns, 800 words. All material, payment rates vary. Pays on publication.

Baton Rouge Parents Magazine

11831 Wentling Avenue
Baton Rouge, LA 70816-6055

Editor: Amy Foreman-Plaisance

Description and Interests
Parents in the Baton Rouge metropolitan area read this monthly magazine for locally-oriented, up-to-date, meaningful articles on family life, plus information on events and resources. Circ: 55,000.
Website: www.brparents.com

Freelance Potential
95% written by nonstaff writers. Publishes 50+ freelance submissions yearly; 15% by unpublished writers, 30% by authors who are new to the magazine.
Submissions and Payment: Guidelines available via email request to brpm@brparents.com. Query with outline, list of potential sources, brief author biography, and two writing samples. Accepts hard copy and email queries to brpm@brparents.com. SASE. Response time varies. First North American serial rights. Written material, word lengths vary; $25–$70. Kill fee, $10. Pays on publication. Provides 2 contributor's copies.

Bay Area Baby

1660 South Amphlett Boulevard, Suite 335
San Mateo, CA 94402

Special Sections Editor

Description and Interests
Expectant and new parents in the San Francisco Bay area comprise the audience of this twice-yearly magazine. Its informative and well-researched articles relate to pregnancy and infant and child care and development. It also features regional baby activities and moms-group news, and lists helpful resources. It is not accepting queries or unsolicited manuscripts at this time, as all articles are currently written on assignment only. Circ: 80,000.
Website: www.bayareaparent.com

Freelance Potential
50% written by nonstaff writers. Publishes 21 freelance submissions yearly; 50% by authors who are new to the magazine.
Submissions and Payment: Guidelines and theme list available. Sample copy, free with 9x12 SASE (5 first-class stamps). All work is assigned.

Beta Journal

National Beta Club
151 Beta Club Way
Spartanburg, SC 29306-3012

Editor: Lori Guthrie

Description and Interests
Targeting elementary and high school students who are members of the National Beta Club, this magazine offers articles on topics such as member accomplishments, community service, academics, and leadership. It is published five times each year. Circ: 400,000.
Website: www.betaclub.org

Freelance Potential
10% written by nonstaff writers. Publishes 2–4 freelance submissions yearly; 80% by unpublished writers. Receives 12 unsolicited mss yearly.
Submissions and Payment: Send complete ms. Accepts hard copy and email submissions to lguthrie@betaclub.org. Availability of artwork improves chance of acceptance. SASE. Responds in 2 months. Rights vary. Articles, 700–1,000 words; $25–$50. B/W prints or transparencies and line art; payment rates vary. Pays on publication. Provides 10 contributor's copies.

The Big Country Peacock Chronicle

RR 1 Box 89K-112
Aspermont, TX 79502

Editor-in-Chief: Audrey Yoeckel

Description and Interests
Striving to preserve American folk cultures and community values, this website offers articles covering traditional arts and crafts, artists, and writers, as well as reviews, resource information, short stories, and poetry. It is interested in seeing more adventure pieces. Hits per month: Unavailable.
Website: http://peacockchronicle.com

Freelance Potential
80% written by nonstaff writers. Publishes 10–12 freelance submissions yearly; 60% by unpublished writers, 80% by authors who are new to the magazine. Receives 100 queries and unsolicited mss yearly.
Submissions and Payment: Sample copy available at website. Query or send complete ms. Accepts email submissions to audrey@peacockchronicle.com. Response time varies. Electronic rights. Articles, word lengths vary. No payment.

Biography Today

615 Griswold Street
Detroit, MI 48226

Managing Editor: Cherie D. Abbey

Description and Interests
Issued six times each year, *Biography Today* profiles authors, musicians, political leaders, sports figures, actors, cartoonists, scientists, astronauts, TV personalities, and other people of interest to readers ages nine and older. Articles take a complete look at a person's life without skirting the controversial aspects. It is especially interested in a subject's early experiences: family, school, and favorite books and activities. Circ: 9,000.
Website: www.biographytoday.com

Freelance Potential
50% written by nonstaff writers. Publishes several freelance submissions yearly. Receives 12 queries yearly.
Submissions and Payment: Sample copy and guidelines available with 9x12 SASE. Query with résumé. SASE. Responds in 2 months. All rights. Articles, 2,000–5,000 words; payment rates vary according to author's experience. Provides 2 contributor's copies.

Black Woman and Child

P.O. Box 47045
300 Borough Drive
Toronto, Ontario M1P 4P0
Canada

Editor: Nicole Osbourne James

Description and Interests
This magazine is dedicated to serving the interests of African American women who are or have been pregnant, or plan to become pregnant. Published quarterly, it seeks articles on birth, diet and nutrition, fashion, health and wellness, spirituality, discipline, safety, and other pregnancy and parenting topics. Circ: Unavailable.
Website: www.blackwomanandchild.com

Freelance Potential
75% written by nonstaff writers. Publishes 25–40 freelance submissions yearly. Receives 75–100 queries, 30 unsolicited mss yearly.
Submissions and Payment: Guidelines available. Query or send ms. Accepts hard copy and email to bwacinfo@ nubeing.com (text files). No simultaneous submissions. SAE/IRC. Response time varies. Rights vary. Articles, 750–1,500 words. Depts/columns, word lengths vary. Written material, payment rates vary. Pays on publication.

Bird Times

7-L Dundas Circle
Greensboro, NC 27407

Executive Editor: Rita Davis

Description and Interests
This magazine is dedicated to covering topics related to birds. Each issue includes articles on health, breeding, new products, training, and basic care. Published six times each year, it is interested in articles on caring for birds, as well as information on the latest bird gadgets and food. Circ: 20,000.
Website: www.birdtimes.com

Freelance Potential
90% written by nonstaff writers. Publishes 30–40 freelance submissions yearly; 10% by unpublished writers, 50% by authors who are new to the magazine.
Submissions and Payment: Sample copy, $5 with 9x12 SASE (4 first-class stamps). Query or send complete ms. SASE. Responds in 1 month. All rights. Articles, 1,200–2,000 words. Depts/columns, 600–800 words. Written material, $.10 per word. Pays on publication. Provides 1 contributor's copy.

B'nai B'rith Magazine

2020 K Street NW, 7th Floor
Washington, DC 20006

Managing Editor: Hiram Reisner

Description and Interests
Members of B'nai B'rith, an international Jewish organization, read this magazine for its objective articles reporting on Jewish life in Israel and North America. It appears quarterly. Circ: 100,000.
Website: www.bnaibrith.org

Freelance Potential
50% written by nonstaff writers. Publishes 12–15 freelance submissions yearly; 10% by unpublished writers, 50% by new authors. Receives 120 queries yearly.
Submissions and Payment: Sample copy and guidelines, $3 with 9x12 SASE (3 first-class stamps). Query with clips. Accepts hard copy and email to bbm@ bnaibrith.org. SASE. Responds in 2–4 weeks. First North American serial rights. Articles, 1,000–3,000 words. Depts/columns, word lengths vary. Written material, payment rates vary. Pays on publication. Provides 2 contributor's copies.

Brain, Child

P.O. Box 714
Lexington, VA 24450

Editors: Jennifer Niesslein & Stephanie Wilkinson

Description and Interests
Celebrating the diversity of mothers and their styles, this quarterly features in-depth articles and personal essays that support thought and debate on topics of interest to mothers. It also includes fiction, cartoons, reviews, humor, and art. It is interested in essays that employ illustrative anecdotes, a personal voice, and a down-to-earth tone. Humor is a big plus. Circ: 30,000+.
Website: www.brainchildmag.com

Freelance Potential
Publishes many freelance submissions yearly.
Submissions and Payment: Sample copy and guidelines, $5. Query or send complete ms. Accepts hard copy, simultaneous submissions, and email to editor@brainchildmag.com. SASE. Responds in 2 months. Electronic rights. Features, 3,000 words. Personal essays, 800–4,500 words. Fiction, 1,500–4,500 words. Written material, payment rates vary. Pays on publication.

Caledonia Times

Box 278
Prince Rupert, British Columbia V8J 3P6
Canada

Editor: Debby Shaw

Description and Interests
This small Christian newsletter is published 10 times each year for Canadian young adults. It contains information on what's going on in each church parish, as well as opinion and personal experience pieces; humor; biography; articles on music, nature, religion, social issues, and multicultural subjects; and inspirational fiction and poetry. All departments are open to submissions from freelance writers. Circ: 1,259.

Freelance Potential
95% written by nonstaff writers. Publishes 10 freelance submissions yearly. Receives 1–2 unsolicited mss each year.
Submissions and Payment: Send complete ms. Accepts hard copy. SAE/IRC. Responds in 2–4 weeks. All rights. Articles and fiction, 500–750 words. Depts/columns, word lengths vary. No payment. Provides 5 contributor's copies.

Calgary's Child

723-105, 150 Crowfoot Cres NW
Calgary, Alberta T3G 3T2
Canada

Editor: Ellen Percival

Description and Interests
Parents, health care professionals, educators, and caregivers living in the Calgary area turn to this magazine, published six times per year, for news and information about current events, health and educational issues, and recreational activities for children and parents alike. Because all of its material features a local slant, writers submitting material to *Calgary's Child* should be familiar with this region of Canada. Circ: 70,000+.
Website: www.calgaryschild.com

Freelance Potential
80–90% written by nonstaff writers. Publishes 30–40 freelance submissions yearly.
Submissions and Payment: Query with outline. Accepts email queries to calgaryschild@shaw.ca. No simultaneous submissions. Response time varies. Rights vary. Articles, 400–500 words; payment negotiable. Provides 2 contributor's copies.

Canoe & Kayak Magazine

10526 NE 68th Street, Suite 3
Kirkland, WA 98033

Editor

Description and Interests
Focusing on flatwater and whitewater boating, this magazine offers articles on techniques and destinations. Published seven times each year, it also includes equipment reviews. Circ: 63,000.
Website: www.canoekayak.com

Freelance Potential
90% written by nonstaff writers. Publishes 25 freelance submissions yearly; 5% by unpublished writers, 25% by authors who are new to the magazine. Receives 240 queries and unsolicited mss yearly.
Submissions and Payment: Sample copy and guidelines, free with 9x12 SASE (7 first-class stamps). Query or send complete ms. Prefers email submissions to editor@canoekayak.com. Responds in 6–8 weeks. All rights. Articles, 400–2,000 words. Depts/columns, 150–750 words. Written material, $.15–$.50 per word. Pays within 30 days after publication. Provides 1 copy.

Caring for Kids

480 North Main Street
Canandaigua, NY 14424

Editor: Isabelle D. Jensen

Description and Interests
Published 11 times each year by the Cornell University Cooperative Extension, this regional newsletter is aimed at all adults who care for and about young children. Articles cover parenting, child care, safety, discipline, nutrition, health, fitness, crafts, current events, nature, the environment, education, early childhood issues, and teaching. Information about local parenting and family programs is also included. It is currently seeking activities for children ages two to ten. Submit seasonal material three months in advance. Circ: 1,000.

Freelance Potential
100% written by nonstaff writers.
Submissions and Payment: Sample copy, free. Query. Accepts hard copy and email queries to idj1@cornell.edu (Microsoft Word attachments). SASE. Response time varies. Articles, 300–500 words. No payment.

Cat Fancy

3 Burroughs
Irvine, CA 92618

Editor: Susan Logan

Description and Interests
Cat lovers, young and old, read this colorful monthly magazine for its mix of informative articles and profiles of other cat fanciers and their felines. Circ: 290,000.
Website: www.catchannel.com

Freelance Potential
95% written by nonstaff writers. Publishes 150 freelance submissions yearly; 10% by unpublished writers, 70% by authors who are new to the magazine. Receives 500+ queries yearly.
Submissions and Payment: Guidelines available. Query with clips between January 1 and May 1 only. Accepts email to query@catfancy.com. Availability of artwork improves chance of acceptance. Responds by August. First rights. Articles, 600–1,000 words. Depts/columns, 600 words. 35mm slides or high resolution digital photos with contact sheets. All material, payment rates vary. Pays on publication. Provides 2 copies.

Catalyst Chicago
Independent Reporting on Urban Schools

332 South Michigan Avenue, Suite 500
Chicago, IL 60604

Editor-in-Chief: Veronica Anderson

Description and Interests
This independent newsmagazine tracks the policies, practices, and problems of urban school improvement in Chicago. Published nine times each year, it is read by teachers and administrators. All material is written on assignment. Education journalists interested in contributing to this magazine are welcome to submit a query or present their credentials. Circ: 9,000.
Website: www.catalyst-chicago.org

Freelance Potential
20% written by nonstaff writers. Publishes 10–20 freelance submissions yearly; 25% by authors who are new to the magazine. Receives 45 queries yearly.
Submissions and Payment: Sample copy and guidelines, $2. Query or send letter of introduction. Accepts hard copy. SASE. Response time varies. All rights. Articles, to 2,300 words; $1,700. Pays on acceptance. Provides 1 contributor's copy.

Chickadee

Bayard Press Canada
10 Lower Spadina Avenue, Suite 400
Toronto, Ontario M4V 2V2
Canada

Submissions Editor

Description and Interests
This sister publication to *Chirp* and *Owl* is published 10 times each year for beginning readers ages six to nine. Interactive content—including articles, stories, puzzles, experiments, and crafts—is designed to enhance children's independent reading and problem-solving skills. Each issue centers around a theme. It does not review queries or unsolicited manuscripts; all material is assigned. Circ: 85,000.
Website: www.owlkids.com

Freelance Potential
5% written by nonstaff writers. Publishes 1 freelance submission yearly.
Submissions and Payment: Sample copy, $4. Guidelines and theme list available. Send résumé only. No unsolicited mss. All rights. Fiction, 650–700 words; $250. Pays on acceptance. Provides 2 contributor's copies.

Childbirth Magazine

375 Lexington Avenue
New York, NY 10017

Managing Editor: Kate Kelly

Description and Interests
Published annually, this magazine features articles on topics related to the third trimester of pregnancy and childbirth, including labor, delivery, and recovery. It also includes information on child care and parenting. Please note that all writing is done by assignment only, and it does not accept unsolicited manuscripts. Writers are welcome to submit a query for a topic related to childbirth or recovery. Circ: 230,000.
Website: www.americanbaby.com

Freelance Potential
55% written by nonstaff writers. Publishes 10 freelance submissions yearly.
Submissions and Payment: Query. Accepts hard copy. SASE. Responds in 6 weeks. First serial rights. Articles, 1,000–2,000 words. Depts/columns, word lengths vary. Written material, payment rates vary. Pays on acceptance. Provides 5 contributor's copies.

Child Life

Children's Better Health Institute
P.O. Box 567
Indianapolis, IN 46206-0567

Editor: Jack Gramling

Description and Interests
Child Life, published six times each year, is written for children ages 9 to 11 with a focus on their health, fitness, nutrition, hygiene, and safety. The 87-year-old magazine is sprinkled with historical features and reprints from its venerable past, along with other stories, articles, puzzles, quizzes, and word games that seek to enrich readers' education. Currently, its editors are seeking only poetry and limericks written by children and related to health and fitness. Circ: 20,000.
Website: www.childlifemag.org

Freelance Potential
15% written by nonstaff writers. Publishes few freelance submissions yearly.
Submissions and Payment: Guidelines available with SASE. Sample copy, $2.95 with 9x12 SASE (4 first-class stamps). Currently not accepting submissions for articles and stories. No payment for children's poetry.

Children's Advocate

Action Alliance for Children
The Hunt Home
1201 Martin Luther King Jr. Way
Oakland, CA 94612-1217

Editor: Jeanne Tepperman

Description and Interests
Published six times each year in both English and Spanish, this newsmagazine covers public policy issues affecting children and families in California. A typical issue contains news articles, resource lists, reviews of children's books, and updates from the Children's Advocates Roundtable. It is currently not accepting freelance submissions. Circ: 15,000.
Website: www.4children.org

Freelance Potential
40% written by nonstaff writers. Publishes 18 freelance submissions yearly.
Submissions and Payment: Sample copy, $3. Guidelines available. Not accepting queries or mss at this time. First North American serial rights. Articles, 500–1,500 words. Depts/columns, 300–1,100 words. Written material, to $.25 per word. Pays on acceptance. Provides 3 contributor's copies.

Chirp

Bayard Press Canada
10 Lower Spadina Avenue, Suite 400
Toronto, Ontario M4V 2V2
Canada

Submissions Editor

Description and Interests
Like its older siblings *Chickadee* and *Owl*, this magazine for children ages two to six is designed to make learning fun. Published nine times each year, it contains puzzles, games, rhymes, stories, and songs that introduce preschoolers to the relationship between words and pictures. It does not review queries or unsolicited manuscripts, as all work is done on assignment only. Circ: 60,000.
Website: www.owlkids.com

Freelance Potential
10% written by nonstaff writers. Publishes 1–3 freelance submissions yearly; 1% by unpublished writers.
Submissions and Payment: Sample copy, $3.50. Guidelines available. Send résumé only. No unsolicited mss. All rights. Written material, 300–400 words; payment rates vary. Pays on acceptance. Provides 2 contributor's copies.

Cincinnati Family Magazine

10945 Reed Hartman Highway, Suite 221
Cincinnati, OH 45242

Editor: Sherry Hang

Description and Interests
This free, regional parenting magazine gives parents of children of all ages the "inside scoop" on raising a family in the Greater Cincinnati area. Published monthly, it is interested in articles on topics such as parenting, travel, careers, and recreation, as well as coverage of regional events and family-oriented activities. Circ: 50,000.
Website: www.cincinnatifamilymagazine.com

Freelance Potential
50% written by nonstaff writers. Publishes 12–20 freelance submissions yearly; 5% by new authors. Receives 240–300 queries and unsolicited mss yearly.
Submissions and Payment: Query or send complete ms. Accepts hard copy and email to sherryh@ daycommail.com. SASE. Response time varies. First rights. Articles, word lengths vary; $75–$125. Depts/columns, word lengths and payment rates vary. Pays 30 days after publication.

Civilized Revolt

107 Crestview Drive
Morgantown, WV 26505

Editor: Derek Wehrwein

Description and Interests
Formerly titled *Virtue Magazine*, this online publication created by high school students as a way to air their concerns targets a politically-minded, conservative audience. It seeks political and social commentary by young people regarding specific, newsworthy events happening today. Content is updated every two weeks. Hits per month: 7,100.
Website: www.civilizedrevolt.com

Freelance Potential
15% written by nonstaff writers. Publishes 20 freelance submissions yearly; 75% by unpublished writers, 33% by authors who are new to the magazine. Receives 20 unsolicited mss yearly.
Submissions and Payment: Guidelines available at website. Send complete ms. Accepts email submissions to editor@civilizedrevolt.com. Responds in 2–3 weeks. All rights. Articles, 400–900 words. No payment.

Classic Toy Trains

21027 Crossroads Circle
Waukesha, WI 53187

Editor: Carl Swanson

Description and Interests
This magazine features articles and photographs covering all aspects of collecting and operating toy trains. Published nine times each year, it seeks how-to articles and reviews. Circ: 55,000.
Website: www.classictoytrains.com

Freelance Potential
60% written by nonstaff writers. Publishes 40–50 freelance submissions yearly; 20% by unpublished writers, 20% by authors who are new to the magazine. Receives 96 queries, 60 unsolicited mss yearly.
Submissions and Payment: Sample copy, $4.95 ($3 postage). Prefers query. Will accept complete ms. Accepts hard copy, disk submissions (Microsoft Word), and email to editor@classictoytrains.com. SASE. Responds in 3 months. All rights. Articles, 500–5,000 words; $75 per page. Depts/columns, word lengths and payment rates vary. Pays on acceptance. Provides 1 author's copy.

Clubhouse

P.O. Box 15
Berrien Springs, MI 49103

President/Editor: Elaine Trumbo

Description and Interests
First appearing in 1951, this monthly publication targets children ages nine to twelve. Each issue contains an editorial mix of fiction in a variety of genres, nonfiction, poetry, crafts, games, activities, and children's artwork. It is currently not accepting any new material. Check its website for any changes regarding this policy. Circ: 500.
Website: www.yourstoryhour.org/clubhouse

Freelance Potential
85% written by nonstaff writers. Publishes several freelance submissions yearly; 75% by unpublished writers, 95% by authors who are new to the magazine.
Submissions and Payment: Sample copy, free with 6x9 SASE (2 first-class stamps). Send complete ms. Accepts hard copy. SASE. Response time varies. All rights. Articles and fiction, 1,500 words. B/W line art. All material, payment rates vary. Pays after publication.

Coastal Family Magazine

340 Eisenhower Drive, Suite 240
Savannah, GA 31406

Managing Editor: Laura Gray

Description and Interests
This magazine offers Savannah-area families plenty of valuable information about the region and beyond. In addition to articles on local concerns, including travel and recreational guides, event news, and profiles, this magazine features articles on a variety of topics such as education, health and fitness, family finances, and parenting. Circ: Unavailable.
Website: www.coastalfamily.com

Freelance Potential
5% written by nonstaff writers. Publishes 24–36 freelance submissions yearly. Receives 100–150 queries each year.
Submissions and Payment: Guidelines available. Query. Accepts hard copy and email queries to editor@coastalfamily.com. SASE. Response time varies. All rights. Articles and depts/columns, word lengths vary; payment rates vary. Payment policy varies.

College and Junior Tennis

Fort Washington Tennis Academy
100 Harbor Road
Fort Washington, NY 11050

Webmaster: Marcia Frost

Description and Interests
Focusing on the national and international junior tennis circuit, this online publication features up-to-date information on tournaments, scores, results, and rankings. In also includes interviews with players, and a comprehensive directory of colleges in the U.S. with tennis programs. Hits per month: 1.5 million.
Website: www.collegeandjuniortennis.com

Freelance Potential
10% written by nonstaff writers. Publishes 5 freelance submissions yearly; 1% by authors who are new to the magazine. Receives 24 unsolicited mss yearly.
Submissions and Payment: Sample copy available at website. Send complete ms. Accepts email submissions to marcia@collegeandjuniortenniscom. Responds in 2–14 days. One-time rights. Articles, to 700 words. Games and 1-page puzzles. No payment.

Coins

700 East State Street
Iola, WI 54990

Editor: Robert Van Ryzin

Description and Interests
Coin collectors and enthusiasts, from novice to expert, read this monthly magazine for its authoritative articles on coins, medals, and tokens. Each issue includes value guides and an events and shows calendar. Also featured are personal experience pieces and profiles of collectors and collections, and how-to information on collecting and buying. Circ: 60,000.
Website: www.collect.com

Freelance Potential
40% written by nonstaff writers. Publishes 70 freelance submissions yearly; 5% by authors who are new to the magazine. Receives 36–60 queries yearly.
Submissions and Payment: Sample copy and guidelines, free. Query. Accepts hard copy. SASE. Responds in 1–2 months. All rights. Articles, 1,500–2,500 words; $.04 per word. Work for hire. Pays on publication. Provides contributor's copies upon request.

Community Education Journal

3929 Old Lee Highway, Suite 91A
Fairfax, VA 22030

Editor

Description and Interests
Published quarterly by the National Community Education Association, this journal serves as a conduit for information about community education opportunities, including adult continuing education and summer school programs for kindergarten through high school. Circ: Unavailable.
Website: www.ncea.com

Freelance Potential
98% written by nonstaff writers. Publishes 24 freelance submissions yearly; 30% by unpublished writers, 60% by authors who are new to the magazine. Receives 12–24 unsolicited mss yearly.
Submissions and Payment: Sample copy, guidelines, and theme list, $5. Send 5 copies of complete ms. Accepts email submissions to ncea@ncea.com. Responds in 1–2 months. All rights. Articles, 1,500–2,000 words. No payment. Provides 5 author's copies.

Cookie

4 Times Square
New York, NY 10036

Acquisitions: Mireille Hyde

Description and Interests

Cookie, which is published ten times each year, is for parents of infants and children up to age six. It differs from other parenting magazines in that its readership has established a sophisticated lifestyle. It offers articles on a wide variety of topics, including health, travel, family life, and parenting issues, all geared toward the busy mom and dad. Queries should include an organization plan for the proposed article. Circ: 400,000.
Website: www.cookiemag.com

Freelance Potential

50% written by nonstaff writers. Receives 600–1,200 queries yearly.
Submissions and Payment: Query. Accepts hard copy and email queries to editor@cookiemag.com (include "Freelance Pitch" in the subject line). SASE. Response time varies. Rights vary. Articles, word lengths and payment rates vary. Pays on publication.

Creative Child Magazine

2505 Anthem Village Drive, Suite E619
Henderson, NV 89052

Editor

Description and Interests

Six times each year, *Creative Child Magazine* provides parents with the latest information and advice on nurturing their child's creativity. It offers articles on topics ranging from health and safety to family travel, as well as holiday and craft activities for children, and book and media reviews. Circ: 50,000.
Website: www.creativechildonline.com

Freelance Potential

25% written by nonstaff writers. Publishes 20 freelance submissions yearly.
Submissions and Payment: Sample copy, free with 9x12 SASE (4 first-class stamps). Query. Accepts hard copy and email queries to info@creativechildonline.com. SASE. Responds in 1–3 months. First print and electronic rights. Articles and depts/columns, word lengths and payment rates vary. Pays on publication. Provides contributor's copies.

Countdown for Kids

Juvenile Diabetes Research Foundation
120 Wall Street, 19th Floor
New York, NY 10005

Submissions Editor: Jason Dineen

Description and Interests

Children and young adults living with Type I diabetes read this quarterly for informative articles on the various social and emotional issues of dealing with their illness. Profiles and self-help and personal experience pieces are also a part of its mix. Circ: Unavailable.
Website: www.jdrf.org

Freelance Potential

50% written by nonstaff writers. Publishes 4–5 freelance submissions yearly; 10% by authors who are new to the magazine. Receives 120 queries and unsolicited mss each year.
Submissions and Payment: Sample copy available. Query or send complete ms. Accepts hard copy. SASE. Response time varies. First North American serial rights. Articles and depts/columns, word lengths and payment rates vary. Pays on publication. Provides 1 contributor's copy.

Curriculum Review

Paperclip Communications
125 Patterson Avenue
Little Falls, NJ 07424

Editor: Susan M. Spangler

Description and Interests

Teachers who are striving to keep up with the challenges of working with young people turn to *Curriculum Review* for its informational articles, teaching techniques, and reviews of educational resources and programs. It is published monthly through the school year, September to May, and prefers submissions from writers with backgrounds in education. Circ: 5,000.
Website: www.curriculumreview.com

Freelance Potential

2% written by nonstaff writers. Publishes 10 freelance submissions yearly. Receives 24 queries yearly.
Submissions and Payment: Sample copy, free with 9x12 SASE (2 first-class stamps). Query. Accepts hard copy. SASE. Responds in 1 month. One-time rights. Articles, to 4,000 words. Depts/columns, word lengths vary. Written material, payment rates vary. Payment policy varies. Provides contributor's copies.

Cyberteens Zeen

Able Minds, Inc.
7509 Alfred Drive
Silver Spring, MD 20910

Editor

Description and Interests
Written by and for teens, this e-zine features their original short stories, essays, poetry, creative nonfiction, and media reviews. All topics will be considered, but upbeat and humorous pieces, especially those with illustrations, have the best chance of being accepted. Authors cannot be older than 19. Please note that we are not accepting submissions at the present time. Hits per month: Unavailable.
Website: www.cyberteens.com

Freelance Potential
100% written by nonstaff writers. Publishes 30 freelance submissions yearly. Receives many unsolicited mss yearly.
Submissions and Payment: Sample copy available at website. Production is temporarily suspended. Please do not send queries or mss at this time. Check website periodically for updated information on status.

Discoveries

WordAction Publishing Company
2923 Troost Avenue
Kansas City, MO 64109

Assistant Editor: Kimberly Adams

Description and Interests
A full-color story paper, *Discoveries* ties directly into the publisher's Sunday school curriculum. It is intended to connect Sunday school lessons to the everyday lives of children ages eight to ten. Writers are advised to use realistic, present day situations to show, not preach, the character building and Scripture application. Circ: 35,000.
Website: www.wordaction.com

Freelance Potential
75% written by nonstaff writers. Of the freelance submissions published yearly, 20% are by unpublished writers.
Submissions and Payment: Theme list available. Query or send complete ms. Accepts hard copy. SASE. Responds in 6–8 weeks. Multiple-use rights. Articles, 150 words; $15. Stories, to 500 words; $25. Pays on acceptance. Provides 2 contributor's copies.

Dirt Rider Magazine

6420 Wilshire Boulevard, 17th Floor
Los Angeles, CA 90048-5515

Editor

Description and Interests
This monthly magazine for dirt bike riders of all ages features riding tips, gear reviews, rider profiles and interviews, industry news, and competition updates, as well as photo-essays. It welcomes freelance contributions. Manuscripts must be typewritten on white paper, and all photographs must be accompanied by captions. Photo model releases are required for all persons depicted in photos. Circ: Unavailable.
Website: www.dirtrider.com

Freelance Potential
20% written by nonstaff writers. Publishes 20 freelance submissions yearly.
Submissions and Payment: Query. Accepts hard copy. SASE. Response time varies. Rights vary. Articles, word lengths vary. 5x5 JPEG images at 300 dpi. All material, payment rates vary. Pays on publication. Provides 1 contributor's copy.

Discovery Girls

4300 Stevens Creek Boulevard, Suite 190
San Jose, CA 95129

Editor: Catherine Lee

Description and Interests
Published six times each year, this magazine strives to inspire confidence in pre-teen girls by offering advice and encouragement on topics such as diet and nutrition, careers, fitness, social issues, sports, fashion, popular culture, volunteering, and entertainment. Created by and for girls ages seven to twelve, it is interested in inspirational articles and essays on friendship, fashion, and other topics of interest to tweens. Material must be positive and age-appropriate. Circ: 120,000.
Website: www.discoverygirls.com

Freelance Potential
75% written by nonstaff writers. Publishes 30 freelance submissions yearly.
Submissions and Payment: Query or send complete ms. Accepts hard copy. SASE. Response time varies. Rights vary. Articles and depts/columns, word lengths vary. No payment.

Dog Fancy

BowTie, Inc.
P.O. Box 6050
Mission Viejo, CA 92690-6050

Managing Editor: Hazel Kelly

Description and Interests
Each monthly issue of *Dog Fancy* magazine is filled with informative and thoroughly researched articles on canine health, behavior, and training. Its readership includes breeders, trainers, and showers, as well as pet owners. Circ: 270,000.
Website: www.dogfancy.com

Freelance Potential
80% written by nonstaff writers. Publishes 20–25 freelance submissions yearly; 25% by authors who are new to the magazine. Receives 1,200 queries yearly.
Submissions and Payment: Guidelines available. Sample copy, $4.50 at newsstands. Query with résumé, outline, and writing samples. No unsolicited mss. Responds in 6–8 weeks. First North American serial rights. Articles, 1,200–1,800 words. Depts/columns, 650 words. All material, payment rates vary. Pays on publication. Provides 2 contributor's copies.

Dolls

217 Passaic Avenue
Hasbrouck, NJ 07604

Editor: Nayda Rondon

Description and Interests
Collectors of contemporary, antique, and reproduction dolls read this magazine, published 10 times each year. Articles cover doll collections and history. Circ: 65,000.
Website: www.dollsmagazine.com

Freelance Potential
50% written by nonstaff writers. Publishes 90 freelance submissions yearly; 5% by unpublished writers, 20% by authors who are new to the magazine. Receives 40 unsolicited mss monthly.
Submissions and Payment: Send complete ms. Accepts hard copy, Macintosh disk submissions, and email submissions to nrdollsmagazine@earthlink.net. Availability of artwork improves chance of acceptance. SASE. Response time varies. All rights. Articles, 1,000–2,000 words. Depts/columns, word lengths vary. Color prints, slides, or transparencies; JPEG files at 300 dpi. All material, payment rates vary. Pays on publication.

Dollhouse Miniatures

420 Boylston Street, 5th Floor
Boston, MA 02116

Editor-in-Chief: Terrence Lynch

Description and Interests
Dollhouse Miniatures is a monthly magazine for enthusiasts of small-scale reproductions. Beginners as well as long-time hobbyists value this publication for its profiles of miniaturists and their collections, instructions for projects, and product reviews. Circ: 25,000.
Website: www.dhminiatures.com

Freelance Potential
75% written by nonstaff writers. Publishes 100 freelance submissions yearly; 10% by unpublished writers, 30% by new authors. Receives 60 queries yearly.
Submissions and Payment: Guidelines available at website. Sample copy, $4.95 with 9x12 SASE ($1.95 postage). Query with outline. Accepts hard copy and email queries to tlynch@madavor.com. SASE. Responds in 2 months. All rights. Articles and depts/columns, word lengths vary; $75 per magazine page. Pays on publication. Provides 1 contributor's copy.

Dyslexia Online Magazine

Editor: John Bradford

Description and Interests
This Internet publication founded in 1998 specializes in articles about children and adults with dyslexia. It is written in equal measure for parents, teachers, and students, and features self-help, informational, and personal experience pieces along with book reviews and teaching techniques. Much of its content is available in both English and Spanish. Due to the online nature of the magazine, published contributions remain permanently available at the website. Hits per month: 150,000.
Website: www.dyslexia-parent.com/magazine

Freelance Potential
50% written by nonstaff writers.
Submissions and Payment: Sample copy and guidelines available at website. Send complete ms. Accepts email submissions to dyslextest@aol.com (no attachments). Responds in 2 weeks. All rights. Articles, word lengths vary. No payment.

Early Years

3035 Valley Avenue, Suite 103
Winchester, VA 22601

Submissions: Jennifer Hutchinson

Description and Interests
Striving to promote parental involvement in school, this newsletter, published nine times each year, includes short articles and tips for parents of children in preschool and kindergarten. It is not in need of freelance material at this time; check its website for updates. Circ: 60,000.
Website: www.rfeonline.com

Freelance Potential
100% written by nonstaff writers. Publishes 80 freelance submissions yearly; 28% by unpublished writers. Receives 36 queries yearly.
Submissions and Payment: Sample copy, free with 9x12 SASE (2 first-class stamps). Query with résumé and clips when submission policy changes. Accepts hard copy. SASE. Responds in 1 month. All rights. Articles, 225–300 words. Depts/columns, 175–200 words. Written material, $.60 per word. Pays on acceptance. Provides 5 contributor's copies.

The Education Revolution

417 Roslyn Road
Roslyn Heights, NY 11577

Executive Director: Jerry Mintz

Description and Interests
Each issue of this quarterly magazine is packed with articles and information about public and private alternative schools and homeschooling. Targeting administrators, teachers, and parents, it reports on successful programs and events and presents essays on vital issues. In addition, it includes contact information, job opportunities, conference details, and international news. Writers experienced in the field of education are welcome to submit a query. Circ: 5,000.
Website: www.educationrevolution.org

Freelance Potential
20% written by nonstaff writers. Publishes 10 freelance submissions yearly; 40% by authors who are new to the magazine. Receives 180 queries yearly.
Submissions and Payment: Query. SASE. Responds in 1 month. Rights vary. Written material, word lengths vary. No payment.

Earthwatch Institute Journal

3 Clock Tower Place, Suite 100
Maynard, MA 01754-0075

Editor: Jennifer Goebel

Description and Interests
This journal is the member publication of Earthwatch Institute, an organization dedicated to "finding solutions for a sustainable future." It is published three times each year and distributed worldwide. It features Earthwatch Institute news, events, and member profiles, as well as articles describing the research undertaken by the Institute. Circ: 25,000.
Website: www.earthwatch.org

Freelance Potential
30% written by nonstaff writers. Publishes 2–3 freelance submissions yearly. Receives 60 queries, 36 unsolicited mss yearly.
Submissions and Payment: Sample copy and guidelines available. Query or send ms. Prefers email submissions to jgoebel@earthwatch.org. Will accept hard copy. SASE. Response time varies. First rights. Articles, 1,500–2,000 words; $500–$1,000. Pays on publication.

EFCA Today

901 East 78th Street
Minneapolis, MN 55420

Editor: Diane McDougall

Description and Interests
This quarterly publication of the Evangelical Free Church of America (EFCA) is read by pastors, church elders, Sunday school teachers, and ministry volunteers. Its goal is to generate conversations over topics pertinent to faith and life in the twenty-first century. Circ: 30,000.
Website: www.efca.org/magazine

Freelance Potential
90% written by nonstaff writers. Publishes several freelance submissions yearly.
Submissions and Payment: Sample copy and guidelines, $1 with 9x12 SASE (5 first-class stamps). Query. Accepts hard copy and email queries to dianemc@ journeygroup.com. SASE. Response time varies. First rights. Articles, 200–700 words. Cover theme articles, 300–1,000 words. Written material, $.23 per word. Pays on acceptance.

The Elementary School Journal

University of Missouri, College of Education
202 London Hall
Columbia, MO 65211-1150

Managing Editor: Gail M. Hinkel

Description and Interests
This peer-reviewed academic journal published five times each year by the University of Chicago Press contains original scholarly studies about elementary and middle school processes, as well as articles on education theory and research and their implications for teaching practice. It occasionally publishes integrative research reviews and in-depth conceptual analyses of schooling. Circ: 2,200.
Website: www.journals.uchicago.edu/ESJ

Freelance Potential
100% written by nonstaff writers. Publishes several freelance submissions yearly.
Submissions and Payment: Sample copy, $13.50. Guidelines available at website. Send 4 copies of complete ms with an abstract of 100–150 words. Accepts hard copy. SASE. Response time varies. Rights vary. Articles, word lengths vary. No payment.

Encyclopedia of Youth Studies

130 Essex Street
South Hamilton, MA 01982

Editor: Dean Borgman

Description and Interests
Anyone who works with young people, including social workers, teachers, youth ministers, and civic youth leaders, finds important information on over 200 topics related to youth issues in this online encyclopedia. It features well-researched articles, training materials, and program ideas. Hits per month: Unavailable.
Website: www.centerforyouth.org

Freelance Potential
20% written by nonstaff writers. Publishes 5–10 freelance submissions yearly; 85% by unpublished writers, 85% by authors who are new to the magazine. Receives 48 queries, 12 unsolicited mss yearly.
Submissions and Payment: Sample copy and guidelines available at website. Query or send complete ms. Accepts email submissions to cys@centerforyouth.org. Responds to queries in 1 week, to mss in 1 month. All rights. Articles, 600 words. No payment.

Entertainment Magazine

P.O. Box 3355
Tucson, AZ 85722

Publisher: Robert Zucker

Description and Interests
This online magazine provides daily updates about community activities in the greater Tucson area, with a focus on families. It will consider submissions for all areas, including health and fitness, music, recreation, regional news, college, and careers. It is not interested in product promotions. Hits per month: 1 million.
Website: www.emol.org

Freelance Potential
90% written by nonstaff writers. Publishes 300+ freelance submissions yearly; 75% by unpublished writers, 25% by authors who are new to the magazine. Receives 3,000+ queries yearly.
Submissions and Payment: Sample copy and guidelines available at website. Query. Accepts email queries to publisher@emol.org. Responds in 1–2 days. Author retains rights. Articles, to 1,000 words. B/W digital prints. No payment.

eSchoolNews

7920 Norfolk Avenue, Suite 900
Bethesda, MD 20814

Editor: Greg Downey

Description and Interests
Appearing both online and in print, *eSchoolNews* provides school administrators and technology educators with comprehensive coverage of technology issues in the kindergarten to college classroom. Each monthly issue includes articles on the latest products, services, and strategies. It also covers news and events relevant to school technology professionals. Circ: Unavailable.
Website: www.eschoolnews.com

Freelance Potential
20% written by nonstaff writers. Publishes 6–8 freelance submissions yearly. Receives 12 unsolicited mss yearly.
Submissions and Payment: Sample copy available at website. Prefers query. Will accept complete ms. Accepts hard copy and email to GDowney@eschoolnews.com. SASE. Response time varies. Rights vary. Articles and depts/columns, word lengths and payment rates vary. Pays on acceptance.

Family-Life Magazine

100 Professional Center Drive, Suite 104
Rohnert Park, CA 94928

Publisher/Editor: Sharon Gowan

Description and Interests
This monthly publication targets parents in California's Sonoma, Mendocino, and Lake counties with articles on the arts, education, child care, health, fitness, home, and family fun. It currently seeks submissions about teen issues and healthy living tips for families. Circ: 40,000.
Website: www.family-life.us

Freelance Potential
40% written by nonstaff writers. Publishes 24–36 freelance submissions yearly; 10% by unpublished writers. Receives 120+ unsolicited mss yearly.
Submissions and Payment: Guidelines and editorial calendar available. Send complete ms. Accepts email submissions to sharon@family-life.us (in body of email or as Microsoft Word attachment). Response time varies. One-time rights. Articles, 650–1,150 words; $.08 per word. Pays on publication.

Family Safety & Health

1121 Spring Lake Drive
Itasca, IL 60143

Editor: Tim Hodson

Description and Interests
This magazine strives to promote home, recreational, and traffic safety, as well as the importance of good nutrition and fitness. It is published four times each year by the National Safety Council and is currently not accepting queries or unsolicited manuscripts. All work is assigned. Circ: 225,000.
Website: www.nsc.org

Freelance Potential
1% written by nonstaff writers. Publishes 5 freelance submissions yearly; 20% by authors who are new to the magazine.
Submissions and Payment: Sample copy, $4 with 9x12 SASE ($.77 postage). No queries or unsolicited mss. All writing is done on a work-for-hire basis. Send résumé only. All rights. Articles, 1,200 words. Written material, payment rates vary. Pays on acceptance. Provides 2 contributor's copies.

FamilyRapp.com

P.O. Box 117
Oxted RH8 OFN
United Kingdom

Submissions: Cathy Baillie & Jane Rouse

Description and Interests
Providing a wealth of information on parenting topics, this weekly online magazine targets parents of children ages three through thirteen. In addition, it covers topics such as health, family traveling, social issues, the holidays, and education. Helpful resources, profiles, and book reviews are also included in its editorial mix. Hits per month: Unavailable.
Website: www.familyrapp.com

Freelance Potential
75% written by nonstaff writers. Publishes 100 freelance submissions yearly. Receives 52 unsolicited mss each year.
Submissions and Payment: Sample copy and guidelines available at website. Send complete ms. Accepts email submissions to info@familyrapp.com. Response time varies. One-time and electronic rights. Articles, 500–1,000 words. No payment.

Farm & Ranch Living

5925 Country Lane
Greendale, WI 53129

Editor: Nick Pabst

Description and Interests
Published six times each year, *Farm & Ranch Living* is a lifestyle magazine "for families who love the land." It seeks photo-illustrated stories about present-day farmers and ranchers. Circ: 350,000.
Website: www.farmandranchliving.com

Freelance Potential
90% written by nonstaff writers. Publishes 36 freelance submissions yearly; 50% by unpublished writers, 50% by authors who are new to the magazine. Receives 120 queries and unsolicited mss yearly.
Submissions and Payment: Sample copy, $2. Query or send complete ms. Accepts hard copy and email to editors@farmandranchliving.com. Artwork improves chance of acceptance. SASE. Responds in 6 weeks. One-time rights. Articles, 1,200 words. Depts/columns, 350 words. Artwork, color prints. Written material, $10–$150. Pays on publication. Provides 1 copy.

FatherMag.com

P.O. Box 231891
Houston, TX 77223

Managing Editor: John Gill

Description and Interests
Since 1995, this online magazine has been providing innovative solutions for men with children. It is always looking for articles, short stories, and any other material of interest to fathers; submissions should be new, exciting, and thought-provoking. No idea is too wild. Writers do not need to be fathers, or even male, to contribute. Hits per month: 1 million.
Website: www.fathermag.com

Freelance Potential
95% written by nonstaff writers. Publishes 50 freelance submissions yearly; 50% by authors who are new to the magazine.
Submissions and Payment: Sample copy and writers' guidelines available at website. Query. Accepts email queries to jgill@fathermag.com. Response time varies. One-time rights. Articles and fiction, word lengths vary. No payment.

FineScale Modeler

21027 Crossroads Circle
P.O. Box 1612
Waukesha, WI 53187

Editor: Matthew Usher

Description and Interests
This magazine for model builders is published 10 times each year. It offers beginner and advanced modelers alike step-by-step how-to articles on technique and every other aspect of model building. Circ: 60,000.
Website: www.finescale.com

Freelance Potential
85% written by nonstaff writers. Publishes 40 freelance submissions yearly; 20% by authors who are new to the magazine. Receives 120–240 unsolicited mss yearly.
Submissions and Payment: Sample copy, $4.95 with 9x12 SASE. Query or send complete ms. Accepts hard copy, disk submissions with hard copy, and email submissions to editor@finescale.com. SASE. Responds in 1–4 months. All rights. Articles, 750–3,000 words. Depts/columns, word lengths vary. Written material, $60–$75 per page. Pays on acceptance. Provides 1 contributor's copy.

Fido Friendly

P.O. Box 10219
Costa Mesa, CA 92627

Editor: Nick Sveslosky

Description and Interests
Focusing on traveling with dogs, this magazine includes personal experience pieces and reviews covering travel destinations, hiking and camping spots, and hotels. It is published six times each year and welcomes articles from new writers about traveling with dogs in different parts of the U.S. and Canada. Circ: 44,000.
Website: www.fidofriendly.com

Freelance Potential
60% written by nonstaff writers. Publishes 6–12 freelance submissions yearly; 10% by unpublished writers, 10% by authors who are new to the magazine. Receives 120 queries yearly.
Submissions and Payment: Sample copy and guidelines, $4.95. Query with sample paragraph. Accepts email queries to nick@fidofriendly.com. Responds in 1 month. First rights. Articles, 800–1,200 words; $.10 per word. Pays on publication. Provides 1 author's copy.

Fort Lauderdale Family Magazine

7045 SW 69th Avenue
South Miami, FL 33143

Publisher: Janet Jupiter

Description and Interests
Residents of Fort Lauderdale and its surrounding communities read this monthly magazine for family-oriented articles and columns. Animal and pet information, movie reviews, local events, and child care issues are a part of every issue. This magazine prefers to work with writers who are familiar with the Fort Lauderdale area. Circ: Unavailable.
Website: www.fortlauderdalefamily.com

Freelance Potential
20% written by nonstaff writers. Publishes 15–20 freelance submissions yearly.
Submissions and Payment: Sample copy available at website. Query. Accepts hard copy and email queries to miamifamily@bellsouth.net. SASE. Response time varies. One-time rights. Articles and depts/columns, word lengths and payment rates vary. Pays on publication. Provides contributor's copies.

Gay Parent Magazine

P.O. Box 750852
Forest Hills, NY 11375-0852

Editor: Angeline Acain

Description and Interests
Gay Parent Magazine, published six times each year, serves as a valuable resource for lesbian and gay families. It provides information on gay-oriented schools, travel, camps, and other activities; and features articles on issues important to them. Circ: 10,000.
Website: www.gayparentmag.com

Freelance Potential
3% written by nonstaff writers. Publishes 6 freelance submissions yearly; 1% by authors who are new to the magazine. Receives 75 unsolicited mss yearly.
Submissions and Payment: Sample copy and guidelines, $3.50. Send complete ms. Accepts email submissions to acain@gis.net. Availability of artwork improves chance of acceptance. SASE. Response time varies. One-time rights. Articles, 500–1,000 words; $.10 per word. Color prints or electronic files. Pays on publication. Provides contributor's copies upon request.

Girlfriend Magazine

35-51 Mitchell Street
McMahons Point, New South Wales 2060
Australia

Editorial Coordinator: Belinda Frizza

Description and Interests
Teenage girls turn to this monthly magazine for articles covering the fashion scene, careers, beauty, boys, and real-life teen issues. It also includes the latest celebrity gossip. Circ: 112,000.
Website: www.girlfriend.com.au

Freelance Potential
30% written by nonstaff writers. Publishes 36 freelance submissions yearly; 25% by unpublished writers, 15% by authors who are new to the magazine.
Submissions and Payment: Sample copy, $4.50. Send complete ms. Accepts hard copy and email submissions to girlfriendonline@pacpubs.com.au. SAE/IRC. Responds in 3 weeks. Exclusive rights. Articles, 1,500–2,000 words. Fiction, 2,000 words. Depts/columns, 500 words. Color prints or transparencies. All material, payment rates vary. Pays on publication. Provides 3 contributor's copies.

Golfer Girl Magazine

12948 Biscayne Cove
Del Mar, CA 92014

Submissions: Libby Hooton

Description and Interests
This new quarterly magazine for girls ages 8 to 17 aims to increase the community of female golfers with interesting, educational, and inspirational articles about junior golfers, famous women golfers, and related topics such as fashion and rules. It is edited in part by teenage girls. Circ: 10,000.
Website: www.golfergirlmagazine.com

Freelance Potential
100% written by nonstaff writers. Publishes many freelance submissions yearly; 40% by authors who are new to the magazine.
Submissions and Payment: Send complete ms, preferably with artwork. Accepts email submissions only to libby@golfergirlmagazine.com; copy claude@golfergirlmagazine.com. Response time varies. Rights vary. Written material, word lengths vary. No payment. Provides a 2-year subscription.

Go! Magazine

2711 S. Loop Drive, Suite 4700
Ames, IA 50010

Editor: Michele Regenold

Description and Interests
This e-magazine is for teens and young adults who are interested in exploring careers in transportation. Appearing six times each year, it features articles about the exciting opportunities in the transportation industry. Past issue themes have included winter work, shipping, and design/engineering. Hits per month: Unavailable.
Website: www.go-explore-trans.org

Freelance Potential
50–75% written by nonstaff writers. Publishes 2 freelance submissions yearly.
Submissions and Payment: Sample copy, guidelines, and theme list available at website. Query. Accepts email queries to editor@go-explore-trans.com. First world electronic and archival rights. Articles, 1,000–1,500 words. Depts/columns, 750–1,250 words. Written material, $50. Artwork, $25.

Good Housekeeping

Hearst Corporation
300 West 57th Street
New York, NY 10019-5288

Executive Editor: Judith Coyne

Description and Interests
This monthly magazine covers topics of interest to women, including family life, careers, and child rearing. Circ: 25 million.
Website: www.goodhousekeeping.com

Freelance Potential
80% written by nonstaff writers. Publishes 50+ freelance submissions yearly. Receives 18,000–24,000 queries yearly.
Submissions and Payment: Guidelines available at website. Sample copy, $2.50 at newsstands. Query with résumé and clips for nonfiction; SASE. Send complete ms for fiction; mss not returned. Accepts hard copy. Responds in 4–6 weeks. All rights for nonfiction; first North American serial rights for fiction. Articles, 750–2,500 words; to $2,000. Essays, to 1,000 words; to $750. Fiction, to 3,000 words; payment rates vary. Pays on acceptance. Provides 1 contributor's copy.

Grandparents Magazine

281 Rosedale Avenue
Wayne, PA 19087

Editor: Katrina Hayday Wester

Description and Interests
This e-zine offers informational articles, profiles, essays, interviews, new product information, and book and toy reviews. In addition, it includes resource information, song lyrics, and links to children's activities. It is interested in articles on family-friendly travel destinations, life lessons, social issues, health and exercise, religion, and recreation, as well as essays that explore fun ways to spend time with grandchildren. Hits per month: Unavailable.
Website: www.grandparentsmagazine.net

Freelance Potential
Publishes several freelance submissions yearly.
Submissions and Payment: Sample copy and guidelines available at website. Query. Accepts email queries to content@grandparentsmagazine.net. Response time varies. Electronic rights. Articles, word lengths vary. No payment.

Grand Rapids Family

549 Ottawa Avenue NW, Suite 201
Grand Rapids, MI 49503

Editor: Carole Valade

Description and Interests
Targeting West Michigan families, this informational magazine includes articles on a variety of topics, including child care, education, child rearing, travel, family issues, adoption, and health, as well as profiles, reviews, and local news. Published monthly, it is interested in profiles of outstanding children from the region, and family-friendly travel pieces. Circ: 30,000.
Website: www.grfamily.com

Freelance Potential
20% written by nonstaff writers. Publishes 15 freelance submissions yearly.
Submissions and Payment: Guidelines available with #10 SASE. Query or send complete ms. Accepts hard copy. SASE. Responds to queries in 2 months, to mss in 6 months. All rights. Articles and depts/columns, word lengths and payment rates vary. B/W or color prints; $25. Kill fee, $25. Pays on publication.

Harford County Kids

P.O. Box 1666
Bel Air, MD 21014

Publisher: Joan Fernandez

Description and Interests
Families in Harford County, Maryland, and its surrounding communities turn to this monthly magazine for articles on exercise and health, pregnancy, area recreational activities and events, education, and family issues. Each issue of *Harford County Kids* also features profiles of area families. Circ: 28,500.
Website: www.harfordcountykids.com

Freelance Potential
100% written by nonstaff writers. Publishes 20 freelance submissions yearly.
Submissions and Payment: Guidelines available. Query. Accepts hard copy and email queries to joanf@aboutdelta.com. SASE. Response time varies. First print and electronic rights. Articles and depts/columns, word lengths and payment rates vary. Pays on publication. Provides 1 contributor's copy.

Highlights High Five

807 Church Street
Honesdale, PA 18431-1895

Editor: Kathleen Hayes

Description and Interests
This new magazine from the publishers of *Highlights for Children*, published monthly for ages two to six, celebrates the early years of childhood with a mix of puzzles, activities, poetry, and read-aloud stories. Its goal is to provide high quality material that supports the social, emotional, physical, and cognitive development of young children. Animal stories, folktales, fantasy, and contemporary fiction are featured. Nonfiction topics include animals, nature, math, crafts, and cooking. At this time its entire content is commissioned or written in-house; interested writers are advised to check the website for changes to this policy. Circ: 100,000.
Website: www.highlights.com

Freelance Potential
Publishes few freelance submissions yearly.
Submissions and Payment: Not seeking unsolicited manuscripts at this time.

The High School Journal

Editorial Office, School of Education
University of North Carolina, CB#3500
Chapel Hill, NC 27599

Submissions: Daniella Cook

Description and Interests
Secondary school educators and administrators read this journal for articles about successful educational practices and programs, and research reports on teacher, administrator, and student interaction in school settings. It is published four times each school year. Circ: 800.
Website: www.uncpress.unc.edu

Freelance Potential
100% written by nonstaff writers. Publishes 20–30 freelance submissions yearly; 25% by unpublished writers, 85% by authors who are new to the magazine. Receives 324 unsolicited mss yearly.
Submissions and Payment: Sample copy, $7.50 with 9x12 SASE. Send 3 copies of complete ms. Accepts email submissions to daniellacook@gmail.com. Responds in 3–4 months. All rights. Articles, 1,500–2,500 words. Depts/columns, 300–400 words. No payment. Provides 3 contributor's copies.

High School Writer Senior

Writer Publications
P.O. Box 718
Grand Rapids, MN 55477-0718

Editor: Emily Benes

Description and Interests
Six times each year this magazine publishes high-quality nonfiction, fiction, and poetry submitted by high school students. Circ: 44,000.
Website: www.writerpublications.com

Freelance Potential
100% written by nonstaff writers. Publishes 300 freelance submissions yearly; 95% by unpublished writers, 75% by authors who are new to the magazine. Receives 36,000 unsolicited mss yearly.
Submissions and Payment: Sample copy, free. Accepts submissions from senior high school students of subscribing teachers only. Send complete ms. Accepts hard copy, email submissions to writers@mx3.com (ASCII attachments), and simultaneous submissions if identified. SASE. Response time varies. One-time rights. Articles and fiction, to 2,000 words. Poetry, no line limits. No payment. Provides 1 author's copy.

High School Years

3035 Valley Avenue, Suite 103
Winchester, VA 22601

Submissions Editor

Description and Interests
Distributed directly by schools to parents, this newsletter includes information on how to help high school students achieve academically. Published monthly, it features practical articles on topics such as homework, careers, jobs, and parenting issues. It is not accepting freelance material at this time. Circ: 300,000.
Website: www.rfeonline.com

Freelance Potential
100% written by nonstaff writers. Publishes 80 freelance submissions yearly; 25% by unpublished writers. Receives 36 unsolicited mss yearly.
Submissions and Payment: Sample copy, guidelines, and editorial calendar, free with 9x12 SASE. Query with résumé and clips when submission policy changes. SASE. Responds in 1 month. All rights. Articles, 225–300 words. Depts/columns, 175–200 words. Written material, $.60 per word. Pays on acceptance. Provides 5 copies.

Hit Parader

210 Route 4 East, Suite 211
Paramus, NJ 07652

Editor

Description and Interests
The world of rock and roll, from classic rock to heavy metal, is covered in this magazine. Profiles of bands and musicians and reviews of instruments and sound equipment are also a part of each monthly issue. Circ: 150,000.
Website: www.hitparader.com

Freelance Potential
10% written by nonstaff writers. Publishes 10 freelance submissions yearly; 50% by authors who are new to the magazine.
Submissions and Payment: Sample copy, $4.99 at newsstands. Query. Accepts hard copy. Availability of artwork improves chance of acceptance. SASE. Responds in 1–3 months. First rights. Articles, 1,000 words; $100–$150. Other material, word lengths and payment rates vary. 3x5 and 5x7 B/W prints and color transparencies. Pays on publication. Provides 1 contributor's copy.

Home Times Family Newspaper

3676 Collin Drive, Suite 16
West Palm Beach, FL 33406

Editor: Dennis Lombard

Description and Interests
This monthly tabloid reports on global, national, and local news; people; and current issues. It takes a biblical worldview and stresses family values. True-to-life stories about ordinary people who do extraordinary things are welcome. Circ: 8,000.
Website: www.hometimes.org

Freelance Potential
90% written by nonstaff writers. Publishes 150 freelance submissions yearly; 25% by unpublished writers, 25% by authors who are new to the magazine. Receives 360 unsolicited mss yearly.
Submissions and Payment: Sample copy, $3. Send complete ms. Accepts hard copy and simultaneous submissions. SASE. Responds in 1 month. One-time and electronic rights. Articles, 500–750 words; $5–$50. Depts/columns, word lengths and payment rates vary. Pays on publication. Provides copies upon request.

304

Home & School Connection

3305 Valley Avenue, Suite 103
Winchester, VA 22601

Submissions: Jennifer Hutchinson

Description and Interests
Since 1989, this monthly newsletter has been providing parents of elementary school children with articles on topics related to promoting success in school. Written in an upbeat, conversational tone, it covers parenting skills, careers, special needs, family issues, health, communication, nature, and science. It is not accepting queries or submissions at this time. Check its website for changes to this policy. Circ: 3 million.
Website: www.rfeonline.com

Freelance Potential
100% written by nonstaff writers. Publishes 80 freelance submissions yearly; 28% by unpublished writers, 14% by authors who are new to the magazine. Receives 36 unsolicited mss yearly.
Submissions and Payment: Sample copy, free with 9x12 SASE (2 first-class stamps). Do not send submissions at this time.

Horse Illustrated

P.O. Box 6050
Mission Viejo, CA 92690

Editor: Elizabeth Moyer

Description and Interests
Horse Illustrated, published monthly, is read by horse owners and riders of English and Western disciplines. Although primarily an adult publication, it is also read by young adults interested in horse care, training, and riding. Circ: 200,000.
Website: www.horseillustrated.com

Freelance Potential
80% written by nonstaff writers. Publishes 10–20 freelance submissions yearly. Receives 480 queries, 240 unsolicited mss yearly.
Submissions and Payment: Guidelines available. Prefers complete ms; will accept detailed query. Accepts hard copy. SASE. Responds in 1+ months. First North American serial rights. Articles, 1,500–1,800 words. Depts/columns, 1,000–1,400 words. Written material, $50–$400. Pays on publication. Provides 2 contributor's copies.

Hot Rod

6420 Wilshire Boulevard
Los Angeles, CA 90048

Editor: David Freiburger

Description and Interests
Articles and photos covering the sport of hot rodding can be found in this magazine. Published monthly, it features articles on custom cars, repairs and maintenance, collecting, and racing, as well as driver profiles and event coverage. Car news and car features offer the best opportunities for new writers. Circ: 680,000.
Website: www.hotrod.com

Freelance Potential
15% written by nonstaff writers. Publishes 24 freelance submissions yearly. Receives 288 queries yearly.
Submissions and Payment: Sample copy, $3.50 at newsstands. Guidelines available. Query. SASE. Response time varies. All rights. Articles, 3,000 characters per page; $250–$300 per page. Depts/columns, word lengths vary; $100 per page. B/W and color prints and 35mm color transparencies; payment rates vary. Pays on publication.

I Love Cats

16 Meadow Hill Lane
Armonk, NY 10504

Editor: Lisa Allmendinger

Description and Interests
This magazine offers a wide variety of cat information, from serious to humorous. It includes interesting stories about cats and their owners, tips for owners, articles covering health issues and behavior problems, show information, and reviews of products of interest to cat lovers. Circ: 25,000.
Website: www.iluvcats.com

Freelance Potential
95% written by nonstaff writers. Publishes 100 freelance submissions yearly; 50% by unpublished writers, 75% by authors who are new to the magazine. Receives 6,000 queries and unsolicited mss yearly.
Submissions and Payment: Sample copy and guidelines, $5 with 9x12 SASE. Query or send complete ms. Accepts hard copy. SASE. Responds in 1–2 months. All rights. Articles and fiction, 500–1,000 words; $25–$100. Pays on publication. Provides 1 author's copy.

I.D.

Cook Communications Ministries
4050 Lee Vance View
Colorado Springs, CO 80918

Editor: Doug Mauss

Description and Interests
Targeting high school students, this weekly Sunday school journal includes stories relating to Bible study on topics such as school, health, careers, sports, nature, recreation, and social issues, followed by a lesson and an activity. While all material should relate to Bible studies, it should not be too preachy. It is not reviewing queries at the present time. Circ: 50,000.
Website: www.cookministries.com

Freelance Potential
30% written by nonstaff writers.
Submissions and Payment: Guidelines available. Send résumé. No queries or unsolicited mss. All articles are assigned. Accepts hard copy. SASE. Responds in 6 months. Rights vary. Articles, 600–1,200 words; $50–$300 depending on experience. B/W and color prints; payment rates vary. Pays on acceptance. Provides 1 contributor's copy.

Indian Life Newspaper

P.O. Box 3765
Redwood Post Office, Redwood Centre
Winnipeg, Manitoba R2L 1L6
Canada

Editor: Jim Uttley

Description and Interests
Inspirational stories of hope that are culturally relevant to Christian North American Natives appear in this publication. Published six times each year, it offers articles on topics such as spirituality and overcoming challenges, as well as news. Writing should have Christian and biblical overtones without being preachy. Circ: 20,000.
Website: www.indianlife.org

Freelance Potential
80% written by nonstaff writers. Publishes 10 freelance submissions yearly; 2% by unpublished writers, 25% by authors who are new to the magazine. Receives 276 unsolicited mss yearly.
Submissions and Payment: Sample copy, $2.50 with #9 SAE. Prefers query. Will accept ms. Accepts hard copy and disk submissions. SAE/IRC. Responds in 1 month. First rights. Articles, 250–2,000 words; $25–$100. Pays on publication. Provides 15 author's copies.

Inside Kung-Fu

Action Pursuit Group
265 South Anita Drive, Suite 120
Orange, CA 92868-3310

Editor: Dave Cater

Description and Interests
For 25 years, this magazine has been offering articles and news covering Chinese-style martial arts. Appearing monthly, it seeks articles on traditional forms of fighting, weapons, and history, as well as profiles of well-known practitioners. Circ: 65,000.
Website: www.insidekung-fu.com

Freelance Potential
80% written by nonstaff writers. Publishes 100 freelance submissions yearly; 50% by unpublished writers, 50% by authors who are new to the magazine. Receives 504 queries yearly.
Submissions and Payment: Sample copy and guidelines, $2.95 with 9x12 SASE. Query. Accepts hard copy and email queries to dave.cater@apg-media.com. SASE. Responds in 4–6 weeks. First rights. Articles, 1,500 words. Depts/columns, 750 words. Written material, payment rates vary. Pays on publication.

Junior Storyteller

P.O. Box 205
Masonville, CO 80541

Editor: Vivian Dubrovin

Description and Interests
This guide for elementary through junior high students features stories, projects, and tips on the art and craft of storytelling. Published quarterly, it is interested in queries from teachers and youth group leaders working with young storytellers about their events, as well as information on storytelling programs. Circ: 500.
Website: www.storycraft.com

Freelance Potential
30% written by nonstaff writers. Receives several queries yearly.
Submissions and Payment: Guidelines available at website. Sample copy, $4 with 6x9 SASE. Query. Accepts hard copy and email queries to jrstoryteller@direcway.com. Availability of artwork may improve chance of acceptance. SASE. Response time varies. First rights. Articles and fiction, 500–1,000 words; $50–$125. Pays on acceptance. Provides 10 copies.

Kahani

P.O. Box 590155
Newton Centre, MA 02459

Editor: Monika Jain

Description and Interests
This quarterly targets children of South Asian descent with its educational articles and adventure, mystery, and humorous fiction stories. Submissions to *Kahani* should complement the upcoming editorial themes that are listed at the website. Circ: Unavailable.
Website: www.kahani.com

Freelance Potential
50% written by nonstaff writers. Publishes several freelance submissions yearly.
Submissions and Payment: Query with clips for articles; send complete ms for fiction. Accepts email submissions to writers@kahani.com. Include either "Feature Query" or "Fiction Submission" in the subject line. Responds only if interested for articles; in 1 month for fiction. Rights vary. Articles, 400–600 words. Fiction, to 950 words. No payment. Provides contributor's copies.

Kansas 4-H Journal

116 Umberger Hall
KSU
Manhattan, KS 66506-3714

Editor: Rhonda Atkinson

Description and Interests
Kansas 4-H members read this magazine. Each issue reports on statewide topics, programs, and issues. In addition, it includes coverage of events, photo-essays, how-to articles, personal experience pieces, and member news. Appearing eight times each year, it welcomes submissions from writers who are involved with 4-H clubs. Circ: 10,000.

Freelance Potential
60% written by nonstaff writers. Publishes 100 freelance submissions yearly; 10% by unpublished writers, 20% by authors who are new to the magazine. Receives 696 queries and unsolicited mss yearly.
Submissions and Payment: Sample copy and editorial calendar, $5. Query or send complete ms. Accepts hard copy. SASE. Response time varies. Rights negotiable. Articles, 500 words; payment rates vary. Payment policy varies.

Keyboard

1111 Bay Hill Drive
San Bruno, CA 94066

Editor-in-Chief: Ernie Rideout

Description and Interests
This monthly magazine offers informational and how-to articles for both professional and amateur keyboardists. It also features artist profiles, product guides, and music reviews. Circ: 61,000.
Website: www.keyboardmag.com

Freelance Potential
25–35% written by nonstaff writers. Publishes 120 freelance submissions yearly; 35% by unpublished writers, 55% by authors who are new to the magazine. Receives 60–120 unsolicited mss yearly.
Submissions and Payment: Sample copy and guidelines available via email request. Send complete ms with résumé. Accepts hard copy and email submissions to keyboard@musicplayer.com. SASE. Responds in 3 months. All rights. Articles, 500–3,000 words. Depts/columns, 400–600 words. All material, payment rates vary. Pays on publication. Provides 5 author's copies.

Kids

341 East Lancaster Avenue
Downingtown, PA 19335

Editor: Bob Ludwick

Description and Interests
Families and educators who live in Chester County, Pennsylvania, read this regional tabloid-style magazine sponsored by the Chester County Intermediate Unit and its public schools. Distributed in the county's elementary and intermediate schools, each monthly issue offers timely information on school programs, events, and news. Teacher and student profiles are also featured regularly. Circ: 45,000.

Freelance Potential
90% written by nonstaff writers. Publishes 120 freelance submissions yearly; 20% by unpublished writers. Receives several queries yearly.
Submissions and Payment: Sample copy and editorial calendar, free with 9x12 SASE. Query with résumé. Accepts hard copy. SASE. Responds in 1 week. All rights. Articles and depts/columns, to 500 words. No payment. Provides 2 contributor's copies.

Kidsandkaboodle.com

1169 Mount Rushmore Way
Lexington, KY 40515

Editor: Jennifer Anderson

Description and Interests
Informative and entertaining articles covering parenting issues, child development, health, and safety can be found in this e-zine. Targeting families residing in central Kentucky, it is interested in research-type articles for expectant parents, as well as articles on fitness and health. Hits per month: 50,000.
Website: www.kidsandkaboodle.com

Freelance Potential
20% written by nonstaff writers. Publishes 20 freelance submissions yearly; 50% by unpublished writers, 50% by authors who are new to the magazine. Receives 36–48 unsolicited mss yearly.
Submissions and Payment: Sample copy available at website. Send complete ms. Accepts email submissions to editor@kidsandkaboodle.com. Response time varies. All rights. Articles, word lengths vary. No payment.

Kids Discover

149 Fifth Avenue, 12th Floor
New York, NY 10010-6801

Editor: Stella Sands

Description and Interests
Each issue of this monthly magazine for children ages six to twelve delves deeply into a particular subject related to science, history, ecology, geography, or architecture; recent issues have centered on the disparate topics of nutrition, volcanoes, and Leonardo da Vinci. Editorial content is enhanced with copious artwork and thought-provoking activities. Currently, *Kids Discover* is not accepting unsolicited submissions. Circ: 400,000.
Website: www.kidsdiscover.com

Freelance Potential
100% written by staff writers. Receives 120 queries each year.
Submissions and Payment: Sample copy available upon email request to editor@kidsdiscover.com. Not accepting queries or unsolicited mss at this time. Rights vary. Written material, word lengths and payment rates vary. Payment policy varies.

The Kids Storytelling Club

Editor: Vivian Dubrovin

Description and Interests
Stories, crafts, activities, and storytelling tips can be found at this award-winning website for children. In addition, it features a parent/teacher page, which includes news and ideas that help promote storytelling. It is interested in information about local storytelling events and actitivies. Hits per month: 4,000+.
Website: www.storycraft.com

Freelance Potential
70% written by nonstaff writers. Publishes many freelance submissions yearly; many by unpublished writers, most by authors who are new to the magazine.
Submissions and Payment: Guidelines and sample copy available at website. Query. Accepts hard copy and email queries to jrstoryteller@storycraft.com. SASE. Response time varies. First rights. Articles, 500 words. Fiction, 250–500 words. Written material, $25. Pays on acceptance.

Kiwibox.com

330 West 38th Street, Suite 1602
New York, NY 10018

Submissions Editor: Josh Maldonado

Description and Interests
Updated weekly, *Kiwibox.com* is a website designed and run by teens. It is a unique Internet forum for teen-written fiction and nonfiction, and publishes hundreds of freelance submissions each year. Topics covered appeal specifically to high school and college students, and content ranges from genre fiction to articles on science and technology. *Kiwibox.com* editors will consider any well-written work of interest to readers between the ages of 14 and 21. Hits per month: 10 million.
Website: www.kiwibox.com

Freelance Potential
90% written by nonstaff writers.
Submissions and Payment: Sample copy available at website. Send complete ms. Accepts email submissions to josh@kiwibox.net. Responds in 2 weeks. All rights. Articles, 350 words. Fiction, word lengths vary. No payment.

Kindred

P.O. Box 971
Mullumbimby, New South Wales 2482
Australia

Editor: Kali Wendorf
U.S. Editorial Contact: Lisa Reagan

Description and Interests
Previously listed as *Byronchild*, this quarterly magazine addresses family life from a sustainability and natural living perspective. It focuses on personal growth, natural parenting, social justice, and environmental health. It seeks articles on topics such as fatherhood, men's issues, gay couples, and gay parenting. Circ: Unavailable.
Website: www.kindredmagazine.com.au

Freelance Potential
90% written by nonstaff writers. Publishes 20 freelance submissions yearly; 95% by unpublished writers, 95% by new authors. Receives 200 queries and mss yearly.
Submissions and Payment: Sample copy and guidelines available. Query or send ms with list of sources. Accepts email to kali@kindredmagazine.com.au (Microsoft Word attachments). Response time varies. First rights. Articles, word lengths vary. No payment.

Knucklebones

N7450 Aanstad Road
P.O. 5000
Iola, WI 54945-5000

Editor: Sarah Gloystein Peterson

Description and Interests
Game enthusiasts read this magazine for its coverage of board games, puzzles, brainteasers, and the kinds of games that encourage them to spend quality time with family and friends. Each issue includes reviews, how-to articles, and profiles. *Knucklebones* is published six times each year. Circ: Unavailable.
Website: www.kbones.com

Freelance Potential
90% written by nonstaff writers. Publishes 150–175 freelance submissions yearly; 5% by unpublished writers, 2% by authors who are new to the magazine.
Submissions and Payment: Guidelines available with SASE or by email request. Prefers query. Will accept ms. Accepts hard copy and email submissions to editor@kbones.com. SASE. Response time varies. First and electronic rights. Articles and depts/columns, word lengths and payment rates vary. Pays on publication.

The Learning Edge

Clonlara School
1289 Jewett
Ann Arbor, MI 48104

Editor: Judy Gelner

Description and Interests
Distributed six times each year to those enrolled in the Clonlara School Home-Based Education Program, this newsletter publishes news, opinions, and resources that illuminate educational rights and freedoms. It also includes material of general interest to home educators. Currently, only contributions from Clonlara families are being considered. Circ: 1,000.
Website: www.clonlara.org

Freelance Potential
25% written by nonstaff writers. Of the freelance submissions published yearly, 10% are by unpublished writers, 1% are by authors who are new to the magazine. Receives 12 queries yearly.
Submissions and Payment: Sample copy available. Accepts queries from Clonlara students only. Accepts hard copy. SASE. Responds in 2 months. All rights. Written material, word lengths vary. No payment.

Learning Through History

P.O. Box 1858
Cranberry Township, PA 16066-1858

Editor: Rebecca Thompson

Description and Interests
This magazine provides historical information with articles and crafts relating to a different theme in each of its six issues yearly. Circ: 10,000.
Website: www.learningthroughhistory.com

Freelance Potential
100% written by nonstaff writers. Publishes 120 freelance submissions yearly; 8% by unpublished writers, 35–40% by authors who are new to the magazine.
Submissions and Payment: Guidelines available at website. Accepts query with synopsis and clips from established writers. Accepts complete ms from less experienced writers. Accepts email submissions only to submissions@learningthroughhistory.com (Microsoft Word or text attachments). Responds in 2 weeks. All rights. Articles, 1,000–1,400 words; $60. Arts and crafts projects, word lengths vary; $30. Kill fee, 50%. Pays on publication. Provides 1 contributor's copy.

Life Learning Magazine

P.O. Box 112
Niagara Falls, NY 14304-0112

Editor: Wendy Priesnitz

Description and Interests
Self-directed, life-based learning is the focus of this magazine that is published six times each year. Its content includes articles on unstructured learning and distance education. Profiles and personal experience accounts from people of all ages who have learned from life experience are desired. Circ: 35,000.
Website: www.lifelearningmagazine.com

Freelance Potential
100% written by nonstaff writers. Publishes 40 freelance submissions yearly; 50% by authors who are new to the magazine.
Submissions and Payment: Sample copy, $4.95. Guidelines available at website. Query. Accepts email queries only to editor@lifelearningmagazine.com. Responds in 3 weeks. Rights vary. Articles and depts/columns, word lengths vary. No payment. Provides contributor's copies.

Literary Mama

Department of English
Pinewood Preparatory School
1114 Orangeburg Road
Summerville, SC 29843

Editor-in-Chief: Amy Hudock

Description and Interests
Articles, fiction, and poetry centered around the many facets of motherhood make up the content of this quarterly online literary magazine. *Literary Mama* strives to honor the difficult job of being a mother through its intellectual and spiritual material. Hits per month: 35,000.
Website: www.literarymama.com

Freelance Potential
75% written by nonstaff writers. Publishes 80–120 freelance submissions yearly; 75% by new authors.
Submissions and Payment: Guidelines available at website. Query for profiles, reviews, and columns. Send complete ms for all other types of submissions. Accepts email submissions only. Check website for appropriate department editor and email address. Responds in 1–4 months. Non-exclusive rights. Articles and fiction, to 6,000 words. Depts/columns, 1,000–1,600 words. Poetry, no line limits. No payment.

Little Rock Family

122 East Second Street
Little Rock, AR 72201

Submissions Editor

Description and Interests
Distributed free to parents living in central Arkansas, this newsletter features timely articles on topics such as parenting, family, health care, fashion, fitness, child care, education, and recreation. Information about regional events and resources and family-oriented activities are also included. Published monthly, it is interested in articles on parenting issues that inform and educate its readers—busy parents who are educated professionals involved in their communities. Circ: 20,000.
Website: www.littlerockfamily.com

Freelance Potential
100% written by nonstaff writers. Publishes many freelance submissions yearly.
Submissions and Payment: Query. Accepts hard copy. SASE. Response time varies. First rights. Articles and depts/columns, word lengths and payment rates vary. Payment policy varies.

Lowcountry Parent

1180 Sam Rittenberg Boulevard
Charleston, SC 29407

Submissions Editor: Shannon Brigham

Description and Interests
Informative articles on parenting topics and family issues are featured in this monthly magazine for families residing in the Charleston, South Carolina, region. It is currently not accepting material. Check its website for updates to this policy. Circ: 38,000.
Website: www.lowcountryparent.com

Freelance Potential
Publishes many freelance submissions yearly; 10% by authors who are new to the magazine. Receives 1,200 queries yearly.
Submissions and Payment: Sample copy, free. Guidelines available. Query with sample pages. Accepts email queries to editor@lowcontryparent.com. Responds in 3 days. One-time rights. Articles and depts/columns, word lengths vary. Written material, $15–$100. Pays on publication. Provides 3 contributor's copies.

Mad Kids

1700 Broadway
New York, NY 10019

Submissions Editor

Description and Interests
A sister publication to *MAD Magazine*, *MAD Kids* targets children ages seven to twelve with its humor, activities, comic strips, and short fiction and nonfiction. Q&As with celebrities are also a part of each quarterly issue. Circ: Unavailable.
Website: www.madmagazine.com

Freelance Potential
20% written by nonstaff writers. Publishes 10–15 freelance submissions yearly.
Submissions and Payment: Sample copy, $4.99 at newsstands. Guidelines available at website. Query or send complete ms. Prefers email submissions to submissions@madmagazine.com; will accept hard copy if submission includes artwork. SASE. Responds if interested. All rights. Written material, word lengths vary; $500 per printed page. Artwork, payment rates vary. Pays on acceptance. Provides 1 contributor's copy.

Mad Magazine

1700 Broadway
New York, NY 10019

Submissions Editor

Description and Interests
Parodies, satire, and silliness fill the pages of *Mad Magazine*, which targets young adults and adults. Published monthly, it features comic strips, short fiction, and short articles highlighting current events, pop culture, and television programs. Circ: Unavailable.
Website: www.madmagazine.com

Freelance Potential
25% written by nonstaff writers. Publishes 25 freelance submissions yearly.
Submissions and Payment: Sample copy, $4.99 at newsstands. Guidelines available at website. Query or send complete ms. Prefers email submissions to submissions@madmagazine.com; will accept hard copy if submission includes artwork. SASE. Responds if interested. All rights. Written material, word lengths vary; $500 per printed page. Artwork, payment rates vary. Pays on acceptance. Provides 1 contributor's copy.

Metro Augusta Parent

700 Broad Street
Augusta, GA 30901

Editor: Amy Christian

Description and Interests
Each month, *Metro Augusta Parent* is the go-to magazine for local recreational activities, dining guides, sports, and general family and parenting information. It also offers articles on schools and after-school programs, as well as book and movie reviews. Writers interested in submitting queries should be familiar with the local area. Circ: Unavailable.
Website: www.augustaparent.com

Freelance Potential
90% written by nonstaff writers. Publishes 10 freelance submissions yearly.
Submissions and Payment: Sample copy, free with SASE. Query. Accepts hard copy and email queries to editor@augustaparent.com. SASE. Response time varies. First rights. Articles and depts/columns, word lengths and payment rates vary. Payment policy varies. Provides 1 contributor's copy.

Metro Parent

P.O. Box 13660
Portland, OR 97213

Editor: Marie Sherlock

Description and Interests
This free monthly magazine is a valuable resource for families in the Portland metropolitan area. It features articles on child development, nutrition, and education, as well as event calendars, and recreation and travel ideas. Note that queries by local authors only will be considered. Circ: 45,000.
Website: www.metro-parent.com

Freelance Potential
75% written by nonstaff writers. Publishes 50 freelance submissions yearly; 20% by unpublished writers. Receives 240 queries yearly.
Submissions and Payment: Sample copy and theme list, $2. Query with outline. Accepts hard copy, simultaneous submissions, and email queries to editor@metro-parent.com. SASE. Responds in 1 month. Rights vary. Articles and depts/columns, word lengths and payment rates vary. Pays on publication.

MetroFamily

306 South Bryant, Suite C-152
Edmond, OK 73034

Editor: Denise Springer

Description and Interests
Billed as "The Essential Resource for Central Oklahoma Families," this monthly publication features articles on parenting, education, health, travel, and various recreational activities. Circ: 35,000.
Website: www.metrofamilymagazine.com

Freelance Potential
60% written by nonstaff writers. Publishes 50–60 freelance submissions yearly; 10% by unpublished writers, 10% by authors who are new to the magazine. Receives 1,000 queries and unsolicited mss yearly.
Submissions and Payment: Sample copy and guidelines, free with 10x13 SASE. Query or send complete ms. Accepts email submissions only to editor@ metrofamilymagazine.com. Responds to queries in 3 weeks, to mss in 1 month. First North American serial rights. Articles, 300–600 words; $25–$50. Kill fee, 100%. Pays on publication. Provides 1 author's copy.

Miami Family Magazine

7045 SW 69th Avenue
South Miami, FL 33143

Publisher: Janet Jupiter

Description and Interests
Published monthly, *Miami Family Magazine* offers parents insightful information for raising their kids and spotlights local family activities, sporting events, and outings. It also features profiles of local residents making a difference in the community. Writers familiar with the Miami area are welcome to submit their queries. Circ: Unavailable.
Website: www.miamifamilymagazine.com

Freelance Potential
20% written by nonstaff writers. Publishes 15–20 freelance submissions yearly.
Submissions and Payment: Sample copy available at website. Query. Accepts hard copy and email queries to miamifamily@bellsouth.net. SASE. Response time varies. One-time rights. Articles and depts/columns, word lengths and payment rates vary. Pays on publication. Provides contributor's copies.

Middle Years

3035 Valley Avenue, Suite104
Winchester, VA 22601

Submissions Editor: Jennifer Hutchinson

Description and Interests
Parents of middle school children read this publication for upbeat articles on topics such as education, health, special education, and parenting. Published monthly, it also offers short articles on parental involvement in education. It is not accepting queries or manuscripts at this time. Circ: 1 million.
Website: www.rfeonline.com.

Freelance Potential
100% written by nonstaff writers. Publishes 80 freelance submissions yearly. Receives 36 queries yearly.
Submissions and Payment: Sample copy and guidelines, free with 9x12 SASE (2 first-class stamps). Query with résumé and 3 clips when submission policy changes. Accepts hard copy. Responds in 1 month. All rights. Articles, 225–300 words. Depts/columns, 175–200 words. Written material, $.60 per word. Pays on acceptance. Provides 5 contributor's copies.

Model Airplane News

Air Age Publishing
20 Westport Road
Wilton, CT 06897

Editor-in-Chief: Debra Cleghorn

Description and Interests
In print since 1929, this monthly magazine offers aeromodelers a wealth of how-to information on building and flying model airplanes, as well as detailed product reviews. It is amply illustrated with full-color photos and many charts and graphs. Circ: 95,000.
Website: www.modelairplanenews.com

Freelance Potential
90% written by nonstaff writers. Publishes 100+ freelance submissions yearly; 33% by authors who are new to the magazine. Receives 144–288 queries yearly.
Submissions and Payment: Sample copy and guidelines, $3.50 with 9x12 SASE. Query with outline and biography describing model experience. Accepts hard copy. Availability of artwork improves chance of acceptance. SASE. Responds in 6 weeks. All North American serial rights. Articles, 1,700–2,000 words; $175–$600. Pays on publication. Provides up to 6 author's copies.

Minnesota Parent

1115 Hennepin Avenue South
Minneapolis, MN 55403

Editor: Tricia Cornell

Description and Interests
Minnesota Parent is a monthly magazine that offers parents the information they need to raise happy, healthy children. Hard-hitting articles on education, relevant legislation, and important social issues are side by side with pieces on travel, new product reviews, and popular culture. All items are aimed at enriching the lives of families within the state. Circ: 70,000.
Website: www.mnparent.com

Freelance Potential
50% written by nonstaff writers. Publishes 50 freelance submissions yearly.
Submissions and Payment: Query only. Accepts hard copy and email queries to tcornell@mnpubs.com. SASE. Response time varies. First serial and electronic rights. Articles and depts/columns, word lengths vary; $50–$350. Pays on publication. Provides 2 contributor's copies.

Mother Verse

222 Third Avenue
Two Harbors, MN 55616

Editor: Melanie Mayo-Laakso

Description and Interests
This quarterly "Journal of Contemporary Motherhood" explores experiences from across cultural, geographical, economic, and political lines. It seeks submissions of radical, challenging, and uncommon works of literature. Circ: 600.
Website: www.motherverse.com

Freelance Potential
95% written by nonstaff writers. Publishes 80 freelance submissions yearly; 10% by unpublished writers, 95% by authors who are new to the magazine. Receives 500 queries and unsolicited mss each year.
Submissions and Payment: Sample copy and guidelines available at website. Query or send ms. Accepts email to submissions@motherverse.com (RTF attachments or in body of email). Responds in 1–2 months. One-time rights. Written material, word lengths vary. No payment. Provides 2 copies or a 1-year subscription.

Motivos Bilingual Magazine

P.O. Box 48215
Philadelphia, PA 19144

Publisher: Jenee Chiznick

Description and Interests
This quarterly bilingual magazine is read by young adults interested in learning about Latino culture. Its socially relevant content includes life issues, college and career information, and ethnic material. Its pages are filled with sources of wisdom, words of courage, and friends to share life's journey. Circ: 45,000.
Website: www.motivosmag.com

Freelance Potential
90% written by nonstaff writers. Publishes 40 freelance submissions yearly; 90% by unpublished writers, 90% by authors who are new to the magazine.
Submissions and Payment: Guidelines available at website. Send complete ms. Accepts hard copy and email submissions to editor@motivosmag.com. SASE. Response time varies. First North American serial rights. Articles, 400–800 words; payment rates vary. Pays on publication. Provides 2 contributor's copies.

Mysteries Magazine

P.O. Box 490
Walpole, NH 03608

Editor: Kim Guarnaccia

Description and Interests
This quarterly magazine publishes articles and book reviews related to historical or ancient mysteries, paranormal events, bizarre scientific breakthroughs, and unusual archaeological finds. Circ: 15,000.
Website: www.mysteriesmagazine.com

Freelance Potential
30% written by nonstaff writers. Publishes 12 freelance submissions yearly; 20% by authors who are new to the magazine. Receives 240 queries yearly.
Submissions and Payment: Sample copy, $8. Guidelines available at website. Query. Accepts email queries to editor@mysteriesmagazine.com. Responds in 1 month. First North American serial rights. Articles, 3,000–5,000 words. Depts/columns, 1,200–1,500 words. Book reviews, 200–500 words. Written material, $.05 per word. Pays on publication. Provides 2 contributor's copies.

Muslim Girl

1179 King Street West, Suite 114
Toronto, Ontario M6K 3G5
Canada

Editor-in-Chief: Ausma Khan

Description and Interests
Positive, life-affirming stories of Canadian Muslim teens can be found in this magazine. It offers a contemporary lifestyle guide within the parameters of the values of girls ages 12 to 19. For future issues, it is interested in material that focuses on the themes of change, Ramadan, and teen girls around the world. Female writers of Muslim background who relate to and understand its editorial vision are welcome to query. Circ: Unavailable.
Website: www.muslimgirlmagazine.com

Freelance Potential
40% written by nonstaff writers. Publishes 20 freelance submissions yearly.
Submissions and Payment: Query. Accepts email queries to submissions@muslimgirlmagazine.com. Response time varies. Rights vary. Articles, word lengths vary. Written material, $150–$1,000.

National Geographic Explorer

1145 17th Street NW
Washington, DC 20036

Editor

Description and Interests
National Geographic Explorer is a classroom magazine for grades two through six that invites students to explore the world and all that is in it. Each issue contains three nonfiction features, which probe curriculum-related topics in science and social studies; articles also provide glossaries with kid-friendly definitions of key terms. The magazine is published seven times throughout each school year. Circ: Unavailable.
Website: http://magma.nationalgeographic.com/ ngexplorer

Freelance Potential
5% written by nonstaff writers. Publishes few freelance submissions yearly.
Submissions and Payment: Send résumé only; all articles are assigned. Accepts hard copy. SASE. Responds only if interested. All rights. Articles and fiction, word lengths and payment rates vary. Pays on acceptance.

Neapolitan Family Magazine

P.O. Box 110656
Naples, FL 34108

Editor: Andrea Breznay

Description and Interests
Parents, grandparents, and educators who reside in Naples, Florida, are the target audience of this monthly magazine. It uses freelance material frequently and welcomes articles and news pertaining to families and children from published as well as unpublished writers. Circ: 11,000.
Website: www.neafamily.com

Freelance Potential
80% written by nonstaff writers. Publishes 12 freelance submissions yearly. Receives 60 queries, 100 mss yearly.
Submissions and Payment: Guidelines and editorial calendar available at website. Sample copy, free with 9x12 SASE. Query or send complete ms. Prefers email submissions to NeapolitanFamily@aol.com. Will accept hard copy. SASE. Responds in 1 month. Rights vary. Articles and depts/columns, word lengths and payment rates vary. Pays on publication.

The New Era

50 East North Temple Street, Room 2414
Salt Lake City, UT 84150

Managing Editor: Richard Romney

Description and Interests
This monthly publication, available in print and online, targets children and young adults with its personal experience stories that show the Gospel of Jesus Christ at work in the lives of young Latter-day Saints. Articles with issues relevant to today's youth, including drug addiction, relationships, and anger, also appear. Circ: 230,000.
Website: www.lds.org

Freelance Potential
20% written by nonstaff writers. Publishes 10–15 freelance submissions yearly. Receives 150 queries yearly.
Submissions and Payment: Sample copy, $1.50 with 9x12 SASE. Query. Accepts hard copy and email queries to newera@ldschurch.org. SASE. Responds in 2 months. All rights. Articles, 200–500 words. Fiction, to 1,500 words. Depts/columns, word lengths vary. Poetry, to 30 lines. Written material, $.03–$.12 per word. Pays on acceptance. Provides 2 author's copies.

New Jersey Family

1122 Route 22 West
Mountainside, NJ 07092

Editor: Farn Dupre

Description and Interests
Distributed monthly in northern and central New Jersey, this publication addresses universal parenting concerns such as health, education, and child development. In addition, it provides information about local events and community resources in an effort to help parents make the best choices for their families. It seeks creative, practical articles from parents and others with expertise in family issues. Circ: Unavailable.
Website: www.njfamily.com

Freelance Potential
20% written by nonstaff writers. Publishes 15–20 freelance submissions yearly.
Submissions and Payment: Guidelines available at website. Query with writing samples. Accepts email queries to editor@njcountyfamily.com. Response time varies. First rights. Articles, 750–1,000 words. Depts/columns, word lengths vary. No payment.

North State Parent

P.O. Box 1602
Mount Shasta, CA 96067

Editorial Department

Description and Interests
North State Parent magazine is a monthly regional publication for families living in Butte, Shasta, Tehama, and southern Siskiyou counties in California. It features informative and uplifting articles on a variety of topics of interest to parents and guardians of all backgrounds, while seeking to promote the health and well-being of children of all ages. Circ: Unavailable.
Website: www.northstateparent.com

Freelance Potential
90% written by nonstaff writers. Publishes 20 freelance submissions yearly.
Submissions and Payment: Guidelines available at website. Send complete ms. Accepts hard copy and email submissions to lisa@northstateparent.com. SASE. Response time varies. First rights. Articles, 700–1,000 words. Depts/columns, 300–500 words. Written material, $35–$75. Pays on publication.

The Numismatist

American Numismatic Association
818 North Cascade Avenue
Colorado Springs, CO 80903-3279

Editor-in-Chief: Barbara J. Gregory

Description and Interests
The Numismatist is a monthly magazine for members of the American Numismatic Association. It features articles and news items of interest to collectors of coins, paper money, medals, and tokens. Circ: 30,500.
Website: www.money.org

Freelance Potential
60% written by nonstaff writers. Publishes 36 freelance submissions yearly; 20% by unpublished writers, 10% by authors who are new to the magazine. Receives 48 unsolicited mss yearly.
Submissions and Payment: Sample copy and guidelines, free with 9x12 SASE ($2.50 postage). Send complete ms with biography. Prefers email submissions to editor@money.org. Will accept hard copy and disk submissions. SASE. Responds in 8–10 weeks. Perpetual nonexclusive rights. Articles, to 3,500 words; $.12 per word. Pays on publication. Provides 5 author's copies.

Owl

Bayard Press Canada
10 Lower Spadina Avenue, Suite 400
Toronto, Ontario M5V 2Z2
Canada

Submissions Editor

Description and Interests
The wise old *Owl*—big sister to *Chickadee* and *Chirp*—is a self-described "discovery magazine" aimed at children ages 8 to 12. Published nine times each year, it teaches kids about the world around them with entertaining articles on animals, natural phenomena, science, conservation, and technology. Do not submit queries or manuscripts; all work is done on assignment only. Circ: 104,000.
Website: www.owlkids.com

Freelance Potential
60% written by nonstaff writers. Publishes 1–3 freelance submissions yearly; 5% by unpublished writers, 10% by authors who are new to the magazine.
Submissions and Payment: Sample copy, $4.28. Guidelines available. Send résumé. No unsolicited mss. All rights. Articles, 500–1,000 words; $200–$500. Pays on acceptance. Provides 1 contributor's copy.

Our Little Friend

Pacific Press Publishing
P.O. Box 5353
Nampa, ID 83653-5353

Editor: Aileen Andres Sox

Description and Interests
For 112 years, this magazine has been providing children ages one through six attending Bible school at Seventh-day Adventist Churches with stories and lessons that focus on God's love and teach Christian values and beliefs. Circ: 35,000.
Website: www.ourlittlefriend.com

Freelance Potential
20% written by nonstaff writers. Publishes 52 freelance submissions yearly; 10% by unpublished writers, 10% by authors who are new to the magazine. Receives 240 unsolicited mss yearly.
Submissions and Payment: Sample copy and guidelines, free with 9x12 SASE (2 first-class stamps). Send ms. Accepts hard copy, simultaneous submissions, and email to ailsox@pacificpress.com. SASE. Responds in 4 months. One-time rights. Articles and fiction, 500–650 words; $25–$50. Pays on acceptance. Provides 3 copies.

Parenting for High Potential

4921 Ringwood Meadow
Sarasota, FL 34235

Editor: Dr. Donald Treffinger

Description and Interests
Published by the National Association for Gifted Children, this quarterly journal is aimed at helping parents develop their children's gifts and talents. Articles are written by experts in the field, or by parents and other individuals with first-hand knowledge of high-ability children and youth. General parenting articles are not accepted. Circ: Unavailable.
Website: www.nagc.org

Freelance Potential
100% written by nonstaff writers. Publishes 10–12 freelance submissions yearly; 50% by authors who are new to the magazine. Receives 20–30 unsolicited mss yearly.
Submissions and Payment: Guidelines available. Send complete ms. Accepts email submissions to don@creativelearning.com. Responds in 6–8 weeks. First rights. Articles and depts/columns, word lengths vary. No payment.

ParentingHumor.com

P.O. Box 2128
Weaverville, NC 28787

Editor

Description and Interests
This weekly updated e-magazine is where parents and child-care workers turn for humorous articles on all aspects of child rearing and family life. From pregnancy, through the tween years, to college-bound young adulthood, parenting is fraught with fun and funny situations. New and experienced writers alike are encouraged to submit their work. Hits per month: Unavailable.
Website: www.parentinghumor.com

Freelance Potential
98% written by nonstaff writers. Publishes 350 freelance submissions yearly. Receives 300 queries yearly.
Submissions and Payment: Sample copy, guidelines, and submission form available at website. Query. Accepts email queries to staff@parentinghumor.com. Response time varies. One-time electronic rights. Articles, word lengths vary. No payment. Offers an author's biography and a link to the author's website.

Parents Express

290 Commerce Drive
Fort Washington, PA 19034

Submissions Editor: Daniel Sean Kaye

Description and Interests
Parents in the greater Philadelphia area—including southern New Jersey—read this monthly magazine for news, information, advice, events, and entertainment coverage. Circ: 49,000.
Website: www.parents-express.net

Freelance Potential
30% written by nonstaff writers. Publishes 25–35 freelance submissions yearly; 25% by unpublished writers, 75% by authors who are new to the magazine. Receives several queries yearly.
Submissions and Payment: Sample copy, free with 10x13 SASE ($2.14 postage). Query with clips or writing samples. Accepts hard copy and email to dkaye@ montgomerynews.com. SASE. Responds in 1 month. One-time rights. Articles, 300–1,000 words; $35–$200. Depts/columns, 600–800 words; payment rates vary. Pays on publication. Provides contributor's copies.

Parents' Choice

Parents' Choice Foundation
201 West Padonia Road, Suite 303
Timonium, MD 21093

Editor: Claire Green

Description and Interests
Striving to bring parents solid information about children's media products and toys to aid them in making informed choices, this e-zine includes reviews and information on products that are safe, fun, age appropriate, and socially sound. Published by the Parents' Choice Foundation, it is updated monthly and appears in newsletter format twice each year. Reviews of toys or television shows are welcome. Hits per month: 1 million+.
Website: www.parentschoice.org

Freelance Potential
80% written by nonstaff writers. Publishes many freelance submissions yearly.
Submissions and Payment: Sample copy available at website. Query or send complete ms. Accepts hard copy and simultaneous submissions if identified. SASE. Response time varies. All rights. Articles, to 1,500 words; payment rates vary. Pays on acceptance.

Parents Magazine

375 Lexington Avenue
New York, NY 10017

Editor

Description and Interests
This national publication appeals to parents interested in reading the best information and advice on raising healthy, well-adjusted children. Each monthly issue covers topics such as child health, education, behavior, and care. *Parents* also covers pregnancy and parent fitness and health. There are articles by noted experts as well as personal experience pieces. Circ: Unavailable.
Website: www.parents.com

Freelance Potential
50% written by nonstaff writers. Publishes 50 freelance submissions yearly. Receives 1,200 queries yearly.
Submissions and Payment: Sample copy, $3.50 with 9x12 SASE (4 first-class stamps). Query with clips. Accepts hard copy. SASE. Responds in 6 weeks. Rights vary. Articles and depts/columns, word lengths and payment rates vary. Pays on publication. Provides 2 contributor's copies.

Plum Magazine

276 Fifth Avenue, Suite 302
New York, NY 10001

Submissions: Mary Jane Horton

Description and Interests
Serving as a comprehensive guide for pregnant women over the age of 35, this magazine features articles on health and well-being, pregnancy, beauty and fashion, home and entertainment, child care, work, and finances. Appearing twice each year, it seeks well-written first-person essays on pregnancy, child care, and infants. Circ: 500,000.
Website: www.plummagazine.com

Freelance Potential
90% written by nonstaff writers. Publishes 25 freelance submissions yearly; 10% by authors who are new to the magazine. Receives 150 queries and mss yearly.
Submissions and Payment: Guidelines available at website. Query or send complete ms. Accepts email submissions to editor@plummagazine.com. Response time varies. All rights. Articles and depts/columns, word lengths vary. No payment. Provides 1 author's copy.

PTO Today

100 Stonewall Boulevard, Suite 3
Wrentham, MA 02093

Editor-in-Chief: Craig Bystrynski

Description and Interests
This magazine, published six times each year, is written for leaders of parent-teacher organizations at elementary and middle schools across the U.S. It seeks articles that provide expert advice on issues such as recruiting and keeping parent volunteers, and on running parent-teacher organizations effectively. Circ: 80,000.
Website: www.ptotoday.com

Freelance Potential
75% written by nonstaff writers. Publishes 40–60 freelance submissions yearly; 5% by unpublished writers, 10% by authors who are new to the magazine. Receives 100–150 queries yearly.
Submissions and Payment: Guidelines available. Query. Accepts email queries to editor@ptotoday.com. Responds in 2 months. First and electronic rights. Articles, word lengths vary; payment rates vary. Pays on publication. Provides 1 contributor's copy.

Prairie Messenger

Box 190, 100 College Drive
Muenster, Saskatchewan S0K 2Y0
Canada

Associate Editor: Maureen Weber

Description and Interests
Catholics living in Saskatchewan and Manitoba turn to this weekly tabloid for local, national, and international religious news and coverage of current affairs. The publication also includes essays on faith along with features and opinion pieces. Circ: 7,100.
Website: www.stpeters.sk.ca/prairie_messenger

Freelance Potential
60% written by nonstaff writers. Publishes 10 freelance submissions yearly. Receives 30 queries and mss yearly.
Submissions and Payment: Sample copy and guidelines, $1 with 9x12 SASE/IRC. Query or send complete ms. Accepts email submissions to pm.canadian@stpeters.sk.ca. Responds in 1 month. First rights. Articles, 700 words; payment rates vary. Depts/columns, 700 words; $50 (Canadian). Color prints or transparencies and line art, payment rates vary. Pays at the end of each month.

Racquetball

1685 West Uintah
Colorado Springs, CO 80904

Executive Assistant: Heather Fender

Description and Interests
Racquetball enthusiasts enjoy this publication for its articles covering techniques and strategies of the sport, as well as tournament coverage and profiles of players. Published six times each year by the United States Racquetball Association, it needs more articles on health and fitness. Circ: 40,000.
Website: www.usaracquetball.com

Freelance Potential
90% written by nonstaff writers. Publishes 100 freelance submissions yearly; 100% by unpublished writers. Receives 100 queries yearly.
Submissions and Payment: Sample copy and guidelines, $4. Prefers query; will accept complete ms. Accepts hard copy. SASE. Responds in 9 weeks. One-time rights. Articles, 1,500–2,000 words. Depts/columns, 500–1,000 words. Written material, $.03–$.07 per word. Pays on publication.

Radio Control Boat Modeler

Air Age Publishing
20 Westport Road
Wilton, CT 06897

Executive Editor: Matt Higgins

Description and Interests
This fully illustrated quarterly magazine is devoted to providing enthusiasts of radio-control model boats plenty of informative how-to articles, product reviews, and racing event coverage. Circ: 55,000.
Website: www.rcboatmodeler.com

Freelance Potential
70% written by nonstaff writers. Publishes 20–25 freelance submissions yearly; 75% by unpublished writers. Receives 180 queries yearly.
Submissions and Payment: Sample copy and guidelines, free with 9x12 SASE. Query with outline and brief biography. Accepts hard copy and email queries to rcboatmodeler@airage.com. Availability of artwork improves chance of acceptance. B/W prints and 35mm slides. SASE. Responds in 1–3 months. All rights. Articles, 1,000–2,000 words; $50–$500. Pays on publication. Provides 2 contributor's copies.

Radio Control Car Action

Air Age Publishing
20 Westport Road
Wilton, CT 06897

Executive Editor: Peter Vieira

Description and Interests
Radio-control car enthusiasts read this widely regarded monthly magazine for expert advice, how-to information, and in-depth product reviews of electric- and gas-powered model cars. All aspects of the hobby are covered, including designing, building, and racing, as well as racer profiles and event news. Circ: 140,000.
Website: www.rccaraction.com

Freelance Potential
30% written by nonstaff writers. Publishes 50 freelance submissions yearly. Receives 410 unsolicited mss each year.
Submissions and Payment: Sample copy and guidelines available. Send complete ms with available artwork. Accepts hard copy and disk submissions (ASCII). SASE. Response time varies. All rights. Articles, word lengths and payment rates vary. 35mm color slides. Pays on acceptance. Provides 2 contributor's copies.

Raising Arizona Kids

7000 E. Shea Boulevard, Suite 1470
Scottsdale, AZ 85254-5257

Assistant Editor: Mary Holden

Description and Interests
Raising Arizona Kids Magazine is targeted to caring, open-minded, and intellectually curious Arizona parents ages 25 to 59. Articles should be written to inform, enlighten, challenge, support, amuse, or touch these parents as they grow within their new roles, seek ways to enhance their children's lives, and face the pressure of combining careers and parenting. Circ: Unavailable.
Website: www.raisingarizonakids.com

Freelance Potential
25–35% written by nonstaff writers. Publishes 50 freelance submissions yearly.
Submissions and Payment: Sample copy and guidelines available at website. Query with clips. Accepts hard copy and email to maryh@raisingarizonakids.com. SASE. Response time varies. Rights vary. Articles, 2,000 words; $125. Journal submissions, 600 words; $100. Pays 30 days after publication.

Read

Weekly Reader
1 Reader's Digest Road
Pleasantville, NY 10570

Managing Editor: Debra Dolan Nevins

Description and Interests
Read, published 18 times during the school year, is read primarily by children ages 12 to 14. Each issue contains a play, a short story or narrative, and other material thought capable of providing the basis for good classroom discussion, teaching possibilities, and enjoyable reading. Circ: 180,000.
Website: www.weeklyreader.com

Freelance Potential
60% written by nonstaff writers. Publishes 8–10 freelance submissions yearly; 10% by authors who are new to the magazine. Receives 900 queries yearly.
Submissions and Payment: Send résumé only. No unsolicited submissions. Responds only if interested. First North American serial and electronic one-time use rights. Articles, 1,000–2,000 words. Written material, payment rates vary. Pays on acceptance. Provides 5 contributor's copies.

Read, America!

3900 Glenwood Avenue
Golden Valley, MN 55422

Editor & Publisher: Roger Hammer

Description and Interests

In print since 1983, this quarterly newsletter is distributed to librarians, teachers, reading program leaders, and others advocating for increased literacy programs. It includes articles and reading-related news, as well as poetry and fiction for children. While poetry and short stories offer the best opportunities for new writers, it is not interested in fantasies, king and queen themes, or prince/princess stories. Circ: 10,000.

Freelance Potential

50% written by nonstaff writers. Publishes 50 freelance submissions yearly; 100% by authors who are new to the magazine. Receives 1,500 unsolicited mss yearly.
Submissions and Payment: Sample copy and guidelines, $7.50. Send complete ms. No simultaneous submissions. SASE. Responds in 2–3 months. All rights. Articles and fiction, to 1,000 words; $50. Pays on acceptance.

Relate Magazine

1254 Greenmar Drive
Fenton, MO 63026

Submissions: Mary Dohack

Description and Interests

Striving to encourage and motivate teens ages 15 to 19, this magazine features articles covering personal development, self-esteem, education, careers, recreation, science, technology, teen designers, decorating, beauty and health, and social issues. Published three times each year, it welcomes detailed queries for articles. While it does not preach Christianity, all material must have a Christian slant. Circ: Unavailable.
Website: www.relatemag.com

Freelance Potential

50% written by nonstaff writers. Publishes 40 freelance submissions yearly.
Submissions and Payment: Query. Accepts email queries to mary@relatemag.com. Response time varies. Rights vary. Articles, 800–1,800 words. Depts/columns, 200–800 words. Written material, $50–$700. Payment policy varies.

Redbook

Hearst Corporation
300 West 57th Street, 22nd Floor
New York, NY 10019

Articles Department

Description and Interests

This glossy covers issues related to marriage, children, and work. Published monthly for women, it includes articles, essays, news stories, and reports on exciting trends. It seeks queries for news stories on contemporary social issues, and marriage articles that focus on strengthening the relationship. Queries should include a list of sources or experts consulted. Circ: 2.3 million.
Website: www.redbookmag.com

Freelance Potential

5% written by nonstaff writers. Publishes 10 freelance submissions yearly; 2% by unpublished writers. Receives 9,960+ queries yearly.
Submissions and Payment: Sample copy, $2.99 at newsstands. Query with clips. Accepts hard copy. SASE. Responds in 3–4 months. All rights. Articles, 1,000–3,000 words; $.75–$1 per word. Depts/columns, 1,000–5,000 words; payment rates vary. Pays on acceptance.

Reptiles

P.O. Box 6050
Mission Viejo, CA 92690

Editor: Russ Case

Description and Interests

Amateur enthusiasts and professionals alike read this monthly magazine on reptiles and amphibians. Readers find articles on keeping, caring for, and breeding these animals. Circ: 40,000.
Website: www.reptilesmagazine.com

Freelance Potential

60% written by nonstaff writers. Publishes 55 freelance submissions yearly; 50% by unpublished writers, 40% by authors who are new to the magazine. Receives 120 queries yearly.
Submissions and Payment: Sample copy, $4.50 at newsstands. Query or send complete ms. Accepts hard copy. No simultaneous submissions. SASE. Responds in 2–3 months. First North American serial rights. Articles and depts/columns, word lengths and payment rates vary. Payment policy varies. Provides 2 contributor's copies.

The Rock

Cook Communications Ministries
4050 Lee Vance View
Colorado Springs, CO 80918

Editor: Doug Mauss

Description and Interests
Published weekly by Cook Communications Ministries, this publication for middle school children attending Sunday school classes includes inspirational stories and lessons that teach children about the Bible, and devotions and activities that reinforce the lessons. Most of its material is created by staff, and it is not reviewing freelance queries or unsolicited manuscripts at this time. Circ: 50,000.
Website: www.cookministries.com

Freelance Potential
10% written by nonstaff writers. Publishes 2–3 freelance submissions yearly; 20% by unpublished writers.
Submissions and Payment: Guidelines available at website. Send résumé or writing samples. SASE. Response time varies. Rights negotiable. Written material, word lengths and payment rates vary. Pays on acceptance. Provides 1 contributor's copy.

Rugby Magazine

33 Kings Highway
Orangeburg, NY 10962

Editor: Ed Hagerty

Description and Interests
Every rugby championship played in the United States is covered in this monthly magazine, along with a roundup of international matches and other news about the sport. It is currently seeking profiles of rugby personalities. Circ: 10,500.
Website: www.rugbymag.com

Freelance Potential
50% written by nonstaff writers. Publishes 400 freelance submissions yearly; 50% by unpublished writers, 50% by authors who are new to the magazine. Receives 600 queries and unsolicited mss yearly.
Submissions and Payment: Sample copy and guidelines, $4 with 9x12 SASE ($1.70 postage). Query or send complete ms. Accepts hard copy and disk submissions. SASE. Responds in 2 weeks. All rights. Written material, word lengths and payment rates vary. Pays on publication. Provides 3 contributor's copies.

Scholastic News

557 Broadway
New York, NY 10012

Submissions Editor, Editions 1–3: Janis Behrens
Submissions Editor, Editions 4–6: Lee Baier

Description and Interests
Each issue of this magazine includes fascinating nonfiction articles that help students develop strong reading and thinking skills while providing information about the culturally, physically, and environmentally diverse world around them. Distributed weekly to students in grades one through six, it presents material that meets state and national standards. It is interested in kid-friendly topics and news articles. Circ: 1 million+.
Website: www.scholastic.com

Freelance Potential
5% written by nonstaff writers.
Submissions and Payment: Query or send complete ms with résumé. Accepts hard copy and simultaneous submissions if identified. Availability of artwork improves chance of acceptance. SASE. Responds in 1–3 months. All rights. Articles, to 500 words; $75–$500. Pays on publication. Provides 3+ author's copies.

Scholastic News English/Español

557 Broadway
New York, NY 10012

Editor: Graciella Vidal

Description and Interests
Scholastic News English/Español is published monthly for Spanish-speaking children in grades one through three. Each flip-format issue contains pages in English and Spanish so students can read the same content in both languages, as well as reading tips that parents can use with their children. Circ: 125,000.
Website: www.scholastic.com

Freelance Potential
10% written by nonstaff writers. Publishes several freelance submissions yearly. Receives many unsolicited mss yearly.
Submissions and Payment: Sample copy and editorial calendar available at website. Query or send complete ms with résumé. Accepts hard copy and simultaneous submissions if identified. SASE. Responds in 1–3 months. All rights. Articles, to 500 words; $75–$500. Pays on publication. Provides 3+ contributor's copies.

Science World

Scholastic Inc.
557 Broadway
New York, NY 10012-3999

Editor: Patricia Jones

Description and Interests
Published by Scholastic, this magazine is distributed to junior high and high school classrooms 14 times each year. It is filled with high-interest, well-researched articles on a variety of topics in the life, Earth, and physical sciences. Circ: 400,000.
Website: www.scholastic.com

Freelance Potential
50% written by nonstaff writers. Publishes 2 freelance submissions yearly; 10% by authors who are new to the magazine. Receives 120 queries yearly.
Submissions and Payment: Sample copy and guidelines, free with 9x12 SASE. All articles are assigned. Query with list of publishing credits and clips or writing samples. Accepts hard copy. SASE. Responds in 2 months. All rights. Articles, to 750 words; $200–$650. Depts/columns, 200 words; $100–$125. Pays on publication. Provides 2 contributor's copies.

Scuola Calcio Soccer Coaching Magazine

P.O. Box 15669
Wilmington, NC 28408

Contributing Writer: Antonio Saviano

Description and Interests
This magazine, published nine times each year, aims to inform youth soccer coaches across the globe of the most effective methods for improving the skills of players ages five and older. Specializing in the Italian style of coaching, it includes articles on player development as well as diagrams of soccer drills. Circ: 350+.
Website: www.soccercoachingmagazine.com

Freelance Potential
10% written by nonstaff writers. Publishes 10 freelance submissions yearly; 5% by unpublished writers, 10% by authors who are new to the magazine.
Submissions and Payment: Guidelines available at website. Query. Accepts hard copy and email queries to magazine@soccercoachingmagazine.com (Microsoft Word attachments). SASE. Response time varies. Worldwide rights. Articles and depts/columns, word lengths, payment rates, and payment policy vary.

Scott Stamp Monthly

Scott Publishing Company
P.O. Box 828
Sidney, OH 45365

Managing Editor: Donna Houseman

Description and Interests
Avid stamp collectors eagerly await their monthly copy of this essential guide, which includes a catalogue of the latest stamp releases as well as "Amazing Stamp Stories" and how-to articles on building and protecting a collection. Circ: 35,000.
Website: www.scottonline.com

Freelance Potential
70% written by nonstaff writers. Publishes 100 freelance submissions yearly; 15% by unpublished writers, 15% by new authors. Receives 180 queries and mss yearly.
Submissions and Payment: Sample copy and guidelines, $3.50 with 9x12 SASE ($2.07 postage). Prefers query. Will accept complete ms. Accepts hard copy and disk submissions (Microsoft Word). SASE. Responds in 1 month. First rights. Articles, 1,000–2,000 words; $75–$150. Depts/columns, word lengths and payment rates vary. Pays on publication. Provides 1 contributor's copy.

Sesame Street Magazine

Sesame Workshop
One Lincoln Plaza
New York, NY 10023

Editor: Rebecca Herman

Description and Interests
This well-known magazine appears 11 times each year, offering fun materials that provide many learning opportunities for young children on subjects such as math, science, reviewing letters and numbers, friendship, and health. Each issue includes a mix of nonfiction, stories, poetry, and activities. *Sesame Street* does not accept unsolicited manuscripts, as all material is written on assignment. Circ: 650,000.
Website: www.sesamestreet.com

Freelance Potential
Receives 48 queries each year.
Submissions and Payment: Query or send résumé only. No unsolicited mss. Accepts hard copy. SASE. Response time varies. All rights. Written material, word lengths and payment rates vary. Pays on publication. Provides contributor's copies.

Shameless

360A Bloor Street W
P.O. Box 68548
Toronto, Ontario M5S 1X1
Canada

Editor: Nicole Cohen

Description and Interests
This unique Canadian publication for teenage girls features insightful, edgy, and engaging articles covering socio-political issues, current events, activism, arts and culture, health, sexuality, and sports. It also includes profiles of outstanding women role models. Published three times each year, it is interested in diverse, creative, and thought-provoking stories. Circ: Unavailable.
Website: www.shamelessmag.com

Freelance Potential
30% written by nonstaff writers. Publishes 25 freelance submissions yearly.
Submissions and Payment: Guidelines available at website. Query with clips. Prefers email to submit@shamlessmag.com. Will accept hard copy. SAE/IRC. Response time varies. First and electronic rights. Articles, 600–2,200 words. Profiles, 300–500 words. No payment.

Six78th

P.O. Box 450
Newark, CA 94560

Features Editor: Carol Rothchild

Description and Interests
With a mission of protecting young girls from growing up before they are ready, this new magazine is published every other month. Its age-appropriate content for girls in the tween age group of 10 to 14 features fashion advice, celebrity interviews, and articles on social issues, health and fitness, current events, and relationships. Circ: Unavailable.
Website: www.six78th.com

Freelance Potential
25% written by nonstaff writers. Publishes 10–20 freelance submissions yearly.
Submissions and Payment: Sample copy, $4.50 with 9x12 SASE. Query. Accepts email queries to features@six78th.com. Responds in 2 months. Rights vary. Articles and depts/columns, word lengths and payment rates vary. Pays on publication. Provides 1 contributor's copy.

Simply You Magazine

P.O. Box 284
Phillips, WI 54555-0284

Editor

Description and Interests
Portions of this online magazine for young adults appear in newsletter form six times each year. With a focus on the body, mind, and spirit, *Simply You* seeks true-life stories about teens, advice from older adults, and articles about coping with loss and overcoming addiction. Hits per month: 10,000.
Website: www.simplyyoumagazine.com

Freelance Potential
25% written by nonstaff writers. Publishes 20–40 freelance submissions yearly; 25% by unpublished writers, 50% by authors who are new to the magazine. Receives 100–125 unsolicited mss yearly.
Submissions and Payment: Sample copy and guidelines, free with #10 SASE. Send complete ms. Accepts email submissions to lynne@simplyyoumagazine.com. Responds in 1–2 months. All rights. Articles, word lengths vary. No payment. Provides 1 author's copy.

Skiing

929 Pearl Street, Suite 200
Boulder, CO 80302

Editor: Scott Gornall

Description and Interests
Entertaining and informative articles covering skiing and other outdoor sports fill the pages of this magazine. Appearing seven times each year, it seeks articles on small ski areas. Circ: 400,000.
Website: www.skinet.com

Freelance Potential
60% written by nonstaff writers. Publishes 50 freelance submissions yearly; 2% by unpublished writers, 5% by new authors. Receives 180 queries yearly.
Submissions and Payment: Sample copy and guidelines, $2.50 with 9x12 SASE ($1 postage). Query with clips or writing samples. No simultaneous submissions. Prefers email to scott.gornall@time4.com. Will accept hard copy. SASE. Responds in 2–4 months. First universal and all media rights. Articles and depts/columns, word lengths vary; $.75 per word. Pays on acceptance. Provides contributor's copies.

Small Town Life Magazine

1046 Barnett Hill Road
Punxsutawney, PA 15767

Editor: Jennifer Forrest

Description and Interests
Readers of *Small Town Life Magazine* enjoy uplifting, interesting articles, in themed issues, on topics such as gardening, holidays, and back to school. This magazine also features profiles of people and places. It provides a great opportunity for new writers and illustrators to get their work published. Circ: 5,000.
Website: www.smalltownlifemagazine.com

Freelance Potential
80% written by nonstaff writers. Publishes 60 freelance submissions yearly; 10% by unpublished writers, 25% by authors who are new to the magazine.
Submissions and Payment: Sample copy, $5. Guidelines available at website. Query or send complete ms. Accepts disk submissions and email submissions to editor@smalltownlifemagazine.com. SASE. Response time varies. First rights. Articles, 3–4 pages. Depts/columns, 500–700 words. No payment.

Socialist Appeal

P.O. Box 4244
St. Paul, MN 55104

Editor: John Peterson

Description and Interests
This self-described "Marxist voice of workers and youth" is published eight times each year by the Workers International League. It contains the latest news and analysis from a Marxist perspective on national, international, labor, and theoretical issues. It seeks politically insightful manuscripts that raise the consciousness of the working class, from details on conditions in the workplace to opinions on current events. Circ: 700.
Website: www.socialistappeal.org

Freelance Potential
5% written by nonstaff writers. Publishes 8 freelance submissions yearly; 100% by authors who are new to the magazine.
Submissions and Payment: Query or send complete ms. Accepts hard copy. SASE. Response time varies. Rights vary. Articles, word lengths vary. No payment.

Spirit

Sisters of St. Joseph of Carondelet
1884 Randolph Avenue
St. Paul, MN 55105-1700

Editor: Joan Mitchell

Description and Interests
Inspirational articles that challenge Catholic teens to work through tough issues and that encourage them to develop a closer relationship with God can be found in this weekly take-home paper. Appearing 28 times each year, it is distributed in religious education classes. While it has depended on freelance material in the past, *Spirit* is not reviewing queries or unsolicited manuscripts at this time. Writers who are interested in this publication are advised to check the website for any changes to this policy. Circ: 25,000.
Website: www.goodgroundpress.com

Freelance Potential
50% written by nonstaff writers. Publishes 6–10 freelance submissions yearly; 50% by unpublished writers.
Submissions and Payment: Sample copy, free. Not accepting queries or unsolicited material at this time.

Sporting Youth GA

P.O. Box 1137
Watkinsville, GA 30677

Editor: Barbara W. Peterson

Description and Interests
Distributed free every other month, this publication covers northeast Georgia's school sports and sporting events. Profiles of area athletes, as well as well-known athletes from across the country, appear in each issue. It targets children and young adults ages 10 to 18 and offers training tips from coaches, college athletes, and professionals. Circ: 5,000.
Website: www.sportingyouthga.com

Freelance Potential
90% written by nonstaff writers. Publishes 25 freelance submissions yearly.
Submissions and Payment: Sample copy available at website. Query or send complete ms. Accepts email submissions to mail@sportingyouthga.com. Responds in 1 month. One-time rights. Articles and depts/columns, word lengths vary. No payment. Provides contributor's copies.

Start

321 North Pine
Lansing, MI 48933

Editor: Bryan Taylor

Description and Interests
A publication of Partnership for Learning, *Start* brings parents and experts together in a magazine-style series containing articles that inspire and inform. Topics include literacy, skill building activities, and the developmental stages of babies, toddlers, and preschoolers. Each issue also features a journal-type story that describes lessons learned as a parent, as well as learning games for children. Circ: 90,000.
Website: www.partnershipforlearning.org

Freelance Potential
85% written by nonstaff writers.
Submissions and Payment: Guidelines available at website. Sample copy, free with 9x12 SASE. Query. Accepts hard copy and email queries to info@ partnershipforlearning.org. SASE. Response time varies. Rights vary. Articles, 150–800 words; $75–$150. Pays on publication.

Supertwins

P.O. Box 306
East Islip, NY 17130

Editor: Maureen Boyle

Description and Interests
This magazine is packed with articles and information on topics related to parenting twins and multiples up to the age of five. It also includes crafts, recipes, and essays from fathers. Published quarterly by MOST (Mothers of Supertwins), it is interested in practical articles that inform parents and support them. Circ: Unavailable.
Website: www.MOSTonline.org

Freelance Potential
100% written by nonstaff writers. Publishes 16 freelance submissions yearly. Receives 100 queries yearly.
Submissions and Payment: Sample copy, $5 with 9x12 SASE. Query or send complete ms. Accepts hard copy and email submissions to info@mostonline.org. SASE. Response time varies. Rights vary. Articles and depts/columns, word lengths and payment rates vary. Pays on publication. Provides 2 contributor's copies.

Storytelling Magazine

National Storytelling Network
132 Boone Street, Suite 5
Jonesborough, TN 37659

Managing Editor: Grace Hawthorne

Description and Interests
For 19 years, this publication has been offering news, resources, read-aloud stories, applications on oral storytelling traditions, and other information on the art of storytelling. It is published six times each year. At this time it is not accepting submissions. Experienced storytellers who wish to contribute are advised to watch the website for changes to this policy. Circ: 6,000.
Website: www.storynet.org

Freelance Potential
50% written by nonstaff writers. Publishes 100 freelance submissions yearly. Receives 48 mss yearly.
Submissions and Payment: Sample copy, $6. Query when submission policy changes. Accepts email queries to ghawthorne@mindspring.com. Response time varies. First North American serial rights. Articles, 1,000–2,000 words. Depts/columns, 500 words. No payment. Provides 2 contributor's copies.

Surfing

950 Calle Amanecer, Suite C
San Clemente, CA 92673

Editor: Evan Slater

Description and Interests
This monthly caters to 13- to 30-year-old experienced surfers with exciting articles about improving skills and enjoying the surfing lifestyle. Circ: 105,000.
Website: www.surfingmagazine.com

Freelance Potential
20% written by nonstaff writers. Publishes 15 freelance submissions yearly; 50% by unpublished writers. Receives 72 unsolicited mss yearly.
Submissions and Payment: Sample copy, $3.99 at newsstands. Guidelines available. Query or send complete ms. Prefers email submissions to surfing@ primedia.com. Will accept hard copy, disk submissions (QuarkXPress or Microsoft Word), and simultaneous submissions if identified. SASE. Responds in 1 month. One-time rights. Articles, 2,000–3,000 words. Depts/ columns, 35–500 words. Written material, $.10–$.25 per word. Pays on publication. Provides 2 copies.

Synchro Swimming USA

201 South Capitol Avenue, Suite 901
Indianapolis, IN 46225

Editor: Taylor D. Payne

Description and Interests
Published quarterly by United States Synchronized Swimming, this magazine features articles and news covering teams, coaches, and judges of the sport. In addition, it includes competition results, member news, and information on the latest in gear and equipment. It is interested in up-to-date information on topics related to synchronized swimming, and event coverage. Hits per month: 7,000.
Website: www.usasynchro.org

Freelance Potential
50% written by nonstaff writers. Publishes 15–18 freelance submissions yearly; 35% by unpublished writers, 50% by authors who are new to the magazine.
Submissions and Payment: Query or send complete ms. Accepts hard copy. SASE. Response time varies. All rights. Articles, word lengths vary. No payment.

Teen Strings

255 West End Avenue
San Rafael, CA 94901

Editorial Director: Greg Cahill

Description and Interests
This quarterly targets children and young adults ages 11 through 18 who play string-bowed instruments including violin, guitar, cello, and viola. It offers tips on getting the most out of practice and performance opportunities, and advice on auditions and training camps and schools. *Teen Strings* is open to working with new writers who have a strong background in the string playing world, and is also open to receiving personal experience pieces from young adults. Circ: Unavailable.
Website: www.teenstrings.com

Freelance Potential
64% written by nonstaff writers. Publishes 15–20 freelance submissions yearly.
Submissions and Payment: Sample copy available. Query. Accepts email queries to greg@stringletter.com. Response time varies. Rights vary. Articles, 1,000 words; $300. Pays on publication.

Teen Times

1910 Association Drive
Reston, VA 20191

Director of Communications: Bana Yahnke

Description and Interests
Launched in 1945, this quarterly publication is for teens who are members of FCCLA (Family, Career, and Community Leaders of America). It includes articles on topics such as careers, leadership, family, community service, communication skills, health and fitness, and recreation. Submissions from freelancers are not being used at this time. Interested writers may check with the editor or visit the website at a future date to determine when and if it will be again open to submissions from writers outside of its established circle of contributors. Circ: 220,000.
Website: www.fcclainc.org

Freelance Potential
50% written by nonstaff writers.
Submissions and Payment: Sample copy available with 9x12 SASE. Not accepting freelance queries or manuscripts at this time.

Teen Trend Magazine

P.O. Box 567
Middle Island, NY 11953-0567

Editor: Candice Cain

Description and Interests
This magazine features interviews, fashion trends, advice, and articles of interest to teens ages 12 to 18. Published six times each year, it also includes stories about school activities and insight into different extracurricular activities for teens. It seeks queries covering the latest trends. All material must be relevant to teens. Writers should familiarize themselves with the publication prior to submitting work. Circ: 75,000.
Website: www.teentrendmagazine.com

Freelance Potential
10% written by nonstaff writers. Publishes 6 freelance submissions yearly; 50% by unpublished writers, 100% by authors who are new to the magazine.
Submissions and Payment: Sample copy, $2.49. Query with résumé. SASE. Response time varies. First rights. Articles and depts/columns, word lengths vary. Written material, $50. Payment policy varies.

Tidewater Parent

258 Granby Street
Norfolk, VA 23510

Editor: Jennifer O'Donnell

Description and Interests
This monthly covers general parenting and child development, and offers information on area resources and events. Distributed at schools, doctors' offices, and other local outlets, the magazine works with writers from the Norfolk region only. Circ: 48,000.
Website: www.tidewaterparent.com

Freelance Potential
90% written by nonstaff writers. Publishes 40 freelance submissions yearly; 10% by unpublished writers, 50% by authors who are new to the magazine. Receives 72 unsolicited mss yearly.
Submissions and Payment: Send complete ms. Will accept previously published mss that can be reprinted. Accepts hard copy. SASE. Response time varies. Rights vary. Articles, 800–1,200 words; $25. Kill fee, 50%. Pays on publication. Provides 1 contributor's copy.

Toy Farmer

7496 106th Avenue SE
LaMoure, ND 58458-9404

Editorial Assistant: Cheryl Hegvik

Description and Interests
Collectors of toy tractors and other farm-themed toys read this monthly magazine to keep up with trends, auctions, shows, and other related events. Features include manufacturer profiles; farm toy histories; and nostalgia. Circ: 27,000.
Website: www.toyfarmer.com

Freelance Potential
100% written by nonstaff writers. Publishes 50 freelance submissions yearly; 20% by unpublished writers, 20% by authors who are new to the magazine. Receives numerous queries yearly.
Submissions and Payment: Sample copy, guidelines, and editorial calendar, $5 with 9x12 SASE. Query with writing samples. Accepts hard copy. SASE. Responds in 1 month. First rights. Articles, 1,500 words. Depts/columns, 800 words. Written material, $.10 per word. Pays on publication. Provides 2 contributor's copies.

Today's Christian

People of Faith, Stories of Hope

465 Gundersen Drive
Carol Stream, IL 60188

Editorial Coordinator: Cynthia Thomas

Description and Interests
This digest-sized magazine published six times each year offers inspirational personal essays and profiles for a broad range of Christians. It seeks real-life drama and high-quality humor pieces. Circ: 85,000.
Website: www.todays-christian.com

Freelance Potential
80% written by nonstaff writers. Publishes 25–30 freelance submissions yearly; 10% by unpublished writers, 10% by authors who are new to the magazine. Receives 1,000 unsolicited mss yearly.
Submissions and Payment: Sample copy, free with 6x9 SASE (4 first-class stamps). Send complete ms. Accepts hard copy and email submissions to tceditor@ christianitytoday.com. SASE. Responds in 2 months. First serial rights. Articles, 700–2,800 words. Depts/columns, word lengths vary. Written material, $.15–$.25 per word. Pays on acceptance. Provides 2 copies.

Turtle Trails

P.O. Box 19623
Reno, NV 89511

Editor: Virginia Castleman

Description and Interests
Turtle Trails bridges the gap between magazine and newsletter with its multicultural articles and personal experience pieces. It also features short stories in the genres of mystery, adventure, and contemporary and historical fiction. All of its material promotes tolerance and understanding while demonstrating sensitivity to other cultures. Circ: 20,000+.

Freelance Potential
40% written by nonstaff writers. Publishes 12 freelance submissions yearly; 80% by unpublished writers. Receives 36 unsolicited mss yearly.
Submissions and Payment: Sample copy, guidelines, and theme list, free with 9x12 SASE ($3 postage). Send complete ms. Accepts hard copy and email submissions to vcastleman@sbcglobal.net. SASE. Responds in 3 months. First rights. Articles and fiction, 750 words; $25. Pays on publication. Provides 1 author's copy.

Vertical Thought

555 Technecenter Drive
Milford, OH 45150

Managing Editor: David Treybig

Description and Interests
Helping teens and young adults to "seek those things which are above, where Christ is" and become tomorrow's leaders is the mission of this quarterly magazine that encourages a Christian worldview and corresponding conduct. Articles must conform to the teachings and doctrines of the United Church of God, which publishes *Vertical Thought*. Circ: 24,000.
Website: www.verticalthought.org

Freelance Potential
5% written by nonstaff writers. Publishes 3–4 freelance submissions yearly; 20% by unpublished writers.
Submissions and Payment: Sample copy and guidelines available via email to info@verticalthought.org. Send complete ms. Accepts hard copy and email submissions to info@verticalthought.org. SASE. Response time varies. One-time rights. Written material, word lengths vary. No payment.

The Village Family

501 40th Street S
Fargo, ND 58103

Editor: Laurie Neill

Description and Interests
In print since 1997, this family oriented magazine targets parents in the Fargo, North Dakota–Moorhead, Minnesota, region. Appearing six times each year, it is interested in articles on grandparents and extended-family issues. Circ: 25,000.
Website: www.thevillagefamily.org

Freelance Potential
80% written by nonstaff writers. Publishes 30 freelance submissions yearly; 60% by unpublished writers. Receives 1,200+ queries and unsolicited mss yearly.
Submissions and Payment: Guidelines available. Query or send ms with author bio. Accepts hard copy and email to magazine@thevillagefamily.org. SASE. Response time varies. First and electronic rights. Articles, to 1,500 words. Depts/columns, word lengths vary. Written material, $.07–$.10 per word. Reprints, $30–$50. Pays on publication.

Vibrant Life

55 West Oak Ridge Drive
Hagerstown, MD 21740

Editor: Charles Mills

Description and Interests
Published six times each year, this magazine promotes physical health, mental clarity, and spiritual balance from a practical, Christian perspective. It seeks articles about spirituality and health, family issues, and community health. Circ: 28,500.
Website: www.vibrantlife.com

Freelance Potential
95% written by nonstaff writers. Publishes 18 freelance submissions yearly; 50% by unpublished writers, 50% by new authors. Receives 480 queries and mss yearly.
Submissions and Payment: Sample copy and guidelines, $1 with 9x12 SASE (3 first-class stamps). Prefers ms. Will accept query. Accepts hard copy and email to vibrantlife@rhpa.org (Microsoft Word attachments). SASE. Responds in 1 month. First world, reprint, and electronic rights. Articles, 450–1,500 words; $75–$300. Pays on acceptance. Provides 3 contributor's copies.

Volta Voices

Alexander Graham Bell Association
for the Deaf and Hard of Hearing
3417 Volta Place NW
Washington, DC 20007-2778

Editor

Description and Interests
Published six times each year, this magazine offers articles and information on hearing loss and spoken language education. It is interested in stories on topics such as new teaching methods; technology; advocacy; psychological, social, and emotional issues relating to children with hearing loss; and events of general interest to people who are deaf. Circ: 5,500.
Website: www.agbell.org

Freelance Potential
90% written by nonstaff writers. Publishes 6–8 freelance submissions yearly; 50% by unpublished writers. Receives 24 unsolicited mss yearly.
Submissions and Payment: Sample copy available at website. Send complete ms. Accepts email submissions to editor@agbell.org (Microsoft Word attachments). Responds in 1–3 months. All rights. Articles, 500–2,000 words. No payment. Provides 3 copies.

Wanna Bet?

North American Training Institute
314 West Superior Street, Suite 508
Duluth, MN 55802

Submissions

Description and Interests
Wanna Bet? is an online magazine by and for kids concerned about gambling. Along with adult and youth advisors, a junior editor looks for articles that address all forms of betting and gambling and the problems that these activities can cause. Its target audience is middle school-aged students who may be worried about parental gambling or who may think that they themselves are addicted. *Wanna Bet?* is updated monthly. Hits per month: 60,000.
Website: www.wannabet.org

Freelance Potential
25% written by nonstaff writers. Publishes many freelance submissions yearly.
Submissions and Payment: Sample copy available at website. Query or send ms. Accepts email submissions to info@wannabet.org. Response time varies. Electronic rights. Articles, word lengths vary. No payment.

West Tennessee Parent and Family

245 West Lafayette Street
Jackson, TN 38301

Editor: Jacque Hillman

Description and Interests
This monthly magazine is distributed throughout the western Tennessee region, and features the work of local writers only. It regularly offers articles on travel, recreation, culture, and education, as well as family health and fitness, nutrition, pets, social issues, and parenting issues. Its content also includes personality profiles, interviews, product reviews, book reviews, event and activity calendars, recipes, craft ideas, and photo-essays. Circ: Unavailable.
Website: www.wtnparent.com

Freelance Potential
100% written by nonstaff writers. Publishes 25 freelance submissions yearly.
Submissions and Payment: Query or send complete ms. SASE. Response time varies. All rights. Articles and depts/columns, word lengths and payment rates vary. Payment policy varies.

The Water Skier

USA Water Ski
1251 Holy Cow Road
Polk City, FL 33868-8200

Editor: Scott Atkinson

Description and Interests
Articles and action photos covering the sport of water skiing can be found in this magazine. As the official publication of the American Water Ski Association, it features articles on techniques and training, competition results, and profiles of teams and athletes. It appears nine times each year. Circ: 35,000.
Website: www.usawaterski.org

Freelance Potential
20% written by nonstaff writers. Publishes 10–12 freelance submissions yearly; 10% by authors who are new to the magazine. Receives 20–30 queries yearly.
Submissions and Payment: Sample copy, $1.25 with 9x12 SASE. Query. Accepts email queries only to usawsmagazine@usawaterski.org. Responds in 1 month. All rights. Articles, 1,000 words. Fiction, 500–1,000 words. Written material, payment rates vary. Provides 1 contributor's copy.

Wild West

Weider History Group
741 Miller Drive SE, Suite D-2
Leesburg, VA 20175

Editor: Greg Lalire

Description and Interests
Published six times each year, this magazine chronicles the history of America's frontier with factual articles that also convey a sense of action and adventure. High school teachers and history buffs comprise its readership. Circ: 80,000.
Website: www.thehistorynet.com

Freelance Potential
80% written by nonstaff writers. Publishes 60 freelance submissions yearly; 10% by unpublished writers, 20% by authors who are new to the magazine. Receives 250 queries yearly.
Submissions and Payment: Sample copy and guidelines, $6. Query with résumé, outline, illustration ideas, source lists, and clips or writing samples. Accepts hard copy. SASE. Responds in 4–6 months. All rights. Articles, to 3,500 words; $300. Depts/columns, to 1,200 words; $150. Pays on publication.

With

The Magazine for Radical Christian Youth

722 Main Street
P.O. Box 347
Newton, KS 67114

Editor: Carol Duerksen

Description and Interests
Christian teens read this magazine for its first-person stories of life-changing experiences, humorous pieces, realistic fiction, and how-to articles. It appears six times each year. Circ: 4,000.
Website: www.withonline.org

Freelance Potential
5% written by nonstaff writers. Publishes 60 freelance submissions yearly; 5% by unpublished writers, 5% by authors who are new to the magazine. Receives 960 queries and mss yearly.
Submissions and Payment: Sample copy, guidelines, and theme list, free with 9x12 SASE (4 first-class stamps). Query with clips or writing samples for how-to and first-person stories. Send ms for other material. Accepts hard copy and simultaneous submissions. SASE. Responds in 1 month. Simultaneous and reprint rights. All material, payment rates vary. Pays on publication.

With Kids

6 High Street
Corsham, Wiltshire SN13 OHB
United Kingdom

Editor: Sarah North

Description and Interests
Not a "parenting magazine," but a magazine for parents, this glossy British monthly targets mothers in their 20s, 30s, and 40s with general lifestyle features. Its readers have largely moved beyond the need for baby advice and seek instead articles that identify with their needs and interests as adults—who also happen to have young kids. Suggestions for features directly related to parenting topics are less likely to be accepted than articles on broader issues. Circ: 30,000.
Website: www.withkidsmagazine.com

Freelance Potential
80% written by nonstaff writers. Publishes several freelance submissions yearly; 50% by authors who are new to the magazine.
Submissions and Payment: Guidelines available via email request to editor@withkidsmagazine.com. First and Internet rights. Articles, £220 per 1,000 words.

Women Today Magazine

Box 300 STN "A"
Vancouver, BC V6C 2X3
Canada

Senior Editor: Claire Colvin

Description and Interests
This online magazine is updated monthly with content that addresses the spiritual, emotional, and physical needs of modern women seeking to be the best version of themselves. It does not publish poetry, fiction, or artwork. Hits per month: Unavailable.
Website: www.womentodaymagazine.com

Freelance Potential
30–50% written by nonstaff writers. Publishes 20–30 freelance submissions yearly; 15% by unpublished writers, 25% by authors who are new to the magazine. Receives 450 unsolicited mss yearly.
Submissions and Payment: Sample copy and guidelines available at website. Send complete ms. Accepts email submissions to info@womentodaymagazine.com. Responds in 4–6 weeks. One-time rights. Articles, 1,000–1,500 words. Depts/columns, 700–1,000 words. No payment.

World Around You

Laurent Clerc National Deaf Education Center
KDES, Suite 3600
800 Florida Avenue NE
Washington, DC 20002

Submissions: Michael Walton

Description and Interests
Published by Gallaudet University, the only undergraduate school in the world designed entirely for deaf students, this online magazine publishes articles on careers and lifestyles of the hearing-impaired, with an emphasis on achievement. It is especially interested in personal experience pieces from writers who are deaf or hard of hearing. Hits per month: Unavailable.
Website: http://clerccenter.gallaudet.edu/ worldaroundyou/

Freelance Potential
10% written by nonstaff writers. Publishes 3–5 freelance submissions yearly. Receives 48 queries yearly.
Submissions and Payment: Sample copy available at website. Query. Accepts hard copy and email queries to michael.walton@gallaudet.edu. SASE. Responds in 1 month. Rights negotiable. Written material, word lengths and payment rates vary. Pays on publication.

Youngbucksoutdoors.com

10350 Highway 80 East
Montgomery, AL 36117

Managing Editor: Dockery Austin

Description and Interests
This online publication for children ages seven and up focuses on the great outdoors with articles covering hunting, fishing, animals, and nature. Short stories about animals and nature are also a part of its editorial mix. Hits per month: 200,000.
Website: www.youngbucksoutdoors.com

Freelance Potential
60% written by nonstaff writers. Publishes 15–20 freelance submissions yearly.
Submissions and Payment: Sample copy available at website. Query with detailed photo information. Availability of artwork improves chance of acceptance. Accepts hard copy and email queries to daustin@buckmasters.com. SASE. Responds in 1 week. First rights. Articles, 400 words. Fiction, to 500 words. Color prints and transparencies. All material, payment rates vary. Pays on publication.

Youthrunner

P.O. Box 1156
Lake Oswego, OR 97035

Editor: Dan Kesterson

Description and Interests
The core readers of *Youthrunner* are children and young adults ages 9 to 15 who are involved in track and field or cross-country running. Published quarterly, it includes interviews with young athletes, coaches, and Olympians and offers training tips and advice from the pros. Fresh talent and ideas are of great interest at this time. Circ: Unavailable.
Website: www.youthrunner.com

Freelance Potential
50% written by nonstaff writers. Publishes 10 freelance submissions yearly; 50% by unpublished writers, 50% by authors who are new to the magazine.
Submissions and Payment: Sample copy available. Send complete ms. Accepts email submissions to dank@youthrunner.com. Response time varies. First rights. Written material, word lengths and payment rates vary. Payment policy varies.

Your Child

155 Fifth Avenue
New York, NY 10010-6802

Editor: Kay E. Pomerantz

Description and Interests
Now appearing as an e-zine, this newsletter focuses on offering solutions to problems and issues involved in raising and educating Jewish children. It includes articles, family projects, holiday ideas, media reviews, and resources. Published three times each year, it is interested in parenting articles with Jewish angles on positive and effective child-raising techniques. Circ: 3,000.
Website: www.uscj.org

Freelance Potential
Of the freelance submissions published yearly, 50% are by unpublished writers.
Submissions and Payment: Sample copy, free with 9x12 SASE ($.55 postage). Send complete ms. Accepts hard copy. Availability of artwork improves chance of acceptance. SASE. Response time varies. All rights. Articles, word lengths vary. 8x10 B/W transparencies; line art. No payment. Provides 1 contributor's copy.

ZooGoer

Friends of the National Zoo Communications Office
National Zoological Park
3001 Connecticut Avenue NW
Washington, DC 20008

Associate Editor: Shannon Lyons

Description and Interests
ZooGoer aims to enlighten and entertain readers from all walks of life with feature stories about natural history, wildlife biology, and conservation. It appears six times each year. Circ: 30,000.
Website: www.fonz.org/zoogoer.htm

Freelance Potential
70% written by nonstaff writers. Publishes 25 freelance submissions yearly; 15% by unpublished writers, 25% by authors who are new to the magazine. Receives 15 queries and unsolicited mss yearly.
Submissions and Payment: Guidelines available. Query with synopsis and clips; or send complete ms. Accepts hard copy, disk submissions (Microsoft Word), and email to shannon@fonz.org. SASE. Responds in 1–2 months. First rights. Articles, 2,500–3,000 words. Depts/columns, 800–1,500 words. Written material, $.50 per word. Pays on publication. Provides 5 author's copies.

 # Contests and Awards

Selected Contests and Awards

Entering a writing contest will provide you with a chance to have your work read by established writers and qualified editors. Winning or placing in a contest or an award program can open the door to publication and recognition of your writing. If you don't win, try to read the winning entry if it is published; doing so will give you some insight into how your work compares with its competition.

For both editors and writers, contests generate excitement. For editors, contests are a source to discover new writers. Entries are more focused because of the contest guidelines, and therefore more closely target an editor's current needs.

For writers, every contest entry is read, often by more than one editor, as opposed to unsolicited submissions that are often relegated to a slush pile.

And you don't have to be the grand-prize winner to benefit—non-winning manuscripts are often purchased by the publication for future issues.

To be considered for the contests and awards that follow, your entry must fulfill all of the requirements mentioned. Most are looking for unpublished article or story manuscripts, while a few require published works. Note special entry requirements, such as whether or not you can submit the material yourself, need to be a member of an organization, or are limited in the number of entries you can send. Also, be sure to submit your article or story in the standard manuscript submission format.

For each listing, we've included the address, the contact, a description, the entry requirements, the deadline, and the prize. In some cases, the 2008 deadlines were not available at press time. We recommend that you write to the addresses provided or visit the websites to request an entry form and the contest guidelines, which usually specify the current deadline.

Amy Writing Awards

The Amy Foundation
P.O. Box 16091
Lansing, MI 48901

Description
Held annually, these awards recognize creative writing that presents the biblical position on issues affecting the world today in a sensitive, thought-provoking manner. The competition is open to all writers and eligible entries will have been published in a secular, non-religious publication, but must contain Scripture.
Website: www.amyfound.org
Length: No length requirements.
Requirements: No entry fee. All entries must contain quotes from the Bible. Manuscripts will not be returned. Send an SASE or visit the website for complete guidelines.
Prizes: First-place winner receives a cash award of $10,000.
Deadline: December 31.

Isaac Asimov Award

University of South Florida
School of Mass Communications
4202 East Fowler
Tampa, FL 33620

Description
Open to undergraduate students, this annual award looks to promote and encourage the writing of high-quality science fiction and fantasy. It accepts previously unpublished entries only.
Website: www.asimovs.com
Length: 1,000–10,000 words.
Requirements: Open to full-time college students only. Entry fee, $10. Limit 3 entries per competition. Entries should include a cover sheet with author's name, address, and university. Author's name should not appear on the entry itself.
Prizes: Winner receives a cash prize of $500 and will be considered for publication in *Asimov's Science Fiction Magazine*.
Deadline: December 15.

Arizona Literary Contest

Arizona Authors Association
P.O. Box 87857
Phoenix, AZ 85080-7857

Description
This literary competition accepts unpublished entries in the categories of short story, essay/article, poetry, and novel.
Website: www.azauthors.com/contest.html
Requirements: Entry fees vary per category, ranging from $10 to $30. Accepts hard copy. Manuscripts will not be returned. Complete guidelines are available at the website.
Prizes: Winners receive publication in *Arizona Literary Magazine*.
Deadline: Entries are accepted between January 1 and July 1.

Baker's Plays High School Playwriting Contest

Baker's Plays
P.O. Box 699222
Quincy, MA 02269-9222

Description
This annual contest accepts submissions from high school students only. It looks to acknowledge playwrights at the high school level and to ensure the future of American theater. Each entry should receive a public reading or production prior to submission.
Website: www.bakersplays.com
Length: No length requirements.
Requirements: No entry fee. Plays must be accompanied by the signature of a sponsoring high school English teacher. Accepts hard copy. Include an SASE for return of manuscript. Visit the website or send an SASE for complete guidelines and entry form.
Prizes: First-place winner receives a cash award of $500 with a royalty-earning contract from Baker's Plays. Second- and third-place winners also receive cash prizes.
Deadline: January 30.

Waldo M. and Grace C. Bonderman Youth Theatre Playwriting Competition

Indiana Repertory Theatre
140 West Washington Street
Indianapolis, IN 46204

Description

This competition looks to encourage writers to create theatrical scripts for young audiences. Playwrights also receive constructive criticism on their entries.
Website: www.indianarep.com/Bonderman
Length: 45-minute running time.
Requirements: No entry fee. Limit one entry per competition. Accepts hard copy. For dramatizations or adaptations, written proof is required that the original work is in the public domain or that permission has been granted by the copyright holder. Send an SASE or visit the website for more details.
Prizes: Awards will be presented to 10 finalists. Four cash awards of $1,000 are also awarded to the playwrights whose plays are selected for development.
Deadline: August 31.

Calliope Fiction Contest

Calliope
P.O. Box 466
Moraga, CA 94556-0466

Description

Calliope sponsors this annual contest that accepts entries of short fiction that display creativity, good storytelling, and appropriate use of language for the target audience.
Length: To 2,500 words.
Requirements: Entry fee, $2 per story for non-subscribers; first entry is free for subscribers. Limit 5 entries per competition. Accepts hard copy. Manuscript will not be returned. Enclose an SASE for winners' list.
Prizes: First-place winner receives a cash award of $75. Second- and third-place winners receive $25 and $10, respectively. All winners are published in Calliope (requires one-time rights). Winners also receive certificates and a 1-year subscription to Calliope.
Deadline: Entries are accepted between April 15 and September 30.

ByLine Magazine Contests

Contests: ByLine Magazine
P.O. Box 111
Albion, NY 14411

Description

ByLine sponsors monthly contests that are presented in several different categories. Past categories include personal memoir, short story, juvenile short story, inspirational article, and poetry.
Website: www.bylinemag.com/contests.html
Length: Lengths vary according to category.
Requirements: Fees vary according to category but range from $3 to $5. Multiple entries are accepted. Accepts hard copy. Send an SASE or visit the website for complete category information and further guidelines.
Prizes: Cash prizes ranging from $10 to $70 are presented to the winners. Runners-up also receive cash awards in each category. Winning entries for the Annual Literary Awards are published in ByLine and receive a cash award of $250.
Deadline: Deadlines vary according to category.

Canadian Writer's Journal Short Fiction Contest

Canadian Writer's Journal
Box 1178
New Liskeard, Ontario P0J 1P0
Canada

Description

Sponsored by Canadian Writer's Journal, this semi-annual contest accepts original, unpublished stories in any genre.
Website: www.cwj.ca
Length: To 1,200 words.
Requirements: Entry fee, $5. Multiple entries are accepted. Accepts hard copy. Author's name should not appear on manuscript. Include a cover sheet with author's name, address, and title of entry. Manuscript will not be returned. Send an SASE or visit the website for further guidelines.
Prizes: First-place winner receives a cash prize of $100. Second- and third-place winners receive cash prizes of $50 and $25, respectively.
Deadline: September 30 or March 31.

CAPA Competition

c/o Daniel Uitti
Connecticut Authors and Publishers
223 Buckingham Street
Oakville, CT 06779

Description
Residents of Connecticut may enter this competition that accepts previously unpublished entries in the categories of children's story, short story, personal essay, and poetry.
Website: http://aboutcapa.com
Length: Children's stories and short stories, to 2,000 words. Personal essays, to 1,500 words. Poetry, to 30 lines.
Requirements: Entry fee, $10 for 1 story or essay or up to 3 poems. Multiple entries are accepted. Accepts hard copy. Submit 4 copies of manuscript. Manuscripts will not be returned. Visit the website or send an SASE for complete guidelines.
Prizes: First-place winners in each category receive a cash prize of $100. Second-place winners receive a cash award of $50.
Deadline: May 31.

Children's Writer Contests

Children's Writer
95 Long Ridge Road
West Redding, CT 06896-1124

Description
Children's Writer sponsors two contests each year with different themes for original, unpublished fiction and nonfiction. Upcoming themes for 2008 are preK seasonal story or article and sports nonfiction article.
Website: www.childrenswriter.com
Length: Requirements vary for each contest; usually 500–1,000 words.
Requirements: Entry fee, $10 for non-subscribers (entry fee includes an 8-month subscription); no entry fee for subscribers. Multiple entries are accepted. Manuscripts are not returned. Visit the website or send an SASE for current themes and further requirements.
Prizes: Cash prizes vary per contest. Winning entries are published in *Children's Writer*.
Deadline: February and October of each year.

CNW/FFWA Florida State Writing Competition

CNW/FFWA
P.O. Box A
North Stratford, NH 03590

Description
Open to all writers, this annual competition presents awards in several categories including children's literature short story, children's nonfiction, novel chapter, nonfiction book chapter, and poetry.
Website: www.writers-editors.com
Length: Lengths vary according to category.
Requirements: Entry fees vary for each category. Multiple entries are accepted, as long as each entry is accompanied by an entry fee. Use paper clips only. Author's name must not appear on manuscript. Send an SASE or visit the website for complete contest guidelines, specific category information, and official entry form.
Prizes: First- through third-place prizes will be awarded in each category. Winners receive cash awards ranging from $50 to $100.
Deadline: March 15.

Kimberly Colen Memorial Grant

Box 20322
Park West Finance Station
New York, NY 10025-1512

Description
This grant is available to new authors or illustrators who have not yet published their first children's book. Grants are offered in early reader/picture book and middle-grade/young adult categories.
Website: www.scbwi.org
Requirements: Applicants should send a 1-page letter (approximately 300 words) describing the work they hope will become their first children's book. It must describe a work-in-progress or completed project. Do not send writing or illustration samples with application letter.
Prizes: A grant of $2,500 will be presented to each of the winners.
Deadline: September 15 through October 31.

Shubert Fendrich Memorial Playwriting Contest

Pioneer Drama Service, Inc.
P.O. Box 4267
Englewood, CO 80155-4267

Description

This annual playwriting contest honors its winners with publication and a royalty advance. Plays may be on any subject that is appropriate for family viewing.
Website: www.pioneerdrama.com
Length: Running time, 20 to 90 minutes.
Requirements: No entry fee. Cover letter must accompany all submissions. Include title, synopsis, cast list breakdown, proof of production, number of sets and scenes, and, if applicable, musical score and tape. Any writers currently published by Pioneer Drama Service are not eligible. Send SASE for contest guidelines and information.
Prizes: Winner receives $1,000 royalty advance in addition to publication.
Deadline: March 1. Winners will be announced in June.

John Gardner Memorial Prize for Fiction

Harpur Palate
English Department, Binghamton University
Box 6000
Binghamton, NY 13902-6000

Description

This annual fiction contest honors John Gardner for his dedication to the creative writing program at Binghamton University. It is open to submissions of previously unpublished short stories in any genre.
Website: http://harpurpalate.binghamton.edu
Length: To 8,000 words.
Requirements: Entry fee, $15 (checks should be made out to *Harpur Palate*). Multiple entries are accepted under separate cover only. Include a cover letter with name, address, phone number, email address, and title. Manuscripts will not be returned. Send an SASE or visit the website for further information.
Prizes: Winner receives a cash award of $500 and publication in *Harpur Palate*.
Deadline: March 1.

Foster City International Writing Contest

Foster City Recreation Dept.
650 Shell Boulevard
Foster City, CA 94404

Description

This annual contest accepts original, unpublished entries in the categories of children's story, fiction, humor, poetry, and personal essay.
Website: www.geocities.com/fostercity_writers/
Length: Children's stories and fiction, to 3,000 words. Humor and personal experience pieces, to 2,000 words. Poetry, to 500 words.
Requirements: Entry fee, $12. Multiple entries are accepted. Accepts hard copy and email submissions to fostercity_writers@yahoo.com (RTF or Microsoft Word attachments). Check website for further category information.
Prizes: First-place winners in each category receive a cash award of $100.
Deadline: December 30.

Paul Gillette Memorial Writing Contest

Pikes Peak Writers
4164 Austin Bluffs Parkway, #246
Colorado Springs, CO 80918

Description

The Paul Gillette Memorial Writing Contest accepts manuscripts from unpublished writers in several different categories including children's, young adult, mystery, historical fiction, and creative nonfiction.
Website: www.ppwc.net
Length: Lengths vary for each category.
Requirements: Entry fee, $30 for members; $40 for non-members. Manuscript critiques are available for an additional $20. Accepts hard copy and email submissions to pgcontest@gmail.com. All entries must be accompanied by an entry form, cover letter, and two copies of manuscript. Guidelines are available with an SASE or at the website.
Prizes: First-place winners in each category receive a cash prize of $100. Second-place winners receive a cash award of $50.
Deadline: November 1.

Lorian Hemingway
Short Story Competition

P.O. Box 993
Key West, FL 33041

Description
Held annually, this competition is open to all writers and has a goal of helping writers who have not yet achieved major success in the world of publishing. All themes will be considered.
Website: www.shortstorycompetition.com
Length: To 3,000 words.
Requirements: Entry fee, $10 postmarked by May 1; $15 per submission postmarked between May 1 and May 15. Multiple entries are accepted. Accepts hard copy only. No electronic submissions. Send an SASE for complete guidelines and further information.
Prizes: First-place winner receives a cash award of $1,000. Second- and third-place winners each receive a cash award of $500.
Deadline: May 15. Winners are announced in July.

Highlights for Children
Fiction Contest

Fiction Contest
803 Church Street
Honesdale, PA 18431

Description
This well-known annual contest has a commitment to raise the quality of writing for children. It looks for well-written short stories for children ages two through twelve. Stories should not contain violence, crime, or derogatory humor.
Website: www.highlights.com
Length: To 500 words.
Requirements: No entry fee. Multiple entries are accepted. Accepts hard copy. Include SASE for manuscript return. Send SASE for further guidelines.
Prizes: Winners receive a cash award of $1,000 and publication in *Highlights for Children* (requires all rights).
Deadline: Entries must be postmarked between January 1 and February 28.

Insight Writing Contest

Insight Magazine
55 West Oak Ridge Drive
Hagerstown, MD 21740-7390

Description
This writing contest puts value on the mechanics of good writing, particularly that with a spiritual message. It accepts entries of short nonfiction and poetry of interest to young people ages 14 to 22.
Website: www.insightmagazine.org
Length: From 1,500 to 2,000 words (no longer than 7 pages).
Requirements: No entry fee. Accepts hard copy and email submissions to insight@rhpa.org. Author's name must not be included on the manuscript. Include cover letter with title, category, name, address, phone number, and Social Security number. Multiple submissions are accepted. Include SASE for return of entry.
Prizes: Winners receive cash awards ranging from $150 to $250 and publication in *Insight*. All other entries will be considered for publication.
Deadline: June 1.

Magazine Merit Awards

The Society of Children's Book Writers & Illustrators
8271 Beverly Boulevard
Los Angeles, CA 90048

Description
These awards look to honor previously published fiction and nonfiction. The purpose of these awards is to recognize outstanding original magazine work for young people published during that calendar year.
Website: www.scbwi.org
Length: No length requirements.
Requirements: No entry fee. SCBWI members only. Submit 4 copies of the published work showing proof of publication date. Include 4 cover sheets with member's name as listed by SCBWI, mailing address, phone number, entry title, category, name of publication, and date of issue.
Prizes: Winners in each category receive a plaque. Honor certificates are also awarded.
Deadline: Entries are accepted between January 31 and December 15 of each year.

Milkweed Fiction Prize

Milkweed Editions
430 First Avenue North, Suite 400
Minneapolis, MN 55401-1473

Description
The Milkweed Fiction Prize is awarded to the best fiction manuscripts received by Milkweed during each calendar year. Manuscripts can be a collection of short stories or individual stories previously published in magazines or anthologies.
Website: www.milkweed.org
Length: No length requirement.
Requirements: No entry fee. Manuscripts previously submitted to Milkweed Editions should not be resubmitted. Individual stories previously published in magazines or anthologies are eligible. Complete guidelines are available at the website.
Prizes: Winner receives a $10,000 cash advance.
Deadline: Ongoing.

New Millennium Writings ☆ Awards

P.O. Box 2463, Room M2
Knoxville, TN 37901

Description
Sponsored by *New Millennium Writings*, an annual literary journal, this competition presents awards in the categories of fiction, short-short fiction, nonfiction, and poetry. There are no restrictions on content or style.
Website: www.newmillenniumwritings.com
Length: Fiction and nonfiction, to 6,000 words. Short-short fiction, to 1,000 words. Poetry, to 5 pages (up to 3 poems).
Requirements: Entry fee, $17. Multiple submissions are accepted. Accepts hard copy. Manuscripts should have author's name, address, phone number, and category listed on the first page.
Prizes: Winners in each category will receive a cash award of $1,000 and publication in *New Millennium Writings.*
Deadline: July 31.

NWA Nonfiction Contest

National Writers Association
10940 S. Parke Road, #508
Parker, CO 80134

Description
The National Writers Association presents this contest that encourages the writing of nonfiction. The competition is open to all writers and looks to encourage writers in this field.
Website: www.nationalwriters.com
Length: To 5,000 words.
Requirements: Entry fee, $18. Multiple entries are accepted under separate cover. Accepts hard copy. All entries must be accompanied by an entry form (available with an SASE or at the website).
Prizes: First-place winner receives $200. Second- and third-place winners receive $100 and $50, respectively.
Deadline: December 31.

NWA Short Story Contest

National Writers Association
10940 S. Parke Road, #508
Parker, CO 80134

Description
This annual contest accepts previously unpublished manuscripts and looks to encourage the development of creative skills, and to recognize and reward outstanding ability in this field.
Website: www.nationalwriters.com
Length: To 5,000 words.
Requirements: Entry fee, $15. Multiple entries are accepted under separate cover. Accepts hard copy. All entries must be accompanied by an entry form (available with an SASE or at the website).
Prizes: First-place winner receives $250. Second- and third-place winners receive $100 and $50, respectively.
Deadline: July 1.

Pacific Northwest Writers Association Literary Contest

P.O. Box 2016
Edmonds, WA 98020-9516

Description
Presenting awards in 11 categories, including juvenile short story or picture book, nonfiction/memoir, young adult novel, and screenwriting, this annual contest is sponsored by the Pacific Northwest Writers Association.
Website: www.pnwa.org
Length: Length limits vary for each category.
Requirements: Entry fee, $35 for members; $45 for non-members. Limit one entry per category. Accepts hard copy. Send 2 copies of manuscript. Author's name should not appear on manuscript. Include a 3x5 index card with author's name, address, and title of entry. Send an SASE or visit the website for guidelines and specific category information.
Prizes: Winners in each category receive a cash prize of $1,000 and publication of their entry.
Deadline: February 28.

Pockets Annual Fiction Contest

Attn: Lynn Gilliam
Box 340004
1908 Grand Avenue
Nashville, TN 37203-0004

Description
This annual contest accepts fiction entries in all categories except historical and biblical fiction. It is open to all writers.
Website: www.pockets.org
Length: From 1,000 to 1,600 words.
Requirements: No entry fee. Multiple entries are accepted. Accepts hard copy. Manuscripts must list accurate word count on cover sheet. Entries not adhering to the contest word lengths will be disqualified. Send an SASE for return of manuscript. Visit the website or send an SASE for complete competition guidelines.
Prizes: Winner receives a cash award of $1,000 and publication in *Pockets Magazine*.
Deadline: Submissions must be postmarked between March 1 and August 15.

San Antonio Writers Guild Writing Contests

P.O. Box 34775
San Antonio, TX 78265

Description
Offering prizes in the categories of children's literature, fiction, nonfiction, and poetry, these contests are sponsored by the San Antonio Writers Guild. The competition is open to all writers and accepts previously unpublished work only.
Website: www.sawritersguild.com
Requirements: Entry fee, $20 for non-members; $10 for members. Submit two copies of each entry. Accepts hard copy. Complete guidelines are available at the website.
Prizes: First-place winners receive $100. Second- and third-place winners receive $50 and $25, respectively.
Deadline: October.

Seventeen Magazine Fiction Contest

Seventeen Magazine
1440 Broadway, 13th Floor
New York, NY 10018

Description
Sponsored by *Seventeen Magazine*, this contest is open to writers between the ages of 13 and 21. It accepts original short story entries that exemplify creativity, originality, and writing ability.
Website: www.seventeen.com
Length: To 2,000 words.
Requirements: No entry fee. Multiple entries are accepted. Accepts hard copy. Send an SASE or visit the website for complete guidelines.
Prizes: Grand-prize winner receives a cash prize of $1,000 and publication in *Seventeen Magazine*. Cash prizes and possible publication are awarded to second- and third-place winners.
Deadline: December 31.

Skipping Stones Awards

Skipping Stones
P.O. Box 3939
Eugene, OR 97403

Description
These awards look to cultivate awareness of our multi-cultural world without perpetuating stereotypes or biases. Entries should promote cooperation, non-violence, and an appreciation of nature. Entries may be published magazine articles, books, or educational videos.
Website: www.efn.org/~skipping
Length: No length requirements.
Requirements: Entry fee, $3. Send 4 copies of each entry. Only entries produced in the preceding year are eligible. Send an SASE, visit the website, or send email to editor@SkippingStones.org for complete guidelines.
Prizes: Cash prizes are awarded to first- through fourth-place winners. Winners are announced in April and reviewed in the summer issue of Skipping Stones.
Deadline: January 20.

Sydney Taylor Manuscript Competition

Association of Jewish Libraries
c/o Aileen Grossberg
67 Park Street
Montclair, NJ 07042

Description
This competition, sponsored by the Association of Jewish Libraries, was established to encourage aspiring writers of Jewish children's books. It looks for fiction manuscripts of interest to children ages 8 to 11. Entries must have a universal appeal and should reveal positive aspects of Jewish life.
Website: www.jewishlibraries.org
Length: From 64 to 200 pages.
Requirements: No entry fee. Limit one entry per competition. Submit 3 copies of manuscript. Accepts hard copy. Send an SASE or visit the website for complete guidelines and submission information.
Prizes: Winner receives a cash award of $1,000 and possible publication.
Deadline: December 31.

Southwest Writers Contests

Southwest Writers Workshop
3721 Morris NE
Albuquerque, NM 87110

Description
Southwest Writers Workshop presents awards in several categories including middle-grade short story, children's picture book, screenplay, genre story, and young adult short story. The competition accepts unpublished material only.
Website: www.southwestwriters.org
Length: Lengths vary according to category.
Requirements: Entry fee, $25 for members; $45 for non-members. Accepts hard copy. Multiple entries are accepted under separate cover. Author's name should only appear on entry form (available at website or with an SASE). Send an SASE or visit the website for category information and further guidelines.
Prizes: Winners receive cash awards ranging from $50 to $150. First-place winners also compete for the $1,000 Storyteller Award.
Deadline: May 1.

Utah Original Writing Competition

617 E. South Temple
Salt Lake City, UT 84102

Description
This competition looks to promote and reward excellence from Utah's finest writers. The competition presents awards in several categories including juvenile book, juvenile essay, short story, biography, and general nonfiction. It accepts previously unpublished work from Utah writers only.
Website: http://arts.utah.gov/literature/comprules.html
Length: Lengths vary for each category.
Requirements: No entry fee. Limit one entry per category. Accepts hard copy. Manuscripts will not be returned. Send an SASE or visit the website for complete category guidelines.
Prizes: Winners receive cash prizes ranging from $200 to $5,000.
Deadline: June 29. Winners are notified in September.

Vegetarian Essay Contest

The Vegetarian Resource Group
P.O. Box 1463
Baltimore, MD 21203

Description
The Vegetarian Resource Group sponsors this competition that awards prizes in three age categories: 14–18; 9–13; and 8 and under. Entrants should base their submissions on interviews, research, or personal opinion. Entrants need not be vegetarian to enter.
Website: www.vrg.org
Length: 2–3 pages.
Requirements: No entry fee. Limit one entry per competition. Accepts hard copy. Send an SASE or visit the website for complete guidelines.
Prizes: Winners in each category receive a $50 savings bond and publication in *The Vegetarian Journal* (requires all rights).
Deadline: May 1. Winners are announced at the end of the year.

Paul A. Witty Short Story Award

International Reading Association
P.O. Box 8139
Newark, DE 19714-8139

Description
The Paul A. Witty Short Story Award is presented annually to the author of an original short story published for the first time during the calendar year. Entries should serve as a literary standard that encourages young readers to read periodicals.
Website: www.reading.org
Length: No length requirements.
Requirements: No entry fee. Accepts hard copy accompanied by a copy of the periodical. No more than 3 entries per magazine. Publishers or authors may nominate a short story and send it to the designated Paul A. Witty Award Subcommittee Chair. For additional information and award guidelines, send an SASE or email exec@reading.org.
Prizes: $1,000 is awarded to winner at the annual IRA Convention.
Deadline: December 1.

Tennessee Williams One-Act Play Competition

Tennessee Williams New Orleans Literary Festival
938 Lafayette Street, Suite 514
New Orleans, LA 70113

Description
This competition looks to celebrate and honor previously unpublished playwrights. Entries should be one-act plays of high literary quality.
Website: www.tennesseewilliams.org
Length: One act; 1-hour in length.
Requirements: Entry fee, $25 per piece. Accepts hard copy. All entries must be typed and must include an entry form, available with an SASE or at the website. Send an SASE or visit the website for guidelines.
Prizes: Winner receives a cash prize of $1,000 and a reading and staging of their winning entry.
Deadline: Entries are accepted between September 1 and November 1.

WOW! Women on Writing ☆ Flash Fiction Contests

Contest Coordinator

Description
Sponsored by WOW! Women on Writing, these contests accept original flash fiction that is geared toward women. Entries should be lighthearted, funny, imaginative, and creative.
Website: www.wow-womenonwriting.com
Length: 250 to 500 words.
Requirements: Entry fee, $5. Accepts email entries to contests@wow-womenonwriting.com and submissions through the website.
Prizes: First-place winner receives a cash award of $200. Second- and third-place winners receive cash awards of $150 and $100, respectively. All winners will be published on the WOW! website (requires electronic rights).
Deadline: February 28; May 31; August 31; and November 30.

Writers at Work Fellowship Competition

P.O. Box 540370
North Salt Lake, UT 84054-0370

Description
The Writers at Work Fellowship Competition is open to emerging writers in the genres of fiction, nonfiction, and poetry. It is open to original, previously unpublished entries only.
Website: www.writersatwork.org
Length: Fiction and nonfiction, to 5,000 words. Poetry, to 10 pages (up to 6 poems).
Requirements: Entry fee, $15. Accepts hard copy and electronic submissions through the website. Multiple entries are accepted under separate cover only. Indicate contest category on outside envelope. Manuscripts will not be returned. Visit the website or send an SASE for complete guidelines.
Prizes: Winners in each category receive a cash prize of $1,500 and publication in *Quarterly West*. Honorable mentions are also awarded.
Deadline: March 1.

The Writing Conference, Inc., Writing Contests

P.O. Box 664
Ottawa, KS 66067-0664

Description
These contests are open to children and young adults and accept entries of short stories, short nonfiction, and poetry. The goal of these contests is to encourage a love of writing among young people.
Website: www.writingconference.com
Length: No length requirements.
Requirements: No entry fee. Limit one entry per competition. Accepts hard copy. Visit the website or send an SASE for further information.
Prizes: Winners in each category receive publication in *The Writer's Slate*.
Deadline: January.

Writer's Digest Annual Writing Competition

4700 East Galbraith Road
Cincinnati, OH 45236

Description
This annual competition accepts works in several categories including children's fiction, feature article, genre short story, memoir/personal essay, and stage play script.
Website: www.writersdigest.com
Length: Children's fiction, to 2,000 words. Other categories, word lengths vary.
Requirements: Entry fee, $12. Multiple submissions are accepted under separate cover. Accepts hard copy. Author's name, address, phone number, and category should appear in the upper left corner of the first page. Manuscripts are not returned. Visit the website or send an SASE for complete category list and guidelines.
Prizes: Winners will be published in a short story collection by Outskirts Press.
Deadline: June 1.

Writing for Children Competition

Writers' Union of Canada
90 Richmond Street, Suite 200
Toronto, Ontario M5E 1C7
Canada

Description
This competition looks to discover, encourage, and promote new and emerging writers. It is open to Canadian residents. Entries must target children, and may be either fiction or nonfiction.
Website: www.writersunion.ca
Length: To 1,500 words.
Requirements: Entry fee, $15 per piece. Multiple entries are accepted. Accepts hard copy. Send an SASE or visit the website for complete competition guidelines.
Prizes: Winner receives a cash prize of $1,500 and the Writers' Union of Canada will submit the winning entry to several children's publishers.
Deadline: April 24.

 **Indexes**

2008 Market News

New Listings ✫

Action Pursuit Games
Advocate
AMomsLove.com
Arizona Literary Contest
Blaze
bNetS@vvy
Calgary's Child Magazine
Caring for Kids
City Parent
Civilized Revolt
Kimberly Colen Memorial
   Grant
Conceive Magazine
Delmarva Youth Magazine
Dirt Rider Magazine
Dolls Magazine
Exchange
Family Magazine/
   La Familia
Fandangle Magazine
Fertility Today
Fort Lauderdale Family
   Magazine
Georgia Family
Golfer Girl Magazine
Highlights High Five
Home Educator's Family
   Times
Horse Illustrated
Inside Out
Kaboose.com

Keeping Family First
   Online Magazine
Kid Zone
Kindred
Life Learning Magazine
Literary Mama
MAD Kids
MAD Magazine
Miami Family Magazine
Mom Magazine
Mom Writer's Literary
   Magazine
Motivos Bilingual
   Magazine
Muslim Girl
National Geographic
   Explorer
National Geographic Little
   Kids
The New Era
New Jersey Family
New Millennium Writings
   Awards
North Star Family Matters
Pageantry Magazine
Parent: Wise Austin
Pocono Parent Magazine
PresenTense Magazine
Raising Arizona Kids
Relate Magazine

San Antonio Writers Guild
   Writing Contests
Santa Barbara Family Life
Sisterhood Agenda
Six78th Magazine
Socialist Appeal
South Jersey Mom
Sporting Youth GA
Teaching Music
Teen Strings
Teen Trend Magazine
Vancouver Family
   Magazine
With Kids
WOW! Women On Writing
   Flash Fiction Contests
YoungBucksOutdoors.com
Youthrunner
Zamoof! Magazine

2008 Market News (cont.)

Deletions and Name Changes

Above & Beyond: Ceased publication

Amazing Journeys Magazine: Ceased publication

American Cheerleader Junior: Ceased publication

Anime: Ceased publication

The Blue Review: Ceased publication

Challenge: Removed at editor's request

Cheat Codes Magazine: Unable to locate

Child: Ceased publication

Club Connection: Ceased publication

CollegeBound Teen Magazine: Ceased publication

Comet: Removed at editor's request

Current Science: Staff written

Dane County Kids: Ceased publication

Disney Magazine: Unable to contact

Dragon: Ceased publication

Explore Magazine: Removed per editor's request

Family Energy: Ceased publication

Fantastic Stories of the Imagination: Suspended publication

Guideposts Sweet 16: Ceased publication

JuniorWay Teacher: Unable to update information

Kids on Wheels: Unable to update information

Kids' Rooms Etc.: Ceased publication

Leading Student Ministry: Ceased publication

Magic the Gathering: Ceased publication

My Friend: Ceased publication

National PAL CopsNKids Chronicles: Ceased publication

Natural Family Online: Unable to locate

Natural Jewish Parenting: Ceased publication

Nick Jr. Family Magazine: Ceased publication

North Texas Teens: Ceased publication

Park & Pipe: Ceased publication

Paws, Claws, Hooves and All: Ceased publication

Pogo Stick: Ceased publication

Positive Teens: Ceased publication

Puget Sound Parent: Ceased publication

Real Sports: Ceased publication

Resource: Ceased publication

SheKnows.com: Ceased publication

Teacher Magazine: Ceased publication

Teaching Elementary Physical Education: Ceased publication

Teen Light: Ceased publication

Teen People: Ceased publication

Theory Into Practice: Unable to contact

Think & Discover: Ceased publication

Three Leaping Frogs: Ceased publication

Tiny Tummies: Ceased publication

Total Reader: Not accepting freelance material

Tuscaloosa Christian Family: Unable to contact

U*S*Kids: Ceased publication

What's Hers: Ceased publication

World Pulse Magazine: Ceased publication

Young Expressions Magazine: Unable to locate

Yu Gi Oh: Ceased publication

Fifty+ Freelance

You can improve your chances of selling by submitting to magazines that fill their pages with freelance material. Of the 636 freelance markets listed in this directory, we have listed 93 markets that buy at least 50% of their freelance material from writers who are new to the magazine. Of course, there are no guarantees; but if you approach these magazines with well-written manuscripts targeted to their subject, age range, and word-limit requirements, you can increase your publication odds.

AIM Magazine
The ALAN Review
Amazing Kids!
American Secondary
  Education
The Apprentice Writer
Big Country Peacock
  Chronicle
Bread For God's Children
Brilliant Star
Capper's
Cat Fancy
Childhood Education
Children and Families
Children's Ministry
Child Welfare Report
Cicada
The Claremont Review
Clubhouse
College Outlook
Community Education
  Journal
Creative Kids
The Dabbling Mum
Dig
Dimensions of Early
  Childhood
Dovetail
East of the Web
Educational Horizons
Education Forum
Education Week
EduGuide
Elementary School Writer
Encyclopedia of Youth
  Studies
Exchange
Face Up
Fandangle Magazine

Fort Myers Magazine
Fuel
Green Teacher
Group
High School Writer
  (Junior High Edition)
High School Writer (Senior)
The Illuminata
I Love Cats
Insight
Instructor
Jack And Jill
Journal of School Health
Kaleidoscope
Kansas School Naturalist
Keyboard
The Lamp-Post
Leadership for Student
  Activities
Leading Edge
Learning and Leading with
  Technology
Look-Look Magazine
Massive Online Gamer
Momentum
Mom Writer's Literary
  Magazine
Moo-Cow Fan Club
Mothering
Mother Verse Magazine
Mr. Marquis' Museletter
No Crime
Our Children
Parentguide News
Parents Express-
  Pennsylvania
Potluck Children's Literary
  Magazine
PresenTense Magazine

Principal
Read, America!
Reunions Magazine
SchoolArts
School Library Journal
Science Activities
Seek
Shine Brightly
Skipping Stones
Socialist Appeal
South Jersey Mom
Sparkle
Stone Soup
Student Leader
Teaching PreK–8
Teen Trend Magazine
Teen Voices
Transitions Abroad
The Universe in the
  Classroom
Voice of Youth Advocates
Voices from the Middle
What If?
What's Up Kids Family
  Magazine
Writers' Journal
Young People's Press
Zamoof! Magazine

Category Index

To help you find the appropriate market for your manuscript or query letter, we have compiled a category and subject index listing magazines according to their primary editorial interests. Pay close attention to the markets that overlap. For example, when searching for a market for your rock-climbing adventure story for 8- to 12-year-old readers, you might look under the categories "Adventure Stories" and "Middle-grade (Fiction)." If you have an idea for an article about blue herons for early readers, look under the categories "Animals/Pets" and "Early Reader (Nonfiction)" to find possible markets. Always check the magazine's listing for explanations of specific needs.

For your convenience, we have listed below all of the categories that are included in this index. If you don't find a category that exactly fits your material, try to find a broader term that covers your topic.

Adventure Stories
Animals (Fiction)
Animals/Pets (Nonfiction)
Audio/Video
Bilingual (Nonfiction)
Biography
Boys' Magazines
Canadian Magazines
Career/College
Child Care
Computers
Contemporary Fiction
Crafts/Hobbies
Current Events
Drama
Early Reader (Fiction)
Early Reader (Nonfiction)
Education/Classroom
Factual/Informational
Fairy Tales
Family/Parenting
Fantasy
Folktales/Folklore
Games/Puzzles/Activities
Geography
Gifted Education
Girls' Magazines
Health/Fitness

Historical Fiction
History
Horror
How-to
Humor (Fiction)
Humor (Nonfiction)
Inspirational Fiction
Language Arts
Mathematics
Middle-grade (Fiction)
Middle-grade (Nonfiction)
Multicultural/Ethnic (Fiction)
Multicultural/Ethnic (Nonfiction)
Music
Mystery/Suspense
Nature/Environment (Fiction)
Nature/Environment (Nonfiction)
Personal Experience
Photo-Essays
Popular Culture
Preschool (Fiction)
Preschool (Nonfiction)
Profile/Interview
Read-aloud Stories

Real-life/Problem-solving
Rebus
Recreation/Entertainment
Regional
Religious (Fiction)
Religious (Nonfiction)
Reviews
Romance
Science Fiction
Science/Technology
Self-help
Services/Clubs
Social Issues
Special Education
Sports (Fiction)
Sports (Nonfiction)
Travel
Western
Writing
Young Adult (Fiction)
Young Adult (Nonfiction)
Young Author (Fiction)
Young Author (Nonfiction)

Magazine and Contest Index

The following codes have been used to indicate each publication's readership: **YA**=Young adults, **A**=Adults, **E**=Educators (including librarians, teachers, administrators, student group leaders, and child-care professionals), **F**=Family (general interest), **P**=Parents. We have listed age ranges when specified by the editor.

If you do not find a particular magazine, turn to Market News on page 344.

★ indicates a newly listed magazine